The Art of OS/2 2.1 C Programming

The Art of OS/2 2.1
C Programming

Kathleen Panov
Larry Salomon, Jr.
Arthur Panov

A Wiley–QED Publication

John Wiley & Sons, Inc.

New York • Chichester • Brisbane • Toronto • Singapore

Library of Congress Cataloging-in-Publication Data

Panov, Kathleen.
    The art of OS/2 2.1 C programming / Kathleen Panov, Arthur Panov, Larry Salomon, Jr.
        p.   cm.
    Includes index.
    ISBN 0-471-58802-4
    1. C (Computer program language)   2. OS/2 (Computer file)   I. Panov, Arthur.   II. Salomon, Larry.   III. Title.
    QA76.73C15P36   1993
    005.4'469—dc20   93-25632
                                                                CIP

Printed in the United States of America

10 9 8 7 6 5 4 3

This book is dedicated to Arthur and Mom & Dad.

Table of Contents

Figures

Preface

In 1992, OS/2 2.0 was released by IBM amid much hype and speculation. Much to the surprise of both the press and IBM, OS/2 sales were extraordinary in the home computer market. This has created both a whole new breed of IBM customers and an untapped market for OS/2 applications.

About the time this book is announced in print, OS/2 2.1 will be available. If you liked 2.0, you'll love 2.1. Super VGA (SVGA) support for Presentation Manager and WINOS/2, enhanced stability, multimedia extensions — all combine for an outstanding product that should sell very well, both for the home desktop as well as for the corporate desktop.

So, you want to learn how to program for OS/2? There are two kinds of OS/2 programmers: those that migrate existing DOS or Windows programs with no regard for the extra power and functionality of OS/2, and those that use imagination and creativity to exploit the full potential of OS/2. This book will lay the foundation work for you to become a "real" OS/2 programmer.

A warning in advance — once you start using OS/2 as a development environment, you'll never go back. Multitasking makes it possible to compile in the background, download your CompuServe mail, and finish writing that letter to the president that you've always wanted to write.

Assumptions About Your Abilities

This book makes some assumptions about your existing knowledge. It assumes you're at least a good C programmer. It is not necessary for you to have programmed under some other GUI environment, although it is beneficial. The purpose of this book is not to explain the design of OS/2; it is intended to be a practical reference guide and how-to book for OS/2 developers.

Your Equipment

You will need the following in order to compile and run the examples in this book:

- OS/2 2.0 or OS/2 2.1
- The OS/2 Developer's Toolkit
- An OS/2 32-bit C-Compiler

All the examples in this book were compiled using the IBM C-Set/2 compiler and OS/2 2.0 and OS/2 2.1. The .MAK files were designed for the C-Set/2 compiler, and will have to be modified if you are using another compiler.

In addition, the Presentation Manager examples were designed for a VGA display. If you have a SVGA system, they may not be "aesthetically pleasing." Feel free to modify the size and positioning to suit the display system you are using.

Contacting the Authors

If you wish to contact the authors of this book, Kathleen and Arthur Panov can be reached at CompuServe ID 71033,1721. Larry Salomon can be reached at Internet os2man@panix.com. Feel free to submit comments, corrections, or questions.

Acknowledgements

There are many people the authors would like to thank. Special thanks go to James Summers, Phil Doragh, Sam Detweiler, David Reich (author of *Designing OS/2 Applications*), Tom Ingram, Bret and Brian Curran, Alan Warren, Jerry Cuomo, John Ponzo, Peter Haggar, and Mark Benge.

We would like to thank Arthur and Lisa for their patience and tolerance.

Lastly, we would like to thank Ed Kerr and Beth Roberts at QED for making this book possible.

Introduction

Once upon a time, when the age of thinking machines was in its infancy, there existed only one large kingdom — the kingdom of Armonk. The Armonkians had a thriving kingdom that was large and prosperous. All the other kingdoms in the country depended on the Armonkians to decide how the machines were to be made, and how the machines should think. The Armonkians were very proud of their accomplishments, and rightly so. Each day they would look to their king and proclaim to each other, "How wise he is. Surely the world of thinking machines depends on his every decision." And each day the king would meet with his elders and make new plans for their thinking machines.

Now, a thinking machine in those days consisted of the machine itself, and the whirligig that ran the thinking machine. A small kingdom outside of Armonk created whirligigs. This was the kingdom of Redmond. The kingdoms of Armonk and Redmond depended on each other, and they worked well together. Redmond was much smaller than Armonk, and was very courteous and courtly to the Armonkians. And each day the Redmondians would go to the other kingdoms and asked if they found the whirligigs acceptable. And each night the Redmondians would confer on their findings of the day.

As time passed, the other kingdoms began to demand better thinking machines and better whirligigs, so the king of Redmond went to the king of Armonk to discuss the other kingdoms' wishes. And the king of Armonk listened attentively to the king of Redmond. When the king of Redmond finished, the king of Armonk nodded his head wisely and said, "I must ponder this new information. If the people want new whirligigs, then we must provide them." And the king of Armonk and the king of Redmond signed a declaration —

together they would work on the design of this whirligig. They agreed to call it "Whirligig/2."

The kingdom of Redmond already had some work done on a new whirligig, but they called their whirligig "Okno." Okno was slow and clumsy, but made it easier for the people to use their thinking machines. The kingdom of Redmond saw the problems with Okno, and put all their energies into redesigning Okno into Whirligig/2.

For many years the Redmondians and the Armonkians toiled away at Whirligig/2. Finally they were ready to present their first work to the people of the other kingdoms. The king of Redmond was very proud of Whirligig/2. He proclaimed to the Redmondians, "This is the most significant event in the history of thinking machines." The king of Armonk was also very proud. The only problem was that Whirligig/2 was not very popular. Most people looked at it and said "Phooey!" and instead began using Okno. The Redmondians were puzzled. They could not understand why the people were not pleased with Whirligig/2. The young leaders of Redmond gathered together and whispered among themselves for many days. Finally, they reached a consensus — they would concentrate their energies on making Okno more powerful. In the meantime, the Armonkians were oblivious to the failures of Whirligig/2. They continued to toil away at newer versions, each being a little better than the previous one.

A time came when the Redmondians were ready to announce the new version of Okno: Okno 3.0. Okno was a tremendous success. All the people involved in thinking machines hailed Okno 3.0 as a miracle. The Redmondians rejoiced and there were tremendous celebrations. And the Redmondians prospered and became as well respected as the Armonkians. Gradually, the Redmondians forgot about Whirligig/2. It became an embarrassment to them. They dropped Whirligig/2 right into the lap of the Armonkians and left it there. And it landed with a thud.

The Armonkians became aware of the brouhaha surrounding Okno 3.0. The elders gathered among themselves and hemmed and hawed and explained to the others why the people were wrong. The people did not understand the power of Whirligig/2. The elders decided not to do anything - the people would soon realize the mistake they made.

Time passed. And more time passed. And still the people did not realize their mistake. The elders of Armonk again came together. The kingdom of Armonk was suffering. The cows were no longer fat, and the village was no longer prosperous. The elders realized they had to do something. They could no longer count on the people coming to their senses. So the elders called all the people of Armonk together. They explained their problems. Experts puzzled and pondered. They showed charts. They analyzed data. And still they could not understand why Whirligig/2 was a failure. A group of young Armonkians were in the crowd. They were from the side of Armonk that sat on the ocean and was surrounded by beaches, the area of Boca. One Bocasite called to the elders, "Let us try. We can do it. We can make a new and better version of Whirligig/2!" And all the Bocasites were joyous. "Yes, we can do it!" "Everyone will want this new version of Whirligig/2!"

The Bocasites had been bound by chains of bureaucracy, and smothered by the endless dronings of the elder lawyers of Armonk. They saw this as their chance. Their chance to prove to the kingdoms everywhere that they could create a whirligig just as great if not greater than the Redmondians. Creativity and confidence abounded by the sunny shores of Boca. The Bocasites toiled for days and nights. They had no time for food, only tomatoes on bread brought in as they slaved over their thinking machines. As they worked, the project became greater and greater. Impossibilities became possibilities, became realities. The people of the other kingdoms saw the tremendous work the Bocasites were doing, and rallied behind them.

The Redmondians were not blind to the new goings-on. Many of the younger, fatted elders of Redmond grumbled and glowered about this new kingdom of Armonk. The king of Redmond became agitated and spent many hours with his elders wondering how to best attack the Armonkians. The Redmondians began to talk to the people of the other kingdoms. They talked about how bad this new Whirligig/2 would be. They told the people the Armonkians were not smart enough to create this new Whirligig/2. And the people waited.

Soon, the Bocasites were done with Whirligig/2. They gave the new version to the elders of Armonk and promptly went home to sleep in their abodes, to which they had become strangers. The elders of Armonk were impressed. This was a fine new whirligig. Surely the people of the other kingdoms would realize now that this was the best whirligig. And the people saw Whirligig/2, and many bought Whirligig/2.

And this is where the story ends — for now. Never count out the Redmondians; they will be back. But Armonk will be ready this time...

Chapter 1

Tools

All the examples in this book were compiled using the IBM C Set/2 compiler and the IBM OS/2 Toolkit. There are other OS/2 compilers available including Watcom, Zortech, and the Borland C++ compiler. The include files and libraries necessary to access the system calls — memory management, multitasking, Presentation Manager, etc. — are found in the Developer's Toolkit. Although you can write a fully functional OS/2 program using only an OS/2 C compiler, you probably want to get the toolkit for any serious development work. Without the toolkit, you will need to delve into the minds of the OS/2 developers to find function prototypes, structure definitions, etc. Suffice it to say, however, that it is an order of magnitude more difficult to do so.

1.1 Dialog Box Editor

The dialog box editor, DLGEDIT, is a very nice program to facilitate the creation of dialog boxes. The interface consists of a screen painter that lets you visually design the dialog boxes for your own applications. The editor will create a resource file (.rc), dialog file (.dlg), and a header file (.h). The dialog box editor is shipped with the Developer's Toolkit for OS/2 2.1.

1.2 Resource Compiler

The resource compiler, RC, is a compiler that takes your application-defined resources — dialogs, menus, messages, etc. — and compiles them to a .RES file. This file can then be bound to your executable so that when the resources are needed, they are pulled into your program. The resource compiler is shipped with the Developer's Toolkit for OS/2 2.1, and also with the operating system.

1.3 NMAKE

NMAKE is a newer version of the MAKE utility provided with most compilers. It is a program that sorts through all the tasks that need to be done to build an OS/2 executable, and dispatches those tasks that should be done when a specific module has been changed. There are many different ways to build makefiles (.MAK). The IBM Workframe/2 environment will automate this process for you. However, the examples in this book contain .MAK files that were built by hand.

1.4 IPFC

The program IPFC is the Information Presentation Facility Compiler. This will take a text-based file and create a .HLP or .IPF file that can be used either with the help facility in Presentation Manager, or using VIEW.EXE, which is shipped with OS/2 2.1. This program has been greatly expanded in OS/2 2.1 to give the programmer and the technical writer a lot of power over the online information displays.

1.5 Libraries

The OS/2 2.1 Developer's Toolkit comes with two libraries, OS2286.LIB and OS2386.LIB. OS2386 contains the system call resolutions for all 32-bit entry-points. OS2286 contains the 16-bit ones. One of these will need to be explicitly linked in with your OS/2 2.1 applications.

1.6 Header (or INCLUDE) Files

The Developer's Toolkit for OS/2 contains lots of different header files, but there is only one, OS2.H, that should be included in your program. However, you must use the #define INCL_xxx statements in order to include the function definitions, structures, data types, etc. necessary for your program. INCL_WIN will include all the necessary information for the Win... functions. INCL_DOS includes all the information for the Dos... functions, and INCL_GPI includes all the information for the Gpi... functions. These INCL_ statements can be broken down even further.

It is a very good idea for you to go snooping through the header files. There is lots of information in them, and also, in many cases the online and hard-copy documentation is just flat-out wrong. The header files are the final authority. One caveat here — the header files are not always complete. For 99 percent of the time they will be adequate for development purposes, and the other 1 percent of the time you will tear your hair out trying to find your mistake. The following table is a road map to the various header files.

FILES	DESCRIPTION
OS2DEF.H	Includes the most common constants, data types, and structures.
PM*.H	Includes the necessary information for the Presentation Manager functions.
BSE*.H	Includes the necessary information for the base (Dos...) functions.
SOM*.H	Includes the System Object Model functions and information.
WP*.H	Includes all the information for the Workplace Object functions.
REXX*.H	Includes the REXX information and functions.

1.7 The Compiler Switches Used in This Book

All examples in this book include their own .MAK files. The compiler and linker switches for the IBM C Set/2 compiler you may see are defined below. Check your compiler documentation for a full discussion of the compiler switches and the equivalents if you are not using the IBM C Set/2 compiler.

SWITCH	MEANING	DEFAULT
C or C+	compile only, no linking	No
Gd-	static linking	Yes
Ge+	build an .EXE file	Yes
Gm-	single-threaded	Yes
Gm+	multi-threaded	No
Kb+	basic diagnostic messages (check for function prototypes)	No
Ms-	use system linkage	No
O-	no optimization	Yes
Re	subsystem development enabled	Yes
S2	SAA Level 2	No
Sa	ANSI C	No
Sp*n*	structure packing along *n* byte boundaries	4 byte boundaries
Ss+	allow use of // comments	No
W3	warning level	Yes

LINKAGE OPTS	MEANING
/MAP	generate MAP file
/A:*n*	align along *n* byte boundaries
/PM:VIO	window-compatible application

Chapter 2

Memory Management

In OS/2 1.3, the memory management scheme was designed to support the Intel segmented architecture. The 80286 could only provide access to memory in segments that were limited in size to 64K. There would be times when more than 64K was necessary. In those cases, elaborate memory management schemes would have to be the product of the developer. This has changed in OS/2 2.0. The amount of memory that developers can access is only limited by three items:

- The physical amount of RAM in the system
- The amount of disk space available on the drive pointed to by the SWAPPATH variable in config.sys
- The absolute limit of 512 Mbytes

By dropping support for the 80286, and supporting only processors capable of supporting a 32-bit engine, OS/2 could have the flat, paged memory architecture of other nonIntel-based chips. Both the Motorola 680x0 chips (base of the Apple Macintosh and other machines) and the RISC-base chips (base for IBM's RS-6000) use the flat, paged architecture. You can probably see where this is leading. Designing a memory model that is portable is the first step in designing a portable operating system. A 32-bit operating system will allow addresses of up to 0xFFFFFFFF, or 4 GB. This also gives programmers the opportunity to allocate memory objects that are as large as the system memory allows.

OS/2 1.x used the 16-bit addressing scheme of the 80286. A location in memory was represented as a 16:16 pointer, in selector-offset fashion. The upper portion of the selector maps into a descriptor table. The entry in the descriptor table maps the absolute location of the memory address.

OS/2 2.x has only three segments that combine to make 4GB total. This means that memory addresses are represented as a 0:32 pointer. All memory resides in these three segments. A normal program will run in the segment that starts at address 0 and covers 480Mb. Protected DLLS see the same 480Mb region plus 32Mb above it. The kernel functions see the full 4Gb region. This is where the big performance boost comes in. Because all memory is in these three segments, when the operating system has to switch memory objects the segment registers do not always have to be loaded. A flat memory management scheme has one more advantage: all pointers are near pointers since all memory can be addressed using a 0:32 pointer. This means no more "FAR" jumps for the operating system. This also means memory models — small, medium, large, and huge — are now obsolete.

The basis of the OS/2 2.x memory management functions is *DosAllocMem*. This function allocates memory in 4096-byte chunks called pages; however, a developer can allocate several contiguous pages in one call. While this means that you can allocate any amount of memory up to the process limit, it also means that you can waste a considerable amount of memory if you're not careful. Consider the following code fragment:

```
for (i=0; i < 1000; i++)
        DosAllocMem(    &p[i],
                        1,
                        PAG_READ | PAG_WRITE | PAG_COMMIT );
```

The first parameter is a PPVOID rather than the PVOID that you might expect. The second parameter is the number of bytes allocated, and the last parameter is the memory flags. We'll see this again soon.

What you see in the code fragment is 1000 1-byte blocks being allocated. What you don't see is the 1000 4095-byte blocks that are not being used because *DosAllocMem* allocates memory as an integral number of pages.

2.1 Committing Memory

 OS/2 2.0 also introduced the concept of committing memory. A call to *DosAllocMem* will reserve an address range for the memory; however, only if the PAG_COMMIT flag is specified will physical memory actually be assigned to the range. (A side note here: in OS/2 2.x, a page is REALLY only assigned to an address when the page is touched.) If you try to access uncommitted memory, otherwise known as sparse memory objects, TRAP-BOOM! If you choose to allocate memory without committing it, you have two ways of having it committed later — *DosSetMem* or *DosSubSetMem*. Also, in OS/2 2.x, memory is guaranteed to be initialized to 0. This prevents the application from having to initialize the memory, thereby touching all the memory, thereby committing all the memory.

The following is a very simple program to allocate memory, and to show a little about what happens to bad programs. Remember that we are seasoned professionals. Do not attempt this at home. Well, you may want to attempt it at home, but if you consistently attempt this at work, it may get you fired.

BADMEM.C

```
#define INCL_DOSMEMMGR

#include <os2.h>
#include <stdio.h>
#include <stdlib.h>

INT main ( VOID )
{
    PBYTE           pbBuffer ;
    APIRET          arReturn ;
    USHORT          usIndex ;

    arReturn = DosAllocMem (( PPVOID ) &pbBuffer,
                              3000,
                              PAG_READ | PAG_WRITE | PAG_COMMIT ) ;

    if ( arReturn == 0 ) {

        for ( usIndex = 0 ; usIndex < 4097 ; usIndex++ ) {

            printf ( "\nNow Writing to %p ( index = %d ) ",
                     &pbBuffer [usIndex] ,
                     usIndex ) ;

            pbBuffer [usIndex] = 1 ;
```

```
    } /* endfor */

  } /* endif */

  return 0 ;
}
```

BADMEM.MAK

```
BADMEM.EXE:                           BADMEM.OBJ
       LINK386 @<<
BADMEM
BADMEM
BADMEM
OS2386
BADMEM
<<

BADMEM.OBJ:                           BADMEM.C
       ICC -C+ -Kb+ -Ss+ BADMEM.C
```

BADMEM.DEF

```
NAME BADMEM WINDOWCOMPAT
DESCRIPTION 'Memory example
             Copyright (c) 1992 by Kathleen Panov.
             All rights reserved.'
```

Now, you may look at this code and say, "But, you're only allocating 3000 bytes, and you're writing to 4098." OK, this is bad code; however, it illustrates that no matter how much you specify as bytes allocated, the operating system will return it to you in 4096-byte pages and you could use them all and never see a protection violation. You'd just end up stomping all over some data that you may need. However, notice that when you try to write to byte 4097, TRAP! This too can happen to you, so be very careful about writing to unallocated, uncommitted memory.

The flags used as the page attributes in the above example were PAG_READ | PAG_WRITE | PAG_COMMIT. The possible page attributes are:

FLAG	DESCRIPTION
PAG_READ	Read access is the only access allowed. A write to the memory location will generate a trap.
PAG_WRITE	Read, write, and execute access is allowed.

PAG_EXECUTE	Execute and read access to the memory is allowed. This will also provide compatibility for future versions of the operating system.
PAG_GUARD	Sets a guard page after the allocated memory object. If any attempt is made to write to that guard page, a guard page fault exception is raised, and the application is given a chance to allocate more memory as needed. (See later section 2.4.).
OBJ_TILE	All memory objects are put into tiled, or compatibility, region in OS/2 2.x. All objects are aligned on 64K boundaries. Provides upward compatibility when applications will be allowed by future versions of the operating system to access regions above the 512MB "16-bit compatibility" barrier.

Often the example programs and manuals will reference the default page attribute, *fALLOC*; this is a symbolic constant, or #define, for OBJ_TILE | PAG_COMMIT | PAG_EXECUTE | PAG_READ | PAG_WRITE.

2.2 Suballocating Memory

DosSubSetMem and *DosSubAllocMem* provide a more efficient way for developers to access chunks of memory smaller than 4096 bytes. An application can use *DosAllocMem* to allocate some number of bytes, called a memory object. *DosSubSetMem* is used to initialize or grow a heap within the memory object. This function has three parameters, PVOID *offset*, ULONG *flags*, and ULONG *size*. The flags parameter is used to provide more details about the heap. The following options are available for this parameter:

- DOSSUB_INIT — You *must* specify this option when first suballocating a memory object. If this bit is not set, the operating system will try to find shared memory from another process. If no shared memory is found, the return code 87 will result.

- DOSSUB_GROW — This option will grow the memory pool to the size specified by the last parameter. Note that this flag will only increase the amount of memory in the memory pool that will be suballocated, and will not increase the size of the memory pool itself.

- DOSSUB_SPARSE_OBJ — This option allows the operating system handle the committing and decommitting of pages as they are needed. Note that all pages in the memory object must be uncommitted.

- DOSSUB_SERIALIZE — Serializes the suballocation of shared memory by multiple processes. If you have two processes sharing memory and suballocating it, use this to make your life easier.

DosSubSetMem has access to all memory in the memory object. The application then calls *DosSubAllocMem* to allocate a smaller chunk of the heap. *DosSubAllocMem* can allocate all but 64 bytes of the heap. The 64 bytes is called a memory pool header. It is used by the operating system to manage the suballocated portion. *DosSubAllocMem* has three parameters, PVOID *Offset*, PPVOID *SmallBlock*, and lastly ULONG *Size*. The amount actually allocated is a multiple of 8 bytes, rounded *up* if not a multiple of 8.

The following program shows you how to handle suballocation of memory:

SUBMEM.C

```
#define INCL_DOSMEMMGR

#include <os2.h>
#include <stdio.h>
#include <stdlib.h>

INT main ( VOID )
{
    PBYTE          pbHeap ;
    PBYTE          pbPtr1 ;
    PBYTE          pbPtr2 ;
    PBYTE          pbPtr3 ;
    PBYTE          pbPtr4 ;
    APIRET         arReturn ;

    arReturn = DosAllocMem(( PPVOID ) &pbHeap,
                        4096,
                        PAG_READ | PAG_WRITE ) ;

    printf ( "\nDosAllocMem ( ) returns %d", arReturn ) ;

    arReturn = DosSubSetMem(( PVOID ) pbHeap,
                        DOSSUB_SPARSE_OBJ | DOSSUB_INIT,
                        4096 ) ;

    printf ( "\nDosSubSetMem ( ) returns %d", arReturn ) ;
```

```
    arReturn = DosSubAllocMem ( pbHeap,
                                ( PPVOID ) &pbPtr1,
                                20 ) ;

    printf ( "\nDosSubAlloc ( ) returns %ld "
             "pbPtr1 size requested = 20",
             arReturn ) ;

    arReturn = DosSubAllocMem ( pbHeap,
                                ( PVOID ) &pbPtr2,
                                15 ) ;

    printf ( "\nDosSubAlloc ( ) returns %ld "
             "pbPtr2 size requested = 15",
             arReturn ) ;

    arReturn = DosSubAllocMem ( pbHeap,
                                ( PVOID ) &pbPtr3,
                                45 ) ;

    printf ( "\nDosSubAlloc ( ) returns %ld "
             "pbPtr3 size requested = 45",
             arReturn ) ;

    arReturn = DosSubAllocMem ( pbHeap,
                                ( PVOID ) &pbPtr4,
                                8 ) ;

    printf ( "\nDosSubAlloc ( ) returns %ld "
             "pbPtr4 size requested = 8",
             arReturn ) ;

    printf ( "\n\nHeader size = %d", pbPtr1 - pbHeap ) ;
    printf ( "\nSize of pbPtr1 ptr = %d", pbPtr2 - pbPtr1 ) ;
    printf ( "\nSize of pbPtr2 ptr = %d", pbPtr3 - pbPtr2 ) ;
    printf ( "\nSize of pbPtr3 ptr = %d", pbPtr4 - pbPtr3 ) ;
    printf ( "\nSize of pbPtr4 undeterminable" ) ;

    DosSubFreeMem ( pbHeap, pbPtr1, 20 ) ;
    DosSubFreeMem ( pbHeap, pbPtr2, 15 ) ;
    DosSubFreeMem ( pbHeap, pbPtr3, 45 ) ;
    DosSubFreeMem ( pbHeap, pbPtr4, 8 ) ;

    arReturn = DosFreeMem ( pbHeap ) ;

    printf ( "\nDosFreeMem ( ) returns %d", arReturn ) ;

    return 0 ;
}
```

SUBMEM.MAK

```
SUBMEM.EXE:                        SUBMEM.OBJ
        LINK386 @<<
SUBMEM
SUBMEM
SUBMEM
OS2386
SUBMEM
<<

SUBMEM.OBJ:                        SUBMEM.C
        ICC -C+ -Kb+ -Ss+ SUBMEM.C
```

SUBMEM.DEF

```
NAME SUBMEM WINDOWCOMPAT
DESCRIPTION 'Memory suballocation example
            Copyright (c) 1992 by Kathleen Panov.
            All rights reserved.'
```

You'll notice when you run this program that all your pointer sizes are rounded up in increments of 8, and that *DosSubAllocMem* starts allocating at the 65th byte of the memory object.

2.3 Guard Pages

Guard pages provide an extra level of protection for two things, data and thread stacks. A guard page is like a traffic cop with a large brick wall as a stop sign. You hit that brick wall and you're going to have some reaction, in this case, a guard page exception. This gives you, the programmer, a chance to clean up the problem. When a page of memory is committed, it can also be marked as a guard page. If the application writes to the edge of the guard page, top or bottom, a guard page exception is generated. The default behavior is designed for dynamic stack growth, and stacks grow downwards. Because of this, the operating system will look to see if the next *lower* page is free, and if so, commit it. However, the programmer is given some flexibility in an exception handler. If the application so chooses, it can commit the next higher page in the exception handler, and then return control back to the function that generated the guard page exception.

2.4 How to Handle an $&@*# Exception

OS/2 provides a way to trap major system errors known as exceptions. Some common system exceptions are guard page violations, access violations, and divide by zero exceptions. The system uses a default exception handler to trap these exceptions. You've probably seen this in action — the black screens that say "General Protection Fault Exception...".

Perhaps you'd like to intercept the exception yourself and put up a message that says something a little more user-friendly. *DosSetExceptionHandler* does just that. It points the default exception handler to an exception handler of your very own. The only parameter is a pointer to the EXCEPTIONREGISTRATIONRECORD structure. This structure is actually a linked list of pointers to exception handler functions, but in this example we only have one, so we set the ExceptionHandler field equal to a pointer to our exception handler function.

When an exception occurs, information about the exception is placed in the EXCEPTIONREPORTRECORD structure, and a pointer to these structures is passed to the exception handler.

```
struct _EXCEPTIONREPORTRECORD
{
  ULONG ExceptionNum;
  ULONG fHandlerFlags;
  struct _EXCEPTIONREPORTRECORD     *NestedExceptionReportRecord;
  PVOID ExceptionAddress;
  ULONG cParameters;
  ULONG ExceptionInfo[EXCEPTION_MAXIMUM_PARAMETERS];
};
```

ExceptionNum is the field that tells you the type of exception that has occurred. In our case, we're looking for a XCPT_GUARD_PAGE_VIOLATION. If the exception is not a guard page, we pass it on through to the system exception handler by returning XCPT_CONTINUE_SEARCH. If a guard page exception occurs, we check to see if we have enough memory to commit one more page. If the memory is available, we commit another page, and set it as a guard page. The last thing we do is return XCPT_CONTINUE_EXECUTION, which tells the system to bypass the other exception handler and continue executing the program. The errant function statement will execute correctly, and your program functions as though no problems had occurred.

GP.C

```
#define INCL_DOSMEMMGR
#define INCL_DOSEXCEPTIONS

#include <os2.h>
#include <stdio.h>

#define NUM_PAGES                   8
#define SZ_PAGE                     4096

ULONG MyExceptionHandler ( PEXCEPTIONREPORTRECORD pTrap ) ;

PBYTE pbBase ;
BOOL bGuardUp ;

INT main ( USHORT usNumArgs, PCHAR apchArgs [] )
{
    LONG        lIndex ;
    EXCEPTIONREGISTRATIONRECORD         errRegister ;
    APIRET          arReturn ;

    pbBase = NULL ;

    if ( usNumArgs > 1 ) {
       bGuardUp = TRUE ;
       printf ( "Guarding up\n" ) ;
    } else {
       bGuardUp = FALSE ;
       printf ( "Guarding down\n" ) ;
    } /* endif */

    errRegister.ExceptionHandler = (_ERR *) &MyExceptionHandler ;
    arReturn = DosSetExceptionHandler ( &errRegister ) ;
    printf ( "DosSetExceptionHandler returns %ld\n", arReturn ) ;

    /* allocate some memory */
    arReturn = DosAllocMem ( (PPVOID) &pbBase,
                             NUM_PAGES * SZ_PAGE,
                             PAG_READ | PAG_WRITE ) ;

    printf ( "DosAllocMem returns %ld ( pbBase = %p ) \n",
        arReturn,
        pbBase ) ;

    if ( !bGuardUp ) {
       //-----------------------------------------------------------
       // Commit last page and set to guard page
       //-----------------------------------------------------------
       arReturn = DosSetMem ( pbBase + (( NUM_PAGES - 1 ) *
                             SZ_PAGE ) ,
                             SZ_PAGE,
                             PAG_COMMIT | PAG_READ |
                             PAG_WRITE | PAG_GUARD ) ;
       printf ( "Return Code from DosSetMem, "
               "%ld - pbBase = %p\n",
               arReturn,
               pbBase ) ;
```

```
        //------------------------------------------------------------
        // Write to pages, from top to bottom
        //------------------------------------------------------------
        for ( lIndex = ( NUM_PAGES * SZ_PAGE ) - 1L ;
            lIndex >= 0L ;
            lIndex -= 0x0010L ) {
            printf ( "\rWriting to offset 0x%08lX", lIndex ) ;
            pbBase [lIndex] = 1 ;
            printf ( "\rWritten to offset 0x%08lX", lIndex ) ;
        } /* endfor */
    } else {
        //------------------------------------------------------------
        // Commit first page and set to guard page
        //------------------------------------------------------------
        arReturn = DosSetMem ( pbBase,
                               SZ_PAGE,
                               PAG_COMMIT | PAG_READ |
                               PAG_WRITE | PAG_GUARD ) ;
        printf ( "Return Code from DosSetMem, "
                "%ld - pbBase = %p\n",
                arReturn,
                pbBase ) ;

        //------------------------------------------------------------
        // Write to pages, from bottom to top
        //------------------------------------------------------------
        for ( lIndex = 0L ;
            lIndex < ( NUM_PAGES * SZ_PAGE ) ;
            lIndex += 0x0010L ) {
            printf ( "\rWriting to offset 0x%08lX", lIndex ) ;
            pbBase [lIndex] = 1 ;
            printf ( "\rWritten to offset 0x%08lX", lIndex ) ;
        } /* endfor */
    } /* endif */

    printf ( "\n" ) ;

    //------------------------------------------------------------
    // Free memory area
    //------------------------------------------------------------
    printf ( "Freeing pbBase = %p\n", pbBase ) ;
    arReturn = DosFreeMem ( pbBase ) ;

    printf ( "Done\n" ) ;
    return 0 ;
}

ULONG MyExceptionHandler ( PEXCEPTIONREPORTRECORD perrTrap )
{
    ULONG       ulReturn ;
    APIRET      arReturn ;
    PBYTE       pbTrap ;

    ulReturn = XCPT_CONTINUE_SEARCH ;
```

```
if ( perrTrap -> ExceptionNum == XCPT_GUARD_PAGE_VIOLATION ) {
   DosBeep ( 300, 100 ) ;
   printf ( "\n *** Guard exception *** \n" ) ;

   pbTrap = ( PBYTE ) perrTrap -> ExceptionInfo [1] ;

   //-----------------------------------------------------------
   // Check that the fault is within our memory zone, so that
   // we won't interfere with system handling of stack growth
   //-----------------------------------------------------------
   if (( pbTrap >= pbBase ) &&
       ( pbTrap < pbBase + NUM_PAGES * SZ_PAGE )) {

      if ( !bGuardUp ) {
         //-----------------------------------------------------
         // Unguard guard page
         //-----------------------------------------------------
         arReturn = DosSetMem ( pbTrap,
                                SZ_PAGE,
                                PAG_READ | PAG_WRITE ) ;

         printf ( "DosSetMem returns %ld "
                  "( pbTrap = 0x%081X ) \n",
                  arReturn,
                  pbTrap ) ;

         //-----------------------------------------------------
         // Commit and guard next page below
         //-----------------------------------------------------
         printf ( "Going down!\n" ) ;
         pbTrap -= SZ_PAGE ;

         if (( pbTrap >= pbBase ) &&
             ( pbTrap < pbBase + NUM_PAGES * SZ_PAGE )) {
            arReturn = DosSetMem ( pbTrap,
                                   SZ_PAGE,
                                   PAG_COMMIT | PAG_READ |
                                   PAG_WRITE | PAG_GUARD ) ;

            printf ( "DosSetMem returns %ld "
                     "( pbTrap = 0x%081X ) \n",
                     arReturn,
                     pbTrap ) ;
         } /* endif */

         //-----------------------------------------------------
         // We can continue execution
         //-----------------------------------------------------
         ulReturn = XCPT_CONTINUE_EXECUTION ;
      } else {
         //-----------------------------------------------------
         // Unguard guard page
         //-----------------------------------------------------
         arReturn = DosSetMem ( pbTrap,
                                SZ_PAGE,
                                PAG_READ | PAG_WRITE ) ;
```

```
                printf ( "DosSetMem returns %ld "
                         "( pbTrap = 0x%081X ) \n",
                         arReturn,
                         pbTrap ) ;

                printf ( "Going up!\n" ) ;
                pbTrap += SZ_PAGE ;

                //------------------------------------------------------
                // Commit and guard next page above
                //------------------------------------------------------
                if (( pbTrap >= pbBase ) &&
                    ( pbTrap < pbBase + NUM_PAGES * SZ_PAGE )) {
                    arReturn = DosSetMem ( pbTrap,
                                           SZ_PAGE,
                                           PAG_COMMIT | PAG_READ |
                                           PAG_WRITE | PAG_GUARD ) ;

                    printf ( "DosSetMem returns %ld "
                             "( pbTrap = 0x%081X ) \n",
                             arReturn,
                             pbTrap ) ;
                } /* endif */

                //------------------------------------------------------
                // We can continue execution
                //------------------------------------------------------
                ulReturn = XCPT_CONTINUE_EXECUTION ;
            } /* endif */
        } /* endif */
    } /* endif */

    return ulReturn ;
}
```

GP.MAK

```
GP.EXE:                         GP.OBJ
        LINK386 @<<
GP
GP
GP
OS2386
GP
<<

GP.OBJ:                         GP.C
        ICC -C+ -Kb+ -Ss+ GP.C
```

GP.DEF

```
NAME GP WINDOWCOMPAT
DESCRIPTION 'Exception handler example
Copyright (c) 1992 by Kathleen Panov.
All rights reserved.'

STACKSIZE 16384
```

2.5 Shared Memory

Shared memory is the fastest method of interprocess communication. There are two types of shared memory, named and unnamed. Shared memory is created by a call to *DosAllocSharedMem*. If creating shared memory, the second parameter to *DosAllocSharedMem* is the name for the memory, in the form of \SHAREMEM\MemName. If using unnamed memory, a NULL is specified. There is one other difference between shared and unnamed memory — the process that allocates an unnamed memory object must declare it as giveable by using *DosGiveSharedMem*, and the process accessing the memory object must call *DosGetSharedMem*. Shared memory can be committed and decommitted just like private memory.

Gotcha!

All the processes involved with the shared memory (both the getting and giving) must free the shared memory before it is available for reuse. If only one process frees the memory, you may begin to notice an increase in your program's memory consumption over time. The system maintains a usage count of shared memory that enables it to keep track of all the processes that have access to the shared memory. You can use the IBM products THESEUS2 and SPM/2 to detect leaks. THESEUS2 is the only tool that can be used to detect memory leakage. These are two excellent tools to monitor the system performance.

The following programs are an example of allocating a named shared memory object. Notice that the memory is being allocated in a downward fashion; private memory is allocated upward from the bottom of the available space.

BATMAN.C

```
#define INCL_DOSMEMMGR

#include <os2.h>
#include <stdio.h>
#include "dynduo.h"

INT main ( VOID )
{
    PBYTE      pchShare ;
    APIRET     arReturn ;

    arReturn = DosGetNamedSharedMem((PPVOID) &pchShare,
                                    SHAREMEM_NAME,
                                    PAG_READ | PAG_WRITE ) ;

    if ( arReturn == 0 ) {
       printf ( "\nString read is: \"%s\"\n", pchShare ) ;
    } /* endif */

    DosFreeMem ( pchShare ) ;
    return 0 ;
}
```

ROBIN.C

```
#define INCL_DOSMEMMGR

#include <os2.h>
#include <stdio.h>
#include <string.h>
#include <conio.h>
#include "dynduo.h"

INT main ( VOID )
{
    PCHAR      pchShare ;
    APIRET     arReturn ;

    arReturn = DosAllocSharedMem((PVOID) &pchShare,
                                 SHAREMEM_NAME,
                                 1024,
                                 PAG_READ |
                                 PAG_WRITE |
                                 PAG_COMMIT ) ;

    if ( arReturn == 0 ) {
       strcpy ( pchShare, "Holy Toledo, Batman" ) ;
       getchar ( ) ;
       DosFreeMem ( pchShare ) ;
    } /* endif */

    return 0 ;
}
```

DYNDUO.H

```
#define SHAREMEM_NAME              "\\SHAREMEM\\BATMAN"
```

DYNDUO.MAK

```
ALL:                        BATMAN.EXE \
                            ROBIN.EXE

BATMAN.EXE:                 BATMAN.OBJ
        LINK386 @<<
BATMAN
BATMAN
BATMAN
OS2386
BATMAN
<<

BATMAN.OBJ:                  BATMAN.C \
                             DYNDUO.H
        ICC -C+ -Kb+ -Ss+ BATMAN.C

ROBIN.EXE:                  ROBIN.OBJ
        LINK386 @<<
ROBIN
ROBIN
ROBIN
OS2386
ROBIN
<<

ROBIN.OBJ:                   ROBIN.C \
                             DYNDUO.H
        ICC -C+ -Kb+ -Ss+ ROBIN.C
```

BATMAN.DEF

```
NAME BATMAN WINDOWCOMPAT

DESCRIPTION 'Shared memory example
Copyright (c) 1992 by Kathleen Panov.
All rights reserved.'

STACKSIZE 16384
```

ROBIN.DEF

```
NAME ROBIN WINDOWCOMPAT

DESCRIPTION 'Shared memory example
Copyright (c) 1992 by Kathleen Panov.
All rights reserved.'

STACKSIZE 16384
```

2.6 *DosAllocMem,* or *malloc?*

DosAllocMem, DosSubSetMem, and *DosSubAllocMem* might seem like a bit of overkill if you would only like to have 20 bytes for a string every now and then. And they are. These functions would be most useful for large programs that allocate large quantities of memory at one time, or allocate shared memory, or have special memory needs. For most smaller applications, *malloc* from the IBM C Set/2 compiler will be just fine. Also, you will probably find that *malloc* is much more portable to other versions of OS/2 running on top of the Workplace OS. The C Set/2 version of *malloc* is the only compiler version of *malloc* that will be compared to *DosAllocMem* and company. In most cases *malloc* will provide memory to the program just as fast as *DosAllocMem*. The C Set/2 compiler uses a special algorithm, designed to provide the expected amount of memory in the fastest time. The following program uses *malloc* to allocate memory, and then displays the amount of memory allocated plus the location of the pointer in memory. You will probably start to notice a pattern emerging, and there is one.

SPEED.C

```
#define INCL_DOSMEMMGR
#define INCL_DOSMISC

#include <os2.h>
#include <stdio.h>
#include <stdlib.h>

INT main ( VOID )
{
   PBYTE apbBuf [1500] ;
   USHORT usIndex ;

   for ( usIndex = 0 ; usIndex < 1500 ; usIndex ++ ) {
      apbBuf [usIndex] = malloc ( usIndex ) ;

      if ( usIndex > 0 ) {
         printf ( "\napbBuf [%d] = %p delta = %ld",
                  usIndex,
                  apbBuf [usIndex] ,
                  (PBYTE) apbBuf [usIndex] -
                     (PBYTE) apbBuf [usIndex - 1] ) ;
      } /* endif */

      if ((( usIndex % 25 ) == 0 ) && ( usIndex != 0 )) {
         printf ( "\nPress ENTER to continue..." ) ;
         fflush ( stdout ) ;
         getchar () ;
      } /* endif */
   } /* endfor */
```

```
    for ( usIndex = 0 ; usIndex < 1500 ; usIndex ++ ) {
        free ( apbBuf [usIndex] ) ;
    } /* endfor */

    return 0 ;
}
```

SPEED.MAK

```
SPEED.EXE:                          SPEED.OBJ
        LINK386 @<<
SPEED
SPEED
SPEED
OS2386
SPEED
<<

SPEED.OBJ:                      SPEED.C
        ICC -C+ -Kb+ -Ss+ SPEED.C
NAME SPEED WINDOWCOMPAT
```

SPEED.DEF

```
DESCRIPTION 'malloc() example
Copyright (c) 1992 by Kathleen Panov.
All rights reserved.'

STACKSIZE 16384
```

By looking at the output of the program, notice that memory allocation starts by using 32 for values between 1 and 16, 64 for values between 17 and 32, 128, 256, and finally 512. You may notice a few "bumps" in the algorithm. This occurs when the C runtime is using some of the memory for its own purposes.

Chapter 3

File I/O and Extended Attributes

File I/O is one of the most important aspects of any operating system. The OS/2 developer is very lucky when it comes to the file system programming because OS/2 makes it very easy to understand and master, yet it still provides the programmer with a great deal of powerful features and flexibility. OS/2 has introduced to DOS developers the new concept of Installable File Systems, which allows various file systems to be installed like device drivers. OS/2 introduces the new High Performance File System (HPFS), which allows greater throughput and security features for servers, workstations, and LAN administrators. The File Allocation Table (FAT) compatibility is preserved, so DOS users are able to manipulate their files without any constraints.

3.1 Extended Attributes

The following examples demonstrate some straightforward file manipulation, yet provide the user with some useful concepts. It is also necessary to introduce the concept of Extended Attributes, which is the lesser-known OS/2 file system feature. One of the examples will show a way to gain access to the various types of Extended Attributes. The Extended Attributes (EAs) appeared in OS/2 1.2 and have remained there through the 16 – 32 bit migration; they are nothing more than additional data that is associated with the file. The user does not see this extra data. It is there only for the applications' and operating system's use. The designers had to be creative in order to implement EA support under FAT due to the fact that DOS, which is the grandfather of FAT, never had support for EAs. The HPFS does not require the same creativity in implementation, thus the FAT implementation is the one that deserves a short explanation. The FAT directory entries take up 32 bytes (20 hex), and are represented by the following chart:

Filename:	00–07
Extension:	08–0A
Attribute:	0B
Reserved:	0C–15
Time:	16–17
Date:	18–19
FAT Cluster :	1A–1B
Size:	1C–1F

Most DOS files will have the reserved bits 0C–15 set to zero. This is the very area that is utilized to attach the Extended Attributes to the files in OS/2. The EA allocation clusters use the 14h and 15h bytes, and thus may appear illegal to some DOS applications. In order to avoid compatibility problems with DOS, another file entry is maintained called EA DATA. SF; this file "pretends" to own all of the loose EA clusters on the hard disk, thus eliminating "lost clusters" messages from chkdsk.exe and similar messages from other disk managing utilities. There exist two references to all EA clusters: one that is maintained with the 14h & 15h byte directory entries, and one that is "assigned" to the EA DATA. SF. This implementation creates a source of confusion for users who are not familiar with EAs. For example, when using EA unaware backup utilities or when copying files from an OS/2 partition under DOS, most users do not know what to do with the EA DATA. SF file. One must realize that the EA clusters referenced by that file belong to several different applications. In order to properly maintain the EAs it is best to use the OS/2 EAUTIL program to separate EAs from their owners, then copy them as separate files, and later reunite them for a happy ending. Generally the EAs take up a substantial amount of disk space, and if the latter is at a premium, one can usually delete the EAs that do not have a critical attribute associated with them. This means that the presence of the EA is not critical to the application's correct execution, and thus can be removed. The user must take care in determining which EAs can be removed, as some applications will not work correctly afterwards.

A more thorough discussion of EA APIs and a detailed discussion of the API structures for the FAT and HPFS can be found in the *OS/2 Programming*

Guide and various other IBM technical publications that are listed in the reference section. The short description that is offered here is merely for the benefit of the programming examples and is supposed to help the programmer understand the syntax of the APIs used in order to attain the EA information. Extended attributes will appear foreign to DOS users and programmers, and their usefulness is generally questioned almost immediately. It is only upon closer inspection that it becomes evident that EAs are quite important and really constitute a must-have feature, especially so in high-end operating systems like OS/2. Basically the Extended Attributes are nothing more than a storage area of information no more than 64K in size that is available to the applications to use as they please. There are several standard types of EAs that are defined by OS/2, and are available for general use. Also, the programmer can define application-specific extended attributes. The only restriction is that the total EA size cannot exceed 64K. The standard EAs are called SEAs and by convention start with a period [.]. They are:

.ASSOCTABLE
.CODEPAGE
.COMMENTS
.HISTORY
.ICON
.KEYPHRASES
.LONGNAME
.SUBJECT
.TYPE
.VERSION

It is a good idea to not use the preceding [.] character in your own applications. The operating system reserves the right to use [.] as the first character of the EA name types. Nothing prevents the user from implementing the same convention, but be aware that if OS/2 designers decide to add another standard type that happens to use your EA name it may cause some unpredictable behavior. The type of data that is stored within an SEA is representative of the SEA name. For example, the .ICON SEA will contain the icon data, while the .TYPE SEA will contain the file object's type. This type can represent an executable, data, metafile, C code, bitmap, icon, resource file, object code, DOS binary, etc. As you might have guessed, the .TYPE SEA is one of the more used attributes a file object has. One point that should be made here is that extended attributes are associated not only with files, but also with subdirectories. As a matter of fact, the subdirectory that contains the Workplace Shell desktop information contains subdirectories that have many, many EAs.

3.2 EAs — Fragile: Handle with Care

There are some steps that a programmer must take while using EAs. First, if the file objects are being moved or copied to a system that does not support EAs, like a DOS-FAT combination, for example, care must be taken not to lose the EAs that may be associated with the particular file object. As an example, one can try uploading a file with EAs to a 370 host and then downloading the same file back. Doing so may result in EAs being lost or misplaced due to the fact that most 370 hosts do not support EAs. Another good example is trying to copy a file that has a long name from an HPFS partition to a FAT partition. Since FAT only supports the 8.3 naming convention the file name may be truncated, but that is not a problem since the correct HPFS name may be stored in the .LONGNAME EA. An application that manipulates files must be EA- and HPFS-aware in order to perform proper file management in an OS/2 environment.

3.3 The LIBPATH.C Example

The first example attempts to find out the value of the LIBPATH environment variable. This cannot be returned from the regular environment SET command, or a DosQuery... API. Occasionally the LIBPATH variable is a handy thing to know. So, a not-so-clean solution is to find the value of the boot drive, find the CONFIG.SYS file, and attempt to extract the LIBPATH string from that file. This will only work in a case where there have been no previous changes to the CONFIG.SYS file since the system has been booted, and specifically no direct manipulations of the LIBPATH value. Although this example is a crude kluge, the method can actually be useful on a number of occasions.

LIBPATH.C

```
#define INCL_DOSFILEMGR
#define INCL_DOSMISC

#include <os2.h>
#include <stdio.h>
#include <stdlib.h>
#include <string.h>
#include <ctype.h>

#define CONFIG_FILE              "?:\\CONFIG.SYS"
#define LIBPATH                  "LIBPATH"
#define CR                       13
#define LF                       10

INT main ( VOID )
{
   APIRET          arReturn ;
   ULONG           ulDrive;
   PCHAR           pchFile ;
   HFILE           hfFile ;
   ULONG           ulAction ;
   ULONG           ulBytesRead ;
   PCHAR           pchBuffer ;
   PCHAR           pchLibpath ;
   USHORT          usIndex ;
   FILESTATUS3     fsStatus ;

   pchBuffer = NULL ;

   arReturn = DosQuerySysInfo ( QSV_BOOT_DRIVE,
                                QSV_BOOT_DRIVE,
                                &ulDrive,
                                sizeof ( ulDrive )) ;

   pchFile = CONFIG_FILE ;
   pchFile [0] = ulDrive + 'A' - 1 ;

   arReturn = DosQueryPathInfo ( pchFile,
                                 FIL_STANDARD,
                                 &fsStatus,
                                 sizeof ( fsStatus )) ;

   pchBuffer = malloc ( fsStatus.cbFile ) ;

   arReturn = DosOpen ( pchFile,
                        &hfFile,
                        &ulAction,
                        0,
                        FILE_NORMAL,
                        FILE_OPEN,
                        OPEN_FLAGS_FAIL_ON_ERROR |
                        OPEN_FLAGS_SEQUENTIAL |
                        OPEN_SHARE_DENYNONE |
                        OPEN_ACCESS_READONLY,
                        NULL ) ;
```

```
    arReturn = DosRead ( hfFile,
                         pchBuffer,
                         fsStatus.cbFile,
                         &ulBytesRead ) ;

    arReturn = DosClose ( hfFile ) ;

    pchBuffer [fsStatus.cbFile] = 0 ;

    pchLibpath = strstr ( pchBuffer, LIBPATH ) ;

    if (pchLibpath == NULL){
/* will only execute this section of code if LIBPATH is */
        /* NOT all caps */
        for ( usIndex = 0; usIndex < strlen (pchBuffer); usIndex++){
        if (toupper(pchBuffer[usIndex]) == 'L')
            if (toupper(pchBuffer[usIndex+1]) == 'I' &&
                toupper(pchBuffer[usIndex+2]) == 'B' &&
                toupper(pchBuffer[usIndex+3]) == 'P' &&
                toupper(pchBuffer[usIndex+4]) == 'A' &&
                toupper(pchBuffer[usIndex+5]) == 'T' &&
                toupper(pchBuffer[usIndex+6]) == 'H'){
            pchLibpath = pchBuffer + usIndex;
            break;
            }
        }
    }

    for ( usIndex = 0 ; usIndex < CCHMAXPATHCOMP ; usIndex++ ){
        if ( pchLibpath [usIndex] == CR ){
            if ( pchLibpath [usIndex + 1] == LF )
            break ;
        } /* endif */
    } /* endfor */

    pchLibpath [usIndex] = 0 ;
    printf ( "\n%s\n", pchLibpath ) ;
    free ( pchBuffer ) ;
    return arReturn ;
}
```

LIBPATH.MAK

```
LIBPATH.EXE:                    LIBPATH.OBJ
      LINK386 @<<
LIBPATH
LIBPATH
LIBPATH
OS2386
LIBPATH
<<

LIBPATH.OBJ:                    LIBPATH.C
      ICC -C+ -Kb+ -Ss+ LIBPATH.C
```

LIBPATH.DEF

```
NAME LIBPATH WINDOWCOMPAT NEWFILES
DESCRIPTION 'LIBPATH Example
             Copyright (c) 1993 by Arthur Panov
             All rights reserved.'
PROTMODE
```

The first step is to find the system boot drive. In order to do this, one can use *DosQuerySysInfo* and specify the arguments corresponding to the boot drive information. *DosQuerySysInfo* takes 3 input parameters and one output parameter, and returns the values of the system's static variables:

```
APIRET = DosQuerySysInfo (   ULONG ulStartIndex,
                             ULONG ulLastIndex,
                             PVOID pDataBuf,
                             ULONG ulDataBufLen);
```

This call can return a single value or a range of values, depending on the *ulStartIndex*, *ulLastIndex*. As is evident by the example, in order to obtain a single value the *ulStartIndex* and *ulLastIndex* are set to the same input value:

```
arReturn = DosQuerySysInfo (  QSV_BOOT_DRIVE,
                              QSV_BOOT_DRIVE,
                              &ulDrive,
                              sizeof ( ulDrive )) ;
```

The QSV_BOOT_DRIVE constant is defined by the bsedos.h header file which is part of the set of standard header files provided by the Programmer's Toolkit. The additional values are defined below. The third parameter is the data buffer that *DosQuerySysInfo* uses to place the returned values into, and the last parameter is the size of the data buffer.

Description	Value	Meaning
QSV_MAX_PATH_LENGTH	1	Maximum path name length in bytes
QSV_MAX_TEXT_SESSIONS	2	Maximum number of text sessions
QSV_MAX_PM_SESSIONS	3	Maximum number of PM sessions
QSV_MAX_VDM_SESSIONS	4	Maximum number of VDM sessions
QSV_BOOT_DRIVE	5	Boot drive value (0=A:, 1=B:, etc.)

QSV_DYN_PRI_VARIATION	6	Dynamic/Absolute priority (0=absolute)
QSV_MAX_WAIT	7	Maximum wait time in seconds
QSV_MIN_SLICE	8	Minimum time slice allowed in milliseconds
QSV_MAX_SLICE	9	Maximum time slice allowed in milliseconds
QSV_PAGE_SIZE	10	Default page size (4K)
QSV_VERSION_MAJOR	11	Major version number
QSV_VERSION_MINOR	12	Minor version number
QSV_VERSION_REVISION	13	Revision version letter
QSV_MS_COUNT	14	The value of a free-running 32-bit counter in milliseconds (value=0 at boot time)
QSV_TIME_LOW	15	Lower 32 bits of time since 01-01-1970 in seconds
QSV_TIME_HIGH	16	Upper 32 bits of time since 01-01-1979 in seconds
QSV_TOTPHYSMEM	17	Total number of pages of physical memory (4K each)
QSV_TOTRESMEM	18	Total number of system resident memory
QSV_TOTAVAILMEM	19	Total number of pages available for allocation to the system at the instance of the call
QSV_MAXPRMEM	20	Total number of pages available for allocation to the process at the instance of the call
QSV_MAXSHMEM	21	Total number of shareable pages available to the caller in the shared area
QSV_TIMER_INTERVAL	22	Timer interval in 1/10 millisecond
QSV_MAX_COMP_LENGTH	23	Maximum length of a component's path name in bytes

Gotcha!

An application that is intended to be used in the HPFS/FAT environment should make the *DosQuerySysInfo* call and determine the maximum value of the legal file name length: QSV_MAX_COMP_LENGTH. For HPFS this value is much greater than FAT (255). The application should issue this call in its initialization section, and remember the pertinent values for future *DosFindFirst*, *DosFindNext* buffer size allocation values.

Once the boot drive is located, the string containing the full path to CONFIG.SYS is created.

3.4 Getting the File Size

```
arReturn = DosQueryPathInfo ( pchFile,
                              FIL_STANDARD,
                              &fsStatus,
                              sizeof ( fsStatus )) ;

pchBuffer = malloc ( fsStatus.cbFileAlloc ) ;
```

DosQueryPathInfo is used to determine the size of CONFIG.SYS. The function is designed to get file information for a file or subdirectory. The first parameter, *pchFile*, is the fully qualified path for the file. The second parameter is the level of information required. All we need for this example is standard file information, FIL_STANDARD. The information level determines the third parameter. If FIL_STANDARD is specified, a pointer to a FILESTATUS3 structure is used. The structure looks like this:

```
typedef struct _FILESTATUS3
{       FDATE   fdateCreation;
        FTIME   ftimeCreation;
        FDATE   fdateLastAccess;
        FTIME   ftimeLastAccess;
        FDATE   fdateLastWrite;
        FTIME   ftimeLastWrite;
        ULONG   cbFile;
        ULONG   cbFileAlloc;
        ULONG   attrFile;
} FILESTATUS3;
```

Among them there are two fields of interest: *cbFile* and *cbFileAlloc*. The *cbFile* element contains the actual size of the file, start to finish, in bytes. The *cbFileAlloc*, on the other hand, contains the file system allocation unit (AU) size, which is a value that has a size that can be a multiple of 512, 2K, 4K, 8K, 16k, 32k, etc., depending on the type of magnetic media. HPFS and diskettes use 512 byte AUs, while the FAT AU size depends on the volume size. Most of the applications will find *cbFileAlloc* of minimal value, and should use the *cbFile* value to allocate the required storage. Thus, it is *cbFile* size value that is used in the next call to allocate the memory buffer needed to read the whole CONFIG.SYS at once.

One does not have to perform this memory allocation. It is possible to read one character at a time and parse the output using a 1-byte storage area. This particular method was used for ease of implementation as well as performance reasons. It is much quicker to read the whole file. Since the CONFIG.SYS is generally smaller than 4K in size it should easily fit into a single page of memory, which is the smallest allocation allowed in 32-bit OS/2. The parsing can be achieved more rapidly as well. Memory operations are much quicker than storage disk I/O.

3.5 Opening a File

Having found the file size, the next step is to attempt to open the CONFIG.SYS file. The *DosOpen* API call is a good example of the flexibility and power of the OS/2 file system interface. There are several flags that are available to the programmer, and he or she can define almost any combination of them in order to provide for maximum system-wide cooperation. In this case, the file is opened in read-only mode, and with full sharing enabled. This means that if another application decided to open and read CONFIG.SYS at the same time, it would be able to do so. Having allowed full sharing rights for other applications also presents a problem of the file data being changed while we are attempting to read it. Although a remote possibility, the risk is still there, and can be easily prevented by using the OPEN_SHARE_DENYWRITE flag instead of OPEN_SHARE_DENYNONE. The OPEN_FLAGS_SEQUENTIAL flag is used to define how we will be reading the file. Lastly, we examine the file in read-only mode by specifying the flag OPEN_ACCESS_READONLY. *DosOpen* is a fairly involved API. We'll go into some more details in just a moment.

```
arReturn = DosOpen ( pchFile,
                     &hfFile,
                     &ulAction,
                     0,
                     FILE_NORMAL,
                     FILE_OPEN,
                     OPEN_FLAGS_FAIL_ON_ERROR |
                     OPEN_FLAGS_SEQUENTIAL |
                     OPEN_SHARE_DENYNONE |
                     OPEN_ACCESS_READONLY,
                     NULL ) ;
```

3.6 Reading a File

```
arReturn = DosRead ( hfFile,
                     pchBuffer,
                     fsStatus.cbFile,
                     &ulBytesRead ) ;
```

DosRead is the function to read not only files but any devices. The first parameter, *hfile,* is the file handle returned from *DosOpen.* The buffer, *pchBuffer*, is the second parameter. The third parameter is the number of bytes to read. In our case, the entire file size is used. The last parameter is a pointer to a ULONG. The number of bytes actually placed into the buffer is returned in a variable, *ulBytesRead.*

Note: It is possible in DOS and OS/2 to get a good return code (*arReturn*=0) and not have the *DosRead/DosWrite* API complete as expected. It is a good idea to check for the return code first, then check for the *BytesRead* value and compare it with the expected number.

Once in memory, the last character of the CONFIG.SYS file is set to NULL. This is done so that string operations can be performed more easily. The last step is parsing the file in order to find the LIBPATH information. Once the LIBPATH is found it is displayed with a straightforward *printf.* The cleanup is accomplished by freeing the memory, and using *DosClose* to close the file.

```
arReturn = DosClose ( hfFile ) ;
printf ( "\n%s\n", pchLibpath ) ;
free ( pchBuffer ) ;
```

3.7 More on *DosOpen*

Prior to continuing with the EA example, it might be beneficial to cover the *DosOpen* API in greater detail:

```
APIRET DosOpen (     PSZ              pszFileName,
                     PHFILE           ppFileHandle,
                     PULONG           pActionTaken,
                     ULONG            ulFileSize,
                     ULONG            ulFileAttribute,
                     ULONG            ulOpenFlag,
                     ULONG            ulOpenMode,
                     PEAOP2  ppEABuf);
```

The first three arguments are clearly identified:

pszFileName	input address of a string containing the file name
ppFileHandle	output address of a returned file handle
pActionTaken	output address of a specified action variable

The action variable on output will have the following useful values:

#define	Value	Meaning
FILE_EXISTED	1	File existed prior to call
FILE_CREATED	2	File was created as the result of the call
FILE_TRUNCATED	3	Existing file was changed by the call

The next three input arguments can create the most confusion:

ulFileAttribute	Double word containing the files attributes
ulOpenFlag	Double word containing the desired open conditions
ulOpenMode	Double word containing the mode/sharing conditions

This is due to the fact that the same *DosOpen* call can be used to open files, disk volumes, pipes, and other devices. For example, if a user wanted to open a named pipe, some of the sharing flags and the *ulFileSize* value are ignored because the pipe's buffer sizes are specified by the *DosCreateNPipe* API. Also, the *ulFileSize* may not make sense if the user is opening a disk volume for direct access. Sometimes, device drivers allow *DosOpen* calls with a device name specified in place of the *pszFileName*. It is still a null-terminated string, but in the case of a device driver the string contains the device name, i.e., "DEVICE$". Specifying *ulFileSize* or other *ulFileAttribute* flags makes no sense, and thus some of the input parameters are ignored. All three input flag parameters are bit-encoded, meaning each bit that is set represents a new or unique flag condition. Most of the bits can be set in combination. All of the flags are 32 bits wide, but not all of the 32 bits are used at this time. Some are reserved for future use and must be set to zero. For example, the *ulFileAttribute* bit values are shown in Figure 3.1.

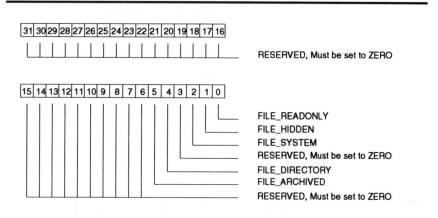

Figure 3.1. File attribute bit flags.

To allow the file read-only access, and to declare the file to be of the system type, one would use the following combination:

```
ulFileAttribute =      FILE_READONLY | FILE_SYSTEM;
```

which will assign it the value of 0x00000005 (= 0x00000001 I 0x00000004).

The *ulOpenFlag* describes the action that the *DosOpen* will perform based on the bit encoding specified by the programmer. These actions deal with conditions of file existence, replacement, and creation. One may want to allow the *DosOpen* API to fail, if the file already exists. If so, specify:

```
ulOpenFlag =   OPEN_ACTION_FAIL_IF_EXISTS;
```

If the user wants the *DosOpen* call to open the file if it exists, and fail if it does not exist, please specify:

```
ulOpenFlag =   OPEN_ACTION_FAIL_IF_NEW |
               OPEN_ACTION_OPEN_IF_EXISTS;
```

For additional file open action flags please look at Figure 3.2.

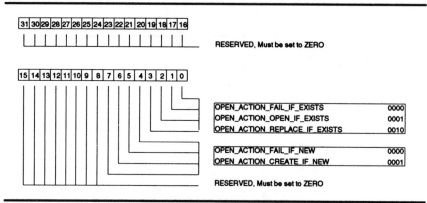

Figure 3.2. File open action flags.

The *ulOpenMode* describes the mode that the open call will set for the file object. This flag will tell the system how to behave when other users request access to the file that is currently in use by someone else. It is here that the system write-through buffering is specified and the error reporting is decided. For example, the user may want to allow the system to use its cache to transfer the data between the application and the file object, but the actual write must complete prior to the return of the call. Also, the user may want to have all of the errors reported directly to his or her application, and not through the system critical-error handler. On top of that, one may want to open this file in read-only mode, and not allow anyone else write access to the file while in use. Wow! Well, for a combination of conditions like that, use the following flags:

```
ulOpenMode =    OPEN_FLAGS_WRITE_THROUGH
                |OPEN_FLAGS_FAIL_ON_ERROR
                |OPEN_SHARE_DENY_WRITE
                |OPEN_ACCESS_READONLY;
```

It becomes obvious that a number of conditions can be specified, and thus management of files is a tedious and time-consuming task for the programmer and the operating system. See Figure 3.3.

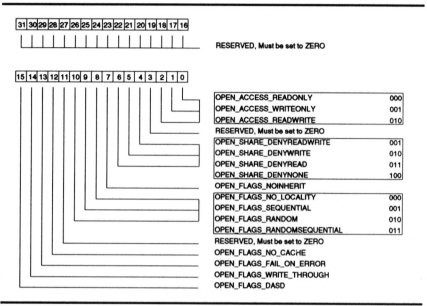

Figure 3.3. Open mode flags.

3.8 An Extended Attribute Example: CHKEA.C

The next example, CHKEA.C, shows a way to find out if the file object has
Extended Attributes associated with it. If so, then the query is made as to the
size of all of the Extended Attributes that are attached. Lastly, the names of the
types of the Extended Attributes are displayed. One can go further and modify
this example to actually display the data stored in the Extended Attributes.
This was left as an exercise for the reader. Most of the error checking in this
and other examples is minimal due to the fact that clarity was the intention
here, not necessarily robustness of the code. Error recovery is a topic that can
easily demand a separate book by itself, and thus was mostly left out of these
examples.

CHKEA.C

```
#define INCL_DOSERRORS
#define INCL_DOSFILEMGR

#include <os2.h>
#include <stdio.h>
#include <stdlib.h>
#include <string.h>

INT main (USHORT usNumArgs,
          PCHAR apchArgs [] )
{

   CHAR           achPath [CCHMAXPATHCOMP] ;
   PCHAR          pchPath ;
   ULONG          ulCount ;
   HDIR           hdFile ;
   APIRET         arReturn ;
   FILEFINDBUF4   ffbFile ;
   CHAR           achFile [CCHMAXPATHCOMP] ;
   PBYTE          pbBuffer ;
   PDENA2         pdAttribute ;

   if ( usNumArgs != 2 ) {

      puts ( "Syntax:  CHKEA [filename]" ) ;
      puts ( "" ) ;
      puts ( "where \'filename\' is the name of a " ) ;
      puts ( "file/directory and can contain wildcards." ) ;
      return 1 ;

   } /* endif */

   DosQueryPathInfo ( apchArgs[1],
                      FIL_QUERYFULLNAME,
                      achPath,
                      CCHMAXPATHCOMP ) ;

   pchPath = strrchr ( achPath, '\\' ) ;

   if ( pchPath != NULL ) {

      pchPath++ ;
      *pchPath = 0 ;

   } /* endif */

   ulCount = 1 ;
   hdFile = HDIR_SYSTEM ;

   arReturn = DosFindFirst ( apchArgs[1],
                             &hdFile,
                             FILE_DIRECTORY,
                             &ffbFile,
                             sizeof ( FILEFINDBUF4 ),
                             &ulCount,
                             FIL_QUERYEASIZE ) ;
```

```
    while ( arReturn == 0 ) {

       sprintf ( achFile, "%s%s", achPath, ffbFile.achName ) ;

       printf ( "\nFile name: %s\n", achFile ) ;
       printf ( "\nTotal bytes allocated for EAs: %ld bytes.\n",
                ffbFile.cbList ) ;

       pbBuffer = malloc ( ffbFile.cbList ) ;

       ulCount = -1 ;

       arReturn = DosEnumAttribute ( ENUMEA_REFTYPE_PATH,
                                     achFile,
                                     1,
                                     pbBuffer,
                                     ffbFile.cbList,
                                     &ulCount,
                                     ENUMEA_LEVEL_NO_VALUE ) ;

       printf ( "\nThis object contains %ld EAs.\n", ulCount ) ;

       pdAttribute = (PDENA2) pbBuffer ;

       while ( ulCount != 0) {

          printf ( "Found EA with name \"%s\"\n",
                   pdAttribute->szName ) ;

          ulCount-- ;
          pdAttribute = (PDENA2) (((PBYTE) pdAttribute ) +
                        pdAttribute->oNextEntryOffset ) ;

       } /* endwhile */

       free ( pbBuffer ) ;

       ulCount = 1 ;
       arReturn = DosFindNext ( hdFile,
                                &ffbFile,
                                sizeof ( ffbFile ),
                                &ulCount ) ;

    } /* endwhile */

    if (( arReturn != 0 ) &&
        ( arReturn != ERROR_NO_MORE_FILES )) {

       printf ( "\nError %ld encountered\n", arReturn ) ;

    } /* endif */

    return arReturn ;

}
```

CHKEA.MAK

```
CHKEA.EXE:                        CHKEA.OBJ
        LINK386 @<<
CHKEA
CHKEA
CHKEA
OS2386
CHKEA
<<

CHKEA.OBJ:                        CHKEA.C
        ICC -C+ -Kb+ -Ss+ CHKEA.C
```

CHKEA.DEF

```
NAME CHKEA WINDOWCOMPAT NEWFILES
DESCRIPTION 'Extended Attribute Example
             Copyright (c) 1993 by Arthur Panov
             All rights reserved.'
PROTMODE
```

CHKEA.EXE expects a command line input argument that is the name of the file of interest. Wildcard characters are accepted. Firstly, a determination is made if the file object can be located on the hard disk, and if successful, the full name of the object is constructed.

```
DosQueryPathInfo ( apchArgs[1],
                   FIL_QUERYFULLNAME,
                   achPath,
                   CCHMAXPATHCOMP ) ;
pchPath = strrchr ( achPath, '\\' ) ;

if ( pchPath != NULL ) {

   pchPath++ ;
   *pchPath = 0 ;

} /* endif */

ulCount = 1 ;
hdFile = HDIR_SYSTEM ;

arReturn = DosFindFirst ( apchArgs[1],
                          &hdFile,
                          FILE_DIRECTORY,
                          &ffbFile,
                          sizeof ( FILEFINDBUF4 ),
                          &ulCount,
                          FIL_QUERYEASIZE ) ;
```

The *DosFindFirst* API is the most useful function call available to a programmer when attempting to locate file objects.

```
APIRET APIENTRY  DosFindFirst(PSZ         pszFileSpec,
                              PHDIR       phdir,
                              ULONG       flAttribute,
                              PVOID       pfindbuf,
                              ULONG       cbBuf,
                              PULONG  pcFileNames,
                              ULONG       ulInfoLevel);
```

The definition for this API can be found in the BSEDOS.H header file, which is part of the OS/2 Developer's Toolkit. The arguments of interest are:

Arguments	Value(s)	Meaning
phdir	0x00000001	HDIR_SYSTEM
phdir	0xFFFFFFFF	HDIR_CREATE
flAttribute	bit encoded	Type of object to search for
pfindbuf	depends on ulInfoLevel	Result of the request
ulInfoLevel	1	FIL_STANDARD
ulInfoLevel	2	FIL_QUERYEASIZE
ulInfoLevel	3	FIL_QUERYEASFROMLIST

phdir is an input/output parameter. On input it specifies the type of file handle required by the application. HDIR_SYSTEM tells the operating system to assign a handle that will always be available to the process. This is a handle for standard output. HDIR_CREATE will cause the system to allocate a handle and return it to the application in *phdir*. Since *pszFileSpec* can accept wildcard characters, the handle returned can be used in conjunction with the *DosFindNext* to find the next file object that matches the *pszFileSpec*.

flAttribute is an input bit-encoded flag that tells *DosFindFirst* what types of file objects to look for. These bits represent conditions that may be true, or must be true. For example, you may want to locate a directory with a particular name that may be hidden, and although there are files that can correspond to the *pszFileSpec* specified, only the directories are of interest. You could use the following bit combination:

```
flAttribute = MUST_HAVE_DIRECTORY | FILE_HIDDEN;
```

The *pfindbuf* is a pointer to the buffer that must be allocated prior to making the *DosFindFirst* call, and it must be passed to the API as a pointer. On output the buffer will contain the information specified by the next parameter *ulInfoLevel*, which can have three valid values associated with it (1, 2, 3). The first one requests *DosFindFirst* to return Level 1 information about the file.

Level 1 information contains the data associated with the FILEFINDBUF3 structure. Level 2 information is requested by specifying 2 for the *ulInfoLevel*, and it returns the data associated with the FILEFINDBUF4 structure. Finally, Level 3 information is obtained by specifying the value 3 for the *ulInfoLevel*, and it returns an EAOP2 data structure. The Level 3 request is slightly different from the previous two levels. On input *pfindbuf* must contain the EAOP2 data structure with the correct names of the EAs to be queried. Since EA data structures are variable in length the *fpGEA2List* must contain a pointer to the GEA2 list, which in turn must have the correct value specified for the *oNextEntryOffset* and *szName*. The *szName* specifies the EA to be returned, and the *oNextEntryOffset* contains the number of bytes from the beginning of the first entry to the ending of the next entry. On output the EAOP2 contains a pointer to the *fpFEA2List*. The *fpFEA2List* points to the list of FEA2 structures that have the actual EA information. All of the input records must be aligned on a two-word boundary, and the last in the list of GEA2 structures *oNextEntryOffset* value must be set to zero. The following are the various data buffers that are returned depending on the level of information requested.

Level 1 Output generally contains the basic file information without EAs.

```
typedef struct _FILEFINDBUF3
        {
        ULONG   oNextEntryOffset;
        FDATE   fdateCreation;
        FTIME   ftimeCreation;
        FDATE   fdateLastAccess;
        FTIME   ftimeLastAccess;
        FDATE   fdateLastWrite;
        FTIME   ftimeLastWrite;
        ULONG   cbFile;
        ULONG   cbFileAlloc;
        ULONG   attrFile;
        UCHAR   cchName;
        CHAR    achName[CCHMAXPATHCOMP];
        }  FILEFINDBUF3;
```

Level 2 Output contains the same information that Level 1 plus EA size.

```
typedef struct _FILEFINDBUF4
        {
        ULONG   oNextEntryOffset;
        FDATE   fdateCreation;
        FTIME   ftimeCreation;
        FDATE   fdateLastAccess;
        FTIME   ftimeLastAccess;
        FDATE   fdateLastWrite;
        FTIME   ftimeLastWrite;
        ULONG   cbFile;
        ULONG   cbFileAlloc;
        ULONG   attrFile;
        ULONG   cbList;
        UCHAR   cchName;
        CHAR    achName[CCHMAXPATHCOMP];
        } FILEFINDBUF4;
```

The *cbList* field contains the size of the entire EA set for this file object, in bytes.

Level 3 Input contains the GEA2 information.
Output contains the FEA2 information.

```
typedef struct _GEA2LIST
        {
        ULONG   cbList;
        GEA2    list[1];
        } GEA2LIST;

typedef GEA2LIST * PGEA2LIST;

typedef struct _GEA2
        {
        ULONG   oNextEntryOffset;
        BYTE    cbName;
        CHAR    szName[1];
        } GEA2;

typedef struct _FEA2LIST
        {
        ULONG   cbList;
        FEA2    list[1];
        } FEA2LIST;
typedef FEA2LIST * PFEA2LIST;
```

```
typedef struct _FEA2
       {
       ULONG   oNextEntryOffset;
       BYTE    fEA;
       BYTE    cbName;
       USHORT  cbValue;
       CHAR    szName[1];
       }  FEA2;

typedef struct _EAOP2
       {
       PGEA2LIST   fpGEA2List;
       PFEA2LIST   fpFEA2List;
       ULONG       oError;
       }  EAOP2;
```

DosFindFirst also accomplishes one other thing. It provides us with the size of the EAs associated with the file. A buffer of this size, *pbBuffer*, is allocated.

DosEnumAttribute is used to identify the names and sizes of the EAs associated with a particular file object.

```
APIRET APIENTRY  DosEnumAttribute(    ULONG   ulRefType,
                                      PVOID   pvFile,
                                      ULONG   ulEntry,
                                      PVOID   pvBuf,
                                      ULONG   cbBuf,
                                      PULONG  pulCount,
                                      ULONG   ulInfoLevel);
```

The *ulRefType* tells the *DosEnumAttribute* about the next input parameter. When the value is 0, the *pvFile* argument contains a file handle, when the value is 1, the *pvFile* argument contains a pointer to a null-terminated string representing the name of the file object.

Description	Value(s)	Meaning
ulRefType	0	ENUM_REFTYPE_HANDLE
ulRefType	1	ENUM_REFTYPE_PATH
ulInfoLevel	1	ENUMEA_LEVEL_NO_VALUE

If the *pvFile* contains a handle, then this handle must be obtained by an earlier call to a *DosOpen*, or similar API.

ulEntry describes the ordinal of the file object's EA entry. This value must be non-zero and positive. The value of 1 is indicative of the first EA entry in the list, 2 of the second one, and so on.

pvBuf is the pointer to the output buffer. Only Level 1 information can be returned, thus the ulInfoLevel is always 1 (ENUMEA_LEVEL_NO_VALUE).

cbBuf is the length of the buffer referenced by the *pvBuf*.

pulCount is an input/output type argument. On input, the value contains the number of EAs for which the information is requested. If the value of -1L is specified all of the EAs are queried, and the information is returned in the *pvBuf*, provided the buffer is of adequate size. On output, this argument contains the actual number of EAs for which the information was returned. If the buffer is big enough, all of the requested EAs for the file will be returned. On output, the buffer contains the list of DENA2 structures each of which is aligned on a two-word boundary. The last structure in the list will have the *oNextEntryOffset* value of zero.

```
typedef struct _FEA2
       {
       ULONG    oNextEntryOffset;
       BYTE     fEA;
       BYTE     cbName;
       USHORT   cbValue;
       CHAR     szName[1];
       }  FEA2;

typedef FEA2   DENA2;

       arReturn = DosEnumAttribute ( ENUMEA_REFTYPE_PATH,
                                     achFile,
                                     1,
                                     pbBuffer,
                                     ffbFile.cbList,
                                     &ulCount,
                                     ENUMEA_LEVEL_NO_VALUE ) ;

       printf ( "\nThis object contains %ld EAs.\n", ulCount ) ;
```

In this example, *DosEnumAttribute* uses a '1' as the EA ordinal, indicating the function is to start enumerating at the first EA. Since *pbBuffer* is big enough to hold all the EA, it should all be placed in the buffer after just one function call to *DosEnumAttribute*.

```
       pdAttribute = (PDENA2) pbBuffer ;

       while ( ulCount != 0) {

          printf ( "Found EA with name \"%s\"\n",
                   pdAttribute->szName ) ;
```

```
        ulCount-- ;
        pdAttribute = (PDENA2) (((PBYTE) pdAttribute ) +
                      pdAttribute->oNextEntryOffset ) ;

} /* endwhile */
```

Once the EAs are enumerated, a *while* loop is used to loop through and list each EA. The next EA is found by adding the *oNextEntryOffset* to the *pbBuffer* pointer. Notice the casting involved here. Remember, you want to add in PBYTE-increments, not in PDENA2-increments.

```
arReturn = DosFindNext ( hdFile,
                         &ffbFile,
                         sizeof ( ffbFile ),
                         &ulCount ) ;
```

Once all theEAs are listed for one file object, *DosFindNext* is used to find the next file object that matches the wildcard criteria.

In order to obtain the values of the EAs you should specify Level 3 information and use one of the following APIs: *DosQueryFileInfo*, or *DosQueryPathInfo*. Also, it is important to remember that while the EA information is being read by one process, it can be changed by another one. To prevent this from becoming a problem the application must open a file with the sharing flag set to the deny-write state. This will prevent another user from changing the information in the EAs while in use. One must realize the DosEnumAttribute may return a different EA for the same specified ordinal number. This is due to the fact that ordinals are assigned only to the existing EAs. An application can delete an EA, then turn around and write another one in its place. The ordinal numbers are not preserved, and thus are not unique. As a final note, it is possible to calculate the required buffer size based on the following information. This was taken from the OS/2 2.1 Control Program Programming Reference manual:

The buffer size is calculated as follows:

Four bytes (for oNextEntryOffset)   +
One   byte (for fEA)   +
One   byte (for cbName)   +
Two   bytes (for cbValue)   +

Value of cbName (for the name of EA)   +
One   byte (for NULL in cbName)   +
Value of cbValue(for the value of EA)

Each entry must start on a double-word boundary.

Chapter 4

Multitasking

The session and task management facilities in OS/2 give the programmer an exceptional opportunity to fully exploit the multitasking features in the operating system. An application can gain a tremendous performance boost by using multiple threads or processes. OS/2 provides a special brand of multitasking, preemptive multitasking, which is different from the multitasking found in either Windows or the Macintosh System 7. Preemptive multitasking is controlled by the operating system. Each process is interrupted when its time to run is over, and the process will never realize it has been interrupted the next time it is running. OS/2 lets your computer walk and chew gum at the same time. With either the Mac or Windows, your computer takes a step, chews the gum, takes a step, chews the gum, and so on.

The task management of OS/2 is divided into three separate entities:

- Threads
- Processes
- Sessions

A thread is the only unit to get its own time-slice of the CPU. All threads belonging to a process are contained within that process, and each thread has its own stack and registers. There is a system-wide limit of 4096 threads; however, CONFIG. SYS contains a THREADS parameter that is usually set at a significantly smaller number — 256 is the default. The base operating system uses approximately 40 threads, so most applications are limited to 216 threads unless the THREADS parameter is changed. Typically, a thread should have one distinct function; for example, file I/O, asynch communications, or heavy number crunching. Each thread has a thread identifier — a TID. Each thread also has a priority. The higher the priority, the more CPU time-slices are given to the thread. A thread is much quicker to create than a process or session and has less system overhead. All threads within a process run in the same virtual address space; therefore, global resources, such as file handles, and global variables are accessible from all threads in the process. Threads are created using *DosCreateThread*, with the first thread created automatically by the operating system. When a thread is created is it assigned the same priority class as the thread that created it..

A process is an application that contains a unique address space in memory. Each process has its own memory area that cannot be accessed by other processes in the system. Two processes can only access the same area in memory by using shared memory. A process also contains file handles, semaphores, and other resources. All processes contain at least one thread, the main thread. A process also contains a unique identifier — a PID. A process contains its own set of memory pages that can be swapped in and out as the kernel switches from one process to the other. A process can create other processes; however, a process can only create processes of the same session type. For instance, a full-screen process can only create other full-screen processes. The five types of processes are OS/2 Full Screen, OS/2 windowed, DOS Full Screen, DOS windowed, and Presentation Manager.

A session is similar to a process except a session also contains ownership of the mouse, keyboard, and video. A session can contain either one process or multiple processes. The task list (accessed by Ctrl-Esc) contains a list of all running sessions. When a process or session creates a new session using *DosStartSession*, the keyboard, screen, and mouse are responsive only to the session with the foreground focus. The session chosen as the background will gain control of the three resources only by switching to the foreground.

4.1 The Scheduler

 The OS/2 Scheduler runs on a round-robin type of disbursement of CPU time. The Scheduler deals only with threads, not processes or sessions. Threads have four different priority levels: time-critical, server-class or fixed-high, regular, and idle time. The first threads to run are the time-critical threads. All time-critical threads will run until there are no more time-critical threads waiting to be run. After all time-critical threads are finished, the server-class threads are run. After server class, the regular class of threads are run. After the regular class of threads are run, idle-time threads are run. Within each class of priorities are 32 sublevels. A thread that is not running is called a "blocked" thread.

The OS/2 Scheduler does a lot of monkeying around with thread priorities. Threads are given "boosts" by the scheduler to make OS/2's multitasking smarter. There are three types of artificial priority boosts that are given to threads:

- Foreground boost
- I/O boost
- Starvation boost

The foreground boost is given to the user interface thread of the process that is in the foreground. This is usually the main thread. The foreground process is the process with which the user is currently interacting. This makes the system respond quickly when the user clicks a mouse button, or types in characters at a keyboard. This boost is a full boost in priority. Also, a Presentation Manager thread has a boost applied to it while it is processing a message.

We'll take this opportunity to get up on our soapbox. Do not throw away all the work the operating system does to provide the enduser with a crisp response time! Any operation that takes any amount of time should be in its own thread. A well-written, multithreaded program running on a 20 MHz 386SX will be blazingly fast to an enduser used to a single-threaded program running on a 486 DX2. Well, maybe that's a little bit of an exaggeration, but you get the idea. Any time you see an hourglass on the screen for more than a second or two, and the user cannot size a window or select a menu item, that program should be put through a serious design review! OK, off the soapbox, and on to our regularly scheduled programming...

An I/O boost is given after an I/O operation is completed. An I/O boost does not change a thread's priority, but will bump it up to level 31 (the highest level) within its own priority class.

A starvation boost is given to a thread in the regular class that has not been able to run. The MAXWAIT parameter in CONFIG.SYS is used to define how long, in seconds, a thread must *not* run before it is given a starvation boost. The default value is 3 seconds.

The time slices for threads that are given a starvation boost or an I/O boost are different from a normal time slice. Because of the tinkering the scheduler does with their priorities, they do not get to run as long as a nonadjusted thread would run. The length of time for the "short" time slices and normal time slices is controlled by the TIMESLICE parameter in CONFIG.SYS. The first value represents the "short" time slice length, and the default amount of time is set to 32 ms. The second value represents the normal time slice length, and the default amount of time is set to 65536.

There are four ways a programmer can refine the way the threads in a program are run:

- *DosSetPriority*
- *DosSuspendThread/DosResumeThread*
- *DosEnterCritSec / DosExitCritSec*
- *DosSleep*

DosSetPriority can be called anytime in a thread's lifetime. It is used to adjust the class and/or the priority level within that class. *DosSetPriority* should be used to adjust threads whose tasks need special timing considerations. For instance, a thread handling communications would probably want to run at a server class. A thread that backs up files in the background should be set at idle-time priority, so that it would run when no other tasks were running. You can change the priority of threads in another process, but only if they were not changed explicitly from the regular class.

DosResumeThread and *DosSuspendThread* are used to change a thread's blocked state. *DosSuspendThread* will cause a thread to be set to a blocked state. *DosResumeThread* is used to cause a suspended thread to be put back in the list of ready-to-run threads.

DosEnterCritSec is used to suspend all other threads in a process. This function should be used when it is vitally important that the running thread not be interrupted until it is good and ready. *DosExitCritSec* will cause all the suspended threads to be put back in a ready-to-run state. A program can nest critical sections within critical sections. A counter is incremented by *DosEnterCritSec* calls and decremented by *DosExitCritSec* calls. Only when this counter is 0 will the critical section exit. Nesting critical sections is probably something you want to avoid unless you absolutely need this functionality. One final note on critical sections: if a thread exits while in a critical section, the critical section automatically ends.

Gotcha!

DosEnterCritSec can be a very dangerous function. If for any reason the single thread running is put in a blocked state and needs some other thread to cause it to be unblocked, your program will go out to lunch and will not return. For example, *DosWait...Sem* are major no-no's in a critical section, because the required *DosPost...Sem* calls will probably exist in a thread that will be put in a suspended state. Also, be very careful calling a function that resides in a .DLL when inside a critical section. It is possible that the function uses semaphores to manage resources, and it may be put in a suspended state while waiting for those resources to be freed.

DosSleep is the most practical function of the group. Using this function you can put a thread in a suspended state until a specified amount of time has passed. *DosSleep* only has one argument, the amount of time to "sleep." This value is specified in milliseconds. A thread cannot suspend other threads using *DosSleep*, only itself. When *DosSleep* is called with an argument of 0, the thread gives up the rest of its time slice. This does not change the thread's priorities, or affect its position in the list of ready-to-run threads.

Gotcha!

There's one small problem with *DosSleep* in OS/2 2.0 and in the Service Pak. An argument of 0 will *not* cause the running thread to give up its time slice. This has been fixed in OS/2 2.1. However, for those users on 2.0 or the Service Pak, specify an argument of 1 instead. It works just as well.

4.2 The Subtleties of Creating a Thread

DosCreateThread is used to create a thread. The following code illustrates this:

```
DosCreateThread( &tidThread, /* thread TID */
                 pfnThreadFunction, /* pointer to fn */
                 ulThreadParameter, /* parameter passed */
                 ulThreadState, /* 0 to run, 1 to suspend */
                 ulStackSize ); /* 4096 at a minimum */
```

The first parameter contains the address of the threads TID, or Thread ID. The next parameter is a pointer to the function that the operating system will call when the thread is running. When using *DosCreateThread*, a typical function prototype of a thread function looks something like this:

```
VOID APIENTRY fnThread( ULONG ulThreadArgs );
```

Notice the APIENTRY keyword. This is used to indicate that this is a function that will be called by the operating system. The *ulThreadParameter* is 4 bytes of data, in the form of a ULONG, that are passed as an argument to the thread function. If you need to pass more than one value, you need to create a structure that contains all the values you want to pass. The first bytes of the structure should contain the size of the structure that is being passed. Also, if you use a structure make sure you pass the address of the structure as the data. The *ulThreadState* parameter indicates whether the thread is started in a running state (with a value of 0) or if the thread is started in a suspended state (with a value of 1). If the thread is started suspended, somebody needs to call *DosResumeThread* to get the thread going. The last parameter is the stack size. The thread's stack is located in memory when the thread is blocked, and is loaded into registers when the thread becomes ready to run. One of the great things that was done in OS/2 2.0 is that the programmer no longer needs to mess with allocating and freeing the memory for the stack. However, it does mean the programmer needs to know the maximum amount of memory that stack will use. This is the value passed as the last parameter. This memory is not committed until it is absolutely necessary. The thread stack uses guard pages to commit a new page as necessary. Also, you may notice that a thread stack grows *downward* rather than upward as normal memory grows.

4.3 Threads and the C Runtime

The C runtime library can cause problems when used within a thread other than the main thread. Because the C runtime uses many internal variables, multiple threads using the C runtime can cause problems unless the runtime library is notified of the other threads. A separate function, *_beginthread*, was provided by C-Set/2 to fix this situation. This function should be used to create threads in which you want to use the C library. The parameters for *_beginthread* are very similar to the parameters for *DosCreateThread*.

```
_beginthread( pfnThreadFunction,
        /* void pointer to thread function */
            pNull,
        /* This is a NOP parameter,  used for migration */
            ulStackSize,
        /* stack size */
            pArgList );
        /* void pointer to argument list */
```

The prototype for a thread function changes a little here. The typical thread function prototype looks something like this:

```
void fnThread(  void *pArgList );
```

Gotcha!

When using the C Set/2 compiler, make sure you specify the multithreaded option, Gm+. Also, either let the compiler link in the proper library for you, or make sure you specify DDE4M*.LIB.

4.4 A Thread Example

The following example creates threads with different priorities. Each thread writes its priority to the screen. In this example, we avoided using *_beginthread* and *printf*, but instead used *DosCreateThread* and *DosWrite*. This gives us the opportunity to start the threads in a suspended state.

THREAD.C

```
#define INCL_DOS

#include <os2.h>
```

```
#include <stdio.h>
#include <stdlib.h>

#define THREAD_SUSPEND            1L
#define STDOUT                    (HFILE) 1

VOID APIENTRY MyThread ( ULONG ulThreadArgs ) ;

INT main ( VOID )
{
   APIRET       arReturn ;
   TID          tidThreadID [5] ;
   USHORT       usIndex ;
   ULONG        ulThreadPriorities [] =
   {
                PRTYC_FOREGROUNDSERVER,
                PRTYC_TIMECRITICAL,
                PRTYC_REGULAR,
                PRTYC_NOCHANGE,
                PRTYC_IDLETIME
   } ;

   for ( usIndex = 0 ; usIndex < 5 ; usIndex ++ ) {
      arReturn = DosCreateThread ( &tidThreadID [usIndex] ,
                                   MyThread,
                                   ulThreadPriorities [usIndex] ,
                                   THREAD_SUSPEND,
                                   4096 ) ;

      arReturn = DosSetPriority ( PRTYS_THREAD,
                                  ulThreadPriorities [usIndex] ,
                                  (LONG) 0,
                                  tidThreadID [usIndex] ) ;

      if ( arReturn ) {
         printf ( "\narReturn = %d", arReturn ) ;
      } /* endif */

      DosResumeThread ( tidThreadID [usIndex] ) ;
   } /* endfor */

   DosSleep ( 2000 ) ;
   return 0 ;
}

VOID APIENTRY MyThread ( ULONG ulThreadArgs )
{
   USHORT       usIndex ;
   CHAR         cChar ;
   ULONG        ulBytesWritten ;

   for ( usIndex = 0 ; usIndex < 200 ; usIndex ++ ) {
      cChar = ( CHAR ) ulThreadArgs + '0' ;

      DosWrite ( STDOUT,
                 (PVOID) &cChar,
                 1,
```

```
                        &ulBytesWritten ) ;
    } /* endfor */

    return ;
}
```

THREAD.MAK

```
THREAD.EXE:                    THREAD.OBJ
        LINK386 @<<
THREAD
THREAD
THREAD
OS2386
THREAD
<<

THREAD.OBJ:                    THREAD.C
        ICC -C+ -Gm+ -Kb+ -Ss+ THREAD.C
```

THREAD.DEF

```
NAME THREAD WINDOWCOMPAT

DESCRIPTION 'Multithread example
Copyright (c) 1992 by Kathleen Panov.
All rights reserved.'

STACKSIZE 16384
```

The first part of the program is the actual creation of the threads. We'll create five almost identical threads. Each thread is started in suspended state by specifying 1 (THREAD_SUSPEND) as *ulThreadFlags*. The thread function, *MyThread*, is assigned to *pfnThreadFunction*. Since the thread function itself is fairly small, the minimum stack size of 4096 is specified.

The one difference between the five threads is their priority. Each thread priority is passed to *MyThread* in the *ulThreadArgs* variable. An array, *ulThreadPriorities[]*, holds all the possible thread priority classes.

DosSetPriority is used to actually change the priority of the threads from regular priority to the respective priority in the *ulThreadPriorities[]* array. The first parameter, PRTYS_THREAD, specifies that only one thread, not all the threads in the process, will have its priority affected. The second parameter is the priority class to use. The third parameter is the delta of the priority level. Within each class are 32 levels that can be used to even further refine a thread's priority. Threads at level 31 of a class will execute before threads at level 0 of the same class. This parameter specifies the change to make to the current level, *not the absolute level value itself.* Values are from −31 to +31. A value of 0 indicates no change, and this is what we use in this example. The last parameter, *tidThreadID[]*, is the thread ID of the thread whose priority is to be changed.

Once the thread is created and its priority has been changed, *DosResumeThread* is called to wake the thread up and have it begin running.

The above steps are repeated for all five threads in a FOR loop. *DosSleep* is used to delay the main thread from ending for 2 seconds. This gives all the threads a chance to complete.

4.5 The Thread Output

Each thread will print out its priority 200 times. Although this example is an elementary program, it will give you some insight into how threads are scheduled. The screen output you see should show the "3" thread (PRTYC_TIMECRITICAL) running first, followed by the "4" thread (PRTYC_FOREGROUNDSERVER). The '2' thread (PRTYC_REGULAR) and the "0" thread (PRTYC_NOCHANGE) are actually running at the same priority and should appear somewhat intermingled. A 0 in the priority class means no change from the existing class. The "1" thread (PRTYC_IDLETIME) should always run after the other priority threads.

4.6 Executing a Program

The function *DosExecPgm* is used to execute a child process from within a parent process. A child process is a very special kind of process. Normally all resources are private to each process; however, because of the parent/child relationship, a child can inherit some of the resources owned by the parent. Most handles can be inherited; however, memory cannot, unless it is shared memory. This protects one process (even if it is a child process) from destroying another process.

The following examples uses *DosExecPgm* to create a new command process session. The command process executes a "dir *.*".

PROG.C

```
#define INCL_DOSPROCESS

#include <os2.h>
```

```
#include <stdio.h>

#define BUFFER_SIZE              200

INT main ( VOID )
{
   APIRET           arReturn ;
   CHAR             achFail [BUFFER_SIZE] ;
   RESULTCODES      rcResult ;

   arReturn = DosExecPgm ( achFail,
                           BUFFER_SIZE,
                           EXEC_ASYNC,
                           "CMD.EXE\0 /C dir *.* \0",
                           (PSZ) NULL,
                           &rcResult,
                           "CMD.EXE" ) ;

   if ( arReturn ) {
      printf ( "\narReturn = %d", arReturn ) ;
   } /* endif */

   printf ( "\nrcResult = %ld", rcResult.codeResult ) ;
   return 0 ;
}
```

PROG.MAK

```
PROG.EXE:                        PROG.OBJ
        LINK386 @<<
PROG
PROG
PROG
OS2386
PROG
<<

PROG.OBJ:                        PROG.C
        ICC -C+ -Kb+ -Ss+ PROG.C
```

PROG.DEF

```
NAME PROG WINDOWCOMPAT

DESCRIPTION 'DosExecPgm example
Copyright (c) 1992 by Kathleen Panov.
All rights reserved.'

STACKSIZE 16384
```

The first parameter of *DosExecPgm* is a buffer that is used to store information if the application being started fails. The size of the buffer is the next parameter. The third parameter is the parameter string to pass to the program name.

The third parameter indicates how you want to the child process to run. A child process can run simultaneously with the parent process (EXEC_ASYNC), or the parent can wait to run until the child has finished (EXEC_SYNC). There are other options, but these are the two most commonly used.

Gotcha!

The parameter string conforms to regular C parameter conventions, where argv[0] is the name of the executing program. After the program name, *you must insert one null character*. Following the null is the regular string of program arguments. These arguments must be terminated by *two null characters*. This is accomplished easily by manually inserting one null at the end of the argument string and letting the normal C string null termination insert the other.

The argument string for this example is:

```
"CMD.EXE\0 /C dir *.*\0";
```

CMD.EXE will execute a new command processor session. The "\0" is the first null character. The argument string "/C dir *.* \0" indicates the session will be closed when it finishes executing the dir *.* command. The "\0" at the end is the first of the last two nulls. The second null is automatically inserted at the end of the string.

The fifth parameter is the environment string to pass to the new program. This is formatted:

```
variable = text \0 variable = text \0\0
```

Each environment variable you want to set must be ended with a null character. The end of the string must be terminated with *two null characters*. A null value in the environment string variable indicates that the child process will inherit its parent's environment.

The next parameter is a RESULTCODES structure. This structure contains two values, a termination code and a result code. The termination code is provided by the operating system to indicate whether the program ended normally or whether some error, for example, a trap, ended the program abruptly. The result code is what is returned by the program itself, either through *DosExitProcess* or through *return*.

The last parameter is the actual name of the program to be executed. A fully qualified path name is necessary only if the executable file is not found in the current directory or in any of the directories specified in the path.

There are several ways to tell whether a child process has terminated, but the easiest by far is *DosCwait*. This function will either wait indefinitely until a child process has ended, or will return immediately with an error, ERROR_CHILD_NOT_COMPLETE.

4.7 Sessions

A session is a process with its own input/output devices (i.e., Presentation Manager/nonPresentation Manager output, keyboard, and mouse). There are several different types of sessions:

- OS/2 window
- OS/2 full screen
- DOS window
- DOS full screen
- Presentation Manager

All are started the same way, using *DosStartSession*.

Gotcha!

There is a little bit of a trick to determine whether to use *DosExecPgm* or *DosStartSession*. The difference lies in whether the newly created process is going to perform *any* input or output. The following table outlines the guidelines. If you need to determine the type of an application (or .DLL), *DosQueryAppType* can be used.

Parent Type	Child Type	Child does I/O ?	Use
PM	PM	—	*DosExecPgm* or *DosStartSession*
Non-PM	PM	—	*DosStartSession*
PM	Non-PM	yes	*DosStartSession*
PM	Non-PM	no	*DosExecPgm* or *DosStartSession*

The following example program is similar to the PROG.C; however, *DosStartSession* is used instead of *DosExecPgm*.

SESSION.C

```
#define INCL_DOSSESMGR

#include <os2.h>
#include <stdio.h>

INT main ( VOID )
{
   APIRET        arReturn ;
   ULONG         ulSession ;
   PID           pidProcess ;
   STARTDATA     sdSession ;
   CHAR          achFail [200] ;

   sdSession.Length = sizeof ( STARTDATA ) ;
   sdSession.Related = SSF_RELATED_INDEPENDENT ;
   sdSession.FgBg = SSF_FGBG_FORE ;
   sdSession.TraceOpt = SSF_TRACEOPT_NONE ;
   sdSession.PgmTitle =  "Directory Test Program" ;
   sdSession.PgmName = 0 ;
   sdSession.PgmInputs = " /C dir *.*" ;
   sdSession.TermQ = 0 ;
   sdSession.Environment = 0 ;
   sdSession.InheritOpt = SSF_INHERTOPT_PARENT ;
   sdSession.SessionType = SSF_TYPE_WINDOWABLEVIO ;
   sdSession.IconFile = 0 ;
   sdSession.PgmHandle = 0 ;
   sdSession.PgmControl = SSF_CONTROL_NOAUTOCLOSE ;
   sdSession.InitXPos = 10 ;
   sdSession.InitYPos = 10 ;
   sdSession.InitXSize = 400 ;
   sdSession.InitYSize = 400 ;
   sdSession.Reserved = 0 ;
   sdSession.ObjectBuffer = achFail ;
   sdSession.ObjectBuffLen = 200 ;

   arReturn = DosStartSession ( &sdSession,
                                &ulSession,
                                &pidProcess ) ;
```

```
   printf ( "\narReturn = %d", arReturn ) ;

   return 0 ;
}
```

SESSION.MAK

```
SESSION.EXE:                       SESSION.OBJ
       LINK386 @<<
SESSION
SESSION
SESSION
OS2386
SESSION
<<

SESSION.OBJ:                SESSION.C
       ICC -C+ -Kb+ -Ss+ SESSION.C
```

SESSION.DEF

```
NAME SESSION WINDOWCOMPAT

DESCRIPTION 'DosStartSession example
Copyright (c) 1992 by Kathleen Panov.
All rights reserved.'

STACKSIZE 16384
```

The *DosStartSession* function itself is actually very small. Most of the preparatory work is done by setting up the STARTDATA structure. The structure looks like this:

```
typedef struct _STARTDATA      /* stdata */
        {
        USHORT  Length;
        USHORT  Related;
        USHORT  FgBg;
        USHORT  TraceOpt;
        PSZ     PgmTitle;
        PSZ     PgmName;
        PBYTE   PgmInputs;
        PBYTE   TermQ;
        PBYTE   Environment;
        USHORT  InheritOpt;
        USHORT  SessionType;
        PSZ     IconFile;
        ULONG   PgmHandle;
        USHORT  PgmControl;
        USHORT  InitXPos;
        USHORT  InitYPos;
        USHORT  InitXSize;
        USHORT  InitYSize;
        USHORT  Reserved;
        PSZ     ObjectBuffer;
        ULONG   ObjectBuffLen;
        } STARTDATA;
 typedef STARTDATA *PSTARTDATA;
```

Length is the length of the structure in bytes.

Related specifies whether the new session will be a child session (field is TRUE), or independent session (field is FALSE).

FgBg defines whether the session is to be started in the foreground (field is FALSE), or in the background (field is TRUE).

TraceOpt specifies whether there is to be any debugging (tracing) of the new session. TRUE indicates debug on, FALSE indicates debug off.

PgmTitle is the name that the program is to be called. This is *not* the name of the executable, only the title for any windows or task list. If a NULL is used, the executable name is used for the title.

PgmName is the fully qualified path name of the program to load.

PgmInputs is a pointer to a string of program arguments (see page 60 for argument formatting).

TermQ is a pointer to a string that specifies the name of a system queue that will be notified when the session terminates.

Environment is a pointer to a string of environment variables (see page 60 for environment variable formatting).

InheritOpt indicates whether the new session will inherit open file handles and an environment from the calling process. TRUE in this field will cause the session to inherit the parent's environment; FALSE will cause the session to inherit the shell's environment.

SessionType specifies the type of session to start. Possible values are:

SSF_TYPE_DEFAULT — uses the program's type as the session type
SSF_TYPE_FULLSCREEN — OS/2 full screen
SSF_TYPE_WINDOWABLEVIO — OS/2 window
SSF_TYPE_PM — Presentation Manager program
SSF_TYPE_VDM — DOS full screen
SSF_TYPE_WINDOWEDVDM — DOS window

IconFile is a pointer to a fully qualified path name of a .ICO file to associate with the new session.

PgmName is a program handle that is returned from either *WinAddProgram*, or *WinQueryProgramHandle*. A 0 can be used if these functions are not used.

PgmControl specifies the initial attributes for either the OS/2 window or DOS window sessions. The following values can be used:

SSF_CONTROL_VISIBLE
SSF_CONTROL_INVISIBLE
SSF_CONTROL_MAXIMIZE
SSF_CONTROL_MINIMIZE
SSF_CONTROL_NOAUTOCLOSE
SSF_CONTROL_SETPOS

Except for SSF_CONTROL_NOAUTOCLOSE and SSF_CONTROL_SETPOS, the values are pretty self-explanatory. SSF_CONTROL_NOAUTOCLOSE is used only for the OS/2 windowed sessions, and will keep the session open after the program has completed. The SSF_CONTROL_SETPOS value indicates that the operating system will use the InitXPos, InitYPos, InitXSize, and InitYSize for the size and placement of the windowed sessions.

The second parameter to *DosStartSession* is the address of a ULONG that will contain the session ID after the function has completed. The last parameter is

the address of a PID (process ID) that will contain the new process's PID after
the session has started.

Chapter 5

Interprocess Communication

OS/2 provides several different methods of interprocess communication, all fairly easy to implement. In OS/2 1.3 there were five distinct ways available for a process to communicate with another process. These communications methods used flags, semaphores, pipes, queues, and shared memory to send and receive messages and signals. In OS/2 2.0 four of the most common methods were retained; the only one that was dropped was the *DosFlagProcess* API. The functionality that was provided by *DosFlagProcess* is now provided by *DosRaiseException* and related APIs.

The easiest IPC method to implement is unnamed and named pipes. An unnamed pipe is a circular memory buffer that can be used to communicate between related processes. The parent process must set the inheritance flags to true in order for the child process to inherit the handles and allow the parent and the child processes to communicate. The communication is bidirectional, and the pipe remains open until both the read handle and the write handle are closed. Named pipes are also an easy way to provide remote communication. You can have a process on the requester workstation communicating with a process running on the server workstation as well as with a process running locally. However, the client-server remote connectivity can only be achieved with the help of some type of LAN server.

5.1 A PIPE.C Example

PIPE.C is written to allow the user to decide the mode of operation: server or client. The program allows remote and local communications and performs simple character redirection. The characters are highlighted in different colors to distinguish server and client modes of operation. As the user types in characters at the server, they immediately echo on the client. Only the server is able to accept keystrokes, display the characters, and echo the same characters to the client, which in turn displays the characters, but in a different color. Pressing the F2 function key on the server will switch modes on the server and the client applications. The server will become the client, and the client will become the server. The user may start typing at the new server only to see the input characters echo on the new client. Pressing the F3 function key will end the application. Remember that, even though the client does not display any keystrokes, if any keys are pressed the buffer is not flushed; therefore, you may see the keystrokes display when you decide to switch modes from client to server and vice versa.

You can start the pipe.exe application by simply typing *pipe* followed by a carriage return from the command line. This will start the pipe program in the default server mode. You must start the pipe server first, since it is the server that creates the named pipe and allows the client to connect to it. After the server starts successfully, start the client by typing *pipe client [ServerName]* followed by a carriage return from the command line. Note that the ServerName is an optional parameter and is only used if you are attempting a remote pipe connection. If you are running the pipe server and the pipe client in the same workstation, and the workstation is capable of running the server software, the server-client communication can be achieved with both local and remote connections. However, if the LAN server is not active, or the user is not logged on to the LAN server domain, attempting a remote connection witll produce an error. The error will tell you that the pipe name was not found. This is correct, and usually points to an inactive server, or an unauthorized user. The best way to look at this example is to open two OS/2 window sessions, and to allow one session to run the pipe server and the other to run the pipe client. This way it will be easier to see the transition from server to client and vice versa.

PIPE.C

```
#define   INCL_DOSNMPIPES

#include <os2.h>
#include <stdlib.h>
#include <string.h>
#include <stdio.h>
#include <conio.h>

#define MAX_INPUT_ARGS          3
#define SERVER_MODE             1
#define CLIENT_MODE             2
#define DISCON_MODE             3
#define BAD_INPUT_ARGS          99
#define MAX_PIPE_NAME_LEN       80
#define MAX_SERV_NAME_LEN       8
#define DEFAULT_PIPE_NAME       "\\PIPE\\MYPIPE"
#define DEFAULT_MAKE_MODE       NP_ACCESS_DUPLEX
#define DEFAULT_PIPE_MODE       NP_WMESG | NP_RMESG | 0x01
#define DEFAULT_OPEN_FLAG       OPEN_ACTION_OPEN_IF_EXISTS
#define DEFAULT_OPEN_MODE       OPEN_FLAGS_WRITE_THROUGH | \
                                OPEN_FLAGS_FAIL_ON_ERROR | \
                                OPEN_FLAGS_RANDOM |        \
                                OPEN_SHARE_DENYNONE |      \
                                OPEN_ACCESS_READWRITE
#define DEFAULT_OUTB_SIZE       0x1000
#define DEFAULT_INPB_SIZE       0x1000
#define DEFAULT_TIME_OUTV       20000L
#define TOKEN_F2_SWITCH         0x0000003CL
#define TOKEN_F3_DISCON         0x0000003DL
#define RETURN_CHAR             0x0D
#define LINE_FEED_CHAR          0x0A
#define FUNC_KEYS_CHAR          0x00
#define EXTD_KEYS_CHAR          0xE0
#define HAND_SHAKE_LEN          0x08
#define HAND_SHAKE_INP          "pIpEtEsT"
#define HAND_SHAKE_OUT          "PiPeTeSt"
#define HAND_SHAKE_ERROR        101
#define PROGRAM_ERROR           999


CHAR    achPipeName [MAX_PIPE_NAME_LEN] ;
HPIPE   hpPipe ;
CHAR    chToken ;

USHORT BadArgs ( USHORT usNumArgs, PCHAR apchArgs [] ) ;
APIRET ConnToClient ( VOID ) ;
APIRET ConnToServer ( VOID ) ;
APIRET SendToClient ( ULONG ulHiLoCh ) ;
APIRET RecvFromServer ( PULONG pulHiLoCh ) ;

INT main ( USHORT usNumArgs, PCHAR apchArgs [] )
{
    USHORT    usHiCh ;
    USHORT    usLoCh ;
    ULONG     ulHiLoCh ;
    APIRET    arReturn ;
```

```
achPipeName [0] = 0 ;
chToken = 0 ;

usHiCh = 0 ;
usLoCh = 0 ;
ulHiLoCh = 0 ;

if ( !BadArgs ( usNumArgs, apchArgs )) {
   if ( chToken == SERVER_MODE ) {
      printf ( "\n□[0;32;40m Starting the program in "
               "Server Mode...\n" ) ;
      printf ( "\n Press F2 to switch to client mode, "
               "F3 to quit \n" ) ;
      strcpy ( achPipeName, DEFAULT_PIPE_NAME ) ;
      arReturn = ConnToClient ( ) ;
   } else

   if ( chToken == CLIENT_MODE ) {
      printf ( "\n□[0;31;40m Starting the program in "
               "Client Mode...\n" ) ;
      printf ( "\n Press F2 to switch to server mode, "
               "F3 to quit \n" ) ;
      if ( usNumArgs == MAX_INPUT_ARGS ) {
         sprintf ( achPipeName, "\\\\%s", apchArgs [2] ) ;
      }
      strcat ( achPipeName, DEFAULT_PIPE_NAME ) ;
      arReturn = ConnToServer ( ) ;

   } else {
      arReturn = PROGRAM_ERROR ;
   }

   while ( !arReturn && ( chToken != DISCON_MODE )) {

      switch ( chToken ) {
      case SERVER_MODE:
         usHiCh = getch ( ) ;
         if (( usHiCh == FUNC_KEYS_CHAR ) ||
             ( usHiCh == EXTD_KEYS_CHAR )) {
            usLoCh = getch ( ) ;
         } else {
            usLoCh = usHiCh ;
         } /* endif */

         ulHiLoCh = (( ULONG ) usHiCh << 16 ) |
                     ( ULONG ) usLoCh ;

         arReturn = SendToClient ( ulHiLoCh ) ;

         if ( ulHiLoCh == TOKEN_F2_SWITCH ) {
            chToken = CLIENT_MODE ;
            printf ( "\n □ [0 ; 31 ; 40m Switching to "
                     "Client Mode...\n" ) ;
            break ;
```

```
            } else
        if ( ulHiLoCh == TOKEN_F3_DISCON ) {
            chToken = DISCON_MODE ;
            break ;
        } /* endif */

        putch ( usHiCh ) ;

        if ( usHiCh == RETURN_CHAR ) {
            putch ( LINE_FEED_CHAR ) ;
        } /* endif */
        break ;

    case CLIENT_MODE:
        arReturn = RecvFromServer ( &ulHiLoCh ) ;

        if ( ulHiLoCh == TOKEN_F2_SWITCH ) {
            chToken = SERVER_MODE ;
            printf ( "\n □ [0 ; 32 ; 40m Switching to "
                     "Server Mode...\n" ) ;
            break ;
        } else
        if ( ulHiLoCh == TOKEN_F3_DISCON ) {
            chToken = DISCON_MODE ;
            break ;
        } /* endif */

        usHiCh = ( USHORT ) ( ulHiLoCh & 0x0000FFFFL ) ;

        putch ( usHiCh ) ;

        if ( usHiCh == RETURN_CHAR ) {
            putch ( LINE_FEED_CHAR ) ;
        } /* endif */
        break ;

    default:
        arReturn = PROGRAM_ERROR ;
        break ;
    } /* endswitch */
  } /* endwhile */
} /* endif */

    if ( arReturn == 0 ) {
        arReturn = DosClose ( hpPipe ) ;
    } /* endif */

    printf ( "\n □ [0 ; 37 ; 40m" ) ;
    return arReturn ;
}

USHORT BadArgs ( USHORT usNumArgs, PCHAR apchArgs [] )
{
    if ( usNumArgs == SERVER_MODE ) {
        chToken = SERVER_MODE ;
```

```
      } else
  if (( usNumArgs == CLIENT_MODE ) &&
      ( apchArgs [1] [0] != '?' )) {
      chToken = CLIENT_MODE ;
   } else
  if (( usNumArgs == MAX_INPUT_ARGS ) &&
      ( strlen ( apchArgs [2] ) <= MAX_SERV_NAME_LEN )) {
      chToken = CLIENT_MODE ;
   } else {
      printf ( "\n  Incorrect command line argument was "
               "entered" ) ;
      printf ( "\n  Please enter:\n" ) ;
      printf ( "\n  □[0;31;40m  pipe CLIENT SERVERNAME "
               " ( use for CLIENT operation ) " ) ;
      printf ( "\n  □[0;32;40m  pipe                    "
               " ( use for SERVER operation ) " ) ;
      printf ( "\n  □[0;37;40m \n" ) ;

      return BAD_INPUT_ARGS ;
   } /* endif */

   return 0 ;
}

APIRET ConnToClient ( VOID )
{
   CHAR         achInitBuf [HAND_SHAKE_LEN + 1] ;
   ULONG        ulOpenMode ;
   ULONG        ulPipeMode ;
   ULONG        ulOutBufSize ;
   ULONG        ulInpBufSize ;
   ULONG        ulTimeOut ;
   USHORT       arReturn ;
   ULONG        ulBytesDone ;

   memset ( achInitBuf, 0, sizeof ( achInitBuf )) ;

   ulOpenMode =    DEFAULT_MAKE_MODE ;
   ulPipeMode =    DEFAULT_PIPE_MODE ;
   ulOutBufSize = DEFAULT_OUTB_SIZE ;
   ulInpBufSize = DEFAULT_INPB_SIZE ;
   ulTimeOut =    DEFAULT_TIME_OUTV ;

   arReturn = DosCreateNPipe ( achPipeName,
                               &hpPipe,
                               ulOpenMode,
                               ulPipeMode,
                               ulOutBufSize,
                               ulInpBufSize,
                               ulTimeOut ) ;

   if ( !arReturn ) {
      arReturn = DosConnectNPipe ( hpPipe ) ;
```

```
        if ( !arReturn ) {
            arReturn = DosRead ( hpPipe,
                                  achInitBuf,
                                  ( ULONG ) HAND_SHAKE_LEN,
                                  &ulBytesDone ) ;

            if ( !strcmp ( achInitBuf, HAND_SHAKE_INP )
                            && !arReturn ) {
                arReturn = DosWrite ( hpPipe,
                                      HAND_SHAKE_OUT,
                                      strlen ( HAND_SHAKE_OUT ) ,
                                      &ulBytesDone ) ;
            } else {
                arReturn = HAND_SHAKE_ERROR ;
            } /* endif */
        } /* endif */
    } /* endif */

    printf ( "\n  The Pipe Creation / Connection API "
             "returned rc = %02X\n\n",
             arReturn ) ;
    return arReturn ;
}

APIRET ConnToServer ( VOID )
{
    CHAR achInitBuf [HAND_SHAKE_LEN + 1] ;
    ULONG ulOpenFlag ;
    ULONG ulOpenMode ;
    ULONG ulActionTaken ;
    INT arReturn ;
    ULONG ulBytesDone ;

    memset ( achInitBuf, 0, sizeof ( achInitBuf )) ;

    ulOpenFlag = DEFAULT_OPEN_FLAG ;
    ulOpenMode = DEFAULT_OPEN_MODE ;

    arReturn = DosOpen ( achPipeName,
                         &hpPipe,
                         &ulActionTaken,
                         0,
                         0,
                         ulOpenFlag,
                         ulOpenMode,
                         0 ) ;

    if ( !arReturn ) {
        arReturn = DosWrite ( hpPipe,
                              HAND_SHAKE_INP,
                              strlen ( HAND_SHAKE_INP ) ,
                              &ulBytesDone ) ;
```

```
        if ( !arReturn ) {
           arReturn = DosRead ( hpPipe,
                                 achInitBuf,
                                 ( ULONG ) HAND_SHAKE_LEN,
                                 &ulBytesDone ) ;

           if ( strcmp ( achInitBuf, HAND_SHAKE_OUT )) {
              arReturn = HAND_SHAKE_ERROR ;
           } /* endif */
        } /* endif */
     } /* endif */

     if ( arReturn ) {
        printf ( "\n  The Pipe Open / Connection API "
                 "returned rc = %02x\n",
                 arReturn ) ;
        printf ( "\n  Make sure the Server is running.\n\n" ) ;
     } /* endif */

     return arReturn ;
}

APIRET SendToClient ( ULONG ulHiLoCh )
{
   ULONG ulBytesDone ;

   return DosWrite ( hpPipe,
                     &ulHiLoCh,
                     sizeof ( ulHiLoCh ) ,
                     &ulBytesDone ) ;
}

APIRET RecvFromServer ( PULONG pulHiLoCh )
{
   ULONG ulBytesDone ;

   return DosRead ( hpPipe,
                    pulHiLoCh,
                    sizeof ( pulHiLoCh ) ,
                    &ulBytesDone ) ;
}
```

PIPE.MAK

```
PIPE.EXE:                       PIPE.OBJ
        LINK386 @<<
PIPE
PIPE
PIPE
OS2386
PIPE
<<

PIPE.OBJ:                       PIPE.C
        ICC -C+ -Gm+ -Kb+ -Sm -Ss+ PIPE.C
```

PIPE.DEF

```
NAME PIPE WINDOWCOMPAT
DESCRIPTION 'Pipe example
             Copyright (c) 1992 by Arthur Panov.
             All rights reserved.'
STACKSIZE 16384
```

Now let us look at the implementation of the PIPE.C. First, a simple argument checking routine *BadArgs* is called, and upon determining the validity of the input arguments, the global variable *chToken* is set to SERVER_MODE or CLIENT_MODE. The argument checking function returns a zero if the arguments are acceptable, or an error BAD_INPUT_ARGS if there is a problem with the input arguments.

```c
USHORT BadArgs ( USHORT usNumArgs, PCHAR apchArgs [] )
{
   if ( usNumArgs == SERVER_MODE ) {
      chToken = SERVER_MODE ;
   } else
   if (( usNumArgs == CLIENT_MODE ) &&
       ( apchArgs [1] [0] != '?' )) {
      chToken = CLIENT_MODE ;
   } else
   if (( usNumArgs == MAX_INPUT_ARGS ) &&
       ( strlen ( apchArgs [2] ) <= MAX_SERV_NAME_LEN )) {
      chToken = CLIENT_MODE ;
   } else {
      printf ( "\n  Incorrect command line argument was "
               "entered" ) ;
      printf ( "\n  Please enter:\n" ) ;
      printf ( "\n  □[0;31;40m  pipe CLIENT SERVERNAME "
               " ( use for CLIENT operation ) " ) ;
      printf ( "\n  □[0;32;40m  pipe                   "
               " ( use for SERVER operation ) " ) ;
      printf ( "\n  □[0;37;40m \n" ) ;

      return BAD_INPUT_ARGS ;
   } /* endif */

   return 0 ;
}
```

Depending on the mode of operation, the corresponding initialization routines are called. The program uses ANSI escape sequences to provide color to the echoed keystrokes.

ConnToClient must issue two calls: *DosCreateNPipe* and *DosConnectNPipe*. Issuing the *DosConnectNPipe* is what allows the client to perform a *DosOpen* successfully. After the first necessary APIs are called successfully, a simple handshake operation is performed by reading a known string from the pipe, and writing a known string back.

```
arReturn = DosCreateNPipe ( achPipeName,
                            &hpPipe,
                            ulOpenMode,
                            ulPipeMode,
                            ulOutBufSize,
                            ulInpBufSize,
                            ulTimeOut ) ;

if ( !arReturn ) {
    arReturn = DosConnectNPipe ( hpPipe ) ;
    if ( !arReturn ) {
        arReturn = DosRead ( hpPipe,
                             achInitBuf,
                             ( ULONG ) HAND_SHAKE_LEN,
                             &ulBytesDone ) ;
```

DosCreateNPipe has seven arguments. The first parameter, *achPipeName*, is an ASCII string that contains the name of the pipe to be created. The second is a pointer to the pipe handle that will be returned when the function returns. The next parameter is the open mode used for the pipe. The flag used in the example is NP_ACCESS_DUPLEX, which provides inbound and outbound communication. The fourth parameter is the pipe mode. This parameter is a set of bit-fields that define the pipe mode. The flags used in this example are NP_WMESG | NP_RMESG | 0x01. These flags indicate the pipe can send and receive messages, and also that only one instance of the pipe can be created. The pipe can only be created in either byte or message mode. If a byte mode pipe is created, then *DosRead* and *DosWrite* must use byte stream mode when reading from or writing to the pipe. If a message mode pipe is created then *DosRead* and *DosWrite* will automatically use the first two bytes of each message, called the header, to determine the size of the message. Message mode pipes can be read from and written to using byte or message streams. Byte mode pipes, on the other hand, can only be used in byte stream mode. If a message stream is used, the operating system will encode the message header without the user having to calculate the value. Care should be taken when deciding on the size of the buffers to be used during communications. It is a good idea for the transaction buffer to be two bytes greater than the largest expected message.

DosConnectNPipe only takes one argument, the named pipe handle.

When the pipe application is started in the client mode, the initialization call is different. *ConnToServer* must perform a *DosOpen* first in order to obtain a pipe handle. Once the pipe handle is obtained, the application can freely read from the pipe and write to the pipe. In this case the first write/read pair is used for primitive handshaking communication.

```
arReturn = DosOpen ( achPipeName,
                     &hpPipe,
                     &ulActionTaken,
                     0,
                     0,
                     ulOpenFlag,
                     ulOpenMode,
                     0 ) ;
```

The parameter *ulOpenFlag* contains the open flag OPEN_ACTION_OPEN_IF_EXISTS. The parameter *ulOpenMode* contains the following flags: OPEN_FLAGS_WRITE_THROUGH | OPEN_FLAGS_FAIL_ON_ERROR | OPEN_FLAGS_RANDOM | OPEN_SHARE_DENYNONE | OPEN_ACCESS_READWRITE.

Next, the *while* loop is entered, and it can only be stopped if an API error is encountered, or if the user presses the F3 function key at the pipe server. Notice that a simple switch-case-break structure is used to implement the different modes of operation of the pipe program. The *SendToClient* and the *RecvFromServer* routines are very straightforward *DosWrite* and *DosRead* API implementation. The buffer that is being transmitted from the server to the client represents the character received from the keyboard buffer attached to the pipe server application. The reason for using a double word is to allow for the F1–F12 function keys translation and some other extended keys translation to occur. The function key keystroke generates two characters; the first is always a 0x00, followed by the 0xYY, where YY is a unique function key identifier.

```
while ( !arReturn && ( chToken != DISCON_MODE )) {

   switch ( chToken ) {
   case SERVER_MODE:
     usHiCh = getch ( ) ;
     if (( usHiCh == FUNC_KEYS_CHAR ) ||
         ( usHiCh == EXTD_KEYS_CHAR )) {
       usLoCh = getch ( ) ;
     } else {
       usLoCh = usHiCh ;
     } /* endif */

     ulHiLoCh = (( ULONG ) usHiCh << 16 ) |
                ( ULONG ) usLoCh ;

     arReturn  = SendToClient ( ulHiLoCh ) ;
```

The remote pipe connection from the client to the server is achieved by starting the pipe client with the following command line *pipe client mysrvr*, where *mysrvr* is the server name. The pipe name that is created inside the client program will have the following format:

local   named pipe name : \PIPE\MYPIPE
remote   named pipe name : \\MYSRVR\PIPE\MYPIPE

The functionality that this example application provides is the same in both remote and local connectivity modes. As a matter of fact, the client does not differentiate between the remote and local connectivity; only the name is significant. This is the beauty of the named pipes IPC!

The main reason for choosing pipes as an IPC method is ease of implementation, but it is not the best choice for all cases. The pipes are only useful when a process has to send information to or receive information from another process. Even though it is possible to allow pipe connections with multiple processes, it is always necessary to implement connect and disconnect algorithms for such situations. The remote connection advantage of named pipes sometimes outweighs the complexity of connect-disconnect algorithms, since it is not possible to communicate remotely with queues, and remote shared memory.

Gotcha!

It is not unusual for an application to receive a return value of ERROR_TOO_MANY_HANDLES when attempting to open additional pipes. The system initially allows 20 file handles per process, and once the limit is reached, the above error will appear. To prevent this from happening, you must issue the *DosSetMaxFH(ULONG ulNumberHandles)* call. This call will be successful provided that the system resources have not been exhausted. It is a good idea to issue this call only when needed since additional file handles consume system resources that may be used elsewhere in the system.

5.2 QUEUE.C Example

This brings us to our next example: QUEUE.C. In the QUEUE.C example the communication process is a little bit more complex than the one in PIPE.C. Here, the point is to show how several different processes can communicate with one central process. The functionality is similar to the PIPE.C program, but with one key difference: the queue server process does not send anything to the queue client processes. In fact, only the queue client process can send information to the server, but this does not mean that the queue server cannot issue a *DosWriteQueue* itself; it is just not part of this example. It is left to the reader to implement this additional functionality. By using the QUEUE.C as the basis you can easily add the *WriteToQue* function call to enhance the QUEUE.C example program to perform the abovementioned operation. The QUEUE.C makes use not only of the OS/2 queues, but also of named shared memory segments.

The concept of an OS/2 queue is somewhat simple. It is in fact an ordered set of elements. The elements are 32-bit values that are passed from the client to the server of the queue. The server of the queue is the process that created the queue by issuing the *DosCreateQueue* API call. Only the server of the queue can read from the queue. When the queue is read, one element is removed from the queue. The server and clients can issue write, query, and close-the-queue calls, but only the server can issue create, read, peek, and purge calls. The queue client must issue a *DosOpenQueue* call prior to attempting to write elements to the queue, or querying the queue elements. The queue elements can be prioritized and processed in particular order. The order depends on the *ulQueueFlags* value used when creating the queue. This value cannot be changed once the queue has been created. There are three values allowed:

0 — First In First Out   (FIFO)
1 — Last In First Out   (LIFO)
2 — Priority   (0–15)

Specifying a priority will cause the *DosReadQueue* API to read the queue elements in descending priority order. Priority 15 is the highest, and 0 is the lowest. FIFO order will be used for the elements with equal priority. The elements of the queue can be used to pass data to the server directly or indirectly. The indirection comes from using pointers to shared memory. When pointers are used, the shared memory can be of two types: named shared memory and unnamed shared memory. The named shared memory is generally used by the related processes, while the unnamed shared memory is used by the rest. In the QUEUE.C the named shared memory method is implemented. OS/2 queues do not perform any data copying. They only pass pointers, and leave the rest of the work for the programmer.

The QUEUE.C example is best illustrated by starting several OS/2 window sessions from the desktop and making all of them visible to the user at the same time. One must start the queue server process first by typing *queue* followed by return from the command line. Once the queue is created and the queue server is started the queue clients can use the queue to pass various information to the queue server. In this case the information that is passed is the keystrokes that are entered by the user from each one of the client processes. This procedure is best described by the Figure 5.1.

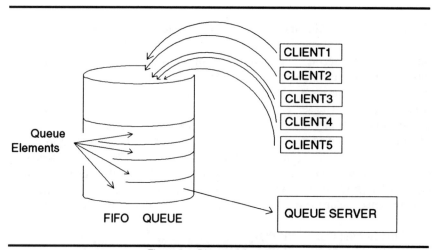

Figure 5.1. Diagram of a queue.

Each one of the queue clients will send keystroke characters to the queue server via FIFO queue. Once the characters are received by the queue server they will be displayed in color depending on the client that sent them. The following table describes the queue client text colors:

NUMBER	COLOR
Client 1	Red
Client 2	Green
Client 3	Yellow
Client 4	Blue
Client 5	Magenta

The QUEUE.C only allows up to five active queue clients at any one time. Once the maximum number of clients has been reached, entering *queue client* followed by a carriage return from the command line will produce a program error message describing the maximum number of clients.

Here is the complete listing of QUEUE.C:

QUEUE.C

```
#define INCL_DOSQUEUES
#define INCL_DOSMEMMGR
#define INCL_DOSPROCESS
#define INCL_DOSERRORS
#define INCL_DOSSEMAPHORES

#include <os2.h>
#include <stdio.h>
#include <stdlib.h>
#include <string.h>
#include <conio.h>

#define MAX_INPUT_ARGS          2
#define MAX_CLIENTS             5
#define SERVER_MODE             1
#define CLIENT_MODE             2
#define DISCON_MODE             3
#define BAD_INPUT_ARGS          99
#define MAX_COLOR_LEN           11
#define DEFAULT_QUE_NAME        "\\QUEUES\\MYQUEUE"
#define DEFAULT_SEM_NAME        "\\SEM32\\EVENTQUE"
#define DEFAULT_PAGE_SIZE       4096
#define DEFAULT_QUE_FLAG        QUE_FIFO | QUE_CONVERT_ADDRESS
#define DEFAULT_SEG_NAME        "\\SHAREMEM\\MYQUEUE.SHR"
#define DEFAULT_SEG_FLAG        PAG_WRITE | PAG_COMMIT
#define TOKEN_F2_SWITCH         0x0000003CL
#define TOKEN_F3_DISCON         0x0000003DL
#define RETURN_CHAR             0x0D
#define LINE_FEED_CHAR          0x0A
#define FUNC_KEYS_CHAR          0x00
#define EXTD_KEYS_CHAR          0xE0
#define CLEAR_HI_WORD           0x0000FFFFL
#define ULONG_NULL              0L
#define PROGRAM_ERROR           999
#define CLIENT0_COLOR           "□[0;31;40m"
#define CLIENT1_COLOR           "□[0;32;40m"
#define CLIENT2_COLOR           "□[0;33;40m"
#define CLIENT3_COLOR           "□[0;34;40m"
#define CLIENT4_COLOR           "□[0;35;40m"

typedef struct  _MYQUEUESTRUC {
   BYTE szColor [MAX_COLOR_LEN] ;
   PID ulPid ;
} MYQUEUESTRUC, * PMYQUEUESTRUC ;

HQUEUE          hqQueue ;
USHORT          usClientIndex = MAX_CLIENTS ;
PVOID           pvData ;
HEV             hsmSem ;
```

```
PMYQUEUESTRUC pmqsClient ;
CHAR          chToken = 0 ;
CHAR          aachColors [MAX_CLIENTS] [MAX_COLOR_LEN] ;

USHORT BadArgs ( USHORT usNumArgs, PCHAR apchArgs [] ) ;
APIRET InitServerQueEnv ( VOID ) ;
APIRET InitClientQueEnv ( VOID ) ;
APIRET ReadFromQue ( PULONG pulHiLoCh ) ;
APIRET WriteToQue ( ULONG ulHiLoCh ) ;

INT main ( USHORT usNumArgs, PCHAR apchArgs [] )
{
    USHORT    usHiCh ;
    USHORT    usLoCh ;
    ULONG     ulHiLoCh ;
    APIRET    arReturn ;

    usHiCh = 0 ;
    usLoCh = 0 ;
    ulHiLoCh = 0 ;

    strcpy ( aachColors [0] , CLIENT0_COLOR ) ;
    strcpy ( aachColors [1] , CLIENT1_COLOR ) ;
    strcpy ( aachColors [2] , CLIENT2_COLOR ) ;
    strcpy ( aachColors [3] , CLIENT3_COLOR ) ;
    strcpy ( aachColors [4] , CLIENT4_COLOR ) ;

    if ( !BadArgs ( usNumArgs, apchArgs )) {

        if ( chToken == SERVER_MODE ) {
            printf ( "\n □ [0 ; 36 ; 40m" ) ;
            printf ( " Server process is creating" ) ;
            printf ( "and initializing the Queue...\n" ) ;
            arReturn = InitServerQueEnv ( ) ;
        } else

        if ( chToken == CLIENT_MODE ) {
            printf ( "\n □ [0 ; 37 ; 40m" ) ;
            printf ( " Client process is initializing" ) ;
            printf ( " and connecting to the Queue...\n" ) ;
            arReturn = InitClientQueEnv ( ) ;

        } else {
            arReturn = PROGRAM_ERROR ;
        } /* endif */

        while ( !arReturn && ( chToken != DISCON_MODE )) {

            switch ( chToken ) {

            case SERVER_MODE:
                if ( kbhit ( )) {
                    usHiCh = getch ( ) ;
                    if (( usHiCh == FUNC_KEYS_CHAR ) ||
                        ( usHiCh == EXTD_KEYS_CHAR )) {
                        usLoCh = getch ( ) ;
```

```
         } else {
           usLoCh = usHiCh ;
         } /* endif */

         ulHiLoCh = ( usHiCh << 16 ) | usLoCh ;

         if ( ulHiLoCh == TOKEN_F3_DISCON ) {
           chToken = DISCON_MODE ;
         } /* endif */

      } /* endif */

      arReturn = ReadFromQue ( &ulHiLoCh ) ;
      if ( !arReturn ) {
         usLoCh = ( USHORT ) ( ulHiLoCh & 0x0000FFFFL ) ;
         usHiCh = ( USHORT ) ( ulHiLoCh >> 16 ) ;

         if ( usHiCh == usLoCh ) {
            putch ( usHiCh ) ;

            if ( usHiCh == RETURN_CHAR ) {
               putch ( LINE_FEED_CHAR ) ;
            } /* endif */
         } /* endif */

      } else
      if ( arReturn == ERROR_QUE_EMPTY ) {
         arReturn = ( SHORT ) NULL ;
      } /* endif */

      break ;

case CLIENT_MODE:
   usHiCh = getch ( ) ;

   if (( usHiCh == FUNC_KEYS_CHAR ) ||
      ( usHiCh == EXTD_KEYS_CHAR )) {
      usLoCh = getch ( ) ;

   } else {
      usLoCh = usHiCh ;
      putch ( usHiCh ) ;

      if ( usHiCh == RETURN_CHAR ) {
         putch ( LINE_FEED_CHAR ) ;
      } /* endif */

   } /* endif */

   ulHiLoCh = (( ULONG ) usHiCh << 16 ) |
      ( ULONG ) usLoCh ;
   if ( ulHiLoCh == TOKEN_F3_DISCON ) {
      chToken = DISCON_MODE ;
      pmqsClient [usClientIndex] .szColor [0] = '\0' ;
      pmqsClient [usClientIndex] .ulPid = 0 ;
```

```
              } else {
                 arReturn = WriteToQue ( ulHiLoCh ) ;
              } /* endif */
              break ;

           default:
              arReturn = PROGRAM_ERROR ;
              break ;
           } /* endswitch */
        } /* endif */
     } /* endif */

     if ( arReturn == 0 ) {
        arReturn = DosCloseQueue ( hqQueue ) ;
     } /* endif */

     printf ( "\n □ [0 ; 37 ; 40m" ) ;
     return arReturn ;
}

USHORT BadArgs ( USHORT usNumArgs, PCHAR apchArgs [] )
{
   if ( usNumArgs == SERVER_MODE ) {
      chToken =  SERVER_MODE ;
   } else
   if (( usNumArgs == CLIENT_MODE ) &&
       ( apchArgs [1] [0] != '?' )) {
      chToken =  CLIENT_MODE ;
   } else {
      printf ( "\n Incorrect command line argument was entered" ) ;
      printf ( "\n  Please enter:\n" ) ;
      printf ( "\n  □ [0 ; 37 ; 40m  QUEUE CLIENT" ) ;
      printf ( "use for CLIENT operation ) " ) ;
      printf ( "\n  □ [0 ; 36 ; 40m  QUEUE" ) ;
      printf ( "         ( use for SERVER operation ) " ) ;
      printf ( "\n  □ [0 ; 37 ; 40m \n" ) ;

      return BAD_INPUT_ARGS ;
   } /* endif */

   return 0 ;
}

APIRET InitServerQueEnv ( VOID )
{
   APIRET arReturn ;
   SHORT sIndex ;

   arReturn = DosAllocSharedMem(( PVOID ) &pmqsClient,
                                 DEFAULT_SEG_NAME,
                                 DEFAULT_PAGE_SIZE,
                                 DEFAULT_SEG_FLAG ) ;
```

```
    if ( !arReturn ) {
        arReturn = DosCreateQueue ( &hqQueue,
                                     DEFAULT_QUE_FLAG,
                                     DEFAULT_QUE_NAME ) ;

        if ( !arReturn ) {
            printf ( "\n  Queue created successfully \n" ) ;
            for ( sIndex = 0 ; sIndex < MAX_CLIENTS ; sIndex ++ ) {
                pmqsClient [sIndex] .szColor [0] = ( BYTE ) NULL ;
                pmqsClient [sIndex] .ulPid = ( PID ) NULL ;
            } /* endfor */

            arReturn = DosCreateEventSem ( DEFAULT_SEM_NAME,
                                           &hsmSem,
                                           ULONG_NULL,
                                           TRUE ) ;
        } else {
            printf ( "\n  DosCreateQueue API returned "
                     "%02d\n",
                     arReturn ) ;
        } /* endif */
    } else {
        printf ( " \n  Could not allocate "
                 "Shared Memory ( %02d ) \n",
                 arReturn ) ;
    } /* endif */

    return arReturn ;
}

APIRET InitClientQueEnv ( VOID )
{
    APIRET arReturn ;
    SHORT sIndex ;
    PID pidOwner ;

    arReturn = DosGetNamedSharedMem(( PVOID ) &pmqsClient,
                                      DEFAULT_SEG_NAME,
                                      PAG_WRITE | PAG_READ ) ;

    if ( !arReturn ) {
        for ( sIndex = 0 ; sIndex <= MAX_CLIENTS ; sIndex ++ ) {
            if (( pmqsClient [sIndex] .szColor [0] == 0 ) &&
                ( sIndex < MAX_CLIENTS )) {
                strcpy ( pmqsClient [sIndex] .szColor,
                         aachColors [sIndex] ) ;
                usClientIndex = sIndex ;
                break ;
            } /* endif */
        } /* endfor */

        if ( sIndex > MAX_CLIENTS ) {
            arReturn = PROGRAM_ERROR ;
            printf ( "\n\n  Maximum number of clients is FIVE !\n" ) ;
        } /* endif */
```

```
        if ( !arReturn ) {
            arReturn = DosOpenQueue ( &pidOwner,
                                      &hqQueue,
                                      DEFAULT_QUE_NAME ) ;
            if ( !arReturn ) {
                printf ( " %s", aachColors [usClientIndex] ) ;
                printf ( "\n Client #%d has connected to the Queue\n",
                         usClientIndex ) ;
            } /* endif */
        } /* endif */
    } /* endif */

    return arReturn ;
}

APIRET ReadFromQue ( PULONG pulHiLoCh )
{
    APIRET          arReturn ;
    REQUESTDATA     rdRequest ;
    ULONG           ulSzData ;
    BYTE            bPriority ;
    SHORT           sIndex ;

    arReturn = DosReadQueue ( hqQueue,
                              &rdRequest,
                              &ulSzData,
                              &pvData,
                              0,
                              DCWW_NOWAIT,
                              &bPriority,
                              hsmSem ) ;

    if ( !arReturn ) {
        pmqsClient [rdRequest.ulData] .ulPid = rdRequest.pid ;
        * pulHiLoCh = ulSzData ;

        for ( sIndex = 0 ; sIndex < MAX_COLOR_LEN - 1 ; sIndex ++ ) {
            putch ( pmqsClient [rdRequest.ulData].szColor [sIndex] ) ;
        } /* endfor */
    } /* endif */

    return arReturn ;
}

APIRET WriteToQue ( ULONG ulHiLoCh )
{
    return DosWriteQueue ( hqQueue,
                           ( ULONG ) usClientIndex,
                           ulHiLoCh,
                           pvData,
                           ULONG_NULL ) ;
}
```

QUEUE.MAK

```
QUEUE.EXE:                        QUEUE.OBJ
      LINK386 @<<
QUEUE
QUEUE
QUEUE
OS2386
QUEUE
<<

QUEUE.OBJ:                        QUEUE.C
      ICC -C+ -Gm+ -Kb+ -Sm -Ss+ QUEUE.C
```

QUEUE.DEF

```
NAME QUEUE WINDOWCOMPAT
DESCRIPTION 'Queue example
            Copyright (c) 1992 by Arthur Panov.
            All rights reserved.'
STACKSIZE 16384
```

Now that you are somewhat familiar with the intended operation of the QUEUE.C, the program itself can be discussed in greater detail. The structure of the program is almost identical to PIPE.C.

The main differences during the initialization are in the *InitServerQueEnv* and *InitClientQueEnv* routines. If the mode of operation is *SERVER_MODE* then the *InitServerQueEnv* is called:

```
APIRET InitServerQueEnv ( VOID )
{
   APIRET arReturn ;
   SHORT sIndex ;

   arReturn = DosAllocSharedMem(( PVOID ) &pmqsClient,
                                DEFAULT_SEG_NAME,
                                DEFAULT_PAGE_SIZE,
                                DEFAULT_SEG_FLAG ) ;

   if ( !arReturn ) {
      arReturn = DosCreateQueue ( &hqQueue,
                                  DEFAULT_QUE_FLAG,
                                  DEFAULT_QUE_NAME ) ;

      if ( !arReturn ) {
         printf ( "\n  Queue created successfully \n" ) ;
         for ( sIndex = 0 ; sIndex < MAX_CLIENTS ; sIndex ++ ) {
            pmqsClient [sIndex] .szColor [0] = ( BYTE ) NULL ;
            pmqsClient [sIndex] .ulPid = ( PID ) NULL ;
         } /* endfor */
```

```
              arReturn = DosCreateEventSem ( DEFAULT_SEM_NAME,
                                             &hsmSem,
                                             ULONG_NULL,
                                             TRUE ) ;
        } else {
           printf ( "\n  DosCreateQueue API returned "
                    "%02d\n",
                    arReturn ) ;
        } /* endif */
    } else {
        printf ( " \n  Could not allocate "
                 "Shared Memory ( %02d ) \n",
                 arReturn ) ;
    } /* endif */

    return arReturn ;
}
```

First the attempt is made to allocate the named shared memory segment in order for all of the clients and the server to be able to communicate with each other. This shared named memory segment contains client-specific information. The MYQUESTRUC structure contains the process ID and a text color ANSI escape sequence.

```
typedef struct  _MYQUEUESTRUC {
   BYTE szColor [MAX_COLOR_LEN] ;
   PID ulPid ;
} MYQUEUESTRUC, * PMYQUEUESTRUC ;
```

The memory map in Figure 5.2 shows the way the shared named memory segment is used:

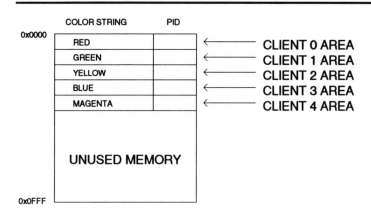

SHARED MEMORY MAP (\SHAREMEM\MYQUEUE.SHR)

Figure 5.2. Shared memory map.

A client area is dedicated to each one of the queue clients and contains the entire *MYQUESTRUC* structure. After the shared memory is allocated, the queue server creates the queue and initializes the named shared segment to nulls. The last API that is called by the initialization routine is *DosCreateEventSem*. Even though the semaphore that is created will not be used as a semaphore during this application, the semaphore handle is required later for the *DosReadQueue*. The reason that the semaphore handle is required in this case is because the queue is read in nonblocking mode, and the API requires a semaphore handle in that case. Choosing to read the queue in nonblocking fashion allows the queue server to scan for keystrokes, and the keystroke that the queue server will be looking for is the F3 function key, which will allow the application to exit. This operation will become clearer as the QUEUE.C discussion is continued.

Next let us look at the initialization of the queue client environment. The *InitClientQueEnv* function call attempts to obtain the named shared memory handle, and once the handle is returned the queue client begins to scan the client areas, checking for the valid color string. The moment the client finds an unused color string area it assumes it is free and copies its color attribute there, and it also saves the unique position identification number in the global *sIndex* variable. If the client determines that five other clients are already active, it will display an error message and exit. On the other hand, if the *sIndex* value is acceptable (less than maximum number of clients), the client will issue the *DosOpenQueue* API call, thus completing the initialization by connecting to the queue.

```
APIRET InitClientQueEnv ( VOID )
{
   APIRET arReturn ;
   SHORT sIndex ;
   PID pidOwner ;

   arReturn = DosGetNamedSharedMem(( PVOID ) &pmqsClient,
                                   DEFAULT_SEG_NAME,
                                   PAG_WRITE | PAG_READ ) ;

   if ( !arReturn ) {
      for ( sIndex = 0 ; sIndex <= MAX_CLIENTS ; sIndex ++ ) {
         if (( pmqsClient [sIndex] .szColor [0] == 0 ) &&
            ( sIndex < MAX_CLIENTS )) {
            strcpy ( pmqsClient [sIndex] .szColor,
                 aachColors [sIndex] ) ;
            usClientIndex = sIndex ;
            break ;
         } /* endif */
      } /* endfor */

      if ( sIndex > MAX_CLIENTS ) {
         arReturn = PROGRAM_ERROR ;
         printf ( "\n\n  Maximum number of clients is FIVE !\n" ) ;
      } /* endif */

      if ( !arReturn ) {
         arReturn = DosOpenQueue ( &pidOwner,
                                   &hqQueue,
                                   DEFAULT_QUE_NAME ) ;
         if ( !arReturn ) {
            printf ( " %s", aachColors [usClientIndex] ) ;
            printf ( "\n Client #%d has connected to the Queue\n",
                 usClientIndex ) ;
         } /* endif */
      } /* endif */
   } /* endif */

   return arReturn ;
}
```

Once the initialization is complete, the main body of the program is a *while* loop:

```
while ( !arReturn && ( chToken != DISCON_MODE )) {

    switch ( chToken ) {

    case SERVER_MODE:
        if ( kbhit ( )) {
            usHiCh = getch ( ) ;
            if (( usHiCh == FUNC_KEYS_CHAR ) ||
                ( usHiCh == EXTD_KEYS_CHAR )) {
                usLoCh = getch ( ) ;

            } else {
                usLoCh = usHiCh ;
            } /* endif */

            ulHiLoCh = ( usHiCh << 16 ) | usLoCh ;

            if ( ulHiLoCh == TOKEN_F3_DISCON ) {
                chToken = DISCON_MODE ;
            } /* endif */

        } /* endif */

        arReturn = ReadFromQue ( &ulHiLoCh ) ;
        if ( !arReturn ) {
            usLoCh = ( USHORT ) ( ulHiLoCh & 0x0000FFFFL ) ;
            usHiCh = ( USHORT ) ( ulHiLoCh >> 16 ) ;

            if ( usHiCh == usLoCh ) {
                putch ( usHiCh ) ;

                if ( usHiCh == RETURN_CHAR ) {
                    putch ( LINE_FEED_CHAR ) ;
                } /* endif */
            } /* endif */

        } else
        if ( arReturn == ERROR_QUE_EMPTY ) {
            arReturn = ( SHORT ) NULL ;
        } /* endif */

        break ;

    case CLIENT_MODE:
        usHiCh = getch ( ) ;

        if (( usHiCh == FUNC_KEYS_CHAR ) ||
            ( usHiCh == EXTD_KEYS_CHAR )) {
            usLoCh = getch ( ) ;

        } else {
            usLoCh = usHiCh ;
            putch ( usHiCh ) ;

            if ( usHiCh == RETURN_CHAR ) {
                putch ( LINE_FEED_CHAR ) ;
            } /* endif */
```

```
      } /* endif */

      ulHiLoCh = (( ULONG ) usHiCh << 16 ) |
         ( ULONG ) usLoCh ;
      if ( ulHiLoCh == TOKEN_F3_DISCON ) {
         chToken = DISCON_MODE ;
         pmqsClient [usClientIndex] .szColor [0] = '\0' ;
         pmqsClient [usClientIndex] .ulPid = 0 ;

      } else {
         arReturn = WriteToQue ( ulHiLoCh ) ;
      } /* endif */
      break ;

   default:
      arReturn = PROGRAM_ERROR ;
      break ;
   } /* endswitch */
} /* endif */
```

The queue server performs a series of simple functions. First, the server checks to see if there is a keyboard character waiting and, if that character corresponds to the F3 function key, the server sets the *uchToken* = DISCON_MODE and exits. Any other characters are ignored. Upon checking the keyboard, the queue server attempts to read the queue; if any elements are present, they are decoded and displayed in their corresponding color, otherwise the server loops to check the keyboard buffer again, and so on. The ERROR_QUE_EMPTY is ignored and reset to zero. For this application, receiving this particular error is part of normal operating procedure. At this point you may ask yourself a question about this particular implementation. Why is it that the queue is read continuously in nonblocking mode when it can be read in blocking mode, which will assure a returned queue element prior to completing the *DosReadQueue* call? The answer is simple. If the *DosReadQueue* API was implemented with the blocking flag set true, it would be difficult to read the keyboard buffer and look for the F3 function key. It is possible to implement a separate thread that will either wait on the event semaphore and only display the characters when the semaphore was posted, or read the keyboard and watch for the F3 function key. Either method would introduce more complexity to this sample program and that is the reasoning behind the current implementation. This does not mean that there is not a better way to implement this example, but the point here is to show the differences between the queues and the pipes.

When the program is operating in the client mode, it does nothing more than read a keystroke character, and write that character to the queue by issuing a *WriteToQue* function call, which in turn calls the *DosWriteQueue* API.

It is clear from this example that queues are somewhat cumbersome to implement, but they are very useful in the situations when several processes have to talk to another single process, even if the processes are unrelated.

Please also note that there exists a potential timing problem in the *InitClientQueEnv* function. If multiple clients decide to initialize concurrently, there will be a race condition. To avoid a potential problem a Mutex semaphore should be installed to protect the access to the shared memory. The implemenation is left as an exercise for the reader.

5.3 Semaphores and SEMFLAG.C Example

There are three different types of semaphores: event, mutex, and muxwait. Event semaphores are used in the following example where a thread needs to notify other threads that some event has occurred. Mutex semaphores enable multiple threads to coordinate their access to some shared resource. Muxwait semaphores enable threads to wait for multiple events to occur.

With this brief introduction here is the last example: SEMFLAG.C. This program uses the concept of semaphores for task or event synchronization, also known as signaling. If a process is waiting for a resource to become available, such as file or port access rights, and the resource is being used by another process, the current task must wait. In the earlier DOS operating system the synchronization was primitively accomplished through the use of flags. One would set a flag, and wait for the flag to be cleared, thus signifying that the resource was free to be used by someone else that needed it. Since only one process could execute at one time under DOS, this was an acceptable form of pseudo-interprocess communication. Under OS/2, however, it is not a good idea to use flags to perform the equivalent semaphore functions. An example of bad flag synchronization processing would be something like this:

```
while (FlagBusy);    /* Wait for flag to clear */
```

If a task requires this type of processing a semaphore should be used. The SEMFLAG.C example demonstrates the difference in machine cycles that is spent waiting for a semaphore to clear as opposed to waiting for a flag to clear. The SEMFLAG.EXE creates several threads, and then decides to wait for a flag/semaphore. While this wait is in process the user is free to type characters at the keyboard, which will be immediately echoed to the console. Using the flags to perform the wait inside the threads will dramatically increase CPU usage, and the keystrokes will appear delayed. On the other hand, using the

semaphore concept, the user is free to type the characters at will with no
noticeable delay between the input-output cycles. This example allows the
user to change the number of threads waiting based on the input command line
argument. Even with as little as 30 threads the difference between waiting on
a flags and waiting on a semaphores is dramatic.

SEMFLAG.C

```
#define INCL_DOSPROCESS
#define INCL_DOSSEMAPHORES

#include <os2.h>
#include <stdio.h>
#include <stdlib.h>
#include <string.h>
#include <conio.h>

#define DEFAULT_THREAD_FLAGS      0
#define DEFAULT_THREAD_STACK      0x4000
#define MY_BEGIN_SEMAPHORE        "\\SEM32\\BEGIN"
#define MAX_SEM_WAIT              - 1L
#define DEFAULT_NUM_THREADS       10
#define MAX_NUM_THREADS           255
#define SEMAPHORE_STATE           1
#define WAIT_FLAG_STATE           0

typedef struct _OPTIONS {
   BYTE       bWait ;
   HEV        hevKillThread ;
   BYTE       usMode ;
} OPTIONS, *POPTIONS ;

VOID APIENTRY MyThreadOne ( POPTIONS poOptions ) ;

INT main ( USHORT usNumArgs, PCHAR apchArgs [] )
{
   USHORT          usNumThreads ;
   OPTIONS         oOptions ;
   USHORT          usIndex ;
   TID             tidThread ;
   INT             iCharRead ;
   USHORT          usReturn ;

   if ( usNumArgs > 1 ) {

      //-----------------------------------------------------------
      // Insure that usNumThreads is in the range 1<<x<<MAX
      //-----------------------------------------------------------

      usNumThreads = max ( min ( atoi ( apchArgs [1] ) ,
                      MAX_NUM_THREADS ) ,
                      1 ) ;
   } else {
      usNumThreads = DEFAULT_NUM_THREADS ;
   } /* endif */
```

```
    if ( usNumArgs > 2 ) {
       oOptions.usMode = SEMAPHORE_STATE ;
       usReturn = DosCreateEventSem ( MY_BEGIN_SEMAPHORE,
                                      &oOptions.hevKillThread,
                                      NULLHANDLE,
                                      FALSE ) ;
    } else {
       oOptions.usMode = WAIT_FLAG_STATE ;
       oOptions.bWait = TRUE ;
    } /* endif */

    for ( usIndex = 0 ; usIndex < usNumThreads ; usIndex ++ ) {
       printf ( " Starting Thread #%2d\n", usIndex + 1 ) ;
       usReturn = DosCreateThread ( &tidThread,
                                    ( PFNTHREAD ) MyThreadOne,
                                    ( ULONG ) &oOptions,
                                    DEFAULT_THREAD_FLAGS,
                                    DEFAULT_THREAD_STACK ) ;
    } /* endfor */

    printf ( "\n Start typing and experience " ) ;
    printf ( "the speed of flags for yourself..." ) ;
    printf ( "\n >> lower case 'x' exits << \n\n" ) ;

    fflush ( stdout ) ;

    iCharRead = getche ( ) ;

    while ( iCharRead != 'x' ) {
       iCharRead = getche ( ) ;
    } /* endwhile */

    usReturn = DosPostEventSem ( oOptions.hevKillThread ) ;
    DosSleep ( 1000L ) ;
    usReturn = DosCloseEventSem ( oOptions.hevKillThread ) ;

    return usReturn ;
}
```

```
VOID APIENTRY MyThreadOne ( POPTIONS poOptions )
{
   if ( poOptions -> usMode == SEMAPHORE_STATE ) {
       DosWaitEventSem ( poOptions -> hevKillThread,
                         MAX_SEM_WAIT ) ;
   } else {
      while ( poOptions -> bWait ) {

         //---------------------------------------------------------
         // This area is left blank to demonstrate the superiority
         // of semaphores!
         //---------------------------------------------------------

      } /* endwhile */
   } /* endif */
   return ;
}
```

SEMFLAG.MAK

```
SEMFLAG.EXE:                        SEMFLAG.OBJ
      LINK386 @<<
SEMFLAG
SEMFLAG
SEMFLAG
OS2386
SEMFLAG
<<

SEMFLAG.OBJ:                        SEMFLAG.C
      ICC -C+ -Gm+ -Kb+ -Sm -Ss+ SEMFLAG.C
```

SEMFLAG.DEF

```
NAME SEMFLAG WINDOWCOMPAT
DESCRIPTION 'Semaphore example
            Copyright (c) 1992 by Arthur Panov.
            All rights reserved.'
STACKSIZE 16384
```

The first command line argument should be a number in the range of 11 – 255. The default number of threads created is 10, and specifying a number less than 10 is unnecessary. The second command line argument, which can be anything so long as one is present, specifies SEMAPHORE_STATE mode. This means that the threads will wait on a semaphore. If the second argument is not present, the threads will wait on a flag. It is not recommended to go over 50 threads with the second command line argument not set, thus designating the WAIT_FLAG_STATE mode condition. Even on a superfast 486 the system is brought down to the point of being useless. For example, once the CTRL-ESC keys are pressed, it may take the system over 5 minutes to paint the PM/WPS screen. One is welcome to experiment, but don't expect performance if the number of threads is 50 or greater, and the WAIT_FLAG_STATE mode is specified. The SEMAPHORE_STATE mode, on the other hand, is perfectly capable of handling 255 threads in the wait state, and will still provide reasonable keyboard and display response.

Once all of the threads have been created, the main thread enters a read-and-display loop. Lower x will cause it to stop reading the keyboard and to proceed directly to the cleanup task.

Depending on the mode of operation, the semaphore is posted and the program waits for one second for the threads to complete their execution. Finally, the semaphore is closed. In the WAIT_FLAG_STATE mode, the value of the flag is changed to FALSE (0), and one second is used to allow the threads to die gracefully.

At the thread level, the input parameter is read, and the mode of operation determination is made. If the mode is WAIT_FLAG_STATE the *while(flag);* loop is used. If the mode is SEMAPHORE_STATE the semaphore condition is used.

```
VOID APIENTRY    MyThreadOne(ULONG ulInputArg)
{
    struct MY_GLOBAL_PTR * PassedFromMain;

    PassedFromMain = (struct MY_GLOBAL_PTR *)ulInputArg;

    if (PassedFromMain->fExeModeFlag == SEMAPHORE_STATE)
        DosWaitEventSem(PassedFromMain->hevBeginSemHandle,
                    MAX_SEM_WAIT);
    else
        while(PassedFromMain->fWaitFlag)
        {
/* This area is left blank to demonstrate sempahore superiority */
        }

}
```

DosWaitEventSem blocks code execution until the semaphore is cleared. Once the semaphore is reset, all of the threads awaken at the same time.

Chapter 6

Windows and Messages

The first thing to understand when beginning Presentation Manager programming is the concept of a window. A window is a graphical image of a rectangle that sits on the screen, and is used to provide a uniform interface with which a user can interact. See Figure 6.1.

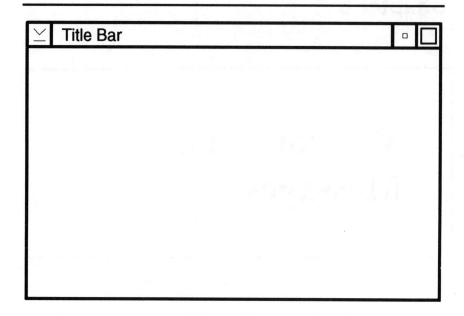

Figure 6.1. A window.

A window can be sized larger or smaller, it can be opened or closed, it can be made visible or invisible. Suffice it to say that there are a lot of things to do with a window.

Figure 6.2 looks like *one* window, but, in reality it is five windows:
- The frame window
- The title bar
- The system menu
- The maximize/minimize buttons
- The client window

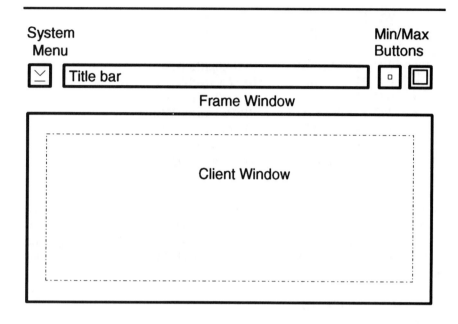

Figure 6.2. Drawing of a window's components.

Each of the five windows has a window procedure associated with it. The window procedure is a function that tells the window how to behave. Windows that share the same window procedure belong to the same window *class*. This is a familiar concept for those readers acquainted with object-oriented programming; however, for those who aren't, an example follows.

Imagine a fast food restaurant. Each item on the menu could be considered one class — a hot dog class, a hamburger class, and a pizza class. Suppose you could get mustard, mayo, relish, or cheese on your hot dog. You could use any combination of these four items. Each of these condiments would be a hot dog *style*.

The same is true for window classes. There are 19 predefined window classes. Some of the classes available for applications are:

- WC_FRAME   ((PSZ)0xffff0001L)
- WC_COMBOBOX   ((PSZ)0xffff0002L)
- WC_BUTTON   ((PSZ)0xffff0003L)
- WC_MENU   ((PSZ)0xffff0004L)

- WC_STATIC   ((PSZ)0xffff0005L)
- WC_ENTRYFIELD   ((PSZ)0xffff0006L)
- WC_LISTBOX   ((PSZ)0xffff0007L)
- WC_SCROLLBAR   ((PSZ)0xffff0008L)
- WC_TITLEBAR   ((PSZ)0xffff0009L)
- WC_MLE   ((PSZ)0xffff000AL)
- WC_SPINBUTTON   ((PSZ)0xffff0020L)
- WC_CONTAINER   ((PSZ)0xffff0025L)
- WC_SLIDER   ((PSZ)0xffff0026L)
- WC_VALUESET   ((PSZ)0xffff0027L)
- WC_NOTEBOOK   ((PSZ)0xffff0028L)

Each window class is very different from the other. Some of these predefined classes will be covered in later chapters. The client window belongs to a user-defined class. Each window class also contains a set of window styles specific to that class. There is a set of class styles available to all classes. The styles are:

- CS_MOVENOTIFY
- CS_SIZEREDRAW
- CS_HITTEST
- CS_PUBLIC
- CS_FRAME
- CS_CLIPCHILDREN
- CS_CLIPSIBLINGS
- CS_PARENTCLIP
- CS_SAVEBITS
- CS_SYNCPAINT

These styles will be covered later in this chapter.

Once you know a little bit about the window class the operating system gives you, you can decide which are best suited for your application, or, as most of us do-it-yourselfers will do, you can create your own. So, let's do just that.

WIN1.C

```
#define INCL_WIN
#define INCL_GPI

#include <os2.h>
#include <stdio.h>
#include <stdlib.h>
#include <string.h>
```

```
#define CLS_CLIENT                "WindowClass"

MRESULT EXPENTRY ClientWndProc ( HWND hwndWnd,
   ULONG ulMsg,
   MPARAM mpParm1,
   MPARAM mpParm2 ) ;

INT main ( VOID )
{
   HAB        habAnchor ;
   HMQ        hmqQueue ;
   ULONG      ulFlags ;
   HWND       hwndFrame ;
   HWND       hwndClient ;
   BOOL       bLoop ;
   QMSG       qmMsg ;

   habAnchor = WinInitialize ( 0 ) ;
   hmqQueue = WinCreateMsgQueue ( habAnchor, 0 ) ;

   WinRegisterClass ( habAnchor,
                      CLS_CLIENT,
                      ClientWndProc,
                      0,
                      0 ) ;

   ulFlags = FCF_TITLEBAR | FCF_SYSMENU | FCF_SIZEBORDER |
             FCF_MINMAX | FCF_SHELLPOSITION | FCF_TASKLIST ;

   hwndFrame = WinCreateStdWindow ( HWND_DESKTOP,
                                    WS_VISIBLE,
                                    &ulFlags,
                                    CLS_CLIENT,
                                    "Titlebar",
                                    0L,
                                    NULLHANDLE,
                                    0,
                                    &hwndClient ) ;

   if ( hwndFrame != NULLHANDLE ) {
      bLoop = WinGetMsg ( habAnchor,
                          &qmMsg,
                          NULLHANDLE,
                          0,
                          0 ) ;
      while ( bLoop ) {
         WinDispatchMsg ( habAnchor, &qmMsg ) ;
         bLoop = WinGetMsg ( habAnchor,
                             &qmMsg,
                             NULLHANDLE,
                             0,
                             0 ) ;
      } /* endwhile */

      WinDestroyWindow ( hwndFrame ) ;
   } /* endif */
```

```
   WinDestroyMsgQueue ( hmqQueue ) ;
   WinTerminate ( habAnchor ) ;
   return 0 ;
}

MRESULT EXPENTRY ClientWndProc ( HWND hwndWnd,
                                 ULONG ulMsg,
                                 MPARAM mpParm1,
                                 MPARAM mpParm2 )
{
   switch ( ulMsg ) {
   case WM_ERASEBACKGROUND:
      return MRFROMSHORT ( TRUE ) ;

   default:
      return WinDefWindowProc ( hwndWnd,
                                ulMsg,
                                mpParm1,
                                mpParm2 ) ;
   } /* endswitch */

   return MRFROMSHORT ( FALSE ) ;
}
```

WIN1.MAK

```
WIN1.EXE:                          WIN1.OBJ
        LINK386 @<<
WIN1
WIN1
WIN1
OS2386
WIN1
<<

WIN1.OBJ:                          WIN1.C
        ICC -C+ -Kb+ -Ss+ WIN1.C
```

WIN1.DEF

```
NAME WIN1 WINDOWAPI

DESCRIPTION 'Simple window example
Copyright (c) 1992 by Kathleen Panov
All rights reserved.'

STACKSIZE 16384
```

6.1 The INCLUDE Files

The OS/2 toolkit provides oodles and oodles of header files. These files contain structure definitions, function prototypes, and many system-defined constants to make OS/2 programs much easier to read. The large size of these files, and the tremendous amount of overhead they create, make it advantageous for you to selectively pick and choose those parts that are applicable to your program. This is done by placing a series of #defines before the inclusion of os2.h. In this program, we will use #define INCL_WIN.

```
#define INCL_WIN
#include <os2.h>
```

This is an all-encompassing define that will include the necessary headers for all the Win... functions. This is overkill in most cases, but for our first example we'll keep things simple.

6.2 The Window Procedure Definition

```
MRESULT EXPENTRY ClientWndProc ( HWND hwndWnd,
    ULONG ulMsg,
    MPARAM mpParm1,
    MPARAM mpParm2 ) ;
```

Window procedures are declared in a very special way, using the prefix MRESULT EXPENTRY. If you search in os2def.h, you will find that these expand to VOID * _System. The return type, MRESULT, gives the window procedure the freedom to return whatever it needs to by using the VOID * type. The _System is the linkage option used for the C-Set/2 compiler when linking with OS/2 APIs. It is a good idea to use the Presentation Manager-defined data types when dealing with window procedures and messages. There is a good probability that some definitions would change when moving to other machine architectures, and by using the defined data types you will save yourself some headaches if you need to port your application to "some other version of OS/2."

The function's parameters are HWND *hwndWnd*, ULONG *msg*, MPARAM *mpParm1*, and MPARAM *mpParm2*. This may look very familiar if you are a Microsoft Windows programmer. The variable type, HWND, is a window handle. Each window has its own unique window handle, and most *Win...* functions will include this as a parameter. In this case, HWND *hwndWnd* is the window to which the message is being sent. The parameter, ULONG *ulmsg*, is the specific message being sent to the window. We will cover messages in more detail later in this chapter.

Gotcha!

This parameter has changed from a USHORT in OS/2 version 1.x to a ULONG in 2.x. The last two parameters are MPARAM *mp1* and MPARAM *mp2*, or message parameter 1 and message parameter 2. These are "shape-shifter" parameters. MPARAM is really a PVOID (pointer to void) in disguise. This gives the operating system two 32-bit spaces to insert whatever data corresponds to the message being sent. These values could be pointers, shorts, or longs. For example, the message WM_MOUSEMOVE is sent whenever the mouse is moved. The first message parameter, mp1, would contain two 16-bit short values. The second message parameter, mp2, also contains two shorts. See Figure 6.3.

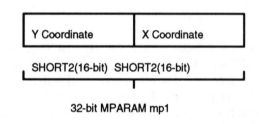

Figure 6.3. Breakdown of a message parameter variable.

6.3 Helper Macros

There are a lot of data type conversions that are necessary in a Presentation Manager application because of the multiple data types that can be used as an MPARAM or MRESULT. A group of helper macros are included in the toolkit to make these conversions easier.

The following are the macros used to convert some standard data type into a MPARAM data type that can be used when sending or posting a window message.

MACRO	CONVERTS INTO MPARAM
MPVOID	0
MPFROMP	ULONG
MPFROMHWND	HWND
MPFROMCHAR	CHAR
MPFROMSHORT	SHORT
MPFROM2SHORT	2 SHORTS
MPFROMSH2CH	2 CHARS
MPFROMLONG	ULONG

The following are the macros used to convert a MPARAM data type into a standard data type that can be used when receiving a window message.

MACRO	CONVERTS FROM MPARAM
PVOIDFROMMP	PVOID
HWNDFROMMP	HWND
CHAR1FROMMP	CHAR
CHAR2FROMMP	SECOND CHAR
CHAR3FROMMP	THIRD CHAR
CHAR4FROMMP	FOURTH CHAR
SHORT1FROMMP	LOW SHORT
SHORT2FROMMP	HIGH SHORT
LONGFROMMP	ULONG

The following are the macros used to convert a MRESULT data type into a standard data type that can be used to examine a return value for the window procedure.

MACRO	CONVERTS FROM MRESULT
PVOIDFROMMR	PVOID
SHORT1FROMMR	LOW SHORT
SHORT2FROMMR	HIGH SHORT
LONGFROMMR	ULONG

The following are the macros used to convert a standard data type into a MRESULT data type that can be used to construct a return value from the window procedure.

MACRO	CONVERTS TO MRESULT
MRFROMP	PVOID
MRFROMSHORT	SHORT
MRFROM2SHORT	2 SHORTS
MRFROMLONG	ULONG

6.4 Initialization

```
habAnchor = WinInitialize ( 0 ) ;
hmqQueue = WinCreateMsgQueue ( habAnchor, 0 ) ;
```

The beginning of your PM program will always start with a few things. First, *WinInitialize* is called to obtain an anchor block handle, or HAB. The only parameter for *WinInitialize* is a ULONG that is initialization options. In a PM environment, only 0 is available. Chances are you won't do much with the HAB except use it in some functions every now and then, but this is primarily designed for "future portability issues."

WinCreateMsgQueue will create a message queue for your program. The message queue is how Presentation Manager communicates back and forth with your windows. The first parameter is the anchor block handle, *habAnchor*. The second parameter is the queue size. A parameter of 0 indicates the default queue size in OS/2 2.1, which holds 10 messages. A full queue will cause your user interface to respond rather slowly and sometimes to stop responding completely. The default queue size should be fine for most applications and, if you find your queue is getting too full, you should probably look at your program to see where your messages are getting backlogged. One of the requirements for a Presentation Manager interface is a crisp response to the user. This means that any response that consumes more than 100 milliseconds should probably be put in a separate thread.

6.5 Creating Your Own Class

```
WinRegisterClass ( habAnchor,
                   CLS_CLIENT,
                   ClientWndProc,
                   0,
                   0 ) ;
```

The function *WinRegisterClass* is used to create a new class of windows, in this case CLS_CLIENT. The first parameter is the anchor block, *habAnchor*.

The next parameter is the class name. This parameter is a null-terminated string. The next parameter is the window procedure the class is assigned to, *ClientWndProc*. The class styles used for the new class is the fourth parameter. We're not going to use any class styles for now; instead a 0 is specified. The last parameter is the number of bytes of storage space that will be tacked on to each window belonging to this class. This piece of space is commonly referred to as "window words." This will be covered in more detail later in this chapter.

6.6 Creating a Window

 By now you're probably thinking, "But I just wanted to create one lousy window." Well, this is it, the function call you've been waiting for — *WinCreateStdWindow*. This function actually creates five windows as stated earlier; but, there are only two that are of any interest to us — the frame window and the client window.

```
ulFlags = FCF_TITLEBAR | FCF_SYSMENU | FCF_SIZEBORDER |
          FCF_MINMAX | FCF_SHELLPOSITION | FCF_TASKLIST ;

hwndFrame = WinCreateStdWindow ( HWND_DESKTOP,
                                 WS_VISIBLE,
                                 &ulFlags,
                                 CLS_CLIENT,
                                 "Titlebar",
                                 0L,
                                 NULLHANDLE,
                                 0,
                                 &hwndClient ) ;
```

The frame window handle is returned by the function. The first parameter specified is the parent of the frame window. We'll discuss parents and owners in a minute. The second parameter is the frame style. There are two sets of styles that a frame can draw from: frame styles, because this is a frame window; and window styles, because the frame class is a subset of the window class "window." The most common window style available is WS_VISIBLE. Yep, you guessed it, this means the window is not only created, but will show up as well.

The third parameter is the frame flags. Frame flags describe how the frame will look. The possible descriptors are OR'ed together. Figure 6.4 is a diagram of all the possible descriptors and the bits that correspond to them.

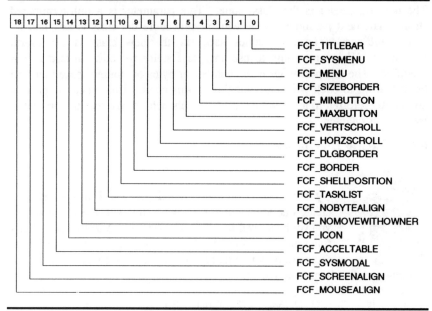

Figure 6.4. Frame creation flags.

FLAG	DESCRIPTION
FCF_TITLEBAR	Creates a title bar on the frame.
FCF_SYSMENU	Creates a system menu on the frame.
FCF_MENU	Creates an application menu on the frame. This is loaded from the resource file or .DLL.
FCF_MINBUTTON	Creates a minimize button on the frame.
FCF_SIZEBORDER	Creates a sizing border on the frame.
FCF_MAXBUTTON	Creates a maximize button on the frame.
FCF_MINMAX	Creates both a minimize and maximize button on the frame.
FCF_HORZSCROLL	Creates a horizontal scroll bar on the frame.
FCF_DLGBORDER	Creates the thick dialog box border on the frame.
FCF_VERTSCROLL	Creates a vertical scroll bar on the frame.
FCF_BORDER	Creates a thin border on the frame.

FCF_SHELLPOSITION	The system determines the initial size and placement of the frame window.
FCF_TASKLIST	Adds the program title to the task list and window title to the window list.
FCF_NOBYTEALIGN	Do not optimize window movements in 8 pel multiples.
FCF_NOMOVEWITHOWNER	The frame window will not move when the owner is moved.
FCF_ICON	An icon is added to the frame. This is loaded from the resource file or .DLL.
FCF_ACCELTABLE	An accelerator table is added to the frame. This is loaded from the resource file or .DLL.
FCF_SYSMODEL	The frame window is system model.
FCF_SCREENALIGN	The frame window is positioned relative to the desktop rather than relative to the owner window.
FCF_MOUSEALIGN	The frame window is positioned relative to the position of the mouse rather than relative to the owner window.
FCF_STANDARD	FCF_TITLEBAR | FCF_SYSMENU | FCF_MINBUTTON | FCF_MAXBUTTON | FCF_SIZEBORDER | FCF_ICON | FCF_MENU | FCF_ACCELTABLE | FCF_SHELLPOSITION | FCF_TASKLIST.
FCF_AUTOICON	A WM_PAINT message will not be sent to the application when the frame window is iconized.
FCF_HIDEBUTTON	Creates "hide" button on the frame.
FCF_HIDEMAX	Creates "hide" and maximize buttons on the frame.

In this example, we'll use the following flags: FCF_TITLEBAR, FCF_SYSMENU, FCF_SIZEBORDER, FCF_TASKLIST, FCF_MINMAX, and FCF_SHELLPOSITION. Be sure to pass a pointer to a ULONG as this parameter.

The fourth parameter is the name of the window class that the client window will belong to, in this case, CLS_CLIENT. The next parameter is the window text for the title bar. The sixth parameter is the the client window style. Since we defined the parent of the client window *hwndFrame* to have the style WS_VISIBLE, the client, as a child of *hwndFrame*, will inherit the WS_VISIBLE style. This means we don't have to specify any window styles here; we'll just leave that a 0.

The next parameter is the resource ID location. If the icons, menus, or other resources were defined in a .DLL file, this parameter would contain the module handle returned from a *DosLoadModule* function. If the resources were defined in a .RC file that was bound to the .EXE file, this parameter would be defined as NULLHANDLE. The next parameter contains the resource ID for the frame window. This one resource ID will point to all the resources that are defined for your frame. This includes the menu, icon, accelerator table, and any other items defined using the frame creation flags.

The last parameter is the address of a window handle. Presentation Manager will place the client window handle into this variable upon the function's return.

If *WinCreateStdWindow* fails, a NULL handle is returned. Before we attempt to do anything else, it is a good idea to check the return handle to make sure it is valid; if not, the application should quit, preferably with some sort of error message.

6.7 Message, Message, Who's Got the Message

```
bLoop = WinGetMsg ( habAnchor,
                    &qmMsg,
                    NULLHANDLE,
                    0,
                    0 ) ;
while ( bLoop ) {
   WinDispatchMsg ( habAnchor, &qmMsg ) ;
   bLoop = WinGetMsg ( habAnchor,
                       &qmMsg,
                       NULLHANDLE,
                       0,
                       0 ) ;
} /* endwhile */
```

The two functions, *WinGetMsg* and *WinDispatchMsg,* are the key to getting the message queue up and running. Without some form of message retrieval and dispatch, the system will respond with a "Program not responding..." error message. The secret to a well-thought-out Presentation Manager application is a message queue that is quick and responsive. *WinGetMsg* will retrieve the message from the message queue and place it into the variable *qmsgMessage.* The QMSG structure is a structure that looks very similar to the variables that are passed to the window procedure. Eventually the QMSG structure will be passed on to *ClientWndProc* or to the window procedure for the window receiving the message. *WinGetMsg* and *WinDispatchMsg* form a post office for messages. They pick up the messages, and then make sure that the messages are delivered to the correct window.

The first parameter of *WinGetMsg* is the anchor block handle. The next one is the address of the QMSG structure that will handle the message information that is retrieved. The next three parameters are not used in this example. These provide a way for *WinGetMsg* to selectively choose which messages to pick out of the queue. By specifying 0s here, *WinGetMsg* will retrieve all messages from the message queue in the order they were placed there. After the message is retrieved from the queue, it is then passed on to *WinDispatchMsg.* It is *WinDispatchMsg*'s job to take the message from the *qmsgMessage* variable and send it on the window procedure associated with the window it is addressed to. For instance, if *qmsgMessage.hwnd* were equal to *hwndWnd,* *WinDispatchMsg* would take *qmsgMessage* and send it on to *ClientWndProc.*

```
/* QMSG structure */
typedef struct _QMSG      /* qmsg */
{
    HWND    hwnd; /* window handle that msg is being sent to */
    ULONG   msg; /* the message itself */
    MPARAM  mp1; /* Message Parameter 1 */
    MPARAM  mp2; /* Message Parameter 2 */
    ULONG   time; /* Time msg was sent */
    POINTL  ptl; /* Mouse position when msg was sent */
    ULONG   reserved;
} QMSG;
typedef QMSG *PQMSG;
```

The QMSG structure contains a lof of very interesting information about the message. The first field in the structure, *hwnd,* is the window handle the message is for. The field, *msg,* is the actual message itself. Some common messages are WM_CREATE, WM_PAINT, WM_QUIT, and WM_SIZE. The next two parameters, *mp1* and *mp2,* are the message parameters. Each message has a set use for these parameters. Usually they are used to convey more information about the message. The *time* field contains the time the message was sent, and the *ptl* field is a structure that contains the mouse position when the message was sent.

6.8 Terminating Your Program

 You may have noticed that *WinGetMsg* and *WinDispatchMsg* were running in a while loop. While *WinGetMsg* returns a TRUE value, this loop continues to process messages. When *WinGetMsg* receives a WM_QUIT, *WinGetMsg* returns FALSE and will fall out of the loop. At this point the user has elected to close the application, and it's time for the final clean-up. There are three things that we have created that need to be destroyed — the frame window *hwndFrame*, *hmqQueue*, and *habAnchor*. Each of these items have their own destroy function. By destroying *hwndFrame*, we are also destroying the client window, the title bar, and all the other windows that were children of the frame.

```
    WinDestroyWindow ( hwndFrame ) ;
} /* endif */

WinDestroyMsgQueue ( hmqQueue ) ;
WinTerminate ( habAnchor ) ;
return 0 ;
```

6.9 The Window Procedure Revisited

You might have looked over *main* and thought, "Is this it?" Well, no. You've only seen the tip of the iceberg. The meat of a Presentation Manager program is the window procedure. A window procedure's sole purpose in life is to respond to the messages for the window that belongs to it. It is also important to realize that multiple windows can and will access the same window procedure. Be very careful with static or global variables or flags. This can come back to haunt you if two windows are accessing the same procedure. It is a good idea to avoid these if at all possible.

Most window procedures are nothing more than a giant *switch* statement, with a case for each message. A window procedure does not have to respond to every message; it can filter the majority of the messages through to a function, *WinDefWindowProc*. This function lets the system handle messages in a system default manner. There are a few messages that are very important to a window procedure. In the next part of this chapter, we will cover those in depth.

In this example, the window procedure, *ClientWndProc,* is very small. It's not quite the smallest window procedure you can have; however, it's pretty close.

```
MRESULT EXPENTRY ClientWndProc ( HWND hwndWnd,
                                 ULONG ulMsg,
                                 MPARAM mpParm1,
                                 MPARAM mpParm2 )
{
   switch ( ulMsg ) {
   case WM_ERASEBACKGROUND:
      return MRFROMSHORT ( TRUE ) ;

   default:
      return WinDefWindowProc ( hwndWnd,
                                ulMsg,
                                mpParm1,
                                mpParm2 ) ;
   } /* endswitch */

   return MRFROMSHORT ( FALSE ) ;
}
```

The only message that is utilized in *ClientWndProc* is WM_ERASEBACKGROUND. This message is used to fill the client window with the system-window background color. If we let this message pass on to *WinDefWindowProc*, the background of our window would be transparent, and the desktop would show through. By returning TRUE, we tell the system to paint the client window with the background color. In some cases, you will not need to process this message if you handle the painting in the WM_PAINT message yourself. In a window procedure, most messages have a default handling of returning FALSE. You can save a few extra function calls if you return FALSE yourself from the messages that you handle instead of calling *WinDefWindowProc*.

6.10 Parents and Owners

Earlier we had mentioned the concept of parents and owners. These are terms you will hear and use often in Presentation Manager programming. It is important to understand each one. Every window has a parent. In some cases the parent will be the desktop, HWND_DESKTOP. In the previous example, the frame window had the desktop as its parent. The frame window was the parent for the client window, the title bar window, and the other windows. What is a parent window?

A parent window performs many of the same duties that parents of human children perform. A parent window controls where the child can go. A child is "clipped" to the parent, and will not be visible outside the parental boundaries. A child window can be partially moved outside these boundaries; however, the portion that is outside the parent window will not be visible. Also, a child will inherit all of the parent's styles. If a parent is visible, a child will be visible; if a parent is not visible, a child will not be visible. If a parent moves, the child moves along with it. However, unlike a human parent, if a parent window is destroyed, all of its children are destroyed as well. If a parent window has two child windows, these children are considered siblings. When a family of windows are all visible at the same time, there is a power struggle for which window will be displayed on top. A child window will always be on top of the parent window. Some surprise, huh? However, siblings, and the whole windowing system as well, use a concept known as "Z-Order" to decide who gets on top. The sibling that is created last will usually be at the top of the "Z-Order." The programmer can change the order using the function *WinSetWindowPos*. This function lets you put a window either on top, or behind its other siblings. Another way the "Z-Order" will be affected is by user interaction. When the user clicks on one of the siblings, that window will become the active window, and it will move to the top of the "Z-Order." The active window is usually the window that either is, or owns, the focus window. There is only one active window in the system at any given time.

The other type of window relationship is an owner window. In the previous example, *hwndFrame* was also the owner of the other windows. An owner shares some of the same duties a parent shares. When an owner is hidden, destroyed, or minimized, the children are also. However, an owned window is not clipped to its owner.

The other interesting features of owners is the level of communication between owners and owned, or "control," windows. When an important event happens to an owned window, the owner is sent a WM_CONTROL message. The mp1 and mp2 parameters tell the owner which control sent the message, and what kind of event has occurred. A window does not have to have an owner.

6.11 Window Stylin'

When a window is created, various descriptors are used to describe how the window will look or act; these descriptors are known as window styles. There are many different kinds of styles: there are window styles and class styles, and each type of control has its own styles as well. In this section we will concentrate on window styles, class styles, and frame styles. The other control styles will be covered in their respective chapters.

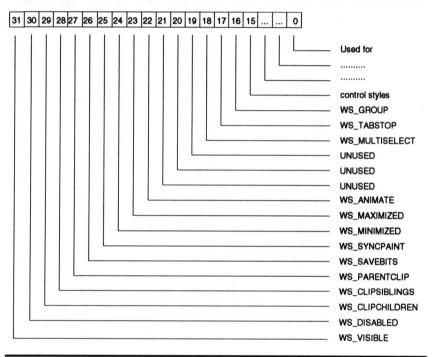

Figure 6.5. Window style flags.

Figure 6.5 shows that the first 16 bits are used for the respective control window styles; the upper 16 bits are used for window styles. Since controls are also windows, both the control window styles and the basic window styles are designed to live together harmoniously. The first three window styles, WS_GROUP, WS_TABSTOP, and WS_MULTISELECT, are to be used as styles for dialog boxes. This is covered in Chapter 7, Dialog Boxes. WS_ANIMATE is a window style that will create "exploding" windows. WS_MAXIMIZED causes the window to be created fully maximized. WS_MINIMIZED causes the window to be created fully minimized.

WS_SYNCPAINT causes a window to have paint messages generated immediately when an area of the window needs to be repainted. Paint messages are usually processed when the system has spare time to process them. WS_SAVEBITS will save the screen area under a window, and will restore the image when a covered area has been uncovered. This saves the programmer from repainting the newly uncovered region. WS_PARENTCLIP will cause the parent's presentation space to be clipped to the child's presentation space. This style enables the child to draw on the parent's presentation space. WS_CLIPSIBLINGS style will prevent siblings from redrawing on top of each other. WS_CLIPCHILDREN will cause the child window area to be excluded from the drawing region.

WS_DISABLED will cause a window to be disabled upon creation. It means that this window will not respond to user input until the window is enabled. WS_VISIBLE will make a window visible at creation time. A default window will be created as invisible.

6.12 Visible, Invisible, Enabled, and Disabled Windows

Presentation Manager supports the idea of a "messy desktop" window arrangement. This means that several windows can be stacked upon each other similar to pieces of paper on a desk. A window that is visible is a window that is either currently visible on the deskop, or that can be uncovered by moving a window that is on top of it. An invisible window is a window with the WS_VISIBLE bit not set, and must be made visible by the programmer before it can be seen. *WinShowWindow* can be used to make an invisible window visible.

A window that is enabled is a window that can respond to user input. An application can disable a window by using *WinEnableWindow*. Items on a dialog box can be disabled from being chosen if the choices are no longer applicable.

6.13 Window Sizing

The CUA (Common User Access) guidelines recommend that a frame window let the user size and position the window to his or her own specifications. Conveniently enough, Presentation Manager can handle most of this auto-magically. The frame control flag, FCF_SIZEBORDER, gives the frame window a "sizing border." The user can shape and size the window to his or her heart's content, and the programmer can kick back, relax, and let Presentation Manager do all the work. But (there's always a but), the programmer should make sure that the WM_PAINT message processing adapts for the change in window real estate. There's a few ways to keep track of the window size:

- In the WM_PAINT processing, call *WinQueryWindowRect* to return the RECTL structure containing the window size.
- Keep track of the window size by processing the WM_SIZE messages, and store these values in a structure pointed to by a window word.

6.14 Saving Window Settings

Now we're ready to expand a little beyond the basic Presentation Manager program. When the user closes down an application, it is only polite to remember all the changes he or she has made to the frame window. In OS/2 2.0, the developers added two new functions to make it super-easy to really impress your customers — *WinStoreWindowPos* and *WinRestoreWindowPos*. These functions store the window size, position, and presentation parameters in the OS2.INI file and then retrieve them on demand.

WINSAVE.C
```
#define INCL_WIN
#include <os2.h>
#include <stdio.h>
#include <stdlib.h>
#include <string.h>

#define CLS_CLIENT              "MyClass"

#define SAVE_NAME               "WINSAVE"
#define SAVE_KEY                "WINDOWPOS"
```

```
MRESULT EXPENTRY ClientWndProc ( HWND hwndWnd,
                                 ULONG ulMsg,
                                 MPARAM mpParm1,
                                 MPARAM mpParm2 ) ;

INT main ( VOID )
{
    HAB         habAnchor ;
    HMQ         hmqQueue ;
    ULONG       ulFlags ;
    HWND        hwndFrame ;
    HWND        hwndClient ;
    BOOL        bReturn ;
    BOOL        bLoop ;
    QMSG        qmMsg ;

    habAnchor = WinInitialize ( 0 ) ;
    hmqQueue = WinCreateMsgQueue ( habAnchor, 0 ) ;

    WinRegisterClass ( habAnchor,
                       CLS_CLIENT,
                       ClientWndProc,
                       0,
                       0 ) ;

    ulFlags = FCF_TITLEBAR | FCF_SYSMENU | FCF_SIZEBORDER |
              FCF_MINMAX | FCF_TASKLIST ;

    hwndFrame = WinCreateStdWindow ( HWND_DESKTOP,
                                     WS_VISIBLE,
                                     &ulFlags,
                                     CLS_CLIENT,
                                     "Titlebar",
                                     0L,
                                     NULLHANDLE,
                                     0,
                                     &hwndClient ) ;

    if ( hwndFrame != NULLHANDLE ) {
        bReturn = WinRestoreWindowPos ( SAVE_NAME,
                                        SAVE_KEY,
                                        hwndFrame ) ;

        if ( bReturn ) {
            WinSetWindowPos ( hwndFrame,
                              HWND_TOP,
                              0,
                              0,
                              0,
                              0,
                              SWP_ACTIVATE | SWP_SHOW ) ;
        } else {
```

```
            WinSetWindowPos ( hwndFrame,
                              NULLHANDLE,
                              10,
                              10,
                              400,
                              300,
                              SWP_ACTIVATE |
                              SWP_MOVE |
                              SWP_SIZE |
                              SWP_SHOW ) ;
        } /* endif */

        bLoop = WinGetMsg ( habAnchor,
                            &qmMsg,
                            NULLHANDLE,
                            0,
                            0 ) ;

        while ( bLoop ) {
            WinDispatchMsg ( habAnchor, &qmMsg ) ;
            bLoop = WinGetMsg ( habAnchor,
                                &qmMsg,
                                NULLHANDLE,
                                0,
                                0 ) ;
        } /* endwhile */

        WinDestroyWindow ( hwndFrame ) ;
    } /* endif */

    WinDestroyMsgQueue ( hmqQueue ) ;
    WinTerminate ( habAnchor ) ;
    return 0 ;
}

MRESULT EXPENTRY ClientWndProc ( HWND hwndWnd,
                                 ULONG ulMsg,
                                 MPARAM mpParm1,
                                 MPARAM mpParm2 )
{
    switch ( ulMsg ) {

    case WM_ERASEBACKGROUND:
        return MRFROMSHORT ( TRUE ) ;

    case WM_SAVEAPPLICATION:
        WinStoreWindowPos ( SAVE_NAME,
                            SAVE_KEY,
                            WinQueryWindow ( hwndWnd, QW_PARENT )) ;
        break ;

    default:
        return WinDefWindowProc ( hwndWnd,
                                  ulMsg,
                                  mpParm1,
                                  mpParm2 ) ;
    } /* endswitch */
```

```
    return MRFROMSHORT ( FALSE ) ;
}
```

WINSAVE.MAK

```
WINSAVE.EXE:                    WINSAVE.OBJ
        LINK386 @<<
WINSAVE
WINSAVE
WINSAVE
OS2386
WINSAVE
<<

WINSAVE.OBJ:                    WINSAVE.C
        ICC -C+ -Kb+ -Ss+ WINSAVE.C
```

WINSAVE.DEF

```
NAME WINSAVE WINDOWAPI

DESCRIPTION 'WinRestoreWindowPos example
Copyright (c) 1992 by Kathleen Panov
All rights reserved.'

STACKSIZE 16384
```

6.15 *WinRestoreWindowPos*

```
        bReturn = WinRestoreWindowPos ( SAVE_NAME,
                                        SAVE_KEY,
                                        hwndFrame ) ;
```

WinRestoreWindowPos is called right after the frame window is created. This enables the saved changes to be visible right when the window is created. The first parameter is the app name, placed in the .INI file. The second is the keyword used in conjunction with the app name. The last parameter is the window to apply the changes to.

If the call completes successfully, *WinSetWindowPos* will make the window visible and make it the active window.

WinSetWindowPos is a very handy function. You can position, size, activate, deactivate, maximize, minimize, hide, or restore a window. One of the nice aspects of *WinSetWindowPos* is the ability to consolidate several function calls into one.

```
WinSetWindowPos ( hwndFrame,
                  HWND_TOP,
                  0,
                  0,
                  0,
                  0,
                  SWP_ACTIVATE | SWP_SHOW ) ;
```

hwndFrame is the window to adjust. The next parameter, HWND_TOP, indicates the position in the Z-order for the window. We've mentioned Z-order before; it's time for a little more detail.

6.16 X,Y,Z-Order

Presentation Manager supports a concept of piling windows (visually) one on top of another, known as Z-order. The active window, and its children, is always the window at the top of the Z-order. Children are ahead of their parents in their position in the Z-order. The window that is at the top of the Z-order is the window in which the user inputs keystrokes, and mouse moves.

The next four parameters of *WinSetWindowPos* are the x coordinate, y coordinate, width, and height of the window. The last parameter is the value of the action flags OR'ed together. If SWP_MOVE is specified, the x, y coordinates are used to move the window to the requested position; if not, these two parameters are ignored. If SWP_SIZE is used, the window is resized to the new height and width; if not, these two parameters are ignored. We'll use SWP_ACTIVATE and SWP_SHOW to show the window, and also to make the frame window the active window.

You may wonder why they call these flags SWP_. There is a structure used in window positioning that is a SWP structure. SWP stands for "set window position." The structure is defined below:

```
typedef struct _SWP
{
   ULONG    fl;
   LONG     cy;
   LONG     cx;
   LONG     y;
   LONG     x;
   HWND     hwndInsertBehind;
   HWND     hwnd;
   ULONG    ulReserved1;
   ULONG    ulReserved2;
} SWP;
typedef SWP *PSWP;
```

After calling *WinRestoreWindowPos* you should either call *WinShowWindow* or *WinSetWindowPos* with the SWP_SHOW flag.

6.17 Saving State

```
case WM_SAVEAPPLICATION:
    WinStoreWindowPos ( SAVE_NAME,
                        SAVE_KEY,
                        WinQueryWindow ( hwndWnd, QW_PARENT )) ;
    break ;
```

Presentation Manager sends a special message at application shutdown time for the sole purpose of giving the programmer a chance to save the options and settings the user has customized to reflect their preferences. This is the WM_SAVEAPPLICATION message. Catchy name. This is the time to call *WinStoreWindowPos*. The parameters for this function are *exactly* the same as *WinRestoreWindowPos*. One little note here: remember to retrieve the settings for the frame window, not the client.

6.18 Another Window Example: WINDOW

The following example program illustrates some of the concepts we've talked about so far. The program, WINDOW, creates a list of all the windows that are children of the frame window and also queries the window style of each window. The information is displayed in the client area.

WINDOW.C

```
#define INCL_WIN
#define INCL_GPI

#include <os2.h>
#include <stdio.h>
#include <stdlib.h>
#include <string.h>

#define CLS_CLIENT              "MyClass"

MRESULT EXPENTRY ClientWndProc ( HWND hwndWnd,
                                 ULONG ulMsg,
                                 MPARAM mpParm1,
                                 MPARAM mpParm2 ) ;
VOID WriteWindowInfo ( HPS hpsPaint,
                       HWND hwndPaint,
                       PRECTL prclRect,
                       ULONG ulCharHeight ) ;
```

```
INT main ( VOID )
{
   HAB          habAnchor ;
   HMQ          hmqQueue ;
   ULONG        ulFlags ;
   HWND         hwndFrame ;
   HWND         hwndClient ;
   BOOL         bLoop ;
   QMSG         qmMsg ;

   habAnchor = WinInitialize ( 0 ) ;
   hmqQueue = WinCreateMsgQueue ( habAnchor, 0 ) ;

   WinRegisterClass ( habAnchor,
                      CLS_CLIENT,
                      ClientWndProc,
                      CS_SIZEREDRAW,
                      0 ) ;

   ulFlags = FCF_TITLEBAR | FCF_SYSMENU | FCF_SIZEBORDER |
             FCF_MINMAX | FCF_SHELLPOSITION | FCF_TASKLIST ;

   hwndFrame = WinCreateStdWindow ( HWND_DESKTOP,
                                    WS_VISIBLE,
                                    &ulFlags,
                                    CLS_CLIENT,
                                    "Titlebar",
                                    0L,
                                    NULLHANDLE,
                                    0,
                                    &hwndClient ) ;

   if ( hwndFrame != NULLHANDLE ) {
      bLoop = WinGetMsg ( habAnchor,
                          &qmMsg,
                          NULLHANDLE,
                          0,
                          0 ) ;
      while ( bLoop ) {
         WinDispatchMsg ( habAnchor, &qmMsg ) ;
         bLoop = WinGetMsg ( habAnchor,
                             &qmMsg,
                             NULLHANDLE,
                             0,
                             0 ) ;
      } /* endwhile */

      WinDestroyWindow ( hwndFrame ) ;
   } /* endif */

   WinDestroyMsgQueue ( hmqQueue ) ;
   WinTerminate ( habAnchor ) ;
   return 0 ;
}
```

```
MRESULT EXPENTRY ClientWndProc ( HWND hwndWnd,
                                 ULONG ulMsg,
                                 MPARAM mpParm1,
                                 MPARAM mpParm2 )
{
   switch ( ulMsg ) {

   case WM_ERASEBACKGROUND:
      return MRFROMSHORT ( TRUE ) ;

   case WM_PAINT:
      {
         HPS               hpsPaint ;
         RECTL             rclRect ;
         RECTL             rclWindow ;
         ULONG             ulCharHeight ;
         HWND              hwndEnum ;
         HWND              hwndFrame ;
         HENUM             heEnum ;
         FONTMETRICS       fmMetrics ;

         hpsPaint = WinBeginPaint ( hwndWnd,
                                    NULLHANDLE,
                                    &rclRect ) ;

         GpiQueryFontMetrics ( hpsPaint,
                               sizeof ( fmMetrics ) ,
                               &fmMetrics ) ;

         ulCharHeight = fmMetrics.lMaxBaselineExt ;

         WinQueryWindowRect ( hwndWnd, &rclWindow ) ;
         rclWindow.yBottom = rclWindow.yTop - ulCharHeight ;

         hwndFrame = WinQueryWindow ( hwndWnd, QW_PARENT ) ;
         WriteWindowInfo ( hpsPaint,
                           hwndFrame,
                           &rclWindow,
                           ulCharHeight ) ;

         heEnum = WinBeginEnumWindows ( hwndFrame ) ;

         hwndEnum = WinGetNextWindow ( heEnum ) ;
         while ( hwndEnum != NULLHANDLE ) {
             WriteWindowInfo ( hpsPaint,
                               hwndEnum,
                               &rclWindow,
                               ulCharHeight ) ;
             hwndEnum = WinGetNextWindow ( heEnum ) ;
         }

         WinEndEnumWindows ( heEnum ) ;
         WinEndPaint ( hpsPaint ) ;
      }
      break ;
   default:
```

```
            return WinDefWindowProc ( hwndWnd,
                                      ulMsg,
                                      mpParm1,
                                      mpParm2 ) ;
   } /* endswitch */

   return MRFROMSHORT ( FALSE ) ;
}

VOID WriteWindowInfo ( HPS hpsPaint,
                       HWND hwndPaint,
                       PRECTL prclRect,
                       ULONG ulCharHeight )
{
   CHAR          achString [ 200 ] ;
   CHAR          achClass [ 65 ] ;
   CHAR          achClassText [ 25 ] ;
   PCHAR         pchStart ;
   USHORT        usIndex ;
   PCHAR         apchClasses [] =
   {
      " ",
      "WC_FRAME",
      "WC_COMBOBOX",
      "WC_BUTTON",
      "WC_MENU",
      "WC_STATIC",
      "WC_ENTRYFIELD",
      "WC_LISTBOX",
      "WC_SCROLLBAR",
      "WC_TITLEBAR"
   } ;

   WinQueryClassName ( hwndPaint,
                       sizeof ( achClass ) ,
                       achClass ) ;
   pchStart = achClass ;

   if ( achClass [ 0 ] == '#' ) {
      usIndex = atoi ( &achClass [ 1 ] ) ;
      strcpy ( achClassText, apchClasses [ usIndex ] ) ;
   } else {
      strcpy ( achClassText, pchStart ) ;
   } /* endif */

   sprintf ( achString,
             "Window 0x%08lX belongs to class \"%s\"",
             hwndPaint, achClassText ) ;

   prclRect -> yTop = prclRect -> yBottom ;
   prclRect -> yBottom = prclRect -> yTop - ulCharHeight ;
```

```
    WinDrawText ( hpsPaint,
                  -1,
                  achString,
                  prclRect,
                  0,
                  0,
                  DT_CENTER | DT_TEXTATTRS ) ;

    sprintf ( achString,
              "  and has style = 0x%08lX",
              WinQueryWindowULong ( hwndPaint, QWL_STYLE )) ;

    prclRect -> yTop = prclRect -> yBottom ;
    prclRect -> yBottom = prclRect -> yTop - ulCharHeight ;

    WinDrawText ( hpsPaint,
                  -1,
                  achString,
                  prclRect,
                  0,
                  0,
                  DT_CENTER | DT_TEXTATTRS ) ;

    return ;
}
```

WINDOW.MAK

```
WINDOW.EXE:                        WINDOW.OBJ
       LINK386 @<<
WINDOW
WINDOW
WINDOW
OS2386
WINDOW
<<

WINDOW.OBJ:                        WINDOW.C
       ICC -C+ -Kb+ -Ss+ WINDOW.C
```

WINDOW.MAK

```
NAME WINDOW WINDOWAPI

DESCRIPTION 'Window list example
Copyright (c) 1992 by Kathleen Panov
All rights reserved.'

STACKSIZE 16384
```

main only has one small difference from *main* in WIN1.C. The class style,
CS_SIZEREDRAW, is used for the client window class. The text on the client
area is centered along the width of the window. We want to ensure that the

text stays centered even when the window is resized, thus: CS_SIZEREDRAW.

6.19 Painting by Numbers

```
hpsPaint = WinBeginPaint ( hwndWnd,
                           NULLHANDLE,
                           &rclRect ) ;
```

It's about time to show some real WM_PAINT processing. *WinBeginPaint* is used to start things off by getting the presentation space we'll use for drawing. *hwndWnd* is the window the presentation space belongs to. The second parameter is used if you already have a presentation space obtained using *WinGetPS* or some other means, and want to use that space for drawing. If a NULLHANDLE is specified, the system will provide a micro-cached presentation space for your use. The last parameter is a pointer to RECTL structure. The coordinates of the invalidated region are placed in the structure. This is the region that needs to be painted.

```
GpiQueryFontMetrics ( hpsPaint,
                      sizeof ( fmMetrics ) ,
                      &fmMetrics ) ;
```

GpiQueryFontMetrics is a function that provides lots of information on the dimensions of the current font. This information is copied into the *fmMetrics* structure. We'll use this information to determine the height of one line of text. The value *lMaxBaselineExt* provides the approximate height of the tallest character. Also, because the text is centered on the window, we need the dimensions of the entire client region. These values are set aside in another RECTL structure, *rclWindow*.

The functions *WinBeginPaint* and *WinEndPaint* are required for all WM_PAINT processing.

6.20 Enumerating Windows

```
heEnum = WinBeginEnumWindows ( hwndFrame ) ;

hwndEnum = WinGetNextWindow ( heEnum ) ;
while ( hwndEnum != NULLHANDLE ) {
    WriteWindowInfo ( hpsPaint,
                      hwndEnum,
                      &rclWindow,
                      ulCharHeight ) ;
```

```
            hwndEnum = WinGetNextWindow ( heEnum ) ;
        }

        WinEndEnumWindows ( heEnum ) ;
```

Presentation Manager lets you query all the descendants of a particular window by using the function *WinBeginEnumWindows* and *WinGetNextWindow*. The window we want to query is the frame window, *hwndFrame*. This window handle is passed to *WinBeginEnumWindows*, which passes back an enumerative handle, *heEnum*. This is a place holder to keep track of the last window that was returned. *WinGetNextWindow* takes *heEnum*, and returns the next window in the window family tree. As each window is found, our own function, *WriteWindowInfo*, is used to display information about the window. The enumeration ends with a call to *WinEndEnumWindows*.

6.21 *WriteWindowInfo*

```
    WinQueryClassName ( hwndPaint,
                        sizeof ( achClass ) ,
                        achClass ) ;
```

The first piece of information we'll retrieve from each window is the class name. Documentation refers to the system-defined class names as WC_FRAME, etc. However, the class name in reality, and returned by *WinQueryClassName*, is a string in the format "#1". Some help, huh? Public window class names are stored in a powerful storage facility known as atom tables. This format helps to check and see if a newly registered window class has the same name as an already registered window class. To help out converting from this cryptic format to something that is more readily deciphered, we define an array, *pszClassNames*, that maps the numeric class names to the documented class names. The string, *pszClass*, returned from *WinQueryClassName* is incremented by one to strip off the "#" and leave a value that can be converted to an integer index into the array.

If *achClass* is a nonnumeric value, we assume this to be an application-defined class, and keep the string whole.

```
    prclRect -> yTop = prclRect -> yBottom ;
    prclRect -> yBottom = prclRect -> yTop - ulCharHeight ;
```

Next, the drawing area *prclRect* is adjusted to drop down one line.

```
WinDrawText ( hpsPaint,
              -1,
              achString,
              prclRect,
              0,
              0,
              DT_CENTER | DT_TEXTATTRS ) ;
```

WinDrawText does the actual drawing on the presentation space. The first parameter is the presentation space. The second parameter is the number of characters to output. A –1 indicates that the entire length of the null-terminated string is to be used. The string to write is *achString*. The size of the text area is defined by passing a pointer to a RECTL structure that contains the designated coordinates.

The next two parameters are the foreground and background colors of the text. The last parameter is the text output flags. DT_CENTER centers the text horizontally, and DT_TEXTATTRS indicates that default window foreground and background colors will be used. If this flag is specified, the two previous parameters are ignored.

```
sprintf ( achString,
          "  and has style = 0x%08lX",
          WinQueryWindowULong ( hwndPaint, QWL_STYLE )) ;
```

The other information we will output to the client area is the window styles. This is a value that is stored in the window word. *WinQueryWindowULong* will retrieve the window styles. The first parameter is the window we're inquiring about. The next parameter is a constant used to identify which piece of the window word we're after. The value QWL_STYLE designates that the window style is the ULONG is question.

When all the windows are enumerated, *WinEndPaint* is used to return the presentation space back to the system.

6.22 Window Words

Window words is a fairly simple concept that is fairly easy to implement, but got a bad rap because it was poorly documented. Every window has a pointer to some memory that contains quite a bit of very interesting information. Such things as window ID, frame flags, window style, and much more are available through window words. There are three sets of functions are used to set and query the information:

Function	Purpose	Data Type Returned
WinQueryWindowUShort	Query	USHORT
WinSetWindowUShort	Set	USHORT
WinQueryWindowULong	Query	ULONG
WinSetWindowULong	Set	ULONG
WinQueryWindowPtr	Query	PVOID
WinSetWindowPtr	Set	PVOID

There is also four bytes of space reserved in the window word for the use of the programmer. These four bytes can contain any data type that will fit in the space. If you need more space, create your own structure and pass a pointer to the structure in the window word.

Specific information from the window word is obtained using QWL_*, QWS_*, and QWP_* values. These values are constants that represent the offset into the window word. The L, S, and P indicates the data type that resides at that offset. The programmer-defined data space resides at offset QWL_USER. One note here: ALL control windows contain the programmer-defined data area.

6.23 Control Windows

At the heart of data input in a Presentation Manager program are many different styles of reusable controls. A control window is a window within a window designed to perform some useful behavior in a consistent manner. The controls available are: buttons, entry-fields, multi-line entry fields (MLEs), combo-boxes, list boxes, spin buttons, and the new controls offered in OS/2 2.x — the value-set, container, notebook, slider, font dialog box, and file dialog box. In later chapters, the programming techniques needed to use these controls will be illustrated.

6.24 Presentation Parameters

Presentation Manager provides a pretty fancy way to set the color and font of a window. These descriptors are called Presentation Parameters. *WinSetPresParam* and *WinQueryPresParam* are used to set and query the presentation parameters respectively. Also, presentation parameters can be passed through *WinCreateWindow*. A presentation parameter has an attribute type (PP_*) and a value for the specified attribute. Valid attribute types are:

ATTRIBUTE TYPE	DATA TYPE FOR ATTRIBUTE VALUE	DESCRIPTION
PP_FOREGROUNDCOLOR	RGB	Foreground window color
PP_BACKGROUNDCOLOR	RGB	Background window color
PP_FOREGROUNDCOLORINDEX	COLOR (LONG)	Foreground window color
PP_BACKGROUNDCOLORINDEX	COLOR (LONG)	Background window color
PP_HILITEFOREGROUNDCOLOR	RGB	Highlighted foreground window color
PP_HILITEBACKGROUNDCOLOR	RGB	Highlighted background window color
PP_HILITEFOREGROUNDCOLORINDEX	COLOR (LONG)	Highlighted foreground window color
PP_HILITEBACKGROUNDCOLORINDEX	COLOR (LONG)	Highlighted background window color
PP_DISABLEDFOREGROUNDCOLOR	RGB	Disabled foreground window color
PP_DISABLEDBACKGROUNDCOLOR	RGB	Disabled background window color
PP_DISABLEDFOREGROUNDCOLORINDEX	COLOR (LONG)	Disabled foreground window color
PP_DISABLEDBACKGROUNDCOLORINDEX	COLOR (LONG)	Disabled background window color
PP_BORDERCOLOR	RGB	Window border color
PP_BORDERCOLORINDEX	COLOR (LONG)	Window border color
PP_FONTNAMESIZE	PSZ	Window font name and point size
PP_ACTIVECOLOR	RGB	Active frame window title bar color
PP_ACTIVECOLORINDEX	COLOR (LONG	Active frame window title bar color

PP_INACTIVECOLOR	RGB	Inactive frame window title bar color
PP_INACTIVECOLORINDEX	COLOR (LONG	Inactive frame window title bar color
PP_ACTIVETEXTFGNDCOLOR	RGB	Active frame window title bar text foreground color
PP_ACTIVETEXTFGNDCOLORINDEX	COLOR (LONG)	Active frame window title bar text foreground color
PP_ACTIVETEXTBGNDCOLOR	RGB	Active frame window title bar text background color
PP_ACTIVETEXTBGNDCOLORINDEX	COLOR (LONG)	Active frame window title bar text background color
PP_INTIVETEXTFGNDCOLOR	RGB	Inactive frame window title bar text foreground color
PP_INTIVETEXTFGNDCOLORINDEX	COLOR (LONG)	Inactive frame window title bar text foreground color
PP_INTIVETEXTBGNDCOLOR	RGB	Inactive frame window title bar text background color
PP_INTIVETEXTBGNDCOLORINDEX	COLOR (LONG)	Inactive frame window title bar text background color
PP_SHADOW	COLOR (LONG)	Color for shadow of certain controls
PP_MENUFOREGROUNDCOLOR	RGB	Color for menu foreground
PP_MENUFOREGROUNDCOLORINDEX	COLOR (LONG)	Color for menu foreground
PP_MENUBACKGROUNDCOLOR	RGB	Color for menu background
PP_MENUBACKGROUNDCOLORINDEX	COLOR (LONG)	Color for menu background
PP_MENUHILITEFOREGROUNDCOLOR	RGB	Color for highlighted menu foreground
PP_MENUHILITEFOREGROUNDCOLORINDEX	COLOR (LONG)	Color for highlighted menu foreground
PP_MENUHILITEBACKGROUNDCOLOR	RGB	Color for highlighted menu background
PP_MENUHILITEBACKGROUNDCOLORINDEX	COLOR (LONG)	Color for highlighted menu background
PP_MENUDISABLEDFOREGROUNDCOLOR	RGB	Color for disabled menu foreground

PP_MENUDISABLEDFOREGROUNDCOLORINDEX	COLOR (LONG)	Color for disabled menu foreground
PP_MENUDISABLEDBACKGROUNDCOLOR	RGB	Color for disabled menu background
PP_MENUDISABLEDBACKGROUNDCOLORINDEX	COLOR (LONG)	Color for disabled menu background

6.25 Resource Files

As your program gets more advanced, there are other items you'll need to add — menus, dialog boxes, icons, accelerator keys, etc. Rather than doing several million *WinCreateWindow*s to create control windows, Presentation Manager supports a system of loading these resources, and nonwindow resources such as ICONs, ACCELTABLEs, and STRINGTABLEs, from a text .RC file known as a resource file.

Gotcha!

The frame window has several resources that can be associated with it, and all that are included in the FCF_* flags *must* be found in either a resource file or a .DLL in order for the frame window to be created. If the resources are not present, *WinCreateStdWindow* will fail. Also, all resources belonging to the frame *must* share the same resource ID.

The Resource Compiler compiles the .RC file into a .RES file and binds this file to the .EXE.

6.26 More on Messages

Presentation Manager windows communicate using a queue message processing system. Each window has its own message queue for processing messages; however, the all message queues are descendants of the Presentation Manager system message queue. This is the reason that one poorly designed Presentation Manager application can freeze up the entire system.

Once a window has a message queue, it can communicate with any other window in the entire system. All it needs is the window handle to send the message to.

A window can send or receive messages. Each message is used to signal some sort of event. Each time a mouse is moved, a window is resized, or a menu item is selected, messages are sent to a window. A window procedure operates like a massive sieve, filtering the messages of interest and passing through those messages that are unimportant. It is important to realize that *all* messages must be processed and replied to, either through your own window procedure or by passing the message to *WinDefWindowProc* or *WinDefDlgProc*. This facility of using events to control the programming flow is known as "event-driven programming." This style is common not only to Presentation Manager programming, but to Windows and Macintosh programming as well.

When a message is sent, it is usually directed to a particular window. For instance, a WM_CHAR message, indicating a key had been pressed, would be sent to the window that was currently active and had the keyboard focus.

There are two ways a message can be dispatched. They can either be sent, using *WinSendMsg*, or posted, using *WinPostMsg*. There is a very subtle difference between these two dispatch methods, and this could cause you problems somewhere down the road. When a message is *sent*, it is not put in a window's message queue; it is *immediately executed*. A message should be sent when it absolutely, positively, has to be there right now. A good example of this is passing pointers in messages when there is no guarantee that the pointer will point to something valid when the message is up for processing. *WinSendMsg* is a viable candidate for this situation.

Gotcha!

One little bit of information about *WinSendMsg:* this function will not return until that message has been processed. Yup, that's right. If you send a message from your window procedure to a window procedure that's asleep at the wheel, or even just a little slow to respond, your window procedure will sit there and wait until it gets some response back from the other window procedure. If you send a message to some window that the system controls the window procedure for, you can pretty much guarantee a zippy response; however, be very careful when using this function to send messages to either your own window procedure or to some other application's window procedure.

WinPostMsg is a much safer method of transmitting messages; however, the message is placed into the receiving window's message queue. It will be processed when that window gets around to it. *WinPostMsg* should be used when you want to communicate some information and do not care about a reply. *WinSendMsg* should be used when it is imperative that you gain some piece of information and have to respond to it now.

6.27 Message Priorities

When messages are retrieved from the message queue, they are not necessarily retrieved on a First In, First Out basis. Instead, messages are retrieved on the basis of priority, similar to threads. The following is a list of messages in the order they will be retrieved:

- WM_SEM1
- Posted messages
- Keyboard or mouse messages
- WM_SEM2
- WM_PAINT
- WM_SEM3
- WM_TIMER
- WM_SEM4

You may be wondering, "What are these WM_SEM messages, and the WM_TIMER message?" Well, on to the next topic...

6.28 Messages and Synchronization of Events

Often an application wants to know when some event has occurred. One way to do this is the use of the WM_SEM1,2,3,4 messages. These messages are totally for your application use. If these messages are passed to *WinDefWindowProc* or *WinDefDlgProc*, it has no effect on the system. For example, suppose you have a worker thread that has finished processing. That thread could post a WM_SEM2 to the main thread to indicate that the thread has finished its work. WM_SEM1 messages should really be reserved for very important, time-critical events.

A way to keep track of an event that is dependent on some function of time is to use the functions *WinStartTimer* and *WinStopTimer*. *WinStartTimer* starts an alarm clock that is set to go off after some application-defined amount of time, in milliseconds. When the timer goes off, the system sends a WM_TIMER message back to your window procedure.

You might consider using semaphores in a window procedure. *DONT'T*!!. Instead, think of using *WinRequestMutexSem*, *WinWaitEventSem*, or *WinWaitMuxWaitSem*. Waiting on a semaphore using the regular *DosWait...Sem* functions can bring a window procedure to a screeching halt. Even the most well-behaved semaphore synchronization can develop a mind of its own every now and then. The special set of window semaphore functions were created to provide the same functionality as the *DosWait...Sem* functions, but not to interrupt the flow of your window procedure. The system will appear to wait in the message processing that this function is called from, but messages posted to the message queue will be processed synchronously. When the semaphore has been posted, the message processing resumes where the *WinWait*...call was executed.

6.29 Window Painting and the WM_PAINT Message

This message is one of the most common messages to handle. A WM_PAINT message is generated whenever some part of the client window needs to be painted. If a user moves one window on top of another window, the bottom window receives a WM_PAINT message when the covered area becomes visible again. When a window region is in need of painting, it is said to be "invalid." Presentation Manager can invalidate a region, or you can invalidate a region yourself using *WinInvalidateRegion* or *WinInvalidateRect*. Presentation Manager is very stingy in sending WM_PAINT messages. Only that piece of the window that needs to be painted will be invalidated, *not* the entire window.

WM_PAINT messages are fairly low on the message priority totem pole. The default window style causes Presentation Manager to "group" invalidated regions together and generate one WM_PAINT message. The window style, WS_SYNCPAINT, or the class style, CS_SYNCPAINT, will stop Presentation Manager from behaving in this independent manner, and each time a region is invalidated, Presentation Manager will very obediently call the WM_PAINT processing immediately. The system does not post this messages, it jumps to the WM_PAINT processing, and then, when painting is completed, jumps back to the call following the region invalidation. Very few times will Presentation Manager dictate what must happen in your message processing, but the WM_PAINT message is the exception. An application must call

WinBeginPaint before painting the region, and *WinEndPaint* after painting is completed.

6.30 Presentation Spaces

A presentation space is similar to an artist's canvas. It is the space where the application draws. However, a presentation space does not have to be a window. It could also be a printer, or even some piece of memory. In reality, a presentation space is a data structure, but to the programmer it is the drawing area.

Presentation Manager will control how much of your window actually belongs in the presentation space. For example, if another window is covering most of your window, who should be able to draw on the intersection of the two windows? The normal answer is the window with the highest value in the Z-order. There are a few exceptions to this rule:

- WS_CLIPCHILDREN — If a window has this style, when the child window overlaps the parent, the parent window cannot draw on any part of the child's window. Normally, a child has a higher place in the Z-order than the parent, anyway, and this style is not necessary.
- WS_CLIPSIBLINGS— When two windows share the same parent, this style will omit a sibling's presentation space from the other sibling's presentation space. This style can be used if you always want to make sure one sibling "comes out on top."
- WS_PARENTCLIP — This gives a child window the ability to draw on its parent. This style can be potentially dangerous, esthetically speaking, because the parent's presentation space is larger than the child's space. However, somebody must have had a use for it somewhere.

6.31 The Class Style, CS_SIZEREDRAW

This style is very beneficial if you have some portion of your WM_PAINT routine that is sensitive to the size of the client area (of course, as good PM programmers we always pay attention to the size of the window, don't we?). If a window is resized, the whole client area is invalidated and a WM_PAINT message is put in the message queue. When you process the WM_PAINT message, simply plug in the new window height and width, and calculate accordingly.

6.32 Window Messages

PL_ALTERED
This message is broadcast to all frame window when the user has altered system settings.

Parameter 1:	HINI hiniNewProfile	handle to new user profile
Parameter 2:	HINI hiniNewSystemProfile	handle to new system profile
Reply:	ULONG ulReserved	reserved, 0

WM_ACTIVATE
This message is sent from the system when a window is being activated or deactivated.

Parameter 1:	USHORT usActive	active? TRUE:FALSE
Parameter 2:	HWND hwndWindow	if *usActive* == TRUE, this is the window being activated, else this is the window being deactivated
Reply:	ULONG ulReserved	reserved, 0

WM_APPTERMINATENOTIFY
This message is posted when a child application is terminated.

Parameter 1:	HAPP happAppHandle	handle to terminating application
Parameter 2:	ULONG ulReturnCode	return code from terminating application
Reply:	ULONG ulReserved	reserved, 0

WM_ADJUSTWINDOWPOS
This message is sent when a window is sized or positioned by *WinSetWindowPos*.

Parameter 1:   PSWP pswpSwap   pointer to new swap structure

```
typedef struct _SWP
{
    ULONG    fl;
    LONG     cy;
    LONG     cx;
    LONG     y;
    LONG     x;
    HWND     hwndInsertBehind;
    HWND     hwnd;
    ULONG    ulReserved1;
    ULONG    ulReserved2;
} SWP;
typedef SWP *PSWP;
```

Parameter 2:   ULONG ulReserved   reserved, 0
Reply: ULONG ulResult   move status
                                               0 — no changes made
                                               AWP_MINIMIZED — window is
                                               minimized
                                               AWP_MAXIMIZED — window is
                                               maximized
                                               AWP_RESTORED — window is
                                               restored
                                               AWP_ACTIVATE — window is
                                               activated
                                               AWP_DEACTIVATE — window
                                               is deactivated

WM_BEGINDRAG
This message is sent when a user starts a drag operation.

Parameter 1:   POINTS structPts   pointer position
```
typedef struct _POINTS         /* pts */
{
    SHORT x;
    SHORT y;
} POINTS;
typedef POINTS *PPOINTS;
```
Parameter 2:   USHORT usPointer   TRUE — input came from mouse
                                               FALSE — input came from
                                               keyboard
Reply: BOOL fProcessed   message processed? TRUE:
                                               FALSE

WM_BEGINSELECT

This message is sent when the user starts a selection operation.

Parameter 1:	USHORT usPointer	TRUE — input came from mouse FALSE — input came from keyboard
Parameter 2:	POINTS structPts	pointer position
Reply:	BOOL fProcessed	message processed? TRUE: FALSE

WM_BUTTON1CLICK

This message is sent when the user clicks on mouse button 1.

Parameter 1:	POINTS structPts	mouse position
Parameter 2:	USHORT usHitTest	hit test result

VALUE	DESCRIPTION
HT_NORMAL	The message belongs to this window
HT_TRANSPARENT	The part of the window underneath the mouse is not visible; keep checking other windows

	USHORT usKeyCode	keyboard control code
Reply:	BOOL fProcessed	message processed? TRUE: FALSE

WM_BUTTON2CLICK

This message is sent when the user clicks on mouse button 2.

Parameter 1:	POINTS ppMousePos	mouse position
Parameter 2:	USHORT usHitTest	hit test result
	USHORT usKeyCode	keyboard control code
Reply:	BOOL fProcessed	message processed? TRUE: FALSE

WM_BUTTON3CLICK
This message is sent when the user clicks on mouse button 3.

Parameter 1:	POINTS structPts	mouse position
Parameter 2:	USHORT usHitTest	hit test result
	USHORT usKeyCode	keyboard control code
Reply:	BOOL fProcessed	message processed? TRUE: FALSE

WM_BUTTON1DBCLK
This message is sent when the user double-clicks on mouse button 1.

Parameter 1:	POINTS structPts	mouse position
Parameter 2:	USHORT usHitTest	hit test result
	USHORT usKeyCode	keyboard control code
Reply:	BOOL fProcessed	message processed? TRUE: FALSE

WM_BUTTON2DBCLK
This message is sent when the user double-clicks on mouse button 2.

Parameter 1:	POINTS structPts	mouse position
Parameter 2:	USHORT usHitTest	hit test result
	USHORT usKeyCode	keyboard control code
Reply:	BOOL fProcessed	message processed? TRUE: FALSE

WM_BUTTON3DBCLK
This message is sent when the user double-clicks on mouse button 3.

Parameter 1:	POINTS structPts	mouse position
Parameter 2:	USHORT usHitTest	hit test result
	USHORT usKeyCode	keyboard control code
Reply:	BOOL fProcessed	message processed? TRUE: FALSE

WM_BUTTON1DOWN
This message is sent when the user presses mouse button 1 down.

Parameter 1:	POINTS structPts	mouse position
Parameter 2:	USHORT usHitTest	hit test result
	USHORT usKeyCode	keyboard control code
Reply:	BOOL fProcessed	message processed? TRUE: FALSE

WM_BUTTON1MOTIONEND
This message is sent when the user finishes a drag operation using mouse button 1.

Parameter 1:	POINTS structPts	mouse position
Parameter 2:	USHORT usHitTest	hit test result
	USHORT usKeyCode	keyboard control code
Reply:	BOOL fProcessed	message processed? TRUE: FALSE

WM_BUTTON1MOTIONSTART
This message is sent when the user starts a drag operation using mouse button 1.

Parameter 1:	POINTS structPts	mouse position
Parameter 2:	USHORT usHitTest	hit test result
	USHORT usKeyCode	keyboard control code
Reply:	BOOL fProcessed	message processed? TRUE: FALSE

WM_BUTTON2DOWN
This message is sent when the user presses mouse button 2 down.

Parameter 1:	POINTS structPts	mouse position
Parameter 2:	USHORT usHitTest	hit test result
	USHORT usKeyCode	keyboard control code
Reply:	BOOL fProcessed	message processed? TRUE: FALSE

WM_BUTTON2MOTIONEND
This message is sent when the user finishes a drag operation using mouse button 2.

Parameter 1:	POINTS structPts	mouse position
Parameter 2:	USHORT usHitTest	hit test result
	USHORT usKeyCode	keyboard control code
Reply:	BOOL fProcessed	message processed? TRUE: FALSE

WM_BUTTON2MOTIONSTART
This message is sent when the user starts a drag operation using mouse button 2.

Parameter 1:	POINTS structPts	mouse position
Parameter 2:	USHORT usHitTest	hit test result
	USHORT usKeyCode	keyboard control code
Reply:	BOOL fProcessed	message processed? TRUE: FALSE

WM_BUTTON3DOWN
This message is sent when the user presses mouse button 3 down.

Parameter 1:	POINTS structPts	mouse position
Parameter 2:	USHORT usHitTest	hit test result
	USHORT usKeyCode	keyboard control code
Reply:	BOOL fProcessed	message processed? TRUE: FALSE

WM_BUTTON3MOTIONEND
This message is sent when the user finishes a drag operation using mouse button 3.

Parameter 1:	POINTS structPts	mouse position
Parameter 2:	USHORT usHitTest	hit test result
	USHORT usKeyCode	keyboard control code
Reply:	BOOL fProcessed	message processed? TRUE: FALSE

WM_BUTTON3MOTIONSTART

This message is sent when the user starts a drag operation using mouse button 3.

Parameter 1:	POINTS structPts	mouse position
Parameter 2:	USHORT usHitTest	hit test result
	USHORT usKeyCode	keyboard control code
Reply:	BOOL fProcessed	message processed? TRUE: FALSE

WM_BUTTON1UP

This message is sent when the user releases mouse button 1.

Parameter 1:	POINTS structPts	mouse position
Parameter 2:	USHORT usHitTest	hit test result
	USHORT usKeyCode	keyboard control code
Reply:	BOOL fProcessed	message processed? TRUE: FALSE

WM_BUTTON2UP

This message is sent when the user releases mouse button 2.

Parameter 1:	POINTS structPts	mouse position
Parameter 2:	USHORT usHitTest	hit test result
	USHORT usKeyCode	keyboard control code
Reply:	BOOL fProcessed	message processed ? TRUE: FALSE

WM_BUTTON3UP

This message is sent when the user releases mouse button 3.

Parameter 1:	POINTS structPts	mouse position
Parameter 2:	USHORT usHitTest	hit test result
	USHORT usKeyCode	keyboard control code
Reply:	BOOL fProcessed	message processed? TRUE: FALSE

WM_CALCFRAMERECT

This message is sent when the window size is calculated using *WinCalcFrameRect*.

Parameter 1:   PRECTL prclWindow   window size

```
typedef struct _RECTL          /* rcl */
{
    LONG  xLeft;
    LONG  yBottom;
    LONG  xRight;
    LONG  yTop;
} RECTL;
typedef RECTL *PRECTL;
```

Parameter 2:   USHORT usFrame   TRUE — calculate client size,
                                         prclWindow is size of frame
                                         FALSE — calculate frame size,
                                         prclWindow is size of client

Reply: BOOL fSuccess   successful? TRUE: FALSE

WM_CALCVALIDRECTS

This message is sent from the system to determine which window region needs to be invalidated if the window is moved or sized.

Parameter 1:   PRECTL prclWindow[2] this is a pointer to two RECTL
                                         structures
                                         the first is the old window size,
                                         the second is the new window size

Parameter 2:   PSWP pswpNewPos   new window position

```
typedef struct _SWP    /* swp */
{
    ULONG   fl;
    LONG    cy;
    LONG    cx;
    LONG    y;
    LONG    x;
    HWND    hwndInsertBehind;
    HWND    hwnd;
    ULONG   ulReserved1;
    ULONG   ulReserved2;
} SWP;
typedef SWP *PSWP;
```

Reply: USHORT usAlign   how to align the window; these values can be OR'ed together

FLAG	DESCRIPTION
CVR_ALIGNLEFT	The valid window region is aligned along with the left edge of the window
CVR_ALIGNBOTTOM	The valid window region is aligned along with the bottom edge of the window
CVR_ALIGNTOP	The valid window region is aligned along with the top edge of the window
CVP_ALIGNRIGHT	The valid window region is aligned along with the right edge of the window
CVR_REDRAW	The whole window is invalidated
0	Use the values specified in the second PRECTL

WM_CHAR

This message is sent to indicate a key has been pressed.

Parameter 1:   USHORT usFlags   keyboard control codes

CODE	MEANING
KC_CHAR	Character key was hit, value is in *usCharCode*
KC_SCANCODE	Value of key is in KC_SCANCODE
KC_VIRTUALKEY	Indicates a virtual key was hit, value is in *usVKeyCode*
KC_KEYUP	Key is released
KC_PREVDOWN	Usually precedes the KC_KEYUP flag
KC_DEADKEY	Key was a dead key
KC_COMPOSITE	Key was a combination of the previous dead key and this key
KC_INVALIDCOMP	Key was an invalid combination
KC_LONEKEY	A key was pressed and released, and no other keys were involved

KC_SHIFT	The SHIFT key was pressed
KC_ALT	The ALT key was pressed
KC_CTRL	The CTRL key was pressed

	UCHAR ucRepeatCt	number of times key was pressed
Parameter 2:	USHORT usCharCode	character code
	USHORT usVKeyCode	virtual key codes
Reply:	BOOL fProcessed	processed? TRUE: FALSE

WM_CHORD

This message is sent when the user presses both mouse button 1 and 2 at the same time.

Parameter 1:	ULONG ulReserved	reserved, 0
Parameter 2:	USHORT usHitTest	hit test result
Reply:	BOOL fProcess	message processed? TRUE: FALSE

WM_CLOSE

This message is sent to a frame when the user is closing the window.

Parameter 1:	ULONG ulReserved	reserved, 0
Parameter 2:	ULONG ulReserved	reserved, 0
Reply:	ULONG ulReply	reserved, 0
Note:	If you intercept this message, make sure to post a WM_QUIT to the appropriate window. This is what the default window procedure does.	

WM_COMMAND

This message is sent from a control to its owner whenever it has to notify its owner about a significant event.

Parameter 1:	USHORT usCommand	application-defined ID of item that generated message
Parameter 2:	USHORT usSourceType	CMDSRC_PUSHBUTTON — pushbutton-generated message CMDSRC_MENU — menu-generated message CMDSRC_ACCELERATOR — accelerator key-generated message

		CMDSRC_FONTDLG — font dialog-generated message CMDSRC_OTHER — some other type of control-generated message
	USHORT usPointer	TRUE — mouse was used to initiate event FALSE — keyboard was used to initiate event
Reply:	ULONG flReply	reserved, 0

WM_CONTEXTMENU

This message is sent when the user performs an operation that initiates a popup menu.

Parameter 1:	USHORT usPoint	TRUE — operation was performed by pointer FALSE — operation was performed by keystroke
Parameter 2:	POINTS ptsMousePos	mouse position if *usPoint* == TRUE
Reply:	BOOL fProcessed	processed? TRUE: FALSE

WM_CONTROL

This message is sent to a control's owner in order to signal a significant event that has occurred to the control.

Parameter 1:	USHORT usId	control ID
	USHORT usNotifyCode	control notify code
Parameter 2:	ULONG ulNotifyInfo	control-specific information
Reply:	ULONG ulReply	reserved, 0

WM_CONTROLPOINTER

This message is sent to a control's owner when the user moves the mouse over the control window.

Parameter 1:	USHORT usID	control ID
Parameter 2:	HPOINTER hptrCurrent	current mouse pointer
Reply:	HPOINTER hptrNew	pointer to new mouse pointer

Note: This message gives you the opportunity to change the standard mouse pointer to something else, for instance, an hourglass pointer. Trap the message when in a wait situation, and return the HPOINTER you want the pointer to change to.

WM_CREATE

This message is sent to a window at the first stage of its creation.

Parameter 1:   PVOID pControlData   data passed from
                                                            WinCreateWindow

Parameter 2:   PCREATESTRUCT pCreateStr   pointer to a create
                                                            structure

```
typedef struct _CREATESTRUCT
{
    PVOID    pPresParams;
    PVOID    pCtlData;
    ULONG    id;
    HWND     hwndInsertBehind;
    HWND     hwndOwner;
    LONG     cy;
    LONG     cx;
    LONG     y;
    LONG     x;
    ULONG    flStyle;
    PSZ      pszText;
    PSZ      pszClass;
    HWND     hwndParent;
} CREATESTRUCT;
typedef CREATESTRUCT *PCREATESTRUCT;
```

Reply: BOOL fContinue   continue creating
                                                            window? TRUE: FALSE

Note: This message is not a good place to do much except transfer data from *WinCreateWindow*. At this point in time a window has no shape, size, or focus, so most changes to any of these qualities will fail. A better idea is to post yourself a message from the WM_CREATE processing. Do all the initialization in the user-defined message.

WM_DESTROY

This message is sent when a window is being destroyed.

Parameter 1:   ULONG ulReserved   reserved, 0
Parameter 2:   ULONG ulReserved   reserved, 0
Reply: ULONG ulReserved   reserved, 0

Note: This is the last message that is sent to a window before it is destroyed. If you have allocated memory for a window word, this is the place to free it.

WM_DRAWITEM
Sent to the owner of a control when an item with *S_OWNERDRAW is to be drawn.

Parameter 1:	USHORT usID	window ID
Parameter 2:	POWNERITEM pownerOwnerItem	pointer to OWNERITEM structure

```
typedef struct _OWNERITEM
{
    HWND    hwnd;
    HPS     hps;
    ULONG   fsState;
    ULONG   fsAttribute;
    ULONG   fsStateOld;
    ULONG   fsAttributeOld;
    RECTL   rclItem;
    LONG    idItem;
    ULONG   hItem;
} OWNERITEM;
typedef OWNERITEM *POWNERITEM;
```

Reply:	BOOL fDrawn	drawn? TRUE:FALSE

WM_ENABLE
This message is sent to enable, or disable, a window.

Parameter 1:	USHORT usEnable	enable window? TRUE: FALSE
Parameter 2:	ULONG ulReserved	reserved, 0
Reply:	ULONG ulReserved	reserved, 0

Note: This is the recommended way to prevent a user from selecting a control. A control window should not be permanently disabled, only disabled while it is not available.

WM_ENDDRAG

This message is sent when a drag operation is completed.

Parameter 1:	USHORT usPoint	TRUE — message came from pointer input FALSE — message came from keyboard input
Parameter 2:	POINTS ptsMousePos	mouse position
Reply:	ULONG ulProcessed	message processed? TRUE: FALSE

WM_ENDSELECT

This message is sent when a select operation is completed.

Parameter 1:	USHORT usPoint	TRUE — message came from pointer input FALSE — message came from keyboard input
Parameter 2:	POINTS ptsMousePos	mouse position
Reply:	ULONG ulProcessed	message processed? TRUE: FALSE

WM_ERASEWINDOW

This message is sent to a window after a region has been invalidated, but before it has been painted.

Parameter 1:	ULONG ulReserved	reserved, 0
Parameter 2:	ULONG ulReserved	reserved, 0
Reply:	BOOL fErase	window region erased? TRUE: FALSE

WM_ERROR

This message is sent when an error is detected.

Parameter 1:	USHORT usErrorCode	error code (list in PMERR.H)
Parameter 2:	ULONG ulReserved	reserved, 0
Reply:	ULONG ulReserved	reserved, 0

WM_FOCUSCHANGE

This message is sent when a window is losing focus or gaining focus.

Parameter 1:	HWND hwndWindow	window handle
Parameter 2:	USHORT usFocus	TRUE — window is gaining focus, *hwndWindow* is window losing focus
		FALSE — window is losing focus, *hwndWindow* is window gaining focus
	USHORT usFocusFlags	focus flags

FLAG	MEANING
FC_NOSETFOCUS	A WM_SETFOCUS message is not sent to the window receiving focus
FC_NOLOSEFOCUS	A WM_SETFOCUS message is not sent to the window losing focus
FC_NOSETACTIVE	A WM_SETACTIVE message is not sent to the window becoming active
FC_NOLOSEACTIVE	A WM_SETACTIVE message is not sent to the window being deactivated
FC_NOSETSELECTION	A WM_SETSELECTION message is not sent to the window being selected
FC_NOLOSESELECTION	A WM_SETSELECTION message is not sent to the window being deselected
FC_NOBRINGTOTOP	No window is brought to the top
FC_NOBRINGTOTOPFIRSTWINDOW	The first frame window is not brought to the top

Reply:	ULONG ulReserved	reserved, 0

WM_FORMATFRAME
This message is sent to the frame to adjust all the frame controls and the client window.

Parameter 1:	PSWP swpSizes	array of sizes and positions of controls
Parameter 2:	PRECTL prclClient	client window size
Reply:	usArrayCount	count of SWP structures returned in swpSizes

Note: This message is used to adjust the sizes and positions of the controls on the frame. If you subclass the frame window and add controls to the frame, you need to intercept this message and add the SWP structures of your controls. You also will need to intercept the WM_QUERYFRAMECTLCOUNT message and increment the return value by the number of the controls you are adding. It is this value that controls the number of SWP structures in the WM_FORMATFRAME. Also, if you put a sizing border on a dialog box, the dialog box does not receive a WM_SIZE message; instead it receives a WM_FORMATFRAME.

WM_HELP
This message is sent to the owner of a control when the user has hit the help key.

Parameter 1:	USHORT usCmd	command value
Parameter 2:	USHORT usCtlType	CMDSRC_PUSHBUTTON CMDSRC_MENU CMDSRC_ACCELERATOR CMDSRC_OTHER
	USHORT usPtr	TRUE — message came from mouse move FALSE — message came from keyboard
Reply:	ULONG ulReserved	reserved, 0

WM_HITTEST
This message is used to find the window that the user was responding to when mouse input occurred.

Parameter 1:	POINTS ptsMousePos	mouse position
Parameter 2:	ULONG ulReserved	reserved, 0

Reply:	ULONG ulResult	HT_NORMAL — message belongs to this window
		HT_TRANSPARENT — message does not belong to this window, keep checking
		HT_DISCARD — discard message
		HT_ERROR — discard message, message resulted from a button down message on a disabled window

WM_HSCROLL

This message is sent to the owner of a horizontal scroll bar when the user initiated some scrolling action.

Parameter 1:	USHORT usID	scroll bar ID
Parameter 2:	SHORT sPos	slider position
	USHORT usCmd	command

COMMAND	MEANING
SB_LINELEFT	The user clicked on left arrow, or a VK_LEFT key was pressed
SB_LINERIGHT	The user clicked on right arrow, or a VK_RIGHT key was pressed
SB_PAGELEFT	The user clicked to the left of the slider or VK_PAGELEFT key was pressed
SB_PAGERIGHT	The user clicked to the right of the slider or VK_PAGERIGHT key was pressed
SB_SLIDERPOSITION	This is the final position of the slider
SB_SLIDERTRACK	The user used the mouse to change the position of the slider
SB_ENDSCROLL	The user has finished scrolling

Reply:	ULONG ulReserved	reserved, 0

WM_INITDLG
Sent when a dialog box is being created.

Parameter 1:	HWND hwndControl	control window to receive focus
Parameter 2:	PVOID pData	application-defined data passed by *WinLoadDlg*, *WinCreateDlg*, or *WinDlgBox*
Reply:	BOOL fFocus	TRUE — focus window has been changed FALSE — focus window has not been changed

WM_INITMENU
This message is sent when a window is becoming active.

Parameter 1:	USHORT usMenuID	menu control ID
Parameter 2:	HWND hwndMenu	menu window handle
Reply:	ULONG ulReserved	reserved, 0

WM_JOURNALNOTIFY
This message is sent during journal playback.

Parameter 1:	ULONG ulCmd	JRN_QUEUESTATUS JRN_PHYSKEYSTATE
Parameter 2:	USHORT usQueueStat	queue status if JRN_QUEUESTATUS
	USHORT usScanCode	key scan code if JRN_PHYSKEYSTATE
	USHORT usKeyState	key state if JRN_PHYSKEYSTATE
Reply:	ULONG ulReserved	reserved, 0

WM_MEASUREITEM
This message is sent to the owner of a control in order to determine the height and width of the specified item.

Parameter 1:	SHORT sControlID	ID of control window
Parameter 2:	ULONG ulInfo	control-specific information

Reply: SHORT sHeight — height of control item of interest
SHORT sWidth — width of control item of interest

WM_MENUEND
This message is sent when a menu is ending.

Parameter 1: USHORT usMenuID — menu control ID
Parameter 2: HWND hwndMenu — menu window handle
Reply: ULONG ulReserved — reserved, 0

WM_MENUSELECT
This message is sent when the user has selected a new menu item.

Parameter 1: UHOSRT usiD — selected menuitem ID
USHORT usCmdMsg — TRUE — a command message will be posted to the owner FALSE — no message will be posted
Parameter 2: HWND hwndMenu — menu window handle
Reply: BOOL fPostMsg — post message? TRUE: FALSE

WM_MINMAXFRAME
This message is sent when a frame is being maximized, minimized, or restored.

Parameter 1: PSWP pswpWinPos — window position
Parameter 2: ULONG ulReserved — reserved, 0
Reply: BOOL fProcess — TRUE — process message FALSE — ignore message

WM_MOUSEMOVE
This mouse has moved.

Parameter 1: POINTS MousePos — mouse position
Parameter 2: USHORT usHitTest — hit test result
USHORT usKeyCode — keyboard control code
Reply: BOOL fProcessed — Message processed? TRUE: FALSE

WM_MOVE
This message is sent when a window has moved.

Parameter 1:	ULONG ulReserved	reserved, 0
Parameter 2:	ULONG ulReserved	reserved, 0
Reply:	ULONG ulReserved	reserved, 0

Note: This message is sent only if the window has the style CS_MOVENOTIFY.

WM_NEXTMENU
This message is sent to the owner of the menu to indicate either the beginning or the end of the menu has been reached.

Parameter 1:	HWND hwndMenu	menu window handle
Parameter 2:	USHORT usBeginning	TRUE — at beginning of menu
		FALSE — at end of menu
Reply:	HWND hwndNextMenu	new menu window handle

WM_NULL
This is a NULL message used for an application-defined purpose.

Parameter 1:	ULONG ulReserved	reserved, 0
Parameter 2:	ULONG ulReserved	reserved, 0
Reply:	ULONG ulReserved	reserved, 0

WM_OPEN
This message is sent when a user opens a window.

Parameter 1:	USHORT usPtr	input source
		TRUE — mouse
		FALSE — keyboard
Parameter 2:	POINTS ptsMousePos	mouse position
Reply:	BOOL fProcess	message processed?
		TRUE: FALSE

WM_PACTIVATE
This is an NLS message sent when a WM_ACTIVATE message is received.

Parameter 1:	USHORT usActive	TRUE — window was made active
		FALSE — window was deactivated
Parameter 2:	HWND hwndWindow	window handle
		if *usActive* == TRUE, this is window handle of window being made active
		if *usActive* == FALSE, this is window handle of window being deactivated
Reply:	ULONG ulReserved	reserved, 0

WM_PAINT
This message is sent when a window needs painting.

Parameter 1:	ULONG ulReserved	reserved, 0
Parameter 2:	ULONG ulReserved	reserved, 0
Reply:	ULONG ulReserved	reserved, 0

WM_PCONTROL
This message is an NLS message sent when a WM_CONTROL message is received.

Parameter 1:	USHORT usID	control window ID
	USHORT usNotifyCode	notification code
Parameter 2:	ULONG ulReserved	reserved, 0
Reply:	ULONG ulReserved	reserved, 0

WM_PPAINT
This is an NLS message sent when a WM_PAINT message is received.

Parameter 1:	ULONG ulReserved	reserved, 0
Parameter 2:	ULONG ulReserved	reserved, 0
Reply:	ULONG ulReserved	reserved, 0

WM_PRESPARAMCHANGED

This message is sent when a window's Presentation Parameters are changed.

Parameter 1:	ULONG ulID	attribute type ID
Parameter 2:	ULONG ulReserved	reserved, 0
Reply:	ULONG ulReserved	reserved, 0

WM_PSETFOCUS

This is an NLS message sent when a WM_SETFOCUS is received.

Parameter 1:	HWND hwndWindow	focus window handle
Parameter 2:	USHORT usFocus	TRUE — window is gaining focus, *hwndWindow* is window losing focus FALSE — window is losing focus, *hwndWindow* is window gaining focus
Reply:	ULONG ulReserved	reserved, 0

WM_PSIZE

This is an NLS message sent when a WM_SIZE is received.

Parameter 1:	SHORT sOldWidth SHORT sOldHeight	old window width old window height
Parameter 2:	SHORT sNewWidth SHORT sNewHeight	new window width new window height
Reply:	ULONG ulReserved	reserved, 0

WM_PSYSCOLORCHANGE

This is an NLS message sent after a WM_SYSCOLORCHANGE message is received.

Parameter 1:	ULONG ulOptions	LCOL_RESET LCOL_PURECOLOR
Parameter 2:	ULONG ulReserved	reserved, 0
Reply:	ULONG ulReserved	reserved, 0

WM_QUERYACCELTABLE
This message is sent to retrieve a handle to a window's accelerator table.

Parameter 1:	ULONG ulReserved	reserved, 0
Parameter 2:	ULONG ulReserved	reserved, 0
Reply:	HACCEL hAccel	accelerator table handle, or NULLHANDLE if not available

WM_QUERYCONVERTPOS
This message is sent to determine whether to begin DBCS character conversion.

Parameter 1:	PRECTL pCursorPos	cursor position
Parameter 2:	ULONG ulParam2	reserved, 0
Reply:	USHORT usCode	QCP_CONVERT — conversion can be performed QCP_NOCONVERT — conversion should not be performed

WM_QUERYHELPINFO
This message is sent to query the help instance associated with a frame window.

Parameter 1:	ULONG ulReserved	reserved, 0
Parameter 2:	ULONG ulReserved	reserved, 0
Reply:	HWND hwndHelp	help instance window handle

WM_QUERYTRACKINFO
This message is sent after a frame receives a WM_TRACKFRAME.

Parameter 1:	USHORT usTrack	tracking flags

FLAG	MEANING
TF_TOP	Track the top of the rectangle
TF_BOTTOM	Track the bottom of the rectangle
TF_RIGHT	Track the right side of the rectangle
TF_LEFT	Track the left side of the rectangle
TF_MOVE	Track all sides
TF_SETPOINTERPOS	Reposition the mouse pointer

TF_GRID	Rectangle is snapped to the grip coordinates in *cxGrid* and *cyGrid*
TF_STANDARD	The grid coordinates are multiples of the border width and height
TF_ALLINBOUNDARY	No part of the tracking is outside the *rclBoundary* rectangle
TF_PARTINBOUNDARY	Some part of the tracking is inside the *rclBoundary* rectangle
TF_VALIDATETRACKRECT	The tracking rectangle is validated

Parameter 2:   PTRACKINFO ptrTrackInfo   pointer to track info structure

```
typedef struct _TRACKINFO      /* ti */
{
    LONG     cxBorder;
    LONG     cyBorder;
    LONG     cxGrid;
    LONG     cyGrid;
    LONG     cxKeyboard;
    LONG     cyKeyboard;
    RECTL    rclTrack;
    RECTL    rclBoundary;
    POINTL   ptlMinTrackSize;
    POINTL   ptlMaxTrackSize;
    ULONG    fs;
} TRACKINFO;
typedef TRACKINFO *PTRACKINFO;
```

Reply: BOOL fContinue   continue moving or sizing: TRUE: FALSE

Note: This message can be used to limit the sizing of a frame window. Adjust the max and min track size POINTL structures and add the TF_ALLINBOUNDARY flag. The IMAGE example of the Developer's Toolkit gives a nice example of the proper processing of the message.

WM_QUERYWINDOWPARAMS
This message is used to query a window's Presentation Parameters

Parameter 1:   PWNDPARAMS pWndParms   pointer to WNDPARAMS structure

```
typedef struct _WNDPARAMS
{
   ULONG   fsStatus;
   ULONG   cchText;
   PSZ     pszText;
   ULONG   cbPresParams;
   PVOID   pPresParams;
   ULONG   cbCtlData;
   PVOID   pCtlData;
} WNDPARAMS;
typedef WNDPARAMS *PWNDPARAMS;
```

Parameter 2:   ULONG ulReserved   reserved, 0
Reply: BOOL fSuccess   successful? TRUE: FALSE

WM_QUIT
This message is used to tell an application to terminate itself.

Parameter 1:   ULONG ulReserved   reserved, 0
Parameter 2:   ULONG ulReserved   reserved, 0
Reply: ULONG ulReserved   reserved, 0
Note: This is the message that causes *WinGetMsg* to return FALSE and end the message processing loop. If you processing this message, do not pass this through to *WinDefWindowProc*.

WM_REALIZEPALETTE
This message is sent when another application changes the display hardware color palette.

Parameter 1:   ULONG ulReserved   reserved, 0
Parameter 2:   ULONG ulReserved   reserved, 0
Reply: ULONG ulReserved   reserved, 0

WM_SAVEAPPLICATION
This message is sent to the application to give the application a chance to save the current state.

Parameter 1:   ULONG ulReserved   reserved, 0

| **Parameter 2:** | ULONG ulReserved | reserved, 0 |
| **Reply:** | ULONG ulReserved | reserved, 0 |

WM_SEM1

This message is sent from the application for its own use.

Parameter 1:	ULONG ulCount	this is a collection of this variable from any other existing WM_SEM1 messages in the queue, OR'ed together
Parameter 2:	ULONG ulReserved	reserved, 0
Reply:	ULONG ulReserved	reserved, 0

Note: This message has a higher priority than any other message, and will be retrieved from the message queue first.

WM_SEM2

This message is sent from the application for its own use.

Parameter 1:	ULONG ulCount	this is a collection of this variable from any other existing WM_SEM2 messages in the queue, OR'ed together
Parameter 2:	ULONG ulReserved	reserved, 0
Reply:	ULONG ulReserved	reserved, 0

Note: This message has a higher priority than WM_PAINT or WM_TIMER, but lower than the user I/O messages.

WM_SEM3

This message is sent from the application for its own use.

Parameter 1:	ULONG ulCount	this is a collection of this variable from any other existing WM_SEM3 messages in the queue, OR'ed together
Parameter 2:	ULONG ulReserved	reserved, 0
Reply:	ULONG ulReserved	reserved, 0

Note: This message has a higher priority than WM_PAINT, but lower than almost all other messages.

WM_SEM4
This message is sent from the application for its own use.

Parameter 1:	ULONG ulCount	this is a collection of this variable from any other existing WM_SEM4 messages in the queue, OR'ed together
Parameter 2:	ULONG ulReserved	reserved, 0
Reply:	ULONG ulReserved	reserved, 0
Note:	This message has a lower priority than all other messages.	

WM_SETACCELTABLE
This message is sent to associate an accelerator table to a window.

Parameter 1:	HACCEL hAccelTable	handle to new accelerator table
Parameter 2:	ULONG ulReserved	reserved, 0
Reply:	BOOL fSuccess	successful? TRUE: FALSE

WM_SETFOCUS
This message is sent when a window is losing or gaining focus.

Parameter 1:	HWND hwndWindow	window handle
Parameter 2:	USHORT usFocus	TRUE — window is gaining focus, *hwndWindow* is window losing focus FALSE — window is losing focus *hwndWindow* is window gaining focus
Reply:	ULONG ulReserved	reserved, 0

WM_SETHELPINFO
This message is sent to associate a help instance with a window.

Parameter 1:	HWND hwndHelp	help instance handle
Parameter 2:	ULONG ulReserved	reserved, 0
Reply:	BOOL fSuccess	successful? TRUE: FALSE

WM_SETSELECTION
This message is sent when a window is selected or deselected.

Parameter 1:	USHORT usSelect	TRUE — window is selected
		FALSE — window is deselected
Parameter 2:	ULONG ulReserved	reserved, 0
Reply:	ULONG ulReserved	reserved, 0

WM_SETWINDOWPARAMS
This message is sent to set the window's Presentation Parameters.

Parameter 1:	PWNDPARAMS ptrWndParams	pointer to WNDPARAMS structure
Parameter 2:	ULONG ulReserved	reserved, 0
Reply:	BOOL fSuccess	successful? TRUE: FALSE

WM_SHOW
This message is sent when a window is to be made visible or invisible.

Parameter 1:	USHORT usShow	TRUE — show window
		FALSE — hide window
Parameter 2:	ULONG ulReserved	reserved, 0
Reply:	ULONG ulReserved	reserved, 0

WM_SINGLESELECT
This message is sent when the user selects an object.

Parameter 1:	USHORT usPtr	TRUE — selection came from mouse
		FALSE — selection came from keyboard
Parameter 2:	POINTS ptsMousePos	mouse position
Reply:	BOOL fProcessed	message processed? TRUE: FALSE

WM_SIZE
This message is sent when a window changes its size.

Parameter 1:	SHORT sOldWidth	old window width

	SHORT sOldHeight	old window height
Parameter 2:	SHORT sNewWidth	new window width
	SHORT sNewHeight	new window height
Reply:	ULONG ulReserved	reserved, 0

WM_SYSCOMMAND

This message is sent from a control to its owner whenever it has to notify its owner about a significant event.

Parameter 1:	USHORT usCommand	one of the following:
		SC_SIZE
		SC_MOVE
		SC_MINIMIZE
		SC_MAXIMIZE
		SC_CLOSE
		SC_NEXT
		SC_APPMENU
		SC_SYSMENU
		SC_RESTORE
		SC_NEXTFRAME
		SC_NEXTWINDOW
		SC_TASKMANAGER
		SC_HELPKEYS
		SC_HELPINDEX
		SC_HELPEXTENDED
		SC_SWITCHPANELIDS
		SC_DBE_FIRST
		SC_DBE_LAST
		SC_BEGINDRAG
		SC_ENDDRAG
		SC_SELECT
		SC_OPEN
		SC_CONTEXTMENU
		SC_CONTEXTHELP
		SC_TEXTEDIT
		SC_BEGINSELECT
		SC_ENDSELECT
		SC_WINDOW
		SC_HIDE
Parameter 2:	USHORT usSourceType	CMDSRC_PUSHBUTTON — pushbutton-generated message

		CMDSRC_MENU — menu-generated message CMDSRC_ACCELERATOR — accelerator key-generated message CMDSRC_FONTDLG — font dialog-generated message CMDSRC_OTHER — some other type of control-generated message
	USHORT usPointer	TRUE — mouse was used to initiate event FALSE — keyboard was used to initiate event
Reply:	ULONG flReply	reserved, 0

WM_SYSVALUECHANGED
This message is sent when a system value (SV_*) has been changed.

Parameter 1:	USHORT usFirstValue	ID of first value that has changed
Parameter 2:	USHORT usLastValue	ID of last value that has changed
Reply:	ULONG ulReserved	reserved, 0

Note: All values between *usFirstValue* and *usLastValue* will have been changed.

WM_TEXTEDIT
This message is sent when a user is doing direct edit.

Parameter 1:	USHORT usPtr	TRUE — selection came from mouse FALSE — selection came from keyboard
Parameter 2:	POINTS ptsMousePos	mouse position
Reply:	BOOL fProcessed	message processed? TRUE: FALSE

WM_TIMER
This message is sent when a timer expires.

Parameter 1:	USHORT usID	timer ID
Parameter 2:	ULONG ulReserved	reserved, 0
Reply:	ULONG ulReserved	reserved, 0

WM_TRACKFRAME
This message is sent when a frame window is moved or sized.

Parameter 1:	USHORT fsFlags	TF_* flags
Parameter 2:	ULONG ulReserved	reserved, 0
Reply:	BOOL fSuccess	successful? TRUE: FALSE

WM_TRANSLATEACCEL
This message is sent to determine if a character key is an accelerator key.

Parameter 1:	PQMSG msg	QMSG structure
Parameter 2:	ULONG ulReserved	reserved, 0
Reply:	BOOL fAccel	character exists in accelerator table? TRUE: FALSE

WM_TRANSLATEMNEMONIC
This message is sent after a WM_TRANSLATEACCEL message.

Parameter 1:	PQMSG msg	pointer to a QMSG structure
Parameter 2:	ULONG ulReserved	reserved, 0
Reply:	BOOL fAccel	key is an accelerator key? TRUE: FALSE

WM_UPDATEFRAME
This message is sent when a frame window needs updating.

Parameter 1:	ULONG ulFrameFlags	the FCF_* flags
Parameter 2:	ULONG ulReserved	reserved, 0
Reply:	BOOL fProcess	processed message? TRUE: FALSE

Note: This message should be sent by the application when the frame window is customized by adding or modifying controls.

WM_VSCROLL
This message is sent when a user modifies the position of a vertical scroll bar.

Parameter 1:	USHORT usID	scroll bar ID

| **Parameter 2:** | SHORT sPos | slider position |
| | USHORT usCmd | command |

COMMAND	MEANING
SB_LINEUP	The user clicked on up arrow, or a VK_UP key was pressed
SB_LINEDOWN	The user clicked on down arrow, or a VK_DOWN key was pressed
SB_PAGEUP	The user clicked to the top of the slider, or VK_PAGEUP key was pressed
SB_PAGEDOWN	The user clicked to the bottom of the slider, or VK_PAGEDOWN key was pressed
SB_SLIDERPOSITION	This is the final position of the slider
SB_SLIDERTRACK	The user used the mouse to change the position of the slider
SB_ENDSCROLL	The user has finished scrolling

| **Reply:** | ULONG ulReserved | reserved, 0 |

WM_WINDOWPOSCHANGED

This message is sent when a window's position is changed.

Parameter 1:	PSWP pswpPosition	pointer to two SWP structures: the first is the new structure, the second is the old structure
Parameter 2:	ULONG ulAdjust	AWF_* flags returned from WM_ADJUSTWINDOWPOS
Reply:	ULONG ulReserved	reserved, 0

Chapter 7

Dialog Boxes

Dialog boxes are designed to gather specific pieces of information from the user. They can be displayed upon selection from a menu item or by pushing a button. Dialogs contain a mix and match of child control windows. A window that pops up and contains such fields as "Name:", "Address", "Phone", "City", "State", etc. is a good example of a fairly common dialog box.

There are two ways to create a dialog box and its child controls — by using a resource file, or by physically calling the *WinCreateWindow* for the dialog box and each of its controls. The resource file is the easiest way to create a dialog box. The Dialog Box Editor shipped with the Toolkit is designed to help facilitate this creation process.

Dialog boxes come in two styles — modal and modeless. A modeless dialog box lets the user interact with all the other windows and controls belonging to the same process. A modal dialog box is more restrictive of the user's input. A user cannot interact with the other windows and controls that are children of the owner of the dialog box, including the owner. A modal dialog box is designed to be used when the user is required to enter some information before proceeding on to the next step in the application.

The following sample program is designed to introduce you to dialog box programming, and also to display the difference between modal and modeless dialog boxes.

DIALOG.C

```
#define INCL_WIN

#include <os2.h>
#include <stdio.h>
#include <stdlib.h>
#include <string.h>
#include "dialog.h"

#define CLS_CLIENT               "MyClass"

MRESULT EXPENTRY ClientWndProc ( HWND hwndWnd,
                                 ULONG ulMsg,
                                 MPARAM mpParm1,
                                 MPARAM mpParm2 ) ;

MRESULT EXPENTRY DlgProc ( HWND hwndWnd,
                           ULONG ulMsg,
                           MPARAM mpParm1,
                           MPARAM mpParm2 ) ;

INT main ( VOID )
{
    HAB           habAnchor ;
    HMQ           hmqQueue ;
    ULONG         ulFlags ;
    HWND          hwndFrame ;
    HWND          hwndClient ;
    QMSG          qmMsg ;
    BOOL          bLoop ;

    habAnchor = WinInitialize ( 0 ) ;
    hmqQueue = WinCreateMsgQueue ( habAnchor, 0 ) ;

    WinRegisterClass ( habAnchor,
                       CLS_CLIENT,
                       ClientWndProc,
                       CS_SIZEREDRAW,
                       0 ) ;

    ulFlags = FCF_STANDARD & ~FCF_SHELLPOSITION & ~FCF_ACCELTABLE &
              ~FCF_TASKLIST ;

    hwndFrame = WinCreateStdWindow ( HWND_DESKTOP,
                                     0,
                                     &ulFlags,
                                     CLS_CLIENT,
                                     "Dialog Box Example",
                                     0,
                                     NULLHANDLE,
                                     IDR_CLIENT,
                                     &hwndClient ) ;
```

```
   if ( hwndFrame != 0 ) {
      WinSetWindowPos ( hwndFrame,
                        NULLHANDLE,
                        50,
                        50,
                        250,
                        150,
                        SWP_SIZE |
                        SWP_MOVE |
                        SWP_ACTIVATE |
                        SWP_SHOW ) ;

      bLoop = WinGetMsg ( habAnchor, &qmMsg, NULLHANDLE, 0, 0 ) ;
      while ( bLoop ) {
         WinDispatchMsg ( habAnchor, &qmMsg ) ;
         bLoop = WinGetMsg ( habAnchor,
                             &qmMsg,
                             NULLHANDLE,
                             0,
                             0 ) ;
      } /* endwhile */

      WinDestroyWindow ( hwndFrame ) ;
   } /* endif */

   WinDestroyMsgQueue ( hmqQueue ) ;
   WinTerminate ( habAnchor ) ;
   return 0 ;
}

MRESULT EXPENTRY DlgProc ( HWND hwndWnd,
                           ULONG ulMsg,
                           MPARAM mpParm1,
                           MPARAM mpParm2 )
{
   switch ( ulMsg ) {

   case WM_INITDLG:
      {
         BOOL bModal ;
         CHAR achMessage [64] ;

         bModal = *(( PBOOL ) PVOIDFROMMP ( mpParm2 )) ;

         WinSetWindowPos ( hwndWnd,
                           NULLHANDLE,
                           10,
                           ( bModal?100:150 ) ,
                           0,
                           0,
                           SWP_MOVE ) ;

         sprintf ( achMessage,
                   "I'm a %s dialog box",
                   ( bModal? ( "modal" ) : ( "modeless" )) ) ;
```

```
            WinSetDlgItemText ( hwndWnd,
                                IDT_DIALOGNAME,
                                achMessage ) ;

         if ( bModal ) {
            strcpy ( achMessage,
                     "Try and click on the main window" ) ;
         } else {
            strcpy ( achMessage, "Click on the main window" ) ;
         } /* endif */

         WinSetDlgItemText ( hwndWnd, IDT_CLICK, achMessage ) ;
      }
      break ;
   case WM_COMMAND:

      switch ( SHORT1FROMMP ( mpParm1 )) {
         case DID_OK:
         case DID_CANCEL:
            WinDismissDlg ( hwndWnd, FALSE ) ;
            break ;

         default:
            return WinDefDlgProc ( hwndWnd,
                                   ulMsg,
                                   mpParm1,
                                   mpParm2 ) ;
      } /* endswitch */
      break ;

   default:
      return WinDefDlgProc ( hwndWnd, ulMsg, mpParm1, mpParm2 ) ;
   } /* endswitch */

   return MRFROMSHORT ( FALSE ) ;
}

MRESULT EXPENTRY ClientWndProc ( HWND hwndWnd,
                                 ULONG ulMsg,
                                 MPARAM mpParm1,
                                 MPARAM mpParm2 )
{
   switch ( ulMsg ) {

   case WM_ERASEBACKGROUND:
      return MRFROMSHORT ( TRUE ) ;

   case WM_COMMAND:

      switch ( SHORT1FROMMP ( mpParm1 )) {
```

```
        case IDM_MODELESS:
            {
                BOOL bModal ;

                bModal = FALSE ;

                WinLoadDlg ( HWND_DESKTOP,
                             hwndWnd,
                             DlgProc,
                             NULLHANDLE,
                             IDD_EXAMPLE,
                             ( PVOID ) &bModal ) ;
            }
            break ;

        case IDM_MODAL:
            {
                BOOL bModal ;

                bModal = TRUE ;

                WinDlgBox ( HWND_DESKTOP,
                            hwndWnd,
                            DlgProc,
                            NULLHANDLE,
                            IDD_EXAMPLE,
                            ( PVOID ) &bModal ) ;
            }
            break ;

        case IDM_EXIT:
            WinPostMsg ( hwndWnd, WM_CLOSE, 0, 0 ) ;
            break ;

        default:
            return WinDefWindowProc ( hwndWnd,
                                      ulMsg,
                                      mpParm1,
                                      mpParm2 ) ;
        } /* endswitch */
        break ;
    default:
        return WinDefWindowProc ( hwndWnd,
                                  ulMsg,
                                  mpParm1,
                                  mpParm2 ) ;
    } /* endswitch */

    return MRFROMSHORT ( FALSE ) ;
}
```

DIALOG.RC

```
#include <os2.h>
#include "dialog.h"

ICON IDR_CLIENT DIALOG.ICO

MENU IDR_CLIENT
{
    SUBMENU "~Dialog", IDM_DIALOG
    {
        MENUITEM "~Modeless dialog...", IDM_MODELESS
        MENUITEM "Modal ~dialog...", IDM_MODAL
        MENUITEM SEPARATOR
        MENUITEM "E~xit", IDM_EXIT
    }
}

DLGTEMPLATE IDD_EXAMPLE LOADONCALL MOVEABLE DISCARDABLE
{
    DIALOG  "Dialog example", IDD_EXAMPLE, 53, 28, 260, 55,
        WS_VISIBLE,
        FCF_SYSMENU | FCF_TITLEBAR
    {
        LTEXT "?", IDT_DIALOGNAME, 10, 40, 240, 8
        LTEXT "?", IDT_CLICK, 10, 30, 240, 8
        DEFPUSHBUTTON "OK", DID_OK, 10, 10, 50, 13
    }
}
```

DIALOG.H

```
#define IDR_CLIENT            256
#define IDD_EXAMPLE           257

#define IDM_DIALOG            320
#define IDM_MODELESS          321
#define IDM_MODAL             322
#define IDM_EXIT              323

#define IDT_DIALOGNAME        512
#define IDT_CLICK             513
```

DIALOG.MAK

```
DIALOG.EXE:                      DIALOG.OBJ \
                                 DIALOG.RES
        LINK386 @<<
DIALOG
DIALOG
DIALOG
OS2386
DIALOG
<<
        RC DIALOG.RES DIALOG.EXE
```

```
DIALOG.RES:                     DIALOG.RC \
                                DIALOG.H
        RC -r DIALOG.RC DIALOG.RES

DIALOG.OBJ:                     DIALOG.C \
                                DIALOG.H
        ICC -C+ -Kb+ -Ss+ DIALOG.C
```

DIALOG.DEF

```
NAME DIALOG WINDOWAPI
DESCRIPTION 'Dialog example.
            Copyright (c) 1992 by Kathleen Panov.
            All rights reserved.'


STACKSIZE 16384
```

The resource file, DIALOG.RC, is the starting point for the sample program. Two items are defined in the file, a menu and the dialog box.

7.1 The Menu Template

The resource file for the window shows the menu that we would like displayed in our client window:

```
MENU IDR_CLIENT
{
    SUBMENU "~Dialog", IDM_DIALOG
    {
        MENUITEM "~Modeless dialog...", IDM_MODELESS
        MENUITEM "Modal ~dialog...", IDM_MODAL
        MENUITEM SEPARATOR
        MENUITEM "E~xit", IDM_EXIT
    }
}
```

The MENU keyword indicates a menu is being defined for our client window. The menu has one submenu, "Dialog", with a resource id, IDM_DIALOG. Two MENUITEMS, or menu choices, "Modeless Dialog" and "Modal Dialog", are available under the submenu.

7.2 The Dialog Box Template

The following is the resource definition to create the dialog boxes used in this program:

```
DLGTEMPLATE IDD_EXAMPLE LOADONCALL MOVEABLE DISCARDABLE
{
   DIALOG  "Dialog example", IDD_EXAMPLE, 53, 28, 260, 55,
      WS_VISIBLE, FCF_SYSMENU | FCF_TITLEBAR
   {
      LTEXT "?", IDT_DIALOGNAME, 10, 40, 240, 8
      LTEXT "?", IDT_CLICK, 10, 30, 240, 8
      DEFPUSHBUTTON "OK", DID_OK, 10, 10, 50, 13
   }
}
```

First, the DLGTEMPLATE keyword is used to indicate that we are defining a dialog box. The resource ID, IDD_EXAMPLE, is specified next. The DIALOG keyword indicates the dialog window. The same resource ID is used for both the dialog box and the dialog window. The next four parameters are the *x* position, *y* position, width, and height of the dialog window, respectively. WS_VISIBLE is used to indicate that we want our dialog window visible when called. FCF_SYSMENU and FCF_TITLEBAR will place a system menu and a title bar on the dialog box.

The next step is to define the controls that are to appear on the dialog box. In this example only an "OK" pushbutton and some static text will be used. The IDT_CLICK text will be used to communicate some instructions to the user. The IDT_DIALOGNAME is used to specify whether this is a modal or modeless dialog box.

7.3 The Client Window Procedure

The client window procedure, *ClientWndProc*, is very small. The WM_ERASEBACKGROUND message is caught and returned TRUE. This keeps the client window from being transparent. The *WinDefWindowProc* processing of WM_ERASEBACKGROUND will return FALSE. We disagree with the system's default processing on this, but hey, we didn't write it.

The processing of the WM_COMMAND message is where the programmatic differences exist between a modal and nonmodal dialog box.

In our WM_COMMAND processing, we first find out who is sending us the WM_COMMAND message. The resource ID for the sender is located in mp1. If the user selected "Modal Dialog Box", IDM_MODAL is returned in mp1. A boolean variable, *Modal*, is used to indicate to the *DlgProc* whether the user selected a modal or modeless dialog box.

7.4 Creating a Modal Dialog Box

```
BOOL bModal ;

bModal = TRUE ;

WinDlgBox ( HWND_DESKTOP,
            hwndWnd,
            DlgProc,
            NULLHANDLE,
            IDD_EXAMPLE,
            ( PVOID ) &bModal ) ;
```

The function *WinDlgBox* is used to create a modal dialog box. When *WinDlgBox* is used to create a dialog box, a message queue is created for that dialog. User interaction with the other message queue (and the client window associated with it) is held up until the dialog box is dismissed and the message queue is destroyed.

The first parameter is the parent, HWND_DESKTOP, and the second parameter is the owner window, *hwndWnd*. The third parameter is the pointer to the dialog process function, in this case *DlgProc*. (HMODULE)0 tells the system that the resources for the dialog process, *DlgProc*, are located in the .EXE file. IDD_DIALOG is the resource ID for the dialog. The last parameter is the data area. This is used to pass programmer-defined data of type PVOID into the DialogProcedure. In this area we will pass a pointer to our boolean variable, *bModal*. *WinDlgBox* is actually a combination of four functions, *WinLoadDlg*, *WinProcessDlg*, *WinDestroyWindow*, and *return*.

Gotcha!

The last parameter to *WinDlgBox* *must* be a pointer. This parameter undergoes a procedure that converts a 32-bit pointer into a pointer that is readable by 16-bit code. This procedure is commonly called "thunking." Thunking will severely damage a value that is not a pointer. The PMWIN.DLL is still 16-bit, and must try and thunk this value.

7.5 Creating a Modeless Dialog Box

```
BOOL bModal ;

bModal = FALSE ;

WinLoadDlg ( HWND_DESKTOP,
             hwndWnd,
             DlgProc,
             NULLHANDLE,
             IDD_EXAMPLE,
             ( PVOID ) &bModal ) ;
```

The function *WinLoadDlg* is used to create a modeless dialog box. This function returns immediately after creating the dialog box. *WinDlgBox* waits until it finishes its processing before returning. It is for this reason that a modeless dialog box permits user interaction with the other windows, and a modal dialog box does not. The parameter list for *WinLoadDlg* is exactly the same as for *WinDlgBox*.

7.6 The Dialog Procedure, *DlgProc*

The dialog procedure, in this case *DlgProc*, is fairly similar to a window procedure. Our program can use the same dialog process for both the modal and modeless dialog boxes. One of the first differences is the appearance of the WM_INITDLG message. This message is provided to give the programmer a place to put the initialization code for the dialog box.

```
bModal = *(( PBOOL ) PVOIDFROMMP ( mpParm2 )) ;

WinSetWindowPos ( hwndWnd,
                  NULLHANDLE,
                  10,
                  ( bModal?100:150 ) ,
                  0,
                  0,
                  SWP_MOVE ) ;

sprintf ( achMessage,
          "I'm a %s dialog box",
          ( bModal? ( "modal" ) : ( "modeless" )) ) ;

WinSetDlgItemText ( hwndWnd,
                    IDT_DIALOGNAME,
                    achMessage ) ;

if ( bModal ) {
   strcpy ( achMessage,
            "Try and click on the main window" ) ;
} else {
   strcpy ( achMessage, "Click on the main window" ) ;
```

```
} /* endif */

WinSetDlgItemText ( hwndWnd, IDT_CLICK, achMessage ) ;
```

In our program, we will look at the boolean variable, *bModal*, to position the two dialog boxes in different places on the client window, and also to adjust the static text in the dialog box to correspond to their choice. For ease of understanding, we set a local boolean variable, *bModal,* equal to the value at the location pointed to by *mpParm2.*

The WM_COMMAND processing is just like the WM_COMMAND processing for the client window. If the user presses the OK pushbutton, the dialog box is canceled with *WinDismissDlg.*

Gotcha!

The other difference between a dialog procedure and a window procedure is the default procedure function. A dialog procedure must call *WinDefDlgProc* instead of *WinDefWindowProc.* If you find your dialog procedure behaving irrationally, check that you have included *WinDefDlgProc.* These two functions often get interchanged.

7.7 Dialog Box Messages

WM_CHAR
This message is sent to the dialog box to indicate that a key has been pressed.
Parameter 1:   USHORT usFlags   Keyboard control codes

CODE	MEANING
KC_CHAR	Character key was hit, value is in *usCharCode*
KC_SCANCODE	Value of key is in KC_SCANCODE
KC_VIRTUALKEY	Indicates a virutal key was hit, and value is in *usVKeyCode*
KC_KEYUP	Key is released
KC_PREVDOWN	Usually precedes the KC_KEYUP flag
KC_DEADKEY	Key was a dead key

KC_COMPOSITE	Key was a combination of the previous dead key and this key
KC_INVALIDCOMP	Key was an invalid combination
KC_LONEKEY	A key was pressed and released, and no other keys were involved
KC_SHIFT	The SHIFT key was pressed
KC_ALT	The ALT key was pressed
KC_CTRL	The CTRL key was pressed

	UCHAR ucRepeatCt	number of times key was pressed
Parameter 2:	USHORT usCharCode	character code
	USHORT usVKeyCode	virtual key codes
Reply:	BOOL fProcessed	processed? TRUE: FALSE

WM_CLOSE

This message is to the dialog box to indicate it is being closed.

Parameter 1:	ULONG ulReserved	reserved, 0
Parameter 2:	ULONG ulReserved	reserved, 0
Reply:	ULONG ulReserved	reserved, 0

WM_COMMAND

This message is sent when a control has to notify its owner of a significant event.

Parameter 1:	USHORT usCommand	application-defined value
Parameter 2:	USHORT usSource	source of command message
	USHORT usPointer	TRUE — command came from mouse; FALSE — command came from the keyboard
Reply:	ULONG ulReserved	reserved, 0

WM_DESTROY

This message is sent when a dialog box is being destroyed.

Parameter 1:	ULONG ulReserved	reserved, 0
Parameter 2:	ULONG ulReserved	reserved, 0
Reply:	ULONG ulReserved	reserved, 0

Note: This is the last message that is sent to a dialog box before it is destroyed. If you have allocated memory for a window word, this is the place to free it.

WM_INITDLG
This message is sent to the dialog at the time of creation.

Parameter 1:	HWND hwndFocus	handle of control window that will receive focus
Parameter 2:	PCREATEPARAMS pCreateData	application-defined data passed through dialog box function
Reply:	BOOL fSetFocus	Focus window is to be changed? TRUE: FALSE

WM_MATCHMNEMONIC
This message is sent by the dialog to the control to determine whether a mnemonic belongs to that control.

Parameter 1:	USHORT usCharacter	character to match
Parameter 2:	ULONG ulReserved	reserved, 0
Reply:	BOOL fMatch	successful match? TRUE: FALSE

WM_QUERYDLGCODE
This message is sent by the dialog box to query what kinds of controls it has.

Parameter 1:	PQMSG Message queue	message queue
Parameter 2:	ULONG ulReserved	reserved, 0
Reply:	ULONG ulControlType	DLGC_ENTRYFIELD
		DLGC_BUTTON
		DLGC_CHECKBOX
		DLGC_RADIOBUTTON
		DLGC_STATIC
		DLGC_DEFAULT
		DLGC_PUSHBUTTON
		DLGC_PUSHBUTTON
		DLGC_SCROLLBAR
		DLGC_MENU
		DLGC_MLE

Chapter 8

Menus

The menu is a control that provides a list of choices to the user. There are four types of menus: the menu bar, pull-down menus, cascaded menus, and popup menus. A menu uses a small amount of screen real estate, and can be very valuable to complex applications as visual clues to the user.

A menu bar is displayed in the area between the title bar and the client area of a window. A menu bar is almost always visible, and contains either specified choices or a description of the choices that are contained by the pull-down menu.

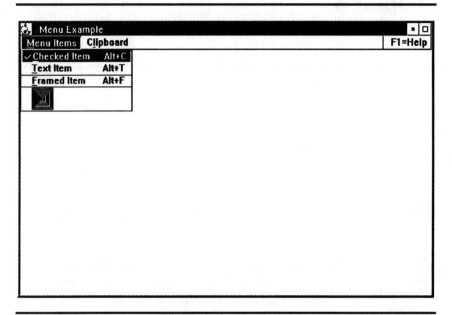

Figure 8.1. A pull-down menu.

Most users are familiar with the traditional pull-down menus (Figure 8.1). This interface is common throughout Macintosh, Windows, and OS/2 1.3 programs. A pull-down menu should contain related choices. These choices extend from the menu bar when a particular menu bar choice is selected.

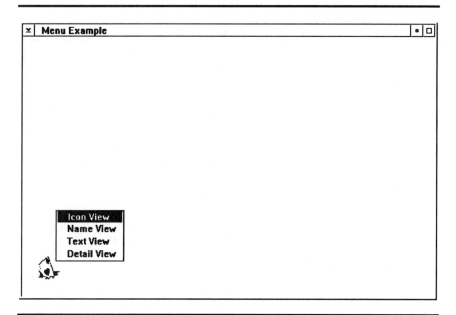

Figure 8.2. A popup menu.

A cascaded menu is a menu that extends from a selected choice in a pull-down menu — kind of a tag-along pull-down menu. Cascaded menus can help to shorten long menus. Presentation Manager indicates the presence of a cascaded menu by a right arrow along the right edge of the pull-down menu.

A popup menu (Figure 8.2) is a menu that pops up a list of choices for an object when some action is performed to trigger the menu. Popup menus are very common in OS/2 2.x, and are an integral part of the object-oriented workplace shell. Popup menus are normally placed to the right of the object they pertain to, unless space does not permit, in which case the menu is placed wherever space permits.

8.1 Menus: The Keyboard and the Mouse

Menus are no good to the user unless they are easy to understand and easy to get to. The mouse provides the easiest interaction with a menu. The user just selects the item by clicking the mouse on any item. If a pull-down menu is available, it will become visible.

The following keys are important keystrokes to access menus:

KEY	ACTION
ALT	Toggles the focus on the menu action bar
Shift + ESC, Alt + spacebar	Causes the system menu to become visible
F10	Jumps to the next higher menu level
↑	If pull-down menu is not visible, causes the pull-down menu to become visible; if the pull-down menu is visible, will move to the previous menu item
↓	If pull-down menu is not visible, causes the pull-down menu to become visible; if the pull-down menu is visible, will move to the next menu item
←	Will move to the next item on the action bar; the system menu is included in the items this key will cycle through
→	Will move to the previous item on the action bar; the system menu is included in the items this key will cycle through
Enter	Selects the current item; if item is on the action bar, the pull-down menu will become visible
Character keys	Will move to menu item that has corresponding mnemonic key

8.2 Mnemosyne's Mnemonics

A mnemonic key is similar to an accelerator key, only not quite as powerful. A mnemonic will select the first menu item with the specified character as its mnemonic key. If the item has a pull-down menu associated with it, the pull-down menu will become visible. A mnemonic key usually corresponds to a character in the menu item text. The first letter is used if possible; otherwise, some meaningful character in the text is used. A mnemonic is indicated by an underlined character.

8.3 Menu Styles

STYLES	DESCRIPTION
MS_ACTIONBAR	This style creates a menu bar
MS_CONDITIONALCASCADE	This style creates a cascaded menu that will only become visible when the arrow to the right of the menu item is selected
MS_TITLEBUTTON	This style creates a push-button along the menu bar
MS_VERTICALFLIP	This style causes a pull-down menu to be placed above the action bar, space permitting; if space is not available, the menu is placed below the action bar

The choices that are available in a menu are known as menu items. These menu items are not really a window, but they do have a special set of styles associated with them.

8.4 Menu Item Styles

ITEM STYLES	DESCRIPTION
MIS_SUBMENU	This style creates a submenu
MIS_SEPARATOR	This style inserts a horizontal bar in the menu; a separator is a dummy item, and cannot be selected, enabled, or disabled
MIS_BITMAP	This menu item is a bitmap instead of text
MIS_TEXT	This menu item is a text string
MIS_BUTTONSEPARATOR	This style creates a menu item that is separate from the other menus. This item will be placed on the far right on a menu bar, and as the last item in a pull-down menu. A separator is drawn between this item and the previous items.
MIS_BREAK	This style will create a new row (on a menu bar) or a new column (on a pull-down menu)

MIS_BREAKSEPARATOR	This style is just like MIS_BREAK, except that a line is drawn between the new row or column
MIS_SYSCOMMAND	This style will notify the owner through a WM_SYSCOMMAND message rather than a WM_COMMAND message
MIS_OWNERDRAW	This style creates an owner-drawn menu item; WM_DRAWITEM messages are sent whenever the menu item is to be drawn
MIS_HELP	This style will send a WM_HELP message to its owner, rather than a WM_COMMAND message
MIS_STATIC	This style creates an unselectable menu item that should be used for information purposes only

The following example program shows how to create a pull-down menu. When the menu item is selected, a message box is displayed containing information about the selected item.

MENU.C

```
#define INCL_WIN
#include <os2.h>
#include <stdio.h>
#include <string.h>
#include "menu.h"

#define CLS_CLIENT              "MyClass"

VOID displayMenuInfo ( HWND hwndMenu,
                       USHORT usMenuItem,
                       HWND hwndClient ) ;
MRESULT EXPENTRY ClientWndProc ( HWND hwndWnd,
                                 ULONG ulMsg,
                                 MPARAM mpParm1,
                                 MPARAM mpParm2 ) ;

INT main ( VOID )
{
    HAB           habAnchor ;
    HMQ           hmqQueue ;
    ULONG         ulFlags ;
    HWND          hwndFrame ;
    HWND          hwndClient ;
    BOOL          bLoop ;
```

```
   QMSG            qmMsg ;

habAnchor = WinInitialize ( 0 ) ;
hmqQueue = WinCreateMsgQueue ( habAnchor, 0 ) ;

WinRegisterClass ( habAnchor,
                   CLS_CLIENT,
                   ClientWndProc,
                   CS_SIZEREDRAW,
                   0 ) ;

ulFlags = FCF_STANDARD & ~FCF_SHELLPOSITION ;

hwndFrame = WinCreateStdWindow ( HWND_DESKTOP,
                                 0,
                                 &ulFlags,
                                 CLS_CLIENT,
                                 "Menu Example",
                                 0,
                                 NULLHANDLE,
                                 RES_CLIENT,
                                 &hwndClient ) ;

if ( hwndFrame != NULLHANDLE ) {
   WinSetWindowPos ( hwndFrame,
                     NULLHANDLE,
                     50,
                     50,
                     250,
                     150,
                     SWP_SIZE |
                     SWP_MOVE |
                     SWP_ACTIVATE |
                     SWP_SHOW ) ;

   bLoop = WinGetMsg ( habAnchor,
                       &qmMsg,
                       NULLHANDLE,
                       0,
                       0 ) ;
   while ( bLoop ) {
      WinDispatchMsg ( habAnchor, &qmMsg ) ;
      bLoop = WinGetMsg ( habAnchor,
                          &qmMsg,
                          NULLHANDLE,
                          0,
                          0 ) ;
   } /* endwhile */

   WinDestroyWindow ( hwndFrame ) ;
} /* endif */

WinDestroyMsgQueue ( hmqQueue ) ;
WinTerminate ( habAnchor ) ;
return 0 ;
}
```

```
MRESULT EXPENTRY ClientWndProc ( HWND hwndWnd,
   ULONG ulMsg,
   MPARAM mpParm1,
   MPARAM mpParm2 )
{

   switch ( ulMsg ) {
   case WM_CREATE:
      {
         HPS          hpsWnd ;
         HBITMAP      hbmBitmap ;
         MENUITEM     miItem ;
         HWND         hwndMenu ;

         hpsWnd = WinGetPS ( hwndWnd ) ;
         hbmBitmap = GpiLoadBitmap ( hpsWnd,
                                     NULLHANDLE,
                                     IDB_BITMAP,
                                     32,
                                     32 ) ;
         WinReleasePS ( hpsWnd ) ;

         miItem.iPosition = 0 ;
         miItem.afStyle = MIS_BITMAP ;
         miItem.afAttribute = 0 ;
         miItem.id = IDM_BITMAP ;
         miItem.hwndSubMenu = NULLHANDLE ;
         miItem.hItem = hbmBitmap ;

         hwndMenu = WinWindowFromID ( WinQueryWindow ( hwndWnd,
                                      QW_PARENT ) ,
                                      FID_MENU ) ;
         WinSendMsg ( hwndMenu,
                      MM_SETITEM,
                      MPFROM2SHORT ( 0, TRUE ) ,
                      MPFROMP ( &miItem )) ;
      }
      break ;
   case WM_ERASEBACKGROUND:
      return MRFROMSHORT ( TRUE ) ;
   case WM_PAINT:
      {
         HPS      hpsPaint ;
         RECTL    rclPaint ;

         hpsPaint = WinBeginPaint ( hwndWnd,
                                    NULLHANDLE,
                                    &rclPaint ) ;
         WinFillRect ( hpsPaint, &rclPaint, SYSCLR_WINDOW ) ;
         WinEndPaint ( hpsPaint ) ;
      }
      break ;
   case WM_COMMAND:
      switch ( SHORT1FROMMP ( mpParm1 )) {
      case IDM_ITEM1:
      case IDM_ITEM2:
      case IDM_ITEM3:
```

```
   case IDM_BITMAP:
   case IDM_CUT:
   case IDM_COPY:
       {
           HWND    hwndFrame ;
           HWND    hwndMenu ;
           USHORT  usAttr ;
           CHAR    achText [64] ;

           hwndFrame = WinQueryWindow ( hwndWnd, QW_PARENT ) ;
           hwndMenu = WinWindowFromID ( hwndFrame, FID_MENU ) ;

           if ( SHORT1FROMMP ( mpParm1 ) == IDM_ITEM1 ) {
               usAttr = SHORT1FROMMR ( WinSendMsg ( hwndMenu,
                                       MM_QUERYITEMATTR,
                                       MPFROM2SHORT ( IDM_ITEM1,
                                                      TRUE ) ,
                                       MPFROMSHORT ( MIA_CHECKED ))) ;
               usAttr ^= MIA_CHECKED ;

               if ( usAttr != 0 ) {
                  strcpy ( achText, " ~Checked item\tAlt + C" ) ;
               } else {
                  strcpy ( achText, " ~Unchecked item\tAlt + C" ) ;
               } /* endif */

               WinSendMsg ( hwndMenu,
                            MM_SETITEMATTR,
                            MPFROM2SHORT ( IDM_ITEM1, TRUE ) ,
                            MPFROM2SHORT ( MIA_CHECKED,
                                           usAttr )) ;

               WinSendMsg ( hwndMenu,
                            MM_SETITEMTEXT,
                            MPFROMSHORT ( IDM_ITEM1 ) ,
                            MPFROMP ( achText )) ;
           } /* endif */

           displayMenuInfo ( hwndMenu,
                             SHORT1FROMMP ( mpParm1 ) ,
                             hwndWnd ) ;
       }
       break ;
   default:
       return WinDefWindowProc ( hwndWnd,
                                 ulMsg,
                                 mpParm1,
                                 mpParm2 ) ;
   } /* endswitch */
   break ;
default:
   return WinDefWindowProc ( hwndWnd,
                             ulMsg,
                             mpParm1,
                             mpParm2 ) ;
} /* endswitch */
```

```
    return MRFROMSHORT ( FALSE ) ;
}

VOID displayMenuInfo ( HWND hwndMenu,
                       USHORT usMenuItem,
                       HWND hwndClient )
{
    USHORT      usAllStyles ;
    USHORT      usAttr ;
    USHORT      usSzText ;
    CHAR        achItemText [32] ;
    CHAR        achText [128] ;

    usAllStyles = MIA_NODISMISS | MIA_FRAMED | MIA_CHECKED |
                  MIA_DISABLED | MIA_HILITED ;

    usAttr = SHORT1FROMMR ( WinSendMsg ( hwndMenu,
                            MM_QUERYITEMATTR,
                            MPFROM2SHORT ( usMenuItem, TRUE ) ,
                            MPFROMSHORT ( usAllStyles )) ) ;

    usSzText = SHORT1FROMMR ( WinSendMsg ( hwndMenu,
                              MM_QUERYITEMTEXT,
                              MPFROM2SHORT ( usMenuItem, 30 ) ,
                              MPFROMP ( achItemText )) ) ;

    sprintf ( achText,
              "Menu Item: \"%s\"\nMenu Item Styles are: 0x%04x",
              usSzText ? achItemText : " (null) ",
              usAttr ) ;

    WinMessageBox ( HWND_DESKTOP,
                    hwndClient,
                    achText,
                    "Menu Information",
                    0,
                    MB_OK ) ;

    return ;
}
```

MENU.RC

```
#include <os2.h>
#include "menu.h"

ICON RES_CLIENT MENU.ICO
BITMAP IDB_BITMAP MENU.BMP

MENU RES_CLIENT
{
   SUBMENU "~Menu", IDM_SUB1
   {
      MENUITEM "~Checked\tAlt+C", IDM_ITEM1, MIS_TEXT, MIA_CHECKED
      MENUITEM "~Framed\tAlt+F", IDM_ITEM2, MIS_TEXT, MIA_FRAMED
      MENUITEM "~Text\tAlt+T", IDM_ITEM3, MIS_TEXT
      MENUITEM SEPARATOR
      MENUITEM "", IDM_BITMAP
   }
   SUBMENU "~Edit", IDM_EDIT
   {
      MENUITEM "~Cut", IDM_CUT
      MENUITEM "C~opy", IDM_COPY
      MENUITEM "~Paste", IDM_PASTE, MIS_TEXT, MIA_DISABLED
   }
   MENUITEM "F1=Help", IDM_HELP, MIS_HELP | MIS_BUTTONSEPARATOR
}

ACCELTABLE RES_CLIENT
{
   "c", IDM_ITEM1, ALT
   "f", IDM_ITEM2, ALT
   "t", IDM_ITEM3, ALT
}
```

MENU.H

```
#define RES_CLIENT          256

#define IDM_SUB1            512
#define IDM_ITEM1           513
#define IDM_ITEM2           514
#define IDM_ITEM3           515
#define IDM_BITMAP          516
#define IDM_EDIT            528
#define IDM_CUT             529
#define IDM_COPY            530
#define IDM_PASTE           531
#define IDM_HELP            544

#define IDB_BITMAP          1024
```

MENU.MAK

```
MENU.EXE:                        MENU.OBJ \
                                 MENU.RES
        LINK386 @<<
MENU
MENU
MENU
OS2386
MENU
<<
        RC MENU.RES MENU.EXE

MENU.RES:                        MENU.RC \
                                 MENU.H
        RC -r MENU.RC MENU.RES

MENU.OBJ:                        MENU.C \
                                 MENU.H
        ICC -C+ -Kb+ -Ss+ MENU.C
```

MENU.DEF

```
NAME MENU WINDOWAPI
DESCRIPTION 'Menu example
Copyright (c) 1992 by Kathleen Panov.
All rights reserved.'

STACKSIZE 16384
```

8.5 The Resource File

The menu for a frame window can be created two ways: either statically, using the resource file, or dynamically, using *WinCreateWindow* with a class WC_WINDOW. The easiest way is to create a window in the resource file, and this example will do just that.

```
MENU RES_CLIENT
```

The MENU keyword in a resource file indicates a menu is being defined. The next word is the resource id, RES_CLIENT. All resources that are attached to the frame window share the same resource ID. This includes icons, accelerator tables, and menus. This resource ID will automatically attach all resources indicated by the FCF_* flags used in *WinCreateStdWindow*. This can cause the function to fail if a resource is defined with the FCF_ flag, and not in the .RC file.

```
{
    SUBMENU "~Menu", IDM_SUB1
    {
        MENUITEM "~Checked\tAlt+C", IDM_ITEM1, MIS_TEXT, MIA_CHECKED
        MENUITEM "~Framed\tAlt+F", IDM_ITEM2, MIS_TEXT, MIA_FRAMED
        MENUITEM "~Text\tAlt+T", IDM_ITEM3, MIS_TEXT
        MENUITEM SEPARATOR
        MENUITEM "", IDM_BITMAP
    }
    SUBMENU "~Edit", IDM_EDIT
    {
        MENUITEM "~Cut", IDM_CUT
        MENUITEM "C~opy", IDM_COPY
        MENUITEM "~Paste", IDM_PASTE, MIS_TEXT, MIA_DISABLED
    }
    MENUITEM "F1=Help", IDM_HELP, MIS_HELP | MIS_BUTTONSEPARATOR
}
```

The keyword SUBMENU is used to define an item on the action bar that will contain a pull-down menu. The { and } characters indicate the start and finish of the menu items that will be placed under the submenu. Each menu item contains the text that will be displayed for that menu item. The tilde character (~) indicates that the character to follow is a mnemonic key. No other definitions are necessary; the menu control processing will handle the action of the mnemonics. The \t characters indicate that a tab is placed between the text and the text that follows. The text following the tab is the information on the accelerator key. Just because we have defined the menu text to indicate an accelerator key does not guarantee its existence.

An accelerator table is defined using the ACCELTABLE keyword. The resource ID is included next. In this example, we prefix the ID with IDM_ to indicate a menu item ID. These IDs are defined in MENU.H. When a WM_COMMAND message is generated, this ID is contained in the lower bytes of message parameter 1.

The options after the resource IDs are the menu item styles. A comma is used to separate the styles from the menu item attributes. Attributes are used to describe the state of a menu item, and are designed to be turned on and off on the fly. The previous example program contains examples of five different kinds of menu items: Checked, Text, Framed, Bitmap, and Disabled. A menu item that is checked or unchecked is an example of a menu item attribute. The following attributes are available.

8.6 Menu Item Attributes

ITEM ATTRIBUTE	DESCRIPTION
MIA_HILITED	The menu item is selected
MIA_CHECKED	A check will appear next to this menu item if TRUE
MIA_DISABLED	The menu item will appear in a greyed, disabled state
MIA_FRAMED	The menu item is enclosed within a frame
MIA_NODISMISS	The pull-down menu containing this menu item will not be dismissed until told to do so

8.7 Defining an Accelerator Table

```
ACCELTABLE RES_CLIENT
{
    "c", IDM_ITEM1, ALT
    "f", IDM_ITEM2, ALT
    "t", IDM_ITEM3, ALT
}
```

The keyword ACCELTABLE defines the accelerator table. The accelerator table is given the same resource IDs as all resources associated with the frame window, RES_CLIENT. The first parameter in the table is the actual character key that will be the accelerator key, in this case, a lowercase c, t, and f. These keys are case-sensitive. If you would like to use a function key or some other noncharacter key as an accelerator key, a full set of #defines are available for use. These are covered in more detail in Chapter 6, Windows and Messages. Each accelerator key is given a command ID. These IDs are sent to the owner as message parameter 1 of a WM_COMMAND message when the accelerator keys are pressed. The IDs used in the example correspond to the menu item resource ID. This prevents the programmer from using two different pieces of code to distinguish between an accelerator key and an actual menu selection. A comma separates the command IDs from the last parameter, accelerator options. This parameter defines the accelerator key. The option ALT indicates that the Alt key will be depressed along with the character key in order to define the accelerator. Other options include: CONTROL, SHIFT, CHAR, HELP, LONEKEY, SCANCODE, SYSCOMMAND, and VIRTUALKEY.

8.8 Creating the Menu Bitmap

There are two ways to use a bitmap as a menu item. One is to include it in the resource file, and the other is to load it during the message processing. In this example, we'll choose the latter.

```
hbmBitmap = GpiLoadBitmap ( hpsWnd,
                            NULLHANDLE,
                            IDB_BITMAP,
                            32,
                            32 ) ;
```

GpiLoadBitmap is used to load the bitmap, MENU.BMP, from the resource file. The first parameter, *hpsWnd*, is the presentation space. The next parameter specifies whether the resource is to be loaded from a .DLL or .EXE. NULLHANDLE indicates the .EXE. The third parameter, IDB_BITMAP, is the resource ID specified in the MENU.RC file. Remember, MENU.RC had the following line:

```
BITMAP IDB_BITMAP MENU.BMP
```

The last two parameters are the width and height of the bitmap. The default size of a bitmap created by the icon editor is 32x32.

The bitmap handle, *hbmBitamp*, is returned from *GpiLoadBitmap*.

```
typedef struct _MENUITEM     /* mi */
{
    SHORT    iPosition;
    USHORT   afStyle;
    USHORT   afAttribute;
    USHORT   id;
    HWND     hwndSubMenu;
    ULONG    hItem;
} MENUITEM;
typedef MENUITEM *PMENUITEM;
```

A menuitem structure is used to tell the menu how this menu item is to appear. As always when passing structures, all fields must be initialized. For the menuitem style, we use MIS_BITMAP. The ID is IDM_BITMAP. *hItem* is the handle to the item, in this case, *hbmBitmap*.

```
miItem.iPosition = 0 ;
miItem.afStyle = MIS_BITMAP ;
miItem.afAttribute = 0 ;
```

```
miItem.id = IDM_BITMAP ;
miItem.hwndSubMenu = NULLHANDLE ;
miItem.hItem = hbmBitmap ;
```

In the MENU.RC file, a spot was created for the IDM_BITMAP menu item. The MM_SETITEM message is sent to finish the job.

```
WinSendMsg ( hwndMenu,
             MM_SETITEM,
             MPFROM2SHORT ( 0, TRUE ) ,
             MPFROMP ( &miItem )) ;
```

The first message parameter is composed of two USHORTS. The first is always 0, and the second is an indication to include submenus in the search. We do want to include submenus. The second message parameter is a pointer to the MENUITEM structure.

8.9 The Client Window Procedure, *ClientWndProc*

The client window procedure is where all of the menu handling is done. The WM_COMMAND message is sent to the owner, *hwndClient*, whenever the user has selected some item from the menu, either using the mouse, keyboard, or accelerator key. The example finds out which menu item is selected, and displays a message box with information about the item. The menu item, IDM_ITEM1, will have the check mark toggled on and off whenever it is selected.

```
case WM_COMMAND:
    switch ( SHORT1FROMMP ( mpParm1 )) {
    case IDM_ITEM1:
    case IDM_ITEM2:
    case IDM_ITEM3:
    case IDM_BITMAP:
    case IDM_CUT:
    case IDM_COPY:
        {
            HWND    hwndFrame ;
            HWND    hwndMenu ;
            USHORT  usAttr ;
            CHAR    achText [64] ;

            hwndFrame = WinQueryWindow ( hwndWnd, QW_PARENT ) ;
            hwndMenu = WinWindowFromID ( hwndFrame, FID_MENU ) ;
```

The menu item ID is contained in message parameter 1 of the WM_COMMAND message. After the ID is obtained, we obtain the menu window handle. The menu handle is used later. *WinWindowFromID* will return the menu window handle when the special ID, FID_MENU, is used. The first parameter is the parent of the menu, the frame window.

```
if ( SHORT1FROMMP ( mpParm1 ) == IDM_ITEM1 ) {
    usAttr = SHORT1FROMMR ( WinSendMsg ( hwndMenu,
                    MM_QUERYITEMATTR,
                    MPFROM2SHORT ( IDM_ITEM1,
                                   TRUE ) ,
                    MPFROMSHORT ( MIA_CHECKED ))) ;
```

If the menu item ID is IDM_ITEM1, we query whether the MIA_CHECKED bit is set, using the message MM_QUERYITEMATTR. The first message parameter consists of two USHORTS. The lower bytes are the menu item ID to query, IDM_ITEM1. The upper bytes indicate whether to include submenus. This is applicable when you want to query all menu items on a pull-down, or sublevel, menu. Message parameter 2 is the attribute mask for the query. We only want to know whether the MIA_CHECKED bit is set, so this will be the mask we use. A mask can be a collection of attributes OR'ed together, or only one. The value of the bit is returned in the variable, *usAttr*.

```
usAttr ^= MIA_CHECKED;
```

Once we know whether the menu item is checked, we want to reverse the state of the MIA_CHECKED bit in order to toggle the check mark. The bitwise exclusive OR (^) is very handy for toggling bits.

```
if ( usAttr != 0 ) {
    strcpy ( achText, " ~Checked item\tAlt + C" ) ;
} else {
    strcpy ( achText, " ~Unchecked item\tAlt + C" ) ;
} /* endif */

WinSendMsg ( hwndMenu,
            MM_SETITEMATTR,
            MPFROM2SHORT ( IDM_ITEM1, TRUE ) ,
            MPFROM2SHORT ( MIA_CHECKED,
                           usAttr )) ;

WinSendMsg ( hwndMenu,
            MM_SETITEMTEXT,
            MPFROMSHORT ( IDM_ITEM1 ) ,
            MPFROMP ( achText )) ;
```

The next thing to do is to set the menu with the new menu item state, and also update the menu item text to reflect the change. The checked state is determined by AND'ing (&) *usAttr* and MIA_CHECKED. The message MM_SETITEMTEXT is used to set the menu item text to the new string.

Message parameter 1 is set to the menu item ID, IDM_ITEM1. Message parameter 2 is a pointer to the text string. The message MM_SETITEMATTR is used to set the menu item attribute to the new value in *usAttr*. The message parameters are equivalent to the MM_QUERYITEMATTR message parameters.

8.10 The User Function, *displayMenuInfo*

After the user selects a menu item, a message box is popped up to display various bits of information about the menu item. The menu item attributes are found using MM_QUERYITEMATTR. Instead of using just one menu item attribute mask, the values MIA_NODISMISS, MIA_FRAMED, MIA_CHECKED, MIA_DISABLED, and MIA_HILITED are OR'ed together.

```
usAllStyles = MIA_NODISMISS | MIA_FRAMED | MIA_CHECKED |
              MIA_DISABLED | MIA_HILITED ;

usAttr = SHORT1FROMMR ( WinSendMsg ( hwndMenu,
                        MM_QUERYITEMATTR,
                        MPFROM2SHORT ( usMenuItem, TRUE ) ,
                        MPFROMSHORT ( usAllStyles )) ) ;

usSzText = SHORT1FROMMR ( WinSendMsg ( hwndMenu,
                          MM_QUERYITEMTEXT,
                          MPFROM2SHORT ( usMenuItem, 30 ) ,
                          MPFROMP ( achItemText )) ) ;
```

The return from the message will yield the state of all these attributes OR'ed together. MM_QUERYITEMTEXT is used to query the menu item text. Message parameter 1 is two USHORTS. The lower bytes contain the menu item ID; the upper bytes contain the length of the text input buffer, *achMenuItemText*. The second message parameter is a pointer to the text input buffer.

The last step is to call *WinMessageBox* to display the menu item information.

8.11 Popup Menus

The following example will demonstrate how to create a popup menu suitable for the OS/2 2.x environment. An icon is created on the client window. If the user clicks the context menu mouse button (the right one by default) on the icon, a popup menu will appear.

POPUP.C

```
#define INCL_WIN
#include <os2.h>
#include "popup.h"
#include "stdlib.h"

MRESULT EXPENTRY ClientWndProc ( HWND hwnd,
                                 ULONG msg,
                                 MPARAM mp1,
                                 MPARAM mp2 ) ;

#define CLS_CLIENT               "MyClass"

typedef struct {
    HWND          hwndMenu ;
    HPOINTER      hptrFileIcon ;
} MENUDATA, *PMENUDATA ;

INT main ( VOID )
{
    HAB           habAnchor ;
    HMQ           hmqQueue ;
    ULONG         ulFlags ;
    HWND          hwndFrame ;
    HWND          hwndClient ;
    BOOL          bLoop ;
    QMSG          qmMsg ;

    habAnchor = WinInitialize ( 0 ) ;
    hmqQueue = WinCreateMsgQueue ( habAnchor, 0 ) ;

    WinRegisterClass ( habAnchor,
                       CLS_CLIENT,
                       ClientWndProc,
                       CS_SIZEREDRAW,
                       sizeof ( PVOID )) ;

    ulFlags = FCF_TASKLIST | FCF_TITLEBAR | FCF_SYSMENU |
              FCF_MINMAX | FCF_SIZEBORDER | FCF_SHELLPOSITION ;

    hwndFrame = WinCreateStdWindow ( HWND_DESKTOP,
                                     WS_VISIBLE,
                                     &ulFlags,
                                     CLS_CLIENT,
                                     "Popup Menu Example",
                                     0,
                                     NULLHANDLE,
                                     0,
                                     &hwndClient ) ;

    if ( hwndFrame != NULLHANDLE ) {
        bLoop = WinGetMsg ( habAnchor,
                            &qmMsg,
                            NULLHANDLE,
                            0,
                            0 ) ;
        while ( bLoop ) {
```

```
                    WinDispatchMsg ( habAnchor, &qmMsg ) ;
                    bLoop = WinGetMsg ( habAnchor,
                                        &qmMsg,
                                        NULLHANDLE,
                                        0,
                                        0 ) ;
            } /* endwhile */

            WinDestroyWindow ( hwndFrame ) ;
        } /* endif */

    WinDestroyMsgQueue ( hmqQueue ) ;
    WinTerminate ( habAnchor ) ;
    return 0 ;
}

MRESULT EXPENTRY ClientWndProc ( HWND hwndWnd,
                                 ULONG ulMsg,
                                 MPARAM mpParm1,
                                 MPARAM mpParm2 )
{
    PMENUDATA       pmdMenuData ;

    pmdMenuData = WinQueryWindowPtr ( hwndWnd, 0 ) ;

    switch ( ulMsg ) {

    case WM_CREATE:
        {
            pmdMenuData = malloc ( sizeof ( MENUDATA )) ;
            WinSetWindowPtr ( hwndWnd, 0, pmdMenuData ) ;

            pmdMenuData -> hwndMenu = WinLoadMenu ( hwndWnd,
                                                    NULLHANDLE,
                                                    IDM_POPUP ) ;
            pmdMenuData -> hptrFileIcon = WinLoadFileIcon (
                                            "POPUP.EXE",
                                            FALSE ) ;
        }
        break ;

    case WM_DESTROY:

        if ( pmdMenuData != NULL ) {
            if ( pmdMenuData -> hptrFileIcon != NULLHANDLE ) {
                WinFreeFileIcon ( pmdMenuData -> hptrFileIcon ) ;
            } /* endif */

            free ( pmdMenuData ) ;
        } /* endif */
        break ;
```

```
    case WM_PAINT:
        {
            HPS         hpsPaint ;
            RECTL       rclInvalid ;

            hpsPaint = WinBeginPaint ( hwndWnd,
                                       NULLHANDLE,
                                       &rclInvalid ) ;
            WinFillRect ( hpsPaint,
                          &rclInvalid,
                          SYSCLR_WINDOW ) ;

            if ( pmdMenuData -> hptrFileIcon != NULLHANDLE ) {
                WinDrawPointer ( hpsPaint,
                                 50,
                                 50,
                                 pmdMenuData -> hptrFileIcon,
                                 DP_NORMAL ) ;
            } /* endif */
            WinEndPaint ( hpsPaint ) ;
        }
        break ;
    case WM_CONTEXTMENU:
        {
            POINTL      ptlMouse ;
            RECTL       rclIcon ;
            HAB         habAnchor ;
            BOOL        bInside ;
            BOOL        bKeyboardUsed ;

            habAnchor = WinQueryAnchorBlock ( hwndWnd ) ;
            bKeyboardUsed = SHORT1FROMMP ( mpParm2 ) ;

            //---------------------------------------------------------
            // If the mouse was used, check to see if the pointer
            // is over the icon, else always display the menu.
            //---------------------------------------------------------
            if ( ! bKeyboardUsed ) {

                rclIcon.xLeft = 50 ;
                rclIcon.xRight = rclIcon.xLeft +
                    WinQuerySysValue ( HWND_DESKTOP, SV_CXICON ) ;

                rclIcon.yBottom = 50 ;
                rclIcon.yTop = rclIcon.yBottom +
                    WinQuerySysValue ( HWND_DESKTOP, SV_CYICON ) ;

                ptlMouse.x = ( LONG ) SHORT1FROMMP ( mpParm1 ) ;
                ptlMouse.y = ( LONG ) SHORT2FROMMP ( mpParm1 ) ;

                bInside = WinPtInRect ( habAnchor,
                                        &rclIcon,
                                        &ptlMouse ) ;
            } else {

                bInside = TRUE ;
                ptlMouse.x = 50 ;
```

```
                ptlMouse.y = 50 ;

        } /* endif */

        if (( bInside ) &&
            ( pmdMenuData -> hwndMenu != NULLHANDLE )) {
            WinPopupMenu ( hwndWnd,
                           hwndWnd,
                           pmdMenuData -> hwndMenu,
                           ptlMouse.x,
                           ptlMouse.y,
                           IDM_ICON,
                           PU_POSITIONONITEM | PU_KEYBOARD |
                           PU_MOUSEBUTTON1 | PU_MOUSEBUTTON2 ) ;
        } /* endif */
    }
    break ;
default:
    return WinDefWindowProc ( hwndWnd,
                              ulMsg,
                              mpParm1,
                              mpParm2 ) ;
} /* endswitch */

return MRFROMSHORT ( FALSE ) ;
}
```

POPUP.RC

```
#include <os2.h>
#include "popup.h"

MENU IDM_POPUP
{
   MENUITEM "~Icon View", IDM_ICON
   MENUITEM "~Name View", IDM_NAME
   MENUITEM "~Text View", IDM_TEXT
   MENUITEM "~Detail View", IDM_DETAIL
}
```

POPUP.H

```
#define IDM_POPUP                256
#define IDM_ICON                 257
#define IDM_NAME                 258
#define IDM_TEXT                 259
#define IDM_DETAIL               260
```

POPUP.MAK

```
POPUP.EXE:                      POPUP.OBJ \
                                POPUP.RES
        LINK386 @<<
POPUP
POPUP
POPUP
OS2386
POPUP
<<
        RC POPUP.RES POPUP.EXE

POPUP.RES:                      POPUP.RC \
                                POPUP.H
        RC -r POPUP.RC POPUP.RES

POPUP.OBJ:                      POPUP.C \
                                POPUP.H
        ICC -C+ -Kb+ -Ss+ POPUP.C
```

POPUP.DEF

```
NAME POPUP WINDOWAPI

DESCRIPTION 'Popup example
Copyright (c) 1992 by Kathleen Panov.
All rights reserved.'

STACKSIZE 16384
```

8.12 Creating a Popup Menu

```
pmdMenuData = malloc ( sizeof ( MENUDATA )) ;
WinSetWindowPtr ( hwndWnd, 0, pmdMenuData ) ;

pmdMenuData -> hwndMenu = WinLoadMenu ( hwndWnd,
                                NULLHANDLE,
                                IDM_POPUP ) ;
```

The popup menu is created almost exactly like a regular menu. The popup template contains the same keywords and definitions as the regular pull-down template. When the client window is being created (the WM_CREATE processing), the menu template is loaded. *WinLoadMenu* returns a menu handle that will be used later in the *WinPopupMenu* function. For now, it is stored in the window word of the client area. One performance note here: we could have used *WinLoadMenu* in the WM_CONTEXTMENU processing, but considering WM_CREATE is called once, and WM_CONTEXTMENU is called as many times as the user chooses, it saves considerable time and system resources if we load the menu in the WM_CREATE processing. Whenever possible, keep your message processing as lean as possible, and be careful of loading resources multiple times.

8.13 I Think I Can, I Think Icon

```
pmdMenuData -> hptrFileIcon = WinLoadFileIcon (
                                "POPUP.EXE",
                                FALSE ) ;
```

One of the functions introduced in OS/2 2.0 is *WinLoadFileIcon*. This is a nifty function to "lift" an icon from some file to use in your program. This example takes the file icon associated with itself and paints it on the client window. *WinLoadFileIcon* has two parameters. The first is the file name. The second is a flag that indicates whether the icon needs to be "public" or "private." A "public" icon is much easier on system resources, but it is a read-only version of the icon. That's all that this example needs. A pointer handle, *hptrFileIcon*, to the icon is returned. Once again, the handle is stored in the client's window word for future use.

```
WinDrawPointer ( hpsPaint,
                 50,
                 50,
                 pmdMenuData -> hptrFileIcon,
                 DP_NORMAL ) ;
```

WinDrawPointer will actually paint the icon on the client window. *WinDrawPointer* can draw bitmaps, icons, and pointers. The first parameter is the presentation space for drawing. The next two parameters are the *x* and *y* coordinates to use for drawing. *hptrFileIcon* is the icon to draw, and the last parameter specifies how the image is drawn. DP_NORMAL draws the image with no changes from the original.

8.14 Popping Up a Menu

```
rclIcon.xLeft = 50 ;
rclIcon.xRight = rclIcon.xLeft +
   WinQuerySysValue ( HWND_DESKTOP, SV_CXICON ) ;

rclIcon.yBottom = 50 ;
rclIcon.yTop = rclIcon.yBottom +
   WinQuerySysValue ( HWND_DESKTOP, SV_CYICON ) ;

ptlMouse.x = ( LONG ) SHORT1FROMMP ( mpParm1 ) ;
ptlMouse.y = ( LONG ) SHORT2FROMMP ( mpParm1 ) ;
```

```
bInside = WinPtInRect ( habAnchor,
                        &rclIcon,
                        &ptlMouse ) ;
```

In this example, when the user clicks the context menu mouse button or uses the context menu keystroke, we'll pop up a menu. The message we'll use to track that event is WM_CONTEXTMENU. A hotspot region is created on the icon. *WinPtInRect* is a function that compares a pair of *x*, *y* coordinates to some region. If the points are contained in that region, the function returns TRUE; if not, the function returns FALSE. If the mouse is contained in the hotspot region, we go ahead and popup the menu.

8.15 The Workhorse Function, *WinPopupMenu*

```
WinPopupMenu ( hwndWnd,
               hwndWnd,
               pmdMenuData -> hwndMenu,
               ptlMouse.x,
               ptlMouse.y,
               IDM_ICON,
               PU_POSITIONONITEM | PU_KEYBOARD |
               PU_MOUSEBUTTON1 | PU_MOUSEBUTTON2 ) ;
```

The popup menu is actually made visible by *WinPopupMenu*. This function handles all the user I/O, and returns WM_COMMAND messages to the owner window, just like a regular pull-down menu. The first and second parameters are the parent and owner windows, respectively. The client window, *hwndWnd*, is used for both. The next parameter is the menu handle of the popup menu. The next two parameters are the *x* and *y* coordinates at which to place the menu. The last two parameters are used to control the initial display state and user interface for the menu. IDM_ICON is the menu item we want to be selected initially.

The last parameter is a collection of flags. PU_POSITIONONITEM will cause the ID specified in the previous parameter to appear directly above where the mouse pointer is. This flag overrides the *x*, *y* coordinates as placement of the menu. This flag also causes the specified menu item ID to appear selected when the popup menu appears. PU_KEYBOARD lets the user use the keyboard keys to traverse the menu choices and select an item. PU_MOUSEBUTTON2 enables the user to use mouse button 2 to select a menu item. PU_MOUSEBUTTON1 enables the user to use mouse button 1 to select a menu item.

8.16 Menu Messages

WM_COMMAND
This message is sent from a menu to its owner whenever it has to notify its owner about a significant event.

Parameter 1:	USHORT usCommand	application-defined ID of item that generated message
Parameter 2:	USHORT usSourceType	CMDSRC_PUSHBUTTON — pushbutton-generated message CMDSRC_MENU — menu-generated message CMDSRC_ACCELERATOR — accelerator key-generated message CMDSRC_FONTDLG — font dialog-generated message CMDSRC_OTHER — some other type of control-generated message
	USHORT usPointer	TRUE — mouse was used to initiate event FALSE — keyboard was used to initiate event
Reply:	ULONG flReply	reserved,0

WM_DRAWITEM
Sent to the owner of a menu when an item with MS_OWNERDRAW is to be drawn.

Parameter 1:	USHORT usID	window ID
Parameter 2:	POWNERITEM pownerOwnerItem	pointer to OWNERITEM structure

```
        typedef struct _OWNERITEM
        {
            HWND    hwnd;
            HPS     hps;
            ULONG   fsState;
            ULONG   fsAttribute;
            ULONG   fsStateOld;
            ULONG   fsAttributeOld;
            RECTL   rclItem;
            LONG    idItem;
/* This field contains idItem for menus, iItem for lb. */
            ULONG   hItem;
        } OWNERITEM;
        typedef OWNERITEM *POWNERITEM;
```

Reply:　　　　　BOOL fDrawn　　　　　　　　　　drawn?
　　　　　　　　　　　　　　　　　　　　　　　　　　TRUE:FALSE

WM_HELP

This message is sent from a menu to its owner whenever the user indicates a need for help.

Parameter 1:	USHORT usCommand	application-defined ID of item that generated message
Parameter 2:	USHORT usSourceType	CMDSRC_PUSHBUTTON — pushbutton-generated message
		CMDSRC_MENU — menu-generated message
		CMDSRC_ACCELERATOR — accelerator key-generated message
		CMDSRC_FONTDLG — font-dialog-generated message
		CMDSRC_OTHER — some other type of control-generated message
	USHORT usPointer	TRUE — mouse was used to initiate event
		FALSE — keyboard was used to initiate event
Reply:	ULONG flReply	reserved, 0

WM_INITMENU
This message is sent when a menu is about to become active.

Parameter 1:   USHORT usMenuID   ID of menu that is becoming active
Parameter 2:   HWND hwndMenu   menu window handle
Reply: ULONG flReply   reserved, 0

WM_MEASUREITEM
This message is sent to the owner of the menu in order to determine the height of a menu item.

Parameter 1:   USHORT usMenuID   menu item ID
Parameter 2:   POWNERITEM pOwnerItem   owner item structure

```
    typedef struct _OWNERITEM
    {
        HWND    hwnd;
        HPS     hps;
        ULONG   fsState;
        ULONG   fsAttribute;
        ULONG   fsStateOld;
        ULONG   fsAttributeOld;
        RECTL   rclItem;
        LONG    idItem;
/* This field contains idItem for menus, iItem for lb. */
        ULONG   hItem;
    } OWNERITEM;
    typedef OWNERITEM *POWNERITEM;
```

Reply: USHORT usHeight   menu item height

WM_MENUEND
This message is sent to the menu's owner to indicate the menu is about to end.

Parameter 1:   USHORT usMenuID   terminating menu ID
Parameter 2:   HWND hwndMenu   menu window handle
Reply: ULONG flReply   reserved, 0

WM_MENUSELECT

This message is sent to the owner of the menu when a menu item has been selected.

Parameter 1:	USHORT usMenuItem	ID of selected menu item
	USHORT usPostMessage	TRUE — indicates a WM_COMMAND, WM_SYSCOMMAND, or WM_HELP message will be posted to the owner FALSE — no message will be posted
Parameter 2:	HWND hwndMenu	menu window handle
Reply:	BOOL fResult	TRUE — indicates the COMMAND messages are to be posted, and menu is dismissed, unless MIA_NODISMISS is set FALSE — indicates no COMMAND messages are to be posted, and the menu is not dismissed

WM_NEXTMENU

This message is sent to the owner of the menu to indicate that either the beginning or the end of the menu has been reached.

Parameter 1:	HWND hwndMenu	menu window handle
Parameter 2:	USHORT usBeginning	TRUE — at beginning of menu FALSE — at end of menu
Reply:	HWND hwndNextMenu	new menu window handle

WM_SYSCOMMAND

This message is sent from a menu to its owner whenever it has to notify its owner about a significant event.

Parameter 1:	USHORT usCommand	menu ID
Parameter 2:	USHORT usSourceType	CMDSRC_PUSHBUTTON — pushbutton-generated message

		CMDSRC_MENU — menu-generated message
		CMDSRC_ACCELERATOR — accelerator key-generated message
		CMDSRC_FONTDLG — font dialog-generated message
		CMDSRC_OTHER — some other type of control-generated message
	USHORT usPointer	TRUE — mouse was used to initiate event
		FALSE — keyboard was used to initiate event
Reply:	ULONG flReply	reserved, 0

MM_DELETEITEM

This message is sent to the window in order to delete a menu item.

Parameter 1:	USHORT usItemID	item ID to delete
	USHORT usIncludeSubMenus	TRUE — search submenus for item ID
		FALSE — do not search the submenus for item ID
Parameter 2:	ULONG ulReserved	reserved, 0
Reply:	SHORT sItemsLeft	number of menu items remaining

WM_ENDMENUMODE

This message is sent to the menu to end the menu.

Parameter 1:	USHORT usDismiss	TRUE — Dismiss the submenu
		FALSE — do not dismiss the submenu
Parameter 2:	ULONG ulReserved	reserved, 0
Reply:	ULONG ulReply	reserved, 0

WM_INSERTITEM

This message is sent to the menu to insert an item into the menu.

Parameter 1:   PMENUITEM pMenuItem   pointer to menu-item
                                                          structure

```
   typedef struct _MENUITEM
   {
      SHORT   iPosition;
/* position in menu or sub-menu */
      USHORT  afStyle;
/* menu item style */
      USHORT  afAttribute;
/* menu item attributes */
      USHORT  id;
/* menu item ID */
      HWND    hwndSubMenu;
/* handle for sub-menu, if item is a member of sub-menu */
      ULONG   hItem;
/* menu item handle */
   } MENUITEM;
   typedef MENUITEM *PMENUITEM;
```

Parameter 2:   PSTRL pText   menu item text
Reply: SHORT sIndex   index of newly inserted
                                                          item

MM_ISITEMVALID

This message is sent to the menu to determine the selectability of a menu item.

Parameter 1:   USHORT usItemID   item ID
                   USHORT usIncludeSubMenus   TRUE — search
                                                      submenus for item ID
                                                      FALSE - do not search
                                                      the submenus for the item
                                                      ID
Parameter 2:   ULONG ulReserved   reserved, 0
Reply: BOOL fSelectable   TRUE — item is
                                                      selectable
                                                      FALSE — item is not
                                                      selectable

MM_ITEMIDFROMPOSITION
This message is sent to the menu to determine the menu item ID from its position in the menu.

Parameter 1:	SHORT sItemIndex	zero-based item index
Parameter 2:	ULONG ulReserved	reserved, 0
Reply:	SHORT sItemID	menu item ID

MM_ITEMPOSITIONFROMID
This message is sent to the menu to determine a menu item's position from its ID.

Parameter 1:	USHORT usItemID	menu item ID
	USHORT usIncludeSubMenus	TRUE — search submenus for item FALSE — do not search submenus for item
Parameter 2:	ULONG ulReserved	reserved, 0
Reply:	SHORT sItemIndex	item index

MM_QUERYITEM
This message is sent to query the definition of a menu item.

Parameter 1:	USHORT usItemID	menu item ID
	USHORT usIncludeSubMenus	TRUE — search submenus for item FALSE — do not search submenus for item
Parameter 2:	PMENUITEM pMenuItem	menu item structure; the menu item definition is copied to this structure on a successful return
Reply:	BOOL fSuccess	successful? TRUE: FALSE

MM_QUERYITEMATTR
This message queries the menu attributes for a menu item.

Parameter 1:	USHORT usItemID	menu item ID

	USHORT usIncludeSubMenus	TRUE — search submenus for item FALSE — do not search submenus for item
Parameter 2:	USHORT usAttributeMask	attributes to return
Reply:	USHORT usState	state of selected attributes

MM_QUERYITEMCOUNT

This message is sent to determine the number of items in a menu.

Parameter 1:	ULONG ulParam1	reserved, 0
Parameter 2:	ULONG ulParam2	reserved, 0
Reply:	SHORT sNumItems	number of menu items

MM_QUERYITEMRECT

This message is sent to determine the rectangle (RECTL) coordinates of a menu item.

Parameter 1:	USHORT usItemID	menu item ID
	USHORT usIncludeSubMenus	TRUE — search submenus for item FALSE — do not search submenus for item
Parameter 2:	PRECTL pBoundingRect	rectangle of the menu item
Reply:	BOOL fSuccess	successful? TRUE: FALSE

MM_QUERYITEMTEXT

This message is sent to the menu to query the menu item text.

Parameter 1:	USHORT usItem	menu item ID
	SHORT sMaxCharCount	size of text input buffer
Parameter 2:	PSTRL pItemText	menu item text buffer
Reply:	SHORT sTextLength	length of text string

MM_QUERYITEMTEXTLENGTH
This message is sent to the menu to determine the length of the specified menu item text.

Parameter 1:	USHORT usItemID	menu item ID
Parameter 2:	ULONG ulParam2	reserved, 0
Reply:	SHORT sLength	length of menu item text, including NULL

MM_QUERYSELITEMID
This message is sent to determine the selected menu item ID.

Parameter 1:	USHORT usReserved	reserved, 0
	USHORT usIncludeSubMenus	TRUE — search submenus for item FALSE — do not search submenus for item
Parameter 2:	ULONG ulParam2	reserved, 0
Reply:	SHORT sSelectedItem	selected item ID

MM_REMOVEITEM
This message is sent to the menu to remove a menu item.

Parameter 1:	USHORT usItemID	menu item ID
	USHORT usIncludeSubMenus	TRUE — search submenus for item FALSE — do not search submenus for item
Parameter 2:	ULONG ulParam2	reserved, 0
Reply:	SHORT sItemsLeft	number of remaining items

MM_SELECTITEM
This message is sent to the menu to select or deselect a menu item.

Parameter 1:	USHORT usItemID	menu item ID of interest MIT_NONE — deselects all menu items
Parameter 2:	USHORT usReserved	reserved, 0

	USHORT usDismiss	TRUE — dismiss menu
		FALSE — do not dismiss the
		menu
Reply:	BOOL fSuccess	successful? TRUE: FALSE

MM_SETITEM

This message is sent to the menu to update the definition of a menu item.

Parameter 1:	USHORT usReserved	reserved, 0
Parameter 2:	PMENUITEM pMenuItem	new menu item structure
Reply:	BOOL fSuccess	successful? TRUE: FALSE

MM_SETITEMATTR

This message is sent to the menu to set a menu item attribute.

Parameter 1:	USHORT usItemID	menu item ID
	USHORT usIncludeSubMenus	TRUE — search submenus for item
		FALSE — do not search submenus for item
Parameter 2:	USHORT usAttributeMask	masks of attributes to set
	USHORT usAttributeData	attribute data
Reply:	BOOL fSuccess	successful? TRUE: FALSE

MM_SETITEMHANDLE

This message is sent to the menu to set an item handle for a menu item. This is used for the menu items that have a style of MIS_BITMAP or MIS_OWNERDRAW.

Parameter 1:	USHORT usItemID	menu item ID
Parameter 2:	ULONG ulItemHandle	item handle
Reply:	BOOL fSuccess	successful? TRUE: FALSE

MM_SETITEMTEXT
This message is sent to the menu to set, or change, the text of a menu item.

Parameter 1:	USHORT usItemID	menu item ID
Parameter 2:	PSTRL pNewText	item text to associate with menu item
Reply:	BOOL fSuccess	successful? TRUE: FALSE

MM_STARTMENUMODE
This message is sent to the menu to begin menu mode.

Parameter 1:	USHORT usShowSub	TRUE — show pull-down menu
		FALSE — do not show pull-down menu
Parameter 2:	USHORT usResume	TRUE — resume where menu had left off
		FALSE — begin new user interaction
Reply:	BOOL fSuccess	successful? TRUE: FALSE

WM_QUERYWINDOWPARAMS
This message is sent to a menu to query its window parameters.

Parameter 1:	PWNDPARAMS pwndParams	Pointer to window parameter structure

```
typedef struct   _WNDPARAMS {
     ULONG   ulStatus;       /* Window parameter selection */
     ULONG   ulText;         /* Length of window text */
     PSZ     pszText;        /* Window text */
     ULONG   ulPresParams;   /* Length of Presentation Parameters
                                structure */
     PVOID   pPresParams;    /* pointer to Presentation Parameters
                                structure */
     ULONG   ulCtlData;      /* Length of control specific data */
     PVOID   pCtlData;       /* Pointer to control specific
                                data /*
} WNDPARAMS;
```

Parameter 2:	ULONG Param2	reserved, 0
Reply:	BOOL fResult	successful? TRUE:FALSE

WM_SETWINDOWPARAMS
This message indicates window parameters have been changed.

Parameter 1:	PWNDPARAMS pwndParams	pointer to window parameter structure.
Parameter 2:	ULONG Param2	reserved, 0
Reply:	BOOL fResult	successful? TRUE: FALSE

Chapter 9

List Boxes

A list box (See Figure 9.1) is a control that provides the user with a list of choices. Single or multiple items can be selected; the default is single. A list box can scroll horizontally, vertically, or both. List boxes, by default, contain only text entries, although owner-drawn list boxes can support bitmaps, icons, or any sort of graphics.

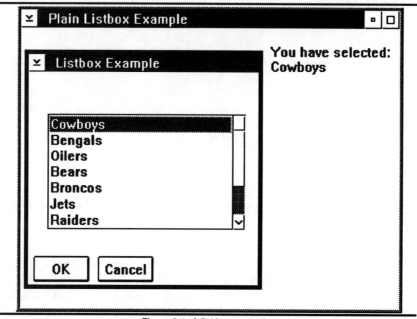

Figure 9.1. A list box control.

The items in a list box should be presented in some order meaningful to the user. A list box should be large enough to have six or eight choices visible at all times. The list box should be wide enough to display an item of average width without horizontal scrolling. If multiple selection is supported, informative text should be provided to indicate the current number of selected items.

9.1 List Box Styles

The following styles can be used when creating a list box:

STYLE	DESCRIPTION
LS_MULTIPLESEL	The list box supports selection of multiple items
LS_OWNERDRAW	The list box generates a WM_DRAWITEM whenever certain parts are to be drawn
LS_NOADJUSTPOS	This list box style will not size the list box
LS_HORZSCROLL	The list box will have a horizontal scroll bar along the bottom, and will support horizontal scrolling

LS_EXTENDEDSEL   This list box style lets the user select more than one item using a point-end point selection technique

9.2 Extended Selection

List boxes also support a selection technique known as extended selection. Extended selection supports a "swiping" technique to select the list box items. The following keystrokes and mouse actions are defined in an extended-selection list box:

MOVEMENT	ACTION
Click mouse button on object	Selects object; all others are deselected
Drag mouse from start point of selection to end point of selection	Selects all objects in area; all other objects are deselected
Press SHIFT key while cursor is at start point, and use ↑ and ↓ keys to move to end point	Selects all objects in area; all other objects are deselected
Click mouse button on object while pressing Ctrl key	Selects object; all other selected objects are left selected
Press Ctrl+spacebar, or spacebar, while cursor is positioned at object	Selects object; all other selected objects are left selected
Press Ctrl key while dragging mouse from start point of selection to end point of selection	Selects all objects in area; all other objects are deselected

Enough of the intro text. The LIST1 example program shows a very introductory list box program. This list box has a LS_MULTIPLESEL style, and communicates with the client area to have the selections displayed in the window.

LIST1.C

```c
#define INCL_WIN
#define INCL_GPI

#include <os2.h>
#include <stdio.h>
#include <stdlib.h>
#include <string.h>
#include "list1.h"

MRESULT EXPENTRY ClientWndProc ( HWND hwndClient,
                                 ULONG ulMsg,
                                 MPARAM mpParm1,
                                 MPARAM mpParm2 ) ;
```

```
MRESULT EXPENTRY DlgProc ( HWND hwndDlg,
                           ULONG ulMsg,
                           MPARAM mpParm1,
                           MPARAM mpParm2 ) ;




#define CLS_CLIENT              "MyClass"
int main ( void ) ;

typedef struct {
    BOOL   fSelectedItems ;
    USHORT ausListBoxSel [10] ;
} LISTBOXINFO, *PLISTBOXINFO ;

int main ( )
{
    HMQ hmqQueue ;
    HAB habAnchor ;
    ULONG ulFlags ;
    HWND hwndFrame ;
    HWND hwndClient ;
    QMSG qmMsg ;

    /* initialization stuff */
    habAnchor = WinInitialize ( 0 ) ;
    hmqQueue = WinCreateMsgQueue ( habAnchor, 0 ) ;

    WinRegisterClass ( habAnchor,
                       CLS_CLIENT,
                       ClientWndProc,
                       CS_SYNCPAINT,
                       sizeof ( PVOID )) ;

    ulFlags = FCF_TITLEBAR | FCF_SYSMENU |
              FCF_SIZEBORDER | FCF_MINMAX | FCF_SHELLPOSITION ;


    hwndFrame = WinCreateStdWindow ( HWND_DESKTOP,
                             WS_VISIBLE,
                             &ulFlags,
                             CLS_CLIENT,
                             "Plain Listbox Example",
                             0,
                             ( HMODULE ) 0,
                             IDM_MENU,
                             &hwndClient ) ;


    if ( hwndFrame != NULLHANDLE ) {
        while ( WinGetMsg ( habAnchor, &qmMsg, NULLHANDLE, 0, 0 ))
            WinDispatchMsg ( habAnchor, &qmMsg ) ;
        WinDestroyWindow ( hwndFrame ) ;
    } /* endif */
```

```
    /* clean - up */
    WinDestroyMsgQueue ( hmqQueue ) ;
    WinTerminate ( habAnchor ) ;
    return 0 ;
}

MRESULT EXPENTRY ClientWndProc ( HWND hwndClient, ULONG ulMsg,
                                 MPARAM mpParm1, MPARAM mpParm2 )

{
    PLISTBOXINFO pliInfo ;


    pliInfo = WinQueryWindowPtr ( hwndClient, 0 ) ;

    switch ( ulMsg ) {
        case WM_ERASEBACKGROUND:
            return ( MRFROMLONG ( TRUE ) ) ;
        case WM_CREATE:
            pliInfo =
            ( PLISTBOXINFO ) malloc ( sizeof ( LISTBOXINFO )) ;
            if ( pliInfo == ( PLISTBOXINFO ) 0 ) {
                WinAlarm ( HWND_DESKTOP,
                           WA_ERROR ) ;
                return (( MRESULT ) TRUE ) ;
            } /* endif */
            WinSetWindowPtr ( hwndClient,
                 0,
                 pliInfo ) ;
            pliInfo -> fSelectedItems = FALSE ;
            WinPostMsg ( hwndClient,
                         UM_LOADDLG,
                         ( MPARAM ) 0,
                         ( MPARAM ) 0 ) ;
            break ;
        case WM_DESTROY:
            if ( pliInfo )
                free ( pliInfo ) ;
            break ;
        case WM_PAINT:
            {
                HPS hpsPresentationSpace ;
                RECTL rectInvalidRect, rclPaintRegion ;
                USHORT i ;

                hpsPresentationSpace = WinBeginPaint (
                                          hwndClient,
                                          NULLHANDLE,
                                          &rectInvalidRect ) ;
                rclPaintRegion.xLeft = rectInvalidRect.xLeft ;
                rclPaintRegion.xRight = rectInvalidRect.xRight ;
                rclPaintRegion.yBottom = rectInvalidRect.yBottom ;
                rclPaintRegion.yTop = rectInvalidRect.yTop ;

                WinFillRect ( hpsPresentationSpace,
                              &rectInvalidRect,
                              CLR_WHITE ) ;
```

```
                    if ( pliInfo -> fSelectedItems == TRUE ) {

                rclPaintRegion.yTop -= 15 ;
                WinDrawText ( hpsPresentationSpace,
                              - 1,
                              "You have selected:",
                              &rclPaintRegion,
                              0,
                              0,
                              DT_LEFT | DT_TEXTATTRS ) ;

                for ( i = 0 ; i < 10 ; i ++ )
                    if ( pliInfo -> ausListBoxSel [i] ==
                            TRUE ) {

                        rclPaintRegion.yTop -= 15 ;
                        WinDrawText ( hpsPresentationSpace,
                                      - 1,
                                      pszListBoxEntry [i] ,
                                      &rclPaintRegion,
                                      0,
                                      0,
                                      DT_LEFT |
                                      DT_TEXTATTRS ) ;

                        pliInfo -> ausListBoxSel [i] = FALSE ;
                    } /* end if selected */
                pliInfo -> fSelectedItems = FALSE ;
            } /* end if */
            WinEndPaint ( hpsPresentationSpace ) ;
            break ;

    }
case UM_LOADDLG:
    WinDlgBox ( hwndClient,
                hwndClient,
                DlgProc,
                ( HMODULE ) 0,
                IDD_LISTBOX,
                NULL ) ;
    return ( MRFROMLONG ( TRUE ) ) ;
case WM_SIZE:
    WinPostMsg ( hwndClient,
                 UM_LISTBOXSEL ,
                 ( MPARAM ) 0,
                 ( MPARAM ) 0 ) ;
    break ;
case UM_LISTBOXSEL:
    {

        SHORT sSelect = 0 ;
        USHORT usIndex = LIT_FIRST ;
        RECTL rclInvalidRegion ;
```

```
                          while ( sSelect != LIT_NONE ) {
                             sSelect = ( SHORT ) WinSendDlgItemMsg (
                                WinWindowFromID (
                                   hwndClient, IDD_LISTBOX ) ,
                                   IDL_LISTBOX,
                                   LM_QUERYSELECTION,
                                   MPFROMSHORT ( usIndex ) ,
                                   ( MPARAM ) 0 ) ;
                                pliInfo -> ausListBoxSel [sSelect] = TRUE ;
                                usIndex = sSelect ;
                             }
                          pliInfo -> fSelectedItems = TRUE ;

                          WinQueryWindowRect ( hwndClient,
                             &rclInvalidRegion ) ;

                          rclInvalidRegion.xLeft =
                             ( rclInvalidRegion.xRight -
                             rclInvalidRegion.xLeft ) / 3 * 2 ;

                          WinInvalidateRect ( hwndClient,
                             &rclInvalidRegion, FALSE ) ;
                          break ;
                       }
              default:
                 return WinDefWindowProc ( hwndClient,
                    ulMsg, mpParm1, mpParm2 ) ;
              } /* endswitch */

     return ( MRFROMLONG ( FALSE )) ;
     }

MRESULT EXPENTRY DlgProc ( HWND hwndDlg, ULONG ulMsg,
     MPARAM mpParm1, MPARAM mpParm2 )

{
     USHORT usNumItems = 10 ;
     USHORT i ;

     switch ( ulMsg ) {

        case WM_INITDLG:
           {
              HWND hwndListBox ;

              hwndListBox = WinWindowFromID ( hwndDlg,
                 IDL_LISTBOX ) ;
              for ( i = 0 ; i < usNumItems ; i ++ )
                 WinInsertLboxItem ( hwndListBox,
                                     LIT_END,
                                     pszListBoxEntry [i] ) ;

              WinSendDlgItemMsg ( hwndDlg,
                                  IDL_LISTBOX,
                                  LM_SELECTITEM,
                                  MPFROMSHORT ( 0 ) ,
                                  MPFROMSHORT ( TRUE )) ;
```

```
                }
            break ;

        case WM_COMMAND:
            {
                SHORT sCommand ;

                HWND hwndClient ;
                RECTL rclRectangle ;

                sCommand = SHORT1FROMMP ( mpParm1 ) ;
                switch ( sCommand ) {
                    case DID_OK:
                        hwndClient = WinQueryWindow ( hwndDlg,
                                                      QW_PARENT ) ;
                        WinPostMsg ( hwndClient,
                                     UM_LISTBOXSEL,
                                     ( MPARAM ) 0,
                                     ( MPARAM ) 0 ) ;
                        return (MRFROMLONG ( TRUE )) ;

                    case DID_CANCEL:
                        hwndClient = WinQueryWindow ( hwndDlg,
                                                      QW_PARENT ) ;
                        WinQueryWindowRect ( hwndClient,
                                             &rclRectangle ) ;
                        WinInvalidateRect ( hwndClient,
                                            &rclRectangle,
                                            FALSE ) ;
                        WinDismissDlg ( hwndDlg, sCommand ) ;
                        break ;

                } /* end switch sCommand */
            break ;
            }
    default:
        return ( WinDefDlgProc ( hwndDlg, ulMsg,
                                 mpParm1, mpParm2 )) ;
} /* endswitch */

return ( MRFROMLONG ( FALSE ) ) ;
}
```

LIST1.RC

```
#include <os2.h>
#include "LIST1.H"

DLGTEMPLATE IDD_LISTBOX LOADONCALL MOVEABLE DISCARDABLE
BEGIN
    DIALOG      "Listbox  Example",  IDD_LISTBOX,  12,  6,  170,  107,
WS_VISIBLE,
            FCF_SYSMENU | FCF_TITLEBAR
            PRESPARAMS PP_BACKGROUNDCOLORINDEX, CLR_WHITE
    BEGIN
        LISTBOX         IDL_LISTBOX, 14, 28, 135, 63,
        LS_MULTIPLESEL
            PRESPARAMS PP_BACKGROUNDCOLORINDEX, CLR_WHITE
        PUSHBUTTON      "OK", DID_OK, 3, 1, 40, 14
        PUSHBUTTON      "Cancel", DID_CANCEL, 48, 1, 40, 14
    END
END
```

LIST1.H

```
#define UM_LOADDLG              (WM_USER+1)
#define UM_LISTBOXSEL           (WM_USER+2)
#define IDD_LISTBOX             200
#define IDL_LISTBOX             201
#define IDM_MENU                202



CHAR *pszListBoxEntry[] = {
        "Cowboys",
        "Bengals",
        "Oilers",
        "Bears",
        "Broncos",
        "Jets",
        "Raiders",
        "Rams",
        "Giants",
        "Redskins" };
```

234 — The Art of OS/2 2.1 C Programming

LIST1.MAK

```
LIST1.EXE:                      LIST1.OBJ \
                                LIST1.RES
        LINK386 @<<
LIST1
LIST1
LIST1
OS2386
LIST1
<<
        RC LIST1.RES LIST1.EXE

LIST1.RES:                      LIST1.RC \
                                LIST1.H
        RC -r LIST1.RC LIST1.RES

LIST1.OBJ:                      LIST1.C \
                                LIST1.H
        ICC -C+ -Kb+ -Ss+ LIST1.C
```

LIST1.DEF

```
NAME LISTBOX WINDOWAPI
DESCRIPTION 'Listbox example.
             Copyright (c) 1992 by Kathleen Panov.
             All rights reserved.'
```

In the LIST1 sample program, the dialog box will post a message, UM_LISTBOXSEL, to the client area when the OK button is pressed. When the client area receives this message, it queries the list box to determine which items have been selected. These items are stored in the user-defined window word area for the client window. Also, a flag, *fSelectedItems*, is set to indicate items have been selected.

The UM_LISTBOXSEL is known as a user-defined message. All user-defined message must use a message ID between 0x1000 (WM_USER) and 0xBFFF. These messages give the programmer the opportunity to create a message for an event that is not a system-defined event.

When the WM_PAINT message is received, the client area is cleared. If the flag, *fSelectedItems*, is set, the items in the window word are written to the client area.

9.3 Initializing the Client Window

The structure LISTBOXINFO is used to hold the list box information.

```
typedef struct {
    BOOL    fSelectedItems ;
    USHORT ausListBoxSel [10] ;
} LISTBOXINFO, *PLISTBOXINFO ;
```

The flag, *fSelectedItems*, is used to indicate that items have been selected from the list box, and the OK button has been pressed. The array, *ausListBoxSel[]*, is used to hold the items that have been selected.

```
pliInfo =
( PLISTBOXINFO ) malloc ( sizeof ( LISTBOXINFO )) ;
if ( pliInfo == ( PLISTBOXINFO ) 0 ) {
    WinAlarm ( HWND_DESKTOP,
               WA_ERROR ) ;
    return (( MRESULT ) TRUE ) ;
} /* endif */
WinSetWindowPtr ( hwndClient,
    0,
    pliInfo ) ;
pliInfo -> fSelectedItems = FALSE ;
WinPostMsg ( hwndClient,
             UM_LOADDLG,
             ( MPARAM ) 0,
             ( MPARAM ) 0 ) ;
```

The WM_CREATE message processing is where the memory is allocated for the structure LISTBOXINFO. *WinSetWindowPtr* is used to assign the pointer to the structure, *pliInfo*, to the window word. After this operation is completed successfully, the message UM_LOADDLG is posted to signify that it is time to load the dialog box containing the list box.

9.4 Initializing the List Box

```
HWND hwndListBox ;

hwndListBox = WinWindowFromID ( hwndDlg,
    IDL_LISTBOX ) ;
for ( i = 0 ; i < usNumItems ; i ++ )
    WinInsertLboxItem ( hwndListBox,
                        LIT_END,
                        pszListBoxEntry [i] ) ;
```

The list box is initialized in the WM_INITDLG message processing of the dialog box. The first step is to obtain the window handle of the list box using *WinWindowFromID*. The parent of all controls in a dialog box is the dialog box. *WinInsertLboxItem* is a new macro that was included starting in OS/2 2.0. The first parameter is the list box window handle, *hwndListBox*. The second parameter indicates the position in the list box to insert the item. Acceptable entries are either an integer value indicating the placement of the item (0 indicates the topmost item), or the constants, LIT_FIRST or LIT_END. Also, the list box control is smart enough to handle sorting the items alphabetically. The constants, LIT_SORTASCENDING and LIT_SORTDESCENDING, can be used to automate this process. This is actually a pretty timely process, so if you can sort the list box items before inserting in the list box you may save some performance hits. The last parameter is the text string to enter into the list box. The array, *pszListBoxEntry*, is defined in the header file, LISTBOX.H.

```
WinSendDlgItemMsg ( hwndDlg,
                    IDL_LISTBOX,
                    LM_SELECTITEM,
                    MPFROMSHORT ( 0 ) ,
                    MPFROMSHORT ( TRUE )) ;
```

One other nit about the list box: you have to manually select the first item. The message, LM_SELECTITEM, will do this for us. The first parameter is the index of the list box item you want selected. The second parameter will show whether the item should be selected (TRUE) or deselected (FALSE). Notice that this time we use the function *WinSendDlgItemMsg*; this is another way to send messages to items in a dialog box.

While we're on the subject of initializing a list box, be aware of the limitation that exists on the number of items that can be inserted into a list box. The list box control is still 16-bit in OS/2 2.1, and thus can hold only 64K worth of data. Much of this space is used for internal housekeeping, and what you will finally be able to fit into the listbox is approximately 32K. Now, according to CUA conventions, you really should never have this many items in your list box, anyway; however, the alternative is to use the container control, which is 32 bit and can hold as many items as your memory will allow. This limit will go away when the PMWIN.DLL (the .DLL that contains the list box control) becomes 32 bit. Hopefully this will occur in the OS/2 version following 2.1

```
hwndClient = WinQueryWindow ( hwndDlg,
                              QW_PARENT ) ;
WinPostMsg ( hwndClient,
             UM_LISTBOXSEL,
             ( MPARAM ) 0,
             ( MPARAM ) 0 ) ;
return (MRFROMLONG ( TRUE )) ;
```

When the user presses either the OK push-button, or the CANCEL push-button, a WM_COMMAND message is sent to the dialog box. The ID of the push-button, either DID_OK or DID_CANCEL, is contained in message parameter 1, *mpParm1*. If the DID_OK button is pressed, a user-defined message, UM_LISTBOXSEL, is sent to the client window.

If the CANCEL button is pressed, the dialog box is destroyed, using *WinDismissDlg*. Also, the client window area is invalidated to cause the client area to repaint itself after the dialog box is gone.

9.5 Processing the UM_LISTBOXSEL Message

```
SHORT sSelect = 0 ;
USHORT usIndex = LIT_FIRST ;
RECTL rclInvalidRegion ;

while ( sSelect != LIT_NONE ) {
    sSelect = ( SHORT ) WinSendDlgItemMsg (
        WinWindowFromID (
        hwndClient, IDD_LISTBOX ) ,
        IDL_LISTBOX,
        LM_QUERYSELECTION,
        MPFROMSHORT ( usIndex ) ,
        ( MPARAM ) 0 ) ;
    pliInfo -> ausListBoxSel [sSelect] = TRUE ;
    usIndex = sSelect ;
}
pliInfo -> fSelectedItems = TRUE ;
```

When the client window receives the UM_LISTBOXSEL message, it is the client's job to find out which items in the list box are selected. Our list box has the style LS_MULTIPLESEL, so the user can select as many items as he or she wants. This makes the procedure to find all these items a little tricky; not difficult, just tricky. The message LM_QUERYSELECTION starts at the list box item specified in message parameter 1, and returns the first selected item it finds. This is a fairly simple procedure to code. A *while* loop is used to continue searching until *sSelect* returns LIT_NONE; in other words, no more items are selected. The LM_QUERYSELECTION message is sent to the list box window. The variable *usIndex* indicates the index of the item at which to start the search. At the start of the loop, this variable is set to LIT_FIRST, the first item in the list box. The first selected item found is returned in the variable, *sSelect*. As the loop traverses through the items in the list box, the starting search point is updated to *sSelect*. As a selected item is found, the corresponding index in the array *ausListBoxSel[]* is set to TRUE. This information is used in the WM_PAINT processing. After all the selected items are found, the flag, *fSelectedItems*, is set to TRUE. This is also used in the WM_PAINT processing.

```
WinQueryWindowRect ( hwndClient,
    &rclInvalidRegion ) ;

rclInvalidRegion.xLeft =
    ( rclInvalidRegion.xRight -
    rclInvalidRegion.xLeft ) / 3 * 2 ;

WinInvalidateRect ( hwndClient,
    &rclInvalidRegion, FALSE ) ;
```

The last part of this message processing is to signal the client window to repaint itself. However, the only part that needs updating is the rightmost third of the client area; this is where the selected items are displayed. A calculation is made to determine the dimensions of this area. The value is placed in the *rclInvalidRegion* structure. Lastly, this structure is passed to *WinInvalidateRect* to actually invalidate the area.

```
hpsPresentationSpace = WinBeginPaint (
                            hwndClient,
                            NULLHANDLE,
                            &rectInvalidRect ) ;
rclPaintRegion.xLeft = rectInvalidRect.xLeft ;
rclPaintRegion.xRight = rectInvalidRect.xRight ;
rclPaintRegion.yBottom = rectInvalidRect.yBottom ;
rclPaintRegion.yTop = rectInvalidRect.yTop ;

WinFillRect ( hpsPresentationSpace,
              &rectInvalidRect,
              CLR_WHITE ) ;
```

The WM_PAINT processing is where the items selected in the list box are actually written to the client area window. *WinFillRect* is used to fill the entire invalidated region with the color CLR_WHITE. Next, a check is made to see if the *fSelectedItems* flag is TRUE. If so, the paint routine has some more work to do.

```
if ( pliInfo -> fSelectedItems == TRUE ) {

    rclPaintRegion.yTop -= 15 ;
    WinDrawText ( hpsPresentationSpace,
                  - 1,
                  "You have selected:",
                  &rclPaintRegion,
                  0,
                  0,
                  DT_LEFT | DT_TEXTATTRS ) ;

    for ( i = 0 ; i < 10 ; i ++ )
        if ( pliInfo -> ausListBoxSel [i] ==
            TRUE ) {

            rclPaintRegion.yTop -= 15 ;
```

```
                              WinDrawText ( hpsPresentationSpace,
                                            - 1,
                                            pszListBoxEntry [i] ,
                                            &rclPaintRegion,
                                            0,
                                            0,
                                            DT_LEFT |
                                            DT_TEXTATTRS ) ;

                              pliInfo -> ausListBoxSel [i] = FALSE ;
                        } /* end if selected */
                 pliInfo -> fSelectedItems = FALSE ;
           } /* end if */
```

If the user has selected some items, *WinDrawText* is used to write a heading on the client area. The array, *ausListBoxSel[]*, is cycled through to find each selected item and write the list box item text to the client area as well.

9.6 Owner-Drawing Controls

An owner-draw style can be used for many of the Presentation Manager controls. This style sends a WM_DRAWITEM message when some portion of the control is to be drawn. This feature lets the programmer customize the control.

The following example program creates an owner-drawn list box that has system bitmaps and their titles as the selectable items.

LISTBOX.C

```
#define INCL_WIN
#define INCL_GPI

#include <os2.h>
#include <stdio.h>
#include <stdlib.h>
#include <string.h>
#include "listbox.h"

#define USRM_LOADDLG                    ( WM_USER + 1 )

typedef struct _BITMAPDATA {
   CHAR    achName [20] ;
   USHORT usNumber ;
} BITMAPDATA, * PBITMAPDATA ;

#define MAX_BITMAPS              9
```

```
BITMAPDATA abdBitmaps [MAX_BITMAPS] = {
   "SBMP_CHILDSYSMENU",        SBMP_CHILDSYSMENU,
   "SBMP_MAXBUTTON",           SBMP_MAXBUTTON,
   "SBMP_MENUATTACHED",        SBMP_MENUATTACHED,
   "SBMP_MINBUTTON",           SBMP_MINBUTTON,
   "SBMP_PROGRAM",             SBMP_PROGRAM,
   "SBMP_RESTOREBUTTON",       SBMP_RESTOREBUTTON,
   "SBMP_SIZEBOX",             SBMP_SIZEBOX,
   "SBMP_SYSMENU",             SBMP_SYSMENU,
   "SBMP_TREEMINUS",           SBMP_TREEMINUS
} ;

#define CLS_CLIENT              "MyClass"

MRESULT EXPENTRY ClientWndProc ( HWND hwndWnd,
                                 ULONG ulMsg,
                                 MPARAM mpParm1,
                                 MPARAM mpParm2 ) ;


BOOL Draw1Bitmap ( HPS hpsDraw,
                   HBITMAP hbmBitmap,
                   PRECTL prclDest ) ;


MRESULT EXPENTRY DlgProc ( HWND hwndWnd,
                           ULONG ulMsg,
                           MPARAM mpParm1,
                           MPARAM mpParm2 ) ;

INT main ( VOID )
{
   HMQ        hmqQueue ;
   HAB        habAnchor ;
   ULONG      ulFlags ;
   HWND       hwndFrame ;
   HWND       hwndClient ;
   BOOL       bLoop ;
   QMSG       qmMsg ;

   habAnchor = WinInitialize ( 0 ) ;
   hmqQueue = WinCreateMsgQueue ( habAnchor, 0 ) ;

   WinRegisterClass ( habAnchor,
                      CLS_CLIENT,
                      ClientWndProc,
                      CS_SIZEREDRAW | CS_SYNCPAINT,
                      0 ) ;

   ulFlags = FCF_TITLEBAR | FCF_SYSMENU |
             FCF_SIZEBORDER | FCF_MINMAX ;
```

```
        hwndFrame = WinCreateStdWindow ( HWND_DESKTOP,
                                          0L,
                                          &ulFlags,
                                          CLS_CLIENT,
                                          "Listbox Example",
                                          0L,
                                          NULLHANDLE,
                                          0,
                                          &hwndClient ) ;

    if ( hwndFrame != NULLHANDLE ) {
        WinSetWindowPos ( hwndFrame,
                          NULLHANDLE,
                          50,
                          50,
                          300,
                          300,
                          SWP_SIZE |
                          SWP_MOVE |
                          SWP_ACTIVATE |
                          SWP_SHOW ) ;

        bLoop = WinGetMsg ( habAnchor, &qmMsg, NULLHANDLE, 0, 0 ) ;
        while ( bLoop ) {
            WinDispatchMsg ( habAnchor, &qmMsg ) ;
            bLoop = WinGetMsg ( habAnchor,
                                &qmMsg,
                                NULLHANDLE,
                                0,
                                0 ) ;
        } /* endwhile */

        WinDestroyWindow ( hwndFrame ) ;
    } /* endif */

    WinDestroyMsgQueue ( hmqQueue ) ;
    WinTerminate ( habAnchor ) ;
    return 0 ;
}

BOOL Draw1Bitmap ( HPS hpsDraw, HBITMAP hbmBitmap, PRECTL prclDest
)
{
    BITMAPINFOHEADER2      bmihHeader ;
    POINTL                 ptlPoint ;
    BOOL                   bRc ;

    bmihHeader.cbFix = 16 ;
    GpiQueryBitmapInfoHeader ( hbmBitmap, &bmihHeader ) ;

    ptlPoint.x = ( prclDest -> xRight -
                   prclDest -> xLeft -
                   bmihHeader.cx ) / 2 +
                   prclDest -> xLeft ;
```

```
    ptlPoint.y = ( prclDest -> yTop -
                   prclDest -> yBottom -
                   bmihHeader.cy ) / 2 +
                   prclDest -> yBottom ;

    bRc = WinDrawBitmap ( hpsDraw,
                          hbmBitmap,
                          NULL,
                          &ptlPoint,
                          0,
                          0,
                          DBM_NORMAL | DBM_IMAGEATTRS ) ;
    return bRc ;
}

MRESULT EXPENTRY DlgProc ( HWND hwndWnd,
                           ULONG ulMsg,
                           MPARAM mpParm1,
                           MPARAM mpParm2 )

{
    switch ( ulMsg ) {

    case WM_INITDLG:
        {
            USHORT usIndex ;

            for ( usIndex = 0 ; usIndex < MAX_BITMAPS ; usIndex ++ ) {
                WinSendDlgItemMsg ( hwndWnd,
                                    IDL_LISTBOX,
                                    LM_INSERTITEM,
                                    MPFROMSHORT ( usIndex ) ,
                                    MPFROMP ( "" )) ;
            } /* endfor */

            WinSendDlgItemMsg ( hwndWnd,
                                IDL_LISTBOX,
                                LM_SELECTITEM,
                                MPFROMSHORT ( 0 ) ,
                                MPFROMSHORT ( TRUE )) ;
        }
        break ;

    case WM_COMMAND:
        switch ( SHORT1FROMMP ( mpParm1 )) {
        case DID_OK:
        case DID_CANCEL:
            WinDismissDlg ( hwndWnd, FALSE ) ;
            break ;

        default:
            return WinDefDlgProc ( hwndWnd,
                                   ulMsg,
                                   mpParm1,
                                   mpParm2 ) ;
        } /* endswitch */
        break ;
```

```
case WM_MEASUREITEM:
    {
        HPS                     hpsChar ;
        FONTMETRICS             fmMetrics ;
        LONG                    lMaxCy ;
        USHORT                  usIndex ;
        HBITMAP                 hbmBitmap ;
        BITMAPINFOHEADER2       bmihHeader ;

        hpsChar = WinGetPS ( hwndWnd ) ;
        GpiQueryFontMetrics ( hpsChar,
                              ( LONG ) sizeof ( fmMetrics ) ,
                              &fmMetrics ) ;
        WinReleasePS ( hpsChar ) ;

        lMaxCy = fmMetrics.lMaxBaselineExt ;

        for ( usIndex = 0 ; usIndex < MAX_BITMAPS ; usIndex ++ ) {
            hbmBitmap = WinGetSysBitmap ( HWND_DESKTOP,
                              abdBitmaps [usIndex].usNumber ) ;

            bmihHeader.cbFix = 16 ;
            GpiQueryBitmapInfoHeader ( hbmBitmap, &bmihHeader ) ;
            lMaxCy = max ( lMaxCy, bmihHeader.cy ) ;

            GpiDeleteBitmap ( hbmBitmap ) ;
        } /* endfor */

        return MRFROMLONG ( lMaxCy + 10 ) ;
    }

case WM_DRAWITEM:
    {
        POWNERITEM      poiItem ;
        HBITMAP         hbmBitmap ;
        RECTL           rclText ;

        poiItem = ( POWNERITEM ) PVOIDFROMMP ( mpParm2 ) ;

        rclText = poiItem -> rclItem ;
        rclText.xLeft = ( rclText.xRight - rclText.xLeft ) / 7 ;

        WinDrawText ( poiItem -> hps,
                      - 1,
                      abdBitmaps [poiItem -> idItem].achName,
                      &rclText,
                      poiItem -> fsState?CLR_YELLOW:CLR_BLUE,
                      poiItem -> fsState?CLR_BLUE:CLR_WHITE,
                      DT_LEFT | DT_VCENTER | DT_ERASERECT ) ;

        rclText = poiItem -> rclItem ;
        rclText.xRight = ( rclText.xRight - rclText.xLeft ) / 7 ;

        WinFillRect ( poiItem -> hps, &rclText, CLR_WHITE ) ;
```

244 — The Art of OS/2 2.1 C Programming

```
            hbmBitmap = WinGetSysBitmap ( HWND_DESKTOP,
                          abdBitmaps [poiItem -> idItem].usNumber ) ;

            Draw1Bitmap ( poiItem -> hps, hbmBitmap, &rclText ) ;

            GpiDeleteBitmap ( hbmBitmap ) ;

            poiItem -> fsState = FALSE ;
            poiItem -> fsStateOld = FALSE ;

            return MRFROMSHORT ( TRUE ) ;
         }

      default:
         return WinDefDlgProc ( hwndWnd, ulMsg, mpParm1, mpParm2 ) ;
      } /* endswitch */

   return MRFROMSHORT ( FALSE ) ;
}

MRESULT EXPENTRY ClientWndProc ( HWND hwndWnd,
                                 ULONG ulMsg,
                                 MPARAM mpParm1,
                                 MPARAM mpParm2 )

{
   switch ( ulMsg ) {

   case WM_CREATE:
      WinPostMsg ( hwndWnd, USRM_LOADDLG, 0L, 0L ) ;
      break ;

   case WM_PAINT:
      {
         HPS hpsPaint ;

         hpsPaint = WinBeginPaint ( hwndWnd, NULLHANDLE, NULL ) ;
         GpiErase ( hpsPaint ) ;
         WinEndPaint ( hpsPaint ) ;
      }
      break ;

   case WM_ERASEBACKGROUND:
      return MRFROMSHORT ( TRUE ) ;

   case USRM_LOADDLG:
      WinDlgBox ( hwndWnd,
                  hwndWnd,
                  DlgProc,
                  NULLHANDLE,
                  IDD_LISTBOX,
                  NULL ) ;
      WinPostMsg ( hwndWnd, WM_CLOSE, 0L, 0L ) ;
      break ;

   default:
```

```
        return WinDefWindowProc ( hwndWnd,
                                  ulMsg,
                                  mpParm1,
                                  mpParm2 ) ;
   } /* endswitch */

   return MRFROMSHORT ( FALSE ) ;
}
```

LISTBOX.RC

```
#include <os2.h>
#include "listbox.h"

DLGTEMPLATE IDD_LISTBOX LOADONCALL MOVEABLE DISCARDABLE
{
    DIALOG "Listbox Example", IDD_LISTBOX, 12, 6, 170, 107,
        WS_VISIBLE,
        FCF_SYSMENU | FCF_TITLEBAR
    {
        LISTBOX IDL_LISTBOX, 14, 33, 135, 63, LS_OWNERDRAW
        DEFPUSHBUTTON "OK", DID_OK, 3, 10, 40, 13, WS_GROUP
        PUSHBUTTON "Cancel", DID_CANCEL, 48, 10, 40, 13
    }
}
```

LISTBOX.H

```
#define IDD_LISTBOX             256
#define IDL_LISTBOX             512
```

LISTBOX.MAK

```
LISTBOX.EXE:                    LISTBOX.OBJ \
                                LISTBOX.RES
        LINK386 @<<
LISTBOX
LISTBOX
LISTBOX
OS2386
LISTBOX
<<
        RC LISTBOX.RES LISTBOX.EXE

LISTBOX.RES:                    LISTBOX.RC \
                                LISTBOX.H
        RC -r LISTBOX.RC LISTBOX.RES

LISTBOX.OBJ:                    LISTBOX.C \
                                LISTBOX.H
        ICC -C+ -Kb+ -Ss+ LISTBOX.C
```

LISTBOX.DEF

```
NAME LISTBOX WINDOWAPI

DESCRIPTION 'Second listbox example
Copyright (c) 1992 by Kathleen Panov
All rights reserved.'

STACKSIZE 16384
```

The beginning of the program is all functions you have seen before. The structure BITMAPDATA is defined:

```
typedef struct _BITMAPDATA {
    CHAR    achName [20] ;
    USHORT usNumber ;
} BITMAPDATA, * PBITMAPDATA ;
```

The first element, *achName*, is the #define'd text string of each system bitmap. The second element, *usNumber*, is the number of the system bitmap. When we draw the bitmaps, we'll use this structure to access the bitmaps we want.

9.7 *DlgProc*

```
        for ( usIndex = 0 ; usIndex < MAX_BITMAPS ; usIndex ++ ) {
            WinSendDlgItemMsg ( hwndWnd,
                                IDL_LISTBOX,
                                LM_INSERTITEM,
                                MPFROMSHORT ( usIndex ) ,
                                MPFROMP ( "" )) ;
        } /* endfor */

        WinSendDlgItemMsg ( hwndWnd,
                            IDL_LISTBOX,
                            LM_SELECTITEM,
                            MPFROMSHORT ( 0 ) ,
                            MPFROMSHORT ( TRUE )) ;
```

The WM_INITDLG message is where the initialization of the dialog box and all its components are done. In this case, we want to initialize the list box. *WinSendDlgItemMsg* can be used to communicate directly with the list box. The message, LM_INSERTITEM, is used to insert items into the list box. If this was not an owner-drawn list box, the actual text strings would be inserted here; however, because this is an owner-drawn list box, the important thing is to tell the list box there will be eight items. The message LM_SELECTITEM is used to set the first item to the selected state.

```
hpsChar = WinGetPS ( hwndWnd ) ;
GpiQueryFontMetrics ( hpsChar,
                        ( LONG ) sizeof ( fmMetrics ) ,
                        &fmMetrics ) ;
WinReleasePS ( hpsChar ) ;

lMaxCy = fmMetrics.lMaxBaselineExt ;

for ( usIndex = 0 ; usIndex < MAX_BITMAPS ; usIndex ++ ) {
    hbmBitmap = WinGetSysBitmap ( HWND_DESKTOP,
                        abdBitmaps [usIndex].usNumber ) ;

    bmihHeader.cbFix = 16 ;
    GpiQueryBitmapInfoHeader ( hbmBitmap, &bmihHeader ) ;
    lMaxCy = max ( lMaxCy, bmihHeader.cy ) ;

    GpiDeleteBitmap ( hbmBitmap ) ;
} /* endfor */

return MRFROMLONG ( lMaxCy + 10 ) ;
```

The WM_MEASUREITEM message must be processed for an owner-drawn list box and also for horizontal scrolling list boxes. This message tells the list box how tall, or in some cases, how wide, each list box item is to be. The tallest, or widest, size should be returned in order for all the list box items to have a consistent look. In our example, all items are the same size. *GpiQueryFontMetrics* is used to get all sorts of information about the selected font. The one piece of the FONTMETRICS structure we are interested in is *fm.FontMetrics.lMaxBaselineExt*. This indicates the maximum height of the font. This is compared to the maximum height of the system bitmap. This information is contained in the BITMAPINFOHEADER structure that is obtained using *GpiQueryBitmapInfoHeader*.

The WM_DRAWITEM is the most complicated message processing in this example. This message is sent to the owner that will be doing the drawing whenever an item needs to be selected, unselected, or drawn. The second parameter in the WM_DRAWITEM message is POWNERITEM. The OWNERITEM structure looks like this:

```
  typedef struct _OWNERITEM
{
    HWND     hwnd;
    HPS      hps;
    ULONG    fsState;
    ULONG    fsAttribute;
    ULONG    fsStateOld;
    ULONG    fsAttributeOld;
    RECTL    rclItem;
    LONG     idItem;
/* This field contains idItem for menus, iItem for lb. */
    ULONG    hItem;
} OWNERITEM;
typedef OWNERITEM *POWNERITEM;
```

This structure has pretty much everything you need to draw a list box item.

```
        poiItem = ( POWNERITEM ) PVOIDFROMMP ( mpParm2 ) ;

        rclText = poiItem -> rclItem ;
        rclText.xLeft = ( rclText.xRight - rclText.xLeft ) / 7 ;

        WinDrawText ( poiItem -> hps,
                      - 1,
                      abdBitmaps [poiItem -> idItem] .achName,
                      &rclText,
                      poiItem -> fsState?CLR_YELLOW:CLR_BLUE,
                      poiItem -> fsState?CLR_BLUE:CLR_WHITE,
                      DT_LEFT | DT_VCENTER | DT_ERASERECT ) ;

        rclText = poiItem -> rclItem ;
        rclText.xRight = ( rclText.xRight - rclText.xLeft ) / 7 ;

        WinFillRect ( poiItem -> hps, &rclText, CLR_WHITE ) ;

        poiItem -> fsState = FALSE ;
        poiItem -> fsStateOld = FALSE ;

        return MRFROMSHORT ( TRUE ) ;
```

The *rclItem* is a RECTL structure that describes the area for the item to be drawn. *WinFillRect* is used to erase the drawing area. The first parameter, hps, is the presentation space handle, returned in the OWNERITEM structure. The second parameter is a pointer to *poiItem->rclText*. This is the area that is to be filled. The last parameter is CLR_WHITE. This is the color to use to fill the specified RECTL.

```
        hbmBitmap = WinGetSysBitmap ( HWND_DESKTOP,
                      abdBitmaps [poiItem -> idItem] .usNumber ) ;

        Draw1Bitmap ( poiItem -> hps, hbmBitmap, &rclText ) ;

        GpiDeleteBitmap ( hbmBitmap ) ;
```

The next thing to do is get a handle to the bitmap we want to draw in our list box item. *WinGetSysBitmap* is used to do this. The first parameter is the desktop window handle, HWND_DESKTOP. The second parameter is the system bitmap number. *poiItem->idItem* is the index of the selected item. We use this index as the index into the *abdBitmaps* structure. *Draw1Bitmap* is a very simple user-defined function we use to actually draw the bitmap. Once the bitmap has been drawn, some cleanup will be necessary. The handle of the bitmap needs to be freed using *GpiDeleteBitmap*.

```
poiItem -> fsState = FALSE ;
poiItem -> fsStateOld = FALSE ;

return MRFROMSHORT ( TRUE ) ;
```

The last step in our message processing is setting all the appropriate variables correctly for the window procedure. If the variable *fsState* is set to TRUE, the window procedure will handle the highlighting of the item. If set to FALSE, the window procedure leaves it alone. We have already done the highlighting ourselves, so we set it to TRUE. The same is true for the variable, *fsStateOld*, which is used to indicate the previous state of the item. A return code of TRUE, *fReturnTrue*, indicates that the item has been drawn already, so please do not draw it again. If FALSE had been returned here, the text " " would be placed over all the wonderful work we've done so far.

9.8 Draw1Bitmap

```
BOOL Draw1Bitmap ( HPS hpsDraw, HBITMAP hbmBitmap, PRECTL prclDest
)
{
    BITMAPINFOHEADER2          bmihHeader ;
    POINTL                     ptlPoint ;
    BOOL                       bRc ;

    bmihHeader.cbFix = 16 ;
    GpiQueryBitmapInfoHeader ( hbmBitmap, &bmihHeader ) ;

    ptlPoint.x = ( prclDest -> xRight -
                   prclDest -> xLeft -
                   bmihHeader.cx ) / 2 +
                   prclDest -> xLeft ;

    ptlPoint.y = ( prclDest -> yTop -
                   prclDest -> yBottom -
                   bmihHeader.cy ) / 2 +
                   prclDest -> yBottom ;
```

```
bRc = WinDrawBitmap ( hpsDraw,
                      hbmBitmap,
                      NULL,
                      &ptlPoint,
                      0,
                      0,
                      DBM_NORMAL | DBM_IMAGEATTRS ) ;
    return bRc ;
}
```

This function is designed to cut down on some repetitive code. The RECTL coordinates have to be changed to POINTLs. *WinDrawBitmap* will draw a bitmap on the specified hps. The second parameter is the bitmap handle, returned from *WinGetSysBitmap*. The next parameter is used to indicate how much of the bitmap to draw. NULL indicates that the whole bitmap is to be drawn. Next, the place to put the bitmap is specified in the PPOINTL structure. The next two parameters are foreground color and background color. 0 is used for both because the flag, DBM_IMAGEATTRS, is used. If this flag is used, the colors are ignored, and the bitmap is drawn using the current foreground and background colors of the presentation space.

9.9 List Box Messages

WM_CONTROL
This message is sent when a list box needs to notify its owner of some significant event.

Parameter 1:	USHORT usID	control window ID
	USHORT usNotifyCode	can be one of the following:
	LN_ENTER	enter or return key has been pressed
	LN_KILLFOCUS	list box is losing focus
	LN_SCROLL	list box is about to scroll horizontally
	LN_SETFOCUS	list box is gaining focus
	LN_SELECT	an item is being selected or deselected
Parameter 2:	HWND hwndControl	window handle of list box
Reply:	ULONG flReply	reserved, 0

WM_DRAWITEM
This message is sent to the drawer each time an item in the list box is to be drawn.

Parameter 1:	USHORT usID	ID of list box sending this message
Parameter 2:	POWNERITEM pOwnerItem	pointer to OWNERITEM structure
Reply:	BOOL fDrawn	TRUE — list box item has already been drawn, system is not to draw it; FALSE — not drawn, system is to draw it

WM_MEASUREITEM
This message is sent to the owner of a list box in order to determine the height and width of the specified item.

Parameter 1:	SHORT sListboxID	ID of list box window
Parameter 2:	SHORT sItemIndex	index of the list box item to determine size
Reply:	SHORT sHeight	height of list box item of interest

Note: This message only needs to be handled when LS_OWNERDRAW or LS_HORZSCROLL styles are specified.

LM_DELETEALL
This message is sent to delete all items in a list box.

Parameter 1:	ULONG ulParam1	reserved, 0
Parameter 2:	ULONG ulParam2	reserved, 0
Reply:	BOOL fSuccessful	successful? TRUE: FALSE

LM_DELETEITEM
This message is sent to a list box to delete a specified item.

Parameter 1:	SHORT sItemIndex	index of list box item to delete
Parameter 2:	ULONG ulParam2	reserved, 0
Reply:	SHORT sItemsRemain	number of items remaining in the list box

LM_INSERTITEM
This message is sent to a list box in order to insert a list box item.

Parameter 1:	SHORT sItemIndex	LIT_END — add item to end of list box LIT_SORTASCENDING — insert item sorted in ascending order LIT_DESCENDING — insert the item sorted in descending order Other — Insert the item at specified index
Parameter 2:	PSZ pItemText	text to enter in list box item
Reply:	SHORT sItemIndex	index of newly inserted item

LM_QUERYITEMCOUNT
This message is sent to the list box to determine the number of items in the list box.

Parameter 1:	ULONG ulParam1	reserved, 0
Parameter 2:	ULONG ulParam2	reserved, 0
Reply:	SHORT sItemCount	number of items in list box

LM_QUERYITEMHANDLE
This message is sent to the list box in order to query the 4 bytes that can be associated with a list box item.

Parameter 1:	SHORT sItemIndex	index of list box item to query
Parameter 2:	ULONG ulParam2	reserved, 0
Reply:	ULONG ulItemHandle	pointer (or any other 4-byte data type) to application-defined data

LM_QUERYITEMTEXT
This message is sent to the list box to query the list box item text.

Parameter 1:	SHORT sItemIndex	index of list box item
	SHORT sMaxLength	length of buffer (including NULL) — 0 returns length of text
Parameter 2:	PSZ pItemText	buffer for list box item text

Reply: SHORT sStringLength   length of text string, minus the
NULL

LM_QUERYITEMTEXTLENGTH

This message is sent to the list box to determine the length of a specified list box item.

Parameter 1:	SHORT sItemIndex	index of list box item
Parameter 2:	ULONG ulParam2	reserved, 0
Reply:	SHORT sTextLength	text length of specified item

LM_QUERYSELECTION

This message is sent to the list box to determine which items are selected.

Parameter 1:	SHORT sItemStart	index of item to start search from; LIT_FIRST — start search at first item
Parameter 2:	ULONG ulParam2	reserved, 0
Reply:	SHORT sItemSelected	index of selected Item; LIT_NONE — no more selected items

LM_QUERYTOPINDEX

This message is sent to the list box to determine the index of the item currently visible at the top of the list box.

Parameter 1:	ULONG ulParam2	reserved, 0
Parameter 2:	ULONG ulParam2	reserved, 0
Reply:	SHORT sItemTop	index of item currently at top of list box

LM_SEARCHSTRING

This message is sent to the list box to find the index of the item that matches the search string.

Parameter 1:	SHORT sSearchCmdd	LSS_CASESENSITIVE — search is case sensitive

		LSS_PREFIX — leading characters of item match the search string
		LSS_SUBSTRING — match if item contains search string
	SHORT sItemSearchStart	index of item to start search from
Parameter 2:	PSZ pSearchString	string to use as search criteria
Reply:	SHORT sItemMatch	index of item that matches string

LM_SELECTITEM

This message is sent to the list box to select or deselect an item.

Parameter 1:	SHORT sItemIndex	index of item to select or deselect; LIT_NONE — all items are deselected
Parameter 2:	SHORT usState	(ignored if *sItemIndex* == LIT_NONE) TRUE — item is selected FALSE — item is deselected
Reply:	BOOL fSuccess	successful? TRUE: FALSE

LM_SETITEMHANDLE

This message is sent to the list box to associate 4 bytes of data with a specific list box item.

Parameter 1:	SHORT sItemIndex	index of list box item
Parameter 2:	ULONG ulItemHandle	application-defined data
Reply:	BOOL fSuccess	successful? TRUE: FALSE

LM_SETITEMHEIGHT

This message is sent to the list box to set the height of the list box items.

Parameter 1:	ULONG ulNewHeight	new height of list box items, in pixels
Parameter 2:	ULONG ulParam2	reserved, 0
Reply:	BOOL fSuccess	successful? TRUE: FALSE

LM_SETITEMTEXT

This message is sent to the list box to set the text of a specified list box item.

Parameter 1:	SHORT sItemIndex	index of list box item
Parameter 2:	PSTRL pItemText	pointer to list box item text
Reply:	BOOL fSuccess	successful? TRUE: FALSE

LM_SETTOPINDEX

This message is sent to the list box to scroll the list box to the specified item.

Parameter 1:	SHORT sItemIndex	index of item to put as currently visible top item
Parameter 2:	ULONG ulParam2	reserved, 0
Reply:	BOOL fSuccess	successful? TRUE: FALSE

WM_QUERYCONVERTPOS

This message is sent to determine whether to begin DBCS character conversion.

Parameter 1:	PRECTL pCursorPos	cursor position
Parameter 2:	ULONG ulParam2	reserved, 0
Reply:	USHORT usCode	QCP_CONVERT — conversion can be performed QCP_NOCONVERT — conversion should not be performed

WM_QUERYWINDOWPARAMS

This message is sent to the list box to query the Presentation Parameters.

Parameter 1:   PWNDPARAMS pWndParams   pointer to WNDPARAMS structure

```
typedef struct _WNDPARAMS   /* wprm */ {
    ULONG fsStatus;          /* can be either WPM_CBCTLDATA
                                or WPM_CTLDATA */
    ULONG cchText;           /* length of window text */
    PSZ   pszText;           /* window text */
    ULONG cbPresParams;      /* Length of presentation
                                parameters */
    PVOID pPresParams;       /* pointer to presentation
                                parameters data */
    ULONG cbCtlData;         /* Length of window class data
                                */
    PVOID pCtlData;          /* Pointer to window class
                                data */
} WNDPARAMS;
typedef WNDPARAMS *PWNDPARAMS;
```

Parameter 2:   ULONG ulParam2   reserved, 0
Reply: BOOL fSuccess   successful?
                                          TRUE:FALSE

WM_SETWINDOWPARAMS

Sent to the list box to set the Presentation Parameters.

Parameter 1:   PWNDPARAMS pWndParams   pointer to WNDPARAMS structure

Parameter 2:   ULONG ulParam2   reserved, 0
Reply: BOOL fSuccess   successful?
                                            TRUE:FALSE

Chapter 10

Buttons

The easiest controls to use are buttons. Buttons belong to the class WC_BUTTON. There are four types of buttons — push-buttons, radio buttons, three-state buttons, and check boxes.

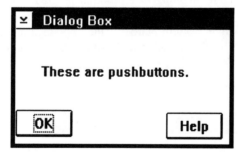

Figure 10.1. Push-buttons.

A push-button (Figure 10.1) sends a WM_COMMAND to its owner immediately when it is pressed. This feature distinguishes the push-button from the other two button types. Push-buttons are commonly used to initiate such actions as "Save", "OK", "Cancel", and "Help".

257

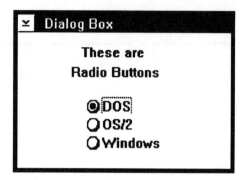

Figure 10.2. Radio buttons.

Radio buttons (Figure 10.2) are designed to be used when only one item in a group should be selectable. For instance, indicating "AM" or "PM" in a time dialog box is a good example of radio buttons. There are two styles of radio buttons: BS_AUTORADIOBUTTON and BS_RADIOBUTTON. When using the BS_RADIOBUTTON, the application must handle the highlighting of the selected button and unhighlighting of the button previously selected. When using the BS_AUTORADIOBUTTON, this is handled automatically by the system. When using radio buttons, the application must send a BM_QUERYCHECKINDEX message to determine which button was selected when the user exited the dialog box.

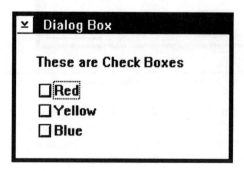

Figure 10.3. Check boxes.

In cases where more than one choice can be selected, check boxes (Figure 10.3) should be used. There are two styles that define check boxes: either BS_CHECKBOX or BS_AUTOCHECKBOX. These styles are similar in manner to their radio button counterparts, BS_RADIOBUTTON and BS_AUTORADIOBUTTON.

10.1 Button Styles

The following styles can be used when creating buttons:

STYLE	DESCRIPTION
BS_3STATE	Creates a three-state check box that can be selected, unselected, or disabled
BS_AUTO3STATE	Creates a three-state check box whose state is set by the system automatically
BS_AUTOCHECKBOX	Creates a check box that the system will automatically toggle between selected and unselected
BS_AUTORADIOBUTTON	Creates a radio button that will automatically disable other radio buttons in the group when it is selected
BS_CHECKBOX	Creates a check box; it is the application's responsibility to select or deselect the check box
BS_DEFAULT	Creates a button with thick border boxes; used with BS_PUSHBUTTON or BS_USERBUTTON
BS_ICON	Creates a push-button, labeled with an icon or bitmap instead of text
BS_HELP	Creates a push-button that sends a WM_HELP message to the owner window; can only be used with push-buttons
BS_NOCURSORSELECT	Creates an auto-radio button that is not automatically selected when the button is moved to with the cursor keys
BS_NOBORDER	Creates a push-button with no border; can only be used with push-buttons
BS_NOPOINTERFOCUS	Creates a radio button or check box that does not receive the keyboard focus when the user selects it
BS_PUSHBUTTON	Creates a push-button

BS_RADIOBUTTON	Creates a radio button
BS_SYSCOMMAND	Creates a button that posts a WM_SYSCOMMAND when selected; can only be used with push-buttons
BS_USERBUTTON	Creates a user-defined button; generates a BN_PAINT notification message, sent to its owner, when painting is needed

10.2 Example Program

The following program will create a simple dialog box that contains various types of buttons. Buttons are created both in the resource file and also by using *WinCreateWindow*.

BUTTON.C

```
#define INCL_WIN

#include <os2.h>
#include <stdio.h>
#include <stdlib.h>
#include "button.h"

#define CLS_CLIENT              "MyClass"

MRESULT EXPENTRY ClientWndProc ( HWND hwndWnd,
                                 ULONG ulMsg,
                                 MPARAM mpParm1,
                                 MPARAM mpParm2 ) ;

MRESULT EXPENTRY DlgProc ( HWND hwndWnd,
                           ULONG ulMsg,
                           MPARAM mpParm1,
                           MPARAM mpParm2 ) ;

INT main ( VOID )
{
    HAB             habAnchor ;
    HMQ             hmqQueue ;
    ULONG           ulFlags ;
    HWND            hwndFrame ;
    HWND            hwndClient ;
    BOOL            bLoop ;
    QMSG            qmMsg ;

    habAnchor = WinInitialize ( 0 ) ;
    hmqQueue = WinCreateMsgQueue ( habAnchor, 0 ) ;
```

```
    WinRegisterClass ( habAnchor,
                       CLS_CLIENT,
                       ClientWndProc,
                       CS_SIZEREDRAW,
                       0 ) ;

  ulFlags = FCF_TITLEBAR | FCF_SYSMENU |
            FCF_MENU | FCF_SIZEBORDER ;

  hwndFrame = WinCreateStdWindow ( HWND_DESKTOP,
                                   0,
                                   &ulFlags,
                                   CLS_CLIENT,
                                   "Button Control Example",
                                   0,
                                   NULLHANDLE,
                                   IDR_CLIENT,
                                   &hwndClient ) ;

  if  ( hwndFrame != NULLHANDLE ) {

    WinSetWindowPos ( hwndFrame,
                      NULLHANDLE,
                      50,
                      50,
                      250,
                      150,
                      SWP_SIZE | SWP_MOVE |
                      SWP_ACTIVATE | SWP_SHOW ) ;

    bLoop = WinGetMsg ( habAnchor, &qmMsg, NULLHANDLE, 0, 0 ) ;
    while  ( bLoop ) {
       WinDispatchMsg ( habAnchor, &qmMsg ) ;
       bLoop = WinGetMsg ( habAnchor,
                           &qmMsg,
                           NULLHANDLE,
                           0,
                           0 ) ;
    } /* endwhile */

    WinDestroyWindow ( hwndFrame ) ;
  } /* endif */

  WinDestroyMsgQueue ( hmqQueue ) ;
  WinTerminate ( habAnchor ) ;
  return 0 ;
}

MRESULT EXPENTRY ClientWndProc ( HWND hwndWnd,
                                 ULONG ulMsg,
                                 MPARAM mpParm1,
                                 MPARAM mpParm2 )
{
   switch ( ulMsg ) {

   case WM_ERASEBACKGROUND:
      return MRFROMSHORT ( TRUE ) ;
```

```
   case WM_COMMAND:
      switch ( SHORT1FROMMP ( mpParm1 )) {

      case IDM_START:
         WinDlgBox ( HWND_DESKTOP,
                     hwndWnd,
                     DlgProc,
                     NULLHANDLE,
                     IDD_BUTTON,
                     NULL ) ;
         break ;

      case IDM_EXIT:
         WinPostMsg ( hwndWnd, WM_CLOSE, 0, 0 ) ;
         break ;

      default:
         return WinDefWindowProc ( hwndWnd,
                                   ulMsg,
                                   mpParm1,
                                   mpParm2 ) ;
      }
      break ;
   default:
      return WinDefWindowProc ( hwndWnd,
                                ulMsg,
                                mpParm1,
                                mpParm2 ) ;
   } /* end switch ulMsg */

   return MRFROMSHORT ( FALSE ) ;
}

MRESULT EXPENTRY DlgProc ( HWND hwndWnd,
                           ULONG ulMsg,
                           MPARAM mpParm1,
                           MPARAM mpParm2 )
{
   switch ( ulMsg ) {

   case WM_INITDLG:
      {
         BTNCDATA bcdData ;

         bcdData.cb = sizeof ( BTNCDATA ) ;
         bcdData.fsCheckState = 0 ;
         bcdData.fsHiliteState = 0 ;
         bcdData.hImage = WinQuerySysPointer (
                           HWND_DESKTOP,
                           SPTR_ICONINFORMATION,
                           FALSE ) ;
```

```
        WinCreateWindow ( hwndWnd,
                          WC_BUTTON,
                          "",
                          WS_VISIBLE |
                          WS_TABSTOP |
                          BS_ICON ,
                          125,
                          55,
                          WinQuerySysValue ( HWND_DESKTOP,
                                             SV_CXICON ) ,
                          WinQuerySysValue ( HWND_DESKTOP,
                                             SV_CYICON ) ,
                          hwndWnd,
                          HWND_TOP,
                          IDR_ICON,
                          ( PVOID ) &bcdData,
                          NULL ) ;

        WinSendDlgItemMsg ( hwndWnd,
                            IDC_AUTOCHECKBOX,
                            BM_SETCHECK,
                            MPFROMSHORT ( TRUE ) ,
                            NULL ) ;

        WinSendDlgItemMsg ( hwndWnd,
                            IDC_AUTO3STATE,
                            BM_SETCHECK,
                            MPFROMSHORT ( 2 ) ,
                            NULL ) ;
    }
    break ;
case WM_COMMAND:

    switch ( SHORT1FROMMP ( mpParm1 )) {

    case DID_OK:
    case DID_CANCEL:
       WinDismissDlg ( hwndWnd, FALSE ) ;
       break ;
    case IDP_NOBORDER:
       break ;
    case IDR_ICON:
       break ;
    default:
       return WinDefDlgProc ( hwndWnd,
                              ulMsg,
                              mpParm1,
                              mpParm2 ) ;
    } /* endswitch */

    break ;
default:
    return WinDefDlgProc ( hwndWnd,
                           ulMsg,
                           mpParm1,
                           mpParm2 ) ;
} /* endswitch */
```

```
      return MRFROMSHORT ( FALSE ) ;
}
```

BUTTON.RC

```
#include <os2.h>
#include "button.h"

MENU IDR_CLIENT
{
   SUBMENU "~File", IDM_FILES
   {
      MENUITEM "~Display dialog...", IDM_START
      MENUITEM "E~xit", IDM_EXIT
   }
}


DLGTEMPLATE IDD_BUTTON PRELOAD MOVEABLE DISCARDABLE
{
   DIALOG "Button dialog", IDD_BUTTON, 28, 23, 258, 110,
           FS_NOBYTEALIGN | WS_VISIBLE,
           FCF_SYSMENU | FCF_TITLEBAR
           PRESPARAMS PP_BACKGROUNDCOLORINDEX, CLR_WHITE
   {
      LTEXT "Radio Button Styles", -1, 135, 95, 86, 8
      LTEXT "Check Box Styles", -1, 11, 95, 76, 8
      LTEXT "Push Button Styles", -1, 55, 48, 82, 8
      AUTOCHECKBOX "BS_AUTOCHECKBOX", IDC_AUTOCHECKBOX,
         11, 81, 106, 10
      AUTOCHECKBOX "BS_AUTO3STATE", IDC_AUTO3STATE,
         11, 66, 89, 10, BS_AUTO3STATE | WS_GROUP
      AUTORADIOBUTTON "BS_AUTORADIOBUTTON", IDR_AUTORADIOBUTTON,
         131, 81, 121, 10
      AUTORADIOBUTTON "BS_NOPOINTERFOCUS", IDR_NOPOINTER,
         131, 66, 116, 10, BS_NOPOINTERFOCUS
      PUSHBUTTON "BS_HELP", IDP_HELP,
         20, 25, 53, 14, BS_HELP
      PUSHBUTTON "BS_NOBORDER", IDP_NOBORDER,
         104, 25, 82, 14, BS_NOBORDER
      DEFPUSHBUTTON "OK", DID_OK, 10, 5, 40, 12 | WS_GROUP
   }
}
```

BUTTON.H

```
#define IDR_CLIENT              256
#define IDD_BUTTON              257

#define IDM_FILES               320
#define IDM_START               321
#define IDM_EXIT                322

#define IDC_AUTOCHECKBOX        512
#define IDC_3STATE              513
```

```
#define IDC_AUTO3STATE          514
#define IDR_AUTORADIOBUTTON     515
#define IDR_NOPOINTER           516
#define IDR_AUTOSIZE            517
#define IDP_HELP                518
#define IDP_NOBORDER            519


#define IDR_ICON                1024
```

BUTTON.MAK

```
BUTTON.EXE:                     BUTTON.OBJ \
                                BUTTON.RES
        LINK386 @<<
BUTTON
BUTTON
BUTTON
OS2386
BUTTON
<<
        RC BUTTON.RES BUTTON.EXE

BUTTON.RES:                     BUTTON.RC \
                                BUTTON.H
        RC -r BUTTON.RC BUTTON.RES

BUTTON.OBJ:                     BUTTON.C \
                                BUTTON.H
        ICC -C+ -Kb+ -Ss+ BUTTON.C
```

BUTTON.DEF

```
NAME BUTTON WINDOWAPI
DESCRIPTION 'Button example.
            Copyright (c) 1992 by Kathleen Panov.
            All rights reserved.'

PROTMODE
STACKSIZE       32768
```

10.3 The Button.rc Resource File

The following is the code used to define the dialog box. The PRESPARAMS PP_BLACKGROUNDCOLORINDEX is set to CLR_WHITE. Presentation Parameters can be set in the resource file by using the keyword PRESPARAMS.

```
DIALOG "Button dialog", IDD_BUTTON, 28, 23, 258, 110,
        FS_NOBYTEALIGN | WS_VISIBLE,
        FCF_SYSMENU | FCF_TITLEBAR
        PRESPARAMS PP_BACKGROUNDCOLORINDEX, CLR_WHITE
```

The creation of the buttons is specified by the keywords PUSHBUTTON, AUTOCHECKBOX, and AUTORADIOBUTTON in the BUTTON.RC resource file.

10.4 *DlgProc*

```
BTNCDATA bcdData ;

bcdData.cb = sizeof ( BTNCDATA ) ;
bcdData.fsCheckState = 0 ;
bcdData.fsHiliteState = 0 ;
bcdData.hImage = WinQuerySysPointer (
                    HWND_DESKTOP,
                    SPTR_ICONINFORMATION,
                    FALSE ) ;
```

The WM_INITDLG message processing is used to create the BS_ICON push-button. The information icon is loaded from the system using *WinQuerySysPointer*. This returns a resource handle (HPOINTER) that is needed in the BTNCDATA structure. The BTNCDATA structure is defined as follows:

```
struct {
        USHORT cb;
        /* control data structure size */
        USHORT fsCheckState;
        /* used to set the initial checked, unchecked state of the
                button */
        USHORT fsHiliteState;
        /* used to set the highlight, unhighlight state of the
                button */
        LHANDLE hImage;
        /* resource handle, in our case, HPOINTER */
} BTNCDATA;
```

Gotcha!

Do not forget to initialize everything in the BTNCDATA structure. If you don't, you will receive an error. The first field is always the size of the BTNCDATA structure. The last field is a handle for a pointer or a bitmap.

```
WinCreateWindow ( hwndWnd,
                  WC_BUTTON,
                  "",
                  WS_VISIBLE |
                  WS_TABSTOP |
                  BS_ICON ,
                  125,
                  55,
                  WinQuerySysValue ( HWND_DESKTOP,
                                     SV_CXICON ) ,
                  WinQuerySysValue ( HWND_DESKTOP,
                                     SV_CYICON ) ,
                  hwndWnd,
                  HWND_TOP,
                  IDR_ICON,
                  ( PVOID ) &bcdData,
                  NULL ) ;
```

WinCreateWindow is used to create the icon push-button. The client area of
the dialog is used as both the parent and owner. The text area is specified as
"". The styles specified for the button are WS_VISIBLE | WS_TABSTOP |
BS_ICON . WS_TABSTOP indicates that the user can press the TAB key to
move to the button. On some button styles this is the default and is not
necessary. Push-buttons and check boxes have this style automatically
associated with them. Icon buttons and radio buttons do not.

The placement of the push-button is specified at 125, 55, and the width and
height are set at the system values for the icon width (SV_CXICON) and icon
height (SV_CYICON), respectively. The dialog window, *hwndWnd,* will be the
owner. HWND_TOP is used to indicate window placement, and IDR_ICON is
the ID of the button. The next parameter is a pointer to the button control data,
in this case *&ButtonData.*

```
WinSendDlgItemMsg ( hwndWnd,
                    IDC_AUTOCHECKBOX,
                    BM_SETCHECK,
                    MPFROMSHORT ( TRUE ) ,
                    NULL ) ;

WinSendDlgItemMsg ( hwndWnd,
                    IDC_AUTO3STATE,
                    BM_SETCHECK,
                    MPFROMSHORT ( 2 ) ,
                    NULL ) ;
```

The last step in the dialog initialization procedure sends a BM_SETCHECK to
both the AUTOCHECKBOX check box and the AUTO3STATE check box.
Also, the three-state check box is started in the indeterminate (or gray-scaled)
state by specifying 2 as parameter 2.

10.5 More on Buttons

The icon button style operates just like a push-button. It is indentical in appearance except for the image on top, and sends a WM_COMMAND message to its owner when it is pressed. Check boxes and radio buttons will only send a WM_CONTROL message to their owners when selected.

10.6 Button Messages

WM_COMMAND
This messages occurs when a control has to notify its owner of an event, or when a keystroke has been translated as an accelerator key.

Parameter 1:	USHORT usCmd	command value
Parameter 2:	USHORT usSource	type of control that generated the message
	USHORT usPointer	pointer device indicator
Reply:	ULONG flReply	reserved, 0

WM_CONTROL
This messages occurs when a control has to notify its owner of an event. The message is sent, whereas the WM_COMMAND message is posted.

Parameter 1:	USHORT idId	button control ID
	USHORT usNotifyCode	notification code
Parameter 2:	ULONG flControlSpec	control-specific information — normally the window handle of the button; however, when *usNotifyCode* equals BN_PAINT, this parameter is PUSERBUTTON
Reply:	ULONG flReply	reserved, 0

WM_HELP
This messages occurs when a control or accelerator key has been used to indicate that help is needed.

Parameter 1:	USHORT usCmd	command value
Parameter 2:	USHORT usSource	source type

	USHORT usPointer	pointer device indicator
Reply:	ULONG flReply	reserved, 0

BM_CLICK
An application sends this message to simulate the clicking of a button.

Parameter 1:	USHORT usUp	up and down indicator
Parameter 2:	ULONG Param2	reserved, 0
Reply:	ULONG flReply	reserved, 0

BM_QUERYCHECK
This message returns whether a button control is checked or not.

Parameter 1:	ULONG Param1	reserved, 0
Parameter 2:	ULONG Param2	reserved, 0
Reply:	USHORT usResult	button checked? TRUE:FALSE

BM_QUERYCHECKINDEX
This message returns the index of a checked radio button with a group of radio buttons (zero-based). A group is defined by the style WS_GROUP.

Parameter 1:	ULONG Param1	reserved, 0
Parameter 2:	ULONG Param2	reserved, 0
Reply:	SHORT sResult	radio button index

BM_QUERYHILITE
This message returns whether a button control is highlighted or not.

Parameter 1:	ULONG Param1	reserved, 0
Parameter 2:	ULONG Param2	reserved, 0
Reply:	BOOL fResult	button highlighted? TRUE:FALSE

BM_SETCHECK
This message checks or unchecks a button control.

Parameter 1:	USHORT usCheck	check button? TRUE:FALSE
Parameter 2:	ULONG Param2	reserved, 0

Reply: USHORT usOldState   previous state of button

BM_SETDEFAULT
This message sets the default state of a button.

Parameter 1:	USHORT usDefault	default state? TRUE:FALSE
Parameter 2:	ULONG Param2	reserved, 0
Reply:	BOOL fSuccess	successful? TRUE:FALSE

BM_SETHILITE
This message either highlights or unhighlights a button.

Parameter 1:	USHORT usHilite	highlighted? TRUE: FALSE
Parameter 2:	ULONG Param2	reserved, 0
Reply:	BOOL fOldState	previously highlighted? TRUE:FALSE

WM_ENABLE
This messages enables or disables a window.

Parameter 1:	USHORT usEnabled	enabled? TRUE:FALSE
Parameter 2:	ULONG Param2	reserved, 0
Reply:	ULONG flReply	reserved, 0

WM_MATCHNEMONIC
Sent to a control window to determine if the keystroke matches that control's mnemonics.

Parameter 1:	USHORT usMatch	keystroke
Parameter 2:	ULONG Param2	reserved, 0
Reply:	BOOL fResult	match? TRUE:FALSE

BM_QUERYCONVERTPOS
Sent to determine if it is OK to convert DBCS characters.

Parameter 1:	PRECTL pCursorPos	cursor position
Parameter 2:	ULONG Param2	reserved, 0

Reply: USHORT usCode   conversion code

WM_QUERYWINDOWPARAMS

This message is sent to a button to query its window parameters.

Parameter 1:   PWNDPARAMS pwndParams   pointer to window
                                                        parameter structure

```
typedef struct _WNDPARAMS {
        ULONG   ulStatus;        /* Window parameter selection */
        ULONG   ulText;          /* Length of window text */
        PSZ     pszText;         /* Window text */
        ULONG   ulPresParams;    /* Length of Presentation Parameters
                                    structure */
        PVOID   pPresParams;     /* pointer to Presentation Parameters
                                    structure */
        ULONG   ulCtlData;       /* Length of control specific data */
        PVOID   pCtlData;        /* Pointer to control specific
                                    data /*
} WNDPARAMS;
```

Parameter 2:   ULONG Param2   reserved, 0
Reply: BOOL fResult   successful? TRUE:FALSE

WM_SETWINDOWPARAMS

This message indicates that window parameters have been changed.

Parameter 1:   PWNDPARAMS pwndParams   pointer to window
                                                      parameter structure
Parameter 2:   ULONG Param2   reserved, 0
Reply: BOOL fResult   successful? TRUE: FALSE

Chapter 11

Notebook

The notebook control is designed to provide the user with a visual organizer of information, similar to a real notebook with dividers. Information can be broken up into categories, with the major tabs representing category headings. Information can then be further broken up using minor tabs as the subcategory headings. The notebook consists of six major parts, as illustrated below: the binding, status line, intersection of pages, forward/backwards page buttons, major tabs, and minor tabs.

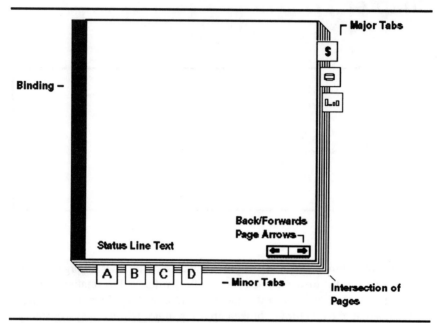

Figure 11.1. Drawing of a notebook.

A notebook (Figure 11.1) should be used to offer the user a choice of settings, or to present data that can be logically organized into categories or groups. Information that can be grouped together should be put into a single tabbed section. Major tabs can be placed at any of the four notebook sides; however, minor tabs are always placed perpendicular to the major tabs. Page buttons are provided to allow the user to page forwards and backwards between the notebook pages. Page buttons are always located in the corner that is flanked by the back pages. The binding can either be spiral-bound or solid-bound, depending on the specified style. A line of status text can be associated with each notebook page. If more than one page exists in a category, the status line should be used to indicate this to the user; for example, "Page 1 of 20." The status line can be left-justified, right-justified, or centered along the bottom of the notebook. The last part of the notebook is the intersection of the back pages. This is used to design a landscape or portrait-mode notebook. This feature gives the appearance of a three-dimensional notebook. It is possible for this intersection to be located at any of the four corners. Figures 11.2 through 11.9 show the eight possible combination of styles.

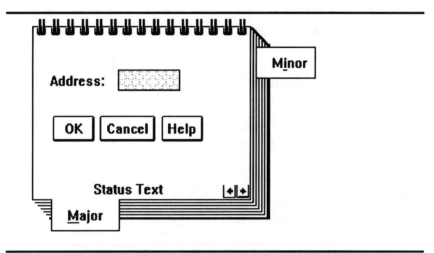

Figure 11.2. BKS_BACKPAGESBR I BKS_MAJORTABBOTTOM.

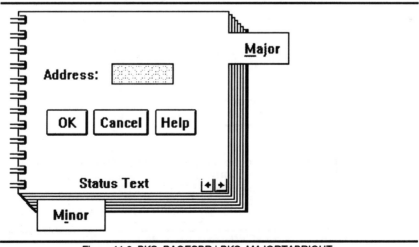

Figure 11.3. BKS_PAGESBR I BKS_MAJORTABRIGHT.

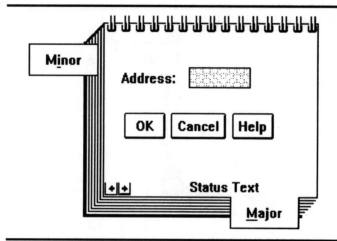

Figure 11.4. BKS_BACKPAGESBL I BKS_MAJORTABBOTTOM.

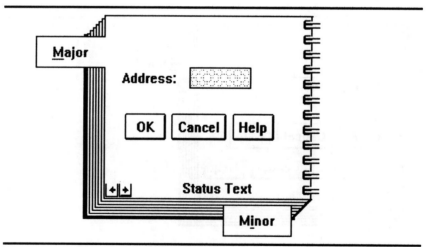

Figure 11.5. BKS_BACKPAGESBL I BKS_MAJORTABLEFT.

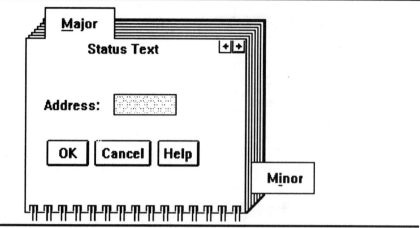

Figure 11.6. BKS_BACKPAGESTR I BKS_MAJORTABTOP.

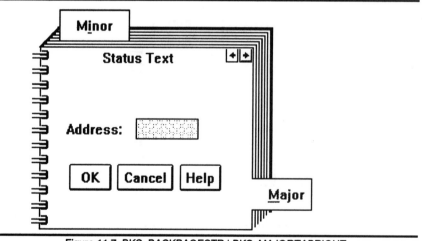

Figure 11.7. BKS_BACKPAGESTR I BKS_MAJORTABRIGHT.

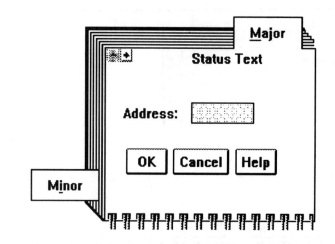

Figure 11.8. BKS_BACKPAGESTL I BKS_MAJORTABTOP.

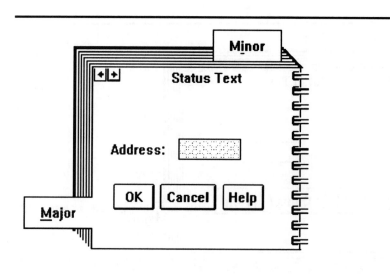

Figure 11.9. BKS_BACKPAGESTL I BKS_MAJORTABLEFT.

The following are the notebook window styles:

STYLE	DESCRIPTION
BKS_BACKPAGESBR	Intersection of pages is located at the bottom right corner
BKS_BACKPAGESBL	Intersection of pages is located at the bottom left corner
BKS_BACKPAGESTR	Intersection of pages is located at the top right corner
BKS_BACKPAGESBR	Intersection of pages is located at the top left corner
BKS_MAJORTABRIGHT	Major tabs are located on the right side
BKS_MAJORTABLEFT	Major tabs are located on the left side
BKS_MAJORTABTOP	Major tabs are located on the top side
BKS_MAJORTABBOTTOM	Major tabs are located on the bottom side
BKS_SQUARETABS	Notebook has squared-edge tabs
BKS_ROUNDEDTABS	Notebook has rounded-edge tabs
BKS_POLYGONTABS	Notebook has polygon-edge tabs
BKS_SOLIDBIND	Notebook has a solid binding
BKS_SPIRALBIND	Notebook has a spiral binding
BKS_STATUSTEXTLEFT	Notebook has the status text left-justified
BKS_STATUSTEXTRIGHT	Notebook has the status text right-justified
BKS_STATUSTEXTCENTER	Notebook has the status text centered
BKS_TABTEXTLEFT	Notebook has the tab text left-justified
BKS_TABTEXTRIGHT	Notebook has the tab text right-justified
BKS_TABTEXTCENTER	Notebook has the tab text centered

The major and minor tabs can be customized somewhat. They can be either square, polygonal, or have rounded corners. A tab can contain either text or bitmaps. The text can be left-justified, right-justified, or centered. If a bitmap is specified for the tab, the bitmap is automatically sized to fill the tab. The dimensions for the tab need to be set using the message BKM_SETDIMENSIONS. There is not automatic sizing of the tab for text.

11.1 Notebook Pages

A notebook page is designed to be associated with a dialog box or window. When a new page is selected in the notebook, the notebook invalidates the new page, causing a WM_PAINT to be sent to the procedure associated with the newly selected page. When a notebook is created, the initialization should handle the insertion of any needed pages. If a page has a major or minor tab associated with it, this is specified in the BKM_INSERTPAGE. The following code segment shows how to insert a page:

```
ULONG ulPageID;
MRESULT Reply;

Reply = WinSendMsg( hwndNotebook,
        BKM_INSERTPAGE,
        (MPARAM)0,
        MPFROM2SHORT ( BKA_MAJOR | BKA_STATUSTEXTON,
        BKA_FIRST ));

ulPageID = LONGFROMMR( Reply );
```

If no major or minor tabs are specified, the new page becomes part of the current section. Each page has a *ulPageID* that is *returned* from the BKM_INSERTPAGE message. This ID is used extensively in the notebook messaging system.

The following example program illustrates the creation of a notebook.

NOTEBOOK.C

```
#define INCL_GPICONTROL
#define INCL_GPILCIDS
#define INCL_WIN

#include <os2.h>
#include <stdio.h>
#include <stdlib.h>
#include <string.h>
#include "notebook.h"

#define WM_LOADDLG                  (WM_USER + 1)
#define CLS_CLIENT                  "MyClass"

BOOL InitializeNotebook ( HWND hwndNotebook,
                          HWND hwndPage1,
                          HWND hwndPage2,
                          LONG lCxChar,
                          LONG lCyChar ) ;

MRESULT EXPENTRY DlgProc ( HWND hwndDlg,
                           ULONG ulMsg,
                           MPARAM mpParm1,
                           MPARAM mpParm2 ) ;
```

```
MRESULT EXPENTRY ClientWndProc ( HWND hwndWnd,
                                 ULONG ulMsg,
                                 MPARAM mpParm1,
                                 MPARAM mpParm2 ) ;

INT main ( VOID )
{
    HAB       habAnchor ;
    HMQ       hmqQueue ;
    ULONG     ulFlags ;
    HWND      hwndFrame ;
    HWND      hwndClient ;
    BOOL      bLoop ;
    QMSG      qmMsg ;

    habAnchor = WinInitialize ( 0 ) ;
    hmqQueue = WinCreateMsgQueue ( habAnchor, 0 ) ;

    WinRegisterClass ( habAnchor,
                       CLS_CLIENT,
                       ClientWndProc,
                       CS_SIZEREDRAW,
                       0 ) ;

    ulFlags = FCF_TITLEBAR | FCF_SYSMENU | FCF_SIZEBORDER |
              FCF_SHELLPOSITION ;

    hwndFrame = WinCreateStdWindow ( HWND_DESKTOP,
                                     0,
                                     &ulFlags,
                                     CLS_CLIENT,
                                     "Notebook Example",
                                     0,
                                     NULLHANDLE,
                                     0,
                                     &hwndClient ) ;

    if ( hwndFrame != 0 ) {
       WinSetWindowPos ( hwndFrame,
                         NULLHANDLE,
                         50,
                         50,
                         550,
                         400,
                         SWP_SIZE | SWP_MOVE |
                         SWP_ACTIVATE | SWP_SHOW ) ;

       bLoop = WinGetMsg ( habAnchor,
                           &qmMsg,
                           NULLHANDLE,
                           0,
                           0 ) ;

       while ( bLoop ) {
          WinDispatchMsg ( habAnchor, &qmMsg ) ;
```

```
                    bLoop = WinGetMsg ( habAnchor,
                                        &qmMsg,
                                        NULLHANDLE,
                                        0,
                                        0 ) ;
        } /* endwhile */

        WinDestroyWindow ( hwndFrame ) ;
    } /* endif */

    WinDestroyMsgQueue ( hmqQueue ) ;
    WinTerminate ( habAnchor ) ;
    return 0 ;
}

MRESULT EXPENTRY ClientWndProc ( HWND hwndWnd,
                                 ULONG ulMsg,
                                 MPARAM mpParm1,
                                 MPARAM mpParm2 )
{
    switch ( ulMsg ) {

    case WM_CREATE:
        {
            HPS             hpsChar ;
            FONTMETRICS     fmMetrics ;
            LONG            lCxChar ;
            LONG            lCyChar ;
            HWND            hwndNotebook ;
            HWND            hwndPage1 ;
            HWND            hwndPage2 ;

            hpsChar = WinGetPS ( hwndWnd ) ;
            GpiQueryFontMetrics ( hpsChar,
                                  sizeof ( fmMetrics ) ,
                                  &fmMetrics ) ;
            WinReleasePS ( hpsChar ) ;

            lCxChar = fmMetrics.lAveCharWidth ;
            lCyChar = fmMetrics.lMaxBaselineExt ;

            hwndNotebook = WinCreateWindow ( hwndWnd,
                                             WC_NOTEBOOK,
                                             "",
                                             BKS_SPIRALBIND |
                                             BKS_SQUARETABS |
                                             BKS_STATUSTEXTCENTER,
                                             0,
                                             0,
                                             0,
                                             0,
                                             hwndWnd,
                                             HWND_TOP,
                                             ID_NOTEBOOK,
                                             NULL,
                                             NULL ) ;
```

```
            hwndPage1 = WinLoadDlg ( hwndWnd,
                                     hwndWnd,
                                     DlgProc,
                                     NULLHANDLE,
                                     IDD_PERSONAL,
                                     NULL ) ;

            hwndPage2 = WinLoadDlg ( hwndWnd,
                                     hwndWnd,
                                     DlgProc,
                                     NULLHANDLE,
                                     IDD_OS2,
                                     NULL ) ;

            InitializeNotebook ( hwndNotebook,
                                 hwndPage1,
                                 hwndPage2,
                                 lCxChar,
                                 lCyChar ) ;

            WinSetFocus ( HWND_DESKTOP,
                         WinWindowFromID ( hwndPage1,
                                          IDE_NAME )) ;
        }
        break ;

    case WM_SIZE:
        WinSetWindowPos ( WinWindowFromID ( hwndWnd, ID_NOTEBOOK ) ,
                         NULLHANDLE,
                         0,
                         0,
                         SHORT1FROMMP ( mpParm2 ) ,
                         SHORT2FROMMP ( mpParm2 ) ,
                         SWP_SIZE | SWP_SHOW ) ;
        break ;

    case WM_CONTROL:
        switch ( SHORT1FROMMP ( mpParm1 )) {
        case ID_NOTEBOOK:
            switch ( SHORT2FROMMP ( mpParm1 )) {
            case BKN_PAGESELECTED:
                {
                    PPAGESELECTNOTIFY       ppsnSelect ;
                    HWND                    hwndPage ;
                    USHORT                  usDlgId ;

                    ppsnSelect =
                        (PPAGESELECTNOTIFY) PVOIDFROMMP ( mpParm2 ) ;

                    hwndPage =
                        (HWND) PVOIDFROMMR (
                            WinSendMsg ( ppsnSelect -> hwndBook,
                                        BKM_QUERYPAGEWINDOWHWND,
                                        MPFROMLONG (
                                        ppsnSelect -> ulPageIdNew ) ,
                                        0 )) ;
```

```
                usDlgId = WinQueryWindowUShort ( hwndPage,
                                                 QWS_ID ) ;

                if ( usDlgId == IDD_PERSONAL ) {
                   WinSetFocus ( HWND_DESKTOP,
                                 WinWindowFromID ( hwndPage,
                                                   IDE_NAME )) ;
                } else {
                   WinSetFocus ( HWND_DESKTOP,
                                 WinWindowFromID ( hwndPage,
                                                   IDE_TEAMOS2 )) ;
                } /* endif */
             }
             break ;

          default:
             return WinDefWindowProc ( hwndWnd,
                                       ulMsg,
                                       mpParm1,
                                       mpParm2 ) ;
          } /* endswitch */
          break ;
       default:
          return WinDefWindowProc ( hwndWnd,
                                    ulMsg,
                                    mpParm1,
                                    mpParm2 ) ;
       } /* endswitch */
       break ;

    case WM_ERASEBACKGROUND:
       return MRFROMSHORT ( TRUE ) ;

    case WM_PAINT:
       {
          HPS hpsPaint ;

          hpsPaint = WinBeginPaint ( hwndWnd,
                                     NULLHANDLE,
                                     NULLHANDLE ) ;
          GpiErase ( hpsPaint ) ;
          WinEndPaint ( hpsPaint ) ;
       }
       break ;

    default:
       return WinDefWindowProc ( hwndWnd,
                                 ulMsg,
                                 mpParm1,
                                 mpParm2 ) ;
    } /* endswitch */

    return MRFROMSHORT ( FALSE ) ;
}
```

```
MRESULT EXPENTRY DlgProc ( HWND hwndDlg,
                           ULONG ulMsg,
                           MPARAM mpParm1,
                           MPARAM mpParm2 )
{
   switch ( ulMsg ) {

   case WM_COMMAND:

      switch ( SHORT1FROMMP ( mpParm1 )) {

      case DID_OK:
      case DID_CANCEL:
         break ;

      default:
         return WinDefDlgProc ( hwndDlg,
                                ulMsg,
                                mpParm1,
                                mpParm2 ) ;
      } /* endswitch */
      break ;

   default:
      return WinDefDlgProc ( hwndDlg,
                             ulMsg,
                             mpParm1,
                             mpParm2 ) ;
   } /* endswitch */

   return MRFROMSHORT ( FALSE ) ;
}

BOOL InitializeNotebook ( HWND hwndNotebook,
                          HWND hwndPage1,
                          HWND hwndPage2,
                          LONG lCxChar,
                          LONG lCyChar )
{
   ULONG        ulIdPage1 ;
   ULONG        ulIdPage2 ;
   ULONG        ulWidth ;
   CHAR         achPage1Text [64] ;
   CHAR         achPage2Text [64] ;

   ulIdPage1 =
      LONGFROMMR ( WinSendMsg ( hwndNotebook,
                                BKM_INSERTPAGE,
                                0,
                                MPFROM2SHORT ( BKA_MAJOR |
                                               BKA_STATUSTEXTON,
                                               BKA_FIRST ))) ;
```

```
    ulIdPage2 =
      LONGFROMMR ( WinSendMsg ( hwndNotebook,
                                BKM_INSERTPAGE,
                                0,
                                MPFROM2SHORT ( BKA_MAJOR |
                                               BKA_STATUSTEXTON,
                                               BKA_LAST ))) ;

    WinSendMsg ( hwndNotebook,
                 BKM_SETSTATUSLINETEXT,
                 MPFROMLONG ( ulIdPage1 ) ,
                 MPFROMP ( "Personal Information for This User" )) ;

    WinSendMsg ( hwndNotebook,
                 BKM_SETSTATUSLINETEXT,
                 MPFROMLONG ( ulIdPage2 ) ,
                 MPFROMP ( "TEAM OS / 2 Information"
                    " for this Location" )) ;

    strcpy ( achPage1Text, " ~Personal" ) ;
    strcpy ( achPage2Text, " ~TEAMOS2" ) ;

    ulWidth = ( max ( strlen ( achPage1Text ) ,
       strlen ( achPage2Text )) + 6 ) * lCxChar ;

    WinSendMsg ( hwndNotebook,
                 BKM_SETDIMENSIONS,
                 MPFROM2SHORT ( ulWidth, lCyChar * 2 ) ,
                 MPFROMSHORT ( BKA_MAJORTAB )) ;

    WinSendMsg ( hwndNotebook,
                 BKM_SETTABTEXT,
                 MPFROMLONG ( ulIdPage1 ) ,
                 MPFROMP ( achPage1Text )) ;

    WinSendMsg ( hwndNotebook,
                 BKM_SETTABTEXT,
                 MPFROMLONG ( ulIdPage2 ) ,
                 MPFROMP ( achPage2Text )) ;

    WinSendMsg ( hwndNotebook,
                 BKM_SETPAGEWINDOWHWND,
                 MPFROMLONG ( ulIdPage1 ) ,
                 MPFROMHWND ( hwndPage1 )) ;

    WinSendMsg ( hwndNotebook,
                 BKM_SETPAGEWINDOWHWND,
                 MPFROMLONG ( ulIdPage2 ) ,
                 MPFROMHWND ( hwndPage2 )) ;

    WinSendMsg ( hwndNotebook,
                 BKM_SETNOTEBOOKCOLORS,
                 MPFROMLONG ( CLR_BLUE ) ,
                 MPFROMSHORT ( BKA_FOREGROUNDMAJORCOLORINDEX )) ;

    return TRUE ;
}
```

NOTEBOOK.RC

```
#include <os2.h>
#include "notebook.h"

DLGTEMPLATE IDD_PERSONAL
{
   DIALOG "Personal Information", IDD_PERSONAL,
        5, 0, 265, 126,
        NOT FS_DLGBORDER
   {
      GROUPBOX "Personal Information", -1, 0, 26, 251, 101
      LTEXT "Name:", -1, 6, 106, 29, 8
      LTEXT "Address:", -1, 6, 85, 39, 8
      LTEXT "City:", -1, 6, 63, 19, 8
      LTEXT "State:", -1, 134, 63, 26, 8
      LTEXT "Zip:", -1, 6, 40, 18, 8
      LTEXT "Phone:", -1, 134, 40, 31, 8
      ENTRYFIELD "", IDE_NAME, 55, 107, 181, 8, ES_MARGIN
      ENTRYFIELD "", IDE_ADDRESS, 55, 85, 181, 8, ES_MARGIN
      ENTRYFIELD "", IDE_CITY, 31, 65, 96, 8, ES_MARGIN
      ENTRYFIELD "", IDE_STATE, 169, 65, 67, 8, ES_MARGIN
      ENTRYFIELD "", IDE_ZIP, 31, 42, 96, 8, ES_MARGIN
      ENTRYFIELD "", IDE_PHONE, 169, 42, 67, 8, ES_MARGIN
   }
}

DLGTEMPLATE IDD_OS2
{
   DIALOG  "TEAMOS2 Information", IDD_OS2, 5, 0, 265, 126,
        NOT FS_DLGBORDER
   {
      GROUPBOX "TEAMOS2 Information", -1, 0, 26, 253, 101
      LTEXT "TEAMOS2 Name:", -1, 6, 106, 74, 8
      LTEXT "User Group:", -1, 6, 85, 53, 8
      LTEXT "Level of OS/2 Experience", -1, 59, 67, 109, 8
      ENTRYFIELD "", IDE_TEAMOS2, 90, 102, 146, 8, ES_MARGIN
      ENTRYFIELD "", IDE_USERGROUP, 90, 85,  146, 8, ES_MARGIN
      AUTORADIOBUTTON "OS/2 Beginner", IDR_BEGIN,
         68, 52, 77, 10, WS_TABSTOP
      AUTORADIOBUTTON "OS/2 Intermediate", IDR_INTERMEDIATE,
         68, 39, 91, 10, WS_TABSTOP
      AUTORADIOBUTTON "OS/2 Expert", IDR_EXPERT,
         68, 27, 65, 10, WS_TABSTOP
   }
}
```

NOTEBOOK.H

```
#define ID_NOTEBOOK          256
#define IDD_PERSONAL         257
#define IDD_OS2              258

#define IDE_NAME             512
#define IDE_ADDRESS          513
#define IDE_CITY             514
#define IDE_STATE            515
#define IDE_ZIP              516
```

```
#define IDE_PHONE                517

#define IDE_TEAMOS2              528
#define IDE_USERGROUP            529
#define IDR_BEGIN                530
#define IDR_INTERMEDIATE         531
#define IDR_EXPERT               532
```

NOTEBOOK.MAK

```
NOTEBOOK.EXE:                    NOTEBOOK.OBJ \
                                 NOTEBOOK.RES

        LINK386 @<<
NOTEBOOK
NOTEBOOK
NOTEBOOK
OS2386
NOTEBOOK
<<
        RC NOTEBOOK.RES NOTEBOOK.EXE

NOTEBOOK.RES:                    NOTEBOOK.RC \
                                 NOTEBOOK.H
        RC -r NOTEBOOK.RC NOTEBOOK.RES

NOTEBOOK.OBJ:                    NOTEBOOK.C \
                                 NOTEBOOK.H
        ICC -C+ -Kb+ -Ss+ NOTEBOOK.C
```

NOTEBOOK.DEF

```
NAME NOTEBOOK WINDOWAPI

DESCRIPTION 'Notebook example
Copyright (c) 1992 by Kathleen Panov.
All rights reserved.'

STACKSIZE 16384
```

11.2 Flipping Pages

```
case WM_CONTROL:
   switch ( SHORT1FROMMP ( mpParm1 )) {
   case ID_NOTEBOOK:
      switch ( SHORT2FROMMP ( mpParm1 )) {
      case BKN_PAGESELECTED:
         {
            PPAGESELECTNOTIFY        ppsnSelect ;
            HWND                     hwndPage ;
            USHORT                   usDlgId ;
```

```
ppsnSelect =
    (PPAGESELECTNOTIFY) PVOIDFROMMP ( mpParm2 ) ;
```

In the **WM_CONTROL** message processing, the BKN_PAGESELECTED notification code is sent each time a new page is selected in the notebook. We'll use this message as a signal to set the focus to the specified dialog control for the selected page.

```
hwndPage =
    (HWND) PVOIDFROMMR (
        WinSendMsg ( ppsnSelect -> hwndBook,
                     BKM_QUERYPAGEWINDOWHWND,
                     MPFROMLONG (
                     ppsnSelect -> ulPageIdNew ) ,
                     0 )) ;

usDlgId = WinQueryWindowUShort ( hwndPage,
                                 QWS_ID ) ;

if ( usDlgId == IDD_PERSONAL ) {
    WinSetFocus ( HWND_DESKTOP,
                  WinWindowFromID ( hwndPage,
                                    IDE_NAME )) ;
} else {
    WinSetFocus ( HWND_DESKTOP,
                  WinWindowFromID ( hwndPage,
                                    IDE_TEAMOS2 )) ;
} /* endif */
}
```

The message BKM_QUERYPAGEWINDOWHWND is sent to get the dialog window handle. The focus is set to the first entry field on the newly selected page.

11.3 WM_CREATE

```
hwndNotebook = WinCreateWindow ( hwndWnd,
                                 WC_NOTEBOOK,
                                 "",
                                 BKS_SPIRALBIND |
                                 BKS_SQUARETABS |
                                 BKS_STATUSTEXTCENTER,
                                 0,
                                 0,
                                 0,
                                 0,
                                 hwndWnd,
                                 HWND_TOP,
                                 ID_NOTEBOOK,
                                 NULL,
                                 NULL ) ;
```

When this message is received, the first thing we do is create the notebook. *hwndWnd*, the client window handle, is specified as the parent in the first parameter of *WinCreateWindow*. The class style is WC_NOTEBOOK. The third parameter is window text, in this case "". The fourth parameter is the notebook style. The style flags specified here are BKS_SPIRALBIND | BKS_SQUARETABS | BKS_STATUSTEXTCENTER. This creates a spiral binding on the notebook, squared-edge tabs, and the status text centered. The next four parameters, 0, 0, 0, 0, designate a notebook position of row 0, column 0 on the client window, a width of 0, and a height of 0. The ninth parameter, *hwndWnd*, is the owner window. The next parameter is window Z-order. Our notebook is to be placed on top of all the other windows, so HWND_TOP is specified. The next parameter is resource ID, ID_NOTEBOOK. The last two parameters are class-specific data and presentation data. In this instance there is none, so NULL is specified for both.

The next few functions are used to find the height and width of a single character. These values are to be used later. The function *GpiQueryFontMetrics* returns the FONTMETRICS structure, which contains loads of information about the current font.

There are two values in the structure we need: *lAveCharWidth* and *lMaxBaselineExt*. These represent the approximate average character width and max character height, respectively. Before calling *GpiQueryFontMetrics*, we will need the presentation space associated with the client window. The function *WinGetPS* is used to get the presentation space handle. *GpiQueryFontMetrics* has three parameters. First is the HPS associated with the window. Next is the size of the FONTMETRICS structure, and last is a pointer to the structure itself. After calling *GpiQueryFontMetrics* and saving the needed values, the HPS is released. The values are saved and passed to the initialization function, *InitializeNotebook*.

The next step is to load the two dialog boxes to be placed in the notebook. The first one is *hwndPage1*. This contains such basic information as "Name" and "Address". The next dialog, *hwndPage2*, contains OS/2-specific information from the user.

Lastly, we set the focus to the first entry field on the first page.

11.4 *InitializeNotebook*

This function performs all the initialization required for our notebook. The first step is to allocate memory for the status text strings on each page. The first messages sent to the notebook are BKM_INSERTPAGE.

```
ulIdPage1 =
    LONGFROMMR ( WinSendMsg ( hwndNotebook,
                              BKM_INSERTPAGE,
                              0,
                              MPFROM2SHORT ( BKA_MAJOR |
                                             BKA_STATUSTEXTON,
                                             BKA_FIRST ))) ;
```

Parameter 1 in the BKM_INSERTPAGE message, in this case (MPARAM)0, is used to indicate a pageID reference point for Parameter 2. In this case, specifying BKA_FIRST or BKA_LAST as page location alleviates the need for a pageID reference. If, for example, BKA_NEXT had been specified, Parameter 1 would have to contain the ID of the page the inserted page is to be placed next to. Parameter 2 contains two SHORTS. The first SHORT is the notebook page styles. In both of the above cases, a major tab is placed on the page, and status text is enabled at the bottom of the page. The second SHORT is the page insertion order. In our case, BKA_FIRST is specified. The page ID of the newly created pages is returned in the Reply, and is stored in *ulIDPage1*.

Since the status text is enabled, the next step is to copy text into it. Each section of the notebook only has one page, so information about that page will suffice. The message BKM_SETSTATUSLINETEXT is used to place text on the status line. Parameter 1 of the message indicates the page ID where the text is to be placed, and Parameter 2 is the text string itself.

```
ulWidth = ( max ( strlen ( achPage1Text ) ,
    strlen ( achPage2Text )) + 6 ) * lCxChar ;

WinSendMsg ( hwndNotebook,
             BKM_SETDIMENSIONS,
             MPFROM2SHORT ( ulWidth, lCyChar * 2 ) ,
             MPFROMSHORT ( BKA_MAJORTAB )) ;
```

After the status text is taken care of, the tabs need to have their dimensions set so that the tab text will not be truncated. The BKM_SETDIMENSIONS message is used to set the size. Parameter 1 of the message is two SHORTs. The first short is tab width. The variable, *ulWidth*, is determined by calculating the maximum number of characters on the tab by the width of each character, *lCxChar*. The second SHORT is height. For this parameter, *lCyChar* * 2 is used. Parameter 2 is the part for which the dimensions are being set, in this case BKA_MAJORTAB.

```
WinSendMsg ( hwndNotebook,
             BKM_SETTABTEXT,
             MPFROMLONG ( ulIdPage1 ) ,
             MPFROMP ( achPage1Text )) ;
```

The tab text is set for each major tab using the message BKM_SETTABTEXT. Parameter 1 is the page ID on which the tab is located. Parameter 2 is the text string that is placed on the tab.

```
WinSendMsg ( hwndNotebook,
             BKM_SETPAGEWINDOWHWND,
             MPFROMLONG ( ulIdPage1 ) ,
             MPFROMHWND ( hwndPage1 )) ;
```

Right now our notebook has two blank pages in it. The next step is to associate something with each page. A window or a dialog box can be associated with a page. Only one item can be associated with each page. The notebook itself is not designed for painting, rather just as a kind of "display device" for windows or dialog boxes.

The message BKM_SETPAGEWINDOWHWND associates a window handle with a page. Parameter 1 is the ID of the page on which the window is to be placed. Parameter 2 is the window handle that will be placed on the specified page of the notebook.

```
WinSendMsg ( hwndNotebook,
             BKM_SETNOTEBOOKCOLORS,
             MPFROMLONG ( CLR_BLUE ) ,
             MPFROMSHORT ( BKA_FOREGROUNDMAJORCOLORINDEX )) ;
```

The last *WinSendMsg* call sends the message BKM_SETNOTEBOOKCOLORS. This is the way to change the presentation parameters on the notebook control. Parameter 1 of the message is the color or color index to use. Parameter 2 is the appropriate Presentation Parameter. Notice that these are different from the normal window Presentation Parameters. This example uses the BKA_FOREGROUNDMAJORCOLORINDEX to change the foreground colors on the major tabs. When using indices into the color palette, only the values CLR_* are acceptable. When specifying the color, RGB representation should be used.

11.5 Notebook Messages

WM_CONTROL
This message is sent when a control has a to notify its owner of a significant event.

Parameter 1:	USHORT usID	control window ID
	USHORT usNotifyCode	BKN_HELP, BKN_NEWPAGESIZE, BKN_PAGESELECTED, BKN_PAGEDELETED
Parameter 2:	ULONG ulNotifyInfo	for BKN_HELP, this is ID of selected page; for BKN_PAGESELECTED, this is pointer to PAGESELECTNOTIFY structure; for BKN_PAGEDELETED, pointer to DELETENOTIFY structure; for BKN_NEWPAGESIZE, notebook window handle
Reply:	ULONG ulReply	reserved, 0

BKM_CALCPAGERECT
This message is used to determine the size of the notebook page, or the application page.

Parameter 1:	PRECTL pRectl	pointer to RECTL structure if *bPage* == TRUE, input will be the coordinates of the notebook window, output will be the size of application page window if *bPage* == FALSE, input will be the coordinates of an application page window, output will be the size of notebook window.

Parameter 2:   BOOL bPage   TRUE — calculate size of application page window FALSE — calculate size of notebook window

Reply: BOOL fSuccess   successful? TRUE:FALSE

BKM_DELETEPAGE
This message is used to delete a page form the notebook.

Parameter 1:   ULONG ulPageID   page identifier

Parameter 2:   USHORT usDeleteFlag   BKA_SINGLE — delete a single page
BKA_TAB — if *ulPageID* is a page that contains a tab, delete all subsequent pages to the next tab
BKA_ALL — delete all pages in the notebook

Reply: BOOL fSuccess   successful? TRUE:FALSE

BKM_INSERTPAGE
This message is sent to insert a page into the notebook.

Parameter 1:   ULONG ulPageID   page ID used as a reference point if BKA_FIRST or BKA_LAST is specified for *usPageOrder*

Parameter 2:   USHORT usPageStyle   BKA_AUTOPAGESIZE — notebook will size the placement and position of page window
BKA_STATUSTEXTON — page will contain status text
BKA_MAJOR — page will have major tab
BKA_MINOR — page will have a minor tab

	USHORT usPageOrder	BKA_FIRST — page is inserted as the first page of the notebook BKA_LAST — page is inserted as the last page of the notebook BKA_NEXT — page is inserted behind the page specified in *ulPageID* BKA_PREV — page is inserted before the page specified in *ulPageID*
Reply:	ULONG ulPageID	page ID for the page inserted, NULL if unsuccessful

BKM_INVALIDATETABS

This message is sent to repaint the notebook tabs.

Parameter 1:	ULONG ulParam1	reserved, 0
Parameter 2:	ULONG ulParam2	reserved, 0
Reply:	BOOL fSuccess	successful repaint? TRUE:FALSE

BKM_QUERYPAGECOUNT

This message is sent to query the number of pages in the notebook.

Parameter 1:	ULONG ulPageID	page identifier to start counting at; 0 indicates to start at first page

Parameter 2:	ULONG usQueryEnd	BKA_MAJOR — returns the number of pages between *ulPageID* and the next page that contains a major tab
		BKA_MINOR — returns the number of pages between *ulPageID* and the next page containing a minor tab
		BKA_END — returns the number of pages between *ulPageID* and the last page
Reply:	USHORT usPageCount	number of pages

BKM_QUERYPAGEDATA

This message is sent to query the data associated with the specified page.

Parameter 1:	ULONG ulPageID	the specified page to retrieve the data
Parameter 2:	ULONG ulParam2	reserved, 0
Reply:	ULONG ulPageData	the 4 bytes of data associated with the page

BKM_QUERYPAGEID

This message is sent to find the page ID for a page in the notebook.

Parameter 1:	ULONG ulPageID	page ID of page used as reference point
Parameter 2:	USHORT usQueryOrder	BKA_FIRST — queries the page ID of the first page
		BKA_LAST — queries the page ID of the last page
		BKA_NEXT — queries the page ID of the page after the page *ulPageID*
		BKA_PREV — queries the page before the page *ulPageID*
		BKA_TOP — queries the page ID of the currently visible page

	USHORT usPageStyle	BKA_MAJOR
		BKA_MINOR
Reply:	ULONG ulPageID	page ID of specified page

BKM_QUERYPAGESTYLE
This message queries the style of a page of interest.

Parameter 1:	ULONG ulPageID	page identifier
Parameter 2:	ULONG ulParam2	reserved, 0
Reply:	USHORT usPageStyle	page style of specified page

BKM_QUERYPAGEWINDOWHWND
This message is used to query the page window handle of the page of interest.

Parameter 1:	ULONG ulPageID	page ID
Parameter 2:	ULONG ulParam2	reserved, 0
Reply:	HWND hwndPage	handle of the page window associated with the page *ulPageID*

BKM_QUERYSTATUSLINETEXT
This message is used to query the status text associated with the specified page.

Parameter 1:	ULONG ulPageID	page ID of page of interest
Parameter 2:	PBOOKTEXT pBookText	pointer to BOOKTEXT structure
Reply:	USHORT usStatusTextLength	length of returned status string

BKM_QUERYTABBITMAP
This message is used to query the bitmap of the page of interest.

Parameter 1:	ULONG ulPageID	page ID of page to retrieve bitmap handle
Parameter 2:	ULONG ulParam2	reserved, 0
Reply:	HBITMAP hbmBitmap	handle of bit map

BKM_QUERYTABTEXT
This message is used to query the text of the tab of the page of interest.

Parameter 1:	ULONG ulPageID	page ID of the page of interest
Parameter 2:	PBOOKTEXT pBookText	pointer to BOOKTEXT structure for page of interest
Reply:	USHORT usTabTextLength	length of the tab text string

BKM_SETDIMENSIONS
This message is used to set the size of the major and minor tabs.

	USHORT usWidth	desired width of tab, in pixels
	USHORT usHeight	desired height of tab, in pixels
Parameter 2:	USHORT usType	BKA_MAJOR — set tab size of major tabs BKA_MINOR — set tab size of minor tabs BKA_PAGEBUTTON — set size of page buttons
Reply:	BOOL fSuccess	successful? TRUE:FALSE

BKM_SETNOTEBOOKCOLORS
This message is used to set the colors of the notebook.

Parameter 1:	ULONG ulColor	color index or RGB value to be used
Parameter 2:	USHORT usBookAttr	notebook region to set

VALUE	REGION
BKA_BACKGROUNDPAGECOLOR	page background
BKA_BACKGROUNDPAGECOLORINDEX	page background
BKA_BACKGROUNDMAJORCOLOR	major tab background
BKA_BACKGROUNDMAJORCOLORINDEX	major tab background
BKA_BACKGROUNDMINORCOLOR	minor tab background
BKA_BACKGROUNDMINORCOLORINDEX	minor tab background
BKA_FOREGROUNDMAJORCOLOR	major tab foreground

BKA_FOREGROUNDMAJORCOLORINDEX	major tab foreground
BKA_FOREGROUNDMINORCOLOR	minor tab foreground
BKA_FOREGROUNDMINORCOLORINDEX	minor tab foreground

| **Reply:** | BOOL fSuccess | successful? TRUE:FALSE |

BKM_SETPAGEDATA

This message is used to associate 4 bytes of data with a page.

Parameter 1:	ULONG ulPageID	page ID of page of interest
Parameter 2:	ULONG ulPageData	four bytes of data to be associated with specified page
Reply:	BOOL fSuccess	successful? TRUE:FALSE

BKM_SETPAGEWINDOWHWND

This message is used to associate a window handle with a page.

Parameter 1:	ULONG ulPageID	page ID to be associated with handle
Parameter 2:	HWND hwndPage	window handle to be associated with specified page
Reply:	BOOL fSuccess	successful? TRUE:FALSE

BKM_SETSTATUSLINETEXT

This message is used to associate a text string with a page's status line.

Parameter 1:	ULONG ulPageID	page ID of page to set status line text
Parameter 2:	PSZ pszString	pointer to text string
Reply:	BOOL fSuccess	successful? TRUE:FALSE

BKM_SETTABBITMAP
This message is used to set a bitmap with a page.

Parameter 1:	ULONG ulPageID	page ID to associate with bitmap
Parameter 2:	HBITMAP hbmBitmap	bitmap handle to be used
Reply:	BOOL fSuccess	successful? TRUE:FALSE

BKM_SETTABTEXT
This message is used to set the text of a major or minor tab.

Parameter 1:	ULONG ulPageID	page containing tab of interest
Parameter 2:	PSZ pszTabTextString	pointer to tab text string
Reply:	BOOL fSuccess	successful? TRUE:FALSE

BKM_TURNTOPAGE
This message is used to set the currently visible notebook page.

Parameter 1:	ULONG ulPageID	page ID to be brought to top
Parameter 2:	ULONG ulParam2	reserved, 0
Reply:	BOOL fSuccess	successful? TRUE:FALSE

Chapter 12

Containers

It was a happy occasion when Tupperware™ was invented. Not only could leftover meatloaf be stored in them, but so could crayons, plants, or almost anything else you desired. The container didn't know about the specifics of the items you stored, nor did it care; it simply stored the items.

OS/2 also has a container that has a similar purpose: to store items. It doesn't care if the items are employee names or sales statistics or the batting averages of the 1929 Yankees. The items to be stored are defined by the application. Additionally, the container control supports multiple views of the objects, in concordance with the CUA 1991 specification. Also, multiple-object selection methods are supported as well as direct editing of text and drag-n-drop. In short, the container can do anything save wash your windows or butter your bread.

This extreme amount of functionality and flexibility is not without its price, unfortunately. The container is a very complex control that demands a fair amount of initialization, and almost every message sent to and from the container references a structure or two. This chapter discusses container basics and will develop a couple of applications to demonstrate the concepts we will learn; the more advanced topics will be left to you for discovery since — should everything be detailed — two or three chapters could easily be devoted to this control.

12.1 LP's or 45's?

The basic data unit of a container is a structure that describes the state of an individual item within the container. Depending on whether or not the CCS_MINIRECORDCORE style bit is specified, this is either a RECORDCORE or MINIRECORDCORE structure. There are advantages to using either; the former requires more setup but is more flexible while the latter requires less setup but is more limiting (for the purposes of this chapter we will always use the RECORDCORE structure in our discussions). Additional bytes at the end of the record can be specified when the record is allocated. Thus, you would typically define your own structure whose first field is the RECORDCORE structure and typecast it to the appropriate structure type for messages sent to or from the container.

```
typedef struct _ITEMINFO {
        MINIRECORDCORE mrcRecord;
        CHAR achItem[256];
        ULONG ulUnitsSold;
        float fRevenue;
} ITEMINFO, *PITEMINFO;
```

Always make sure you specify the style bit that corresponds to the type of object record you decide to use.

Records are allocated using the CM_ALLOCRECORD message with the extra bytes needed beyond the RECORDCORE structure specified in the first parameter and the number of records to allocate specified in the second parameter. Obviously, for performance reasons, you want to avoid allocating one record at a time. Instead, if at all possible, determine how many records you will need and allocate them in one call. If you are allocating more than one record, the head of a linked list of records is returned, with the link specified in the *preccNextRecord* field. It should be noted that allocating memory for the records is not equivalent to inserting the records into the container. This is done using the CM_INSERTRECORD message and, as before, should be done with as many records as possible to increase performance.

The CM_INSERTRECORD message requires the first parameter to contain the head of the linked list of the (one or more) records to insert. The second parameter points to a RECORDINSERT structure.

```
typedef struct _RECORDINSERT {
        ULONG cb;
        PRECORDCORE pRecordOrder;
        PRECORDCORE pRecordParent;
        ULONG fInvalidateRecord;
        ULONG zOrder;
        ULONG cRecordsInsert;
} RECORDINSERT;
```

cb is the size of the structure in bytes. *pRecordOrder* specifies the record after which the record(s) are to be inserted. CMA_FIRST or CMA_END can also be specified to indicate that the record(s) should go at the front or end of the record list. *pRecordParent* specifies the parent record and can be NULL to indicate a top-level record. This field is only valid for tree view. *fInvalidateRecord* is TRUE if the records are to be invalidated (and thus redrawn) after being inserted. *zOrder* specifies the z-order of the record and can be either CMA_TOP or CMA_BOTTOM to specify the top and bottom of the z-order. *cRecordsInsert* specifies the number of records that are being inserted.

12.2 Half Full or Half Empty?

It was stated before that the container supports multiple views of its objects, and this is a perfect time to elaborate because it introduces us to the CNRINFO structure, which is used to control a variety of characteristics of the container.

```
typedef struct _CNRINFO {
        ULONG cb;
        PVOID pSortRecord;
        PFIELDINFO pFieldInfoLast;
        PFIELDINFO pFieldInfoObject;
        PSZ pszCnrTitle;
        ULONG flWindowAttr;
        POINTL ptlOrigin;
        ULONG cDelta;
        ULONG cRecords;
        SIZEL slBitmapOrIcon;
        SIZEL slTreeBitmapOrIcon;
        HBITMAP hbmExpanded;
        HBITMAP hbmCollapsed;
        HPOINTER hptrExpanded;
        HPOINTER hptrCollapsed;
        LONG cyLineSpacing;
        LONG cxTreeIndent;
        LONG cxTreeLine;
        ULONG cFields;
        LONG xVertSplitbar;
} CNRINFO;
```

There are a large number of fields in the CNRINFO structure, so we'll state first that you do not need to initialize every one of them. Instead, you initialize only the fields you need and specify which fields were initialized as a combination of flags specified in the second parameter of the CM_SETCNRINFO message. To change the view to icon view, for example:

```
CNRINFO ciInfo;
ciInfo.cb=sizeof(CNRINFO);
ciInfo.flWindowAttr=CV_ICON;
        WinSendMsg(pcdData->hwndCnr,
                    CM_SETCNRINFO,
                    MPFROMP(&ciInfo),
                    MPFROMLONG(CMA_FLWINDOWATTR));
```

Since we're talking about views of an object, let's look at the various combinations of view flags to specify the different view types.

VIEWS	DESCRIPTION
CV_ICON	Specifies that the icon or bitmap should be displayed with the text below it.
CV_NAME	Specifies that the icon should be displayed with the text to the right. This can be combined with the CV_FLOW flag.
CV_TEXT	Specifies that the text alone should be displayed. This can be combined with the CV_FLOW flag.
CV_TREE	Used for records that have children. The tree view has three view types that can be used with it (see Section 12.4). The tree view shows a hierarchical view of the data.
CV_DETAIL	The details view shows data in a columnar format. This is discussed in more detail later in this chapter.
CV_FLOW	The CV_FLOW flag specifies that, once a column is filled, the list should continue in an adjacent column.

The following sections below look at each view type in more detail.

12.3 Icon, Name, and Text Views

The icon view is perhaps the most widely known because it is the default view for the folders on the desktop. It consists of an icon or bitmap representing the object, with text directly beneath it. The text can be "directly edited," i.e., the user can — using the mouse and/or keyboard — directly edit the text (whether or not the container retains the changes is controlled by the application).

If the container was created with the CCS_AUTOPOSITION style, the objects are automatically arranged whenever any of the following events occur:

- The window size changes
- Container items are inserted, removed, sorted, invalidated, or filtered
- The font or font size changes
- The window title text changes

This arranging occurs as if the container was sent a CM_ARRANGE message.

The name view consists of the icon or bitmap representing the object with the text immediately to the right. As with the icon view, the text can be directly edited. If CV_FLOW is not specified, objects are arranged vertically in a single column. If CV_FLOW is specified, a new column is created to the right if the objects extend beyond the bottom of the container.

The text view consists of the text only and the objects are arranged in the same manner as the name view, with the same semantics regarding the specification of the CV_FLOW flag.

The application below illustrates these three views of a container's contents.

CONTAIN1.C

```
#define INCL_WINPOINTERS
#define INCL_WINSTDCNR
#define INCL_WINSYS
#define INCL_WINWINDOWMGR

#include <os2.h>
#include <stdio.h>
#include <stdlib.h>
#include <string.h>
#include <ctype.h>
#include "contain1.h"

#define CLS_CLIENT              "SampleClass"

#define MAX_YEARS               10
#define MAX_MONTHS              12
#define MAX_COLUMNS             4

#define CX_SPLITBAR             120
```

```
typedef struct _CLIENTDATA {
   HWND      hwndCnr ;
   HPOINTER hptrIcon ;
} CLIENTDATA, *PCLIENTDATA ;

typedef struct _SALESINFO {
   MINIRECORDCORE mrcStd ;
   ULONG          ulNumUnits ;
   float          fSales ;
   PCHAR          pchSales ;
} SALESINFO, * PSALESINFO ;



MRESULT EXPENTRY clientWndProc ( HWND hwndClient,
                                 ULONG ulMsg,
                                 MPARAM mpParm1,
                                 MPARAM mpParm2 ) ;

INT main ( VOID )
{
    HAB           habAnchor ;
    HMQ           hmqQueue ;
    ULONG         ulFlags ;
    HWND          hwndFrame ;
    BOOL          bLoop ;
    QMSG          qmMsg ;

    habAnchor = WinInitialize ( 0 ) ;
    hmqQueue = WinCreateMsgQueue ( habAnchor, 0 ) ;

    WinRegisterClass ( habAnchor,
                       CLS_CLIENT,
                       clientWndProc,
                       0,
                       sizeof ( PVOID )) ;

    ulFlags = FCF_SIZEBORDER | FCF_TITLEBAR |
              FCF_TASKLIST | FCF_SHELLPOSITION |
              FCF_SYSMENU | FCF_MENU ;

    hwndFrame = WinCreateStdWindow ( HWND_DESKTOP,
                                     WS_VISIBLE,
                                     &ulFlags,
                                     CLS_CLIENT,
                                     "Container Sample",
                                     0,
                                     NULLHANDLE,
                                     RES_CLIENT,
                                     NULL ) ;

    if ( hwndFrame != NULLHANDLE ) {
       bLoop = WinGetMsg ( habAnchor, &qmMsg, NULLHANDLE, 0, 0 ) ;
       while ( bLoop ) {
          WinDispatchMsg ( habAnchor, &qmMsg ) ;
```

```
           bLoop = WinGetMsg ( habAnchor,
                               &qmMsg,
                               NULLHANDLE,
                               0,
                               0 ) ;
       } /* endwhile */

       WinDestroyWindow ( hwndFrame ) ;
   } /* endif */

   WinDestroyMsgQueue ( hmqQueue ) ;
   WinTerminate ( habAnchor ) ;
   return 0 ;
}

VOID initSalesInfo ( PCLIENTDATA pcdData,
                     PSALESINFO psiSales,
                     USHORT usIndex )
{
   PCHAR pchPos ;

   psiSales -> mrcStd.cb = sizeof ( MINIRECORDCORE ) ;

   psiSales -> mrcStd.pszIcon = malloc ( 256 ) ;
   if ( psiSales -> mrcStd.pszIcon != NULL ) {
      sprintf ( psiSales -> mrcStd.pszIcon,
                "Year 19%02d",
                usIndex + 84 ) ;

   } /* endif */

   psiSales -> mrcStd.hptrIcon = pcdData -> hptrIcon ;
   psiSales -> ulNumUnits = usIndex * usIndex ;
   psiSales -> fSales = ( float ) psiSales -> ulNumUnits * 9.95 ;

   psiSales -> pchSales = malloc ( 16 ) ;
   if ( psiSales -> pchSales != NULL ) {
      sprintf ( psiSales -> pchSales,
                "$% - 10.2f",
                psiSales -> fSales ) ;

      pchPos = psiSales -> pchSales ;
      while ( !isspace ( *pchPos ) && ( *pchPos != 0 )) {
         pchPos ++ ;
      } /* endwhile */

      * pchPos = 0 ;
   } /* endif */
   return ;
}
```

```
VOID freeYearInfo ( PCLIENTDATA pcdData )
{
   PSALESINFO psiYear ;

   psiYear = ( PSALESINFO ) PVOIDFROMMR (
       WinSendMsg ( pcdData -> hwndCnr,
                    CM_QUERYRECORD,
                    0,
                    MPFROM2SHORT ( CMA_FIRST,
                    CMA_ITEMORDER )) ) ;


   while ( psiYear != NULL ) {
      if ( psiYear -> mrcStd.pszIcon != NULL ) {
         free ( psiYear -> mrcStd.pszIcon ) ;
      } /* endif */

      if ( psiYear -> pchSales != NULL ) {
         free ( psiYear -> pchSales ) ;
      } /* endif */

      psiYear = ( PSALESINFO ) PVOIDFROMMR (
         WinSendMsg ( pcdData -> hwndCnr,
                      CM_QUERYRECORD,
                      MPFROMP ( psiYear ) ,
                      MPFROM2SHORT ( CMA_NEXT,
                      CMA_ITEMORDER )) ) ;
   } /* endwhile */
   return ;
}

MRESULT EXPENTRY clientWndProc ( HWND hwndClient,
                                 ULONG ulMsg,
                                 MPARAM mpParm1,
                                 MPARAM mpParm2 )
{
   PCLIENTDATA pcdData ;

   pcdData = ( PCLIENTDATA ) WinQueryWindowPtr ( hwndClient, 0 ) ;

   switch ( ulMsg ) {
   case WM_CREATE:
      {
         ULONG ulExtra ;
         RECORDINSERT riRecord ;
         PSALESINFO psiYears ;
         PSALESINFO psiCYear ;
         USHORT usIndex ;

         pcdData = ( PCLIENTDATA ) calloc ( 1,
                 sizeof ( CLIENTDATA )) ;
         if ( pcdData == NULL ) {
            WinAlarm ( HWND_DESKTOP, WA_ERROR ) ;
```

```
        WinMessageBox ( HWND_DESKTOP,
                        HWND_DESKTOP,
                        "No memory is available",
                        "Error",
                        0,
                        MB_ICONEXCLAMATION | MB_OK ) ;
     return MRFROMSHORT ( TRUE ) ;
} /* endif */

WinSetWindowPtr ( hwndClient, 0, pcdData ) ;

pcdData -> hwndCnr = NULLHANDLE ;
pcdData -> hptrIcon = NULLHANDLE ;

pcdData -> hwndCnr = WinCreateWindow ( hwndClient,
                                       WC_CONTAINER,
                                       "",
                                       CCS_MINIRECORDCORE|
                                       CCS_EXTENDSEL |
                                       WS_VISIBLE,
                                       0,
                                       0,
                                       0,
                                       0,
                                       hwndClient,
                                       HWND_TOP,
                                       WND_CONTAINER,
                                       NULL,
                                       NULL ) ;

if ( pcdData -> hwndCnr == NULLHANDLE ) {
   free ( pcdData ) ;
   WinAlarm ( HWND_DESKTOP, WA_ERROR ) ;
   WinMessageBox ( HWND_DESKTOP,
                   HWND_DESKTOP,
                   "Cannot create container",
                   "Error",
                   0,
                   MB_ICONEXCLAMATION | MB_OK ) ;
   return MRFROMSHORT ( TRUE ) ;
} /* endif */

pcdData -> hptrIcon = WinLoadPointer ( HWND_DESKTOP,
                                       NULLHANDLE,
                                       ICO_ITEM ) ;

ulExtra = sizeof ( SALESINFO ) -
          sizeof ( MINIRECORDCORE ) ;

riRecord.cb = sizeof ( RECORDINSERT ) ;
riRecord.pRecordOrder = ( PRECORDCORE ) CMA_END ;
riRecord.fInvalidateRecord = FALSE ;
riRecord.zOrder = CMA_TOP ;
```

```
            psiYears = ( PSALESINFO ) PVOIDFROMMR (
                   WinSendMsg ( pcdData -> hwndCnr,
                                CM_ALLOCRECORD,
                                MPFROMLONG ( ulExtra ) ,
                                MPFROMSHORT ( MAX_YEARS )) ) ;


         psiCYear = psiYears ;

         for ( usIndex = 0 ; usIndex < MAX_YEARS ; usIndex ++ ) {
            initSalesInfo ( pcdData, psiCYear, usIndex ) ;

            riRecord.pRecordParent = NULL ;
            riRecord.cRecordsInsert = 1 ;

            WinSendMsg ( pcdData -> hwndCnr,
                         CM_INSERTRECORD,
                         MPFROMP ( psiCYear ) ,
                         MPFROMP ( &riRecord )) ;

            psiCYear =
                ( PSALESINFO ) psiCYear -> mrcStd.preccNextRecord ;
         } /* endfor */

         WinSendMsg ( hwndClient,
                      WM_COMMAND,
                      MPFROMSHORT ( MI_ICON ) ,
                      0 ) ;
      }
      break ;
case WM_DESTROY:
   freeYearInfo ( pcdData ) ;

   if ( pcdData -> hwndCnr != NULLHANDLE ) {
      WinDestroyWindow ( pcdData -> hwndCnr ) ;
   } /* endif */

   if ( pcdData -> hptrIcon != NULLHANDLE ) {
      WinDestroyPointer ( pcdData -> hptrIcon ) ;
   } /* endif */

   free ( pcdData ) ;
   break ;
case WM_SIZE:
   if ( pcdData -> hwndCnr != NULLHANDLE ) {
      WinSetWindowPos ( pcdData -> hwndCnr,
                        NULLHANDLE,
                        0,
                        0,
                        SHORT1FROMMP ( mpParm2 ) ,
                        SHORT2FROMMP ( mpParm2 ) ,
                        SWP_MOVE | SWP_SIZE ) ;
   } /* endif */
   break ;
```

```
case WM_COMMAND:
    switch ( SHORT1FROMMP ( mpParm1 )) {
    case MI_ICON:
        {
            CNRINFO ciInfo ;

            ciInfo.cb = sizeof ( CNRINFO ) ;
            ciInfo.flWindowAttr = CV_ICON ;

            WinSendMsg ( pcdData -> hwndCnr,
                         CM_SETCNRINFO,
                         MPFROMP ( &ciInfo ) ,
                         MPFROMLONG ( CMA_FLWINDOWATTR )) ;

            WinSendMsg ( pcdData -> hwndCnr,
                         CM_ARRANGE,
                         NULL,
                         NULL ) ;
        }
        break ;

    case MI_NAMEFLOWED:
        {
            CNRINFO ciInfo ;

            ciInfo.cb = sizeof ( CNRINFO ) ;
            ciInfo.flWindowAttr = CV_NAME | CV_FLOW ;

            WinSendMsg ( pcdData -> hwndCnr,
                         CM_SETCNRINFO,
                         MPFROMP ( &ciInfo ) ,
                         MPFROMLONG ( CMA_FLWINDOWATTR )) ;

            WinSendMsg ( pcdData -> hwndCnr,
                         CM_ARRANGE,
                         NULL,
                         NULL ) ;

        }
        break ;

    case MI_TEXTFLOWED:
        {
            CNRINFO ciInfo ;

            ciInfo.cb = sizeof ( CNRINFO ) ;
            ciInfo.flWindowAttr = CV_TEXT | CV_FLOW ;

            WinSendMsg ( pcdData -> hwndCnr,
                         CM_SETCNRINFO,
                         MPFROMP ( &ciInfo ) ,
                         MPFROMLONG ( CMA_FLWINDOWATTR )) ;
```

```
                WinSendMsg ( pcdData -> hwndCnr,
                             CM_ARRANGE,
                             NULL,
                             NULL ) ;
        }
        break ;

    case MI_EXIT:
        WinPostMsg ( hwndClient,
                     WM_CLOSE,
                     0,
                     0 ) ;
        break ;

    case MI_RESUME:
        break ;

    default:
        return WinDefWindowProc ( hwndClient,
                                  ulMsg,
                                  mpParm1,
                                  mpParm2 ) ;
    } /* endswitch */
    break ;

case WM_PAINT:
    {
        HPS hpsPaint ;
        RECTL rclPaint ;

        hpsPaint = WinBeginPaint ( hwndClient,
                                   NULLHANDLE,
                                   &rclPaint ) ;
        WinFillRect ( hpsPaint,
                      &rclPaint,
                      SYSCLR_WINDOW ) ;
        WinEndPaint ( hpsPaint ) ;
    }
    break ;

default:
    return WinDefWindowProc ( hwndClient,
                              ulMsg,
                              mpParm1,
                              mpParm2 ) ;
} /* endswitch */

return MRFROMSHORT ( FALSE ) ;
}
```

CONTAIN1.RC

```
#include <os2.h>
#include "contain1.h"

ICON ICO_ITEM CONTAIN1.ICO

MENU RES_CLIENT
{
    SUBMENU "~Views", M_VIEWS
    {
        MENUITEM "~Icon", MI_ICON
        MENUITEM "~Name/flowed", MI_NAMEFLOWED
        MENUITEM "Te~xt/flowed", MI_TEXTFLOWED
    }
    SUBMENU "E~xit", M_EXIT
    {
        MENUITEM "E~xit", MI_EXIT
        MENUITEM "~Resume", MI_RESUME
    }
}
```

CONTAIN1.H

```
#define RES_CLIENT          256
#define WND_CONTAINER       257
#define ICO_ITEM            258
#define M_VIEWS             320
#define MI_ICON             321
#define MI_DETAIL           322
#define MI_TREE             323
#define MI_NAMEFLOWED       324
#define MI_TEXTFLOWED       325
#define M_EXIT              336
#define MI_EXIT             337
#define MI_RESUME           338
```

CONTAIN1.MAK

```
CONTAIN1.EXE:                   CONTAIN1.OBJ \
                                CONTAIN1.RES
        LINK386 @<<
CONTAIN1
CONTAIN1
CONTAIN1
OS2386
CONTAIN1
<<
        RC CONTAIN1.RES CONTAIN1.EXE

CONTAIN1.RES:                   CONTAIN1.RC \
                                CONTAIN1.H
        RC -r CONTAIN1.RC CONTAIN1.RES

CONTAIN1.OBJ:                   CONTAIN1.C \
                                CONTAIN1.H
        ICC -C+ -Kb+ -Ss+ CONTAIN1.C
```

CONTAIN1.DEF

```
NAME   CONTAIN1  WINDOWAPI

DESCRIPTION 'First container example
            Copyright 1992 by Larry Salomon
            All rights reserved.'
STACKSIZE 32768
```

12.4 Tree View

The tree view is next in the list in order of complexity. It offers three different variations, which are described below:

VIEW	DESCRIPTION
Tree icon view	Objects in the tree are represented by icons or bitmaps with the text to the right. If an item is expandable, a separate bitmap is drawn to the left of the object. This view is specified by adding the CV_ICON and CV_TREE flags to the *flWindowAttr* field.
Tree name view	This is the same as the tree icon view except that the expandability of an object is shown on the icon or bitmap of the object, and not as a separate bitmap; the TREEITEMDESC structure contains the bitmap or icon handles for both expanded and collapsed views. The caveat here is that the TREEITEMDESC structure is pointed to by the RECORDCORE structure but *not* the MINIRECORDCORE structure. This view is specified by adding the CV_NAME and CV_TREE flags to the *flWindowAttr* field.
Tree text view	Objects in the tree are represented by text only. The feedback on the expandability of an object is represented by a separate bitmap to the left of the text. This view is specified by adding the CV_TEXT and CV_TREE flags to the *flWindowAttr* field.

In addition to specifying the view type, you may specify the amount of space (in pels) for indentation and the thickness of the tree lines when CA_TREELINE is specified. These are specified in the *cxTreeIndent* and *cxTreeLine* fields of the CNRINFO structure. If you specify a value less than 0 for either field, the default for that field is used.

12.5 Details View

The details view is by far the most difficult of the five view types to program, but its ability to show a lot of information at once overshadows this complexity. This view supports the following data types: bitmap/icon, string, unsigned long integer, date, and time. For the latter three, national language support (NLS) is enabled, meaning that the proper thousands separator character is used, the time information is ordered correctly, etc. Note that there is no support for decimal types, so you'll have to convert any decimals to their string equivalents to display numbers of this type.

The major item of interest when using the details view is the FIELDINFO structure, which describes a single column that is displayed in this view. As with the object records, memory for the FIELDINFO structures is allocated via a message: CM_ALLOCDETAILFIELDINFO. The first parameter specifies the number of FIELDINFO structures to allocate, and a pointer to the first structure is returned. As with CM_ALLOCRECORD, this is the head of a linked list of structures if more than one are allocated and the link to the next record is specified in the *pNextFieldInfo* field.

```
typedef struct _FIELDINFO {
        ULONG cb;
        ULONG flData;
        ULONG flTitle;
        PVOID pTitleData;
        ULONG offStruct;
        PVOID pUserData;
        struct _FIELDINFO *pNextFieldInfo;
        ULONG cxWidth;
} FIELDINFO;
```

cb specifies the size of the structure in bytes. *flData* specifies the type of the data in this field and any associated attributes of the column.

flTitle specifies attributes about the heading for this column and is a combination of CFA_* constants. *pTitleData* points to the column title data; this is a a bitmap or icon if CFA_BITMAPORICON is specified in *flTitle*, otherwise it is a pointer to a string. *offStruct* specifies the offset from the beginning of the RECORDCORE structure to where the data resides. *pUserData* points to any application specific data for this column. *pNextFieldInfo* points to the next FIELDINFO structure in the linked list. *cxWidth* specifies the width of the column. If 0, the column will be autosized to be the width of its widest element.

The fields *cb*, *pNextFieldInfo*, and *cxWidth* are initialized by the container in the CM_ALLOCDETAILINFO processing. The application is responsible for initializing the remaining fields.

Gotcha!

If *flData* specifies CFA_STRING, then *offStruct* specifies the offset of the *pointer to the text* and not the text itself.

Gotcha!

The column heading data is not copied into the container's workspace. Thus they must be global, static, or dynamically allocated data.

12.6 Splitbars

In details view you also have the option of having a single split bar between columns. A splitbar is a vertical bar that can be moved with the mouse. This is useful if the data displayed in a column extends beyond the space available. If a splitbar is used, horizontal scrollbars are displayed on the bottom of the container for each subsection bounded by a container edge or a splitbar.

As you might expect, a splitbar is added to the details view using the CM_SETCNRINFO message. The fields that you initialize in the CNRINFO structure are the *pFieldInfoLast* and *xVertSplitbar* fields. The former points to the FIELDINFO structure to the immediate left of the splitbar and the latter specifies where the splitbar is to be positioned initially. After initializing these fields, send the CM_SETCNRINFO message, specifying CMA_PFIELDINFOLAST | CMA_XVERTSPLITBAR as the second parameter.

Below is a sample application that adds tree and details view to the sample application, CONTAIN1 . Additionally, it demonstrates the use of a splitbar in the details view.

CONTAIN2.C

```c
#define INCL_WINPOINTERS
#define INCL_WINSTDCNR
#define INCL_WINSYS
#define INCL_WINWINDOWMGR

#include <os2.h>
#include <stdio.h>
#include <stdlib.h>
#include <string.h>
#include <ctype.h>
#include "contain2.h"

#define CLS_CLIENT              "SampleClass"

#define MAX_YEARS               10
#define MAX_MONTHS              12
#define MAX_COLUMNS             4

#define CX_SPLITBAR             120

typedef struct _CLIENTDATA {
    HWND      hwndCnr ;
    HPOINTER hptrIcon ;
} CLIENTDATA, *PCLIENTDATA ;

typedef struct _SALESINFO {
    MINIRECORDCORE mrcStd ;
    ULONG          ulNumUnits ;
    float          fSales ;
    PCHAR          pchSales ;
} SALESINFO, *PSALESINFO ;


MRESULT EXPENTRY clientWndProc ( HWND hwndClient,
                                 ULONG ulMsg,
                                 MPARAM mpParm1,
                                 MPARAM mpParm2 ) ;


INT main ( VOID    )
{
    HAB           habAnchor ;
    HMQ           hmqQueue ;
    ULONG         ulFlags ;
    HWND          hwndFrame ;
    BOOL          bLoop ;
    QMSG          qmMsg ;

    habAnchor = WinInitialize ( 0 ) ;
    hmqQueue = WinCreateMsgQueue ( habAnchor, 0 ) ;

    WinRegisterClass ( habAnchor,
                       CLS_CLIENT,
                       clientWndProc,
                       0,
                       sizeof ( PVOID )) ;
```

```
    ulFlags = FCF_SIZEBORDER | FCF_TITLEBAR | FCF_TASKLIST
            | FCF_SHELLPOSITION | FCF_SYSMENU | FCF_MENU ;


    hwndFrame = WinCreateStdWindow ( HWND_DESKTOP,
                                     WS_VISIBLE,
                                     &ulFlags,
                                     CLS_CLIENT,
                                     "Container Sample",
                                     0,
                                     NULLHANDLE,
                                     RES_CLIENT,
                                     NULL ) ;

    if ( hwndFrame != NULLHANDLE ) {
       bLoop = WinGetMsg ( habAnchor, &qmMsg, NULLHANDLE, 0, 0 ) ;
       while ( bLoop ) {
          WinDispatchMsg ( habAnchor, &qmMsg ) ;
          bLoop = WinGetMsg ( habAnchor, &qmMsg, NULLHANDLE, 0, 0 );
       } /* endwhile */

       WinDestroyWindow ( hwndFrame ) ;
    } /* endif */

    WinDestroyMsgQueue ( hmqQueue ) ;
    WinTerminate ( habAnchor ) ;
    return 0 ;
}

VOID initSalesInfo ( PCLIENTDATA pcdData,
                     PSALESINFO psiParent,
                     PSALESINFO psiSales,
                     USHORT usIndex )
{
    PCHAR pchPos ;

    psiSales -> mrcStd.cb = sizeof ( MINIRECORDCORE ) ;

    psiSales -> mrcStd.pszIcon = malloc ( 256 ) ;
    if ( psiSales -> mrcStd.pszIcon != NULL ) {
       if ( psiParent != NULL ) {
          sprintf ( psiSales -> mrcStd.pszIcon,
                  "Month %d",
                  usIndex + 1 ) ;
       } else {
          sprintf ( psiSales -> mrcStd.pszIcon,
                  "Year 19%02d",
                  usIndex + 84 ) ;
       } /* endif */
    } /* endif */

    psiSales -> mrcStd.hptrIcon = pcdData -> hptrIcon ;

    if ( psiParent != NULL ) {
       psiSales -> ulNumUnits = psiParent -> ulNumUnits / 12 ;
    } else {
```

```
      psiSales -> ulNumUnits = usIndex * usIndex ;
   } /* endif */

   psiSales -> fSales = ( float ) psiSales -> ulNumUnits * 9.95 ;

   psiSales -> pchSales = malloc ( 16 ) ;
   if ( psiSales -> pchSales != NULL ) {
      sprintf ( psiSales -> pchSales,
                "$% - 10.2f",
                psiSales -> fSales ) ;

      pchPos = psiSales -> pchSales ;
      while ( !isspace ( *pchPos ) && ( *pchPos != 0 )) {
         pchPos ++ ;
      } /* endwhile */

      *pchPos = 0 ;
   } /* endif */
   return ;
}

VOID freeYearInfo ( PCLIENTDATA pcdData )
{
   PSALESINFO          psiYear ;
   PSALESINFO          psiMonth ;

   psiYear = ( PSALESINFO ) PVOIDFROMMR (
               WinSendMsg ( pcdData -> hwndCnr,
                            CM_QUERYRECORD,
                            0,
                            MPFROM2SHORT ( CMA_FIRST,
                                           CMA_ITEMORDER )) ) ;
   while ( psiYear != NULL ) {
      psiMonth = ( PSALESINFO ) PVOIDFROMMR (
                  WinSendMsg ( pcdData -> hwndCnr,
                               CM_QUERYRECORD,
                               MPFROMP ( psiYear ) ,
                               MPFROM2SHORT ( CMA_FIRSTCHILD,
                                              CMA_ITEMORDER )) ) ;

      while ( psiMonth != NULL ) {
         if ( psiMonth -> mrcStd.pszIcon != NULL ) {
            free ( psiMonth -> mrcStd.pszIcon ) ;
         } /* endif */

         if ( psiMonth -> pchSales != NULL ) {
            free ( psiMonth -> pchSales ) ;
         } /* endif */

         psiMonth = ( PSALESINFO ) PVOIDFROMMR (
                     WinSendMsg ( pcdData -> hwndCnr,
                                  CM_QUERYRECORD,
                                  MPFROMP ( psiMonth ) ,
                                  MPFROM2SHORT ( CMA_NEXT,
                                                 CMA_ITEMORDER )));
      } /* endwhile */
```

```
        if ( psiYear -> mrcStd.pszIcon != NULL ) {
          free ( psiYear -> mrcStd.pszIcon ) ;
        } /* endif */

        if ( psiYear -> pchSales != NULL ) {
          free ( psiYear -> pchSales ) ;
        } /* endif */

        psiYear = ( PSALESINFO ) PVOIDFROMMR (
                    WinSendMsg ( pcdData -> hwndCnr,
                                 CM_QUERYRECORD,
                                 MPFROMP ( psiYear ) ,
                                 MPFROM2SHORT ( CMA_NEXT,
                                                CMA_ITEMORDER )) ) ;
    } /* endwhile */
    return ;
}

VOID initColumns ( PCLIENTDATA pcdData )
{
    CNRINFO               ciInfo ;
    PFIELDINFO            pfiCurrent ;
    PFIELDINFO            pfiInfo ;
    PFIELDINFO            pfiLefty ;
    FIELDINFOINSERT       fiiInfo ;

    pfiInfo = ( PFIELDINFO ) PVOIDFROMMR (
                WinSendMsg ( pcdData -> hwndCnr,
                             CM_ALLOCDETAILFIELDINFO,
                             MPFROMLONG ( MAX_COLUMNS ) ,
                             0 )) ;

    pfiCurrent = pfiInfo ;

    pfiCurrent -> flData = CFA_BITMAPORICON |
                           CFA_HORZSEPARATOR |
                           CFA_CENTER |
                           CFA_SEPARATOR ;

    pfiCurrent -> flTitle = CFA_STRING | CFA_CENTER ;
    pfiCurrent -> pTitleData = "Icon" ;
    pfiCurrent -> offStruct = FIELDOFFSET ( SALESINFO,
                                            mrcStd.hptrIcon ) ;

    pfiCurrent = pfiCurrent -> pNextFieldInfo ;
    pfiCurrent -> flData = CFA_STRING |
                           CFA_CENTER |
                           CFA_HORZSEPARATOR ;

    pfiCurrent -> flTitle = CFA_STRING | CFA_CENTER ;
    pfiCurrent -> pTitleData = "Year" ;
    pfiCurrent -> offStruct = FIELDOFFSET ( SALESINFO,
                                            mrcStd.pszIcon ) ;

    pfiLefty = pfiCurrent ;

    pfiCurrent = pfiCurrent -> pNextFieldInfo ;
```

```
    pfiCurrent -> flData = CFA_ULONG |
                           CFA_CENTER |
                           CFA_HORZSEPARATOR |
                           CFA_SEPARATOR ;

    pfiCurrent -> flTitle = CFA_STRING | CFA_CENTER ;
    pfiCurrent -> pTitleData = "Units Sold" ;
    pfiCurrent -> offStruct = FIELDOFFSET ( SALESINFO,
                                            ulNumUnits ) ;

    pfiCurrent = pfiCurrent -> pNextFieldInfo ;
    pfiCurrent -> flData = CFA_STRING |
                           CFA_RIGHT |
                           CFA_HORZSEPARATOR ;

    pfiCurrent -> flTitle = CFA_STRING | CFA_CENTER ;
    pfiCurrent -> pTitleData = "Sales" ;
    pfiCurrent -> offStruct = FIELDOFFSET ( SALESINFO, pchSales ) ;

    fiiInfo.cb = sizeof ( fiiInfo ) ;
    fiiInfo.pFieldInfoOrder = ( PFIELDINFO ) CMA_FIRST ;
    fiiInfo.cFieldInfoInsert = MAX_COLUMNS ;
    fiiInfo.fInvalidateFieldInfo = TRUE ;

    WinSendMsg ( pcdData -> hwndCnr,
                 CM_INSERTDETAILFIELDINFO,
                 MPFROMP ( pfiInfo ) ,
                 MPFROMP ( &fiiInfo )) ;

    memset ( &ciInfo, 0, sizeof ( ciInfo )) ;
    ciInfo.cb = sizeof ( CNRINFO ) ;
    ciInfo.pFieldInfoLast = pfiLefty ;
    ciInfo.xVertSplitbar = CX_SPLITBAR ;

    WinSendMsg ( pcdData -> hwndCnr,
                 CM_SETCNRINFO,
                 MPFROMP ( &ciInfo ) ,
                 MPFROMLONG ( CMA_PFIELDINFOLAST |
                              CMA_XVERTSPLITBAR )) ;

    return ;
}

MRESULT EXPENTRY clientWndProc ( HWND hwndClient,
                                 ULONG ulMsg,
                                 MPARAM mpParm1,
                                 MPARAM mpParm2 )
{
    PCLIENTDATA         pcdData ;

    pcdData = ( PCLIENTDATA ) WinQueryWindowPtr ( hwndClient, 0 ) ;

    switch ( ulMsg ) {

    case WM_CREATE:
        {
            ULONG               ulExtra ;
```

```
RECORDINSERT        riRecord ;
PSALESINFO          psiYears ;
PSALESINFO          psiCYear ;
USHORT              usIndex1 ;
PSALESINFO          psiMonths ;
PSALESINFO          psiCMonth ;
USHORT              usIndex2 ;

pcdData = ( PCLIENTDATA ) malloc ( sizeof ( CLIENTDATA ));

if ( pcdData == NULL ) {
   WinAlarm ( HWND_DESKTOP, WA_ERROR ) ;
   WinMessageBox ( HWND_DESKTOP,
                   HWND_DESKTOP,
                   "No memory is available",
                   "Error",
                   0,
                   MB_ICONEXCLAMATION | MB_OK ) ;
   return MRFROMSHORT ( TRUE ) ;
} /* endif */

WinSetWindowPtr ( hwndClient, 0, pcdData ) ;

pcdData -> hwndCnr = NULLHANDLE ;
pcdData -> hptrIcon = NULLHANDLE ;

pcdData -> hwndCnr = WinCreateWindow ( hwndClient,
                   WC_CONTAINER,
                   "",
                   CCS_MINIRECORDCORE |
                   CCS_EXTENDSEL |
                   WS_VISIBLE,
                   0,
                   0,
                   0,
                   0,
                   hwndClient,
                   HWND_TOP,
                   WND_CONTAINER,
                   NULL,
                   NULL ) ;

if ( pcdData -> hwndCnr == NULLHANDLE ) {
   free ( pcdData ) ;
   WinAlarm ( HWND_DESKTOP, WA_ERROR ) ;
   WinMessageBox ( HWND_DESKTOP,
                   HWND_DESKTOP,
                   "Cannot create container",
                   "Error",
                   0,
                   MB_ICONEXCLAMATION | MB_OK ) ;
   return MRFROMSHORT ( TRUE ) ;
} /* endif */

pcdData -> hptrIcon = WinLoadPointer ( HWND_DESKTOP,
                                       NULLHANDLE,
                                       ICO_ITEM ) ;
```

```
    ulExtra = sizeof ( SALESINFO ) -
             sizeof ( MINIRECORDCORE ) ;

    riRecord.cb = sizeof ( RECORDINSERT ) ;
    riRecord.pRecordOrder = ( PRECORDCORE ) CMA_END ;
    riRecord.fInvalidateRecord = FALSE ;
    riRecord.zOrder = CMA_TOP ;

    psiYears = ( PSALESINFO ) PVOIDFROMMR (
                    WinSendMsg ( pcdData -> hwndCnr,
                               CM_ALLOCRECORD,
                               MPFROMLONG ( ulExtra ) ,
                             MPFROMSHORT ( MAX_YEARS ))) ;

    psiCYear = psiYears ;

    for ( usIndex1 = 0 ; usIndex1 < MAX_YEARS ; usIndex1 ++ ){
       initSalesInfo ( pcdData, NULL, psiCYear, usIndex1 ) ;

       riRecord.pRecordParent = NULL ;
       riRecord.cRecordsInsert = 1 ;

       WinSendMsg ( pcdData -> hwndCnr,
                  CM_INSERTRECORD,
                  MPFROMP ( psiCYear ) ,
                  MPFROMP ( &riRecord )) ;

       psiMonths = ( PSALESINFO ) PVOIDFROMMR (
                       WinSendMsg ( pcdData -> hwndCnr,
                                  CM_ALLOCRECORD,
                                 MPFROMLONG ( ulExtra ) ,
                                 MPFROMSHORT ( MAX_MONTHS ))) ;

       psiCMonth = psiMonths ;

       for ( usIndex2 = 0 ; usIndex2 < MAX_MONTHS ;
                usIndex2 ++ ) {

          initSalesInfo ( pcdData,
                        psiCYear,
                        psiCMonth,
                        usIndex2 ) ;

          psiCMonth =
          ( PSALESINFO ) psiCMonth->mrcStd.preccNextRecord;
       } /* endfor */

       riRecord.pRecordParent = ( PRECORDCORE ) psiCYear ;
       riRecord.cRecordsInsert = MAX_MONTHS ;

       WinSendMsg ( pcdData -> hwndCnr,
                  CM_INSERTRECORD,
                  MPFROMP ( psiMonths ) ,
                  MPFROMP ( &riRecord )) ;
```

```
                psiCYear =
                ( PSALESINFO ) psiCYear -> mrcStd.preccNextRecord ;
          } /* endfor */

          initColumns ( pcdData ) ;

          WinSendMsg ( hwndClient,
                       WM_COMMAND,
                       MPFROMSHORT ( MI_ICON ) ,
                       0 ) ;
      }
      break ;

   case WM_DESTROY:
      freeYearInfo ( pcdData ) ;

      if ( pcdData -> hwndCnr != NULLHANDLE ) {
         WinDestroyWindow ( pcdData -> hwndCnr ) ;
      } /* endif */

      if ( pcdData -> hptrIcon != NULLHANDLE ) {
         WinDestroyPointer ( pcdData -> hptrIcon ) ;
      } /* endif */

      free ( pcdData ) ;
      break ;

   case WM_SIZE:
      if ( pcdData -> hwndCnr != NULLHANDLE ) {

         WinSetWindowPos ( pcdData -> hwndCnr,
                           NULLHANDLE,
                           0,
                           0,
                           SHORT1FROMMP ( mpParm2 ) ,
                           SHORT2FROMMP ( mpParm2 ) ,
                           SWP_MOVE | SWP_SIZE ) ;
      } /* endif */
      break ;

   case WM_COMMAND:
      switch ( SHORT1FROMMP ( mpParm1 )) {

      case MI_ICON:
         {
            CNRINFO ciInfo ;

            ciInfo.cb = sizeof ( CNRINFO ) ;
            ciInfo.flWindowAttr = CV_ICON ;

            WinSendMsg ( pcdData -> hwndCnr,
                         CM_SETCNRINFO,
                         MPFROMP ( &ciInfo ) ,
                         MPFROMLONG ( CMA_FLWINDOWATTR )) ;
```

```
                WinSendMsg ( pcdData -> hwndCnr,
                             CM_ARRANGE,
                             NULL,
                             NULL ) ;
        }
        break ;

    case MI_DETAIL:
        {
            CNRINFO ciInfo ;

            ciInfo.cb = sizeof ( CNRINFO ) ;
            ciInfo.flWindowAttr = CV_DETAIL |
                                  CA_DETAILSVIEWTITLES ;

            WinSendMsg ( pcdData -> hwndCnr,
                         CM_SETCNRINFO,
                         MPFROMP ( &ciInfo ) ,
                         MPFROMLONG ( CMA_FLWINDOWATTR )) ;
        }
        break ;

    case MI_TREE:
        {
            CNRINFO ciInfo ;

            ciInfo.cb = sizeof ( CNRINFO ) ;
            ciInfo.flWindowAttr = CV_TREE |
                                  CV_ICON |
                                  CA_TREELINE ;
            ciInfo.cxTreeIndent = - 1 ;
            ciInfo.cxTreeLine = - 1 ;

            WinSendMsg ( pcdData -> hwndCnr,
                         CM_SETCNRINFO,
                         MPFROMP ( &ciInfo ) ,
                         MPFROMLONG ( CMA_FLWINDOWATTR )) ;
        }
        break ;

    case MI_NAMEFLOWED:
        {
            CNRINFO ciInfo ;

            ciInfo.cb = sizeof ( CNRINFO ) ;
            ciInfo.flWindowAttr = CV_NAME | CV_FLOW ;

            WinSendMsg ( pcdData -> hwndCnr,
                         CM_SETCNRINFO,
                         MPFROMP ( &ciInfo ) ,
                         MPFROMLONG ( CMA_FLWINDOWATTR )) ;

            WinSendMsg ( pcdData -> hwndCnr,
                         CM_ARRANGE,
                         NULL,
                         NULL ) ;
        }
```

```
              break ;

     case MI_TEXTFLOWED:
         {
             CNRINFO ciInfo ;

             ciInfo.cb = sizeof ( CNRINFO ) ;
             ciInfo.flWindowAttr = CV_TEXT | CV_FLOW ;

             WinSendMsg ( pcdData -> hwndCnr,
                          CM_SETCNRINFO,
                          MPFROMP ( &ciInfo ) ,
                          MPFROMLONG ( CMA_FLWINDOWATTR )) ;

             WinSendMsg ( pcdData -> hwndCnr,
                          CM_ARRANGE,
                          NULL,
                          NULL ) ;
         }
         break ;

     case MI_EXIT:
         WinPostMsg ( hwndClient, WM_CLOSE, 0, 0 ) ;
         break ;

     case MI_RESUME:
         break ;

     default:
         return WinDefWindowProc ( hwndClient,
                                   ulMsg,
                                   mpParm1,
                                   mpParm2 ) ;
     } /* endswitch */
     break ;

 case WM_PAINT:
     {
         HPS hpsPaint ;
         RECTL rclPaint ;

         hpsPaint = WinBeginPaint ( hwndClient,
                                    NULLHANDLE,
                                    &rclPaint ) ;

         WinFillRect ( hpsPaint, &rclPaint, SYSCLR_WINDOW ) ;
         WinEndPaint ( hpsPaint ) ;
     }
     break ;

 default:
     return WinDefWindowProc ( hwndClient,
                               ulMsg,
                               mpParm1,
                               mpParm2 ) ;
 } /* endswitch */
```

```
    return MRFROMSHORT ( FALSE ) ;
}
```

CONTAIN2.RC

```
#include <os2.h>
#include "contain2.h"

ICON ICO_ITEM CONTAIN1.ICO

MENU RES_CLIENT
{
    SUBMENU "~Views", M_VIEWS
    {
        MENUITEM "~Icon", MI_ICON
        MENUITEM "~Detail", MI_DETAIL
        MENUITEM "~Tree", MI_TREE
        MENUITEM "~Name/flowed", MI_NAMEFLOWED
        MENUITEM "Te~xt/flowed", MI_TEXTFLOWED
    }
    SUBMENU "E~xit", M_EXIT
    {
        MENUITEM "E~xit", MI_EXIT
        MENUITEM "~Resume", MI_RESUME
    }
}
```

CONTAIN2.H

```
#define RES_CLIENT              256
#define WND_CONTAINER           257
#define ICO_ITEM                258
#define M_VIEWS                 320
#define MI_ICON                 321
#define MI_DETAIL               322
#define MI_TREE                 323
#define MI_NAMEFLOWED           324
#define MI_TEXTFLOWED           325
#define M_EXIT                  336
#define MI_EXIT                 337
#define MI_RESUME               338
```

CONTAIN2.MAK

```
CONTAIN2.EXE:                   CONTAIN2.OBJ \
                                CONTAIN2.RES
        LINK386 @<<
CONTAIN2
CONTAIN2
CONTAIN2
OS2386
CONTAIN2
<<
        RC CONTAIN2.RES CONTAIN2.EXE
```

```
CONTAIN2.RES:                    CONTAIN2.RC \
                                 CONTAIN2.H
        RC -r CONTAIN2.RC CONTAIN2.RES

CONTAIN2.OBJ:                    CONTAIN2.C \
                                 CONTAIN2.H
        ICC -C+ -Kb+ -Ss+ CONTAIN2.C
```

CONTAIN2.DEF

```
NAME   CONTAIN2  WINDOWAPI

DESCRIPTION 'Second container example
            Copyright 1992 by Larry Salomon
            All rights reserved.'
STACKSIZE 32768
```

12.7 Of Emphasis and Popups

Object emphasis is a visual cue to the user that something about the object is different from the norm. Cursored, selected, in-use, and source emphasis are the four types defined by the container. Of these four types, defined below, only the first two are set automatically by the container. The latter two must be explicitly set by the application via the CM_SETRECORDEMPHASIS message.

EMPHASIS	DESCRIPTION
Cursored	Set whenever the input focus belongs to the object. This is shown as a dotted-line rectangle around the object.
Selected	Set whenever the object was selected using the mouse button or the spacebar. How records previously selected behave when a new record is selected is defined by the selection style of the container. This is shown as an inverted background around the object.
In-use	Set whenever the object is defined to be in use by the application. This is shown as a crosshatch pattern in the background of the object.
Source	Set whenever the object is a source of some action. This record could also be in the selected state, but this is not required. This is shown as a dashed-line rectangle with rounded corners around the object.

Gotcha!

While the CM_SETRECORDEMPHASIS has CRA_* constants for the cursored, selected, and in-use emphasis types, the Toolkit header files in OS/2 2.0 are missing the source emphasis constant. CRA_SOURCE should be defined as 0x00004000L. It should also be noted that it is possible for the entire container to have source emphasis, in which case NULL should be specified for the record pointer.

CONTAIN3.C

```
#define INCL_WINFRAMEMGR
#define INCL_WINMENUS
#define INCL_WINPOINTERS
#define INCL_WINSTDCNR
#define INCL_WINSYS
#define INCL_WINWINDOWMGR

#include <os2.h>
#include <stdio.h>
#include <stdlib.h>
#include <string.h>
#include <ctype.h>

#include "CONTAIN3.H"

#define CLS_CLIENT              "SampleClass"

#define MAX_YEARS               10
#define MAX_MONTHS              12
#define MAX_COLUMNS             4

#define CX_SPLITBAR             120

//---------------------------------------------------
// For the GA 2.0 toolkit, CRA_SOURCE is not defined,
// but it should be.
//---------------------------------------------------

#ifndef CRA_SOURCE
#define CRA_SOURCE              0x00004000L
#endif

typedef struct _CLIENTDATA {
   HWND       hwndCnr ;
   HPOINTER   hptrIcon ;
   HWND       hwndMenu ;
   BOOL       bCnrSelected ;
} CLIENTDATA, *PCLIENTDATA ;
```

```
typedef struct _SALESINFO {
   MINIRECORDCORE mrcStd ;
   BOOL           bEmphasized ;
   ULONG          ulNumUnits ;
   float          fSales ;
   PCHAR          pchSales ;
} SALESINFO, *PSALESINFO ;

MRESULT EXPENTRY clientWndProc ( HWND hwndClient,
                                 ULONG ulMsg,
                                 MPARAM mpParm1,
                                 MPARAM mpParm2 ) ;


INT main ( VOID )
{
   HAB         habAnchor ;
   HMQ         hmqQueue ;
   ULONG       ulFlags ;
   HWND        hwndFrame ;
   BOOL        bLoop ;
   QMSG        qmMsg ;

   habAnchor = WinInitialize ( 0 ) ;
   hmqQueue = WinCreateMsgQueue ( habAnchor, 0 ) ;

   WinRegisterClass ( habAnchor,
                      CLS_CLIENT,
                      clientWndProc,
                      0,
                      sizeof ( PVOID )) ;

   ulFlags = FCF_SIZEBORDER | FCF_TITLEBAR |
             FCF_TASKLIST | FCF_SHELLPOSITION |
             FCF_SYSMENU ;

   hwndFrame = WinCreateStdWindow ( HWND_DESKTOP,
                                    WS_VISIBLE,
                                    &ulFlags,
                                    CLS_CLIENT,
                                    "Container Sample",
                                    0,
                                    NULLHANDLE,
                                    RES_CLIENT,
                                    NULL ) ;

   if ( hwndFrame != NULLHANDLE ) {
      bLoop = WinGetMsg ( habAnchor, &qmMsg, NULLHANDLE, 0, 0 ) ;
      while ( bLoop ) {
         WinDispatchMsg ( habAnchor, &qmMsg ) ;
         bLoop = WinGetMsg ( habAnchor,
                             &qmMsg,
                             NULLHANDLE,
                             0,
                             0 ) ;
      } /* endwhile */
```

```
        WinDestroyWindow ( hwndFrame ) ;
    } /* endif */

    WinDestroyMsgQueue ( hmqQueue ) ;
    WinTerminate ( habAnchor ) ;
    return 0 ;
}

VOID initSalesInfo ( PCLIENTDATA pcdData,
                     PSALESINFO psiParent,
                     PSALESINFO psiSales,
                     USHORT usIndex )
{
    PCHAR pchPos ;

    psiSales -> mrcStd.cb = sizeof ( MINIRECORDCORE ) ;

    psiSales -> mrcStd.pszIcon = malloc ( 256 ) ;
    if ( psiSales -> mrcStd.pszIcon != NULL ) {

        if ( psiParent != NULL ) {
            sprintf ( psiSales -> mrcStd.pszIcon,
                      "Month %d",
                      usIndex + 1 ) ;
        } else {
            sprintf ( psiSales -> mrcStd.pszIcon,
                      "Year 19%02d",
                      usIndex + 84 ) ;
        } /* endif */
    } /* endif */

    psiSales -> mrcStd.hptrIcon = pcdData -> hptrIcon ;
    psiSales -> bEmphasized = FALSE ;

    if ( psiParent != NULL ) {
        psiSales -> ulNumUnits = psiParent -> ulNumUnits / 12 ;
    } else {
        psiSales -> ulNumUnits = usIndex * 100 ;
    } /* endif */

    psiSales -> fSales = ( float ) psiSales -> ulNumUnits * 9.95 ;

    psiSales -> pchSales = malloc ( 16 ) ;

    if ( psiSales -> pchSales != NULL ) {
        sprintf ( psiSales -> pchSales,
                  "$% - 10.2f",
                  psiSales -> fSales ) ;

        pchPos = psiSales -> pchSales ;
        while ( !isspace ( *pchPos ) && ( *pchPos != 0 )) {
            pchPos ++ ;
        } /* endwhile */

        *pchPos = 0 ;
    } /* endif */
    return ;
```

```
}
VOID emphasizeRecs ( HWND hwndCnr, BOOL bEmphasize )
{
    SHORT           sFlag ;
    PSALESINFO      psiYear ;

    sFlag = (( bEmphasize ) ? CRA_SELECTED : CRA_SOURCE ) ;

    psiYear = ( PSALESINFO ) PVOIDFROMMR (
                WinSendMsg ( hwndCnr,
                             CM_QUERYRECORDEMPHASIS,
                             MPFROMP ( CMA_FIRST ) ,
                             MPFROMSHORT ( sFlag )) ) ;

    while ( psiYear != NULL ) {
        if ( bEmphasize ) {
            WinSendMsg ( hwndCnr,
                         CM_SETRECORDEMPHASIS,
                         MPFROMP ( psiYear ) ,
                         MPFROM2SHORT ( TRUE, CRA_SOURCE )) ;

            psiYear -> bEmphasized = TRUE ;
        } else {
            WinSendMsg ( hwndCnr,
                         CM_SETRECORDEMPHASIS,
                         MPFROMP ( psiYear ) ,
                         MPFROM2SHORT ( FALSE, CRA_SOURCE )) ;

            psiYear -> bEmphasized = FALSE ;
        } /* endif */

        psiYear = ( PSALESINFO ) PVOIDFROMMR (
                    WinSendMsg ( hwndCnr,
                                 CM_QUERYRECORDEMPHASIS,
                                 MPFROMP ( psiYear ) ,
                                 MPFROMSHORT ( sFlag ))) ;
    } /* endwhile */
    return ;
}

VOID freeCnrInfo ( HWND hwndCnr )
{
    PSALESINFO psiYear ;
    PSALESINFO psiMonth ;

    psiYear = ( PSALESINFO ) PVOIDFROMMR (
                WinSendMsg ( hwndCnr,
                             CM_QUERYRECORD,
                             0,
                             MPFROM2SHORT ( CMA_FIRST,
                                            CMA_ITEMORDER ))) ;
```

```
   while ( psiYear != NULL ) {
      psiMonth = ( PSALESINFO ) PVOIDFROMMR (
                    WinSendMsg ( hwndCnr,
                                 CM_QUERYRECORD,
                                 MPFROMP ( psiYear ) ,
                                 MPFROM2SHORT ( CMA_FIRSTCHILD,
                                                CMA_ITEMORDER ))) ;
      while ( psiMonth != NULL ) {
         if ( psiMonth -> mrcStd.pszIcon != NULL ) {
            free ( psiMonth -> mrcStd.pszIcon ) ;
         } /* endif */

         if ( psiMonth -> pchSales != NULL ) {
            free ( psiMonth -> pchSales ) ;
         } /* endif */

         psiMonth = ( PSALESINFO ) PVOIDFROMMR (
                       WinSendMsg ( hwndCnr,
                                    CM_QUERYRECORD,
                                    MPFROMP ( psiMonth ) ,
                                    MPFROM2SHORT ( CMA_NEXT,
                                                   CMA_ITEMORDER ))) ;
      } /* endwhile */

      if ( psiYear -> mrcStd.pszIcon != NULL ) {
         free ( psiYear -> mrcStd.pszIcon ) ;
      } /* endif */

      if ( psiYear -> pchSales != NULL ) {
         free ( psiYear -> pchSales ) ;
      } /* endif */

      psiYear = ( PSALESINFO ) PVOIDFROMMR (
                    WinSendMsg ( hwndCnr,
                                 CM_QUERYRECORD,
                                 MPFROMP ( psiYear ) ,
                                 MPFROM2SHORT ( CMA_NEXT,
                                                CMA_ITEMORDER ))) ;
   } /* endwhile */
   return ;
}

VOID initColumns ( PCLIENTDATA pcdData )
{
   CNRINFO         ciInfo ;
   PFIELDINFO      pfiCurrent ;
   PFIELDINFO      pfiInfo ;
   PFIELDINFO      pfiLefty ;
   FIELDINFOINSERT fiiInfo ;

   pfiInfo = ( PFIELDINFO ) PVOIDFROMMR (
                 WinSendMsg ( pcdData -> hwndCnr,
                              CM_ALLOCDETAILFIELDINFO,
                              MPFROMLONG ( MAX_COLUMNS ) ,
                              0 )) ;

   pfiCurrent = pfiInfo ;
```

```
pfiCurrent -> flData = CFA_BITMAPORICON | CFA_HORZSEPARATOR |
                       CFA_CENTER | CFA_SEPARATOR ;

pfiCurrent -> flTitle = CFA_STRING | CFA_CENTER ;
pfiCurrent -> pTitleData = "Icon" ;
pfiCurrent -> offStruct = FIELDOFFSET ( SALESINFO,
                             mrcStd.hptrIcon ) ;

pfiCurrent = pfiCurrent -> pNextFieldInfo ;

pfiCurrent -> flData = CFA_STRING |
                       CFA_CENTER |
                       CFA_HORZSEPARATOR ;

pfiCurrent -> flTitle = CFA_STRING | CFA_CENTER ;
pfiCurrent -> pTitleData = "Year" ;
pfiCurrent -> offStruct = FIELDOFFSET ( SALESINFO,
                                    mrcStd.pszIcon ) ;

pfiLefty = pfiCurrent ;

pfiCurrent = pfiCurrent -> pNextFieldInfo ;
pfiCurrent -> flData = CFA_ULONG | CFA_CENTER |
                       CFA_HORZSEPARATOR | CFA_SEPARATOR ;

pfiCurrent -> flTitle = CFA_STRING | CFA_CENTER ;
pfiCurrent -> pTitleData = "Units Sold" ;
pfiCurrent -> offStruct = FIELDOFFSET ( SALESINFO,
                                    ulNumUnits ) ;

pfiCurrent = pfiCurrent -> pNextFieldInfo ;
pfiCurrent -> flData = CFA_STRING |
                       CFA_RIGHT |
                       CFA_HORZSEPARATOR ;

pfiCurrent -> flTitle = CFA_STRING | CFA_CENTER ;
pfiCurrent -> pTitleData = "Sales" ;
pfiCurrent -> offStruct = FIELDOFFSET ( SALESINFO, pchSales ) ;

fiiInfo.cb = sizeof ( fiiInfo ) ;
fiiInfo.pFieldInfoOrder = ( PFIELDINFO ) CMA_FIRST ;
fiiInfo.cFieldInfoInsert = MAX_COLUMNS ;
fiiInfo.fInvalidateFieldInfo = TRUE ;

WinSendMsg ( pcdData -> hwndCnr,
             CM_INSERTDETAILFIELDINFO,
             MPFROMP ( pfiInfo ) ,
             MPFROMP ( &fiiInfo )) ;

memset ( &ciInfo, 0, sizeof ( ciInfo )) ;
ciInfo.cb = sizeof ( CNRINFO ) ;
ciInfo.pFieldInfoLast = pfiLefty ;
ciInfo.xVertSplitbar = CX_SPLITBAR ;
```

```
    WinSendMsg ( pcdData -> hwndCnr,
                 CM_SETCNRINFO,
                 MPFROMP ( &ciInfo ) ,
                 MPFROMLONG ( CMA_PFIELDINFOLAST |
                              CMA_XVERTSPLITBAR )) ;
    return ;
}

MRESULT EXPENTRY clientWndProc ( HWND hwndClient,
                                 ULONG ulMsg,
                                 MPARAM mpParm1,
                                 MPARAM mpParm2 )
{
    PCLIENTDATA pcdData ;

    pcdData = ( PCLIENTDATA ) WinQueryWindowPtr ( hwndClient, 0 ) ;

    switch ( ulMsg ) {
    case WM_CREATE:
        {
            MENUITEM miItem ;
            ULONG ulStyle ;
            ULONG ulExtra ;
            RECORDINSERT riRecord ;
            PSALESINFO psiYears ;
            PSALESINFO psiCYear ;
            USHORT usIndex1 ;
            PSALESINFO psiMonths ;
            PSALESINFO psiCMonth ;
            USHORT usIndex2 ;

            pcdData = ( PCLIENTDATA ) malloc ( sizeof ( CLIENTDATA ));
            if ( pcdData ==  NULL ) {
                WinAlarm ( HWND_DESKTOP, WA_ERROR ) ;
                WinMessageBox ( HWND_DESKTOP,
                                HWND_DESKTOP,
                                "No memory is available",
                                "Error",
                                0,
                                MB_ICONEXCLAMATION | MB_OK ) ;
                return MRFROMSHORT ( TRUE ) ;
            } /* endif */

            WinSetWindowPtr ( hwndClient, 0, pcdData ) ;

            pcdData -> hwndCnr = NULLHANDLE ;
            pcdData -> hptrIcon = NULLHANDLE ;
            pcdData -> hwndMenu = NULLHANDLE ;
            pcdData -> bCnrSelected = FALSE ;
```

```
        pcdData -> hwndCnr = WinCreateWindow (
                                hwndClient,
                                WC_CONTAINER,
                                "",
                                CCS_MINIRECORDCORE |
                                CCS_EXTENDSEL |
                                WS_VISIBLE,
                                0,
                                0,
                                0,
                                0,
                                hwndClient,
                                HWND_TOP,
                                WND_CONTAINER,
                                NULL,
                                NULL ) ;

    if ( pcdData -> hwndCnr ==  NULLHANDLE ) {
        free ( pcdData ) ;
        WinAlarm ( HWND_DESKTOP, WA_ERROR ) ;
        WinMessageBox ( HWND_DESKTOP,
                        HWND_DESKTOP,
                        "Cannot create container",
                        "Error",
                        0,
                        MB_ICONEXCLAMATION | MB_OK ) ;
        return MRFROMSHORT ( TRUE ) ;
    } /* endif */

    pcdData -> hptrIcon = WinLoadPointer ( HWND_DESKTOP,
                            NULLHANDLE,
                            ICO_ITEM ) ;

    pcdData -> hwndMenu = WinLoadMenu ( hwndClient,
                            NULLHANDLE,
                            RES_CLIENT ) ;
    WinSendMsg ( pcdData -> hwndMenu,
            MM_QUERYITEM,
            MPFROM2SHORT ( M_VIEWS, TRUE ) ,
            MPFROMP ( &miItem )) ;

    ulStyle = WinQueryWindowULong ( miItem.hwndSubMenu,
                            QWL_STYLE ) ;

    ulStyle |= MS_CONDITIONALCASCADE ;
    WinSetWindowULong ( miItem.hwndSubMenu,
                    QWL_STYLE,
                    ulStyle ) ;

    WinSendMsg ( miItem.hwndSubMenu,
            MM_SETDEFAULTITEMID,
            MPFROMSHORT ( MI_ICON ) ,
            0 ) ;

    ulExtra = sizeof ( SALESINFO ) -
            sizeof ( MINIRECORDCORE ) ;
```

```
riRecord.cb = sizeof ( RECORDINSERT ) ;
riRecord.pRecordOrder = ( PRECORDCORE ) CMA_END ;
riRecord.fInvalidateRecord = FALSE ;
riRecord.zOrder = CMA_TOP ;

psiYears = ( PSALESINFO ) PVOIDFROMMR (
             WinSendMsg ( pcdData -> hwndCnr,
                          CM_ALLOCRECORD,
                          MPFROMLONG ( ulExtra ) ,
                          MPFROMSHORT ( MAX_YEARS ))) ;

psiCYear = psiYears ;

for ( usIndex1 = 0 ; usIndex1 < MAX_YEARS ;
        usIndex1 ++ ) {

   initSalesInfo ( pcdData, NULL, psiCYear, usIndex1 ) ;

   riRecord.pRecordParent = NULL ;
   riRecord.cRecordsInsert = 1 ;

   WinSendMsg ( pcdData -> hwndCnr,
                CM_INSERTRECORD,
                MPFROMP ( psiCYear ) ,
                MPFROMP ( &riRecord )) ;

   psiMonths = ( PSALESINFO ) PVOIDFROMMR (
                  WinSendMsg ( pcdData -> hwndCnr,
                               CM_ALLOCRECORD,
                               MPFROMLONG ( ulExtra ) ,
                               MPFROMSHORT ( MAX_MONTHS ))) ;

   psiCMonth = psiMonths ;

   for ( usIndex2 = 0 ; usIndex2 < MAX_MONTHS ;
           usIndex2 ++ ) {

      initSalesInfo ( pcdData,
                      psiCYear,
                      psiCMonth,
                      usIndex2 ) ;

      psiCMonth =
         (PSALESINFO) psiCMonth->mrcStd.preccNextRecord ;
   } /* endfor */

   riRecord.pRecordParent = ( PRECORDCORE ) psiCYear ;
   riRecord.cRecordsInsert = MAX_MONTHS ;

   WinSendMsg ( pcdData -> hwndCnr,
                CM_INSERTRECORD,
                MPFROMP ( psiMonths ) ,
                MPFROMP ( &riRecord )) ;

   psiCYear =
      (PSALESINFO) psiCYear->mrcStd.preccNextRecord ;
} /* endfor */
```

```
         initColumns ( pcdData ) ;

         WinSendMsg ( hwndClient,
                      WM_COMMAND,
                      MPFROMSHORT ( MI_ICON ) ,
                      0 ) ;
      }
      break ;

case WM_DESTROY:
   freeCnrInfo ( pcdData -> hwndCnr ) ;

   if ( pcdData -> hwndCnr != NULLHANDLE ) {
      WinDestroyWindow ( pcdData -> hwndCnr ) ;
   } /* endif */

   if ( pcdData -> hptrIcon != NULLHANDLE ) {
      WinDestroyPointer ( pcdData -> hptrIcon ) ;
   } /* endif */

   free ( pcdData ) ;
   break ;

case WM_SIZE:
   if ( pcdData -> hwndCnr != NULLHANDLE ) {

      WinSetWindowPos ( pcdData -> hwndCnr,
                        NULLHANDLE,
                        0,
                        0,
                        SHORT1FROMMP ( mpParm2 ) ,
                        SHORT2FROMMP ( mpParm2 ) ,
                        SWP_MOVE | SWP_SIZE ) ;
   } /* endif */
   break ;

case WM_MENUEND:
   switch ( SHORT1FROMMP ( mpParm1 )) {
   case FID_MENU:
      if ( pcdData -> bCnrSelected ) {
         WinSendMsg ( pcdData -> hwndCnr,
                      CM_SETRECORDEMPHASIS,
                      0,
                      MPFROM2SHORT ( FALSE, CRA_SOURCE )) ;
         pcdData -> bCnrSelected = FALSE ;
      } else {
         emphasizeRecs ( pcdData -> hwndCnr, FALSE ) ;
      } /* endif */
      break ;

   default:
      return WinDefWindowProc ( hwndClient,
                                ulMsg,
                                mpParm1,
                                mpParm2 ) ;
   } /* endswitch */
```

```
        break ;

case WM_CONTROL:
    switch ( SHORT1FROMMP ( mpParm1 )) {
    case WND_CONTAINER:
        switch ( SHORT2FROMMP ( mpParm1 )) {
        case CN_CONTEXTMENU:
            {
                PSALESINFO psiSales ;
                POINTL ptlMouse ;

                psiSales = ( PSALESINFO ) PVOIDFROMMP ( mpParm2 ) ;
                if ( psiSales != NULL ) {
                    if (( psiSales -> mrcStd.flRecordAttr &
                      CRA_SELECTED ) == 0 )
                    {
                        WinSendMsg ( pcdData -> hwndCnr,
                                     CM_SETRECORDEMPHASIS,
                                     MPFROMP ( psiSales ) ,
                                 MPFROM2SHORT ( TRUE, CRA_SOURCE )) ;
                        psiSales -> bEmphasized = TRUE ;
                    } else {
                        emphasizeRecs ( pcdData -> hwndCnr, TRUE ) ;
                    } /* endif */
                } else {
                    WinSendMsg ( pcdData -> hwndCnr,
                                 CM_SETRECORDEMPHASIS,
                                 0,
                                 MPFROM2SHORT ( TRUE, CRA_SOURCE )) ;
                    pcdData -> bCnrSelected = TRUE ;
                } /* endif */

                WinQueryPointerPos ( HWND_DESKTOP, &ptlMouse ) ;
                WinMapWindowPoints ( HWND_DESKTOP,
                                     hwndClient,
                                     &ptlMouse,
                                     1 ) ;
                WinPopupMenu ( hwndClient,
                               hwndClient,
                               pcdData -> hwndMenu,
                               ptlMouse.x,
                               ptlMouse.y,
                               M_VIEWS,
                               PU_HCONSTRAIN |
                               PU_VCONSTRAIN |
                               PU_KEYBOARD |
                               PU_MOUSEBUTTON1 |
                               PU_MOUSEBUTTON2 |
                               PU_NONE ) ;
            }
            break ;

        default:
            return WinDefWindowProc ( hwndClient,
                                      ulMsg,
                                      mpParm1,
                                      mpParm2 ) ;
```

```
            } /* endswitch */
            break ;

        default:
            return WinDefWindowProc ( hwndClient,
                                      ulMsg,
                                      mpParm1,
                                      mpParm2 ) ;
        } /* endswitch */
        break ;

    case WM_COMMAND:
        switch ( SHORT1FROMMP ( mpParm1 )) {
        case MI_ICON:
            {
                CNRINFO ciInfo ;

                ciInfo.cb = sizeof ( CNRINFO ) ;
                ciInfo.flWindowAttr = CV_ICON ;

                WinSendMsg ( pcdData -> hwndCnr,
                             CM_SETCNRINFO,
                             MPFROMP ( &ciInfo ) ,
                             MPFROMLONG ( CMA_FLWINDOWATTR )) ;

                WinSendMsg ( pcdData -> hwndCnr,
                             CM_ARRANGE,
                             NULL,
                             NULL ) ;
            }
            break ;

        case MI_DETAIL:
            {
                CNRINFO ciInfo ;

                ciInfo.cb = sizeof ( CNRINFO ) ;
                ciInfo.flWindowAttr = CV_DETAIL |
                                      CA_DETAILSVIEWTITLES ;

                WinSendMsg ( pcdData -> hwndCnr,
                             CM_SETCNRINFO,
                             MPFROMP ( &ciInfo ) ,
                             MPFROMLONG ( CMA_FLWINDOWATTR )) ;
            }
            break ;

        case MI_TREE:
            {
                CNRINFO ciInfo ;

                ciInfo.cb = sizeof ( CNRINFO ) ;
                ciInfo.flWindowAttr = CV_TREE | CV_ICON | CA_TREELINE ;
                ciInfo.cxTreeIndent = - 1 ;
                ciInfo.cxTreeLine = - 1 ;
```

```
                WinSendMsg ( pcdData -> hwndCnr,
                             CM_SETCNRINFO,
                             MPFROMP ( &ciInfo ) ,
                             MPFROMLONG ( CMA_FLWINDOWATTR )) ;
            }
        break ;

    case MI_NAMEFLOWED:
        {
            CNRINFO ciInfo ;

            ciInfo.cb = sizeof ( CNRINFO ) ;
            ciInfo.flWindowAttr = CV_NAME | CV_FLOW ;

            WinSendMsg ( pcdData -> hwndCnr,
                         CM_SETCNRINFO,
                         MPFROMP ( &ciInfo ) ,
                         MPFROMLONG ( CMA_FLWINDOWATTR )) ;

            WinSendMsg ( pcdData -> hwndCnr,
                         CM_ARRANGE,
                         NULL,
                         NULL ) ;
        }
        break ;

    case MI_TEXTFLOWED:
        {
            CNRINFO ciInfo ;

            ciInfo.cb = sizeof ( CNRINFO ) ;
            ciInfo.flWindowAttr = CV_TEXT | CV_FLOW ;

            WinSendMsg ( pcdData -> hwndCnr,
                         CM_SETCNRINFO,
                         MPFROMP ( &ciInfo ) ,
                         MPFROMLONG ( CMA_FLWINDOWATTR )) ;

            WinSendMsg ( pcdData -> hwndCnr,
                         CM_ARRANGE,
                         NULL,
                         NULL ) ;
        }
        break ;

    case MI_EXIT:
        WinPostMsg ( hwndClient, WM_CLOSE, 0, 0 ) ;
        break ;

    case MI_RESUME:
        break ;

    default:
        return WinDefWindowProc ( hwndClient,
                                  ulMsg,
                                  mpParm1,
                                  mpParm2 ) ;
```

```
        } /* endswitch */
      break ;

   case WM_PAINT:
      {
         HPS hpsPaint ;
         RECTL rclPaint ;

         hpsPaint = WinBeginPaint ( hwndClient,
                                    NULLHANDLE,
                                    &rclPaint ) ;

         WinFillRect ( hpsPaint, &rclPaint, SYSCLR_WINDOW ) ;
         WinEndPaint ( hpsPaint ) ;
      }
      break ;

   default:
      return WinDefWindowProc ( hwndClient,
                                ulMsg,
                                mpParm1,
                                mpParm2 ) ;
   } /* endswitch */

   return MRFROMSHORT ( FALSE ) ;
}
```

CONTAIN3.RC

```
#include <os2.h>
#include "contain3.h"

ICON ICO_ITEM CONTAIN3.ICO

MENU RES_CLIENT
{
   SUBMENU "~Views    ", M_VIEWS
   {
      MENUITEM "~Icon", MI_ICON
      MENUITEM "~Detail", MI_DETAIL
      MENUITEM "~Tree", MI_TREE
      MENUITEM "~Name/flowed", MI_NAMEFLOWED
      MENUITEM "Te~xt/flowed", MI_TEXTFLOWED
   }
   SUBMENU "E~xit", M_EXIT
   {
      MENUITEM "E~xit", MI_EXIT
      MENUITEM "~Resume", MI_RESUME
   }
}
```

CONTAIN3.H

```
#define RES_CLIENT           256
#define WND_CONTAINER        257
#define ICO_ITEM             258
#define M_VIEWS              320
```

```
#define MI_ICON                      321
#define MI_DETAIL                    322
#define MI_TREE                      323
#define MI_NAMEFLOWED                324
#define MI_TEXTFLOWED                325
#define M_EXIT                       336
#define MI_EXIT                      337
#define MI_RESUME                    338
```

CONTAIN3.MAK

```
CONTAIN3.EXE:                       CONTAIN3.OBJ \
                                    CONTAIN3.RES
         LINK386 $(LINKOPTS) @<<
CONTAIN3
CONTAIN3
CONTAIN3
OS2386
CONTAIN3
<<
         RC CONTAIN3.RES CONTAIN3.EXE

CONTAIN3.RES:                       CONTAIN3.RC \
                                    CONTAIN3.H
         RC -r CONTAIN3.RC CONTAIN3.RES

CONTAIN3.OBJ:                       CONTAIN3.C \
                                    CONTAIN3.H
         ICC -C+ -Kb+ -Ss+ CONTAIN3.C
```

CONTAIN3.DEF

```
NAME    CONTAIN3   WINDOWAPI

DESCRIPTION 'Third container example
            Copyright 1992 by Larry Salomon
            All rights reserved.'
STACKSIZE 32768
```

The records that have a particular emphasis are queried using the CM_QUERYRECORDEMPHASIS message. This message will return the record with the specified emphasis type that follows the record specified in the first parameter. The first parameter may be CMA_FIRST to mean the first record should be returned with the desired emphasis type. The appropriate CRA_* constant is specified in the second parameter.

The sample application, CONTAIN3, removes the action bar and uses a popup menu to provide the same functionality. Source emphasis is also provided.

12.8 Direct Editing

As stated before, direct editing can be accomplished by the user with a mouse click. The application must therefore be aware of this and be able to process this event properly. When the user selects the proper combination of mouse clicks or keystrokes, the container sends the application a WM_CONTROL message with a CN_BEGINEDIT notification code. The data in the second parameter is a pointer to the CNREDITDATA structure:

```
typedef struct _CNREDITDATA {
        ULONG cb;
        HWND hwndCnr;
        PRECORDCORE pRecord;
        PFIELDINFO pFieldInfo;
        PSZ *ppszText;
        ULONG cbText;
        ULONG id;
} CNREDITDATA;
```

cb is the size of the structure in bytes. *hwndCnr* is the handle of the container window. *pRecord* is a pointer to the RECORDCORE structure of the object being edited. If the container titles are being edited, this field is NULL. *pFieldInfo* is a pointer to the FIELDINFO structure if the current view is detail view and the column titles are not being edited. Otherwise, this field is NULL. *ppszText* points to the pointer to the current text if the notification code is CN_BEGINEDIT or CN_REALLOCPSZ. For CN_ENDEDIT notification, this points to the pointer to the new text. *cbText* specifies the number of bytes in the text. id is the identifier of the window being edited and is a CID_* constant.

The CN_BEGINEDIT notification allows the application to perform any pre-edit processing such as setting a limit on the text length. After the direct editing is finished by the user, the container sends a CN_REALLOCPSZ notification to the owner of the container before copying the new text into the application's text string to allow the application to adjust the buffer size if needed. Finally, a CN_ENDEDIT notification is sent to allow any post-edit processing to be done.

Gotcha!

The application must return TRUE from the CN_REALLOCPSZ notification, or else the container will discard the editing changes.

12.9 Container Styles

The following list describes the container styles and their meanings:

STYLE	DESCRIPTION
CCS_EXTENDSEL	Specifies that the extended selection model is to be used according to the CUA 91 guidelines.
CCS_MULTIPLESEL	Specifies that one or more items can be selected at any time.
CCS_SINGLESEL	Specifies that only a single item may be selected at any time. This is the default.
CCS_AUTOPOSITION	Specifies that the container should automatically position items when one of a specific set of events occurs. This is valid for icon view only.
CCS_MINIRECORDCORE	Specifies that the object records are of the type MINIRECORDCORE (instead of RECORDCORE).
CCS_READONLY	Specifies that no text should be editable.
CCS_VERIFYPOINTERS	Specifies that the container should verify that all pointers used belong to the object list. It does not validate the accessibility of the pointers. This should be used only during debugging, since it affects the performance of the container.

12.10 Summary

The container control, while cumbersome at times to initialize and interact with, is a very useful addition to the library of standard controls provided with PM. It is very flexible, providing many different viewing methods, and supports the CUA 91 user interface guidelines. With a little imagination and a great deal of programming, you could greatly enhance the user interface of your application using this control.

12.11 Container Messages

WM_CONTROL/CN_BEGINEDIT
This message is sent when a container is about to be edited.

Parameter 1:	USHORT usID	container ID
	USHORT usCode	CN_BEGINEDIT
Parameter 2:	PCNREDITDATA pcnrEditData	pointer to CNREDITDATA structure

```
typedef struct _CNREDITDATA
{
    ULONG       cb;
    HWND        hwndCnr;
    PRECORDCORE pRecord;
    PFIELDINFO  pFieldInfo;
    PSZ *ppszText;
    ULONG       cbText;
    ULONG       id;
} CNREDITDATA;
typedef CNREDITDATA *PCNREDITDATA;
```

Reply:	ULONG ulReserved	reserved, 0

WM_CONTROL/CN_COLLAPSETREE
This message is sent to the container's owner whenever a parent item in the container is collapsed.

Parameter 1:	USHORT usID	container ID
	USHORT usCode	CN_COLLAPSETREE
Parameter 2:	PRECORDCORE prcCode	pointer to RECORDCORE structure

```
typedef struct _RECORDCORE
{
   ULONG        cb;
   ULONG        flRecordAttr;
   POINTL       ptlIcon;
   struct _RECORDCORE *preccNextRecord;
   PSZ          pszIcon;
   HPOINTER     hptrIcon;
   HPOINTER     hptrMiniIcon;
   HBITMAP      hbmBitmap;
   HBITMAP      hbmMiniBitmap;
   PTREEITEMDESC pTreeItemDesc;
   PSZ          pszText;
   PSZ          pszName;
   PSZ          pszTree;
} RECORDCORE;
typedef RECORDCORE *PRECORDCORE;
```

Reply: ULONG ulReserved   reserved, 0

WM_CONTROL/CN_CONTEXTMENU

This message is sent to the container's owner when a container receives a WM_CONTEXTMENU message.

Parameter 1:	USHORT usID	container ID
	USHORT usCode	CN_CONTEXTMENU
Parameter 2:	PRECORDCORE prcCode	pointer to RECORDCORE structure
Reply:	ULONG ulReserved	reserved, 0

WM_CONTROL/CN_DRAGAFTER

This message is sent to the container's owner whenever the container receives a DM_DRAGOVER message.

Parameter 1:	USHORT usID	container ID
	USHORT usCode	CN_DRAGAFTER
Parameter 2:	PCNRDRAGINFO pcnrDragInfo	pointer to CNRDRAGINFO structure

```
typedef struct _CNRDRAGINFO    /* cdrginfo */
{
   PDRAGINFO   pDragInfo;
   PRECORDCORE pRecord;
} CNRDRAGINFO;
typedef CNRDRAGINFO *PCNRDRAGINFO;
```

Reply: USHORT usDrop   drop flag

FLAG	MEANING
DOR_DROP	Drop operation OK.
DOR_NODROP	Drop operation not OK at current time. Type of drop operation is OK.
DOR_NODROPOP	Drop operation not OK. Type of drop operation is not acceptable.
DOR_NEVERDROP	Drop operation not OK, now or ever.

USHORT usOperation   default drop operation

OPERATION	MEANING
DO_COPY	Copy operation
DO_LINK	Link operation
DO_MOVE	Move operation
Other	User-defined operation

WM_CONTROL/CN_DRAGLEAVE

This message is sent to the container's owner whenever the container receives a DM_DRAGLEAVE message.

Parameter 1:	USHORT usID	container ID
	USHORT usCode	CN_DRAGLEAVE
Parameter 2:	PCNRDRAGINFO pcnrDragInfo	pointer to CNRDRAGINFO structure
Reply:	ULONG ulReserved	reserved, 0

WM_CONTROL/CN_DRAGOVER

This message is sent to the container's owner whenever the container receives a DM_DRAGOVER message.

Parameter 1:	USHORT usID	container ID
	USHORT usCode	CN_DRAGOVER
Parameter 2:	PCNRDRAGINFO pcnrDragInfo	pointer to CNRDRAGINFO structure
Reply:	USHORT usDrop	drop flag

FLAG	MEANING
DOR_DROP	Drop operation OK.
DOR_NODROP	Drop operation not OK at current time. Type of drop operation is OK.
DOR_NODROPOP	Drop operation not OK. Type of drop operation is not acceptable.
DOR_NEVERDROP	Drop operation not OK, now or ever.

USHORT usOperation   default drop operation

OPERATION	MEANING
DO_COPY	Copy operation
DO_LINK	Link operation
DO_MOVE	Move operation
Other	User-defined operation

WM_CONTROL/CN_DROP

This message is sent to the container's owner whenever the container receives a DM_DROP message.

Parameter 1:	USHORT usID	container ID
	USHORT usCode	CN_DROP
Parameter 2:	PCNRDRAGINFO pcnrDragInfo	pointer to CNRDRAGINFO structure
Reply:	ULONG ulReserved	reserved, 0

WM_CONTROL/CN_DROPHELP

This message is sent to the container's owner whenever the container receives a DM_DROPHELP message.

Parameter 1:	USHORT usID	container ID
	USHORT usCode	CN_DROPHELP
Parameter 2:	PCNRDRAGINFO pcnrDragInfo	pointer to CNRDRAGINFO structure
Reply:	ULONG ulReserved	reserved, 0

WM_CONTROL/CN_EMPHASIS
This message is sent to the container's owner whenever a record in the container changes its emphasis attribute.

Parameter 1:   USHORT usID   container ID
          USHORT usCode   CN_DROPEMPHASIS
Parameter 2:   PNOTIFYRECORDEMPHASIS prcdEmphasis
          pointer
          to NOTIFYRECORDEMPHASIS

```
typedef struct _NOTIFYRECORDEMPHASIS
{
  HWND        hwndCnr;
  PRECORDCORE pRecord;
  ULONG       fEmphasisMask;
} NOTIFYRECORDEMPHASIS;
typedef NOTIFYRECORDEMPHASIS *PNOTIFYRECORDEMPHASIS;
```

Reply: ULONG ulReserved   reserved, 0

WM_CONTROL/CN_ENDEDIT
This message is sent when a container's direct editing of text has ended.

Parameter 1:   USHORT usID   container ID
          USHORT usCode   CN_ENDEDIT
Parameter 2:   PCNREDITDATA pcnrEditData pointer to CNREDITDATA structure
Reply: ULONG ulReserved   reserved, 0

WM_CONTROL/CN_ENTER
This message is sent when the Enter key is pressed while the container window has the focus, or the select button is double-clicked while the pointer is over the container window.

Parameter 1:   USHORT usID   container ID
          USHORT usCode   CN_ENTER
Parameter 2:   PNOTIFYRECORDENTER pNotifyRcd
          pointer to NOTIFYRECORDENTER structure

```
typedef struct _NOTIFYRECORDENTER
{
   HWND        hwndCnr;
   ULONG       fKey;
   PRECORDCORE pRecord;
} NOTIFYRECORDENTER;
typedef NOTIFYRECORDENTER *PNOTIFYRECORDENTER;
```

Reply: ULONG ulReserved   reserved, 0

WM_CONTROL/CN_EXPANDTREE

This message is sent when a subtree is expanded in the tree view.

Parameter 1:	USHORT usID	container ID
	USHORT usCode	CN_EXPANDTREE
Parameter 2:	PRECORDCORE pRecordCode	pointer to RECORDCORE structure
Reply:	ULONG ulReserved	reserved, 0

WM_CONTROL/CN_HELP

This message is sent to the owner of the container whenever the container receives a WM_HELP message.

Parameter 1:	USHORT usID	container ID
	USHORT usCode	CN_HELP
Parameter 2:	PRECORDCORE pRecordCode	pointer to RECORDCORE structure
Reply:	ULONG ulReserved	reserved, 0

WM_CONTROL/CN_INITDRAG

Sent when the system-defined drag button was pressed and the pointer was moved while the pointer was over the container control.

Parameter 1:	USHORT usID	container ID
	USHORT usCode	CN_INITDRAG
Parameter 2:	PCNRDRAGINIT pDragInit	pointer to CNRDRAGINIT structure

```
typedef struct _CNRDRAGINIT
{
   HWND         hwndCnr;
   PRECORDCORE  pRecord;
   LONG         x;
   LONG         y;
   LONG         cx;
   LONG         cy;
} CNRDRAGINIT;
typedef CNRDRAGINIT *PCNRDRAGINIT;
```

Reply: ULONG ulReserved   reserved, 0

WM_CONTROL/CN_KILLFOCUS

This message is sent when the container loses the focus.

Parameter 1:	USHORT usID	container ID
	USHORT usCode	CN_KILLFOCUS
Parameter 2:	HWND hwndContainer	container window handle
Reply:	ULONG ulReserved	reserved, 0

WM_CONTROL/CN_QUERYDELTA

This message is sent to query for more data when a user scrolls to a preset delta value. This value is set via the CNRINFO structure in the *cDelta* field.

Parameter 1:	USHORT usID	container ID
	USHORT usCode	CN_QUERYDELTA
Parameter 2:	PNOTIFYDELTA ptrNotifyDelta	pointer to NOTIFYDELTA

```
typedef struct _NOTIFYDELTA
{
   HWND     hwndCnr;
   ULONG    fDelta;
} NOTIFYDELTA;
typedef NOTIFYDELTA *PNOTIFYDELTA;
```

Reply: ULONG ulReserved   reserved, 0

WM_CONTROL/CN_REALLOCPSZ

This message is sent after container text is edited. In order for the changed text to be saved, this message must be processed and TRUE returned. The container then copies the changed text into the new memory area before destroying the MLE.

Parameter 1:	USHORT usID	Container ID
	USHORT usCode	CN_REALLOCPSZ
Parameter 2:	PCNREDITDATA pcnrEditData	pointer to CNREDITDATA structure
Reply:	BOOL fMemStatus	TRUE — memory is sufficient for copy; go ahead and do it FALSE — memory is insufficient for copy; don't copy string

WM_CONTROL/CN_SCROLL

This message is sent when the container window scrolls.

Parameter 1:	USHORT usID	container ID
	USHORT usCode	CN_SCROLL
Parameter 2:	PNOTIFYSCROLL pNotifyScroll	pointer to NOTIFYSCROLL structure

```
typedef struct _NOTIFYSCROLL
{
   HWND        hwndCnr;
   LONG        lScrollInc;
   ULONG       fScroll;
} NOTIFYSCROLL;
typedef NOTIFYSCROLL *PNOTIFYSCROLL;
```

Reply:	ULONG ulReserved	reserved, 0

WM_CONTROL/CN_SETFOCUS

This message is sent when the container receives the focus.

Parameter 1:	USHORT usID	container ID

	USHORT usCode	CN_SETFOCUS
Parameter 2:	HWND hwndContainer	container
		window handle
Reply:	ULONG ulReserved	reserved, 0

WM_CONTROLPOINTER

This message is sent to a container's owner when the user moves the mouse over the control window.

	USHORT usID	container ID
Parameter 1:	USHORT usID	container ID
Parameter 2:	HPOINTER hptrCurrent	current mouse
		pointer
Reply:	HPOINTER hptrNew	pointer to new
		mouse pointer

WM_DRAWITEM

Sent to the owner of a container when an item with CA_OWNERDRAW is to be drawn.

	USHORT usID	window ID
Parameter 1:	USHORT usID	window ID
Parameter 2:	POWNERITEM pownerOwnerItem	pointer to
		OWNERITEM
		structure

```
typedef struct _OWNERITEM
{
    HWND    hwnd;
    HPS     hps;
    ULONG   fsState;
    ULONG   fsAttribute;
    ULONG   fsStateOld;
    ULONG   fsAttributeOld;
    RECTL   rclItem;
    LONG    idItem;
    ULONG   hItem;
} OWNERITEM;
typedef OWNERITEM *POWNERITEM;
```

Reply:	BOOL fDrawn	drawn?
		TRUE:FALSE

CM_ALLOCDETAILFIELDINFO

This message is sent to the container to allocate memory for the FIELDINFO structures for its details view.

Parameter 1:	USHORT usNumStructs	number of FIELDINFO structures to allocate
Parameter 2:	ULONG ulReserved	reserved, 0
Reply:	PFIELDINFO pFieldInfo	pointer to FIELDINFO structures

```
typedef struct _FIELDINFO
 {
    ULONG      cb;
    ULONG      flData;
    ULONG      flTitle;
    PVOID      pTitleData;
    ULONG      offStruct;
    PVOID      pUserData;
    struct _FIELDINFO *pNextFieldInfo;
    ULONG      cxWidth;
 } FIELDINFO;
typedef FIELDINFO *PFIELDINFO;
```

CM_ALLOCRECORD

This message is sent to allocate memory for the RECORDCORE or MINIRECORDCORE structures.

Parameter 1:	ULONG ulExtraData	number of bytes of data to allocate for application-defined use
Parameter 2:	USHORT usNumStruct	number of structures to allocate
Reply:	PRECORDCORE pRecordCore	pointer to RECORDCORE or MINIRECORDCORE structures that have been allocated

```
typedef struct _RECORDCORE      /* recc */
{
   ULONG       cb;
   ULONG       flRecordAttr;
   POINTL      ptlIcon;
   struct _RECORDCORE *preccNextRecord;
   PSZ         pszIcon;
   HPOINTER    hptrIcon;
   HPOINTER    hptrMiniIcon;
   HBITMAP     hbmBitmap;
   HBITMAP     hbmMiniBitmap;
   PTREEITEMDESC pTreeItemDesc;
   PSZ         pszText;
   PSZ         pszName;
   PSZ         pszTree;
} RECORDCORE;
typedef RECORDCORE *PRECORDCORE;

typedef struct _MINIRECORDCORE
{
   ULONG       cb;
   ULONG       flRecordAttr;        /
   POINTL      ptlIcon;
   struct _MINIRECORDCORE *preccNextRecord;
   PSZ         pszIcon;
   HPOINTER    hptrIcon;
} MINIRECORDCORE;
typedef MINIRECORDCORE *PMINIRECORDCORE;
```

Note: If CCS_MINIRECORD is specified as the container style, the return is a PMINIRECORDCORE. If it is not specified, the return is a PRECORDCORE.

CM_ARRANGE
This message is sent to the container to have it arrange the records in the icon view.

Parameter 1:	ULONG ulReserved	reserved, 0
Parameter 2:	ULONG ulReserved	reserved, 0
Reply:	ULONG ulReserved	reserved, 0

CM_CLOSEEDIT
This message is sent to close the MLE window that is used to edit the container text.

Parameter 1:	ULONG ulReserved	reserved, 0
Parameter 2:	ULONG ulReserved	reserved, 0

| **Reply:** | BOOL fSuccess | successful edit? TRUE: FALSE |

CM_COLLAPSETREE

This message is sent to the container to tell it to collapse a specified item in the tree view.

Parameter 1:	PRECORDCORE pRecordCore	pointer to RECORDCORE structure that is to be collapsed
Parameter 2:	ULONG ulReserved	reserved, 0
Reply:	BOOL fSuccess	successful collapse? TRUE: FALSE

Note: If the style CCS_MINIRECORD is specified, parameter 1 is a PMINIRECORDCORE.

CM_ERASERECORD

This message is sent to erase a record from the current view.

Parameter 1:	PRECORDCORE pRecordCore	pointer to RECORDCORE structure to erase
Parameter 2:	ULONG ulReserved	reserved, 0
Reply:	BOOL fSuccess	successful erase? TRUE: FALSE

Note: If the style CCS_MINIRECORD is specified, parameter 1 is a PMINIRECORDCORE. Erasing a record does not delete the record, or free the RECORDCORE structure; instead the record is only visually erased.

CM_EXPANDTREE

This message is sent to the container to expand a parent item in the tree view.

Parameter 1:	PRECORDCORE pRecordCore	pointer to RECORDCORE structure to expand
Parameter 2:	ULONG ulReserved	reserved, 0
Reply:	BOOL fSuccess	successful expansion? TRUE: FALSE

Note: If the style CCS_MINIRECORD is specified, parameter 1 is a PMINIRECORDCORE.

CM_FILTER
This message is sent to the container items, so the subset becomes viewable.

Parameter 1:   PFN pFilterFunction   pointer to user-defined filter function

Parameter 2:   PVOID pExtraData   pointer to application data space

Reply: BOOL fSuccess   successful? TRUE: FALSE

Note: The filter function should be prototyped:

```
BOOL PFN pFilterFunction( PRECORDCORE pRecord, PVOID pExtra );
```

If the style CCS_MINIRECORD is specified, *pRecord* is a PMINIRECORDCORE.

CM_FREEDETAILFIELDINFO
This message is sent to the container to free the FIELDINFO structures.

Parameter 1:   PVOID pFieldArray   pointer to an array of FIELDINFO structures to be freed

Parameter 2:   USHORT usNumStruct   number of structures to free

Reply: BOOL fSuccess   successful? TRUE: FALSE

CM_FREERECORD
This message is sent to the container to free the memory associated with the RECORDCORE structures.

Parameter 1:   PVOID pRecordArray   pointer to an array of RECORDCORE or MINIRECORDCORE structures

Parameter 2:   USHORT usNumStruct   number of structures to free

Reply: BOOL fSuccess   successful? TRUE: FALSE

CM_HORZSCROLLSPLITWINDOW
This message is sent to the container when the user scrolls a split window in the details view.

Parameter 1:   USHORT usWndow   CMA_LEFT — the left window is being scrolled

		CMA_RIGHT — the right window is being scrolled
Parameter 2:	LONG lScroll	the number of pixels to scroll the window; this can be a plus or minus value
Reply:	BOOL fSuccess	successful scroll? TRUE: FALSE

CM_INSERTDETAILFIELDINFO

This message is sent to the container to insert a FIELDINFO structure.

Parameter 1:	PFIELDINFO pFieldInfo	pointer to FIELDINFO structures to insert

```
typedef struct _FIELDINFO
{
    ULONG       cb;
    ULONG       flData;
    ULONG       flTitle;
    PVOID       pTitleData;
    ULONG       offStruct;
    PVOID       pUserData;
    ULONG       cxWidth;
} FIELDINFO;
typedef FIELDINFO *PFIELDINFO;
```

Parameter 2:	PFIELDINFOINSERT pFieldInsert	pointer to FIELDINFOINSERT

```
typedef struct _FIELDINFOINSERT
{
    ULONG       cb;
    PFIELDINFO  pFieldInfoOrder;
    ULONG       fInvalidateFieldInfo;
    ULONG       cFieldInfoInsert;
} FIELDINFOINSERT;
typedef FIELDINFOINSERT *PFIELDINFOINSERT;
```

Reply:	USHORT usNumStruct	number of FIELDINFO structures in the container

CM_INSERTRECORD

This message is sent to insert RECORDCORE structures into the container.

Parameter 1:   PRECORDCORE pRecordCore   pointer to RECORDCORE structure

Parameter 2:   PRECORDINSERT pRecordInsert

pointer to RECORDINSERT structure

```
typedef struct _RECORDINSERT
{
    ULONG       cb;
    PRECORDCORE pRecordOrder;
    PRECORDCORE pRecordParent;
    ULONG       fInvalidateRecord;
    ULONG       zOrder;
    ULONG       cRecordsInsert;
} RECORDINSERT;
typedef RECORDINSERT *PRECORDINSERT;
```

Reply: ULONG ulNumStruct   number of RECORDCORE structure in the container

Note: If the style CCS_MINIRECORD is specified, parameter 1 is a PMINIRECORDCORE.

CM_INVALIDATEDETAILFIELDINFO

This message is sent to the container to indicate that not all of the FIELDINFO structures are valid and the details view should be refreshed.

Parameter 1:   ULONG ulReserved   reserved, 0
Parameter 2:   ULONG ulReserved   reserved, 0
Reply: BOOL fSuccess   successful? TRUE: FALSE

CM_INVALIDATERECORD
This message is sent to the container to indicate that some of the RECORDCORE structures are invalid and should be refreshed.

Parameter 1:	PVOID pRecordArray	pointer to an array of pointers to RECORDCORE structures that should be refreshed
Parameter 2:	USHORT usNumRec	number of records to be refreshed; 0 indicates all records are to be refreshed
	USHORT usFlags	flags used to optimize the memory refresh

FLAG	MEANING
CMA_ERASE	Erase the background when the display is refreshed in the icon view. Default is no erase.
CMA_REPOSITION	Used to indicate that the RECORDCORE structures need to be reordered within the container.
CMA_NOREPOSITION	Used to indicate that the RECORDCORE structures do not need to be reordered within the container.
CMA_TEXTCHANGED	Used to indicate the text within the container records has changed.

Reply: BOOL fSuccess   successful? TRUE: FALSE
Note: If the style CCS_MINIRECORD is specified, parameter 1 is a PMINIRECORDCORE.

CM_OPENEDIT
This message is sent to open the MLE window to edit the container.

Parameter 1:	PCNREDITDATA pEditData	pointer to CNREDITDATA structure
Parameter 2:	ULONG ulReserved	reserved, 0
Reply:	BOOL fSuccess	successful? TRUE: FALSE

CM_PAINTBACKGROUND
This message is sent whenever the container's background is painted.

Parameter 1:   POWNERBACKGROUND pOwnBack

pointer to
OWNERBACKGROUND
structure

```
typedef struct _OWNERBACKGROUND
{
    HWND     hwnd;
    HPS      hps;
    RECTL    rclBackground;
    LONG     idWindow;
} OWNERBACKGROUND;
typedef OWNERBACKGROUND *POWNERBACKGROUND;
```

Parameter 2:   ULONG ulReserved   reserved, 0

Reply: BOOL fDrawn   background drawn? TRUE:
FALSE

CM_QUERYCNRINFO
This message is sent to the container to query the CNRINFO structure.

Parameter 1:   PCNRINFO pCnrInfo   pointer to CNRINFO structure

```
typedef struct _CNRINFO      /* ccinfo */
{
    ULONG        cb;
    PVOID        pSortRecord;
    PFIELDINFO   pFieldInfoLast;
    PFIELDINFO   pFieldInfoObject;
    PSZ          pszCnrTitle;
    ULONG        flWindowAttr;
    POINTL       ptlOrigin;
    ULONG        cDelta;
    ULONG        cRecords;
    SIZEL        slBitmapOrIcon;
    SIZEL        slTreeBitmapOrIcon;
    HBITMAP      hbmExpanded;
    HBITMAP      hbmCollapsed;
    HPOINTER     hptrExpanded;    /
    HPOINTER     hptrCollapsed;
    LONG         cyLineSpacing;
    LONG         cxTreeIndent;
    LONG         cxTreeLine;
    ULONG        cFields;
    LONG         xVertSplitbar;
} CNRINFO;
typedef CNRINFO *PCNRINFO;
```

| **Parameter 2:** | USHORT usSizeCnrInfo | size of CNRINFO structure |
| **Reply:** | USHORT usNumBytes | number of bytes copied |

CM_QUERYDETAILFIELDINFO

This message is sent to the container to return a FIELDINFO structure.

Parameter 1:	PFIELDINFO pFieldInfo	pointer to FIELDINFO structure to use as reference if CMA_NEXT or CMA_PREV is specified
Parameter 2:	USHORT usCmd	CMA_FIRST, CMA_LAST, CMA_NEXT, or CMA_PREV
Reply:	PFIELDINFO pFieldInto	pointer to requested FIELDINFO structures

CM_QUERYDRAGIMAGE

This message is sent to the container to query the image displayed for a specified record in the container.

Parameter 1:	PRECORDCORE pRecordCore	pointer to RECORDCORE structure to be queried
Parameter 2:	ULONG ulReserved	reserved, 0
Reply:	LHANDLE hImage	handle of icon or bit map
Note:	If the style CCS_MINIRECORD is specified, parameter 1 is a PMINIRECORDCORE.	

CM_QUERYRECORD
This message is sent to the container to return a specified RECORDCORE structure.

Parameter 1:   PRECORDCORE pRecordCore   pointer to RECORDCORE structure used as search criteria; ignored if CMA_FIRST or CMA_LAST is specified

Parameter 2:   USHORT usCmd   search command

COMMAND	MEANING
CMA_FIRST	Retrieve first record in the container
CMA_FIRSTCHILD	Retrieve first child record of record specified in Parameter 1
CMA_LAST	Retrieve last record in the container
CMA_LASTCHILD	Retrieve last child record of record specified in Parameter 1
CMA_NEXT	Retrieve next record after record specified in Parameter 1
CMA_PARENT	Retrieve parent of record specified in Parameter 1
CMA_PREV	Retrieve record previous to record specified in Parameter 1

USHORT usOrder   CMA_ITEMORDER — records evaluated in item order
CMA_ZORDER — records evaluated in Z-order

Reply: PRECORDCORE pRecordCore   pointer to RECORDCORE structure of interest

Note: If the style CCS_MINIRECORD is specified, parameter 1 and Reply are PMINIRECORDCOREs.

CM_QUERYRECORDEMPHASIS

This message is sent to the container to find the record with a specified emphasis.

Parameter 1:	PRECORDCORE pRecordCore	pointer to RECORDCORE structure of record to start searching with, or CMA_FIRST to start searching with the first record
Parameter 2:	USHORT usEmphasis	emphasis attribute to find: CRA_CURSORED CRA_INUSE CRA_SELECTED
Reply:	PRECORDCORE pRecordCore	pointer to record satisfying search

Note: If the style CCS_MINIRECORD is specified, parameter 1 and Reply are PMINIRECORDCOREs.

CM_QUERYRECORDFROMRECT

This message is sent to the container to find the record that is contained in a specified rectangle.

Parameter 1:	PRECORDCORE pRecordCore	pointer to RECORDCORE structure of record to start searching with, or CMA_FIRST to start searching with the first record
Parameter 2:	QUERYRECFROMRECT pQueryRect	pointer to QUERYRECFROMRECT structure

```
typedef struct _QUERYRECFROMRECT
{
    ULONG   cb;
    RECTL   rect;
    ULONG   fsSearch;
} QUERYRECFROMRECT;
typedef QUERYRECFROMRECT *PQUERYRECFROMRECT;
```

Reply: PRECORDCORE pRecordCore pointer to record
satisfying search

Note: If the style CCS_MINIRECORD is specified, parameter 1
and Reply are PMINIRECORDCOREs.

CM_QUERYRECORDINFO
This message is sent to the container to update the specified records.

Parameter 1: PVOID pRecordArray pointer to array of
RECORDCORE structures that the
container will copy information
into

Parameter 2: USHORT usNumStruct number of structures in parameter
1

Reply: BOOL fSuccess successful? TRUE: FALSE

Note: If the style CCS_MINIRECORD is specified, parameter 1 is
a pointer to an array of PMINIRECORDCOREs.

CM_QUERYRECORDRECT
This message is sent to the container to query the bounding rectangle of the
specified record.

Parameter 1: PRECTL prclRecord bounding rectangle coordinates

Parameter 2: PQUERYRECORDRECT pQueryRecord
pointer to QUERYRECORDRECT
structure of record that is queried

```
typedef struct _QUERYRECORDRECT
{
   ULONG        cb;
   PRECORDCORE  pRecord;
   ULONG        fRightSplitWindow;
   ULONG        fsExtent;
} QUERYRECORDRECT;
typedef QUERYRECORDRECT *PQUERYRECORDRECT;
```

Reply: BOOL fSuccess successful? TRUE: FALSE

CM_QUERYVIEWPORTRECT

This message is sent to the container to query the rectangle that contains the container's entire coordinates.

Parameter 1:	PRECTL prclContainer	pointer to RECTL that contains the container's coordinates
Parameter 2:	USHORT usSize	CMA_WINDOW — return the client window relative to the container window CMA_WORKSPACE — return the client window relative to the desktop
	BOOL fSplitWindow	TRUE — get size of right split window FALSE — get size of left split window
Reply:	BOOL fSuccess	successful? TRUE: FALSE

CM_REMOVEDETAILFIELDINFO

This message is sent to the container to remove one or several FIELDINFO structures.

Parameter 1:	PVOID pFieldArray	pointer to array of PFIELDINFO that are to be removed
Parameter 2:	USHORT usNumStruct	number of structures in Parameter 1
	USHORT usFlag	CMA_FREE — structures are removed from container, and memory is freed CMA_INVALIDATE — structures are removed from container and container is invalidated; no memory is freed
Reply:	SHORT sStruct	number of structures left in container

CM_REMOVERECORD

This message is sent to the container to remove one or more RECORDCORE structures.

Parameter 1:	PVOID pFieldArray	pointer to array of PRECORDCORE that are to be removed
Parameter 2:	USHORT usNumStruct	number of structures in Parameter 1
	USHORT usFlag	CMA_FREE — structures are removed from container, and memory is freed CMA_INVALIDATE — structures are removed from container and container is invalidated; no memory is freed
Reply:	SHORT sStruct	number of structures left in container

Note: If the style CCS_MINIRECORD is specified, parameter 1 is a PMINIRECORDCORE array.

CM_SCROLLWINDOW

This message is sent to the container to scroll the container window.

Parameter 1:	USHORT usDirection	direction to scroll CMA_VERTICAL — vertical scroll CMA_HORIZONTAL — horizontal scroll
Parameter 2:	LONG lInc	amount to scroll; this can be a plus or minus value
Reply:	BOOL fSuccess	successful? TRUE: FALSE

CM_SEARCHSTRING

This message is sent to the container to find the record that contains a specified string.

Parameter 1:	PSEARCHSTRING pString	pointer to SEARCHSTRING structure

```
typedef struct _SEARCHSTRING
{
    ULONG  cb;
    PSZ    pszSearch;
    ULONG  fsPrefix;
    ULONG  fsCaseSensitive;
    ULONG  usView;
} SEARCHSTRING;
typedef SEARCHSTRING *PSEARCHSTRING;
```

Parameter 2:   PRECORDCORE pRecord   pointer to RECORDCORE structure to start search with

Reply: PRECORDCORE pMatch   pointer to RECORDCORE that contains the string

Note: If the style CCS_MINIRECORD is specified, parameter 2 and Reply are PMINIRECORDCORE.

CM_SETCNRINFO
This message is sent to the container to change the data in the container.

Parameter 1:   PCNRINFO pCnrInfo   pointer to CNRIFO
Parameter 2:   ULONG ulFlags   flags indicating which data is to be changed

FLAG	MEANING
CMA_PSORTRECORD	pointer to sort function
CMA_PFIELDINFOLAST	pointer to last column in details view left window
CMA_PFIELDINFOOBJECT	pointer to object column in details view
CMA_CNRTITLE	pointer to container text title
CMA_FLWINDOWATTR	container attributes
CMA_PTLORIGIN	position of container window
CMA_DELTA	number of records used in delta operations
CMA_SLBITMAPORICON	size of bitmap or icon
CMA_SLTREEBITMAPORICON	size of expand/collapse bitmap or icon
CMA_TREEBITMAP	expand/collapse bitmaps in tree view
CMA_TREEICON	expand/collapse icons in tree view

CMA_LINESPACING	amount of space between records
CMA_CXTREEINDENT	amount of space between levels in tree view
CMA_CXTREELINE	width of lines in tree view
CMA_XVERTSPLITBAR	initial position of splitbar in container window in details view

Reply:	BOOL fSuccess	successful? TRUE: FALSE

CM_SETRECORDEMPHASIS
This message is sent to change emphasis on the specified container record.

Parameter 1:	PRECORDCORE pRecord	pointer to RECORDCORE structure to change
Parameter 2:	USHORT usOn	TRUE — set emphasis attribute ON FALSE — set emphasis attribute OFF
	USHORT usAttribute	CRA_CURSORED, CRA_INUSE, CRA_SELECTED
Reply:	BOOL fSuccess	successful? TRUE: FALSE

Note: If the style CCS_MINIRECORD is specified, parameter 1 is a PMINIRECORDCORE.

CM_SORTRECORD
This message is sent to the container to sort the container records.

Parameter 1:	PFN pfnSort	pointer to sort function
Parameter 2:	PVOID pExtra	application-defined space
Reply:	BOOL fSort	sorted? TRUE: FALSE

WM_PRESPARAMCHANGED
This message is sent when a container's Presentation Parameters are changed.

Parameter 1:	ULONG ulID	attribute-type ID
Parameter 2:	ULONG ulReserved	reserved, 0
Reply:	ULONG ulReserved	reserved, 0

Chapter 13

Value Set

A value set is a control that provides a way for a user to select from several graphically illustrated choices. Only one choice can be selected at a time. A value set can use icons, bitmaps, colors, text, or numbers. However, it is optimal to use only graphical images and/or short text. Other controls should be used if a choice of only text or numbers is offered. The value set is designed to show setting choices, not action choices. A push-button or menu should be used to designate an action choice. A value set must contain at least two items. A value set choice that is unavailable should be disabled. If a value set has text choices, a letter for each choice should be designated as a mnemonic. A value set can be used as a tool palette, also; however, the pointer should be changed to represent the current "tool" selected. For instance, if a "paint" tool is selected, the cursor could be changed to represent a paint brush. See Figure 13.1.

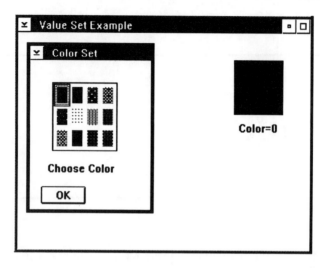

Figure 13.1. Example of the value set control.

13.1 Value Set Styles

STYLE	DESCRIPTION
VS_BITMAP	Default all value set items to bitmaps
VS_ICON	Default all value set items to icons
VS_TEXT	Default all value set items to text strings
VS_RGB	Default all value set items to RGB values
VS_COLORINDEX	Default all value set items to color indices
VS_BORDER	Add a border to the value set control
VS_ITEMBORDER	Add a border around each value set item
VS_SCALEBITMAPS	Scale bitmaps to fit in cell region
VS_RIGHTTOLEFT	Support right-to-left ordering
VS_OWNERDRAW	Owner-drawn value set control

The following example program shows the creation of a value set control with the style VS_COLORINDEX.

VALUE.C

```
#define INCL_WIN
#include <os2.h>
#include <stdio.h>
#include <stdlib.h>
#include <string.h>
#include "value.h"

#define CLS_CLIENT              "MyClass"
#define USRM_LOADDLG            ( WM_USER )

static LONG alColors [] = {
   CLR_BLUE,
   CLR_PINK,
   CLR_GREEN,
   CLR_CYAN,
   CLR_YELLOW,
   CLR_NEUTRAL,
   CLR_DARKGRAY,
   CLR_DARKBLUE,
   CLR_DARKRED,
   CLR_DARKPINK,
   CLR_DARKGREEN,
   CLR_DARKCYAN
} ;

typedef struct {
   SHORT        sColor ;
   HWND         hwndDlg ;
} WNDDATA, * PWNDDATA ;

MRESULT EXPENTRY DlgProc ( HWND hwndDlg,
                           ULONG  ulMsg,
                           MPARAM mpParm1,
                           MPARAM mpParm2 ) ;

MRESULT EXPENTRY ClientWndProc ( HWND hwndWnd,
                                 ULONG ulMsg,
                                 MPARAM mpParm1,
                                 MPARAM mpParm2 ) ;

INT main ( VOID )
{
   HAB          habAnchor ;
   HMQ          hmqQueue ;
   ULONG        ulFlags ;
   HWND         hwndFrame ;
   BOOL         bLoop ;
   QMSG         qmMsg ;

   habAnchor = WinInitialize ( 0 ) ;
   hmqQueue = WinCreateMsgQueue ( habAnchor, 0 ) ;
```

```
    WinRegisterClass ( habAnchor,
                       CLS_CLIENT,
                       ClientWndProc,
                       CS_SIZEREDRAW | CS_CLIPCHILDREN,
                       sizeof ( PVOID )) ;

  ulFlags =    FCF_TITLEBAR | FCF_SYSMENU | FCF_SIZEBORDER |
               FCF_MINMAX ;

  hwndFrame = WinCreateStdWindow ( HWND_DESKTOP,
                                   0,
                                   &ulFlags,
                                   CLS_CLIENT,
                                   "Value Set Example",
                                   0,
                                   NULLHANDLE,
                                   0,
                                   NULL ) ;

  if ( hwndFrame != ( HWND ) NULL ) {
     WinSetWindowPos ( hwndFrame,
                       NULLHANDLE,
                       50,
                       50,
                       400,
                       250,
                       SWP_SIZE |
                       SWP_MOVE |
                       SWP_ACTIVATE |
                       SWP_SHOW ) ;

     bLoop = WinGetMsg ( habAnchor,
                         &qmMsg,
                         NULLHANDLE,
                         0,
                         0 ) ;
     while ( bLoop ) {
        WinDispatchMsg ( habAnchor, &qmMsg ) ;
        bLoop = WinGetMsg ( habAnchor,
                            &qmMsg,
                            NULLHANDLE,
                            0,
                            0 ) ;
     } /* endwhile */

     WinDestroyWindow ( hwndFrame ) ;
  } /* endif */

  WinDestroyMsgQueue ( hmqQueue ) ;
  WinTerminate ( habAnchor ) ;
  return 0 ;
}
```

```
MRESULT EXPENTRY ClientWndProc ( HWND   hwndWnd,
                                 ULONG  ulMsg,
                                 MPARAM mpParm1,
                                 MPARAM mpParm2 )
{
   PWNDDATA        pwdData ;

   pwdData = WinQueryWindowPtr ( hwndWnd, 0 ) ;

   switch ( ulMsg ) {

   case WM_CREATE:
      pwdData = (PWNDDATA) malloc ( sizeof ( WNDDATA )) ;
      if ( pwdData == NULL ) {
         WinAlarm ( HWND_DESKTOP, WA_ERROR ) ;
         return MRFROMSHORT ( TRUE ) ;
      } /* endif */

      WinSetWindowPtr ( hwndWnd, 0, pwdData ) ;

      pwdData -> sColor = - 1 ;

      WinPostMsg ( hwndWnd, USRM_LOADDLG, 0, 0 ) ;
      break ;

   case WM_DESTROY:
      WinDestroyWindow ( pwdData -> hwndDlg ) ;
      free ( pwdData ) ;
      break ;

   case WM_ERASEBACKGROUND:
      return MRFROMSHORT ( TRUE ) ;

   case WM_PAINT:
      {
         RECTL        rclWnd ;
         HPS          hpsPaint ;
         RECTL        rclPaint ;
         CHAR         achMsg [32] ;
         RECTL        rclBox ;

         WinQueryWindowRect ( hwndWnd, &rclWnd ) ;

         hpsPaint = WinBeginPaint ( hwndWnd,
                                    NULLHANDLE,
                                    &rclPaint ) ;
         GpiErase ( hpsPaint ) ;

         if ( pwdData -> sColor != - 1 ) {

            rclBox.xLeft = rclWnd.xRight / 8 * 6 ;
            rclBox.xRight = rclWnd.xRight / 16 * 15 ;
            rclBox.yTop = rclWnd.yTop / 8 * 7 ;
            rclBox.yBottom = rclWnd.yTop / 8 * 4 ;
```

```
                    WinFillRect ( hpsPaint,
                                  &rclBox,
                                  alColors [pwdData -> sColor] ) ;

                    sprintf ( achMsg,
                              "Color: %d",
                              pwdData -> sColor + 1 ) ;

                    rclBox.xLeft = rclWnd.xRight / 8 * 6 ;
                    rclBox.xRight = rclWnd.xRight / 16 * 15 ;
                    rclBox.yBottom = rclWnd.yTop / 8 * 4 ;
                    rclBox.yTop = rclWnd.yTop / 8 * 5 ;

                    WinDrawText ( hpsPaint,
                                  strlen ( achMsg ) ,
                                  achMsg,
                                  &rclBox,
                                  0,
                                  0,
                                  DT_CENTER | DT_VCENTER | DT_TEXTATTRS |
                                  DT_ERASERECT ) ;
                } /* endif */

                WinEndPaint ( hpsPaint ) ;
            }
            break ;

        case USRM_LOADDLG:
            pwdData -> hwndDlg = WinLoadDlg ( hwndWnd,
                                             hwndWnd,
                                             DlgProc,
                                             NULLHANDLE,
                                             IDD_VALUE,
                                             NULL ) ;
            break ;

        default:
            return WinDefWindowProc ( hwndWnd,
                                      ulMsg,
                                      mpParm1,
                                      mpParm2 ) ;
    } /* endswitch */

    return MRFROMSHORT ( FALSE ) ;
}

MRESULT EXPENTRY DlgProc ( HWND hwndDlg,
                           ULONG ulMsg,
                           MPARAM mpParm1,
                           MPARAM mpParm2 )
{
    PWNDDATA pwdData ;

    pwdData = WinQueryWindowPtr ( WinQueryWindow ( hwndDlg,
                                                   QW_PARENT ) ,
                                  0 ) ;
```

```
switch ( ulMsg ) {
case WM_INITDLG:
    {
        SHORT       sColor ;
        USHORT      usX ;
        USHORT      usY ;
        HWND        hwndParent ;

        sColor = 0 ;

        for ( usX = 1 ; usX <= 3 ; usX ++ ) {
            for ( usY = 1 ; usY <= 4 ; usY ++ ) {
                WinSendDlgItemMsg ( hwndDlg,
                                    IDV_VALUE,
                                    VM_SETITEM,
                                    MPFROM2SHORT ( usX, usY ) ,
                                    MPFROMLONG (
                                      alColors [sColor ++ ] )) ;
            } /* endfor */
        } /* endfor */

        WinSendDlgItemMsg ( hwndDlg,
                            IDV_VALUE,
                            VM_SELECTITEM,
                            MPFROM2SHORT ( 1, 1 ) ,
                            NULL ) ;

        pwdData -> sColor = 0 ;
        hwndParent = WinQueryWindow ( hwndDlg, QW_PARENT ) ;
        WinInvalidateRect ( hwndParent, NULL, FALSE ) ;
        WinUpdateWindow ( hwndParent ) ;
    }
    break ;

case WM_CONTROL:
    switch ( SHORT1FROMMP ( mpParm1 )) {
    case IDV_VALUE:
        switch ( SHORT2FROMMP ( mpParm1 )) {
        case VN_SELECT:
            {
                MRESULT     mrReply ;
                HWND        hwndParent ;

                mrReply = WinSendDlgItemMsg ( hwndDlg,
                                              IDV_VALUE,
                                              VM_QUERYSELECTEDITEM,
                                              0,
                                              0 ) ;

                pwdData -> sColor = ( SHORT1FROMMR ( mrReply ) - 1 )
                    * 4 + SHORT2FROMMR ( mrReply ) - 1 ;

                hwndParent = WinQueryWindow ( hwndDlg, QW_PARENT ) ;
                WinInvalidateRect ( hwndParent, NULL, FALSE ) ;
                WinUpdateWindow ( hwndParent ) ;
            }
            break ;
```

```
            default:
                return WinDefDlgProc ( hwndDlg,
                                       ulMsg,
                                       mpParm1,
                                       mpParm2 ) ;
            } /* endswitch */
            break ;

        default:
            return WinDefDlgProc ( hwndDlg,
                                   ulMsg,
                                   mpParm1,
                                   mpParm2 ) ;
        } /* endswitch */
        break ;

    case WM_SYSCOMMAND:
        switch ( SHORT1FROMMP ( mpParm1 )) {

        case SC_CLOSE:
            WinPostMsg ( WinQueryWindow ( hwndDlg, QW_PARENT ) ,
                         WM_CLOSE,
                         0,
                         0 ) ;
            break ;

        default:
            return WinDefDlgProc ( hwndDlg,
                                   ulMsg,
                                   mpParm1,
                                   mpParm2 ) ;
        } /* endswitch */
        break ;

    case WM_COMMAND:
        switch ( SHORT1FROMMP ( mpParm1 )) {
        case DID_OK:
        case DID_CANCEL:
            break ;

        default:
            return WinDefDlgProc ( hwndDlg,
                                   ulMsg,
                                   mpParm1,
                                   mpParm2 ) ;
        } /* endswitch */
        break ;

    default:
        return WinDefDlgProc ( hwndDlg,
                               ulMsg,
                               mpParm1,
                               mpParm2 ) ;
    } /* endswitch */
    return MRFROMSHORT ( FALSE ) ;
}
```

VALUE.RC

```
#include <os2.h>
#include "value.h"

DLGTEMPLATE IDD_VALUE
{
    DIALOG  "Color Set", IDD_VALUE, 58, 36, 105, 75,
       WS_VISIBLE, FCF_TITLEBAR | FCF_SYSMENU
    {
       LTEXT "Choose Color", -1, 10, 10, 85, 8
       CONTROL "", IDV_VALUE, 12, 27, 81, 41, WC_VALUESET,
          VS_COLORINDEX | VS_BORDER | WS_TABSTOP | WS_VISIBLE
          CTLDATA 8, 0, 3, 4
    }
}
```

VALUE.H

```
#define IDD_VALUE            256
#define IDV_VALUE            512
```

VALUE.MAK

```
VALUE.EXE:                    VALUE.OBJ \
                              VALUE.RES

       LINK386 @<<
VALUE
VALUE
VALUE
OS2386
VALUE
<<
       RC VALUE.RES VALUE.EXE

VALUE.RES:                    VALUE.RC \
                              VALUE.H
       RC -r VALUE.RC VALUE.RES

VALUE.OBJ:                    VALUE.C \
                              VALUE.H
       ICC -C+ -Kb+ -Ss+ VALUE.C
```

VALUE.DEF

```
NAME VALUE WINDOWAPI

DESCRIPTION 'Value-set example
Copyright (c) 1992 by Kathleen Panov.
All rights reserved.'

STACKSIZE 16384
```

13.2 The VALUE.RC Resource File

The value.rc file contains two items: a menu and a dialog with the value set control. The dialog is created with the following code:

```
DLGTEMPLATE IDD_VALUE
BEGIN
    DIALOG   "Color Set", IDD_VALUE, 58, 36, 105, 94, WS_VISIBLE,
             FCF_SYSMENU | FCF_TITLEBAR
             PRESPARAMS PP_BACKGROUNDCOLORINDEX, CLR_WHITE
    BEGIN
        CONTROL        "", IDV_VALUE, 20, 37, 58, 43, WC_VALUESET,
                       VS_COLORINDEX | VS_BORDER | WS_TABSTOP |
                       WS_VISIBLE
                       CTLDATA 8, 0, 3, 4
        LTEXT          "Choose Color", -1, 16, 22, 66, 8
                       PRESPARAMS PP_BACKGROUNDCOLORINDEX,
                       CLR_WHITE
        PUSHBUTTON     "OK", DID_OK, 10, 3, 40, 12
    END
END
```

Notice the CONTROL statement after BEGIN. This is the statement used to define the value set. The first parameter is the text for the value set control. In our case, this is blank. The second parameter is the resource id for the control. The next two parameters are the *x,y* coordinates of the value set control on the dialog box. The next two parameters define the height and width of the control, respectively. The seventh parameter is the window class, in this case WC_VALUESET. The eighth parameter is the combination of window and control styles. In this case, we specify VS_COLORINDEX, indicating that the choices of the value set are the indices into the color index table. We also use VS_BORDER, which draws a border around the value set. The window styles used are WS_TABSTOP and WS_VISIBLE. The last parameter is the CTLDATA statement. In this case, this represents the VSCDATA structure. The VSCDATA structure is defined as:

```
typedef struct _VSCDATA /* vscd */
{
    ULONG   cbSize;        /* Size of control block          */
    USHORT  usRowCount;    /* Number of rows in value set    */
    USHORT  usColumnCount;/* Number of columns in value set  */
} VSCDATA;
typedef VSCDATA *PVSCDATA;
```

The CTLDATA key word sees each parameter as a SHORT, so a LONG is represented as two parameters. The first two parameters correspond to the *cbSize* structure member. They are specified in low-byte, high-byte order. The third parameter, 3, represents *usRowCount*. Our value set will contain three rows. The fourth parameter, 4, represents *usColumnCount*. Our value set will contain four columns.

There is a structure defined at the top of the program that is used for the window word. It is:

```
typedef struct {
    SHORT         sColor ;
    HWND          hwndDlg ;
} WNDDATA, * PWNDDATA ;
```

In the structure, the first element SHORT *sColor* represents the currently selected color in the value set. The second element is the window handle for the dialog box.

After the definition of the structures, the array *alColor* is declared. This is the array of color-index values that are used in the value set.

13.3 *ClientWndProc*

```
PWNDDATA pwdData;
pwdData=WinQueryWindowPtr(hwndWnd,0);
```

In the client window procedure, the first variable declared is the pointer to our window word structure, PWNDDATA *pwdData*. Most of the messages in the switch statement will use this data, so this pointer will be visible to the entire function. *WinQueryWindowPtr* is put at the top of the window procedure for the same reason.

```
case WM_PAINT:
    {
        RECTL         rclWnd ;
        HPS           hpsPaint ;
        RECTL         rclPaint ;
        CHAR          achMsg [32] ;
        RECTL         rclBox ;

        WinQueryWindowRect ( hwndWnd, &rclWnd ) ;

        hpsPaint = WinBeginPaint ( hwndWnd,
                                   NULLHANDLE,
                                   &rclPaint ) ;
        GpiErase ( hpsPaint ) ;

        if ( pwdData -> sColor != - 1 ) {

            rclBox.xLeft = rclWnd.xRight / 8 * 6 ;
            rclBox.xRight = rclWnd.xRight / 16 * 15 ;
```

```
                    rclBox.yTop = rclWnd.yTop / 8 * 7 ;
                    rclBox.yBottom = rclWnd.yTop / 8 * 4 ;

                    WinFillRect ( hpsPaint,
                                  &rclBox,
                                  alColors [pwdData -> sColor] ) ;

                    sprintf ( achMsg,
                              "Color: %d",
                              pwdData -> sColor + 1 ) ;

                    rclBox.xLeft = rclWnd.xRight / 8 * 6 ;
                    rclBox.xRight = rclWnd.xRight / 16 * 15 ;
                    rclBox.yBottom = rclWnd.yTop / 8 * 4 ;
                    rclBox.yTop = rclWnd.yTop / 8 * 5 ;

                    WinDrawText ( hpsPaint,
                                  strlen ( achMsg ) ,
                                  achMsg,
                                  &rclBox,
                                  0,
                                  0,
                                  DT_CENTER | DT_VCENTER | DT_TEXTATTRS |
                                  DT_ERASERECT ) ;
                 } /* endif */

              WinEndPaint ( hpsPaint ) ;
           }
           break ;
```

The WM_PAINT message starts with *WinQueryWindowRect* to determine the
size of the client window. Next, the usual *WinBeginPaint* is called. *GpiErase*
is used to erase the entire invalidated region. Before a color has been selected
from the value set, *sColor* is set to –1. A check is made to see if a color has
been selected from the value set. If so, we draw the color box, and print some
text to indicate the currently selected color.

13.4 The Dialog Procedure, *DlgProc*

```
case WM_CONTROL:
    switch ( SHORT1FROMMP ( mpParm1 )) {
    case IDV_VALUE:
        switch ( SHORT2FROMMP ( mpParm1 )) {
        case VN_SELECT:
            {
                MRESULT      mrReply ;
                HWND         hwndParent ;

                mrReply = WinSendDlgItemMsg ( hwndDlg,
                                              IDV_VALUE,
                                              VM_QUERYSELECTEDITEM,
                                              0,
                                              0 ) ;
```

```
        pwdData -> sColor = ( SHORT1FROMMR ( mrReply ) - 1 )
           * 4 + SHORT2FROMMR ( mrReply ) - 1 ;

        hwndParent = WinQueryWindow ( hwndDlg, QW_PARENT ) ;
        WinInvalidateRect ( hwndParent, NULL, FALSE ) ;
        WinUpdateWindow ( hwndParent ) ;
      }
      break ;
```

The WM_CONTROL message is where the value set will indicate when a new color has been selected. We check for the notification code VN_SELECT from the WM_CONTROL message. If this is the case, the first thing we do is determine which item has been selected. The message VM_QUERYSELECTEDITEM is sent to perform this function. The return *mrReply* is a set of two SHORTS that contain the row and column of the selected item.

Gotcha!

There is a discrepancy between the documentation and what actually happens with the VN_SELECT message in OS/2 2.0 GA. The docs indicate that *mpParm2* contains the row and column of the selected item. This is the case in 2.1, but in 2.0 GA, *mpParm2* does not contain these values.

Once we determine which item is selected, we set *sColor* to the new value, invalidate the client window, and force a repaint using *WinUpdateWindow*.

13.5 Initializing the Value Set

```
SHORT        sColor ;
USHORT       usX ;
USHORT       usY ;
HWND         hwndParent ;

sColor = 0 ;

for ( usX = 1 ; usX <= 3 ; usX ++ ) {
   for ( usY = 1 ; usY <= 4 ; usY ++ ) {
      WinSendDlgItemMsg ( hwndDlg,
                          IDV_VALUE,
                          VM_SETITEM,
                          MPFROM2SHORT ( usX, usY ) ,
                          MPFROMLONG (
                            alColors [sColor ++ ] )) ;
```

```
        } /* endfor */
    } /* endfor */

    WinSendDlgItemMsg ( hwndDlg,
                        IDV_VALUE,
                        VM_SELECTITEM,
                        MPFROM2SHORT ( 1, 1 ) ,
                        NULL ) ;

    pwdData -> sColor = 0 ;
    hwndParent = WinQueryWindow ( hwndDlg, QW_PARENT ) ;
    WinInvalidateRect ( hwndParent, NULL, FALSE ) ;
    WinUpdateWindow ( hwndParent ) ;
}
break ;
```

The value set initialization is a very simple process of sending a VM_SETITEM for each item in the value set. Because this value set is of style VS_COLORINDEX, *mpParm2* will contain a CLR_* value. *mpParm1* is a collection of two SHORTS that make up the row and column of the item. Notice that there is no row or column 0; these values start at 1.

Once all the items are in place, we want to select the first item. This is done using the message VM_SELECTITEM. *mpParm1* is the row and column of the item to be selected. The color index to this item, 0, is set equal to *sColor*.

The last step is to invalidate the client window region and force a repaint.

13.6 Value Set Messages

WM_CONTROL
Sent when a control is to notify its owner of a significant event.

Parameter 1:	USHORT usID	value set control ID
	USHORT usNotifyCode	VN_DRAGLEAVE, VN_DRAGOVER, VN_DROP, VN_DROPHELP, VN_ENTER, VN_HELP, VN_INITDRAG, VN_KILLFOCUS, VN_SELECT, VN_SETFOCUS
Parameter 2:	ULONG ulNotifyInfo	for VN_DRAGOVER, VN_DRAGLEAVE, VN_DROP, or VN_DROPHELP pointer to VSDRAGINFO structure

```
typedef struct _VSDRAGINFO {
        PDRAGINFO pDragInfo; /* pointer to DRAGINFO structure */
        USHORT usRow;              /* Row */
        USHORT usColumn;           /* Column */
} VSDRAGINFO

typedef struct _DRAGINFO {
        ULONG ulDraginfo;          /* structure size */
        ULONG usDragitem;          /* DRAGITEM structures sizes */
        SHORT usOperation;         /* modified drag operations */
        HWND hwndSource;           /* window handle */
        SHORT xDrop;               /* x-coordinate */
        SHORT yDrop;               /* y-coordinate */
        USHORT cditem;             /* count of DRAGITEM structures */
        USHORT usReserved;         /* reserved */
} DRAGINFO;
```

for VN_INITDRAG, pointer to
VSDRAGINIT structure

```
typedef struct _VSDRAGINIT {
        HWND hwndVS;               /* value set window handle */
        LONG x;                    /* x-coordinate */
        LONG y;                    /* y-coordinate */
        LONG cx;                   /* x-offset */
        LONG cy;                   /* y-offset */
        USHORT usRow;              /* row */
        USHORT usColumn;           /* column */
} VSDRAGINIT;
```

for VN_ENTER, VN_HELP, or
VN_SELECT, contains row and
column of selected item; low byte
is row, and high byte is column

Reply: ULONG ulReply   reserved, 0

WM_CONTROLPOINTER

Sent to an owner of a control when the mouse pointer moves over the control
window, allowing the pointer to be set.

Parameter 1:	USHORT usIdCtrl	control ID
Parameter 2:	HPOINTER hptrNew	handle of new pointer to be set
Reply:	HPOINTER hptrReturn	handle of actual pointer that is in use

WM_DRAWITEM
Sent to the owner of a value set when an item with VIA_OWNERDRAW is to be drawn, or when the value set window of style VS_OWNERDRAW is to be drawn.

Parameter 1:	USHORT usID	window ID
Parameter 2:	POWNERITEM pownerOwnerItem	pointer to OWNERITEM structure
Reply:	BOOL fDrawn	drawn? TRUE:FALSE

VM_QUERYITEM
Queries the contents of the specified item.

Parameter 1:	USHORT usRow	row
	USHORT usColumn	column
Parameter 2:	PVSTEXT pvsText	pointer to VSTEXT structure

```
typedef struct _VSTEXT {
      PSZ pszItemText;        /* pointer */
      USHORT usBufLen;        /* buffer size */
} VSTEXT;
```

Reply:	ULONG ulItemID	item information

VM_QUERYITEMATTR
Queries the attribute(s) of the item specified.

Parameter 1:	USHORT usRow	row
	USHORT usColumn	column
Parameter 2:	ULONG ulParm2	reserved, 0
Reply:	USHORT usItemAttr	VIA_BITMAP, VIA_COLORINDEX, VIA_ICON, VIA_RGB, VIA_TEXT, VIA_DISABLED, VIA_DRAGGABLE, VIA_DROPONABLE, VIA_OWNERDRAW

VM_QUERYMETRICS
Queries for the current size of each value set item, or the spacing between them.

Parameter 1:	USHORT usMetric	control metrics VMA_ITEMSIZE or VMA_ITEMSPACING
Parameter 2:	ULONG ulParm2	reserved, 0
Reply:	ULONG ulMetric	*usWidth*, in pixels, and *usHeight*, in pixels

VM_QUERYSELECTEDITEM
Queries for the currently selected item in the value set.

Parameter 1:	ULONG ulParam1	reserved, 0
Parameter 2:	ULONG ulParam2	reserved, 0
Reply:	USHORT usRow	row
	USHORT usCol	column

VM_SELECTITEM
Selects the specified value, deselecting the previously selected item.

Parameter 1:	USHORT usRow	row
	USHORT usColumn	column
Parameter 2:	ULONG ulParm2	reserved, 0
Reply:	BOOL fSuccess	successful? TRUE:FALSE

VM_SETITEM
Specifies type of information contained by an item.

Parameter 1:	USHORT usRow	row
	USHORT usColumn	column
Parameter 2:	ULONG ulItemInfo	item information if VIA_TEXT, will be pszItemTextString if VIA_BITMAP, will be HBITMAP hbmItemBitamp if VIA_ICON, will be HPOINTER hptrItemPointer

		if VIA_RGB, will be ULONG rbgItem
		if VIA_COLORINDEX, will be ulColorIndex
Reply:	BOOL fSuccess	successful? TRUE:FALSE

VM_SETITEMATTR

Sets the attribute(s) of the specified item.

Parameter 1:	USHORT usRow	row
	USHORT usColumn	column
Parameter 2:	USHORT usItemAttr	item attributes VIA_BITMAP, VIA_ICON, VIA_TEXT, VIA_RGB, VIA_COLORINDEX, VIA_OWNERDRAW, VIA_DISABLED, VIA_DRAGGABLE, VIA_DROPONABLE
	USHORT fSet	set? TRUE:FALSE
Reply:	BOOL fSuccess	successful? TRUE:FALSE

VM_SETMETRICS

Sets the size of the value set items, or the spacing between them.

Parameter 1:	USHORT fMetric	VMA_ITEMSIZE, or VMA_ITEMSPACING
Parameter 2:	USHORT usWidth	width of item if VMA_ITEMSIZE, space between horizontal if VMA_ITEMSPACING
	USHORT usHeight	height of item if VMA_ITEMSIZE, space between vertical if VMA_ITEMSPACING
Reply:	BOOL fSuccess	successful? TRUE:FALSE

WM_CHAR

Sent when a key is pressed.

Parameter 1:	USHORT usFlags	keyboard control code

	UCHAR ucRepeat	repeat count
	UCHAR ucScanCode	hardware scan code
Parameter 2:	USHORT usChar	character code
	USHORT usVK	virtual key code
Reply:	BOOL fResult	processed? TRUE:FALSE

WM_PREPARAMCHANGED

Sent whenever a Presentation Parameter is set or removed. Also sent to all windows owned by the window whose parameter was changed.

Parameter 1:	ULONG ulAttrType	PP_FOREGROUNDCOLOR,
		PP_FOREGROUNDCOLORINDEX,
		PP_BACKGROUNDCOLOR,
		PP_BACKGROUNDCOLORINDEX,
		PP_HILITEBACKGROUNDCOLOR,
		PP_HILITEBACKGROUNDCOLORINDEX,
		PP_BORDERCOLOR,
		PP_BORDERCOLORINDEX
Parameter 2:	ULONG ulReserved	reserved, 0
Reply:	ULONG ulReply	reserved, 0

WM_QUERYWINDOWPARAMS

Sent when an application queries the window parameters.

Parameter 1:	PWNDPARAMS ptrWndParams	pointer to
		WNDPARAMS structure

```
typedef struct _WNDPARAMS     /* wprm */
{
     ULONG    fsStatus; /* value value are WPM_CBCTLDATA or
              WPM_CTLDATA */
     ULONG    cchText;
     PSZ      pszText;
     ULONG    cbPresParams;
     PVOID    pPresParams;
     ULONG    cbCtlData;
     PVOID    pCtlData;
  } WNDPARAMS;
  typedef WNDPARAMS *PWNDPARAMS;

typedef struct _VSCDATA /* vscd */
{
     ULONG cbSize; /* size of control block */
     USHORT usRowCount; /* number of rows in value set */
     USHORT usColumnCount; /* number of columns in value set */
}
```

Parameter 2:	ULONG ulReserved	reserved, 0
Reply:	BOOL fSuccess	successful? TRUE:FALSE

WM_SETWINDOWPARAMS

Sent when an application sets or changes the window parameters.

Parameter 1:	PWNDPARAMS ptrWindowParams	pointer to WNDPARAMS structure (see above)
Parameter 2:	ULONG ulReserved	reserved, 0
Reply:	BOOL fSuccess	successful? TRUE:FALSE

WM_SIZE

Sent when a window changes its size.

Parameter 1:	SHORT sCxOld	old window width
	SHORT sCyOld	old window height
Parameter 2:	SHORTsCxNew	new window width
	SHORT sCyNew	new window height
Reply:	ULONG ulReply	reserved, 0

Chapter 14

Spin Buttons

A spin button is a button that will display a list of choices to the user. Up and down arrows are displayed to the right of the button, and are used to "spin" through the choices. Spin buttons should be used when the choices can be organized into some logical, consecutive order. For example, a list of days of the week would be a good use for a spin button. A spin button can be read-only, or can be edited similar to an entry-field.

14.1 Spin Button Styles

STYLE	DESCRIPTION
SPBS_ALLCHARACTERS	All characters are accepted into spin button
SPBS_NUMERICONLY	Only the characters 0–9 are accepted into spin button
SPBS_READONLY	No characters are allowed into spin button
SPBS_MASTER	Spin button will have arrows displayed to the right
SPBS_SERVANT	Spin button has no arrows, but is attached to a set of spin buttons that share one set of arrows

SPBS_JUSTLEFT	Left-justify the spin button text
SPBS_JUSTRIGHT	Right-justify the spin button text
SPBS_JUSTCENTER	Center the spin button text
SPBS_NOBORDER	No border will be drawn around spin button
SPBS_FASTSPIN	Spin button can skip over numbers, when arrows are held down
SPBS_PADWITHZEROS	Pad the number with zeros

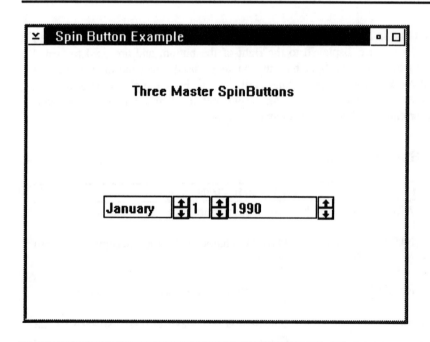

Figure 14.1 The SPBS_MASTER Style.

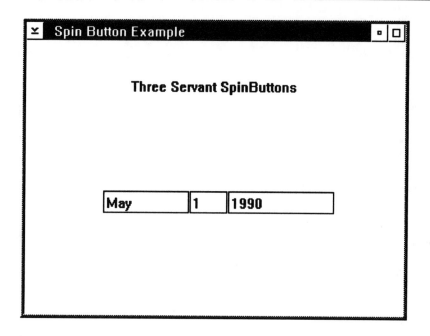

Figure 14.2 The SPBS_SERVANT style.

Figure 14.1 illustrates three master spin buttons, and Figure 14.2 illustrates three servant spin buttons.

The following example program shows how to use a spin button in a program.

SPIN.C

```
#define INCL_WIN
#include <os2.h>
#include <stdio.h>
#include <stdlib.h>
#include "spin.h"

#define CLS_CLIENT              "MyClass"

PCHAR achMonthArray [] = {
    "January",
    "February",
    "March",
    "April",
    "May",
    "June",
```

```
    "July",
    "August",
    "September",
    "October",
    "November",
    "December"
} ;

PCHAR achDayArray [] = {
    "1",
    "2",
    "3",
    "4",
    "5",
    "6",
    "7",
    "8",
    "9",
    "10",
    "11",
    "12",
    "13",
    "14",
    "15",
    "16",
    "17",
    "18",
    "19",
    "20",
    "21",
    "22",
    "23",
    "24",
    "25",
    "26",
    "27",
    "28",
    "29",
    "30",
    "31"
} ;

PCHAR achYearArray [] = {
    "1990",
    "1991",
    "1992",
    "1993",
    "1994",
    "1995",
    "1996",
    "1997",
    "1998",
    "1999",
    "2000"
} ;
```

```
MRESULT EXPENTRY ClientWndProc ( HWND hwndWnd,
                                 ULONG ulMsg,
                                 MPARAM mpParm1,
                                 MPARAM mpParm2 ) ;

INT main ( VOID )
{
   HAB          habAnchor ;
   HMQ          hmqQueue ;
   ULONG        ulFlags ;
   LONG         lHeight ;
   LONG         lWidth ;
   HWND         hwndFrame ;
   HWND         hwndClient ;
   BOOL         bLoop ;
   QMSG         qmMsg ;

   habAnchor = WinInitialize ( 0 ) ;
   hmqQueue = WinCreateMsgQueue ( habAnchor, 0 ) ;

   WinRegisterClass ( habAnchor,
                      CLS_CLIENT,
                      ClientWndProc,
                      CS_SIZEREDRAW | CS_SYNCPAINT,
                      0 ) ;

   ulFlags = FCF_TITLEBAR | FCF_SYSMENU | FCF_SIZEBORDER |
             FCF_MINMAX | FCF_ACCELTABLE ;

   hwndFrame = WinCreateStdWindow ( HWND_DESKTOP,
                                    0,
                                    &ulFlags,
                                    CLS_CLIENT,
                                    "Spin Button Example",
                                    0,
                                    NULLHANDLE,
                                    ID_WINDOW,
                                    &hwndClient ) ;

   if ( hwndFrame != NULLHANDLE ) {

      lHeight = WinQuerySysValue ( HWND_DESKTOP, SV_CYSCREEN ) ;
      lWidth  = WinQuerySysValue ( HWND_DESKTOP, SV_CXSCREEN ) ;

      WinSetWindowPos ( hwndFrame,
                        NULLHANDLE,
                        lWidth  / 4,
                        lHeight / 4,
                        lWidth  / 2,
                        lHeight / 2,
                        SWP_SIZE | SWP_MOVE |
                        SWP_ACTIVATE | SWP_SHOW ) ;
```

```
        bLoop = WinGetMsg ( habAnchor,
                            &qmMsg,
                            NULLHANDLE,
                            0,
                            0 ) ;
     while ( bLoop ) {
        WinDispatchMsg ( habAnchor, &qmMsg ) ;
        bLoop = WinGetMsg ( habAnchor,
                            &qmMsg,
                            NULLHANDLE,
                            0,
                            0 ) ;
     } /* endwhile */

     WinDestroyWindow ( hwndFrame ) ;
  } /* endif */

  WinDestroyMsgQueue ( hmqQueue ) ;
  WinTerminate ( habAnchor ) ;
  return 0 ;
}

MRESULT EXPENTRY ClientWndProc ( HWND hwndWnd,
                                 ULONG ulMsg,
                                 MPARAM mpParm1,
                                 MPARAM mpParm2 )
{
  switch ( ulMsg ) {

  case WM_CREATE:
     {
        ULONG       ulMonthStyle ;
        ULONG       ulDayStyle ;
        ULONG       ulYearStyle ;
        LONG        lWidth ;
        LONG        lHeight ;
        LONG        xPosition ;
        LONG        yPosition ;
        LONG        yHeight ;

        ulMonthStyle = SPBS_SERVANT | SPBS_READONLY |
                       SPBS_JUSTLEFT | SPBS_FASTSPIN |
                       WS_VISIBLE ;

        ulDayStyle =   SPBS_SERVANT | SPBS_READONLY |
                       SPBS_JUSTLEFT | SPBS_FASTSPIN |
                       WS_VISIBLE ;

        ulYearStyle =  SPBS_MASTER | SPBS_READONLY |
                       SPBS_JUSTLEFT | SPBS_FASTSPIN |
                       WS_VISIBLE ;

        lHeight = WinQuerySysValue ( HWND_DESKTOP,
                                 SV_CYSCREEN ) / 2 ;
        lWidth  = WinQuerySysValue ( HWND_DESKTOP,
                                 SV_CXSCREEN ) / 2 ;
```

```
     xPosition = lWidth / 5 ;
     yPosition = lHeight / 3 ;
     yHeight = 50 ;

WinCreateWindow ( hwndWnd,
                    WC_SPINBUTTON,
                    NULL,
                    ulMonthStyle,
                    xPosition,
                    yPosition,
                    90,
                    yHeight,
                    hwndWnd,
                    HWND_TOP,
                    ID_SPINBUTTONMONTH,
                    NULL,
                    NULL ) ;

WinCreateWindow ( hwndWnd,
                    WC_SPINBUTTON,
                    NULL,
                    ulDayStyle,
                    xPosition + 90,
                    yPosition,
                    40,
                    yHeight,
                    hwndWnd,
                    HWND_TOP,
                    ID_SPINBUTTONDAY,
                    NULL,
                    NULL ) ;

WinCreateWindow ( hwndWnd,
                    WC_SPINBUTTON,
                    NULL,
                    ulYearStyle,
                    xPosition + 90 + 40,
                    yPosition,
                    110,
                    yHeight,
                    hwndWnd,
                    HWND_TOP,
                    ID_SPINBUTTONYEAR,
                    NULL,
                    NULL ) ;

WinSendDlgItemMsg ( hwndWnd,
                    ID_SPINBUTTONMONTH,
                    SPBM_SETARRAY,
                    MPFROMP ( achMonthArray ) ,
                    MPFROMSHORT ( 12 )) ;
```

```
            WinSendDlgItemMsg ( hwndWnd,
                                ID_SPINBUTTONMONTH,
                                SPBM_SETMASTER,
                                MPFROMHWND ( WinWindowFromID (
                                                 hwndWnd,
                                                 ID_SPINBUTTONYEAR )),
                                0 ) ;

            WinSendDlgItemMsg ( hwndWnd,
                                ID_SPINBUTTONDAY,
                                SPBM_SETARRAY,
                                MPFROMP ( achDayArray ) ,
                                MPFROMSHORT ( 31 ) ) ;

            WinSendDlgItemMsg ( hwndWnd,
                                ID_SPINBUTTONDAY,
                                SPBM_SETMASTER,
                                MPFROMHWND ( WinWindowFromID (
                                                 hwndWnd,
                                                 ID_SPINBUTTONYEAR )),
                                0 ) ;

            WinSendDlgItemMsg ( hwndWnd,
                                ID_SPINBUTTONYEAR,
                                SPBM_SETARRAY,
                                MPFROMP ( achYearArray ) ,
                                MPFROMSHORT ( 11 ) ) ;

            WinSetFocus ( HWND_DESKTOP,
                          WinWindowFromID ( hwndWnd,
                                            ID_SPINBUTTONMONTH ) ) ;
        }
        break ;

    case WM_CONTROL:
        {
        USHORT        usID ;
        USHORT        usNotifyCode ;
        RECTL         rclWindow ;

        usID = SHORT1FROMMP ( mpParm1 ) ;
        usNotifyCode = SHORT2FROMMP ( mpParm1 ) ;

        if ( usID == ID_SPINBUTTONDAY ||
             usID == ID_SPINBUTTONMONTH ||
             usID == ID_SPINBUTTONYEAR ) {

            if ( usNotifyCode == SPBN_ENDSPIN ) {

                WinQueryWindowRect ( hwndWnd, &rclWindow ) ;
                rclWindow.yBottom = ( rclWindow.yTop -
                                      rclWindow.yBottom ) / 3 * 2 ;

                WinInvalidateRect ( hwndWnd,
                                    &rclWindow,
                                    FALSE ) ;
```

```
            } else {
               return WinDefWindowProc ( hwndWnd,
                                         ulMsg,
                                         mpParm1,
                                         mpParm2 ) ;
            } /* endif */
         } else {
            return WinDefWindowProc ( hwndWnd,
                                      ulMsg,
                                      mpParm1,
                                      mpParm2 ) ;
         } /* endif */
      }
   break ;
case WM_COMMAND:
   {
      HWND          hwndActive ;
      USHORT        usFocusID ;

      if ( SHORT1FROMMP ( mpParm2 ) == CMDSRC_ACCELERATOR ) {

         hwndActive = WinQueryFocus ( HWND_DESKTOP ) ;
         usFocusID = WinQueryWindowUShort ( hwndActive,
                                            QWS_ID ) ;

         if ( SHORT1FROMMP ( mpParm1 ) == IDK_TAB ) {
            usFocusID ++ ;

            if ( usFocusID > LAST_CONTROL ) {
               usFocusID = FIRST_CONTROL ;
            } /* endif */

            hwndActive = WinWindowFromID ( hwndWnd,
                                           usFocusID ) ;
            WinSetFocus ( HWND_DESKTOP, hwndActive ) ;

         } else

         if ( SHORT1FROMMP ( mpParm1 ) == IDK_BACKTAB ) {
            usFocusID -- ;

            if ( usFocusID < FIRST_CONTROL ) {
               usFocusID = LAST_CONTROL ;
            } /* endif */

            hwndActive = WinWindowFromID ( hwndWnd,
                                           usFocusID ) ;
            WinSetFocus ( HWND_DESKTOP, hwndActive ) ;

         } /* endif */
      } /* endif */
   }
   break ;
```

```
case WM_PAINT:
    {
        HPS         hpsPaint ;
        RECTL       rclBox ;
        CHAR        achMonth [15] ;
        CHAR        achDay [3] ;
        CHAR        achYear [5] ;
        CHAR        achMsg [128] ;

        hpsPaint = WinBeginPaint ( hwndWnd,
                                   NULLHANDLE,
                                   NULL ) ;

        WinQueryWindowRect ( hwndWnd, &rclBox ) ;

        rclBox.yBottom = ( rclBox.yTop - rclBox.yBottom ) / 3 *
                           2 ;

        WinFillRect ( hpsPaint, &rclBox, CLR_WHITE ) ;

        WinSendDlgItemMsg ( hwndWnd,
                            ID_SPINBUTTONMONTH,
                            SPBM_QUERYVALUE,
                            MPFROMP ( achMonth ) ,
                            MPFROM2SHORT ( sizeof ( achMonth ) ,
                              SPBQ_DONOTUPDATE )) ;

        WinSendDlgItemMsg ( hwndWnd,
                            ID_SPINBUTTONDAY,
                            SPBM_QUERYVALUE,
                            MPFROMP ( achDay ) ,
                            MPFROM2SHORT ( sizeof ( achDay ) ,
                              SPBQ_DONOTUPDATE )) ;

        WinSendDlgItemMsg ( hwndWnd,
                            ID_SPINBUTTONYEAR,
                            SPBM_QUERYVALUE,
                            MPFROMP ( achYear ) ,
                            MPFROM2SHORT ( sizeof ( achYear ) ,
                              SPBQ_DONOTUPDATE )) ;

        sprintf ( achMsg,
                "SpinButton's set to: %s %s, %s",
                achMonth,
                achDay,
                achYear ) ;

        WinDrawText ( hpsPaint,
                      -1,
                      achMsg,
                      &rclBox,
                      0,
                      0,
                      DT_CENTER | DT_VCENTER | DT_TEXTATTRS ) ;

        WinEndPaint ( hpsPaint ) ;
    }
```

```
        break ;
    case WM_ERASEBACKGROUND:
        return MRFROMSHORT ( TRUE ) ;

    default:
        return WinDefWindowProc ( hwndWnd,
                                  ulMsg,
                                  mpParm1,
                                  mpParm2 ) ;
    } /* endswitch */

    return MRFROMSHORT ( FALSE ) ;
}
```

SPIN.RC

```
#include <os2.h>
#include "spin.h"

ACCELTABLE ID_WINDOW
{
    VK_TAB, IDK_TAB, VIRTUALKEY
    VK_BACKTAB, IDK_BACKTAB, VIRTUALKEY
}
```

SPIN.H

```
#define ID_WINDOW               101
#define ID_SPINBUTTONMONTH      102
#define ID_SPINBUTTONDAY        103
#define ID_SPINBUTTONYEAR       104
#define IDK_TAB                 105
#define IDK_BACKTAB             106
#define FIRST_CONTROL           ID_SPINBUTTONMONTH
#define LAST_CONTROL            ID_SPINBUTTONYEAR
```

SPIN.MAK

```
SPIN.EXE:                       SPIN.OBJ \
                                SPIN.RES
        LINK386 @<<
SPIN
SPIN
SPIN
OS2386
SPIN
<<
        RC SPIN.RES SPIN.EXE

SPIN.RES:                       SPIN.RC \
                                SPIN.H
        RC -r SPIN.RC SPIN.RES

SPIN.OBJ:                       SPIN.C \
                                SPIN.H
        ICC -C+ -Kb+ -Ss+ SPIN.C
```

SPIN.DEF

```
NAME SPIN WINDOWAPI

DESCRIPTION 'Spin button example
Copyright (c) 1992 by Kathleen Panov
All rights reserved.'

STACKSIZE 16384
```

14.2 Device Independence, Almost

One new feature will be added to *main* in this example — a mini form of device independence. SVGA is becoming very popular, and supporting both 1024x768 and 640x480 screen resolutions in your programs can be quite painful. Unfortunately, Presentation Manager does not guarantee that your programs will be dimensioned proportionally at both resolutions. The best way to make your program look great at any resolution is to size your windows according to the screen size. "But how will I know how big the screen is?", you may ask. The answer: Presentation Manager knows all, and you just have to know which questions to ask. *WinQuerySysValue* is used for exactly that reason.

```
lHeight = WinQuerySysValue( HWND_DESKTOP, SV_CYSCREEN );
lWidth  = WinQuerySysValue( HWND_DESKTOP, SV_CXSCREEN );
```

This function will provide lots of information about the dimensions of various system components. The values we are interested in are the height and width of the screen, SV_CXSCREEN and SV_CYSCREEN. The value returned from the function is the answer to your query. The first parameter to *WinQuerySysValue* is the desktop handle, HWND_DESKTOP. The second value is the system-value identity. These values are listed in the documentation for *WinQuerySysValue*.

Once we know the screen height and width, we use *WinSetWindowPos* to size and position the window accordingly.

```
WinSetWindowPos ( hwndFrame,
                  NULLHANDLE,
                  lWidth  / 4,
                  lHeight / 4,
                  lWidth  / 2,
                  lHeight / 2,
                  SWP_SIZE | SWP_MOVE |
                  SWP_ACTIVATE | SWP_SHOW ) ;
```

The first parameter to *WinSetWindowPos* is the window to be sized, *hwndFrame*. By sizing the parent, the children, in particular the client area, are sized accordingly. The second parameter is the window handle of the placement window. This is the window that the frame window would be positioned relative to, if SWP_ZORDER was specified as the last parameter. This is ignored in our case, so NULLHANDLE is used. The next two parameters are the *x* and *y* coordinates to move the window to. The *x* coordinate is set to 1/4 the total screen width. The *y* coordinate is set to 1/4 the total screen height. The fifth parameter is the window width. This window will have a width of 1/2 the screen width. The next parameter is window height. This window will have a height of 1/2 the screen height. The last variable is the option-flags variable. The options we will specify are:

> SWP_SIZE — change the window size
> SWP_MOVE — change the window position
> SWP_ACTIVATE — make this window the active window
> SWP_SHOW — make the window visible

14.3 Accelerator Keys

In this example, we create three spin buttons directly on the client window. However, the big drawback to using a client window as the parent, and not a dialog box, is that you lose a lot of the keyboard handling of the dialog box. The dialog box procedure automates the moving from control to control when the user hits the TAB and BACKTAB key. We want our spin buttons to do this also, so we will emulate the TAB key handling using accelerator keys.

Accelerator keys are a shortcut keystroke that causes some action to happen immediately. In Presentation Manager programming lingo, a WM_COMMAND message is posted whenever an accelerator key is pressed. Accelerator keys are covered in more detail in Chapter 8, Menus.

```
ACCELTABLE ID_WINDOW
{
    VK_TAB, IDK_TAB, VIRTUALKEY
    VK_BACKTAB, IDK_BACKTAB, VIRTUALKEY
}
```

Accelerator keys can be created dynamically or in a resource file. This example uses a resource file. Our resource file only defines two accelerator keys, VK_TAB and VK_BACKTAB.

14.4 WM_CREATE Processing

In this example, we want to create the spin buttons directly on the client area of the window. The ideal time to create them is at the same time the window is created, in the WM_CREATE processing.

```
ulYearStyle =  SPBS_MASTER | SPBS_READONLY |
               SPBS_JUSTLEFT | SPBS_FASTSPIN |
               WS_VISIBLE ;
```

The variables *ulMonthStyle, ulDayStyle,* and *ulYearStyle* are used to hold the spin button styles. Each button is fairly similar. SPBS_READONLY indicates this spin button will be read-only. SPBS_JUSTLEFT will left-justify the spin button text. SPBS_FASTSPIN lets the user spin the buttons quickly by holding down the arrow keys. Two of the spin buttons will be servant spin buttons. The Year spin button will be the master, and the up and down arrows are located to the right of that button.

```
lHeight = WinQuerySysValue ( HWND_DESKTOP,
                             SV_CYSCREEN ) / 2 ;
lWidth  = WinQuerySysValue ( HWND_DESKTOP,
                             SV_CXSCREEN ) / 2 ;
```

The next step is to determine where we will place the spin buttons in the client area. In the WM_CREATE message, the client area has a size of 0, 0. This can make it very difficult to try to guess the size. However, in this case we can cheat. We know what proportion the client window is of the screen size; so, we use the screen height and width, and divide by two.

```
xPosition = lWidth / 5;
yPosition = lHeight / 3;
yHeight = 50;
```

The *x* and *y* coordinates are calculated by using 1/5 the client area width, and 1/3 the client area height.

```
WinCreateWindow ( hwndWnd,
                  WC_SPINBUTTON,
                  NULL,
                  ulYearStyle,
                  xPosition + 90 + 40,
                  yPosition,
                  110,
                  yHeight,
                  hwndWnd,
                  HWND_TOP,
                  ID_SPINBUTTONYEAR,
                  NULL,
                  NULL ) ;
```

WinCreateWindow is used to create the three spin buttons. The first parameter is the parent window, *hwndWnd*. The next parameter is the window class that the new window will belong to, in this case WC_SPINBUTTON. The third parameter is the window text. We'll leave the buttons blank for now, and assign data to them later. The spin button style variables are the next parameter. The next parameters are the *x* and *y* coordinates of the spin buttons. The spin button height and width are set in the next two parameters. The ninth parameter is the owner window. We want the spin buttons to keep open communications with the client area, so *hwndWnd* is our owner window as well. The next parameter is the window placement variable. We want the spin buttons to sit on top of all the other siblings (there are no other siblings in this example), so HWND_TOP is specified. The next parameter is the resource ID for the spin buttons. The next parameter is the control data. The window class WC_SPINBUTTON does not have any control data associated with it, so this variable is set to NULL. The last parameter is the presentation parameter data. This is also unused for these spin buttons.

```
WinSendDlgItemMsg ( hwndWnd,
                    ID_SPINBUTTONDAY,
                    SPBM_SETARRAY,
                    MPFROMP ( achDayArray ) ,
                    MPFROMSHORT ( 31 ) ) ;

WinSendDlgItemMsg ( hwndWnd,
                    ID_SPINBUTTONDAY,
                    SPBM_SETMASTER,
                    MPFROMHWND ( WinWindowFromID (
                                 hwndWnd,
                                 ID_SPINBUTTONYEAR )),
                    0 ) ;
```

The last step in creating the spin buttons is to initialize them. The buttons, ID_SPINBUTTONDAY and ID_SPINBUTTONMONTH, need to be told exactly who their master is, since they are only servant spin buttons. The message SPBM_SETMASTER will do this. The message parameter 1 is the master window handle, and message parameter 2 is unused. Each different button also has an array of data that needs to be associated with it. These arrays are defined in SPIN.H. To associate the array, we will send the spin button the message SPBM_SETARRAY. The message parameter 1 is a pointer to the array, and message parameter 2 is the number of items in the array.

14.5 WM_CONTROL Processing

The owner of control windows will receive a WM_CONTROL message when something important has happened. It just so happens that one of these messages will be able to tell the client window that the spin button has finished spinning. When that happens, we want to update the status string at the top of the client window.

```
usID = SHORT1FROMMP ( mpParm1 ) ;
usNotifyCode = SHORT2FROMMP ( mpParm1 ) ;

if ( usID == ID_SPINBUTTONDAY ||
     usID == ID_SPINBUTTONMONTH ||
     usID == ID_SPINBUTTONYEAR ) {

   if ( usNotifyCode == SPBN_ENDSPIN ) {

      WinQueryWindowRect ( hwndWnd, &rclWindow ) ;
      rclWindow.yBottom = ( rclWindow.yTop -
                            rclWindow.yBottom ) / 3 * 2 ;

      WinInvalidateRect ( hwndWnd,
                          &rclWindow,
                          FALSE ) ;
```

Message parameter 1 in the WM_CONTROL message contains all the information we need to know about the spin buttons. The first SHORT is the ID of the control that sent the WM_CONTROL message. The second SHORT is a notification code that is specific to that type of control. It's a good idea to look at the IDs of the window sending the message in order to make sure you've got the right window. The only notification code that we're interested in is SPBN_ENDSPIN. If we receive that message, we want to make the client area repaint the status area. This area takes up the top 1/3 of the client window. First we find the rectangle we want to repaint, then we use *WinInvalidateRect* to force a repaint of that area.

14.6 WM_COMMAND Processing

The WM_COMMAND processing is where we handle the processing of the accelerator keys.

```
if ( SHORT1FROMMP ( mpParm2 ) == CMDSRC_ACCELERATOR ) {

    hwndActive = WinQueryFocus ( HWND_DESKTOP ) ;
    usFocusID = WinQueryWindowUShort ( hwndActive,
                                       QWS_ID ) ;
```

The lower bytes of *mpParm2* contain the command type ID. This can contain values such as: CMDSRC_PUSHBUTTON, CMDSRC_MENU, CMDSRC_FONTDLG, CMDSRC_FILEDLG, CMDSRC_OTHER, or the value that we're interested in, CMDSRC_ACCELERATOR. The lower bytes of *mpParm1* contains the accelerator key command ID that we specified as the *cmd* element of the ACCEL structures. This information tells us whether the user hit the TAB key or BACKTAB key. *WinQueryFocus* is used to determine what spin button to use as a starting point. The window ID is retrieved using *WinQueryWindowUShort*. Our window IDs are consecutive numbers, so it is a simple matter to determine which spin button should have the focus next.

```
if ( SHORT1FROMMP ( mpParm1 ) == IDK_TAB ) {
    usFocusID ++ ;

    if ( usFocusID > LAST_CONTROL ) {
        usFocusID = FIRST_CONTROL ;
    } /* endif */

    hwndActive = WinWindowFromID ( hwndWnd,
                                   usFocusID ) ;
    WinSetFocus ( HWND_DESKTOP, hwndActive ) ;

} else
```

If the accelerator key was a TAB key, we're moving forward. If the current spin button is the last one in the chain, or if the window ID received is out of the bounds of the spin buttons, we set the variable *usFocusID* to the first spin button, or else we just increment *usFocusD*.

```
if ( SHORT1FROMMP ( mpParm1 ) == IDK_BACKTAB ) {
    usFocusID -- ;

    if ( usFocusID < FIRST_CONTROL ) {
        usFocusID = LAST_CONTROL ;
    } /* endif */

    hwndActive = WinWindowFromID ( hwndWnd,
                                   usFocusID ) ;
```

```
                    WinSetFocus ( HWND_DESKTOP, hwndActive ) ;

        } /* endif */
    } /* endif */
```

The same logic, reversed, is used if the accelerator key is the BACKTAB. Once the new window ID is determined, *WinSetFocus* will set the keyboard focus to the new window.

14.7 WM_PAINT Processing

The text displaying the current selection of the spin buttons is displayed in the top 1/3 of the window. *WinQueryWindowRect* determines the size of the window, and then *WinFillRect* fills this part of the window with the color white, CLR_WHITE, effectively erasing this part of this window.

```
        WinSendDlgItemMsg ( hwndWnd,
                            ID_SPINBUTTONYEAR,
                            SPBM_QUERYVALUE,
                            MPFROMP ( achYear ) ,
                            MPFROM2SHORT ( sizeof ( achYear ) ,
                                SPBQ_DONOTUPDATE )) ;

        sprintf ( achMsg,
                  "SpinButton's set to: %s %s, %s",
                  achMonth,
                  achDay,
                  achYear ) ;

        WinDrawText ( hpsPaint,
                      -1,
                      achMsg,
                      &rclBox,
                      0,
                      0,
                      DT_CENTER | DT_VCENTER | DT_TEXTATTRS ) ;
```

The message SPBM_QUERYVALUE will determine what the spin buttons are currently set at. All three spin buttons are queried, and their values are returned in a character string. These strings are used to create one string that will be displayed in the text portion of the window. *WinDrawText* is used to display the text, centered both horizontally and vertically, in the text portion of the window.

14.8 Spin Button Messages

WM_CONTROL
This message is sent when a control has to notify its owner of a significant event.

Parameter 1:	USHORT usID	spin button ID
	USHORT usNotifyCode	SPBN_UPARROW, SPBN_DOWNARROW, SPBN_SETFOCUS, SPBN_KILLFOCUS, SPBN_ENDSPIN, SPBN_CHANGE
Parameter 2:	HWND hwndWindow	for SPBN_UPARROW, SPBN_DOWNARROW, and SPBN_ENDSPIN this is handle of active spin button for SPBN_SETFOCUS this is handle of current active spin button; for SPBN_KILLFOCUS, this is NULLHANDLE
Reply:	ULONG ulReply	reserved, 0

SPBM_OVERRIDESETLIMITS
This message is sent to the spin button to change the upper or lower limit.

Parameter 1:	LONG lUpperLimit	upper limit
Parameter 2:	LONG lLowerLimit	lower limit
Reply:	BOOL fSuccess	successful? TRUE:FALSE

SPBM_QUERYLIMITS
This message is sent to the spin button to query the limits of a numeric spin field.

Parameter 1:	LONG lUpperLimit	upper limit
Parameter 2:	LONG lLowerLimit	lower limit

Reply: BOOL fSuccess   successful? TRUE:FALSE

SPBM_QUERYVALUE

This message is sent to the spin button to query the current value of the spin button.

Parameter 1:	PVOID pStorage	storage for returned value
Parameter 2:	USHORT usBufSize	size of buffer; if 0, *pStorage* is assumed to be address of a long variable
	USHORT usValue	SPBQ_UPDATEIFVALID — accept contents of spin button field if within limits
		SPBN_ALWAYSUPDATE — update contents of the field, even if not valid
		SPBN_DONOTUPDATE — do not change the current value of the spin button field
Reply:	BOOL fSuccess	successful? TRUE:FALSE

SPBM_SETARRAY

This message is sent to the spin button to set or reset a data array.

Parameter 1:	PSZ pszString	pointer to data array
Parameter 2:	USHORT usNumItems	number of items in array
Reply:	BOOL fSuccess	successful? TRUE:FALSE

SPBM_SETCURRENTVALUE

This message is sent to the spin button to set the current value to either a numeric value or to a data array index.

Parameter 1:	LONG lValue	array index or numeric value
Parameter 2:	ULONG ulReserved	reserved, 0
Reply:	BOOL fSuccess	successful? TRUE:FALSE

SPBM_SETLIMITS
This message is sent to the spin button to set or reset numeric limits.

Parameter 1:	LONG lUpperLimit	upper limit
Parameter 2:	LONG lLowerLimit	lower limit
Reply:	BOOL fSuccess	successful? TRUE:FALSE

SPBM_SETMASTER
This message is sent to the spin button to set the master of that spin button.

Parameter 1:	HWND hwndMaster	window handle of master
Parameter 2:	ULONG ulReserved	reserved, 0
Reply:	BOOL fSuccess	successful? TRUE:FALSE

SPBM_SETTEXTLIMIT
This message is sent to the spin button to set the maximum number of characters allowed.

Parameter 1:	USHORT usCharLimit	number of characters allowed
Parameter 2:	ULONG ulReserved	reserved, 0
Reply:	BOOL fSuccess	successful? TRUE:FALSE

SPBM_SPINDOWN
This message is sent to the spin button to spin backward.

Parameter 1:	ULONG ulItems	number of items to spin
Parameter 2:	ULONG ulReserved	reserved, 0
Reply:	BOOL fSuccess	successful? TRUE:FALSE

SPBM_SPINUP
This message is sent to the spin button to spin forward.

Parameter 1:	ULONG ulItems	number of items to spin
Parameter 2:	ULONG ulReserved	reserved, 0
Reply:	BOOL fSuccess	successful? TRUE:FALSE

Chapter 15

Slider

A slider control is a control designed for two purposes:

(1) To let a user adjust some value on a graduated scale

(2) To serve as a progress indicator of a process

The slider is similar in function to an air conditioning thermostat. It can be adjustable, or read-only. Figure 15.1 illustrates the different slider components.

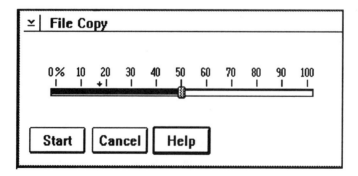

Figure 15.1. Slider control.

The slider arm is the "handle" that is used to select new values along the slider shaft. The arm can be dragged with a mouse, or moved with the cursor keys.

415

The piece of color that sits to the right or left of the slider arm (depending on slider orientation) is called a ribbon-strip.

The graduations marked along the slider shaft are called tick marks. They can be labeled with text, or left blank.

A detent is a little arrow that marks some level of interest along the scale.

A slider scale can sit above or below the slider shaft, or a slider can use two scales. The following are the available slider styles:

STYLE	DESCRIPTION
SLS_HORIZONTAL	This is the default orientation of the slider. When is slider is of style SLS_HORIZONTAL, the slider arm will move left and right. The scale is placed either above the shaft, below the shaft, or above and below the shaft.
SLS_VERTICAL	This slider is positioned vertically. The arm will move up and down the shaft, and the scale(s) are placed vertically along the shaft, similar to a thermometer.
SLS_CENTER	The slider is centered in the slider window. Default position.
SLS_BOTTOM	This style will position the slider at the bottom of the slider window. Not valid for vertical sliders.
SLS_TOP	This style will position the slider at the top of the slider window. Not valid for vertical sliders.
SLS_LEFT	This style will position the slider at the left of the slider window. Not valid for horizontal sliders.
SLS_RIGHT	This style will position the slider at the right of the slider window. Not valid for horizontal sliders.
SLS_PRIMARYSCALE1	This style will position the scale above the slider for a horizontal slider, and to the right of the slider for a vertical slider. The increments and detents are also positioned correspondingly. This is the default style.

SLS_PRIMARYSCALE2	This style is the inverse of the previous style. Scales for horizontal sliders are placed on the bottom, and scales for vertical sliders are placed on the left.
SLS_HOMELEFT	This style will cause the slider arm to be placed on the left edge of the slider when it is in base, or zero, position. This style can only be used with horizontal sliders.
SLS_HOMERIGHT	This style will case the slider arm to be placed on the right edge of the slider when it is in base, or zero, position. This style can only be used with horizontal sliders.
SLS_HOMEBOTTOM	This style will cause the slider arm to be placed on the bottom of the slider when it is in base, or zero, position. This style can only be used with vertical sliders.
SLS_HOMETOP	This style will cause the slider arm to be placed on the top of the slider when it is in base, or zero, position. This style can only be used with vertical sliders.
SLS_BUTTONSLEFT	This style will include slider buttons that will be placed to the left of the slider. Clicking on the buttons move the slider arm one position in the specified direction. This style can only be used with horizontal sliders.
SLS_BUTTONSRIGHT	This style will include slider buttons that will be placed to the right of the slider. Clicking on the buttons move the slider arm one position in the specified direction. This style can only be used with horizontal sliders.
SLS_BUTTONSBOTTOM	This style will include slider buttons that will be placed on the bottom of the slider. Clicking on the buttons move the slider arm one position in the specified direction. This style can only be used with vertical sliders.
SLS_BUTTONSTOP	This style will include slider buttons that will be placed on the top of the slider. Clicking on the buttons move the slider arm one position in the specified direction. This style can only be used with vertical sliders.

SLS_SNAPTOINCREMENT	This style will cause the slider arm to snap to the nearest scale increment as it is moved.
SLS_READONLY	This style prevents the user from interacting with the slider. The slider will contain no slider buttons, no detents, and the slider arm is narrower than non-read-only sliders.
SLS_OWNDERDRAW	This style will cause WM_DRAWITEM messages to be sent to the application when the slider needs to be painted.
SLS_RIBBONSTRIP	Provides a ribbon-strip in the middle of the slider shaft.

15.1 Creating a Slider

 A slider can be created by either using *WinCreateWindow* or by specifying a slider control in the resource file. The following code demonstrates using the function *WinCreateWindow* to create a slider:

```
SLDCDATA structSliderData;
HWND hwndSlider;
ULONG ulSliderStyle;

structSliderData.cbSize = sizeof( SLDCDATA);
/* size of control data structure */
structSliderData.usScale1Increments = 10;
/* number of increments on Scale 1 */
structSliderData.usScale1Spacing = 6;
/* number of pixels between Scale 1 increments */
structSliderData.usScale2Increments = 0;
/* number of increments on Scale2 */
structSliderData.usScale2Spacing = 0;
/* number of pixels between Scale 2 increments */
ulSliderStyle    =      WS_VISIBLE       |       SLS_BUTTONSLEFT     |
SLS_SNAPTOINCREMENT;
```

```
hwndSlider = WinCreateWindow(
        hwndParent,    /* parent window  */
        WC_SLIDER,     /* slider class */
        (PSZ)0,        /* window text - none here */
        ulSliderStyle, /* slider styles */
        50,            /* x */
        50,            /* y */
        240,           /* cx */
        50,            /* cy */
        hwndOwner,     /* owner window */
        HWND_TOP,      /* Z-order */
        IDS_SLIDER,    /* slider ID */
        &structSliderData,    /* pointer to SLDCDATA structure */
        NULL ); /* presentation parameters */
```

When specifying a slider in a resource file, the following statements are necessary:

```
CONTROL        "", IDS_SLIDER, 50, 50, 240, 50, WC_SLIDER,
               SLS_SNAPTOINCREMENT |
               SLS_BUTTONSLEFT | WS_VISIBLE
               CTLDATA 12, 0, 11, 0, 0, 0
```

The CTLDATA line represents the Slider Control Data structure. The first two numbers represent the ULONG value that is the size of the structure. The next number is the number of divisions on scale one. The next number indicates auto-spacing. The last two numbers represent the number of divisions on scale 2 and spacing on scale two, respectively.

Gotcha!
In OS/2 2.x, auto-sizing for the increments between the tick marks is not ideal. The slider divides the number of increments into the size of the slider. This means that long tick mark text will fall off the edges. Unless you have short tick mark text, it's best to size the slider increments yourself.

The following program is an example of a read-only slider that is used as a progress indicator. The slider is owner-drawn (SLS_OWNERDRAW) in order to change the ribbon strip color from ordinary gray to blue. The program is designed to create a backup copy of the source code. This program does not create a standard window as the parent of the dialog; instead, a dialog is created at program startup. HWND_DESKTOP is used as the parent and owner of the dialog. This is a perfectly legitimate way of designing small programs that don't need the extra functionality of a client window space or menu.

SLIDER.C

```
#define INCL_DOSFILEMGR
#define INCL_DOSMEMMGR
#define INCL_WINDIALOGS
#define INCL_WINMENUS
#define INCL_WINSTDSLIDER
#define INCL_WINSYS

#include <os2.h>
#include <stdio.h>
#include <stdlib.h>
#include <string.h>
#include "slider.h"

#define COPY_FILE               "SLIDER.C"
#define BACKUP_FILE             "SLIDER.BAK"

BOOL CopyFile ( HWND hwndSlider ) ;
MRESULT EXPENTRY DlgProc ( HWND hwndDlg,
                           ULONG ulMsg,
                           MPARAM mpParm1,
                           MPARAM mpParm2 ) ;

INT main ( VOID )
{
    HAB         habAnchor ;
    HMQ         hmqQueue ;

    habAnchor = WinInitialize ( 0 ) ;
    hmqQueue = WinCreateMsgQueue ( habAnchor, 0 ) ;

    WinDlgBox ( HWND_DESKTOP,
                HWND_DESKTOP,
                DlgProc,
                NULLHANDLE,
                IDD_FCOPYDLG,
                NULL ) ;

    WinDestroyMsgQueue ( hmqQueue ) ;
    WinTerminate ( habAnchor ) ;
    return 0 ;
}

MRESULT EXPENTRY DlgProc ( HWND hwndDlg,
    ULONG ulMsg,
    MPARAM mpParm1,
    MPARAM mpParm2 )
{
    switch ( ulMsg ) {
    case WM_INITDLG:
        {
            CHAR        achFont [16] ;
            USHORT      usIndex ;
            CHAR        achMessage [64] ;
```

```
        //---------------------------------------------------------
        // Set the size of the tick marks
        //---------------------------------------------------------

        WinSendDlgItemMsg ( hwndDlg,
                            IDS_SLIDER,
                            SLM_SETTICKSIZE,
                            MPFROM2SHORT ( SMA_SETALLTICKS, 7 ) ,
                            0 ) ;

        strcpy ( achFont, "8.Tms Rmn" ) ;
        WinSetPresParam ( WinWindowFromID ( hwndDlg, IDS_SLIDER ),
                          PP_FONTNAMESIZE,
                          strlen ( achFont ) + 1,
                          achFont ) ;

        for ( usIndex = 0 ; usIndex < 11 ; usIndex ++ ) {
            sprintf ( achMessage, "%d%%", usIndex * 10 ) ;

            WinSendDlgItemMsg ( hwndDlg,
                                IDS_SLIDER,
                                SLM_SETSCALETEXT,
                                MPFROMSHORT ( usIndex ) ,
                                MPFROMP ( achMessage )) ;
        } /* endfor */
    }
    break ;

case WM_COMMAND:
    switch ( SHORT1FROMMP ( mpParm1 )) {
    case IDP_START:
        CopyFile ( WinWindowFromID ( hwndDlg, IDS_SLIDER )) ;

        WinAlarm ( HWND_DESKTOP, WA_NOTE ) ;
        WinMessageBox ( HWND_DESKTOP,
                        hwndDlg,
                        "Backup is Complete",
                        "Status",
                        0,
                        MB_OK | MB_INFORMATION ) ;
        break ;

    case IDP_CANCEL:
        WinDismissDlg ( hwndDlg, FALSE ) ;
        break ;

    default:
        return WinDefDlgProc ( hwndDlg,
                               ulMsg,
                               mpParm1,
                               mpParm2 ) ;
    } /* endswitch */
    break ;
```

```
    case WM_DRAWITEM:
        {
            POWNERITEM poiItem ;

            //----------------------------------------------------------
            // get the OWNERITEM structure from mpParm2
            //----------------------------------------------------------

            poiItem = (POWNERITEM) PVOIDFROMMP ( mpParm2 ) ;

            switch ( poiItem -> idItem ) {
            case SDA_RIBBONSTRIP:
               WinFillRect ( poiItem -> hps,
                             &poiItem -> rclItem,
                             CLR_BLUE ) ;
               return MRFROMSHORT ( TRUE ) ;
            default:
               return WinDefDlgProc ( hwndDlg,
                                      ulMsg,
                                      mpParm1,
                                      mpParm2 ) ;
            } /* endswitch */
        }

    default:
        return WinDefDlgProc ( hwndDlg,
                               ulMsg,
                               mpParm1,
                               mpParm2 ) ;
    } /* endswitch */

    return MRFROMSHORT ( FALSE ) ;
}

BOOL CopyFile ( HWND hwndSlider )
{
    APIRET          arRc ;
    FILESTATUS3     fsStatus ;
    PBYTE           pbBuffer ;
    HFILE           hfRead ;
    ULONG           ulAction ;
    HFILE           hfWrite ;
    ULONG           ulSzBlock ;
    USHORT          usIndex ;
    ULONG           ulBytesRead ;
    ULONG           ulBytesWritten ;

    arRc = DosQueryPathInfo ( COPY_FILE,
                              FIL_STANDARD,
                              (PVOID) &fsStatus,
                              sizeof ( fsStatus )) ;

    if ( !arRc ) {
        ulSzBlock = fsStatus.cbFile / 10 + 1 ;

        pbBuffer = (PBYTE) malloc ( ulSzBlock ) ;
```

```
//------------------------------------------------------------
// Open up the file for reading
//------------------------------------------------------------

arRc = DosOpen ( COPY_FILE,
                 &hfRead,
                 &ulAction,
                 0,
                 FILE_NORMAL,
                 FILE_OPEN,
                 OPEN_ACCESS_READONLY | OPEN_SHARE_DENYWRITE,
                 0 ) ;

//------------------------------------------------------------
// Open up the backup file for write
//------------------------------------------------------------

arRc = DosOpen ( BACKUP_FILE,
                 &hfWrite,
                 &ulAction,
                 0,
                 FILE_NORMAL,
                 FILE_CREATE,
                 OPEN_ACCESS_WRITEONLY |
                 OPEN_SHARE_DENYREADWRITE,
                 0 ) ;

for ( usIndex = 1 ; usIndex < 11 ; usIndex ++ ) {

   //---------------------------------------------------------
   // Read a block
   //---------------------------------------------------------

   DosRead ( hfRead,
             pbBuffer,
             ulSzBlock,
             &ulBytesRead ) ;

   //---------------------------------------------------------
   // Write a block
   //---------------------------------------------------------

   DosWrite ( hfWrite,
              pbBuffer,
              ulBytesRead,
              &ulBytesWritten ) ;

   //---------------------------------------------------------
   // Tell the slider to move
   //---------------------------------------------------------

   WinSendMsg ( hwndSlider,
                SLM_SETSLIDERINFO,
                MPFROM2SHORT ( SMA_SLIDERARMPOSITION,
                  SMA_INCREMENTVALUE ) ,
                MPFROMSHORT ( usIndex )) ;
```

```
    } /* endfor */

    //-----------------------------------------------------------
    // Clean up
    //-----------------------------------------------------------

    DosClose ( hfRead ) ;
    DosClose ( hfWrite ) ;
    free ( pbBuffer ) ;
    return TRUE ;
  } else {
    return FALSE ;
  } /* endif */
}
```

SLIDER.RC

```
#include <os2.h>
#include "slider.h"

DLGTEMPLATE IDD_FCOPYDLG LOADONCALL MOVEABLE DISCARDABLE
{
   DIALOG  "File Copy", IDD_FCOPYDLG, 67, 80, 324, 104,
      WS_VISIBLE,
      FCF_SYSMENU | FCF_TITLEBAR
   {
      LTEXT "Progress Indicator", -1, 115, 30, 80, 12
      CONTROL  "", IDS_SLIDER, 12, 43, 300, 46, WC_SLIDER,
         SLS_HORIZONTAL | SLS_OWNERDRAW | SLS_CENTER |
         SLS_SNAPTOINCREMENT | SLS_READONLY | SLS_RIBBONSTRIP |
         SLS_HOMELEFT | SLS_PRIMARYSCALE1 | WS_GROUP | WS_TABSTOP |
         WS_VISIBLE
         CTLDATA 12, 0, 11, 26, 0, 0
      PUSHBUTTON "~Start", IDP_START, 6, 4, 40, 14
      PUSHBUTTON "Cancel", IDP_CANCEL, 49, 4, 40, 14
   }
}
```

SLIDER.H

```
#define IDD_FCOPYDLG        256
#define IDS_SLIDER          512
#define IDP_START           513
#define IDP_CANCEL          514
```

SLIDER.MAK

```
SLIDER.EXE:                      SLIDER.OBJ \
                                 SLIDER.RES
        LINK386 @<<
SLIDER
SLIDER
SLIDER
OS2386
SLIDER
<<
        RC SLIDER.RES SLIDER.EXE

SLIDER.RES:                      SLIDER.RC \
                                 SLIDER.H
        RC -r SLIDER.RC SLIDER.RES

SLIDER.OBJ:                      SLIDER.C \
                                 SLIDER.H
        ICC -C+ -Kb+ -Ss+ SLIDER.C
```

SLIDER.DEF

```
NAME SLIDER WINDOWAPI

DESCRIPTION 'Slider example
Copyright (c) 1992 by Kathleen Panov
All rights reserved.'

STACKSIZE 16384
```

```
        WinSendDlgItemMsg ( hwndDlg,
                            IDS_SLIDER,
                            SLM_SETTICKSIZE,
                            MPFROM2SHORT ( SMA_SETALLTICKS, 7 ) ,
                            0 ) ;
```

In the WM_INITDLG, a SLM_SETTICKSIZE message is sent to the slider window to set the height of the tick marks. This is different from the item in the CTRLDATA statement in the resource file that sets the width between the tick marks.

```
        strcpy ( achFont, "8.Tms Rmn" ) ;
        WinSetPresParam ( WinWindowFromID ( hwndDlg, IDS_SLIDER ),
                          PP_FONTNAMESIZE,
                          strlen ( achFont ) + 1,
                          achFont ) ;
```

WinSetPresParam is used to change the system font of the slider to something nicer, "8.Tms Rmn".

```
for ( usIndex = 0 ; usIndex < 11 ; usIndex ++ ) {
   sprintf ( achMessage, "%d%%", usIndex * 10 ) ;

   WinSendDlgItemMsg ( hwndDlg,
                       IDS_SLIDER,
                       SLM_SETSCALETEXT,
                       MPFROMSHORT ( usIndex ) ,
                       MPFROMP ( achMessage )) ;
```

Next, the tick marks are labeled with eleven percentage markers by sending the message SLM_SETSCALETEXT. The first parameter is the division number to set, and the second parameter is the string to use. One little note here: SLM_SETSCALETEXT does not recognize SMA_SETALLTICKS in Parameter 2. (Not that you will want to set all the tick marks with the same text very often, but, just in case you did.)

The WM_COMMAND processing is very simple: when the user pushes the START button, a WM_COMMAND message is sent to the dialog process. The function *CopyFile* is called to back up the file. If the CANCEL button is pressed the dialog is dismissed, and the process exits.

Because the slider is of style SLS_OWNERDRAW, the dialog procedure will also receive the WM_DRAWITEM message. Message parameter 2 contains a pointer to the owneritem structure. The structure is shown here:

```
typedef struct _OWNERITEM             {
    HWND    hwnd;           /* window handle */
    HPS     hps;            /* presentation space handle */
    ULONG   fsState;        /* Slider control style */
    ULONG   fsAttribute;    /* attribute state of control */
    ULONG   fsStateOld;     /* previous state of control */
    ULONG   fsAttributeOld; /* previous state of attribute */
    RECTL   rclItem;        /* RECTL structure of drawing area */
    LONG    idItem;         /* id of item to be drawn, for slider -
            /* SDA_RIBBONSTRIP, SDA_SLIDERSHAFT, SDA_BACKGROUND,
                    SDA_SLIDERARM */
    ULONG   hItem;          /* Resource handle */
} OWNERITEM;
typedef OWNERITEM *POWNERITEM;


    poiItem = (POWNERITEM) PVOIDFROMMP ( mpParm2 ) ;

    switch ( poiItem -> idItem ) {
    case SDA_RIBBONSTRIP:
       WinFillRect ( poiItem -> hps,
                     &poiItem -> rclItem,
                     CLR_BLUE ) ;
       return MRFROMSHORT ( TRUE ) ;
```

In this case, the program checks to see if the item needing to be drawn, *poiItem->rclItem*, is SDA_RIBBONSTRIP. If it isn't, we break out of the switch statement. If it is SDA_RIBBONSTRIP, *WinFillRect* is called to fill the RECTL structure with CLR_BLUE. After the area is filled we return TRUE, to indicate that we've already drawn the area, and there's no drawing left to do.

The last part of the program is the function *CopyFile*, which is used to copy the file, SLIDER.C, to the file SLIDER.BAK. This example copies the file in ten equal increments, in order to demonstrate a progress indicator. Please note that there is an OS/2 function, *DosCopy*, that will do all this in one function call, but for this example, we'll do our own copying. First, *DosQueryPathInfo* is used to make sure the file exists, and to find the file size. A buffer, Buffer, is allocated to serve as the holding place for bytes read, and then written. Next, *DosOpen* is called to open both files. The file functions are covered in more detail in Chapter 3, File I/O and Extended Attributes; see this chapter for more information on the parameters used in *DosOpen, DosQueryPathInfo* and *DosFindFirst*.

```
WinSendMsg ( hwndSlider,
             SLM_SETSLIDERINFO,
             MPFROM2SHORT ( SMA_SLIDERARMPOSITION,
                SMA_INCREMENTVALUE ) ,
             MPFROMSHORT ( usIndex )) ;
```

We will copy the file in ten pieces. As each piece is copied, a message is sent to the slider to set the progress indicator to the next value. The message is SLM_SETSLIDERINFO. The first parameter is made up of two SHORTS. The first value is the type of information that is being set. Possible values are:

- SMA_SHAFTDIMENSIONS
- SMA_SHAFTPOSITION
- SMA_SLIDERARMDIMENSIONS
- SMA_SLIDERARMPOSITION.

We will use SMA_SLIDERARMPOSITION. The second value, SMA_INCREMENTVALUE, tells the slider to change the slider arm position using tick marks instead of pixels. The second parameter indicates the number of the tick mark at which to set the slider arm.

15.2 Making a Better Slider Program

The example program, SLIDER, is an excellent target for a multithreaded Presentation Manager application. The following program, SLIDERTH, incorporates the use of semaphores and threads to make the example a little bit more responsive to the user.

SLIDERTH.C

```
#define INCL_DOSFILEMGR
#define INCL_DOSMEMMGR
#define INCL_DOSSEMAPHORES
#define INCL_WINDIALOGS
#define INCL_WINMENUS
#define INCL_WINSTDSLIDER
#define INCL_WINSYS

#include <os2.h>
#include <stdio.h>
#include <stdlib.h>
#include <string.h >
#include "sliderth.h"

#define COPY_FILE                "SLIDERTH.C"
#define BACKUP_FILE              "SLIDERTH.BAK"

#define SZ_STACK                 16384

typedef struct _SLIDERINFO {
    ULONG        ulSzStruct ;
    HWND         hwndDlg ;
    HEV          hevStartCopy ;
} SLIDERINFO, *PSLIDERINFO ;

typedef VOID ( * _Optlink PFNCOPY ) ( PVOID ) ;

BOOL CopyFile ( HWND hwndSlider ) ;
VOID _Optlink CopyThread ( PSLIDERINFO psiSlider ) ;
MRESULT EXPENTRY DlgProc ( HWND hwndDlg,
                           ULONG ulMsg,
                           MPARAM mpParm1,
                           MPARAM mpParm2 ) ;

INT main ( VOID )
{
    HAB        habAnchor ;
    HMQ        hmqQueue ;

    habAnchor = WinInitialize ( 0 ) ;
    hmqQueue = WinCreateMsgQueue ( habAnchor, 0 ) ;
```

```
    WinDlgBox ( HWND_DESKTOP,
                HWND_DESKTOP,
                DlgProc,
                NULLHANDLE,
                IDD_FCOPYDLG,
                NULL ) ;

    WinDestroyMsgQueue ( hmqQueue ) ;
    WinTerminate ( habAnchor ) ;
    return 0 ;
}

MRESULT EXPENTRY DlgProc ( HWND hwndDlg,
                           ULONG ulMsg,
                           MPARAM mpParm1,
                           MPARAM mpParm2 )
{
    switch ( ulMsg ) {

    case WM_INITDLG:
        {
            CHAR        achFont [16] ;
            USHORT      usIndex ;
            CHAR        achMessage [64] ;

            //---------------------------------------------------------
            // Set the size of the tick marks
            //---------------------------------------------------------
            WinSendDlgItemMsg ( hwndDlg,
                                IDS_SLIDER,
                                SLM_SETTICKSIZE,
                                MPFROM2SHORT ( SMA_SETALLTICKS, 7 ) ,
                                0 ) ;

            strcpy ( achFont, "8.Tms Rmn" ) ;
            WinSetPresParam ( WinWindowFromID ( hwndDlg, IDS_SLIDER )
,
                              PP_FONTNAMESIZE,
                              strlen ( achFont ) + 1,
                              achFont ) ;

            for ( usIndex = 0 ; usIndex < 11 ; usIndex ++ ) {
                sprintf ( achMessage, "%d%%", usIndex * 10 ) ;

                WinSendDlgItemMsg ( hwndDlg,
                                    IDS_SLIDER,
                                    SLM_SETSCALETEXT,
                                    MPFROMSHORT ( usIndex ) ,
                                    MPFROMP ( achMessage )) ;
            } /* endfor */
        }
        break ;

    case WM_COMMAND:
        switch ( SHORT1FROMMP ( mpParm1 )) {
```

```
    case IDP_START:
        {
        PSLIDERINFO        psiSlider ;

        psiSlider = (PSLIDERINFO) malloc (
            sizeof ( SLIDERINFO )) ;

        if ( psiSlider == NULL ) {
            WinMessageBox ( HWND_DESKTOP,
                            hwndDlg,
                            "Out of memory !",
                            "Error",
                            0,
                            MB_ICONEXCLAMATION | MB_OK ) ;
            return MRFROMSHORT ( FALSE ) ;
        } /* endif */

        psiSlider -> ulSzStruct = sizeof ( SLIDERINFO ) ;
        psiSlider -> hwndDlg = hwndDlg ;

        DosCreateEventSem ( NULL,
                            &psiSlider -> hevStartCopy,
                            0,
                            0 ) ;

        if ( _beginthread(( PFNCOPY ) CopyThread,
                            NULL,
                            SZ_STACK,
                            ( PVOID ) psiSlider ) == - 1 ) {

            WinMessageBox ( HWND_DESKTOP,
                hwndDlg,
                "Cannot create thread!",
                "Error",
                0,
                MB_ICONEXCLAMATION | MB_OK ) ;

            DosCloseEventSem ( psiSlider -> hevStartCopy ) ;
            free ( psiSlider ) ;
            return MRFROMSHORT ( FALSE ) ;
        } /* endif */

        DosPostEventSem ( psiSlider -> hevStartCopy ) ;
        }
        break ;

    case IDP_CANCEL:
        WinDismissDlg ( hwndDlg, FALSE ) ;
        break ;

    default:
        return WinDefDlgProc ( hwndDlg,
                               ulMsg,
                               mpParm1,
                               mpParm2 ) ;
    } /* endswitch */
    break ;
```

```
    case WM_DRAWITEM:
        {
            POWNERITEM poiItem ;

            //--------------------------------------------------------
            // get the OWNERITEM structure from mpParm2
            //--------------------------------------------------------

            poiItem = ( POWNERITEM ) PVOIDFROMMP ( mpParm2 ) ;

            switch ( poiItem -> idItem ) {
            case SDA_RIBBONSTRIP:
                WinFillRect ( poiItem -> hps,
                              &poiItem -> rclItem,
                              CLR_BLUE ) ;
                return MRFROMSHORT ( TRUE ) ;
            default:
                return WinDefDlgProc ( hwndDlg,
                                       ulMsg,
                                       mpParm1,
                                       mpParm2 ) ;
            } /* endswitch */
        }

    default:
        return WinDefDlgProc ( hwndDlg,
                               ulMsg,
                               mpParm1,
                               mpParm2 ) ;
    } /* endswitch */

    return MRFROMSHORT ( FALSE ) ;
}

VOID _Optlink CopyThread ( PSLIDERINFO psiSlider )
{
    HAB habAnchor ;
    HMQ hmqQueue ;

    habAnchor = WinInitialize ( 0 ) ;
    hmqQueue = WinCreateMsgQueue ( habAnchor, 0 ) ;

    DosWaitEventSem ( psiSlider -> hevStartCopy, -1 ) ;
    DosCloseEventSem ( psiSlider -> hevStartCopy ) ;

    CopyFile ( WinWindowFromID ( psiSlider -> hwndDlg,
               IDS_SLIDER )) ;

    WinAlarm ( HWND_DESKTOP, WA_NOTE ) ;

    WinMessageBox ( HWND_DESKTOP,
                    psiSlider -> hwndDlg,
                    "Backup is Complete",
                    "Status",
                    0,
                    MB_OK | MB_INFORMATION ) ;
```

```
    free ( psiSlider ) ;

    WinDestroyMsgQueue ( hmqQueue ) ;
    WinTerminate ( habAnchor ) ;
    return ;
}

BOOL CopyFile ( HWND hwndSlider )
{
    APIRET           arRc ;
    FILESTATUS3      fsStatus ;
    PBYTE            pbBuffer ;
    HFILE            hfRead ;
    ULONG            ulAction ;
    HFILE            hfWrite ;
    ULONG            ulSzBlock ;
    USHORT           usIndex ;
    ULONG            ulBytesRead ;
    ULONG            ulBytesWritten ;

    arRc = DosQueryPathInfo ( COPY_FILE,
                              FIL_STANDARD,
                              (PVOID) &fsStatus,
                              sizeof ( fsStatus )) ;

    if ( !arRc ) {

        ulSzBlock = fsStatus.cbFile / 10 + 1 ;

        pbBuffer = ( PBYTE ) malloc ( ulSzBlock ) ;

        //-----------------------------------------------------------
        // Open up the file for reading
        //-----------------------------------------------------------

        arRc = DosOpen ( COPY_FILE,
                         &hfRead,
                         &ulAction,
                         0,
                         FILE_NORMAL,
                         FILE_OPEN,
                         OPEN_ACCESS_READONLY | OPEN_SHARE_DENYWRITE,
                         0 ) ;

        //-----------------------------------------------------------
        // Open up the backup file for write
        //-----------------------------------------------------------
```

```
    arRc = DosOpen ( BACKUP_FILE,
                     &hfWrite,
                     &ulAction,
                     0,
                     FILE_NORMAL,
                     FILE_CREATE,
                     OPEN_ACCESS_WRITEONLY |
                     OPEN_SHARE_DENYREADWRITE,
                     0 ) ;

    for ( usIndex = 1 ; usIndex < 11 ; usIndex ++ ) {

      //----------------------------------------------------------
      // Read a block
      //----------------------------------------------------------

      DosRead ( hfRead,
                pbBuffer,
                ulSzBlock,
                &ulBytesRead ) ;

      //----------------------------------------------------------
      // Write a block
      //----------------------------------------------------------

      DosWrite ( hfWrite,
                 pbBuffer,
                 ulBytesRead,
                 &ulBytesWritten ) ;

      //----------------------------------------------------------
      // Tell the slider to move
      //----------------------------------------------------------

      WinSendMsg ( hwndSlider,
                   SLM_SETSLIDERINFO,
                   MPFROM2SHORT ( SMA_SLIDERARMPOSITION,
                     SMA_INCREMENTVALUE ) ,
                   MPFROMSHORT ( usIndex )) ;
    } /* endfor */

    //----------------------------------------------------------
    // Clean up
    //----------------------------------------------------------

    DosClose ( hfRead ) ;
    DosClose ( hfWrite ) ;
    free ( pbBuffer ) ;
    return TRUE ;
  } else {
    return FALSE ;
  } /* endif */
}
```

SLIDERTH.RC

```
#include <os2.h>
#include "sliderth.h"

DLGTEMPLATE IDD_FCOPYDLG LOADONCALL MOVEABLE DISCARDABLE
{
    DIALOG  "File Copy", IDD_FCOPYDLG, 67, 80, 324, 104,
        WS_VISIBLE,
        FCF_SYSMENU | FCF_TITLEBAR
    {
        LTEXT "Progress Indicator", -1, 115, 30, 80, 12
        CONTROL  "", IDS_SLIDER, 12, 43, 300, 46, WC_SLIDER,
            SLS_HORIZONTAL | SLS_OWNERDRAW | SLS_CENTER |
            SLS_SNAPTOINCREMENT | SLS_READONLY | SLS_RIBBONSTRIP |
            SLS_HOMELEFT | SLS_PRIMARYSCALE1 | WS_GROUP | WS_TABSTOP |
            WS_VISIBLE
            CTLDATA 12, 0, 11, 26, 0, 0
        PUSHBUTTON "~Start", IDP_START, 6, 4, 40, 14
        PUSHBUTTON "Cancel", IDP_CANCEL, 49, 4, 40, 14
    }
}
```

SLIDERTH.H

```
#define IDD_FCOPYDLG          256
#define IDS_SLIDER            512
#define IDP_START             513
#define IDP_CANCEL            514
```

SLIDERTH.MAK

```
SLIDERTH.EXE:                    SLIDERTH.OBJ \
                                 SLIDERTH.RES
        LINK386 @<<
SLIDERTH
SLIDERTH
SLIDERTH
OS2386
SLIDERTH
<<
        RC SLIDERTH.RES SLIDERTH.EXE

SLIDERTH.RES:                    SLIDERTH.RC \
                                 SLIDERTH.H
        RC -r SLIDERTH.RC SLIDERTH.RES

SLIDERTH.OBJ:                    SLIDERTH.C \
                                 SLIDERTH.H
        ICC -C+ -Gm+ -Kb+ -Ss+ SLIDERTH.C
```

SLIDERTH.DEF

```
NAME SLIDER WINDOWAPI

DESCRIPTION 'Multithread slider example
Copyright (c) 1992 by Kathleen Panov.
All rights reserved.'

STACKSIZE 16384
```

There is only one spot in the dialog procedure that is different from
SLIDER.C. This is in the WM_COMMAND processing.

```
DosCreateEventSem ( NULL,
                    &psiSlider -> hevStartCopy,
                    0,
                    0 ) ;
```

When the user clicks the IDP_START push-button, we'll spawn off a worker
thread to perform the file backup. We use an event semaphore to signal the
worker thread to start working. In this example, an event semaphore is a little
bit of overkill; however, in most programs you will want to do this to
coordinate the timing between the two threads.

```
if ( _beginthread(( PFNCOPY ) CopyThread,
                   NULL,
                   SZ_STACK,
                   ( PVOID ) psiSlider ) == - 1 ) {
```

We need to make sure the worker thread has the semaphore handle and the
window handle for the slider window. We use this information to create a
structure that is passed in the last argument of _beginthread. When passing a
pointer to a structure, your first structure argument should be the size of the
structure. The operating system expects this. The first parameter to
_beginthread is the thread function, CopyThread. The next parameter is a
bogus parameter that is left over from OS/2 1.x to ease migration woes. The
thread parameter is the stack size. Once the thread is created,
DosPostEventSem is used to raise the flag on our worker thread, and let it start
working.

15.3 The Thread Function

```
VOID _Optlink CopyThread ( PSLIDERINFO psiSlider )
{
   HAB habAnchor ;
   HMQ hmqQueue ;

   habAnchor = WinInitialize ( 0 ) ;
   hmqQueue = WinCreateMsgQueue ( habAnchor, 0 ) ;

   DosWaitEventSem ( psiSlider -> hevStartCopy, -1 ) ;
   DosCloseEventSem ( psiSlider -> hevStartCopy ) ;

   CopyFile ( WinWindowFromID ( psiSlider -> hwndDlg,
           IDS_SLIDER )) ;

   WinAlarm ( HWND_DESKTOP, WA_NOTE ) ;

   WinMessageBox ( HWND_DESKTOP,
                   psiSlider -> hwndDlg,
                   "Backup is Complete",
                   "Status",
                   0,
                   MB_OK | MB_INFORMATION ) ;

   free ( psiSlider ) ;

   WinDestroyMsgQueue ( hmqQueue ) ;
   WinTerminate ( habAnchor ) ;
   return ;
}
```

The other new addition to our SLIDER program is the thread function, *CopyThread*. The first thing we do is a little initialization. We create a message queue and anchor block for our worker thread. If we had chosen to post a message back to the main thread, these functions would not have been necessary; however, we'll call *WinMessageBox* from within the thread, so it is necessary.

The event semaphore is used to signal the start of the copy procedure. Once the function completes, the *psiSlider* structure is freed, and the anchor block and message queue are destroyed.

15.4 Making an Even Better Slider Program

Well, our multithreaded slider program was pretty good, but let's explore one more aspect of Presentation Manager programming, object windows. An object window is similar to a regular window, only it is not a relation to HWND_DESKTOP. A window whose parent is HWND_OBJECT will not be visible, and will never inherit the keyboard or mouse focus. The main advantages to creating an object window are:

- Object windows can send and receive messages.
- Object windows can take as long as they want to process messages, so long as they are operating independently of the main thread.

Gotcha!

This last point needs a little explanation. The message queue for an object window operates as a separate entity from the desktop. Because of this, the object window can handle tasks that take a large amount of time without hanging the system, or receiving the infamous "System Not Responding..." dialog box. However, if for some reason the main thread is awaiting a response from the object window thread, the desktop is still going to lock up. So, the moral to this story is: don't use *WinSendMsg* to communicate from the main thread to the object window thread unless you're really, really sure you want to. Also, avoid having the main thread wait on a semaphore that is being posted by the object window thread. Finally, a very useful piece of information to know about object windows: object windows *only* respond to WM_CREATE, WM_DESTROY, and user-defined messages.

SLIDEROB.C

```
#define INCL_DOS
#define INCL_WINDIALOGS
#define INCL_WINMENUS
#define INCL_WINSTDSLIDER
#define INCL_WINSYS
#define INCL_WINWINDOWMGR

#include <os2.h>
#include <stdio.h>
#include <stdlib.h>
#include <string.h>
#include "sliderob.h"

#define CLS_OBJECT              "ObjectClass"

#define UM_STARTCOPY            ( WM_USER )
#define UM_COPYDONE             ( WM_USER + 1 )

#define COPY_FILE               "SLIDEROB.C"
#define BACKUP_FILE             "SLIDEROB.BAK"

#define SZ_STACK                16384
```

```
typedef struct _SLIDERINFO {
   ULONG          ulStructSize ;
   HWND           hwndSlider ;
   HWND           hwndObject ;
   HWND           hwndDialog ;
} SLIDERINFO, * PSLIDERINFO ;

typedef VOID ( * _Optlink PFNCOPY ) ( PVOID ) ;

BOOL CopyFile ( HWND hwndSlider ) ;
MRESULT EXPENTRY ObjectWndProc ( HWND hwndWnd,
                                 ULONG ulMsg,
                                 MPARAM mpParm1,
                                 MPARAM mpParm2 ) ;


VOID CopyThread ( PSLIDERINFO psiSlider ) ;

MRESULT EXPENTRY DlgProc ( HWND hwndDlg,
                           ULONG ulMsg,
                           MPARAM mpParm1,
                           MPARAM mpParm2 ) ;

INT main ( VOID )
{
   HAB                habAnchor ;
   HMQ                hmqQueue ;
   PSLIDERINFO        pSliderInfo ;

   habAnchor = WinInitialize ( 0 ) ;
   hmqQueue = WinCreateMsgQueue ( habAnchor, 0 ) ;

   pSliderInfo = (PSLIDERINFO) malloc ( sizeof ( SLIDERINFO )) ;
   if ( pSliderInfo == NULL ) {
      WinMessageBox ( HWND_DESKTOP,
                      HWND_DESKTOP,
                      "Out of memory !",
                      "Error",
                      0,
                      MB_ICONEXCLAMATION | MB_OK ) ;
      WinDestroyMsgQueue ( hmqQueue ) ;
      WinTerminate ( habAnchor ) ;
      return 0 ;
   } /* endif */

   pSliderInfo -> ulStructSize = sizeof ( SLIDERINFO ) ;

   if ( _beginthread(( PFNCOPY ) CopyThread,
                     0,
                     SZ_STACK,
                     ( PVOID ) pSliderInfo ) == - 1 ) {

      WinMessageBox ( HWND_DESKTOP,
                      HWND_DESKTOP,
                      "Cannot create thread !",
                      "Error",
                      0,
                      MB_ICONEXCLAMATION | MB_OK ) ;
```

```
        free ( pSliderInfo ) ;
        WinDestroyMsgQueue ( hmqQueue ) ;
        WinTerminate ( habAnchor ) ;
        return 0 ;
    } /* endif */

    WinDlgBox ( HWND_DESKTOP,
                HWND_DESKTOP,
                DlgProc,
                NULLHANDLE,
                IDD_FCOPYDLG,
                pSliderInfo ) ;

    WinDestroyMsgQueue ( hmqQueue ) ;
    WinDestroyWindow ( pSliderInfo -> hwndObject ) ;
    free ( pSliderInfo ) ;
    WinTerminate ( habAnchor ) ;
    return 0 ;
}

MRESULT EXPENTRY DlgProc ( HWND hwndDlg,
                           ULONG ulMsg,
                           MPARAM mpParm1,
                           MPARAM mpParm2 )
{
    PSLIDERINFO psiSlider ;

    psiSlider = WinQueryWindowPtr ( hwndDlg, 0 ) ;

    switch ( ulMsg ) {

    case WM_INITDLG:
        {
            CHAR        achFont [16] ;
            USHORT      usIndex ;
            CHAR        achMessage [64] ;

            psiSlider = (PSLIDERINFO) PVOIDFROMMP ( mpParm2 ) ;
            WinSetWindowPtr ( hwndDlg, 0, psiSlider ) ;

            psiSlider -> hwndDialog = hwndDlg ;
            psiSlider -> hwndSlider = WinWindowFromID ( hwndDlg,
                                                        IDS_SLIDER ) ;

            //-------------------------------------------------------
            // Set the size of the tick marks
            //-------------------------------------------------------

            WinSendDlgItemMsg ( hwndDlg,
                                IDS_SLIDER,
                                SLM_SETTICKSIZE,
                                MPFROM2SHORT ( SMA_SETALLTICKS, 7 ) ,
                                0 ) ;

            strcpy ( achFont, "8.Tms Rmn" ) ;
            WinSetPresParam ( WinWindowFromID( hwndDlg, IDS_SLIDER ) ,
```

```
                                 PP_FONTNAMESIZE,
                                 strlen ( achFont ) + 1,
                                 achFont ) ;

          for ( usIndex = 0 ; usIndex < 11 ; usIndex ++ ) {
             sprintf ( achMessage, "%d%%", usIndex * 10 ) ;

             WinSendDlgItemMsg ( hwndDlg,
                                 IDS_SLIDER,
                                 SLM_SETSCALETEXT,
                                 MPFROMSHORT ( usIndex ) ,
                                 MPFROMP ( achMessage )) ;
          } /* endfor */
       }
       break ;


   case WM_COMMAND:

       switch ( SHORT1FROMMP ( mpParm1 )) {

          case IDP_START:
             WinPostMsg ( psiSlider -> hwndObject,
                          UM_STARTCOPY,
                          0,
                          0 ) ;
             WinEnableWindow ( WinWindowFromID ( hwndDlg,
                                                 IDP_START ) ,
                               FALSE ) ;
             break ;

          case IDP_CANCEL:
             WinDismissDlg ( hwndDlg, FALSE ) ;
             break ;

          default:
             return WinDefDlgProc ( hwndDlg,
                                    ulMsg,
                                    mpParm1,
                                    mpParm2 ) ;
       } /* endswitch */
       break ;

   case WM_DRAWITEM:
       {
          POWNERITEM poiItem ;

          //----------------------------------------------------------
          // get the OWNERITEM structure from mpParm2
          //----------------------------------------------------------

          poiItem = ( POWNERITEM ) PVOIDFROMMP ( mpParm2 ) ;

          switch ( poiItem -> idItem ) {
```

```
           case SDA_RIBBONSTRIP:
               WinFillRect ( poiItem -> hps,
                             &poiItem -> rclItem,
                             CLR_BLUE ) ;
               return MRFROMSHORT ( TRUE ) ;

           default:
               return WinDefDlgProc ( hwndDlg,
                                      ulMsg,
                                      mpParm1,
                                      mpParm2 ) ;
           } /* endswitch */
       }

   case UM_COPYDONE:
       {
           USHORT      usState ;
           CHAR        achMessage [60] ;

           WinEnableWindow ( WinWindowFromID ( hwndDlg,
                                               IDP_START ) ,
                             TRUE ) ;

           usState = SHORT1FROMMP ( mpParm1 ) ;
           if ( usState == TRUE ) {
               strcpy ( achMessage, "Copy completed Successfully" ) ;
               WinAlarm ( HWND_DESKTOP, WA_NOTE ) ;
           } else {
               strcpy ( achMessage, "Copy failed" ) ;
               WinAlarm ( HWND_DESKTOP, WA_ERROR ) ;
           } /* endif */

           WinMessageBox ( HWND_DESKTOP,
                           hwndDlg,
                           achMessage,
                           "Copy Status",
                           0,
                           MB_OK | MB_INFORMATION ) ;
       }
       break ;

   default:
       return WinDefDlgProc ( hwndDlg,
                              ulMsg,
                              mpParm1,
                              mpParm2 ) ;
   } /* endswitch */

   return MRFROMSHORT ( FALSE ) ;
}
```

```
VOID CopyThread ( PSLIDERINFO psiSlider )
{
   HAB         habAnchor ;
   HMQ         hmqQueue ;
   BOOL        bLoop ;
   QMSG        qmMsg ;

   habAnchor = WinInitialize ( 0 ) ;
   hmqQueue = WinCreateMsgQueue ( habAnchor, 0 ) ;

   WinRegisterClass ( habAnchor,
                      CLS_OBJECT,
                      ObjectWndProc,
                      0,
                      sizeof ( PVOID )) ;

   psiSlider -> hwndObject = WinCreateWindow ( HWND_OBJECT,
                                               CLS_OBJECT,
                                               NULL,
                                               0,
                                               0,
                                               0,
                                               0,
                                               0,
                                               NULLHANDLE,
                                               HWND_TOP,
                                               ID_OBJECT,
                                               psiSlider,
                                               NULL ) ;

   if ( psiSlider -> hwndObject != NULLHANDLE ) {
      bLoop = WinGetMsg ( habAnchor,
                          &qmMsg,
                          NULLHANDLE,
                          0,
                          0 ) ;

      while ( bLoop ) {
         WinDispatchMsg ( habAnchor, &qmMsg ) ;
         bLoop = WinGetMsg ( habAnchor,
                             &qmMsg,
                             NULLHANDLE,
                             0,
                             0 ) ;
      } /* endwhile */

      WinDestroyWindow ( psiSlider -> hwndObject ) ;
   } /* endif */

   WinDestroyMsgQueue ( hmqQueue ) ;
   WinTerminate ( habAnchor ) ;
   return ;
}
```

```
MRESULT EXPENTRY ObjectWndProc ( HWND hwndWnd,
                                 ULONG  ulMsg,
                                 MPARAM mpParm1,
                                 MPARAM mpParm2 )
{
   switch ( ulMsg ) {

      case WM_CREATE:
         WinSetWindowPtr ( hwndWnd, 0, PVOIDFROMMP ( mpParm1 )) ;
         break ;

      case UM_STARTCOPY:
         {
            PSLIDERINFO pSliderInfo ;

            pSliderInfo = WinQueryWindowPtr ( hwndWnd, 0 ) ;

            if ( CopyFile ( pSliderInfo -> hwndSlider )) {
               WinPostMsg ( pSliderInfo -> hwndDialog,
                            UM_COPYDONE,
                            MPFROMSHORT ( TRUE ) ,
                            0 ) ;
            } else {
               WinPostMsg ( pSliderInfo -> hwndDialog,
                            UM_COPYDONE,
                            MPFROMSHORT ( FALSE ) ,
                            0 ) ;
            } /* endif */
         }
         break ;

      default:
         return WinDefWindowProc ( hwndWnd,
                                   ulMsg,
                                   mpParm1,
                                   mpParm2 ) ;
   } /* endswitch */

   return MRFROMSHORT ( FALSE ) ;
}

BOOL CopyFile ( HWND hwndSlider )
{
   APIRET            arRc ;
   FILESTATUS3       fsStatus ;
   PBYTE             pbBuffer ;
   HFILE             hfRead ;
   ULONG             ulAction ;
   HFILE             hfWrite ;
   ULONG             ulSzBlock ;
   USHORT            usIndex ;
   ULONG             ulBytesRead ;
   ULONG             ulBytesWritten ;
```

```
   arRc = DosQueryPathInfo ( COPY_FILE,
                             FIL_STANDARD,
                             (PVOID) &fsStatus,
                             sizeof ( fsStatus )) ;

if ( !arRc ) {

   ulSzBlock = fsStatus.cbFile / 10 + 1 ;

   pbBuffer = (PBYTE) malloc ( ulSzBlock ) ;

   //------------------------------------------------------------
   // Open up the file for reading
   //------------------------------------------------------------

   arRc = DosOpen ( COPY_FILE,
                    &hfRead,
                    &ulAction,
                    0,
                    FILE_NORMAL,
                    FILE_OPEN,
                    OPEN_ACCESS_READONLY | OPEN_SHARE_DENYWRITE,
                    0 ) ;

   //------------------------------------------------------------
   // Open up the backup file for write
   //------------------------------------------------------------

   arRc = DosOpen ( BACKUP_FILE,
                    &hfWrite,
                    &ulAction,
                    0,
                    FILE_NORMAL,
                    FILE_CREATE,
                    OPEN_ACCESS_WRITEONLY |
                    OPEN_SHARE_DENYREADWRITE,
                    0 ) ;

   for ( usIndex = 1 ; usIndex < 11 ; usIndex ++ ) {

      //------------------------------------------------------------
      // Read a block
      //------------------------------------------------------------

      DosRead ( hfRead,
                pbBuffer,
                ulSzBlock,
                &ulBytesRead ) ;

      //------------------------------------------------------------
      // Write a block
      //------------------------------------------------------------
```

```
          DosWrite ( hfWrite,
                     pbBuffer,
                     ulBytesRead,
                     &ulBytesWritten ) ;

       //------------------------------------------------------------
       // Tell the slider to move
       //------------------------------------------------------------

       WinSendMsg ( hwndSlider,
                    SLM_SETSLIDERINFO,
                    MPFROM2SHORT ( SMA_SLIDERARMPOSITION,
                          SMA_INCREMENTVALUE ) ,
                    MPFROMSHORT ( usIndex )) ;
    } /* endfor */

    //------------------------------------------------------------
    // Clean up
    //------------------------------------------------------------

    DosClose ( hfRead ) ;
    DosClose ( hfWrite ) ;
    free ( pbBuffer ) ;
    return TRUE ;
  } else {
    return FALSE ;
  } /* endif */
}
```

SLIDEROB.RC

```
#include <os2.h>
#include "sliderob.h"

DLGTEMPLATE IDD_FCOPYDLG LOADONCALL MOVEABLE DISCARDABLE
{
   DIALOG  "File Copy", IDD_FCOPYDLG, 67, 80, 324, 104,
      WS_VISIBLE,
      FCF_SYSMENU | FCF_TITLEBAR
   {
      LTEXT "Progress Indicator", -1, 115, 30, 80, 12
      CONTROL  "", IDS_SLIDER, 12, 43, 300, 46, WC_SLIDER,
         SLS_HORIZONTAL | SLS_OWNERDRAW | SLS_CENTER |
         SLS_SNAPTOINCREMENT | SLS_READONLY | SLS_RIBBONSTRIP |
         SLS_HOMELEFT | SLS_PRIMARYSCALE1 | WS_GROUP | WS_TABSTOP |
         WS_VISIBLE
         CTLDATA 12, 0, 11, 26, 0, 0
      PUSHBUTTON "~Start", IDP_START, 6, 4, 40, 14
      PUSHBUTTON "Cancel", IDP_CANCEL, 49, 4, 40, 14
   }
}
```

SLIDEROB.H

```
#define IDD_FCOPYDLG                256
#define ID_OBJECT                   257
```

```
#define IDS_SLIDER              512
#define IDP_START               513
#define IDP_CANCEL              514
```

SLIDEROB.MAK

```
SLIDEROB.EXE:                   SLIDEROB.OBJ \
                                SLIDEROB.RES
        LINK386 @<<
SLIDEROB
SLIDEROB
SLIDEROB
OS2386
SLIDEROB
<<
        RC SLIDEROB.RES SLIDEROB.EXE

SLIDEROB.RES:                   SLIDEROB.RC \
                                SLIDEROB.H
        RC -r SLIDEROB.RC SLIDEROB.RES

SLIDEROB.OBJ:                   SLIDEROB.C \
                                SLIDEROB.H
        ICC -C+ -Gm+ -Kb+ -Ss+ SLIDEROB.C
```

SLIDEROB.DEF

```
NAME SLIDER WINDOWAPI

DESCRIPTION 'Object window slider example
Copyright (c) 1992 by Kathleen Panov.
All rights reserved.'

STACKSIZE 16384
```

15.5 In the Beginning...

```
    pSliderInfo = (PSLIDERINFO) malloc ( sizeof ( SLIDERINFO )) ;
```

The beginning of this program immediately differentiates itself from the
SLIDERTH program. We're going to allocate some memory and let both
threads read and write to it.

```
    if ( _beginthread(( PFNCOPY ) CopyThread,
                        0,
                        SZ_STACK,
                        ( PVOID ) pSliderInfo ) == - 1 ) {
```

```
WinDlgBox ( HWND_DESKTOP,
            HWND_DESKTOP,
            DlgProc,
            NULLHANDLE,
            IDD_FCOPYDLG,
            pSliderInfo ) ;
```

It is passed to the worker thread as a thread argument to *_beginthread*. It is also passed to the dialog procedure as the last parameter to *WinDlgBox*, the user-defined data area.

```
            pSliderInfo = PVOIDFROMMP( mp2 );
```

In the WM_INITDLG processing, the pointer to the PSLIDERINFO structure is retrieved from message parameter 2.

```
        psiSlider = (PSLIDERINFO) PVOIDFROMMP ( mpParm2 ) ;
        WinSetWindowPtr ( hwndDlg, 0, psiSlider ) ;

        psiSlider -> hwndDialog = hwndDlg ;
        psiSlider -> hwndSlider = WinWindowFromID ( hwndDlg,
                                              IDS_SLIDER ) ;
```

At the end of the slider initialization, the window handles for the slider and the dialog box are written to *psiSlider*. In order to keep this data handy, we use *WinSetWindowPtr* to store it in the user-defined area of the window word.

15.6 Creating the Object Window

The *CopyThread* function looks quite a bit different from the previous example. First, we retrieve the PSLIDERINFO structure from the thread args. The next few lines of code look just like a normal window initialization procedure. An anchor block and message queue are created. A new class of window is created, CLS_OBJECT. This class is assigned to the window procedure *ObjectWndProc*. We specify the size of a PVOID for the user-defined window word area.

```
psiSlider -> hwndObject = WinCreateWindow ( HWND_OBJECT,
                                            CLS_OBJECT,
                                            NULL,
                                            0,
                                            0,
                                            0,
                                            0,
                                            0,
                                            NULLHANDLE,
                                            HWND_TOP,
                                            ID_OBJECT,
                                            psiSlider,
                                            NULL ) ;
```

The *WinCreateWindow* call is the easiest version of this function you will ever see. The window text, *x* and *y* coordinates, height and width, and owner are all set to 0 or NULL. The Z-order is immaterial. The control data parameter is where we slip the pointer to the PSLIDERINFO structure into the object window procedure.

15.7 Meanwhile, Back in the Dialog Procedure...

There are two user-defined messages in this example: UM_STARTCOPY and UM_COPYDONE. When the user presses the IDP_START push-button, the first thing we do is to post a UM_STARTCOPY message to the object window.

```
WinPostMsg ( psiSlider -> hwndObject,
             UM_STARTCOPY,
             0,
             0 ) ;

WinEnableWindow ( WinWindowFromID ( hwndDlg,
                                    IDP_START ) ,
                  FALSE ) ;
```

This is the object window's signal to start the file copy. Next, we'll disable the IDP_START push-button. This is one of those end-user niceties that the CUA police recommend. The button will stay disabled until the UM_COPYDONE message is received from the object window.

```
WinEnableWindow ( WinWindowFromID ( hwndDlg,
                                    IDP_START ) ,
                  TRUE ) ;

usState = SHORT1FROMMP ( mpParm1 ) ;
if ( usState == TRUE ) {
   strcpy ( achMessage, "Copy completed Successfully" ) ;
   WinAlarm ( HWND_DESKTOP, WA_NOTE ) ;
} else {
   strcpy ( achMessage, "Copy failed" ) ;
```

```
    WinAlarm ( HWND_DESKTOP, WA_ERROR ) ;
} /* endif */

WinMessageBox ( HWND_DESKTOP,
                hwndDlg,
                achMessage,
                "Copy Status",
                0,
                MB_OK | MB_INFORMATION ) ;
```

When the UM_COPYDONE message is received, we go ahead and enable the
IDP_START push-button. Next we update the user with a status report on the
file copy, using *WinMessageBox*. An OK or NOTOK flag is contained in
message parameter 1.

15.8 Meanwhile, Back in the Object Window Procedure...

The object window procedure only processes two messages, WM_CREATE
and UM_STARTCOPY. The WM_CREATE message processing retrieves the
control data parameters, in this case, the *pSliderInfo* pointer, out of message
parameter 1. Next, this pointer is stored in the user-defined window word
storage area using *WinSetWindowPtr*.

The UM_STARTCOPY message processing is where the file copy is actually
performed. As the file copy is being performed, the object thread posts
messages to update the slider. When the copy is done, a UM_COPYDONE
message is posted back with either an OK or NOTOK return code in message
parameter 1.

15.9 Slider Messages

WM_CONTROL
This message is sent to a control's owner, in order to signal a significant event
that has occurred to the control.

Parameter 1: USHORT usId   slider control ID
                  USHORT usNotifyCode   notification code — can be any of
                                          the following for the slider control:
                                          SLN_CHANGE — slider arm
                                          position changed
                                          SLN_KILLFOCUS — slider is
                                          losing focus

		SLN_SETFOCUS — slider is receiving the focus SLN_SLIDERTRACK — slider arm is being dragged, but not released
Parameter 2:	ULONG ulNotifyInfo	when *usNotifyCode* is SLN_CHANGE, or SLN_SLIDERTRACK, this equals the new arm position, in pixels when *usNotifyCode* is SLN_SETFOCUS, or SLN_KILLFOCUS, this is *hwndSlider*
Reply:	ULONG ulReply	reserved, 0

WM_CONTROLPOINTER

This message is sent to the owner of a control when the mouse pointer moves over the control.

Parameter 1:	USHORT usControlID	control ID
Parameter 2:	HPOINTER hptrCurrent	current pointer handle
Reply:	HPOINTER hptrNew	pointer handle to be used

WM_DRAWITEM

Sent when the slider is of style SLS_OWNERDRAW. Sent to the control's owner whenever the slider shaft, slider arm, ribbon-strip, or background need to be drawn.

Parameter 1:	USHORT usID	window ID
Parameter 2:	POWNERITEM pOwneritem	pointer to OWNERITEM structure (see page 426)
Reply:	BOOL fDrawn	drawn? TRUE:FALSE

SLM_QUERYDETENTPOS

Queries the slider for the text on a specific tick mark.

Parameter 1:	USHORT usTickNum	tick mark number
	USHORT usBufLen	length of *pszTickText*

Parameter 2:	PSZ pszTickText	pointer to tick text buffer
Reply:	SHORT sBufLen	count of bytes returned

SLM_QUERYSLIDERINFO

Sends a query to the slider for the position or size of some part of the slider.

Parameter 1:	USHORT usType	SMA_SHAFTDIMENSIONS,
		SMA_SHAFTPOSITION,
		SMA_SLIDERARMDIMENSIONS,
		SMA_SLIDERARMPOSITION
	USHORT usVal	SMA_RANGEVALUE —
		reply represents number of pixels
		between home and current arm
		position in low byte; high byte is
		pixel length of slider
		SMA_INCREMENTVALUE —
		represents position as
		increment value
Parameter 2:	ULONG ulMP2	reserved, 0
Reply:	ULONG ulInfo	see *usVal*

SLM_QUERYTICKPOS

This message is used to query the slider for the current position of a specified tick mark.

Parameter 1:	USHORT usTickNumber	tick mark number
Parameter 2:	ULONG ulParam2	reserved, 0
Reply:	USHORT usXTickPos	*x* - coordinate
	USHORT usYTickPos	*y* - coordinate

SLM_QUERYTICKSIZE

This message is used to query the slider for the size of the tick mark.

Parameter 1:	USHORT usTickNumber	tick mark number
Parameter 2:	ULONG ulParam2	reserved, 0
Reply:	USHORT usTickSize	tick mark length

SLM_REMOVEDETENT
This message is used to remove a detent.

Parameter 1:	ULONG ulDetentID	detent ID
Parameter 2:	ULONG ulParam2	reserved, 0
Reply:	BOOL fSuccess	successful?
		TRUE:FALSE

SLM_SETSCALETEXT
This message is sent to the slider to set the text above a tick mark. Text is centered on the tick mark.

Parameter 1:	USHORT usTickNumber	tick mark number
Parameter 2:	PSZ pszTickMarkText	pointer to tick mark text
Reply:	BOOL fSuccess	successful?
		TRUE:FALSE

SLM_SETSLIDERINFO
This message is sent to set the current position or dimensions of a specific part of the slider.

Parameter 1:	USHORT usInfoType	information attribute
	USHORT usArmPosType	format attribute
Parameter 2:	ULONG ulNewInfo	new value
Reply:	BOOL fSuccess	successful?TRUE:FALSE

SLM_SETTICKSIZE
This message is used to set the size of a tick mark.

Parameter 1:	USHORT usTickNumber	tick mark number
	USHORT usTickSize	tick mark length
Parameter 2:	ULONG ulParam2	reserved, 0
Reply:	BOOL fSuccess	successful?
		TRUE:FALSE

WM_CHAR

This message is sent when the user presses a key.

Parameter 1:	USHORT fsFlags	keyboard control code
	UCHAR ucRepeat	repeat count
	UCHAR usScanCode	scan code
Parameter 2:	USHORT usCharCode	character code
	USHORT usVirtualKey	virtual key
Reply:	BOOL fResult	key processed?
		TRUE:FALSE

WM_PRESPARAMCHANGED

This message is sent to indicate a change in the slider's Presentation Parameters.

Parameter 1:	ULONG ulAttributeType	attribute type
Parameter 2:	ULONG ulParam2	reserved, 0
Reply:	ULONG ulReply	reserved, 0

WM_QUERYWINDOWPARAMS

This message is sent to the slider to query the Presentation Parameters.

Parameter 1:	PWNDPARAMS pWndParams	pointer to
		WNDPARAMS structure

```
typedef struct _WNDPARAMS  /* wprm */ {
    ULONG fsStatus;         /* can be either WPM_CBCTLDATA
                               or WPM_CTLDATA */
    ULONG cchText;          /* length of window text */
    PSZ   pszText;          /* window text */
    ULONG cbPresParams;     /* Length of presentation
                               parameters */
    PVOID pPresParams;      /* pointer to presentation
                               parameters data */
    ULONG cbCtlData;        /* Length of window class data
                               */
    PVOID pCtlData;         /* Pointer to window class
                               data */
} WNDPARAMS;
typedef WNDPARAMS *PWNDPARAMS;
```

window class data structure for slider:

```
typedef struct _SLDCDATA  /* sldcd */ {
      ULONG  cbSize;            /* Size of control block   */
      USHORT usScale1Increments;  /* # of divisions on
                            scale   */
       USHORT  usScale1Spacing; /* Space in pels between
                          increments */
      USHORT  usScale2Increments;  /* # of divisions on
                          scale   */
       USHORT  usScale2Spacing; /* Space in pels between
                          increments  */
    } SLDCDATA;
  typedef SLDCDATA *PSLDCDATA;
```

Parameter 2:	ULONG ulParam2	reserved, 0
Reply:	BOOL fSuccess	successful? TRUE:FALSE

WM_SETWINDOWPARAMS

Sent to the slider window to set the Presentation Parameters.

Parameter 1:	PWNDPARAMS pWndParams	pointer to WNDPARAMS structure
Parameter 2:	ULONG ulParam2	reserved, 0
Reply:	BOOL fSuccess	successful? TRUE:FALSE

Chapter 16

Font and File Dialogs

The Font Dialog and File Dialog were introduced in OS/2 2.0 to provide two high-level functions that perform tasks that most programmers had previously written by hand at one time or another. The Font Dialog is a dialog box with a listing of fonts and an example of each. The File Dialog is a dialog box that contains a list of files on the enduser's available drives (see Figure 16.1). Both functions can be extensively reconfigured by the programmer.

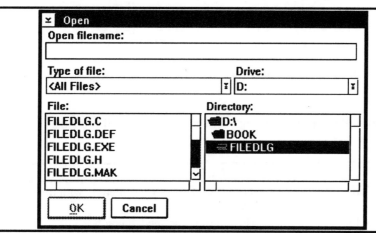

Figure 16.1. A file dialog box.

16.1 The File Dialog

The file dialog can either be created as a "Save As..." or "Open" dialog. A list of all the controls in the file dialog is included so that you can add your own, or remove some of those you feel are unnecessary.

The meat of creating a file dialog structure is the FILEDLG structure. This structure includes all the configurable options for the file dialog. The structure is shown below:

```
typedef struct _FILEDLG      /* filedlg */
{
    ULONG     cbSize;
    ULONG     fl;
    ULONG     ulUser;
    LONG      lReturn;
    LONG      lSRC;
    PSZ       pszTitle;
    PSZ       pszOKButton;
    PFNWP     pfnDlgProc;
    PSZ       pszIType;
    PAPSZ     papszITypeList;
    PSZ       pszIDrive;
    PAPSZ     papszIDriveList;
    HMODULE   hMod;
    CHAR      szFullFile[CCHMAXPATH];
    PAPSZ     papszFQFilename;
    ULONG     ulFQFCount;
    USHORT    usDlgId;
    SHORT     x;
    SHORT     y;
    SHORT     sEAType;
} FILEDLG;
    typedef FILEDLG *PFILEDLG;
```

The *cbSize* field is the size of the FILEDLG structure. This field *must* be filled in.

The *fl* field is the File Dialog flags used to describe the file dialog. The possible values are:

FLAG	MEANING
FDS_CENTER	The file dialog is centered within its owner.
FDS_CUSTOM	Use a custom-defined dialog box.
FDS_FILTERUNION	Use a union of EAs and file name filter.
FDS_HELPBUTTON	Include a HELP push-button on the file dialog.

FDS_APPLYBUTTON	Include an APPLY push-button on the file dialog.
FDS_PRELOAD_VOL_INFO	Load the volume inf. on the file dialog initialization. This can cause lengthy processing at startup.
FDS_MODELESS	The file dialog is modeless.
FDS_INCLUDE_EAS	Load the EA information.
FDS_OPEN_DIALOG	File dialog is the "Open" dialog.
FDS_SAVEAS_DIALOG	File dialog is the "Save As..." dialog.
FDS_MULTIPLESEL	Multiple files can be selected from the list box.
FDS_ENABLEFILELB	If file dialog is the "Save As..." style, the list box of files is enabled, not disabled (the default).

This field *must* be filled in.

The *ulUser* field is 4 bytes of space that are available for the programmer to use.

The *lReturn* field is the return code from the file dialog. This can be DID_OK, DID_CANCEL, or 0 if an error occurs.

The *lSRC* field contains an FDS_ERR return code if an error occurs in the file dialog.

The *pszTitle* field is a pointer to a string that contains the title of the file dialog box window. If this is NULL, the title of the owner window is used.

The *pszOKButton* field is a pointer to a string that contains the text for the OK push-button. If this is NULL, "OK" is used.

The *pfnDlgProc* field is a pointer to a user-defined dialog procedure. The function *WinDefFileDlgProc* can be used to call the default dialog procedure from the user-defined procedure.

The *pszIType* field is a pointer to a string containing a type of EA (extended attribute). Only files that contain this EA type will be shown in the list of available files.

The field *papszlDriveList* is an array of pointers that contain a list of EA types for filtering the available file list. This array must end with a NULL pointer. The *pszlDrive* field is a pointer to a string that contains the selected drive when the dialog is first made visible.

The field *papszlDriveList* is an array of pointers to strings that contain a list of drives to use as available drives. A NULL in this field will cause all available drives to be included in the list. This array must end with a NULL pointer.

The *hMod* field is the handle of a .DLL that contains the dialog box resource to be used if a FDS_CUSTOM flag is specified.

The character array *szFullFile* contains the file name of the initially selected file. On return, this field contains the fully qualified file name selected by the enduser.

The field *papszFQFilename* is an array of pointers to fully qualified file names. On return from the *WinFileDlg* function, this array contains all the files that the enduser selected.

The field *ulFQFCount* is the number of files selected by the user.

The field *usDlgID* is the dialog resource ID of a file dialog to use as a replacement for the default file dialog. This field is used if FDS_CUSTOM is specified.

The fields *x* and *y* are the *x,y* coordinates to be used to place the file dialog. These fields are ignored when FDS_CENTER is used.

The field *sEAType* is an index into the *papszlTypeList* array that contains the EA type of the file that was selected.

16.2 Special Considerations for Multiple File Selections

When a file dialog has the style FDS_MULTIPLESEL, multiple files can be selected from the file dialog. This causes a few events to happen:

- The number of files selected is returned in the field *ulFQFCount*.
- An array of pointers to the selected files' names are returned in the *papszFQFilename* field.

- If the file dialog has allocated memory for these strings, the *lSRC* field will contain FDS_ERR_DEALLOCATE_MEMORY (1). This is a signal to the programmer that they need to free the memory allocated for these strings with the *WinFreeFileDlgList* api.
- The first file selected will be contained in the *szFullFile* array.

16.3 The FILEDLG Example Program

The example program FILEDLG creates a file dialog and prints the file name of the selected file on the client area.

FILEDLG.C

```
#define INCL_WINSTDFILE
#define INCL_WINSYS
#define INCL_WINWINDOWMGR

#include <os2.h>
#include <stdio.h>
#include <stdlib.h>
#include <string.h>
#include "filedlg.h"

MRESULT EXPENTRY ClientWndProc ( HWND hwndWnd,
                                 ULONG ulMsg,
                                 MPARAM mpParm1,
                                 MPARAM mpParm2 ) ;

BOOL FindFile ( HWND hwndWnd, CHAR * pchFile ) ;

#define CLS_CLIENT              "MyClass"

INT main ( VOID )
{
    HAB         habAnchor ;
    HMQ         hmqQueue ;
    ULONG       ulFlags ;
    HWND        hwndFrame ;
    HWND        hwndClient ;
    BOOL        bLoop ;
    QMSG        qmMsg ;

    habAnchor = WinInitialize ( 0 ) ;
    hmqQueue = WinCreateMsgQueue ( habAnchor, 0 ) ;

    WinRegisterClass ( habAnchor,
                       CLS_CLIENT,
                       ClientWndProc,
                       CS_SIZEREDRAW,
                       sizeof ( PVOID )) ;
```

```
    ulFlags = FCF_TITLEBAR | FCF_SYSMENU | FCF_MENU |
              FCF_MINMAX | FCF_SIZEBORDER | FCF_SHELLPOSITION |
              FCF_TASKLIST ;

    hwndFrame = WinCreateStdWindow ( HWND_DESKTOP,
                                     0,
                                     &ulFlags,
                                     CLS_CLIENT,
                                     "File Dialog Example",
                                     0,
                                     NULLHANDLE,
                                     RES_CLIENT,
                                     &hwndClient ) ;

    if ( hwndFrame != NULLHANDLE ) {

        WinSetWindowPos ( hwndFrame,
                          NULLHANDLE,
                          50,
                          50,
                          500,
                          250,
                          SWP_SIZE |
                          SWP_MOVE |
                          SWP_ACTIVATE |
                          SWP_SHOW ) ;

        bLoop = WinGetMsg ( habAnchor, &qmMsg, NULLHANDLE, 0, 0 ) ;

        while ( bLoop ) {
            WinDispatchMsg ( habAnchor, &qmMsg ) ;
            bLoop = WinGetMsg ( habAnchor,
                                &qmMsg,
                                NULLHANDLE,
                                0,
                                0 ) ;
        } /* endwhile */

        WinDestroyWindow ( hwndFrame ) ;
    } /* endif */

    WinDestroyMsgQueue ( hmqQueue ) ;
    WinTerminate ( habAnchor ) ;
    return 0 ;
}

MRESULT EXPENTRY ClientWndProc ( HWND hwndWnd,
                                 ULONG ulMsg,
                                 MPARAM mpParm1,
                                 MPARAM mpParm2 )
{
    PCHAR pchFile ;

    pchFile = WinQueryWindowPtr ( hwndWnd, 0 ) ;

    switch ( ulMsg ) {
```

```
case WM_CREATE:
    pchFile = ( PCHAR ) malloc ( CCHMAXPATH ) ;
    if ( pchFile == NULL ) {
        WinAlarm ( HWND_DESKTOP, WA_ERROR ) ;
        WinMessageBox ( HWND_DESKTOP,
                        hwndWnd,
                        "No memory could be allocated !",
                        "Error",
                        0,
                        MB_INFORMATION | MB_OK ) ;
        return MRFROMSHORT ( TRUE ) ;
    } /* endif */

    WinSetWindowPtr ( hwndWnd, 0, pchFile ) ;
    pchFile [0] = 0 ;
    break ;

case WM_DESTROY:
    if ( pchFile != NULL ) {
        free ( pchFile ) ;
    } /* endif */
    break ;

case WM_PAINT:
    {
        HPS   hpsPaint ;
        RECTL rclInvalid ;
        CHAR  achText [CCHMAXPATH] ;

        hpsPaint = WinBeginPaint ( hwndWnd,
                                   NULLHANDLE,
                                   &rclInvalid ) ;

        WinFillRect ( hpsPaint, &rclInvalid, SYSCLR_WINDOW ) ;

        if ( pchFile [0] != 0 ) {

            WinQueryWindowRect ( hwndWnd, &rclInvalid ) ;
            sprintf ( achText,
                      "You have selected file %s",
                      pchFile ) ;
            WinDrawText ( hpsPaint,
                          - 1,
                          achText,
                          &rclInvalid,
                          0,
                          0,
                          DT_CENTER | DT_VCENTER | DT_TEXTATTRS ) ;
        } /* endif */

        WinEndPaint ( hpsPaint ) ;
    }
    break ;

case WM_COMMAND:

    switch ( SHORT1FROMMP ( mpParm1 )) {
```

```
        case IDM_OPEN:
           if ( pchFile ) {
              FindFile ( hwndWnd, pchFile ) ;
           } /* endif */

           WinInvalidateRect ( hwndWnd, NULL, TRUE ) ;
           WinUpdateWindow ( hwndWnd ) ;
           break ;

        case IDM_EXIT:
           WinPostMsg ( hwndWnd, WM_QUIT, 0, 0 ) ;
           break ;

        default:
           return WinDefWindowProc ( hwndWnd,
                                     ulMsg,
                                     mpParm1,
                                     mpParm2 ) ;
        } /* endswitch */
        break ;

     default:
        return WinDefWindowProc ( hwndWnd,
                                  ulMsg,
                                  mpParm1,
                                  mpParm2 ) ;
     } /* endswitch */

     return MRFROMSHORT ( FALSE ) ;
}

BOOL FindFile ( HWND hwndWnd, CHAR * pchFile )
{
   FILEDLG       fdFileDlg ;

   memset ( &fdFileDlg, 0, sizeof ( FILEDLG )) ;

   fdFileDlg.cbSize = sizeof ( FILEDLG ) ;
   fdFileDlg.fl = FDS_CENTER | FDS_PRELOAD_VOLINFO |
                  FDS_OPEN_DIALOG ;

   if ( WinFileDlg ( HWND_DESKTOP,
                     hwndWnd,
                     &fdFileDlg ) != DID_OK ) {
      WinAlarm ( HWND_DESKTOP, WA_ERROR ) ;
      return FALSE ;
   } /* endif */

   strcpy ( pchFile, fdFileDlg.szFullFile ) ;
   return TRUE ;
}
```

FILEDLG.RC

```
#include <os2.h>
#include "filedlg.h"

MENU RES_CLIENT
{
    SUBMENU "~File", IDM_SUB1
    {
        MENUITEM "~New" , IDM_NEW
        MENUITEM "~Open File...", IDM_OPEN
        MENUITEM "~Close File", IDM_CLOSE
        MENUITEM "E~xit" , IDM_EXIT
    }
}
```

FILEDLG.H

```
#define RES_CLIENT          256
#define IDM_SUB1            512
#define IDM_NEW             513
#define IDM_OPEN            514
#define IDM_CLOSE           515
#define IDM_EXIT            516
```

FILEDLG.MAK

```
FILEDLG.EXE:                    FILEDLG.OBJ \
                                FILEDLG.RES
        LINK386 @<<
FILEDLG
FILEDLG
FILEDLG
OS2386
FILEDLG
<<
        RC FILEDLG.RES FILEDLG.EXE

FILEDLG.RES:                    FILEDLG.RC \
                                FILEDLG.H
        RC -r FILEDLG.RC FILEDLG.RES

FILEDLG.OBJ:                    FILEDLG.C \
                                FILEDLG.H
        ICC -C+ -Kb+ -Ss+ FILEDLG.C
```

FILEDLG.DEF

```
NAME FILEDLG WINDOWAPI
DESCRIPTION 'File dialog example
            Copyright (c) 1992 by Kathleen Panov.
            All rights reserved.'
STACKSIZE 16384
```

16.4 The Window Word

```
pchFile = ( PCHAR ) malloc ( CCHMAXPATH ) ;
if ( pchFile == NULL ) {
    WinAlarm ( HWND_DESKTOP, WA_ERROR ) ;
    WinMessageBox ( HWND_DESKTOP,
                    hwndWnd,
                    "No memory could be allocated !",
                    "Error",
                    0,
                    MB_INFORMATION | MB_OK ) ;
    return MRFROMSHORT ( TRUE ) ;
} /* endif */

WinSetWindowPtr ( hwndWnd, 0, pchFile ) ;
pchFile [0] = 0 ;
```

In the FILEDLG example, a standard window is created with a menu. In the WM_CREATE processing, memory is allocated to hold the selected file name. The pointer to this memory is attached as a window word using *WinSetWindowPtr*. This memory is freed when the WM_DESTROY message is received.

When the user selects the "Open" selection from the menu, a WM_COMMAND message is sent. When the message is received, the user function *FindFile* is called. After this function returns, the client area is invalidated to force a repaint.

16.5 Putting It All Together, *FindFile*

The *FindFile* function is a user-defined function where the FILEDLG structure is initialized, and *WinFileDlg* is called. When the FILEDLG structure is declared, it is important to initialize the entire structure to 0.

Gotcha!

The FILEDLG structure is a very particular beast. There are several fields in the structure that are pointers, or arrays of pointers. You can get very bad results if these pointers are not set to NULL if unused, but to some arbitrary garbage. This will occur if the FILEDLG structure is declared as an automatic structure variable and is left uninitialized. Also, note that most of these fields in the FILEDLG structure are *pointers*, not arrays. This means it is your responsibility to provide the memory. There is only one character array, *szFullFile*, of size CCHMAXFILEPATH. This is the only string field you can copy data directly into!

16.6 Initializing the FILEDLG Structure

```
fdFileDlg.cbSize = sizeof ( FILEDLG ) ;
fdFileDlg.fl = FDS_CENTER | FDS_PRELOAD_VOLINFO |
               FDS_OPEN_DIALOG ;
```

The mandatory *cbSize* field is set to the size of the FILEDLG structure. The file dialog box in this example has the styles FDS_CENTER, FDS_PRELOAD_INFO, and FDS_OPEN_DIALOG. This centers the dialog, loads all the drive volume info on startup, and creates the "File Open..." dialog. These styles are OR'ed together in the *fl* field. This is also a mandatory field.

```
if ( WinFileDlg ( HWND_DESKTOP,
                  hwndWnd,
                  &fdFileDlg ) != DID_OK ) {
```

WinFileDlg has three parameters. The first parameter is the parent window handle, in this case HWND_DESKTOP. The second parameter is the owner window handle, in this case *hwndClient*. The last parameter is a pointer to a FILEDLG structure.

```
strcpy ( pchFile, fdFileDlg.szFullFile ) ;
```

Once the user has closed the file dialog, *szFullFile* is copied into the window word, *pchFileName*, and the function returns.

16.7 The Font Dialog

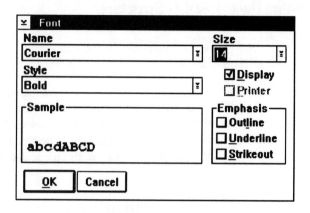

Figure 16.2. The font dialog.

The font dialog (see Figure 16.2) is created using *WinFontDlg*. This function is very similar to *WinFileDlg* in its setup. The structure FONTDLG is used to design the font dialog box layout. The structure is shown below:

```
typedef struct _FONTDLG
{
    ULONG    cbSize;
    HPS      hpsScreen;
    HPS      hpsPrinter;
    PSZ      pszTitle;
    PSZ      pszPreview;
    PSZ      pszPtSizeList;
    PFNWP    pfnDlgProc;
    PSZ      pszFamilyname;
    FIXED    fxPointSize;
    ULONG    fl;
    ULONG    flFlags;
    ULONG    flType;
    ULONG    flTypeMask;
    ULONG    flStyle;
    ULONG    flStyleMask;
    LONG     clrFore;
    LONG     clrBack;
    ULONG    ulUser;
    LONG     lReturn;
    LONG     lSRC;
    LONG     lEmHeight;
    LONG     lXHeight;
    LONG     lExternalLeading;
    HMODULE  hMod;
    FATTRS   fAttrs;
    SHORT    sNominalPointSize;
    USHORT   usWeight;
    USHORT   usWidth;
    SHORT    x;
    SHORT    y;
    USHORT   usDlgId;
    USHORT   usFamilyBufLen;
    USHORT   usReserved;
} FONTDLG;
typedef FONTDLG *PFONTDLG;
```

The field *cbSize* is the size of the FONTDLG structure.

The field *hpsScreen* is the presentation space for the screen. If this field is NULL, no screen fonts will be used as available fonts.

The field *hpsPrinter* is the presentation space for the printer. If this field is NULL, no printer fonts will be used as available fonts.

The field psz*Title* is a pointer to a string that is the title of the file dialog box window. If this is NULL, the title of the owner window is used.

The field *pszPreview* is a pointer to a string that is the text to be used in the preview window.

The field *pszPtSizeList* is a pointer to a string that is the list of font sizes that the font dialog will use as available fonts. The string is in the format "8 10 12", where each font size is separated by a space.

The field *pfnDlgProc* is a pointer to a user-defined dialog procedure. The function *WinDefFontDlgProc* can be used to call the default dialog procedure from the user-defined dialog procedure.

The field *pszFamilyname* is a pointer to a string that contains the font family name. On input, this field is used to determine the selected font when the font dialog is first started. When the user closes the dialog box, this field contains the family name of the font the user selected.

The field *fxPointSize* is the point size of the selected font. On input, this field is the point size of the default-selected font. When the user closes the dialog box, this field contains the point size of the font the user selected.

The field *fl* is the font dialog styles flag. This field is a collection of styles OR'ed together. The following styles are available:

STYLE	DESCRIPTION
FNTS_CENTER	The dialog is centered on the owner window.
FNTS_CUSTOM	Uses a custom-defined dialog template.
FNTS_OWNERDRAWPREVIEW	The preview box is owner-drawn.
FNTS_HELPBUTTON	A HELP button is included in the font dialog.
FNTS_APPLYBUTTON	An APPLY button is included in the font dialog.
FNTS_RESETBUTTON	A RESET button is included in the font dialog.
FNTS_MODELESS	The font dialog box is modeless.
FNTS_INITFROMFATTRS	The font dialog will choose the initially selected font by matching the values in the FATTRS structure.
FNTS_BITMAPONLY	Only bitmapped fonts will be used as available fonts.
FNTS_VECTORONLY	Only vector fonts will be used as available fonts.

FNTS_FIXEDWIDTHONLY	Only monospaced fonts will be used as available fonts.
FNTS_PROPORTIONALONLY	Only proportional fonts will be used as available fonts.
FNTS_NOSYNTHESIZEDFONTS	Fonts will not be synthesized.

The field *flFlags* is a collection of font flags OR'ed together. The following flags are available:

FLAG	DESCRIPTION
FNTF_NOVIEWPRINTERFONTS	This flag is an input flag. If specified, and both *hpsScreen* and *hpsPrinter* are used, the printer fonts will not be included in the list of available fonts.
FNTF_NOVIEWSCREENFONTS	This flag is an input flag. If specified, and both *hpsScreen* and *hpsPrinter* are used, the screen fonts will not be included in the list of available fonts.
FNTF_PRINTERFONTSELECTED	This flag is an output flag. It indicates that the user selected a printer font.
FNTF_SCREENFONTSELECTED	This flag is an output flag. It indicates that the user selected a screen font.

The field *flType* contains the additional characteristics of the font the user selected. The following types are available:

TYPE	DESCRIPTION
FTYPE_ITALIC	The font selected was italic.
FTYPE_ITALIC_DONT_CARE	The font selected was not italic.
FTYPE_OBLIQUE	The font selected was oblique.
FTYPE_OBLIQUE_DONT_CARE	The font selected was not oblique.
FTYPE_ROUNDED	The font selected was rounded.
FTYPE_ROUNDED_DONT_CARE	The font selected was not rounded.

The field *flTypeMask* is a mask of which font types to use.

The field *flStyle* is the font styles the user selected. The following styles are available:

STYLE	DESCRIPTION
FATTR_SEL_ITALIC	The font selected was italic.
FATTR_SEL_UNDERSCORE	The font selected was underscore.
FATTR_SEL_BOLD	The font selected was bold.
FATTR_SEL_STRIKEOUT	The font selected was strikeout.
FATTR_SEL_OUTLINE	The font selected was outline.

The field *flStyleMask* is a mask of which font styles to use.

The field *clrFore* is the font foreground color index.

The field *clrBack* is the font background color index.

The field *ulUser* is 4 bytes of user-defined storage space.

The field *lReturn* is the ID of the push-button the user pushed to close the dialog; DID_OK, DID_CANCEL, or 0 if an error occurred.

The field *lSRC* is the system return code if the font dialog fails. Possible values are:

FNTS_SUCCESSFUL	0
FNTS_ERR_INVALID_DIALOG	3
FNTS_ERR_ALLOC_SHARED_MEM	4
FNTS_ERR_INVALID_PARM	5
FNTS_ERR_OUT_OF_MEMORY	7
FNTS_ERR_INVALID_VERSION	10
FNTS_ERR_DIALOG_LOAD_ERROR	12

The field *lEmHeight* is the point size of the font converted into world coordinates. This field multiplied by 1.2 is often a good gauge for the vertical spacing between rows of text.

The field *lXHeight* is the height in pixels of the character x.

The field *lExternalLeading* is the recommended vertical spacing between rows of text. This value is the maximum spacing, not the actual spacing to use.

The field *hMod* is the module handle to use for loading a custom font dialog. This field is only used if FNTS_CUSTOM is set in the *fl* field. If FNTS_CUSTOM is set, and this field is NULL, the resource is drawn from the executable.

The field *fAttrs* is a FATTRS structure for the selected font.

The field *sNominalPointSize* is the font point size. This field is meaningful for bitmap fonts only.

The field *usWeight* is the weight of the font. Possible values are:

WEIGHT	DESCRIPTION
FWEIGHT_DONT_CARE	Any font weight is applicable.
FWEIGHT_ULTRA_LIGHT	The font is ultra-light.
FWEIGHT_EXTRA_LIGHT	The font is extra light.
FWEIGHT_LIGHT	The font is light.
FWEIGHT_SEMI_LIGHT	The font is semi-light.
FWEIGHT_NORMAL	The font is normal weight.
FWEIGHT_SEMI_BOLD	The font is semi-bold.
FWEIGHT_BOLD	The font is bold.
FWEIGHT_EXTRA_BOLD	The font is extra-bold.
FWEIGHT_ULTRA_BOLD	The font is ultra-bold.

The field *usWidth* is the width class of the font the user selects. Possible values are:

WIDTH	DESCRIPTION
FWIDTH_DONT_CARE	Any font width is applicable.
FWIDTH_ULTRA_CONDENSED	The selected font has an aspect ratio 50 percent of the normal ratio.
FWIDTH_EXTRA_CONDENSED	The selected font has an aspect ratio 62.5 percent of the normal ratio.
FWIDTH_CONDENSED	The selected font has an aspect ratio 75 percent of the normal ratio.
FWIDTH_SEMI_CONDENSED	The selected font has an aspect ratio 87.5 percent of the normal ratio.
FWIDTH_NORMAL	The selected font has an aspect ratio 100 percent of the normal ratio.
FWIDTH_SEMI_EXPANDED	The selected font has an aspect ratio 112.25 percent of the normal ratio.

FWIDTH_EXPANDED	The selected font has an aspect ratio 125 percent of the normal ratio.
FWIDTH_EXTRA_EXPANDED	The selected font has an aspect ratio 150 percent of the normal ratio.
FWIDTH_ULTRA_EXPANDED	The selected font has an aspect ratio 200 percent of the normal ratio.

The field *x* is the x-coordinate for the font dialog box. This field is unused if the *fl* flag has FNTS_CENTER set.

The field *y* is the y-coordinate for the font dialog box. This field is unused if the *fl* flag has FNTS_CENTER set.

The field *usDlgID* is the resource ID of the dialog box to be used if the FNTS_CUSTOM flag in the *fl* field is set.

The field *usFamilyBufLen* is the length of the *pszFamilyname* buffer. This field is mandatory.

Gotcha!

There are several fields that are *mandatory* in the font dialog control. These fields are: *cbSize*, *hpsScreen* or *hpsPrinter*, *pszFamilyname*, and *fl*. Also, all of the string fields in the FONTDLG structure are pointers. It is the programmer's responsibility to provide the space for these fields.

16.8 An Example Program: FONTDLG

FONTDLG.C

```
#define INCL_WIN
#define INCL_STDDLG
#define INCL_GPI

#include <os2.h>
#include <stdio.h>
#include <stdlib.h>
#include <string.h>
#include "fontdlg.h"

typedef struct {
   FONTDLG fdFontDlg ;
   USHORT  bInit ;
} MYFONTINFO, *PMYFONTINFO ;

MRESULT EXPENTRY ClientWndProc ( HWND hwndWnd,
                                 ULONG ulMsg,
                                 MPARAM mpParm1,
                                 MPARAM mpParm2 ) ;

VOID SetFont ( HWND hwndWnd, PMYFONTINFO pmfiFont ) ;

#define CLS_CLIENT              "MyClass"

INT main ( VOID )
{
   HAB    habAnchor ;
   HMQ    hmqQueue ;
   ULONG  ulFlags ;
   HWND   hwndFrame ;
   HWND   hwndClient ;
   BOOL   bLoop ;
   QMSG   qmMsg ;

   habAnchor = WinInitialize ( 0 ) ;
   hmqQueue = WinCreateMsgQueue ( habAnchor, 0 ) ;

   WinRegisterClass ( habAnchor,
                      CLS_CLIENT,
                      ClientWndProc,
                      CS_SIZEREDRAW,
                      sizeof ( PVOID )) ;

   ulFlags = FCF_STANDARD & ~FCF_ACCELTABLE & ~FCF_ICON ;
```

```
      hwndFrame = WinCreateStdWindow ( HWND_DESKTOP,
                                        0,
                                        &ulFlags,
                                        CLS_CLIENT,
                                        "Font Dialog Example",
                                        0,
                                        NULLHANDLE,
                                        RES_CLIENT,
                                        &hwndClient ) ;

   if ( hwndFrame != NULLHANDLE ) {

      WinSetWindowPos ( hwndFrame,
                        NULLHANDLE,
                        50,
                        50,
                        500,
                        250,
                        SWP_SIZE |
                        SWP_MOVE |
                        SWP_ACTIVATE |
                        SWP_SHOW ) ;

      bLoop = WinGetMsg ( habAnchor, &qmMsg, NULLHANDLE, 0, 0 ) ;
      while ( bLoop ) {
         WinDispatchMsg ( habAnchor, &qmMsg ) ;
         bLoop = WinGetMsg ( habAnchor, &qmMsg, NULLHANDLE, 0, 0 )
;
      } /* endwhile */

      WinDestroyWindow ( hwndFrame ) ;
   } /* endif */

   WinDestroyMsgQueue ( hmqQueue ) ;
   WinTerminate ( habAnchor ) ;
   return 0 ;
}

MRESULT EXPENTRY ClientWndProc ( HWND hwndWnd,
                                 ULONG ulMsg,
                                 MPARAM mpParm1,
                                 MPARAM mpParm2 )
{
   PMYFONTINFO pmfiFont ;

   pmfiFont = WinQueryWindowPtr ( hwndWnd, 0 ) ;

   switch ( ulMsg ) {

   case WM_CREATE:

      pmfiFont = malloc ( sizeof ( MYFONTINFO )) ;
      if ( pmfiFont == NULL ) {
         WinAlarm ( HWND_DESKTOP, WA_ERROR ) ;
```

```
                WinMessageBox ( HWND_DESKTOP,
                                hwndWnd,
                                "No memory could be allocated !",
                                "Error",
                                0,
                                MB_INFORMATION | MB_OK ) ;
            return MRFROMSHORT ( TRUE ) ;
        } /* endif */

        WinSetWindowPtr ( hwndWnd, 0, pmfiFont ) ;

        memset ( pmfiFont, 0, sizeof ( MYFONTINFO )) ;
        pmfiFont -> bInit = FALSE ;
        break ;
    case WM_DESTROY:
        if ( pmfiFont != NULL ) {
            free ( pmfiFont ) ;
        } /* endif */
        break ;

    case WM_PAINT:
        {
            HPS   hpsPaint ;
            ULONG ulReturn ;
            RECTL rclPaint ;
            CHAR  achFontName [200] , achMsg [256] ;

            hpsPaint = WinBeginPaint ( hwndWnd,
                                       NULLHANDLE,
                                       &rclPaint ) ;

            ulReturn = WinQueryPresParam ( hwndWnd,
                                           PP_FONTNAMESIZE,
                                           0,
                                           NULL,
                                           256,
                                           achFontName,
                                           0 ) ;
            if ( ulReturn ) {
                sprintf ( achMsg,
                          "The font selected is \"%s\"",
                          achFontName ) ;
            } else {
                strcpy ( achMsg, "No font selected" ) ;
            } /* endif */

            WinFillRect ( hpsPaint, &rclPaint, SYSCLR_WINDOW ) ;
            WinQueryWindowRect ( hwndWnd, &rclPaint ) ;

            WinDrawText ( hpsPaint,
                          - 1,
                          achMsg,
                          & rclPaint,
                          0,
                          0,
                          DT_VCENTER | DT_CENTER | DT_TEXTATTRS ) ;
```

```
                    WinEndPaint ( hpsPaint ) ;
                }
                break ;

        case WM_COMMAND:

            switch ( SHORT1FROMMP ( mpParm1 )) {

            case IDM_FONT:
                SetFont ( hwndWnd , pmfiFont ) ;
                WinInvalidateRect ( hwndWnd, NULL, TRUE ) ;
                WinUpdateWindow ( hwndWnd ) ;
                break ;

            case IDM_EXIT:
                WinPostMsg ( hwndWnd, WM_CLOSE, 0, 0 ) ;
                break ;

            default:
                return WinDefWindowProc ( hwndWnd,
                                          ulMsg,
                                          mpParm1,
                                          mpParm2 ) ;

            } /* endswitch */
            break ;

        default:
            return WinDefWindowProc ( hwndWnd,
                                      ulMsg,
                                      mpParm1,
                                      mpParm2 ) ;
        } /* endswitch */

        return MRFROMSHORT ( FALSE ) ;
}

VOID SetFont ( HWND hwndWnd, PMYFONTINFO pmfiFont )
{
    FATTRS  faAttrs ;
    FIXED   fxSzFont ;
    CHAR    achFamily [256] ;
    CHAR    achFont [256] ;


    faAttrs = pmfiFont -> fdFontDlg.fAttrs ;
    fxSzFont = pmfiFont -> fdFontDlg.fxPointSize ;

    memset ( &pmfiFont -> fdFontDlg, 0, sizeof ( FONTDLG )) ;
    memset ( achFont, 0, 256 ) ;

    pmfiFont -> fdFontDlg.cbSize = sizeof ( FONTDLG ) ;
    pmfiFont -> fdFontDlg.hpsScreen = WinGetPS ( hwndWnd ) ;
    pmfiFont -> fdFontDlg.pszFamilyname = achFamily ;
    pmfiFont -> fdFontDlg.usFamilyBufLen = sizeof ( achFamily ) ;
    pmfiFont -> fdFontDlg.fl = FNTS_CENTER | FNTS_INITFROMFATTRS ;
    pmfiFont -> fdFontDlg.clrFore = CLR_BLACK ;
```

```
   pmfiFont -> bInit = TRUE ;

if ( pmfiFont -> bInit ) {
   pmfiFont -> fdFontDlg.fAttrs = faAttrs ;
   pmfiFont -> fdFontDlg.fxPointSize = fxSzFont ;
} /* endif */

if ( WinFontDlg ( HWND_DESKTOP,
                  hwndWnd,
                  &pmfiFont -> fdFontDlg ) != DID_OK ) {
   WinAlarm ( HWND_DESKTOP, WA_ERROR ) ;
   return ;
} /* endif */

WinReleasePS ( pmfiFont -> fdFontDlg.hpsScreen ) ;

sprintf ( achFont,
          "%d.%s",
          FIXEDINT ( pmfiFont -> fdFontDlg.fxPointSize ) ,
          pmfiFont -> fdFontDlg.fAttrs.szFacename ) ;

if ( pmfiFont -> fdFontDlg.fAttrs.fsSelection &
     FATTR_SEL_ITALIC ) {
   strcat ( achFont, ".Italic" ) ;
} /* endif */

if ( pmfiFont -> fdFontDlg.fAttrs.fsSelection &
     FATTR_SEL_UNDERSCORE ) {
   strcat ( achFont, ".Underscore" ) ;
} /* endif */

if ( pmfiFont -> fdFontDlg.fAttrs.fsSelection &
     FATTR_SEL_STRIKEOUT ) {
   strcat ( achFont, ".Strikeout" ) ;
} /* endif */

if ( pmfiFont -> fdFontDlg.fAttrs.fsSelection &
     FATTR_SEL_BOLD ) {
   strcat ( achFont, ".Bold" ) ;
} /* endif */

if ( pmfiFont -> fdFontDlg.fAttrs.fsSelection &
     FATTR_SEL_OUTLINE ) {
   strcat ( achFont, ".Outline" ) ;
} /* endif */

WinSetPresParam ( hwndWnd,
                  PP_FONTNAMESIZE,
                  strlen ( achFont ) + 1,
                  achFont ) ;

return ;
}
```

FONTDLG.RC

```
#include <os2.h>
#include "fontdlg.h"

MENU RES_CLIENT
{
    SUBMENU "~Fonts", IDM_SUB1
    {
        MENUITEM "~Change font...", IDM_FONT
        MENUITEM "E~xit", IDM_EXIT
    }
}
```

FONTDLG.H

```
#define RES_CLIENT              256
#define IDM_SUB1                512
#define IDM_FONT                513
#define IDM_EXIT                514
```

FONTDLG.MAK

```
FONTDLG.EXE:                    FONTDLG.OBJ \
                                FONTDLG.RES
        LINK386 /CO @<<
FONTDLG
FONTDLG
FONTDLG
OS2386
FONTDLG
<<
        RC FONTDLG.RES FONTDLG.EXE

FONTDLG.RES:                    FONTDLG.RC \
                                FONTDLG.H
        RC -r FONTDLG.RC FONTDLG.RES

FONTDLG.OBJ:                    FONTDLG.C \
                                FONTDLG.H
        ICC -C+ -Kb+ -Ss+ -Ti FONTDLG.C
```

FONTDLG.DEF

```
NAME FONTDLG WINDOWAPI
DESCRIPTION 'Font dialog example
            Copyright (c) 1992 by Kathleen Panov.
            All rights reserved.'
STACKSIZE 32768
```

16.9 Customizing the Font Dialog

The font dialog does not use the current font of a window as the default-selected font. If you want the default font to be the current font of a selected window, there are two ways to do this:

- Query the current font characteristics, place these in the appropriate spots in the FONTDLG structure, and use the FNTS_INITFROMATTRS flag. You must use this method if you want to use the current font of a selected window and it is this first time *WinFontDlg* has been called.
- Store the FONTDLG structure that was the output from *WinFontDlg*, and reuse it the next time *WinFontDlg* is called.

The first option is a real pain to implement, so in this example we use the second method. We create a special structure, MYFONTINFO.

```
typedef struct {
    FONTDLG fdFontDlg ;
    USHORT  bInit ;
} MYFONTINFO, *PMYFONTINFO ;
```

This structure contains a FONTDLG structure, and a flag to indicate whether the structure has been initialized or not.

In the WM_CREATE processing, space is allocated for the MYFONTINFO structure. This pointer is stored in a window word of the client window. This memory is freed in the WM_DESTROY message processing.

```
ulReturn = WinQueryPresParam ( hwndWnd,
                               PP_FONTNAMESIZE,
                               0,
                               NULL,
                               256,
                               achFontName,
                               0 ) ;
```

When a WM_PAINT message is received, *WinQueryPresParam* is used to determine the current font. The first parameter is the window to query. The next parameter is the attribute ID. PP_FONTNAMESIZE will retrieve the font name and point size. The third parameter is used if you would like to query a second type of presentation parameter. The next parameter is used to determine which presentation parameter, the first or second, was found first. The fifth parameter is the length of the results buffer. The buffer, *achFontName*, is the next parameter. The last parameter, the query options, is unused in this example. The number of characters placed in the *achFontName* buffer is returned from *WinQueryPresParam*. The fontname is copied into a character array, and *WinDrawText* outputs the result onto the client window.

16.10 Bringing Up the Font Dialog

SetFont is a user-defined function to initialize the font dialog, bring it up, and change the client window font to the newly selected font.

The MYFONTINFO structure that contains the FONTDLG structure is retrieved from the window word, and is passed to *SetFont*

```
faAttrs = pmfiFont -> fdFontDlg.fAttrs ;
fxSzFont = pmfiFont -> fdFontDlg.fxPointSize ;

memset ( &pmfiFont -> fdFontDlg, 0, sizeof ( FONTDLG )) ;
memset ( achFont, 0, 256 ) ;

pmfiFont -> fdFontDlg.cbSize = sizeof ( FONTDLG ) ;
pmfiFont -> fdFontDlg.hpsScreen = WinGetPS ( hwndWnd ) ;
pmfiFont -> fdFontDlg.pszFamilyname = achFamily ;
pmfiFont -> fdFontDlg.usFamilyBufLen = sizeof ( achFamily ) ;
pmfiFont -> fdFontDlg.fl = FNTS_CENTER | FNTS_INITFROMFATTRS ;
pmfiFont -> fdFontDlg.clrFore = CLR_BLACK ;
pmfiFont -> bInit = TRUE ;

if ( pmfiFont -> bInit ) {
   pmfiFont -> fdFontDlg.fAttrs = faAttrs ;
   pmfiFont -> fdFontDlg.fxPointSize = fxSzFont ;
} /* endif */
```

The first time *SetFont* is called, the FONTDLG structure is initialized. The *cbSize* is the size of the structure. The screen presentation space is found using *WinGetPS*. *pszFamilyname* is set equal to the buffer *achFamily*. The length of the buffer is placed in the field *usFamilyBufLen*. The font style flags used are FNTS_CENTER and FNTS_INITFROMFATTRS. We set the foreground color to CLR_BLACK. If you do not specify a foreground color, you lose the font preview in the lefthand corner of the font dialog.

```
if ( WinFontDlg ( HWND_DESKTOP,
                  hwndWnd,
                  &pmfiFont -> fdFontDlg ) != DID_OK ) {
```

WinFontDlg has three parameters. The first is the parent window, HWND_DESKTOP. The next is the owner window, and the last is a *pointer* to the FONTDLG structure.

The *fxPointSize* variable in the FONTDLG structure is a FIXED data type. This is a long integer that is used to represent a fractional integer. To obtain the actual point size, the macro FIXEDINT is used to find the integer position of the fixed type. This value is the actual font point size.

```
sprintf ( achFont,
          "%d.%s",
          FIXEDINT ( pmfiFont -> fdFontDlg.fxPointSize ) ,
          pmfiFont -> fdFontDlg.fAttrs.szFacename ) ;
```

The *szFacename* array in the *fAttrs* structure is where we get the font style from. This array contains a bit more descriptive font style than the *pszFamilyname* pointer. (The authors had mixed results using the *pszFamilyname* variable but got 100% accuracy using *szFacename*.)

```
if ( pmfiFont -> fdFontDlg.fAttrs.fsSelection &
     FATTR_SEL_ITALIC ) {
   strcat ( achFont, ".Italic" ) ;
} /* endif */

if ( pmfiFont -> fdFontDlg.fAttrs.fsSelection &
     FATTR_SEL_UNDERSCORE ) {
   strcat ( achFont, ".Underscore" ) ;
} /* endif */

if ( pmfiFont -> fdFontDlg.fAttrs.fsSelection &
     FATTR_SEL_STRIKEOUT ) {
   strcat ( achFont, ".Strikeout" ) ;
} /* endif */

if ( pmfiFont -> fdFontDlg.fAttrs.fsSelection &
     FATTR_SEL_BOLD ) {
   strcat ( achFont, ".Bold" ) ;
} /* endif */

if ( pmfiFont -> fdFontDlg.fAttrs.fsSelection &
     FATTR_SEL_OUTLINE ) {
   strcat ( achFont, ".Outline" ) ;
} /* endif */
```

The *fsSelection* flag contains more information about the font type. A comparison is made, and if the result is TRUE, the strong is concatenated with a ".Descriptor" string. The presentation parameter string can take multiple instances of these descriptors. For example, "10.Tms Rmn Bold.Italic.Underline".

```
WinSetPresParam ( hwndWnd,
                  PP_FONTNAMESIZE,
                  strlen ( achFont ) + 1,
                  achFont ) ;
```

WinSetPresParam will change the font of the client window to the user-selected font. The first parameter is the window to apply the changes to, *hwndClient*. The next parameter is the presentation attribute, PP_FONTNAMESIZE, to change. The third parameter is the size of the Presentation Parameter.

 **Gotcha!**

If the type variable containing the Presentation Parameter is a string, the size of the variable is the length of the string, *including the terminating '\0'*. Thus, if you use *strlen*, add one extra byte. If one is not added, *WinSetPresParam* will function unreliably.

The last parameter is a pointer to the variable itself. A small note here: if the presentation parameter is a color, this value is the *address* of a LONG, or RGB, structure.

16.11 File Dialog Messages

FDM_ERROR
This message is sent from the file dialog before the dialog displays an error message.

Parameter 1:	USHORT usErrorID	error message ID
Parameter 2:	ULONG ulReserved	reserved, 0
Reply:	USHORT usProcReply	if 0, bring up error message dialog; else no error message dialog is brought up, and the following values can be returned to the file dialog: MBID_OK, MBID_CANCEL, or MBID_RETRY

FDM_FILTER
This message is sent from the file dialog before a file that meets the filtering criteria is added to the list of selectable files.

Parameter 1:	PSZ pszFilename	pointer to the file name
Parameter 2:	PSZ pszEAType	pointer to the .TYPE EA
Reply:	BOOL fAddFile	add file? TRUE: FALSE

FDM_VALIDATE
This message is sent from the file dialog when the user has selected a file and presses OK.

Parameter 1:	PSZ pszFileName	name of selected file
Parameter 2:	USHORT usSelType	either FDS_EFSELECTION for an entry field selection, or FDS_LBSELECTION for a selection from the list box
Reply:	BOOL bValid	valid file? TRUE: FALSE

16.12 Font Dialog Messages

WM_DRAWITEM
This message is sent from the font dialog if the style FNTS_OWNERDRAWPREVIEW style is specified, when the preview window area is to be drawn.

Parameter 1:	USHORT usWindowID	DID_SAMPLE
Parameter 2:	POWNERITEM pOwnerItem	pointer to owner item structure
Reply:	BOOL bDrawn	draw item? FALSE: TRUE

FNTM_FACENAMECHANGED
This message is sent from the font dialog whenever the font name is changed by the user.

Parameter 1:	PSZ pszFamilyName	pointer to selected font name
Parameter 2:	ULONG ulReserved	reserved, 0
Reply:	ULONG ulReserved	reserved, 0

FNTM_FILTERLIST
This message is sent from the font dialog whenever a new font name is to be added to the list.

Parameter 1:	PSZ pszFamilyName	font family name
Parameter 2:	USHORT usField ID	FNTI_FAMILYNAME
		FNTI_STYLENAME
		FNTI_POINTISZE
	USHORT usFontType	FNTI_BITMAPFONT
		FNTI_VECTORFONT
		FNTI_SYNTHESIZED
		FNTI_FIXEDWIDTHFONT
		FNTI_PROPORTIONALFONT
		FNTI_DEFAULTLIST
Reply:	BOOL fAcceptName	accept new font? TRUE: FALSE

FNTM_POINTSIZECHANGED

This message is sent from the font dialog when the user has changed the selected point size.

Parameter 1:	PSZ pszPointSize	pointer to point size string
Parameter 2:	FIXED fxPointSize	point size as FIXED data type
Reply:	USHORT ulReserved	reserved, 0

FNTM_STYLECHANGED

This message is sent from the font dialog whenever the user changes the font style attributes.

Parameter 1:   PSTYLECHANGE   pointer to style change structure

```
typedef struct _STYLECHANGE      /* stylc */
{
    USHORT      usWeight;
    USHORT      usWeightOld;
    USHORT      usWidth;
    USHORT      usWidthOld;
    ULONG       flType;
    ULONG       flTypeOld;
    ULONG       flTypeMask;
    ULONG       flTypeMaskOld;
    ULONG       flStyle;
    ULONG       flStyleOld;
    ULONG       flStyleMask;
    ULONG       flStyleMaskOld;
} STYLECHANGE;
typedef STYLECHANGE *PSTYLECHANGE;
```

Parameter 2:	ULONG ulReserved	reserved, 0
Reply:	ULONG ulReserved	reserved, 0

FNTM_UPDATEPREVIEW

This message is sent from the font dialog whenever the preview window needs to be changed.

Parameter 1:	HWND hwndPreview	preview window handle
Parameter 2:	ULONG ulReserved	reserved, 0
Reply:	ULONG ulReserved	reserved, 0

Chapter 17

Subclassing
Windows

 Subclassing windows is the ability to intercept and process messages sent to the window procedure of an established window class. A message is normally sent to a window procedure where it is either processed and returned to the calling window, processed and returned to *WinDefWindowProc*, or passed directly to *WinDefWindowProc*. A subclassed procedure is placed in the calling chain directly above the window procedure. This also allows the subclassed procedure to sort through the messages and process only the ones it wishes to modify.

The flowchart shown in Figure 17.1 illustrates the normal calling chain for window messages.

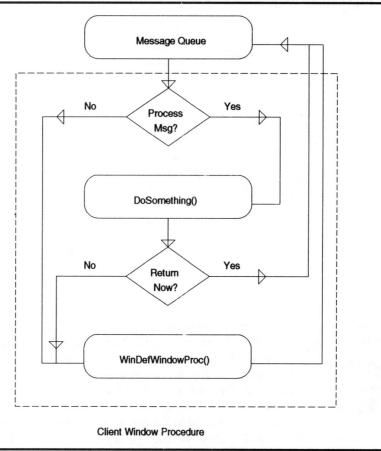

Figure 17.1. Diagram of normal window procedure.

The flowchart shown in Figure 17.2 illustrates what happens to the calling chain when a window is subclassed.

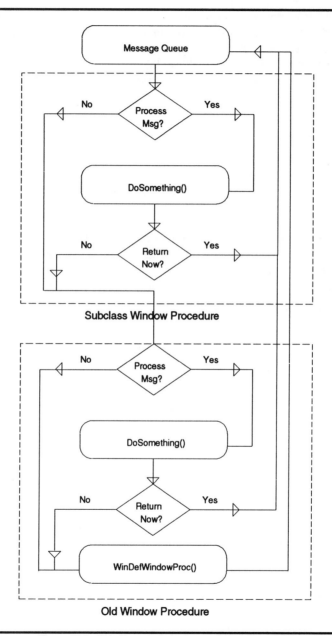

Figure 17.2. Subclassed window procedure calling chain.

Subclassing is a very easy way to modify the behavior of a window class. The subclassed procedure should be kept small to keep the window's behavior responsive to the user. A long and complex subclass procedure will cause a performance hit (you're now calling three functions for every message generated from the window). The following code will define the subclassed procedure:

```
MRESULT EXPENTRY pfnwpOldProc;
pfnwpOldProc = WinSubclassWindow( hwndWindowToSubclass,
        pfnwpNewProc);
```

The previous window procedure is returned from the function as *pfnwpOldProc*. This provides the subclassed procedure a way to call the previous window procedure.

Now let's put subclassing to use. Suppose we want an entry-field that only handles numbers, say, for Zip Codes. There's not an existing numerics-only entry-field, so let's create one.

SUBCLASS.C

```
#define INCL_WIN
#define INCL_GPILCIDS
#include <os2.h>
#include <string.h>
#include <ctype.h>

#define CLS_CLIENT              "MyClass"
#define IDE_ENTRYFIELD          256
#define STR_TEXT                "Zip code:"

MRESULT EXPENTRY newEntryWndProc ( HWND hwndWnd,
    ULONG ulMsg,
    MPARAM mpParm1,
    MPARAM mpParm2 ) ;
MRESULT EXPENTRY clientWndProc ( HWND hwndWnd,
    ULONG ulMsg,
    MPARAM mpParm1,
    MPARAM mpParm2 ) ;

INT main ( VOID )
{
    HAB             habAnchor ;
    HMQ             hmqQueue ;
    ULONG           ulFlags ;
    HWND            hwndFrame ;
    HWND            hwndClient ;
    BOOL            bLoop ;
    QMSG            qmMsg ;

    habAnchor = WinInitialize ( 0 ) ;
    hmqQueue = WinCreateMsgQueue ( habAnchor, 0 ) ;
```

```
    WinRegisterClass ( habAnchor,
       CLS_CLIENT,
       clientWndProc,
       CS_SIZEREDRAW,
       0 ) ;

    ulFlags = FCF_TITLEBAR | FCF_SYSMENU | FCF_SIZEBORDER |
              FCF_MINMAX | FCF_SHELLPOSITION | FCF_TASKLIST ;

    hwndFrame = WinCreateStdWindow ( HWND_DESKTOP,
                                     0,
                                     &ulFlags,
                                     CLS_CLIENT,
                                     "Subclass Example",
                                     0,
                                     NULLHANDLE,
                                     0,
                                     &hwndClient ) ;

    if ( hwndFrame != NULLHANDLE ) {
       WinSetWindowPos ( hwndFrame,
                         HWND_TOP,
                         50,
                         50,
                         250,
                         250,
                         SWP_SIZE |
                         SWP_MOVE |
                         SWP_ACTIVATE |
                         SWP_SHOW ) ;

       bLoop = WinGetMsg ( habAnchor,
                           &qmMsg,
                           NULLHANDLE,
                           0,
                           0 ) ;
       while ( bLoop ) {
          WinDispatchMsg ( habAnchor, &qmMsg ) ;
          bLoop = WinGetMsg ( habAnchor,
                              &qmMsg,
                              NULLHANDLE,
                              0,
                              0 ) ;
       } /* endwhile */

       WinDestroyWindow ( hwndFrame ) ;
    } /* endif */

    WinDestroyMsgQueue ( hmqQueue ) ;
    WinTerminate ( habAnchor ) ;
    return 0 ;
}
```

```
MRESULT EXPENTRY clientWndProc ( HWND hwndWnd,
                                 ULONG ulMsg,
                                 MPARAM mpParm1,
                                 MPARAM mpParm2 )
{
   switch ( ulMsg ) {

   case WM_CREATE:
       {
           HPS                 hpsChar ;
           FONTMETRICS         fmMetrics ;
           ENTRYFDATA          edEntry ;
           HWND                hwndEntry ;
           PFNWP               pfnOldEntryProc ;

           hpsChar = WinGetPS ( hwndWnd ) ;
           GpiQueryFontMetrics ( hpsChar,
                                 sizeof ( fmMetrics ) ,
                                 &fmMetrics ) ;
           WinReleasePS ( hpsChar ) ;

           edEntry.cb = sizeof ( edEntry ) ;
           edEntry.cchEditLimit = 9 ;
           edEntry.ichMinSel = 0 ;
           edEntry.ichMaxSel = 0 ;

           hwndEntry = WinCreateWindow ( hwndWnd,
                                         WC_ENTRYFIELD,
                                         "",
                                         WS_VISIBLE |
                                         ES_MARGIN |
                                         ES_AUTOSIZE,
                                         10,
                                         50,
                                         75,
                                         fmMetrics.lMaxBaselineExt,
                                         hwndWnd,
                                         HWND_TOP,
                                         IDE_ENTRYFIELD,
                                         &edEntry,
                                         NULL ) ;

           pfnOldEntryProc = WinSubclassWindow ( hwndEntry,
                                                 newEntryWndProc ) ;

           WinSetWindowPtr ( hwndEntry,
                             0,
                             (PVOID) pfnOldEntryProc ) ;

           WinSetFocus ( HWND_DESKTOP, hwndEntry ) ;
       }
       break ;

   case WM_DESTROY:
       WinDestroyWindow ( WinWindowFromID ( hwndWnd,
                          IDE_ENTRYFIELD )) ;
       break ;
```

```
        case WM_ERASEBACKGROUND:
           return MRFROMSHORT ( TRUE ) ;

        case WM_PAINT:
           {
               HPS          hpsPaint ;
               SWP          swpEntry ;
               POINTL       ptlText ;

               hpsPaint = WinBeginPaint ( hwndWnd,
                                          NULLHANDLE,
                                          NULL ) ;

               GpiErase ( hpsPaint ) ;
               WinQueryWindowPos ( WinWindowFromID ( hwndWnd,
                                   IDE_ENTRYFIELD ) ,
                                   &swpEntry ) ;

               ptlText.x = swpEntry.x ;
               ptlText.y = swpEntry.y + swpEntry.cy + 10 ;

               GpiCharStringAt ( hpsPaint,
                                 &ptlText,
                                 strlen ( STR_TEXT ) ,
                                 STR_TEXT ) ;

               WinEndPaint ( hpsPaint ) ;
           }
           break ;
        default:
           return WinDefWindowProc ( hwndWnd,
                                     ulMsg,
                                     mpParm1,
                                     mpParm2 ) ;
    } /* endswitch */

    return MRFROMSHORT ( FALSE ) ;
}

MRESULT EXPENTRY newEntryWndProc ( HWND hwndWnd,
                                   ULONG ulMsg,
                                   MPARAM mpParm1,
                                   MPARAM mpParm2 )
{
    PFNWP pfnOldEntryProc ;

    pfnOldEntryProc = (PFNWP) WinQueryWindowPtr ( hwndWnd, 0 ) ;

    switch ( ulMsg ) {
    case WM_CHAR:
        if ( CHARMSG ( &ulMsg ) -> fs & KC_CHAR ) {
            if ( !isdigit ( CHARMSG ( &ulMsg ) -> chr ) &&
                ( CHARMSG ( &ulMsg ) -> chr != '\b' )) {
```

```
                WinMessageBox ( HWND_DESKTOP,
                                HWND_DESKTOP,
                                "Only numeric characters are allowed "
                                "in this field",
                                "Numeric Field",
                                0,
                                MB_OK | MB_ERROR ) ;

            return MRFROMSHORT ( TRUE ) ;
        } /* endif */
    } /* endif */
    break ;
case EM_PASTE:
    {
        HAB habAnchor ;
        PCHAR pchText ;
        CHAR achText [1024] ;
        USHORT usIndex ;

        habAnchor = WinQueryAnchorBlock ( hwndWnd ) ;
        WinOpenClipbrd ( habAnchor ) ;
        pchText = (PCHAR) WinQueryClipbrdData ( habAnchor,
                                                CF_TEXT ) ;

        if ( pchText ) {

            strcpy ( achText, pchText ) ;
            WinCloseClipbrd ( habAnchor ) ;

            usIndex = 0 ;
            while ( achText [usIndex] ) {
                if ( !isdigit ( achText [usIndex ++ ] )){

                    WinMessageBox ( HWND_DESKTOP,
                                    HWND_DESKTOP,
                                    "Only numeric characters are "
                                    "allowed in this field",
                                    "Numerical Field",
                                    0,
                                    MB_OK | MB_ERROR ) ;

                    return MRFROMSHORT ( TRUE ) ;
                } /* endif */
            } /* endwhile */
        } else {
            WinCloseClipbrd ( habAnchor ) ;
        } /* endif */
    }
    break ;
default:
    break ;
} /* endswitch */
```

```
    return ( *pfnOldEntryProc ) ( hwndWnd,
                                   ulMsg,
                                   mpParm1,
                                   mpParm2 ) ;
}
```

SUBCLASS.MAK

```
SUBCLASS.EXE:                   SUBCLASS.OBJ
        LINK386 @<<
SUBCLASS
SUBCLASS
SUBCLASS
OS2386
SUBCLASS
<<

SUBCLASS.OBJ:                   SUBCLASS.C
        ICC -C+ -Kb+ -Ss+ SUBCLASS.C
```

SUBCLASS.DEF

```
NAME SUBCLASS WINDOWAPI

DESCRIPTION 'Subclass example
Copyright (c) 1992 by Kathleen Panov
All rights reserved.'

STACKSIZE 16384
```

The first part of the program should look fairly familiar by now; we're just creating a basic client window. In the WM_CREATE portion of the client window procedure, we create an entry-field using *WinCreateWindow*. After the window is created, *WinSubclassWindow* is called to subclass the default window procedure for an entry-field.

```
pfnOldEntryProc = WinSubclassWindow ( hwndEntry,
                                       newEntryWndProc ) ;

WinSetWindowPtr ( hwndEntry,
                  0,
                  (PVOID) pfnOldEntryProc ) ;
```

The first parameter is the window to subclass, *hwndEntryField*. The second parameter is a pointer to the procedure that messages to the window will be sent to. *WinSubclassWindow* returns the old window procedure, and this pointer is stored in the window word for the entry field.

newEntryWndProc is designed to handle only two messages, WM_CHAR and EM_PASTE. All the other messages will be passed to the normal window procedure for entry-fields.

```
case WM_CHAR:
   if ( CHARMSG ( &ulMsg ) -> fs & KC_CHAR ) {
      if ( !isdigit ( CHARMSG ( &ulMsg ) -> chr ) &&
         ( CHARMSG ( &ulMsg ) -> chr != '\b' )) {

         WinMessageBox ( HWND_DESKTOP,
                         HWND_DESKTOP,
                         "Only numeric characters are allowed "
                         "in this field",
                         "Numeric Field",
                         0,
                         MB_OK | MB_ERROR ) ;

            return MRFROMSHORT ( TRUE ) ;
      } /* endif */
   } /* endif */
   break ;
```

The WM_CHAR processing is fairly straightforward. We will look at all the KC_CHAR keys. The only character keys we want to allow are the digits 0–9 and the Backspace key. The other editing keys set the KC_VIRTUALKEY flag, not the KC_CHAR flag, so they will be allowed. If a nonnumeric character is entered, *WinMessageBox* is called to pop up an error message, telling the user that only numeric keys are allowed in this field. Next, we return TRUE in order to prevent the character from being processed by the next procedure called for the entry-field.

The other message we want to intercept is EM_PASTE. This message is generated whenever text is pasted into the entry-field from the clipboard. Remember, the keyboard is not the only method of entering text in an entry-field. To determine if the data is valid, we have to take a peek at what is in the clipboard.

```
habAnchor = WinQueryAnchorBlock ( hwndWnd ) ;
WinOpenClipbrd ( habAnchor ) ;
pchText = (PCHAR) WinQueryClipbrdData ( habAnchor,
                                        CF_TEXT ) ;
```

The clipboard is opened by calling *WinOpenClipbrd*. There is only one parameter for the function, the anchor block. This gives ownership of the clipboard to the application window. No other window can open the clipboard while it is open. This is potentially a very dangerous situation. If the clipboard is already open when *WinOpenClipbrd* is called, the function will not return until the clipboard can be opened. Hopefully, most programs out there are well behaved, and will close the clipboard as soon as they are done, but beware: if they aren't, this will freeze your message queue unless you open the clipboard in another thread. Once the clipboard is opened, *WinQueryClipbrdData* is called. This function has two parameters, the anchor block and the clipboard data format that is to be retrieved. In our case, we are only concerned with text, so the format CF_TEXT is used. The function returns a string of the text contained in the clipboard. If no text is in the clipboard, the string will be NULL.

```
if ( pchText ) {

    strcpy ( achText, pchText ) ;
    WinCloseClipbrd ( habAnchor ) ;

    usIndex = 0 ;
    while ( achText [usIndex] ) {
       if ( !isdigit ( achText [usIndex ++ ] )){

            WinMessageBox ( HWND_DESKTOP,
                            HWND_DESKTOP,
                            "Only numeric characters are "
                            "allowed in this field",
                            "Numerical Field",
                            0,
                            MB_OK | MB_ERROR ) ;

            return MRFROMSHORT ( TRUE ) ;
          } /* endif */
       } /* endwhile */
} else {
    WinCloseClipbrd ( habAnchor ) ;
} /* endif */
```

After we have the string, we check each digit to see if it is a numeric character. If not, the error message box is again displayed, and we return TRUE to avoid further processing.

```
return ( *pfnOldEntryProc ) ( hwndWnd,
                              ulMsg,
                              mpParm1,
                              mpParm2 ) ;
```

If the characters entered are valid, or if the message is something other than WM_CHAR or EM_PASTE, it will fall through the switch statement. At this point, we want to call the old procedure for the entry-field.

Subclassing is a very easy way to modify the existing controls in Presentation Manager to work the way you want them to.

Chapter 18

Drag and Drop

While the capability to drag and drop an icon from one window to another has been present since OS/2 1.1, a standardized, robust method for providing this essential function was not introduced until OS/2 1.3 with the Drg*() functions and their associated DM_* messages. But what is drag and drop, really?

Drag and drop is the capability of using the mouse to directly manipulate the transfer and placement of data within single or multiple applications. Objects can either be "moved" or "copied" from a source window to a target window ("moved" and "copied" are application-defined concepts and are accomplished by holding down the ALT or CTRL key, respectively).

Drag and drop can be seen from two viewpoints: it can be looked at from the viewpoint of the source, who initiates the drag; and it can be seen from the aspect of the target, which can accept or reject a dragging operation. We will examine both of these as well as what to do once the target is established.

18.1 Tennis, Anyone?

In a nutshell, the source window is responsible for determining that the user is attempting to drag an object, initializing the appropriate data structures, and finally calling either *DrgDrag* or *DrgDragFiles* (a version of *DrgDrag* specifically for file objects). Determining that the user is attempting to drag an object is the easiest part, since the system will send you a WM_BEGINDRAG message with the pointer position in *mpParm1*.

Gotcha!

The documentation in OS/2 2.0 for WM_BEGINDRAG has the message parameters reversed. It incorrectly states that the pointer position is in *mpParm2*; it is instead in *mpParm1*. This has been fixed in the OS/2 2.1 documentation.

After it has been decided that a drag operation is necessary, there are three structure types that the application needs to allocate and initialize: the DRAGINFO, DRAGITEM, and DRAGIMAGE structures (there are actually four; the DRAGTRANSFER structure is used once a target has been established). The DRAGINFO structure contains information about the drag as an entity. The DRAGITEM structures describe each object being dragged. Finally, the DRAGIMAGE structures each describe the appearance of the object under the pointer while it is being dragged.

```
(PDRAGINFO)DrgAllocDraginfo(ULONG ulItems);
(BOOL)DrgSetDragitem(PDRAGINFO pdinfo,
                     PDRAGITEM pditem,
                     USHORT cbBuffer,
                     USHORT iItem);
```

It is important to realize that, because the target will more likely than not exist as part of another process, simple allocation of these structures will not suffice, due to OS/2's memory protection features. They must be allocated in shared memory through the use of the *DrgAllocDraginfo* and *DrgAddStrHandle* functions. The former accepts the number of items being dragged and returns a pointer to the shared DRAGINFO structure, whose individual DRAGITEM structures must be initialized using the *DrgSetDragitem* function. The latter takes a pointer to a string and returns a "string handle," i.e., a pointer to a shared memory block containing (among other things) the string passed to the function.

18.2 Initialization Code for Drag and Drop Source

This is the typical initialization code used in a Presentation Manager application to initiate a drag and drop operation.

```
        HWND hwndWindow;
        PDRAGINFO pdiDrag;
        DRAGITEM diItem;
        pdiDrag=DrgAllocDraginfo(1);
//-----------------------------------------------------------//
Note that DrgAllocDraginfo() initializes all of the DRAGINFO
// fields
// *except* hwndSource.
//-----------------------------------------------------------
pdiDrag->hwndSource=hwndWindow;
        diItem.hwndItem=hwndWindow;
diItem.ulItemID=1L;                    // Unique identifier
diItem.hstrType=DrgAddStrHandle(DRT_TEXT);
diItem.hstrRMF=DrgAddStrHandle("<DRM_OS2FILE,DRF_TEXT>");
diItem.hstrContainerName=DrgAddStrHandle("C:\");
diItem.hstrSourceName=DrgAddStrHandle("CONFIG.SYS");
diItem.hstrTargetName=DrgAddStrHandle("CONFIG.BAK");
diItem.cxOffset=0;
        diItem.cyOffset=0;
        diItem.fsControl=0;
        diItem.fsSupportedOps=DO_COPYABLE;
        DrgSetDragItem(pdiDrag,&diItem,sizeof(diItem),0);
```

Before you begin scratching your scalp, let me state that there are a lot of things illustrated in the above example that haven't been explained, so don't attempt to "adjust your TV set." Instead, keep reading...

18.3 Things You Were Never Told (But Should Have Been)

Before actually taking our forceps to the code, a few concepts need to be introduced. The first is that of the "type" and the "true type" of an object being dragged. The "type" is just that; it is a string that describes what the object consists of. The "true type" is a "type" that more accurately describes the object, if such a true type exists. For example, a file that contains C source code might have the type "Plain Text" but have a true type of "C Code". An object can have more than one type, with each separated by commas and the true type appearing as the first type listed. Thus, the *hstrType* field for the C source code would be initialized as *DrgAddStrHandle*("C Code, Plain Text"). OS/2 defines a set of standard types in the form of DRT_* constants.

The second concept that needs to be discussed is the "rendering mechanism and format" (RMF). The "rendering mechanism" is the method by which the data will be communicated from the source to the target. The "format" is the format of the data if the corresponding rendering mechanism were used to transfer the data. These RMF pairs take the form "<rendering_mechanism, format>", with multiple RMF pairs separated by commas. OS/2 also defines a set of rendering mechanisms, although no constants are defined for them.

Note that if you have a fully populated set of RMF pairs ("fully populated" meaning that for every rendering mechanism, every format is available), you can use a shorthand cross-product notation. For example, if you have the rendering mechanisms RA, RB, and RC and the formats FA, FB, and FC, and the following RMF pairs are available:

"<RA,FA>,<RA,FB>,<RA,FC>,<RB,FA>,<RB,FB>,<RB,FC>,<RC,FA>, <RC,FB>,<RC,FC>"

then this can be represented as "(RA,RB,RC)X(FA,FB,FC)". Obviously, this is a much more concise way of describing the mess above. If the thought of having to parse such a monster with so many different combinations just to discover if <RD,FD> is supported drives you crazy, have no fear; Drg*() functions exist that will determine this for you.

Analogous to the relationship between "type" and "true type," there also exists a "native RMF," which describes the preferred RMF for this object. It is always the first RMF pair listed or the first RMF pair generated in a cross-product. This might employ faster data transfer algorithms or other such performance boosters, so the native RMF should be used by the target whenever possible.

Just because OS/2 defines sets of types, rendering mechanisms, and formats doesn't mean you are limited to those sets. If an application has a new format that it needs to use, it is free to register the appropriate strings describing this using the *DrgAddStrHandle* function. However, the transfer protocol for the rendering mechanisms and the corresponding data formats should also be published so that other applications can understand the new type or RMF.

The next concepts are that of source name, source container, and target name. The "source name" is the name of the object being dragged. This is useful because it is possible that the target application can perform the requested operation without the need to interact with the source application. Typically, this is used when dealing with files. The "source container" describes where the object resides. This, again, is useful to the target when deciding how to complete the action. When dealing with files, for example, this would be the directory name containing the file. Finally, the "target name" is actually a suggested name, since the target could determine that an object with that name already exists and that the object will receive a new, unique name.

Now that these concepts have been explained, the sample code at the beginning of this section should be easier to understand. We are dragging one item, as evidenced in the *DrgAllocDraginfo* call. The one item is of type "text" and will be transferred via the file system using the format "unknown". The file system object resides in the container/directory "C:\" and has the name "CONFIG.SYS". The suggested target name is "CONFIG.BAK", although the target application is free to select a different name. If you still don't understand what's going on (this is understandable, since direct manipulation is more an abstract set of ideas then anything else), then either you should reread the chapter up to this point or the authors should try doing something else for a living.

18.4 Direct Manipulation Is a Real Drag

Assuming you understood the last section and have successfully (and correctly) initialized the DRAGINFO structure and each DRAGITEM structure for each object, we are now ready to call the function that makes all of this hard work worthwhile: *DrgDrag*.

```
(HWND)DrgDrag(HWND hwndSource,
              PDRAGINFO pdiDragInfo,
              PDRAGIMAGE pdiDragImage,
              ULONG ulNumImages,
              ULONG ulTerminateKey,
              PVOID pvReserved);
```

hwndSource is the handle of the window initiating the drag operation. *pdiDragInfo* points to the DRAGINFO structure returned from *DrgAllocDraginfo*. *pdiDragImage* points to an array of one or more DRAGIMAGE structures (see below), and *ulNumImages* specifies how many images the array contains. *ulTerminateKey* is either VK_BUTTON1, VK_BUTTON2, VK_BUTTON3, or VK_ENDDRAG, and describes the manner by which the drag is ended; the VK_BUTTON constants specify a mouse button and VK_ENDDRAG specifies the mouse button defined in the "System Setup" folder to end a drag. VK_ENDDRAG should be used when dragging is performed in response to a WM_BEGINDRAG message.

The DRAGIMAGE structure describes the image to be displayed as the object is being dragged. Since only the *DrgDrag* function needs to access this, and since the *DrgDrag* function executes in the context of the process calling it, this structure is not part of the DRAGITEM structure (although it would have made things slightly less complicated).

```
typedef struct _DRAGIMAGE {
        USHORT cb;                  // size of this structure
        USHORT cptl;                // number of points in hImage if
                                    // DRG_POLYGON
        LHANDLE hImage;             // array of POINTL or HBITMAP
        SIZEL sizlStretch;          // size to stretch hImage to
        ULONG fl;                   // flags
        SHORT cxOffset;             // x offset from pointer
                                    // to display at
        SHORT cyOffset;             // y offset from pointer to display
                                    // at
        } DRAGIMAGE;
```

cb is the size of the structure in bytes. *cptl* specifies the number of points pointed to by *hImage* and is ignored unless *fl* specifies DRG_POLYGON. *hImage* points to the image itself, which is interpreted according to the setting of *fl* — DRG_ICON indicates it is an icon handle, DRG_BITMAP indicates it is a bitmap handle, and DRG_POLYGON indicates that it points to an array of POINTL structures. *sizlStretch* specifies the size that the DRG_ICON or DRG_BITMAP *hImage* should be stretched to if DRG_STRETCH is specified in *fl*. *cxOffset* and *cyOffset* specify the offset in pels to the origin of the image from the pointer hotspot. For DRG_POLYGON, the first point must be (0,0), and this is defined to be the origin of the image. For DRG_ICON and DRG_BITMAP, the lower left is the origin of the image, as you would expect.

DrgDrag returns the window handle of the target window, if one is established. If the user pressed either the ESC key (to end the drag) or the F1 key (to get help for dropping on the current target), NULLHANDLE is returned, and the source is responsible for returning any shared resources consumed by calling *DrgDeleteDraginfoStrHandles* to delete all of the string handles in the DRAGINFO structure, *DrgDeleteStrHandle* for each HSTR allocated that is not present in the DRAGINFO structure, and *DrgFreeDraginfo* to free the DRAGINFO structure. If this were the frequent case the chapter would now end, so we will instead assume that the user selected a target window and released the appropriate mouse button to initiate the transfer.

18.5 And Now a Word from Our Sponsor

Since the data transfer actively involves both the source and target windows, now is a good time to view the target's perspective from the beginning. Remember that it is the target's responsibility to provide visual feedback to the user during the drag operation and to initiate the data transfer once the drop has occurred. Visual feedback is accomplished by responding to the appropriate DM_* messages that are sent to the target during the drag.

DM_DRAGOVER — This message is sent whenever the pointer enters the target window space to allow it the opportunity to add "target emphasis" to the destination of the drag. This is also sent whenever a key is pressed or released. The message contains a pointer to the DRAGINFO structure, which can be accessed by calling *DrgAccessDraginfo*.

DM_DRAGLEAVE — This message is sent to any window previously sent a DM_DRAGOVER message whenever the pointer leaves the target window space to allow it the opportunity to remove any "target emphasis" previously drawn. Note that since this occurs only for a window, the target is responsible for monitoring the mouse position of the DM_DRAGOVER messages when it is a container for other items. This message is not sent if the object(s) are dropped on the window.

DM_DROP — This message is sent to the target window when the user drops the object(s) on it. As with DM_DRAGLEAVE, any target emphasis should be removed once this message is received. This message is normally responded to before any data transfer takes place so that the source can learn the window handle of the target.

DM_DROPHELP — This message is sent whenever the user presses F1 during a drag operation. The target should respond by displaying help on the actions that would occur if the object(s) were dropped at the point where F1 was pressed.

Whenever a DM_DRAGOVER message is received, the potential target must determine if the drag operation is valid. For example, you would be able to drop a C source file on a C compiler object, but not a Pascal source file; or you would be able to copy (by holding down the CTRL key) a file to the printer, but it is (probably) unlikely that you can move a file to the printer. At a minimum, the following two conditions must be met for a drop to be possible:

(1) Both the source and target must understand at least one common type of each object being dragged.

(2) Both the source and target must understand at least one common RMF for each object being dragged.

When determining the state of these conditions, the functions *DrgVerifyType*, *DrgVerifyRMF*, *DrgVerifyTrueType*, and *DrgVerifyNativeRMF* help considerably. The first two determine if a type or RMF specified on the call is valid for the specified object being dragged, while the latter two only check the true type and native RMF.

The target can respond to the DM_DRAGOVER message in one of four ways: DOR_DROP, DOR_NODROP, DOR_NODROPOP, and DOR_NEVERDROP. DOR_DROP is returned whenever the drag is acceptable. DOR_NODROP is returned whenever the location of the object(s) in the target window is unacceptable. DOR_NODROPOP is returned whenever the operation (copy or move) is unacceptable; this implies that the drag might be valid if the operation is changed. DOR_NEVERDROP is returned whenever a drag is never acceptable; no further DM_DRAGOVER messages will be sent to the application until the mouse leaves the window and returns. DOR_DROP is the only response that can be equated with a "Yes, you can drop here."

Gotcha!

Although the DRAGINFO structure is allocated in shared memory and the pointer is passed to the target, the target cannot access the structure until *DrgAccessDraginfo* is called.

18.6 Data Transfer

Okay, let's assume that the user selected one or more objects, depressed the appropriate mouse button, dragged the object(s) over a window, received the feedback that the target is willing to accept the object(s), and let go of the mouse button. What happens next? The answer to this depends on the RMF chosen to transfer the data with. For example, if DRM_OS2FILE is chosen, the target could choose to render the data itself, or maybe it doesn't know the name of the source data (e.g., for security reasons, the source window didn't fill this in), so it must ask the source window to render the data before it can complete the drop operation.

Let us consider each of the three system-defined rendering mechanisms to see the possible chain of events with each:

DRM_OS2FILE — This mechanism would be used to transfer the data via the file system. The data does not have to already exist in this form, but could be placed there by the source after receiving a DM_RENDER message from the target.

If the target understands the native RMF and if the true type of the object is a file object, then the target has the ability to render the operation without the intervention of the source. However, it could be possible that this is not feasible and a DM_RENDER message would need to be sent to the source so that it can perform the operation (this could occur if the source does not know the name of the file containing the data to be transferred). If this is so, the target needs to allocate a DRAGTRANSFER structure (via *DrgAllocDragtransfer*) and fill in the *hstrRenderToName* field; the source sends back a DM_RENDERCOMPLETE message to indicate that the operation is done.

DRM_PRINT — This mechanism would be used when the data is dropped onto a printer, and should only be used if the source understands and can process the DM_PRINT message that will be sent to it by the target. In this message is the name of the print queue to which the operation is to be performed.

Gotcha!

The OS/2 2.0 online documentation incorrectly states that for a DM_PRINTOBJECT *mpParm1* message, *mpParm1* pointers to a DRAGINFO structure. In reality, this points to a DRAGITEM structure for the item to be printed. This has been corrected for OS/2 2.1.

Gotcha!

The authors have experienced trouble using the *pdriv* field of the *pdosData* field of the PRINTDEST structure passed in as a pointer in *mpParm2* for the DM_PRINTOBJECT message; the printer consistently rejects the data as being invalid when we call *DevOpenDC*. Unfortunately, one cannot simply call *DevPostDeviceModes* (see Chapter 20, Presentation Manager Printing, for more information) to get a good set of driver data, because the device name is not specified anywhere. The workaround is to call *SplQueryQueue* first using the queue name in *pszLogAddress* field of the *pdosData* field of the PRINTDEST structure to get the PRQINFO3 structure containing the device name.

DRM_DDE — This mechanism could be used when the other two do not provide the capability to complete the desired operation. While this is the most flexible of the three mechanisms, it is also the most cumbersome.

The source must understand and be able to process the appropriate WM_DDE_* messages sent to it by the target. Note that a WM_DDE_INITIATE is not required since the target already has the window handle with which it wishes to converse.

Since the topic of DDE could fill an entire chapter by itself, we will not present any more information on this type of data transfer in this chapter.

18.7 A Concrete Example

A lot of material has been explained so far, and an example is sorely needed to cross the boundary from the abstract to the applied. Below is an application that can act as both source and target for direct manipulation. While it is a simple program, it demonstrates the concepts previously described.

DRAG1.C

```
#define INCL_DOSFILEMGR
#define INCL_WININPUT
#define INCL_WINPOINTERS
#define INCL_WINSTDDRAG
#define INCL_WINSYS
#define INCL_WINWINDOWMGR

#include <os2.h>
#include <stdio.h>
#include <stdlib.h>
#include <string.h>

#define CLS_CLIENT              "SampleClass"

#define DRAG_METHOD             "DRM_OS2FILE"
#define DRAG_FORMAT             "DRF_UNKNOWN"
#define DRAG_RMF                " < "DRAG_METHOD", "DRAG_FORMAT" > "

#define DRAG_TEMPNAME           "DRAGDROP.TMP"
#define MYM_DEWDROP             ( WM_USER )

typedef struct _CLIENTINFO {
   PDRAGINFO pdiDrag ;
   BOOL bDragging ;
   BOOL bEmphasis ;
   CHAR achLine [256] ;
} CLIENTINFO, *PCLIENTINFO ;
```

```
VOID fileFromDragItem ( PDRAGITEM pdiItem, PCHAR pchFile ) ;

VOID paintClient ( HPS hpsClient,
                   HWND hwndClient,
                   PCLIENTINFO pciInfo ) ;

MRESULT doSource ( HWND hwndClient,
                   ULONG ulMsg,
                   MPARAM mpParm1,
                   MPARAM mpParm2 ) ;
MRESULT doTarget ( HWND hwndClient,
                   ULONG ulMsg,
                   MPARAM mpParm1,
                   MPARAM mpParm2 ) ;

MRESULT EXPENTRY clientWndProc ( HWND hwndClient,
                                 ULONG ulMsg,
                                 MPARAM mpParm1,
                                 MPARAM mpParm2 ) ;

INT main ( VOID )
{
   HAB          habAnchor ;
   HMQ          hmqQueue ;
   ULONG        ulFlags ;
   HWND         hwndFrame ;
   BOOL         bLoop ;
   QMSG         qmMsg ;

   habAnchor = WinInitialize ( 0 ) ;
   hmqQueue = WinCreateMsgQueue ( habAnchor, 0 ) ;

   WinRegisterClass ( habAnchor,
                      CLS_CLIENT,
                      clientWndProc,
                      CS_SIZEREDRAW,
                      sizeof ( PVOID )) ;

   ulFlags = FCF_SIZEBORDER | FCF_TITLEBAR |
             FCF_TASKLIST | FCF_SHELLPOSITION |
             FCF_SYSMENU ;

   hwndFrame = WinCreateStdWindow ( HWND_DESKTOP,
                                    WS_VISIBLE,
                                    &ulFlags,
                                    CLS_CLIENT,
                                    "Drag - n - Drop Sample"
                                    " Application",
                                    0,
                                    NULLHANDLE,
                                    0,
                                    NULL ) ;

   bLoop = WinGetMsg ( habAnchor, &qmMsg, NULLHANDLE, 0, 0 ) ;
   while ( bLoop ) {
      WinDispatchMsg ( habAnchor, &qmMsg ) ;
      bLoop = WinGetMsg ( habAnchor, &qmMsg, NULLHANDLE, 0, 0 ) ;
```

```
      } /* endwhile */

   WinDestroyWindow ( hwndFrame ) ;
   WinDestroyMsgQueue ( hmqQueue ) ;
   WinTerminate ( habAnchor ) ;
   return ( 0 ) ;
}

VOID fileFromDragItem ( PDRAGITEM pdiItem, PCHAR pchFile )
{
   CHAR        achPath [CCHMAXPATH] ;
   CHAR        achFile [CCHMAXPATH] ;

   DrgQueryStrName ( pdiItem -> hstrContainerName,
                     sizeof ( achPath ) ,
                     achPath ) ;

   DosQueryPathInfo ( achPath,
                      FIL_QUERYFULLNAME,
                      achPath,
                      sizeof ( achPath )) ;

   if ( achPath [strlen ( achPath ) - 1] != '\\' ) {
      strcat ( achPath, "\\" ) ;
   } /* endif */

   DrgQueryStrName ( pdiItem -> hstrSourceName,
                     sizeof ( achFile ) ,
                     achFile ) ;

   sprintf ( pchFile, "%s%s", achPath, achFile ) ;
   return ;
}

VOID paintClient ( HPS hpsClient,
                   HWND hwndClient,
                   PCLIENTINFO pciInfo )

//----------------------------------------------------------------
// This function paints the client window according its current
// status.
//
// Input:  hpsClient - handle to the presentation space.
//         hwndClient - handle to the client window.
//         pciInfo - pointer to the CLIENTINFO structure
//           describing the client window.
//----------------------------------------------------------------

{
   RECTL        rclWindow ;
   USHORT       usIndex ;
   POINTL       ptlPaint ;

   WinQueryWindowRect ( hwndClient, &rclWindow ) ;
   WinFillRect ( hpsClient, &rclWindow, SYSCLR_WINDOW ) ;
```

```
//------------------------------------------------------------
// Draw the dividing line
//------------------------------------------------------------

ptlPaint.x = rclWindow.xRight / 2 ;
ptlPaint.y = rclWindow.yBottom ;
GpiMove ( hpsClient, &ptlPaint ) ;

ptlPaint.y = rclWindow.yTop ;
GpiLine ( hpsClient, &ptlPaint ) ;

    //------------------------------------------------------------
    // Set the color to indicate emphasized or
    // non-emphasized state
    //------------------------------------------------------------

if ( pciInfo -> bEmphasis ) {
   GpiSetColor ( hpsClient, CLR_BLACK ) ;
} else {
   GpiSetColor ( hpsClient, SYSCLR_WINDOW ) ;
} /* endif */

    //------------------------------------------------------------
    // Draw/erase the emphasis
    //------------------------------------------------------------

for ( usIndex = 1 ; usIndex < 5 ; usIndex ++ ) {
   ptlPaint.x = rclWindow.xRight / 2 + usIndex ;
   ptlPaint.y = rclWindow.yBottom + usIndex ;
   GpiMove ( hpsClient, &ptlPaint ) ;

   ptlPaint.x = rclWindow.xRight - usIndex ;
   ptlPaint.y = rclWindow.yTop - usIndex ;
   GpiBox ( hpsClient, DRO_OUTLINE, &ptlPaint, 0, 0 ) ;
} /* endfor */

    //------------------------------------------------------------
    // Draw the instructing text
    //------------------------------------------------------------

WinQueryWindowRect ( hwndClient, &rclWindow ) ;
rclWindow.xRight /= 2 ;

WinDrawText ( hpsClient,
              - 1,
              "Drag me",
              &rclWindow,
              CLR_BLACK,
              0,
              DT_CENTER | DT_VCENTER ) ;

if ( pciInfo -> achLine [0] != 0 ) {

    //------------------------------------------------------------
    // Draw the text received if we've been dropped on
    //------------------------------------------------------------
```

```
        WinQueryWindowRect ( hwndClient, &rclWindow ) ;
        rclWindow.xLeft = rclWindow.xRight / 2 ;

        WinDrawText ( hpsClient,
                      - 1,
                      pciInfo -> achLine,
                      &rclWindow,
                      CLR_BLACK,
                      0,
                      DT_CENTER | DT_VCENTER ) ;
    } /* endif */
    return ;
}

MRESULT doSource ( HWND hwndClient,
                   ULONG ulMsg,
                   MPARAM mpParm1,
                   MPARAM mpParm2 )

//---------------------------------------------------------------
// This function handles the direct-manipulation messages
//
// sent to the source part of the window.
//
// Input, output, returns:  as a window procedure
//---------------------------------------------------------------
{
    PCLIENTINFO pciInfo ;

    pciInfo = WinQueryWindowPtr ( hwndClient, 0 ) ;

    switch ( ulMsg ) {

    case WM_BEGINDRAG:
        {
            RECTL           rclWindow ;
            FILE            *pfFile ;
            DRAGITEM        diItem ;
            DRAGIMAGE       diImage ;
            HWND            hwndTarget ;

            WinQueryWindowRect ( hwndClient, &rclWindow ) ;

            //-------------------------------------------------
            // If we're in the right half, return
            //-------------------------------------------------

            if ( SHORT1FROMMP ( mpParm1 ) > rclWindow.xRight / 2 ) {
                return MRFROMSHORT ( FALSE ) ;
            } /* endif */

            //-------------------------------------------------
            // Write the text to be dragged to a file,
            // since the type is
            // DRT_OS2FILE.
            //-------------------------------------------------
```

```
      pfFile = fopen ( DRAG_TEMPNAME, "w" ) ;
      if ( pfFile == NULL ) {
         return MRFROMSHORT ( FALSE ) ;
      } /* endif */

      fprintf ( pfFile, "Dropped text" ) ;
      fclose ( pfFile ) ;

      //-------------------------------------------------------
      // Allocate the DRAGITEM/DRAGINFO structures and
      // initialize them
      //-------------------------------------------------------

      pciInfo -> pdiDrag = DrgAllocDraginfo ( 1 ) ;
      pciInfo -> pdiDrag -> hwndSource = hwndClient ;

      diItem.hwndItem = hwndClient ;
      diItem.ulItemID = 1 ;
      diItem.hstrType = DrgAddStrHandle ( DRT_TEXT ) ;
      diItem.hstrRMF = DrgAddStrHandle ( DRAG_RMF ) ;
      diItem.hstrContainerName = DrgAddStrHandle ( "." ) ;
      diItem.hstrSourceName = DrgAddStrHandle (
                                  DRAG_TEMPNAME ) ;

      diItem.hstrTargetName = diItem.hstrSourceName ;
      diItem.cxOffset = 0 ;
      diItem.cyOffset = 0 ;
      diItem.fsControl = 0 ;
      diItem.fsSupportedOps = DO_MOVEABLE ;

      DrgSetDragitem ( pciInfo -> pdiDrag,
                       &diItem,
                       sizeof ( diItem ) ,
                       0 ) ;

      //-------------------------------------------------------
      // Initialize the DRAGIMAGE structure
      //-------------------------------------------------------

      diImage.cb = sizeof ( diImage ) ;
      diImage.cptl = 0 ;
      diImage.hImage = WinQuerySysPointer ( HWND_DESKTOP,
                                            SPTR_FILE,
                                            FALSE ) ;
      diImage.sizlStretch.cx = 0 ;
      diImage.sizlStretch.cy = 0 ;
      diImage.fl = DRG_ICON | DRG_TRANSPARENT ;
      diImage.cxOffset = 0 ;
      diImage.cyOffset = 0 ;

      //-------------------------------------------------------
      // Set the bDragging flag and call DrgDrag().
      //-------------------------------------------------------

      pciInfo -> bDragging = TRUE ;
```

```
                hwndTarget = DrgDrag ( hwndClient,
                                       pciInfo -> pdiDrag,
                                       &diImage,
                                       1L,
                                       VK_ENDDRAG,
                                       NULL ) ;

            if ( hwndTarget == NULLHANDLE ) {

                DrgDeleteDraginfoStrHandles ( pciInfo -> pdiDrag ) ;
                DrgFreeDraginfo ( pciInfo -> pdiDrag ) ;
                pciInfo -> pdiDrag = NULL ;
                pciInfo -> bDragging = FALSE ;
                remove ( DRAG_TEMPNAME ) ;

                WinInvalidateRect ( hwndClient, NULL, FALSE ) ;
                WinUpdateWindow ( hwndClient ) ;
            } /* endif */
        }
        break ;

    case DM_ENDCONVERSATION:
        {
            PDRAGITEM pdiItem ;
            CHAR achFullFile [CCHMAXPATH] ;

            //-------------------------------------------------------
            // Query the item dragged for cleanup purposes
            //-------------------------------------------------------

            pdiItem = DrgQueryDragitemPtr ( pciInfo -> pdiDrag,
                                            0 ) ;

            //-------------------------------------------------------
            // Delete the file used to transfer the data
            //-------------------------------------------------------

            fileFromDragItem ( pdiItem, achFullFile ) ;
            remove ( achFullFile ) ;

            //-------------------------------------------------------
            // Cleanup
            //-------------------------------------------------------

            DrgDeleteDraginfoStrHandles ( pciInfo -> pdiDrag ) ;
            DrgFreeDraginfo ( pciInfo -> pdiDrag ) ;
            pciInfo -> pdiDrag = NULL ;
            pciInfo -> bDragging = FALSE ;
        }
        break ;

    default:
        break ;
    } /* endswitch */

    return MRFROMSHORT ( FALSE ) ;
}
```

```
MRESULT doTarget ( HWND hwndClient,
                   ULONG ulMsg,
                   MPARAM mpParm1,
                   MPARAM mpParm2 )

//----------------------------------------------------------------
// This function handles the direct-manipulation messages
// sent to the target part of the window.
//
// Input, output, returns:  as a window procedure
//----------------------------------------------------------------

{
    PCLIENTINFO pciInfo ;

    pciInfo = WinQueryWindowPtr ( hwndClient, 0 ) ;

    switch ( ulMsg ) {
    case DM_DRAGOVER:
        {
            PDRAGINFO pdiDrag ;
            POINTL ptlDrop ;
            RECTL rclWindow ;
            HPS hpsWindow ;
            PDRAGITEM pdiItem ;

            //--------------------------------------------------
            // Get the pointer to the DRAGINFO structure
            //--------------------------------------------------

            pdiDrag = ( PDRAGINFO ) PVOIDFROMMP ( mpParm1 ) ;
            DrgAccessDraginfo ( pdiDrag ) ;

            //--------------------------------------------------
            // Since the drop position is in screen coordinates,
            // map them to our window and check if it is
            // in the right half of the window.  If not, return.
            //--------------------------------------------------

            ptlDrop.x = SHORT1FROMMP ( mpParm2 ) ;
            ptlDrop.y = SHORT2FROMMP ( mpParm2 ) ;

            WinMapWindowPoints ( HWND_DESKTOP,
                                 hwndClient,
                                 &ptlDrop,
                                 1 ) ;

            WinQueryWindowRect ( hwndClient, &rclWindow ) ;

            if ( ptlDrop.x < rclWindow.xRight / 2 ) {
                if ( pciInfo -> bEmphasis ) {
                    pciInfo -> bEmphasis = FALSE ;

                    hpsWindow = DrgGetPS ( hwndClient ) ;
                    paintClient ( hpsWindow, hwndClient, pciInfo ) ;
                    DrgReleasePS ( hpsWindow ) ;
```

```
                  } /* endif */

               return MRFROMSHORT ( DOR_NODROP ) ;
            } /* endif */

            //---------------------------------------------------
            // Check to see if we've already turned emphasis on.
            //---------------------------------------------------

            if ( !pciInfo -> bEmphasis ) {
               pciInfo -> bEmphasis = TRUE ;

               hpsWindow = DrgGetPS ( hwndClient ) ;
               paintClient ( hpsWindow, hwndClient, pciInfo ) ;
               DrgReleasePS ( hpsWindow ) ;
            } /* endif */

            //---------------------------------------------------
            // We should only be dragging one item.
            //---------------------------------------------------

            if ( DrgQueryDragitemCount ( pdiDrag ) != 1 ) {
               return MRFROMSHORT ( DOR_NODROP ) ;
            } /* endif */

            //---------------------------------------------------
            // Check the true type and native RMF
            //---------------------------------------------------

            pdiItem = DrgQueryDragitemPtr ( pdiDrag, 0 ) ;

            if ( !DrgVerifyTrueType ( pdiItem, DRT_TEXT )) {
               return MRFROMSHORT ( DOR_NODROP ) ;
            } else

            if ( !DrgVerifyNativeRMF ( pdiItem, DRAG_RMF )) {
               return MRFROMSHORT ( DOR_NODROP ) ;
            } /* endif */

            return MRFROM2SHORT ( DOR_DROP, DO_MOVE ) ;
         }
         break ;
      case DM_DRAGLEAVE:
         if ( pciInfo -> bEmphasis ) {
            HPS hpsWindow ;

            //---------------------------------------------------
            // Turn off the emphasis
            //---------------------------------------------------
            pciInfo -> bEmphasis = FALSE ;

            hpsWindow = DrgGetPS ( hwndClient ) ;
            paintClient ( hpsWindow, hwndClient, pciInfo ) ;
            DrgReleasePS ( hpsWindow ) ;
         } /* endif */
         break ;
```

```
case DM_DROP:
   WinPostMsg ( hwndClient, MYM_DEWDROP, mpParm1, mpParm2 ) ;
   break ;

case DM_DROPHELP:
   WinMessageBox ( HWND_DESKTOP,
                   hwndClient,
                   "This is the drag - n - drop help."
                   "  Great, isn't it?",
                   "Help",
                   0,
                   MB_INFORMATION | MB_OK ) ;
   break ;

case MYM_DEWDROP:
   {
      PDRAGINFO      pdiDrag ;
      PDRAGITEM      pdiItem ;
      CHAR           achFullFile [CCHMAXPATH] ;
      FILE           *pfFile ;
      HPS            hpsDrop ;

      //------------------------------------------------------
      // Get the pointer to the DRAGINFO structure
      //------------------------------------------------------

      pdiDrag = ( PDRAGINFO ) PVOIDFROMMP ( mpParm1 ) ;
      DrgAccessDraginfo ( pdiDrag ) ;

      //------------------------------------------------------
      // Since we can render the object ourselves,
      // get the filename and read in the line
      //------------------------------------------------------

      pdiItem = DrgQueryDragitemPtr ( pdiDrag, 0 ) ;
      fileFromDragItem ( pdiItem, achFullFile ) ;

      pfFile = fopen ( achFullFile, "r" ) ;
      if ( pfFile != NULL ) {
         fgets ( pciInfo -> achLine,
                 sizeof ( pciInfo -> achLine ) ,
                 pfFile ) ;
         fclose ( pfFile ) ;
      } /* endif */

      //------------------------------------------------------
      // Turn the emphasis off and repaint ourselves to
      // show the dropped text
      //------------------------------------------------------

      pciInfo -> bEmphasis = FALSE ;

      hpsDrop = DrgGetPS ( hwndClient ) ;
      paintClient ( hpsDrop, hwndClient, pciInfo ) ;
      DrgReleasePS ( hpsDrop ) ;
```

```
            //----------------------------------------------------
            // Tell the source that we're done with the object
            //----------------------------------------------------

            WinSendMsg ( pdiDrag -> hwndSource,
                         DM_ENDCONVERSATION,
                         MPFROMSHORT ( pdiItem -> ulItemID ) ,
                         0 ) ;

            //----------------------------------------------------
            // Cleanup
            //----------------------------------------------------

            if ( !pciInfo -> bDragging ) {
               DrgDeleteDraginfoStrHandles ( pdiDrag ) ;
               DrgFreeDraginfo ( pdiDrag ) ;
            } /* endif */
         }
      break ;

   default:
      break ;

   } /* endswitch */

   return MRFROMSHORT ( FALSE ) ;
}

MRESULT EXPENTRY clientWndProc ( HWND hwndClient,
                                 ULONG ulMsg,
                                 MPARAM mpParm1,
                                 MPARAM mpParm2 )
//------------------------------------------------------------------
// This function handles the messages sent to the client window.
//
// Input, output, returns:  as a window procedure
//------------------------------------------------------------------

{
   PCLIENTINFO pciInfo ;

   pciInfo = WinQueryWindowPtr ( hwndClient, 0 ) ;

   switch ( ulMsg ) {
   case WM_CREATE:

      //----------------------------------------------------
      // Allocate memory for the instance data structure
      // and initialize it
      //----------------------------------------------------

      pciInfo = malloc ( sizeof ( CLIENTINFO )) ;
```

```
        if ( pciInfo == NULL ) {
            WinMessageBox ( HWND_DESKTOP,
                            hwndClient,
                            "There is not enough memory.",
                            "Error",
                            0,
                            MB_ICONHAND | MB_OK ) ;
            return MRFROMSHORT ( TRUE ) ;
        } /* endif */

        WinSetWindowPtr ( hwndClient, 0, pciInfo ) ;

        pciInfo -> bDragging = FALSE ;
        pciInfo -> bEmphasis = FALSE ;
        pciInfo -> achLine [0] = 0 ;
        break ;

    case WM_DESTROY:

        //---------------------------------------------------------
        // Free the memory used by the instance data
        //---------------------------------------------------------

        free ( pciInfo ) ;
        WinSetWindowPtr ( hwndClient, 0, NULL ) ;
        break ;

    case WM_PAINT:
        {
            HPS hpsPaint ;

            hpsPaint = WinBeginPaint ( hwndClient,
                                       NULLHANDLE,
                                       NULL ) ;

            paintClient ( hpsPaint, hwndClient, pciInfo ) ;
            WinEndPaint ( hpsPaint ) ;
        }
        break ;

    case WM_BEGINDRAG:
    case DM_ENDCONVERSATION:
        return doSource ( hwndClient, ulMsg, mpParm1, mpParm2 ) ;

    case DM_DRAGOVER:
    case DM_DRAGLEAVE:
    case DM_DROP:
    case DM_DROPHELP:
    case MYM_DEWDROP:
        return doTarget ( hwndClient, ulMsg, mpParm1, mpParm2 ) ;

    default:
        return WinDefWindowProc ( hwndClient,
                                  ulMsg,
                                  mpParm1,
                                  mpParm2 ) ;

    } /* endswitch */
```

```
    return MRFROMSHORT ( FALSE ) ;
}
```

DRAG1.MAK

```
DRAG1.EXE:                       DRAG1.OBJ
        LINK386 @<<
DRAG1
DRAG1
DRAG1
OS2386
DRAG1
<<

DRAG1.OBJ:                       DRAG1.C
        ICC -C+ -Kb+ -Ss+ DRAG1.C
```

DRAG1.DEF

```
NAME DRAG1 WINDOWAPI

DESCRIPTION 'Drag example 1
Copyright (c) 1992 by Larry Salomon
All rights reserved.'

STACKSIZE 16384
```

Since *main* is fairly standard, we'll ignore it except for the fact that we're reserving space for a pointer in the call to *WinRegisterClass*. This will be used to store a pointer to the client's instance data, so that we can avoid global variables. This instance data is allocated and initialized in the WM_CREATE message and is freed in the WM_DESTROY message.

```
        typedef struct _CLIENTINFO {
                PDRAGINFO pdiDrag;
                BOOL bDragging;
                BOOL bEmphasis;
                CHAR achLine[256];
        } CLIENTINFO, *PCLIENTINFO;
```

The *pdiDrag* field is used only by the source window and points to the DRAGINFO structure allocated via *DrgAllocDraginfo*. *bDragging* and *bEmphasis* specify whether a dragging operation is in progress and whether or not the client is displaying emphasis, respectively. *achLine* is used only by the target window and contains the line of text that was dropped on the window. For clarity, the processing of the direct-manipulation messages has been separated into those usually associated with the source and target windows (see *doSource* and *doTarget*).

What the program does is allow the dragging of text from the left half of the window into either the right half of this window or another instance of this window (try starting two copies of SAMPLE1.EXE to do this). Whenever a WM_BEGINDRAG message is received by the source, the appropriate data structures are initialized and *DrgDrag* is called. The target adds emphasis whenever it receives a DM_DRAGOVER message and returns the appropriate DOR_* value. After the object has been dropped, the target completely renders the data provided by the source and sends the source a DM_ENDCONVERSATION message to terminate the dragging operation.

You are probably wondering why we return DOR_NODROP from the DM_DRAGOVER message when we find that we cannot accept the drop because the objects are in an unrecognized type or use an unrecognized RMF. It is true that you would normally return DOR_NEVERDROP, but remember that we only allow dropping on the right half of the window; once the pointer moves into the left half, we must remove the target emphasis. However, if we return DOR_NEVERDROP, we never receive another DM_DRAGOVER message until the mouse moves out of the window and then back into the window. This technique is required for container windows (where "container" is a concept and not meant specifically for the WC_CONTAINER window class) when the potential targets are not child windows.

18.8 More Cement, Please

Let's complicate things by modifying our program to have the source window render the data.

DRAG2.C

```
#define INCL_DOSFILEMGR
#define INCL_WININPUT
#define INCL_WINPOINTERS
#define INCL_WINSTDDRAG
#define INCL_WINSYS
#define INCL_WINWINDOWMGR

#include <os2.h>
#include <stdio.h>
#include <stdlib.h>
#include <string.h>

#define CLS_CLIENT              "SampleClass"

#define DRAG_METHOD             "DRM_OS2FILE"
#define DRAG_FORMAT             "DRF_UNKNOWN"
#define DRAG_RMF                " <"DRAG_METHOD", "DRAG_FORMAT"> "
```

```
#define DRAG_TEMPNAME                "DRAGDROP.TMP"

#define MYM_DEWDROP                  ( WM_USER )

typedef struct _CLIENTINFO {
    PDRAGINFO pdiSource ;             // Used by source
    BOOL      bDragging ;             // Used by source
    BOOL      bEmphasis ;             // Used by source
    PDRAGINFO pdiTarget ;             // Used by source
    CHAR      achLine [256] ;         // Used by target
} CLIENTINFO, *PCLIENTINFO ;


VOID fileFromDragItem ( PDRAGITEM pdiItem, PCHAR pchFile ) ;
VOID paintClient ( HPS hpsClient,
                   HWND hwndClient,
                   PCLIENTINFO pciInfo ) ;

MRESULT doSource ( HWND hwndClient,
                   ULONG ulMsg,
                   MPARAM mpParm1,
                   MPARAM mpParm2 ) ;

MRESULT doTarget ( HWND hwndClient,
                   ULONG ulMsg,
                   MPARAM mpParm1,
                   MPARAM mpParm2 ) ;

MRESULT EXPENTRY clientWndProc ( HWND hwndClient,
                                 ULONG ulMsg,
                                 MPARAM mpParm1,
                                 MPARAM mpParm2 ) ;

INT main ( VOID )
{
    HAB            habAnchor ;
    HMQ            hmqQueue ;
    ULONG          ulFlags ;
    HWND           hwndFrame ;
    BOOL           bLoop ;
    QMSG           qmMsg ;

    habAnchor = WinInitialize ( 0 ) ;
    hmqQueue = WinCreateMsgQueue ( habAnchor, 0 ) ;

    WinRegisterClass ( habAnchor,
                       CLS_CLIENT,
                       clientWndProc,
                       CS_SIZEREDRAW,
                       sizeof ( PVOID )) ;

    ulFlags = FCF_SIZEBORDER | FCF_TITLEBAR |
              FCF_TASKLIST | FCF_SHELLPOSITION |
              FCF_SYSMENU ;
```

```
   hwndFrame = WinCreateStdWindow ( HWND_DESKTOP,
                                     WS_VISIBLE,
                                     &ulFlags,
                                     CLS_CLIENT,
                                     "Drag - n - Drop"
                                     " Sample Application 2",
                                     0,
                                     NULLHANDLE,
                                     0,
                                     NULL ) ;

   bLoop = WinGetMsg ( habAnchor, &qmMsg, NULLHANDLE, 0, 0 ) ;
   while ( bLoop ) {
      WinDispatchMsg ( habAnchor, &qmMsg ) ;
      bLoop = WinGetMsg ( habAnchor, &qmMsg, NULLHANDLE, 0, 0 ) ;
   } /* endwhile */

   WinDestroyWindow ( hwndFrame ) ;
   WinDestroyMsgQueue ( hmqQueue ) ;
   WinTerminate ( habAnchor ) ;
   return ( 0 ) ;
}

VOID fileFromDragItem ( PDRAGITEM pdiItem, PCHAR pchFile )

//---------------------------------------------------------------
// This function composes a filename from the DRAGITEM structure
//  and returns it in pchFile.  It is assumed that pchFile
//  points to a buffer of size CCHMAXPATH.
//
//
// Input:  pdiItem - points to the DRAGITEM structure containing
//                   the necessary information.
// Output:  pchFile - points to the variable containing the
//                    filename.
//---------------------------------------------------------------
{
   CHAR       achPath [CCHMAXPATH] ;
   CHAR       achFile [CCHMAXPATH] ;

   DrgQueryStrName ( pdiItem -> hstrContainerName,
                     sizeof ( achPath ) ,
                     achPath ) ;

   DosQueryPathInfo ( achPath,
                      FIL_QUERYFULLNAME,
                      achPath,
                      sizeof ( achPath )) ;

   if ( achPath [strlen ( achPath ) - 1] != '\\' ) {
      strcat ( achPath, "\\" ) ;
   } /* endif */

   DrgQueryStrName ( pdiItem -> hstrSourceName,
                     sizeof ( achFile ) ,
                     achFile ) ;
```

```
      sprintf ( pchFile, "%s%s", achPath, achFile ) ;
      return ;
}

VOID paintClient ( HPS hpsClient,
                   HWND hwndClient,
                   PCLIENTINFO pciInfo )

//-------------------------------------------------------------
// This function paints the client window according
//     its current status.
//
// Input:  hpsClient - handle to the presentation space.
//         hwndClient - handle to the client window.
//         pciInfo - pointer to the CLIENTINFO structure
//                      describing the client window.
//-------------------------------------------------------------

{
   RECTL          rclWindow ;
   USHORT         usIndex ;
   POINTL         ptlPaint ;

   WinQueryWindowRect ( hwndClient, &rclWindow ) ;
   WinFillRect ( hpsClient, &rclWindow, SYSCLR_WINDOW ) ;

   //----------------------------------------------------------
   // Draw the dividing line
   //----------------------------------------------------------

   ptlPaint.x = rclWindow.xRight / 2 ;
   ptlPaint.y = rclWindow.yBottom ;
   GpiMove ( hpsClient, &ptlPaint ) ;

   ptlPaint.y = rclWindow.yTop ;
   GpiLine ( hpsClient, &ptlPaint ) ;

   //----------------------------------------------------------
   // Set the color to indicate emphasized or
   // non-emphasized state
   //----------------------------------------------------------

   if ( pciInfo -> bEmphasis ) {
      GpiSetColor ( hpsClient, CLR_BLACK ) ;
   } else {
      GpiSetColor ( hpsClient, SYSCLR_WINDOW ) ;
   } /* endif */

   //----------------------------------------------------------
   // Draw/erase the emphasis
   //----------------------------------------------------------

   for ( usIndex = 1 ; usIndex < 5 ; usIndex ++ ) {
      ptlPaint.x = rclWindow.xRight / 2 + usIndex ;
      ptlPaint.y = rclWindow.yBottom + usIndex ;
      GpiMove ( hpsClient, &ptlPaint ) ;
```

```
      ptlPaint.x = rclWindow.xRight - usIndex ;
      ptlPaint.y = rclWindow.yTop - usIndex ;
      GpiBox ( hpsClient, DRO_OUTLINE, &ptlPaint, 0, 0 ) ;
   } /* endfor */

   //-------------------------------------------------------------
   // Draw the instructing text
   //-------------------------------------------------------------

   WinQueryWindowRect ( hwndClient, &rclWindow ) ;
   rclWindow.xRight /= 2 ;

   WinDrawText ( hpsClient,
                 - 1,
                 "Drag me",
                 &rclWindow,
                 CLR_BLACK,
                 0L,
                 DT_CENTER | DT_VCENTER ) ;

   if ( pciInfo -> achLine [0] != 0 ) {

      //-------------------------------------------------------------
      // Draw the text received if we've been dropped on
      //-------------------------------------------------------------

      WinQueryWindowRect ( hwndClient, &rclWindow ) ;
      rclWindow.xLeft = rclWindow.xRight / 2 ;

      WinDrawText ( hpsClient,
                    - 1,
                    pciInfo -> achLine,
                    &rclWindow,
                    CLR_BLACK,
                    0L,
                    DT_CENTER | DT_VCENTER ) ;
   } /* endif */
   return ;
}

MRESULT doSource ( HWND hwndClient,
                   ULONG ulMsg,
                   MPARAM mpParm1,
                   MPARAM mpParm2 )

//-------------------------------------------------------------
// This function handles the direct-manipulation messages
// sent to the source part of the window.
//
// Input, output, returns:  as a window procedure
//-------------------------------------------------------------

{
   PCLIENTINFO pciInfo ;

   pciInfo = WinQueryWindowPtr ( hwndClient, 0 ) ;
```

```
    switch ( ulMsg ) {

case WM_BEGINDRAG:
    {
        RECTL rclWindow ;
        DRAGITEM diItem ;
        DRAGIMAGE diImage ;
        HWND hwndTarget ;

        WinQueryWindowRect ( hwndClient, &rclWindow ) ;

        //-------------------------------------------------------
        // If we're in the right half, return
        //-------------------------------------------------------

        if ( SHORT1FROMMP ( mpParm1 ) >
             rclWindow.xRight / 2 ) {

           return MRFROMSHORT ( FALSE ) ;
        } /* endif */

        //-------------------------------------------------------
        // Allocate the DRAGITEM/DRAGINFO structures and
        // initialize them
        //-------------------------------------------------------

        pciInfo -> pdiSource = DrgAllocDraginfo ( 1 ) ;
        pciInfo -> pdiSource -> hwndSource = hwndClient ;

        diItem.hwndItem = hwndClient ;
        diItem.ulItemID = 1 ;
        diItem.hstrType = DrgAddStrHandle ( DRT_TEXT ) ;
        diItem.hstrRMF = DrgAddStrHandle ( DRAG_RMF ) ;
        diItem.hstrContainerName = DrgAddStrHandle ( "." ) ;
        diItem.hstrSourceName = NULLHANDLE ;
        diItem.hstrTargetName = NULLHANDLE ;
        diItem.cxOffset = 0 ;
        diItem.cyOffset = 0 ;
        diItem.fsControl = 0 ;
        diItem.fsSupportedOps = DO_MOVEABLE ;

        DrgSetDragitem ( pciInfo -> pdiSource,
                         &diItem,
                         sizeof ( diItem ) ,
                         0 ) ;

        //-------------------------------------------------------
        // Initialize the DRAGIMAGE structure
        //-------------------------------------------------------

        diImage.cb = sizeof ( diImage ) ;
        diImage.cptl = 0 ;
        diImage.hImage = WinQuerySysPointer ( HWND_DESKTOP,
                                              SPTR_FILE,
                                              FALSE ) ;
        diImage.sizlStretch.cx = 0 ;
        diImage.sizlStretch.cy = 0 ;
```

```
        diImage.fl = DRG_ICON | DRG_TRANSPARENT ;
        diImage.cxOffset = 0 ;
        diImage.cyOffset = 0 ;

        //-------------------------------------------------------
        // Set the bDragging flag and call DrgDrag().
        //-------------------------------------------------------
        pciInfo -> bDragging = TRUE ;

        hwndTarget = DrgDrag ( hwndClient,
                               pciInfo -> pdiSource,
                               &diImage,
                               1L,
                               VK_ENDDRAG,
                               NULL ) ;
        if ( hwndTarget == NULLHANDLE ) {
            DrgDeleteDraginfoStrHandles ( pciInfo -> pdiSource ) ;
            DrgFreeDraginfo ( pciInfo -> pdiSource ) ;
            pciInfo -> pdiSource = NULL ;
            pciInfo -> bDragging = FALSE ;
            remove ( DRAG_TEMPNAME ) ;

            WinInvalidateRect ( hwndClient, NULL, FALSE ) ;
            WinUpdateWindow ( hwndClient ) ;
        } /* endif */
    }
    break ;

case DM_RENDERPREPARE:
    return MRFROMSHORT ( TRUE ) ;

case DM_RENDER:
    {
        PDRAGTRANSFER pdtXfer ;
        CHAR          achFile [CCHMAXPATH] ;
        FILE          *pfFile ;

        pdtXfer = ( PDRAGTRANSFER ) PVOIDFROMMP ( mpParm1 ) ;

        DrgQueryStrName ( pdtXfer -> hstrRenderToName,
                          sizeof ( achFile ) ,
                          achFile ) ;
        DrgFreeDragtransfer(( PDRAGTRANSFER )
                            PVOIDFROMMP ( mpParm1 )) ;

        //-------------------------------------------------------
        // Write the text to be dragged to a file, since the
        // type is DRT_OS2FILE.
        //-------------------------------------------------------

        pfFile = fopen ( achFile, "w" ) ;
        if ( pfFile != NULL ) {
            fprintf ( pfFile, "Dropped text" ) ;
            fclose ( pfFile ) ;

            return MRFROMSHORT ( TRUE ) ;
        } else {
```

```
                    return MRFROMSHORT ( FALSE ) ;
                } /* endif */
            }

    case DM_ENDCONVERSATION:

        //----------------------------------------------------------
        // Cleanup
        //----------------------------------------------------------

        DrgDeleteDraginfoStrHandles ( pciInfo -> pdiSource ) ;
        DrgFreeDraginfo ( pciInfo -> pdiSource ) ;
        pciInfo -> pdiSource = NULL ;
        pciInfo -> bDragging = FALSE ;
        break ;

    default:
        break ;
    } /* endswitch */

    return MRFROMSHORT ( FALSE ) ;
}

MRESULT doTarget ( HWND hwndClient,
                   ULONG ulMsg,
                   MPARAM mpParm1,
                   MPARAM mpParm2 )

//----------------------------------------------------------------
// This function handles the direct-manipulation messages
// sent to the target part of the window.
//
// Input, output, returns:  as a window procedure
//----------------------------------------------------------------

{
    PCLIENTINFO pciInfo ;

    pciInfo = WinQueryWindowPtr ( hwndClient, 0 ) ;

    switch ( ulMsg ) {
    case DM_DRAGOVER:
        {
            PDRAGINFO pdiDrag ;
            POINTL ptlDrop ;
            RECTL rclWindow ;
            HPS hpsWindow ;
            PDRAGITEM pdiItem ;

            //----------------------------------------------------
            // Get the pointer to the DRAGINFO structure
            //----------------------------------------------------

            pdiDrag = ( PDRAGINFO ) PVOIDFROMMP ( mpParm1 ) ;
            DrgAccessDraginfo ( pdiDrag ) ;
```

```
//-----------------------------------------------------
// Since the drop position is in screen coordinates,
// map them to our window and check if it is in the
// right half of the window.  If not, return.
//-----------------------------------------------------

ptlDrop.x = SHORT1FROMMP ( mpParm2 ) ;
ptlDrop.y = SHORT2FROMMP ( mpParm2 ) ;
WinMapWindowPoints ( HWND_DESKTOP,
                     hwndClient,
                     &ptlDrop,
                     1 ) ;

WinQueryWindowRect ( hwndClient, &rclWindow ) ;

if ( ptlDrop.x < rclWindow.xRight / 2 ) {
   if ( pciInfo -> bEmphasis ) {
      pciInfo -> bEmphasis = FALSE ;

      hpsWindow = DrgGetPS ( hwndClient ) ;
      paintClient ( hpsWindow, hwndClient, pciInfo ) ;
      DrgReleasePS ( hpsWindow ) ;
   } /* endif */

   return MRFROMSHORT ( DOR_NODROP ) ;
} /* endif */

//-----------------------------------------------------
// Check to see if we've already turned emphasis on.
//-----------------------------------------------------

if ( !pciInfo -> bEmphasis ) {

   pciInfo -> bEmphasis = TRUE ;

   hpsWindow = DrgGetPS ( hwndClient ) ;
   paintClient ( hpsWindow, hwndClient, pciInfo ) ;
   DrgReleasePS ( hpsWindow ) ;

} /* endif */

//-----------------------------------------------------
// We should only be dragging one item.
//-----------------------------------------------------

if ( DrgQueryDragitemCount ( pdiDrag ) != 1 ) {
   return MRFROMSHORT ( DOR_NODROP ) ;
} /* endif */

//-----------------------------------------------------
// Check the true type and native RMF
//-----------------------------------------------------

pdiItem = DrgQueryDragitemPtr ( pdiDrag, 0 ) ;

if ( !DrgVerifyTrueType ( pdiItem, DRT_TEXT )) {
   return MRFROMSHORT ( DOR_NODROP ) ;
```

```
            } else
            if ( !DrgVerifyNativeRMF ( pdiItem, DRAG_RMF )) {
                return MRFROMSHORT ( DOR_NODROP ) ;
            } /* endif */

            return MRFROM2SHORT ( DOR_DROP, DO_MOVE ) ;
        }

    case DM_DRAGLEAVE:
        if ( pciInfo -> bEmphasis ) {
            HPS hpsWindow ;

            //----------------------------------------------------
            // Turn off the emphasis
            //----------------------------------------------------

            pciInfo -> bEmphasis = FALSE ;

            hpsWindow = DrgGetPS ( hwndClient ) ;
            paintClient ( hpsWindow, hwndClient, pciInfo ) ;
            DrgReleasePS ( hpsWindow ) ;
        } /* endif */
        break ;

    case DM_DROP:
        WinPostMsg ( hwndClient, MYM_DEWDROP, mpParm1, mpParm2 ) ;
        break ;

    case DM_RENDERCOMPLETE:
        break ;

    case DM_DROPHELP:
        WinMessageBox ( HWND_DESKTOP,
                        hwndClient,
                        "This is the drag - n - drop help."
                        "  Great, isn't it?",
                        "Help",
                        0,
                        MB_INFORMATION | MB_OK ) ;
        break ;

    case MYM_DEWDROP:
        {
            HPS              hpsDrop ;
            PDRAGITEM        pdiItem ;
            CHAR             achRMF [256] ;
            PDRAGTRANSFER    pdtXfer ;
            CHAR             achFile [CCHMAXPATH] ;
            FILE             *pfFile ;

            //----------------------------------------------------
            // Get the pointer to the DRAGINFO structure
            //----------------------------------------------------

            pciInfo -> pdiTarget = ( PDRAGINFO )
                                   PVOIDFROMMP ( mpParm1 ) ;
```

```
      DrgAccessDraginfo ( pciInfo -> pdiTarget ) ;

   //------------------------------------------------------
   // Turn the emphasis off
   //------------------------------------------------------

   pciInfo -> bEmphasis = FALSE ;

   hpsDrop = DrgGetPS ( hwndClient ) ;
   paintClient ( hpsDrop, hwndClient, pciInfo ) ;
   DrgReleasePS ( hpsDrop ) ;

   //------------------------------------------------------
   // If the source did not render the data previously,
   // we need to allocate a DRAGTRANSFER structure and
   // send the source a DM_RENDER message.
   //------------------------------------------------------

   pdiItem = DrgQueryDragitemPtr ( pciInfo -> pdiTarget,
                                   0 ) ;

   if ( pdiItem -> hstrSourceName == NULLHANDLE ) {
      DrgQueryNativeRMF ( pdiItem,
                          sizeof ( achRMF ) ,
                          achRMF ) ;

      pdtXfer = DrgAllocDragtransfer ( 1 ) ;
      pdtXfer -> cb = sizeof ( DRAGTRANSFER ) ;
      pdtXfer -> hwndClient = hwndClient ;
      pdtXfer -> pditem = pdiItem ;
      pdtXfer -> hstrSelectedRMF = DrgAddStrHandle (
                                   achRMF ) ;
      pdtXfer -> hstrRenderToName = DrgAddStrHandle (
                                    DRAG_TEMPNAME ) ;
      pdtXfer -> ulTargetInfo = 0 ;
      pdtXfer -> usOperation =
         pciInfo -> pdiTarget -> usOperation ;

      pdtXfer -> fsReply = 0 ;

      //---------------------------------------------------
      // Does the source need to prepare the item?
      // If so, send a DM_RENDERPREPARE message.
      //---------------------------------------------------

      if (( pdiItem -> fsControl & DC_PREPARE ) != 0 ) {

         if ( !SHORT1FROMMR (
                  DrgSendTransferMsg (
                     pciInfo -> pdiTarget -> hwndSource,
                     DM_RENDERPREPARE,
                     MPFROMP ( pdtXfer ) ,
                     0L )) ) {

            DrgDeleteStrHandle (
               pdtXfer -> hstrSelectedRMF ) ;
```

```
              DrgDeleteStrHandle (
                 pdtXfer -> hstrRenderToName ) ;

              DrgFreeDragtransfer ( pdtXfer ) ;
              return MRFROMSHORT ( FALSE ) ;

           } /* endif */
        } /* endif */

        //----------------------------------------------------
        // Render the object
        //----------------------------------------------------

        if ( !SHORT1FROMMR (
              DrgSendTransferMsg (
                    pciInfo -> pdiTarget -> hwndSource,
                    DM_RENDER,
                    MPFROMP ( pdtXfer ) ,
                    0L )) ) {

           DrgDeleteStrHandle ( pdtXfer ->hstrSelectedRMF ) ;
           DrgDeleteStrHandle ( pdtXfer ->hstrRenderToName ) ;
           DrgFreeDragtransfer ( pdtXfer ) ;
           return MRFROMSHORT ( FALSE ) ;

        } /* endif */

        strcpy ( achFile, DRAG_TEMPNAME ) ;

     } else {

        //----------------------------------------------------
        // The source already rendered the object, so we
        // can simply read from the file.
        //----------------------------------------------------

        pdtXfer = NULL ;
        fileFromDragItem ( pdiItem, achFile ) ;
     } /* endif */

     pfFile = fopen ( achFile, "r" ) ;
     if ( pfFile != NULL ) {
        fgets ( pciInfo -> achLine,
                sizeof ( pciInfo -> achLine ) ,
                pfFile ) ;
        fclose ( pfFile ) ;

        if ( pdtXfer != NULL ) {
           remove ( achFile ) ;
        } /* endif */

        //----------------------------------------------------
        // Repaint ourselves again to show the dropped text
        //----------------------------------------------------

        hpsDrop = DrgGetPS ( hwndClient ) ;
        paintClient ( hpsDrop, hwndClient, pciInfo ) ;
```

```
                DrgReleasePS ( hpsDrop ) ;
            } /* endif */

        //-------------------------------------------------
        // Tell the source that we're done rendering
        //-------------------------------------------------

        WinSendMsg ( pciInfo -> pdiTarget -> hwndSource,
                     DM_ENDCONVERSATION,
                     MPFROMSHORT ( pdiItem -> ulItemID ) ,
                     0L ) ;

        //-------------------------------------------------
        // Cleanup
        //-------------------------------------------------

        if ( pdtXfer != NULL ) {
            DrgDeleteStrHandle ( pdtXfer -> hstrSelectedRMF ) ;
            DrgDeleteStrHandle ( pdtXfer -> hstrRenderToName ) ;
            DrgFreeDragtransfer ( pdtXfer ) ;
        } /* endif */

        if ( !pciInfo -> bDragging ) {
            DrgDeleteDraginfoStrHandles ( pciInfo -> pdiTarget ) ;
            DrgFreeDraginfo ( pciInfo -> pdiTarget ) ;
        } /* endif */
        }
        break ;
    default:
        break ;
    } /* endswitch */

    return MRFROMSHORT ( FALSE ) ;
}

MRESULT EXPENTRY clientWndProc ( HWND hwndClient,
                                 ULONG ulMsg,
                                 MPARAM mpParm1,
                                 MPARAM mpParm2 )

{
    PCLIENTINFO pciInfo ;

    pciInfo = WinQueryWindowPtr ( hwndClient, 0 ) ;

    switch ( ulMsg ) {

    case WM_CREATE:

        //-------------------------------------------------
        // Allocate memory for the instance data structure
        // and initialize it
        //-------------------------------------------------

        pciInfo = malloc ( sizeof ( CLIENTINFO )) ;
```

```
        if ( pciInfo == NULL ) {
          WinMessageBox ( HWND_DESKTOP,
                          hwndClient,
                          "There is not enough memory.",
                          "Error",
                          0,
                          MB_ICONHAND | MB_OK ) ;
          return MRFROMSHORT ( TRUE ) ;
        } /* endif */

        WinSetWindowPtr ( hwndClient, 0, pciInfo ) ;

        pciInfo -> pdiSource = NULL ;
        pciInfo -> bDragging = FALSE ;
        pciInfo -> bEmphasis = FALSE ;
        pciInfo -> pdiTarget = NULL ;
        pciInfo -> achLine [0] = 0 ;
        break ;

    case WM_DESTROY:

        //-----------------------------------------------------------
        // Free the memory used by the instance data
        //-----------------------------------------------------------
        free ( pciInfo ) ;
        WinSetWindowPtr ( hwndClient, 0, NULL ) ;
        break ;

    case WM_PAINT:
        {
          HPS hpsPaint ;

          hpsPaint = WinBeginPaint ( hwndClient,
                                     NULLHANDLE,
                                     NULL ) ;

          paintClient ( hpsPaint, hwndClient, pciInfo ) ;
          WinEndPaint ( hpsPaint ) ;
        }
        break ;

    case WM_BEGINDRAG:
    case DM_RENDERPREPARE:
    case DM_RENDER:
    case DM_ENDCONVERSATION:
        return doSource ( hwndClient, ulMsg, mpParm1, mpParm2 ) ;

    case DM_DRAGOVER:
    case DM_DRAGLEAVE:
    case DM_DROP:
    case DM_RENDERCOMPLETE:
    case DM_DROPHELP:
    case MYM_DEWDROP:
        return doTarget ( hwndClient, ulMsg, mpParm1, mpParm2 ) ;

    default:
```

```
        return WinDefWindowProc ( hwndClient,
                                   ulMsg,
                                   mpParm1,
                                   mpParm2 ) ;
    } /* endswitch */

    return MRFROMSHORT ( FALSE ) ;
}
```

DRAG2.MAK

```
DRAG2.EXE:                      DRAG2.OBJ
        LINK386 @<<
DRAG2
DRAG2
DRAG2
OS2386
DRAG2
<<


DRAG2.OBJ:                      DRAG2.C
        ICC -C+ -Kb+ -Ss+ DRAG2.C
```

DRAG2.DEF

```
NAME DRAG2 WINDOWAPI

DESCRIPTION 'Drag example 2
Copyright (c) 1992 by Larry Salomon
All rights reserved.'

STACKSIZE 16384
```

As you can see, there is a bit more work to do to handle the case when the source does not render the data prior to calling *DrgDrag*. This is communicated to the target by not specifying the source name in *hstrSourceName*. After determining that this did not happen, the program allocates another shared structure — DRAGTRANSFER — via a call to *DrgAllocDragtransfer* and sends the source a DM_RENDER message with the target name in the DRAGTRANSFER structure.

The obvious question here is why use *DrgSendTransferMsg* instead ol' reliable *WinSendMsg?* The answer is that the DRAGTRANSFER structure, like the DRAGINFO structure, is allocated in shared memory but is not automatically accessible by the other process. The *DrgSendTransferMsg* ensures that the recipient of the message can access the DRAGTRANSFER message in addition to calling *WinSendMsg* on behalf of the source.

Since it hasn't been said before, resources must be freed via the appropriate Drg functions by both the source and target windows, with the exception of the two HSTR handles in the DRAGTRANSFER structure. Freeing these handles is the responsibility of the target window.

18.9 *DrgDragFiles*

For drag operations involving only files, a much simplified version of *DrgDrag* can be used: *DrgDragFiles*.

```
(BOOL)DrgDragFiles(HWND hwndSource,
                        PSZ *apszFiles,
                        PSZ *apszTypes,
                        PSZ *apszTargets,
                        ULONG ulNumFiles,
                        HPOINTER hptrDrag,
                        ULONG ulTerminateKey,
                        BOOL bRender,
                        ULONG ulReserved);
```

hwndSource is the handle of the window calling the function. *apszFiles*, *apszTypes*, and *apszTargets* are arrays of pointers to the file names, file types, and target file names, respectively. *ulNumFiles* specifies the number of pointers in the *apszFiles*, *apszTypes*, and *apszTargets* arrays. *hptrDrag* is the handle to the pointer to display while dragging. *ulTerminateKey* has the same meaning as in *DrgDrag*. *bRender* specifies whether or not the caller needs to render the files before the transfer can take place. If so, a DM_RENDERFILE message is sent for each file.

That's it! The system takes care of the rest, since files are the only allowed object type.

18.10 From the Top, Now

The following table details the chain of events from the beginning of the drag notification to the end of the data transfer.

Source	Target
1. Receives a WM_BEGINDRAG message	
2. Allocates the DRAGINFO/DRAGITEM structures (*DrgAllocDraginfo*)	
3. Creates the strings for the type and RMF (*DrgAddStrHandle*)	
4. Initializes the appropriate number of DRAGIMAGE structures	
5. Calls *DrgDrag*	
	6. Receives DM_DRAGOVER
	7. Calls *DrgAccessDraginfo*
	8. Decides if objects are acceptable (both type and RMF)
	9. Returns the appropriate DOR_* value; if not DOR_DROP, go to step 20
	10. If user presses F1, target receives a DM_DROPHELP; after providing help, go to step 20
	11. If user presses ESC, go to step 20
	12. User drops objects on target
	13. If the target can render the objects on its own, do so. Go to step 18.
	14. Allocates DRAGTRANSFER structures for each object (*DrgAllocDragtransfer*) and sends a DM_RENDER for each object (*DrgSendTransferMsg*)
15. Renders the objects	
	16. Copies the objects and deletes them from the source

	17. Frees HSTRs for DRAGTRANSFER and DRAGTRANSFER structures (*DrgDeleteStrHandle* and *DrgFreeDragtransfer*)
	18. Frees HSTRs for DRAGINFO and DRAGINFO structure (*DrgDeleteDraginfoStrHandles* and *DrgFreeDragtransfer*)
	19. Sends source a DM_ENDCONVERSATION message
20. Frees HSTRs for DRAGINFO and DRAGINFO structure (*DrgDeleteDraginfoStrHandles* and *DrgFreeDragtransfer*)	

18.11 Drag and Drop Messages

DM_DISCARDOBJECT
This message is sent to a source object if DRM_DISCARD rendering is allowed.

Parameter 1:   PDRAGINFO pDrgInfo   pointer to DRAGINFO structure

```
typedef struct _DRAGINFO      /* dinfo */
{
   ULONG    cbDraginfo;
   USHORT   cbDragitem;
   USHORT   usOperation;
   HWND     hwndSource;
   SHORT    xDrop;
   SHORT    yDrop;
   USHORT   cditem;
   USHORT   usReserved;
} DRAGINFO;
typedef DRAGINFO *PDRAGINFO;
```

Parameter 2:   ULONG ulReserved   reserved, 0

| **Reply:** | ULONG ulAction | DRR_SOURCE — source takes action on object
DRR_TARGET — target takes action on object
DRR_ABORT — abort action |

DM_DRAGERROR

This message is sent when an error occurs during a move or copy file operation.

Parameter 1:	USHORT usError	error code
	USHORT usFailFunct	failing function
		DFF_MOVE — *DosMove*
		DFF_COPY — *DosCopy*
		DFF_DELETE — *DosDelete*
Parameter 2:	HSTR hstrErrFile	file with problem
Reply:	ULONG ulReply	action

CODE	MEANING
DME_IGNORECONTINUE	No retry on this file, continue with the rest
DME_IGNOREABORT	No retry on this file, abort operation
DME_RETRY	Retry
DME_REPLACE	Replace the file at target
Other	New file name to try; this is a HSTR variable

DM_DRAGFILECOMPLETE

This message is sent when a file operation is complete.

| **Parameter 1:** | HSTR hstrFile | file handle |
| **Parameter 2:** | USHORT usAction | result flags OR'ed together |

CODE	MEANING
DF_MOVE	Operation was move operation. If not set, operation was copy.
DF_SOURCE	Receiving window was source. If not set, receiving window was target.
DF_SUCCESSFUL	Operation was successful. It not set, operation was not successful.

Reply: ULONG ulReserved reserved, 0

DM_DRAGLEAVE

This message is sent when an object that was being dragged over a window's boundaries is now either outside those boundaries, or else the operation was aborted.

Parameter 1: PDRAGINFO pdrgInfo pointer to DRAGINFO structure
Parameter 2: ULONG ulReserved reserved, 0
Reply: ULONG ulReserved reserved, 0

DM_DRAGOVER

This message is sent to determine whether objects can be dropped at current destination.

Parameter 1: PDRAGINFO pdrgInfo pointer to DRAGINFO structure
Parameter 2: SHORT x mouse *x* position in desktop coordinates
  SHORT y mouse *y* position in desktop coordinates
Reply: USHORT usDrop drop flag
  USHORT usOperation default drop operation

DROP FLAG	MEANING
DOR_DROP	Drop operation OK.
DOR_NODROP	Drop operation not OK at current time. Type of drop operation is OK.
DOR_NODROPOP	Drop operation not OK. Type of drop operation is not acceptable.
DOR_NEVERDROP	Drop operation not OK, now or ever.

OPERATION	MEANING
DO_COPY	Copy operation
DO_LINK	Link operation
DO_MOVE	Move operation
Other	User-defined operation

DM_DRAGOVERNOTIFY

This message is sent to source after DM_DRAGOVER message has been sent.

Parameter 1:   PDRAGINFO pdrgInfo   pointer to DRAGINFO structure
Parameter 2:   USHORT usDrop   drop flag

FLAG	MEANING
DOR_DROP	Drop operation OK
DOR_NODROP	Drop operation not OK at current time. Type of drop operation is OK.
DOR_NODROPOP	Drop operation not OK. Type of drop operation is not acceptable.
DOR_NEVERDROP	Drop operation not OK, now or ever.

    USHORT usOperation   default drop operation

OPERATION	MEANING
DO_COPY	Copy operation
DO_LINK	Link operation
DO_MOVE	Move operation
Other	User-defined operation
Reply: ULONG ulReserved	reserved, 0

DM_DROP

This message is sent when an object is being dropped on a target.

Parameter 1:   PDRAGINFO pdrgInfo   pointer to DRAGINFO structure
Parameter 2:   ULONG ulReserved   reserved, 0
Reply: ULONG ulReserved   reserved, 0

DM_DROPHELP

This message is sent when a user requests help for the drag operation.

Parameter 1:	PDRAGINFO pdrgInfo	pointer to DRAGINFO structure
Parameter 2:	ULONG ulReserved	reserved, 0
Reply:	ULONG ulReserved	reserved, 0

DM_EMPHASIZETARGET

This message is sent to the target to inform it to either add or remove emphasis from itself.

Parameter 1:	SHORT x	*x* coordinate of mouse in window coordinates
	SHORT y	*y* coordinate of mouse in window coordinates
Parameter 2:	USHORT usAply	TRUE — apply emphasis FALSE — remove emphasis
Reply:	ULONG ulReserved	reserved, 0

DM_ENDCONVERSATION

This message is sent to the source to indicate that the drop operation is over.

Parameter 1:	ULONG ulID	item ID that was dropped
Parameter 2:	ULONG ulSuccess	DMFL_TARGETSUCCESSFUL — successful DMFL_TARGETFAIL — failed
Reply:	ULONG ulReserved	reserved, 0

DM_FILERENDERED

This message is sent when a rendering operation is complete.

Parameter 1:	PRENDERFILE prndFile	pointer to RENDERFILE structure

```
typedef struct _RENDERFILE     /* rndf */
{
    HWND    hwndDragFiles;
    HSTR    hstrSource;
    HSTR    hstrTarget;
    USHORT  fMove;
    USHORT  usRsvd;
} RENDERFILE;
typedef RENDERFILE *PRENDERFILE;
```

Parameter 2: USHORT usSuccess   operation successful?
TRUE: FALSE

Reply: ULONG ulReserved   reserved, 0

DM_PRINTOBJECT
This message is sent when a object is dropped on the printer object.

Parameter 1: PDRAGINFO pdrgInfo   pointer to DRAGINFO structure

```
typedef struct _DRAGINFO     /* dinfo */
{
    ULONG   cbDraginfo;
    USHORT  cbDragitem;
    USHORT  usOperation;
    HWND    hwndSource;
    SHORT   xDrop;
    SHORT   yDrop;
    USHORT  cditem;
    USHORT  usReserved;
} DRAGINFO;
typedef DRAGINFO *PDRAGINFO;
```

Parameter 2: PPRINTDEST pprtDest   pointer to PRINTDEST structure

```
typedef struct _PRINTDEST     /* prntdst */
{
    ULONG       cb;
    LONG        lType;
    PSZ         pszToken;
    LONG        lCount;
    PDEVOPENDATA pdopData;
    ULONG       fl;
    PSZ         pszPrinter;
} PRINTDEST;
typedef PRINTDEST *PPRINTDEST;
```

Reply: ULONG ulAction   action flag

FLAG	MEANING
DRR_SOURCE	Source takes responsiblity for printing object
DRR_TARGET	Target (printer object) takes responsibility for printing object
DRR_ABORT	Abort the operation

DM_RENDER

This message is used to request that an object render another object.

Parameter 1:   PDRAGTRANSFER   pointer to DRAGTRANSFER structure

```
typedef struct _DRAGTRANSFER
  {
    ULONG      cb;
    HWND       hwndClient;
    PDRAGITEM  pditem;
    HSTR       hstrSelectedRMF;
    HSTR       hstrRenderToName;
    ULONG      ulTargetInfo;
    USHORT     usOperation;
    USHORT     fsReply;
  } DRAGTRANSFER;
  typedef DRAGTRANSFER *PDRAGTRANSFER;
```

Parameter 2:   ULONG ulReserved   reserved, 0
Reply: BOOL fSuccess   successful? TRUE: FALSE

DM_RENDERCOMPLETE

This message is sent to the source when a rendering operation is complete.

Parameter 1:   PDRAGTRANSFER pdrgTransfer pointer to DRAGTRANSFER structure
Parameter 2:   USHORT usAction   action flag

FLAG	MEANING
DMFL_RENDERFAIL	This source cannot render the operation.
DMFL_RENDEROK	The source has completed the rendering successfully.
DMFL_RENDEDRRETRY	The source has completed the rendering and will allow the target to retry if the target portion of the operation fails.

Reply:	ULONG ulReserved	reserved, 0

DM_RENDERFILE

This message is sent to tell an object to render a file.

Parameter 1:	PRENDERFILE prndFile	pointer to RENDERFILE structure
Parameter 2:	ULONG ulReserved	reserved, 0
Reply:	BOOL fHandler	TRUE — receiver handles rendering FALSE — caller handles rendering

DM_RENDERPREPARE

This message is sent to tell the source object to prepare for a rendering on an object.

Parameter 1:	PDRAGTRANSFER pdrgTrans	pointer to DRAGTRANSFER structure
Parameter 2:	ULONG ulReserved	reserved, 0
Reply:	BOOL fSuccess	successful? TRUE: FALSE

Chapter 19

Help Manager

Beginning with OS/2 1.2, IBM introduced an addition to the Presentation
Manager interface (touted as the "Help Manager") that allowed an application
to add both general help and field help online (and with 1.3, IBM published the
previously undocumented method for creating online books, which are viewed
using the system-supplied utility VIEW.EXE). It should be noted, however,
that while this capability is a very appealing one, it is by no means added to an
application quickly; in fact, well-written online help can take on the average of
1 day/3000 lines of code to complete (this figure is based on personal
experience) for the text alone. The up-side of this is that, for the majority of
the Presentation Manager applications you will write, no forethought need be
given to this aspect of development when you are designing your programs;
online help can be added at any time, providing you have the source code to
the application.

19.1 Application Components

There are a minimum of three parts to the help component of any application:
the source code, the HELPTABLEs, and the definitions of the help panels.
The source code is obviously part of the application source, and includes the
corresponding Win* calls and HM_ messages sent to and received from the
Help Manager. The HELPTABLEs (and HELPSUBTABLEs) are part of the
resource file, and they define the relationships between the various windows
and the corresponding help panels. Finally, the help panel definitions describe
the look as well as the text of the help panels and are written using a "general

markup language"(GML)-like language (SCRIPT and Bookmaster users will recognize the help panel definition language as a subset of the Bookmaster macros they are familiar with). Let us take a closer look at each of these three parts in more detail.

19.2 The Application Source

The source code is usually the smallest component of the three, only because it typically consists of an initialization section and the processing of a few messages. The initialization section normally goes in your *main* routine after the main window is created and follows the example below:

This is the typical initialization code used in a Presentation Manager application to create a help instance.

```
#define HELP_CLIENT 256

HELPINIT hiInit;
CHAR achHelpTitle[256];
HAB habAnchor;
HWND hwndHelp;
HWND hwndFrame;

     : // WinInitialize, etc. goes here

// We need to initialize the HELPINIT structure before calling
// WinCreateHelpInstance.  See the online technical reference
// for an explanation of the individual fields.

hiInit.cb=sizeof(HELPINIT);
hiInit.ulReturnCode=0L;
hiInit.pszTutorialName=NULL;

// By specifying 0xFFFF in the high word of phtHelpTable, we are
// indicating that the help table is in the resource tables with
// the id specified in the low word.

hiInit.phtHelpTable=(PHELPTABLE)MAKEULONG(HELP_CLIENT,0xFFFF);

hiInit.hmodHelpTableModule=NULLHANDLE;
hiInit.hmodAccelActionBarModule=NULLHANDLE;
hiInit.idAccelTable=0;
hiInit.idActionBar=0;
hiInit.pszHelpWindowTitle=achHelpTitle;
hiInit.fShowPanelId=CMIC_HIDE_PANEL_ID;
hiInit.pszHelpLibraryName="MYAPPL.HLP";
```

```
hwndHelp=WinCreateHelpInstance(habAnchor,&hiInit);
if ((hwndHelp!=NULLHANDLE) && (hiInit.ulReturnCode!=0)) {
    WinDestroyHelpInstance(hwndHelp);
    hwndHelp=NULLHANDLE;
} /* endif */

    :
    :   // Message loop goes here
    :

if (hwndHelp!=(HWND)NULL) {
    WinDestroyHelpInstance(hwndHelp);
    hwndHelp=NULLHANDLE;
} /* endif */
```

As with the relationship between window classes and window instances, there exists a help manager class of which you create an instance by calling *WinCreateHelpInstance*. This function can have one of three outcomes:

(1) The call can complete successfully, and the return value is the handle of the help instance.
(2) The function can partially complete, returning a help instance handle and specifying an error code in the ulReturnCode field.
(3) The function can fail returning NULL. Because of the subtle difference between (1) and (2), it is not sufficient to simply check the return value.

If the help instance is successfully created, it becomes the recipient of any messages that you send and the originator of any messages that are sent to the active window.

Since a help instance is associated with a "root" window and all of its descendants, you need to indicate what the root window is. This is done using the *WinAssociateHelpInstance* function.

```
(BOOL)WinAssociateHelpInstance(HWND hwndHelp,
            // Help instance
        HWND hwndWindow);
            // "Root" window
```

When you specify a non-NULL value for *hwndHelp*, it indicates that this is the active window that should be used when determining which help panel to display. Specifying NULL for this parameter removes the current association between the help instance and the window specified. We will see how this is used shortly.

Gotcha!

Note that the call to *WinAssociateHelpInstance* will not work if you call it within the WM_CREATE message of the window with which it is associated. *WinAssociateHelpInstance* needs a valid window handle, and when the WM_CREATE message is received, the window handle is not yet valid.

19.3 Messages

The next piece of source code that you will use in most of your applications deals with the "Help" pull-down menu and "Help" push-buttons (obviously, if your application does not contain an action bar or any dialogs, you need not read this). According, to IBM's guidelines on developing a application user interface, there should exist on the action bar a pull-down titled "Help" that contains the following four items:

- "Using help..."
- "General help..."
- "Keys help..."
- "Help index..."

There can also be an optional fifth item — labeled "Product information..." — that displays an "About" box when selected. Fortunately, the Help Manager has four messages that can be sent to it to process these four menu items. Each of them take no parameters and are listed below:

MESSAGE	DESCRIPTION
HM_DISPLAY_HELP	Displays help on using online help
HM_EXT_HELP	Displays the "extended" help for the current window
HM_KEYS_HELP	Displays the keys help for the current window
HM_HELP_INDEX	Displays the help index

With the exception of HM_KEYS_HELP, all that needs to be done is send the appropriate message to the help instance. Sending HM_KEYS_HELP results in the help instance sending the window a HM_QUERY_KEYS_HELP message back to determine which "keys help" panel to display. You should return the panel resource id in response to this message.

The behavior of a "Help" push-button is left somewhat up to you. The official IBM response is that it should display field help, i.e., a panel that describes what the purpose is of the control containing the cursor. We have also seen and follow this strategy in our applications; it results in the displaying of the extended help for the frame or dialog. For the former, one should define the push-button with the BS_NOPOINTERFOCUS style to avoid receiving the input focus, and should send the help instance a HM_DISPLAY_HELP message (this time with either the panel resource id or the panel name in parameter 1 and either HM_RESOURCEID or HM_PANELNAME in parameter 2) to display the help panel for the current control with the focus. For the latter, you simply need to send an HM_EXT_HELP message to the help instance.

19.4 Message Boxes

When your application needs to give the user some information, one of the ways it can do so is by using the *WinMessageBox* function. This displays a window that contains application-specified title and text, as well as an optional icon to the left and one or more predefined push-buttons (e.g., "OK", "Yes", "Abort", etc.).

```
(USHORT)WinMessageBox(HWND hwndParent,
        // parent window
                HWND hwndOwner,
        // owning window
                PSZ pszMessage,
        // pointer to the text
                PSZ pszTitle,
         // pointer to the title
                USHORT usHelpId,
        // help topic id
                ULONG ulStyle);
        // message box style
```

hwndParent defines the bounding area of the message box; typically, this is HWND_DESKTOP. *hwndOwner* specifies the window that "owns" the message box; this window is disabled while the message box is displayed and is reactivated when the call returns. *pszMessage* and *pszTitle* point to the message box text and title, respectively. *usHelpId* is used when MB_HELP is specified in *ulStyle* (see below), and *ulStyle* is a combination of MB_* constants.

This function returns a constant that specifies the push-button selected on the message box (e.g., MBID_OK, MBID_NO, MBID_RETRY, etc.). As you can imagine, you can only say so much in a small dialog box. Often, the text is enough for most people to figure out what's you're trying to say. However, it would be nice to provide another level of detail for those who would like more information (i.e., online help). There is a constant, MB_HELP, which specifies that a "Help" push-button is requested; this is the only button that does not cause the function to return. Unfortunately, since a message box doesn't have to have an application window as the owner (HWND_DESKTOP will work fine for *hwndOwner;* this could be used in, for example, a program that simply calls *WinMessageBox* with the command line for the message for CMD files), it cannot simply send the owner a message saying that the help button was pressed. To circumvent this, we need a help hook.

19.5 Fishing, Anyone?

A "hook" is a function that PM calls whenever a certain event occurs. There can be more than one hook for a particular event, and these hooks are called before passing the event on to the rest of the system. There are currently 16 events that can be hooked, ranging from "code page changed" to "DLL has been loaded with *WinLoadLibrary*" to "mouse moved or key pressed". Of course, there is also one for "help requested".

Hooks are installed with *WinSetHook* and are released with *WinReleaseHook*. Both take the same parameters, listed below:

```
(BOOL)WinSetHook(HAB habAnchor,
        // HAB of the calling thread
HMQ hmqQueue,
        // HMQ of the calling thread,
        // HMQ_CURRENT for current
        // thread or NULL for
        // system-wide hook
USHORT usHookType,
        // HK_* constant
PFN pfnHookProc,
        // pointer to the hook
        // procedure
HMODULE hmodProc);
        // HMODULE containing
        // pfnHookProc
```

Each of the procedures for the different hook types take different parameters and return different values. Since we're interested in the HK_HELP hook, the prototype of the hook function is shown below:

```
(BOOL)pfnHookProc(HAB habAnchor,
        // HAB of the calling thread
SHORT sMode,
        // HLPM_* constant
USHORT usTopic,
        // Topic number
USHORT usSubTopic,
        // Subtopic number
PRECTL prclPosition);
```

The help hook returns TRUE if the next hook in the help hook chain should not be called and FALSE if the next hook should be called. The only parameter we are interested in is *usTopic*, which is the help identifier passed to *WinMessageBox* as *usHelpId*. The typical function of the help hook when used in this context is to send the help instance a HM_DISPLAY_HELP message to display the specified help panel.

Gotcha!

Note that the documentation states that the help hook should be installed before creating the help instance. However, since *WinSetHook* installed the hook at the head of the hook chain, this information is backwards. The call to *WinSetHook* should be placed after the call to *WinAssociateHelpInstance* for this to work properly.

19.6 The Help Tables

The help tables define the relationship between the control windows and the help panels to be displayed when the user requests help. To help understand what the help tables are, visualize them as a two-dimensional array of help panel ids. The first index into this array is the id of the window that has been associated with a help instance via *WinAssociateHelpInstance,* and the second index is either a menu item id or an id of a child window that can receive the input focus. To understand how the help tables are used, we need to understand the sequence of events beginning with the user pressing F1 and the displaying of the help panel.

1. The user presses F1.
2. The help instance determines the id of the window that it is currently associated with.

3. The HELPITEM for the given window id is referenced, and the appropriate HELPSUBTABLE is determined.
4. The menu item id (or the id of the window with the focus) is used to look up in the HELPSUBTABLE the id of the help panel to display.
5. The help panel definition is retrieved from the compiled help file.
6. The help panel is displayed.

There are obviously many places where errors can occur; the most frequent one is when the menu item id/child window id is not in the HELPSUBTABLE. When this occurs, the owner window-chain is searched (steps 3 – 6) and if it is still not found, the parent window-chain is also searched. If the id has not been found after both searches, the current window is sent a HM_HELPSUBITEM_NOT_FOUND message, giving it the opportunity to remedy the situation (via a HM_DISPLAY_HELP message). The default action is to display the extended help for the current window.

When the id is found in a HELPSUBTABLE but the panel definition does not exist, or when any other error occurs (with the exception of HELPSUBITEM not found described above and when the extended help panel cannot be determined), the application is sent an HM_ERROR message. This message contains an error code in the first parameter that describes the condition causing the error. The typical response to receiving this is to display a message and then disable the help manager by calling *WinDestroyHelpInstance*.

Given this logical view of the help tables, let us look at a sample definition in a resource file.

19.7 Sample HELPTABLE

The tables below describe the online help panels that correspond to the child windows and menuitems in the application and its associated dialogs.

```
HELPTABLE HELP_CLIENT
{
        HELPITEM HELP_CLIENT, SUBHELP_CLIENT, EXTHELP_CLIENT
        HELPITEM DLG_OPEN, SUBHELP_OPEN, EXTHELP_OPEN
        HELPITEM DLG_PRODUCTINFO,
                SUBHELP_PRODUCTINFO, EXTHELP_PRODUCTINFO
}
```

```
HELPSUBTABLE SUBHELP_CLIENT
{
        HELPSUBITEM M_FILE, HELP_M_FILE
        HELPSUBITEM MI_NEW, HELP_MI_NEW
        HELPSUBITEM MI_OPEN, HELP_MI_OPEN
        HELPSUBITEM MI_SAVE, HELP_MI_SAVE
        HELPSUBITEM MI_CLOSE, HELP_MI_CLOSE
        HELPSUBITEM MI_EXIT, HELP_MI_EXIT
        HELPSUBITEM M_HELP, HELP_M_HELP
        HELPSUBITEM MI_USINGHELP, HELP_MI_USINGHELP
        HELPSUBITEM MI_GENERALHELP, HELP_MI_GENERALHELP
        HELPSUBITEM MI_KEYSHELP, HELP_MI_KEYSHELP
        HELPSUBITEM MI_HELPINDEX, HELP_MI_HELPINDEX
        HELPSUBITEM MI_PRODINFO, HELP_MI_PRODINFO
}
HELPSUBTABLE SUBHELP_SETOPTIONS
{
        HELPSUBITEM DOPEN_EF_FILENAME, HELP_DOPEN_EF_FILENAME
        HELPSUBITEM DLG_PB_OK, HELP_DLG_PB_OK
        HELPSUBITEM DLG_PB_CANCEL, HELP_DLG_PB_CANCEL
        HELPSUBITEM DLG_PB_HELP, HELP_DLG_PB_HELP
}

HELPSUBTABLE SUBHELP_PRODINFO
{
        HELPSUBITEM DLG_PB_CANCEL,  HELP_DLG_PB_CANCEL
        HELPSUBITEM DLG_PB_HELP, HELP_DLG_PB_HELP
}
```

We can see from the sample that our application has two dialogs with online help and their resource identifiers are DLG_OPEN and DLG_PRODUCTINFO, and that there are twelve child windows or menuitems that belong to the client window. In each of the HELPSUBITEMS, the window id is on the left and the corresponding help panel resource id is on the right.

Gotcha!

In the event that the resource id specified in the *WinCreateStdWindow* call is different from that used as the resource id of the HELPTABLE, the first parameter to the HELPITEM that refers to the main window should be the same as the HELPTABLE resource id and not the id for the frame resources.

19.8 The Help Panels

Now that we've seen how easy the code and resource definitions are, it is time to tackle the most difficult (to do well) and time-consuming aspect of this development phase — writing the help panels. While the definition of the language is large, it is fairly easy to digest. We will look at only the rudiments of the language; the full language definition can be gleamed from the online document entitled "IPF Reference" that is included with the OS/2 2.1 Programmer's Toolkit.

The help file (whose file extension is usually ".IPF") is compiled by the "Information Presentation Facility Compiler" (a.k.a. IPFC) to produce a ".HLP" file that is read by the Help Manager when *WinCreateHelpInstance* is called. The source file contains a collection of "tags," which begin with a colon (:), followed by the tag name, an optional set of attributes, and end with a period. Some tags also require a matching "end tag" (e.g., a "begin list" and "end list" tag), which have no attributes and whose name usually matches the beginning tag name preceded by an e (e.g., ":sl." and ":esl."). The common tags and their meanings are described below:

Tag	Meaning
:h1. through :h6.	Heading tag. Headings 1 – 3 also have an entry in the table of contents.
:p.	New paragraph.
:fn. :efn.	Footnote and ending tag.
:hp1. through :hp9.	Emphasis tag. This requires the matching ending tag (:ehp1. through :ehp9.).
:link.	Hypertext link.
:sl. :esl.	Simple list and ending tag.
:ul. :eul.	Unordered list and ending tag.
:ol. :eol.	Ordered list and ending tag.
:li.	List item. Used between the list tags to describe the items in the list.
:dl. :edl.	Definition list and ending tag. Whereas the other lists consist of a single element, definition lists consist of a "data term" and "data definition" (:dt. and :dd., respectively).
:dt. :dd.	Data term and data definition tags.
:dthd. :ddhd.	Data term heading and data definition heading tags. Also, there are a few special tags that are used only once in a help file.
:userdoc. :euserdoc.	Beginning and ending of the document.
:title.	The text to be placed in the title bar of the help panels.

While most of these tags have attributes, the ones you'll use most are the resource and id attributes. The resource attribute allows you to assign a numerical value to a heading tag (e.g., ":h1 res=2048.Help panel"), and this is what the HELPSUBITEMs reference. The id attribute allows you to assign a alphanumeric name for use in hypertext links (e.g., ":h2 id='MYPANEL'.Help panel"). The id attribute can be used on both heading and footnote tags, while the resource attribute can only be used on heading tags. Heading ids are referenced using the "refid" attribute of a hypertext link, while a footnote is referenced also using the "refid" attribute of a ":fnref" (footnote reference) tag.

In addition to the tags, certain symbols that are either translated into different values in other languages, not easily enterable using the keyboard, or are also used by IPF are defined. These are referenced by symbol name substitution, beginning with an ampersand (&), including the symbol name, and ending with a period. Some commonly used symbols are listed below:

Symbol	Meaning
&amp.	Ampersand
&cdq.	Close double quote
&colon.	Colon
&csq.	Close single quote
&lbrk.	Left bracket
&odq.	Open double quote
&osq.	Open single quote
&rbrk.	Right bracket
&vbar.	Vertical bar

A help panel begins with a heading 1, 2, or 3 tag and ends with either the next heading 1, 2, or 3 tag or the end of the document. Everything that is in between is shown when the panel is displayed. A sample panel showing how some of the tags are used is shown below.

19.9 Sample Help Panel

```
:h1 id='MYPANEL' res=1000.My help panel
:p.When adding online help to your PM application, the following
steps must be taken
:fnref refid='MYFN'.&colon.
:ul compact.
:li.Initialization code must be written
:li.Messages must be processed
:li.Resources must be defined
:li.Help panels must be compiled
```

```
:eul.
:fn id='MYFN'.
Footnotes start on an implied paragraph.
:efn.
```

It should be noted that the minimum number of tags that are required in a valid
IPF file are the :userdoc., :title., :h1., :p., and :euserdoc., in that order.

19.10 Putting It All Together

We now have enough information to write a simple application to illustrate the
points made in this chapter. The application, HELP, contains a few menuitems
and dialog boxes, but otherwise does nothing. Its sole purpose is to allow the
user to display the online help.

HELP.C

```c
#define INCL_WINHELP
#define INCL_WINHOOKS
#define INCL_WINSYS

#include <os2.h>
#include "help.h"

#define CLS_CLIENT               "SampleClass"

HWND hwndHelp ;

MRESULT EXPENTRY clientWndProc ( HWND hwndClient,
                                 ULONG ulMsg,
                                 MPARAM mpParm1,
                                 MPARAM mpParm2 ) ;


BOOL EXPENTRY helpHook ( HAB habAnchor,
                         SHORT sMode,
                         USHORT usTopic,
                         USHORT usSubTopic,
                         PRECTL prclPos ) ;

int main ( VOID )
{
    HAB            habAnchor ;
    HMQ            hmqQueue ;
    ULONG          ulFlags ;
    HWND           hwndFrame ;
    HELPINIT       hiInit ;
    BOOL           bLoop ;
    QMSG           qmMsg ;

    habAnchor = WinInitialize ( 0 ) ;
    hmqQueue = WinCreateMsgQueue ( habAnchor, 0 ) ;
```

```
      WinRegisterClass ( habAnchor,
                         CLS_CLIENT,
                         clientWndProc,
                         0,
                         0 ) ;

      ulFlags = FCF_SIZEBORDER | FCF_TITLEBAR |
                FCF_TASKLIST | FCF_SHELLPOSITION |
                FCF_SYSMENU | FCF_MENU ;

      hwndFrame = WinCreateStdWindow ( HWND_DESKTOP,
                                       WS_VISIBLE,
                                       &ulFlags,
                                       CLS_CLIENT,
                                       "Help Manager"
                                       " Sample Application",
                                       0,
                                       NULLHANDLE,
                                       RES_CLIENT,
                                       NULL ) ;

      hiInit.cb = sizeof ( HELPINIT ) ;
      hiInit.ulReturnCode = 0 ;
      hiInit.pszTutorialName = NULL ;
      hiInit.phtHelpTable = ( PHELPTABLE ) MAKEULONG (
                                           HELP_CLIENT,
                                           0xFFFF ) ;
      hiInit.hmodHelpTableModule = NULLHANDLE ;
      hiInit.hmodAccelActionBarModule = NULLHANDLE ;
      hiInit.idAccelTable = 0 ;
      hiInit.idActionBar = 0 ;
      hiInit.pszHelpWindowTitle = "Help Manager Sample Help File" ;
      hiInit.fShowPanelId = CMIC_HIDE_PANEL_ID ;
      hiInit.pszHelpLibraryName = "HELP.HLP" ;

      hwndHelp = WinCreateHelpInstance ( habAnchor,
                                         &hiInit ) ;

      if ( ( hwndHelp != NULLHANDLE ) &&
         ( hiInit.ulReturnCode != 0 )) {

         WinDestroyHelpInstance ( hwndHelp ) ;
         hwndHelp = NULLHANDLE ;

      } else {

         WinAssociateHelpInstance ( hwndHelp, hwndFrame ) ;

      } /* endif */

      WinSetHook ( habAnchor,
                   hmqQueue,
                   HK_HELP,
                   ( PFN ) helpHook,
                   NULLHANDLE ) ;
```

```
   bLoop = WinGetMsg ( habAnchor, &qmMsg, NULLHANDLE, 0, 0 ) ;
   while ( bLoop ) {
      WinDispatchMsg ( habAnchor, &qmMsg ) ;
      bLoop = WinGetMsg ( habAnchor, &qmMsg, NULLHANDLE, 0, 0 ) ;
   } /* endwhile */

   WinReleaseHook ( habAnchor,
                    hmqQueue,
                    HK_HELP,
                    ( PFN ) helpHook,
                    NULLHANDLE ) ;

   if ( hwndHelp != ( HWND ) NULL ) {
      WinAssociateHelpInstance ( NULLHANDLE ,
                                 hwndFrame ) ;
      WinDestroyHelpInstance ( hwndHelp ) ;
      hwndHelp = NULLHANDLE ;
   } /* endif */

   WinDestroyWindow ( hwndFrame ) ;
   WinDestroyMsgQueue ( hmqQueue ) ;
   WinTerminate ( habAnchor ) ;
   return ( 0 ) ;

}


BOOL EXPENTRY helpHook ( HAB habAnchor,
                         SHORT sMode,
                         USHORT usTopic,
                         USHORT usSubTopic,
                         PRECTL prclPos )
{
   if ( ( sMode == HLPM_WINDOW ) && ( hwndHelp != NULLHANDLE )) {
      WinSendMsg ( hwndHelp,
                   HM_DISPLAY_HELP,
                   MPFROMLONG ( MAKELONG ( usTopic, 0 ) ) ,
                   MPFROMSHORT ( HM_RESOURCEID ) ) ;
      return TRUE ;
   } else {
      return FALSE ;
   } /* endif */
}

MRESULT EXPENTRY clientWndProc ( HWND hwndClient,
                                 ULONG ulMsg,
                                 MPARAM mpParm1,
                                 MPARAM mpParm2 )
{
   switch ( ulMsg ) {
```

```
   case WM_PAINT:
      {
         HPS         hpsPaint ;
         RECTL       rclPaint ;

         hpsPaint = WinBeginPaint ( hwndClient,
                                    NULLHANDLE,
                                    &rclPaint ) ;
         WinFillRect ( hpsPaint, &rclPaint, SYSCLR_WINDOW ) ;
         WinEndPaint ( hpsPaint ) ;
      }
      break ;

case WM_COMMAND:
   switch ( SHORT1FROMMP ( mpParm1 ) ) {
      case MI_HELPINDEX:
         WinSendMsg ( hwndHelp,
                      HM_HELP_INDEX,
                      ( MPARAM ) 0,
                      ( MPARAM ) 0 ) ;
         break ;

      case MI_GENERALHELP:
         WinSendMsg ( hwndHelp,
                      HM_EXT_HELP,
                      ( MPARAM ) 0,
                      ( MPARAM ) 0 ) ;
         break ;

      case MI_HELPFORHELP:
         WinSendMsg ( hwndHelp,
                      HM_DISPLAY_HELP,
                      ( MPARAM ) 0,
                      ( MPARAM ) 0 ) ;
         break ;

      case MI_KEYSHELP:
         WinSendMsg ( hwndHelp,
                      HM_KEYS_HELP,
                      ( MPARAM ) 0,
                      ( MPARAM ) 0 ) ;
         break ;

      case MI_PRODINFO:
         WinMessageBox ( HWND_DESKTOP,
                         hwndClient,
                         "Copyright 1992"
                         " by Larry Salomon, Jr.",
                         "Help Sample",
                         HLP_MESSAGEBOX,
                         MB_OK | MB_HELP | MB_INFORMATION ) ;
         break ;
      default:
         return WinDefWindowProc ( hwndClient,
                                   ulMsg,
                                   mpParm1,
                                   mpParm2 ) ;
```

```
      } /* endswitch */
      break ;

   case HM_QUERY_KEYS_HELP:
      return MRFROMSHORT ( KEYSHELP_CLIENT ) ;

   default:
      return WinDefWindowProc ( hwndClient, ulMsg,
         mpParm1, mpParm2 ) ;
   } /* endswitch */

   return MRFROMSHORT ( FALSE ) ;
}
```

HELP.IPF

```
:userdoc.
:title.Help Manager Sample Help File

:h1 res=259.Extended help
:p.Normally, you would write a longer panel here describing an
overview of the function of the active window.  Diagrams, etc.
are certainly welcome, since this is usually called when the
user has no idea of what is going on at the moment.

:h1 res=260.Keys help
:p.A list of the accelerator keys in use is appropriate here.
Do not forget the &odq.hidden&cdq. accelerators in dialog
boxes and elsewhere such as :hp2.enter:ehp2., :hp2.escape:ehp2.,
and :hp2.F1:ehp2..

:h1 res=321.Help for menuitem &odq.Help index...&cdq.
:p.Selecting this menuitem will display a help index.  Note that
 the system has its own help index, while we can add our own
entries using the &colon.i1. and &colon.i2. tags.

:h1 res=322.Help for menuitem &odq.General help...&cdq.
:p.Selecting this menuitem will display the general help panel.

:h1 res=323.Help for menuitem &odq.Using help...&cdq.
:p.Selecting this menuitem will display the system help panel on
how to use the Help Manager.

:h1 res=324.Help for menuitem &odq.Keys help...&cdq.
:p.Selecting this menuitem will display the active key list.

:h1 res=325.Help for menuitem &odq.Product information...&cdq.
:p.Selecting this menuitem will display a message box with a
help button in it, to demonstrate the use of a help hook to
provide message box help.

:h1 res=326.Message box help
:p.This application demonstrates the use of the Help Manager to
provide online help for an application.  Help for both menuitems
 and message boxes is shown.
:euserdoc.
```

HELP.RC

```
#include <os2.h>
#include "rc.h"

MENU RES_CLIENT
{
    SUBMENU "~Help", M_HELP
    {
        MENUITEM "Help ~index...", MI_HELPINDEX
        MENUITEM "~General help...", MI_GENERALHELP
        MENUITEM "~Using help...", MI_HELPFORHELP
        MENUITEM "~Keys help...", MI_KEYSHELP
        MENUITEM SEPARATOR
        MENUITEM "~Product information...", MI_PRODINFO
    }
}

HELPTABLE HELP_CLIENT
{
    HELPITEM RES_CLIENT, SUBHELP_CLIENT, EXTHELP_CLIENT
}

HELPSUBTABLE SUBHELP_CLIENT
{
    HELPSUBITEM MI_HELPINDEX, MI_HELPINDEX
    HELPSUBITEM MI_GENERALHELP, MI_GENERALHELP
    HELPSUBITEM MI_HELPFORHELP, MI_HELPFORHELP
    HELPSUBITEM MI_KEYSHELP, MI_KEYSHELP
    HELPSUBITEM MI_PRODINFO, MI_PRODINFO
}
```

HELP.H

```
#define RES_CLIENT              256
#define HELP_CLIENT             257
#define SUBHELP_CLIENT          258
#define EXTHELP_CLIENT          259
#define KEYSHELP_CLIENT         260
#define M_HELP                  320
#define MI_HELPINDEX            321
#define MI_GENERALHELP          322
#define MI_HELPFORHELP          323
#define MI_KEYSHELP             324
#define MI_PRODINFO             325
#define HLP_MESSAGEBOX          326
```

HELP.MAK

```
HELP.EXE:                     HELP.OBJ HELP.RES HELP.HLP
        LINK386 @<<
HELP,
HELP,
HELP,
OS2386
HELP
<<
        RC HELP.RES HELP.EXE

HELP.OBJ:                     HELP.C HELP.H
        ICC -C+ -Kb+ -Ss+ HELP.C

HELP.RES:                     HELP.RC HELP.H
        RC -r HELP.RC HELP.RES

HELP.HLP:                     HELP.IPF
        IPFC HELP.IPF
```

HELP.DEF

```
NAME   HELP   WINDOWAPI

DESCRIPTION 'Help Example
Copyright 1992 by Larry Salomon.
All rights reserved.'

STACKSIZE 32768
```

19.11 Restrictions

You might have noticed by now that while the HELPSUBITEMs use manifest
constants (those that have been #define'd), the help panels must hard-code their
resource ids. This is a nasty problem that can only be solved by a preprocessor
that can accept C include files; there are a few good public domain ones that
you can get for only the cost of connecting to Compuserve or the Internet.

19.12 Help Manager Messages

HM_ACTIONBAR_COMMAND
This message is sent to the active window by the help manager when the user selects an action bar help item.

Parameter 1:	USHORT usMenuItemID	ID of selected action bar item
Parameter 2:	ULONG ulReserved	reserved, 0
Reply:	ULONG ulReserved	reserved, 0

HM_CONTROL
This message is sent by the help manager to the application to add a control in the control area of a window.

Parameter 1:	USHORT usReserved	reserved, 0
	USHORT usControlID	res ID of selected control
Parameter 2:	ULONG ulReserved	reserved, 0
Reply:	ULONG ulReserved	reserved, 0

HM_CREATE_HELP_TABLE
This message is sent to the help manager to create a new help table.

Parameter 1:	PHELPTABLE pHelpTable	pointer to HELPTABLE structure
Parameter 2:	ULONG ulReserved	reserved, 0
Reply:	ULONG ulSuccess	successful? 0 : error code

HM_DISMISS_WINDOW
This message is sent to the help manager to remove the active help window.

Parameter 1:	ULONG ulReserved	reserved, 0
Parameter 2:	ULONG ulReserved	reserved, 0
Reply:	ULONG ulSuccess	successful? 0 : error code

HM_DISPLAY_HELP
This message is sent to the help manager to display a specified help window.

Parameter 1:	USHORT usPanelID	ID of help panel to display if usFlag == HM_RESOURCEID or
	PSTRL pPanelName	pointer to the name of help panel to display if usFlag == HM_PANELNAME
Parameter 2:	USHORT usFlag	HM_RESOURCEID or HM_PANELNAME
Reply:	ULONG ulSuccess	successful? 0 : error code

HM_ERROR
This message is sent by the help manager when an error has occurred.

Parameter 1: ULONG ulErrorCode   error code

ERROR CODE	CAUSE
HMERR_LOAD_DLL	Resource DLL could not be loaded
HMERR_NO_FRAME_WND_IN_CHAIN	A frame window in the window chain could not be found to set the associated help instance
HMERR_INVALID_ASSOC_APP_WND	The window hwnd specified in *WinAssociateHelpInstance* is not a valid window handle
HMERR_INVALID_ASSOC_HELP_INST	The help instance handle specified in *WinAssociateHelpInstance* is not a valid help instance
HMERR_INVALID_DESTROY_HELP_INST	The help instance window to destroy is not a help instance class object
HMERR_NO_HELP_INST_IN_CHAIN	The parent of the application window specified does not have a help manager instance

HMERR_INVALID_HELP_INSTANCE_HDL	The handle of the help manager instance does not belong to the help instance class
HMERR_INVALID_QUERY_APP_WND	The window handle specified in *WinQueryHelpInstance* is not a valid window handle
HMERR_HELP_INST_CALLED_INVALID	The help instance handle does not belong to the help instance class
HMERR_HELPTABLE_UNDEFINE	There is no help table provided for context-sensitive help
HMERR_HELP_INSTANCE_UNDEFINE	The help instance handle is invalid
HMERR_HELPITEM_NOT_FOUND	The specified help item ID was not found in the help table
HMERR_INVALID_HELPSUBITEM_SIZE	The help subtable has less than two items
HMERR_INDEX_NOT_FOUND	The index is not in the help library file
HMERR_CONTENT_NOT_FOUND	The libary file does not have any content
HMERR_OPEN_LIB_FILE	The help library file cannot be opened
HMERR_READ_LIB_FILE	The help library file cannot be read
HMERR_CLOSE_LIB_FILE	The help library file cannot be closed
HMERR_INVALID_LIB_FILE	The help library file is improper
HMERR_NO_MEMORY	The help manager is unable to allocate the necessary memory
HMERR_ALLOCATE_SEGMENT	The help manager is unable to allocate the necessary memory segments
HMERR_FREE_MEMORY	The help manager cannot free the requested memory

HMERR_PANEL_NOT_FOUND	The help manager is unable to find the specified help panel
HMERR_DATABASE_NOT_OPEN	Unable to read the unopened database

Parameter 2: ULONG ulReserved   reserved, 0
Reply: ULONG ulReserved   reserved, 0

HM_EXT_HELP

This message is sent to the help manager to display the extended help panel.

Parameter 1: ULONG ulReserved   reserved, 0
Parameter 2: ULONG ulReserved   reserved, 0
Reply: ULONG ulSuccess   successful? 0 : error code

HM_EXT_HELP_UNDEFINED

This message is sent from the help manager to indicate that the extended help has not been defined.

Parameter 1: ULONG ulReserved   reserved, 0
Parameter 2: ULONG ulReserved   reserved, 0
Reply: ULONG ulReserved   reserved, 0

HM_GENERAL_HELP

This message is sent to the help manager to display the general help window.

Parameter 1: ULONG ulReserved   reserved, 0
Parameter 2: ULONG ulReserved   reserved, 0
Reply: ULONG ulSuccess   successful? 0 : error code

HM_GENERAL_HELP_UNDEFINED

This message is sent from the help manager to indicate that the general help has not been defined.

Parameter 1: ULONG ulReserved   reserved, 0
Parameter 2: ULONG ulReserved   reserved, 0

Reply: ULONG ulReserved   reserved, 0

HM_HELP_CONTENTS
This message is sent to the help manager to display the help contents.

Parameter 1: ULONG ulReserved   reserved, 0
Parameter 2: ULONG ulReserved   reserved, 0
Reply: ULONG ulSuccess   successful? 0 : error code

HM_HELP_INDEX
This message is sent to the help manager to display the help index.

Parameter 1: ULONG ulReserved   reserved, 0
Parameter 2: ULONG ulReserved   reserved, 0
Reply: ULONG ulSuccess   successful? 0 : error code

HM_HELPSUBITEM_NOT_FOUND
This message is sent from the help manager when the user requested help on a field that has no related entry in the help subtable.

Parameter 1: USHORT usWindowType — HLPM_WINDOW — help was requested on an application window; HLPM_FRAME — help was requested on a frame window; HLPM_MENU — help was requested on a menu window

Parameter 2: SHORT sTopicID — window or menu ID requesting help

SHORT sSubTopicID — control or menuitem ID

Reply: BOOL fAction — FALSE — display extended help; TRUE — do nothing

HM_INFORM

This message is sent by the help manager that the user selected a help field with the reftype = inform.

Parameter 1:	USHORT usWindowID	res ID of the help field
Parameter 2:	ULONG ulReserved	reserved, 0
Reply:	ULONG ulReserved	reserved, 0

HM_INVALIDATE_DDF_DATA

This message is sent to the help manager to indicate that the previous dynamic data formatting data is no longer valid.

Parameter 1:	ULONG ulResCount	count of DDFs tobe invalidated
Parameter 2:	PUSHORT pDDFArray	array of USHORTs that indicate the DDFs to be invalidated
Reply:	ULONG ulSuccess	successful? 0 : error code

HM_KEYS_HELP

This message is sent to the help manager to display the keys help.

Parameter 1:	ULONG ulReserved	reserved, 0
Parameter 2:	ULONG ulReserved	reserved, 0
Reply:	ULONG ulSuccess	successful? 0 : error code

HM_LOAD_HELP_TABLE

This message is sent to the help manager to load a new help table.

Parameter 1:	USHORT usTableID	ID of the help table
	USHORT usReserved	reserved, 0
Parameter 2:	HMODULE hmodResource	handle of DLL that contains help table, NULL for .EXE
Reply:	ULONG ulSuccess	successful? 0 : error code

HM_NOTIFY

This message is sent from the help manager to notify the application of events it may which to subclass.

| **Parameter 1:** | USHORT usResID | selected control ID, if *usEvent* is CONTROL_SELECTED or HELP_REQUESTED |
| | USHORT usEvent | event |

EVENT	MEANING
CONTROL_SELECTED	A control was selected
HELP_REQUESTED	The user requested help
OPEN_COVERPAGE	The coverpage was displayed
OPEN_PAGE	The coverpage child was displayed
SWAP_PAGE	The coverpage child was swapped
OPEN_INDEX	The index was opened
OPEN_TOC	The table of contents was opened
OPEN_HISTORY	The history window was opened
OPEN_LIBRARY	The library was opened
OPEN_SEARCH_HIT_LIST	The search list was displayed

| **Parameter 2:** | HWND hwndWindow | window handle |
| **Reply:** | BOOL fResult | TRUE — help manager will not format the controls FALSE — help manager will process as normal |

HM_QUERY

This message to sent to the help manager to query help manager-specific information.

| **Parameter 1:** | USHORT usMessageID | message ID |

ID	DESCRIPTION
HMQW_INDEX	Query the index window handle
HMQW_TOC	Query the table of contents window handle
HMQW_SEARCH	Query the search hitlist window handle

HMQW_VIEWEDPAGES	Query the viewed pages window handle
HMQW_LIBRARY	Query the library list window handle
HMQW_OBJCOM_WINDOW	Query the handle of the active communication window
HMQW_INSTANCE	Query the handle of the help instance
HMQW_COVERPAGE	Query the handle of the coverpage
HMQW_VIEWPORT	Query the handle of the viewport window specified in param2
HMQW_GROUP_VIEWPORT	Query the group number of the window specified in param2
HMQW_RES_VIEWPORT	Query the res number of the window specified in param2
HMQW_ACTIVEVIEWPORT	Query the handle of the active window
USERDATA	Query the user data

	USHORT usSelType	HMQVP_NUMBER HMQVP_NAME HMQVP_GROUP
Parameter 2:	PVOID param2	if *usMessageID* is HMQW_VIEWPORT, this is a pointer to either a res number, ID, or group ID
		if usMessageID is HMQW_GROUP_VIEWPORT, this is a pointer to the viewport window of interest
		if usMessageID is HMQW_RES_VIEWPORT, this is a viewport handle of interest
Reply:	ULONG ulReturn	0 if error, else a window handle, group ID, res number, group number, or user data

HM_QUERY_DDF_DATA

This message is sent from the help manager when it sees the :ddf. tag in the help file.

Parameter 1:	HWND hwndClient	client window handle
Parameter 2:	ULONG ulResID	res ID
Reply:	HDDF hddfHandle	DDF handle to be displayed, or 0 if error

HM_QUERY_KEYS_HELP

This message is sent from the help manager when the user selects keys help.

Parameter 1:	ULONG ulReserved	reserved, 0
Parameter 2:	ULONG ulReserved	reserved, 0
Reply:	USHORT usPanelID	ID of keys help panel to display

HM_REPLACE_HELP_FOR_HELP

This message is sent to the help manager to display the application-defined Help for Help instead of the regular Help for Help.

Parameter 1:	USHORT usPanelID	ID of application-defined Help for Help panel
Parameter 2:	ULONG ulReserved	reserved, 0
Reply:	ULONG ulReserved	reserved, 0

HM_REPLACE_USING_HELP

This message is sent to the help manager to display the application-defined Using Help instead of the regular Using Help.

Parameter 1:	USHORT usPanelID	ID of application-defined Using Help panel
Parameter 2:	ULONG ulReserved	reserved, 0
Reply:	ULONG ulReserved	reserved, 0

HM_SET_ACTIVE_WINDOW

This message is sent to the help manager to indicate the window with which the help manager should communicate.

Parameter 1:	HWND hwndActWnd	the handle of the window to be made active
Parameter 2:	HWND hwndPlaceWnd	the handle of the window to position help window next to
Reply:	ULONG ulReturn	successful? 0 : error code

HM_SET_COVERPAGE_SIZE

This message is sent to the help manager to set the coverpage size.

Parameter 1:	PRECTL prclNewSize	pointer to RECTL structure containing the coverpage size
Parameter 2:	ULONG ulReserved	reserved, 0
Reply:	ULONG ulReturn	successful? 0 : error code

HM_SET_LIBRARY_NAME

This message is sent to the help manager to define a list of help manager libraries (.HLP files).

Parameter 1:	PSTRL pLibName	list of help manager files, each name separated by a blank
Parameter 2:	ULONG ulReserved	reserved, 0
Reply:	ULONG ulRetrun	successful? 0 : error code

HM_SET_HELP_WINDOW_TITLE

This message is sent to the help manager to change the help window title.

Parameter 1:	PSTRL pWindowText	new help window title
Parameter 2:	ULONG ulReserved	reserved, 0
Reply:	ulReturn	successful? 0 : error code

HM_SET_OBJCOM_WINDOW

This message is sent to the help manager to identify the window to which the help manager is to send the HM_INFORM and HM_QUERY_DDF_DATA messages.

Parameter 1:	HWND hwndComWnd	handle of communication window
Parameter 2:	ULONG ulReserved	reserved, 0
Reply:	ULONG hwndPrevWnd	handle of previous communication window

HM_SET_SHOW_PANEL_ID

This message is sent to the help manager to display or not display the panel id of the help manager windows.

Parameter 1:	USHORT usShowID	CMIC_HIDE_PANEL_ID — hides panel ID CMIC_SHOW_PANEL_ID — shows panel ID CMIC_TOGGLE_PANEL_ID — changes hide/show state of panel ID
Parameter 2:	ULONG ulReserved	reserved, 0
Reply:	ULONG ulReturn	successful? 0 : error code

HM_SET_USERDATA

This message is sent to the help manager to store data in the help manager user-defined data area.

Parameter 1:	ULONG ulReserved	reserved, 0
Parameter 2:	PVOID pData	4 bytes of user-defined data
Reply:	ULONG ulReturn	successful? TRUE: FALSE

HM_TUTORIAL

This message is sent from the help manager to indicate the user selected tutorial.

Parameter 1:	PSTRL pName	default tutorial name
Parameter 2:	ULONG ulReserved	reserved, 0
Reply:	ULONG ulReturn	reserved, 0

HM_UPDATE_OBJCOM_WINDOW_CHAIN
This message is sent from the help manager to the active communication window when a communication object wants to withdraw from the window chain.

Parameter 1:	HWND hwndOutObject	handle of withdrawing object
Parameter 2:	HWND hwndOutWidow	window that contains withdrawing object
Reply:	ULONG ulReserved	reserved, 0

Chapter 20

Presentation Manager Printing

One of the more profound limitations of DOS was that if your application needed to support many different screens and/or printers, you had to write display- and/or printer-specific code for each type of device. Even though the better programmers could make the job easier with a good design, the effort required to code and support the multitude of output devices was often disheartening enough to dissuade all but the commercial developers from attempting the feat.

When the Presentation Manager was added to OS/2 1.1, the concept of "output device independence" finally became an attainable reality because of the layer of abstraction that a presentation space (HPS) provides; the HPS contains only the settings of the current logical attributes (color, fill type, line type, etc.) that were set by default or by the application. The binding of this (and thus the mapping of the logical attributes to their physical counterparts) to a specific device is done by associating the HPS to a "device context." The device context (HDC) contains the actual attributes being used and other things such as the size of the displayable area. This association between HPS and HDC is done either with the *GpiAssociate* call or when the HPS is created by using the GPIA_ASSOC flag in the *GpiCreatePS* call.

Knowing this, you can probably deduce that by associating the HPS with an HDC that corresponds to the appropriate device, your application can create output on that device without any changes to your code. This is almost correct; PM is more attuned to the display device than the printer, since the display is used significantly more than the printer. Thus, when drawing to the screen, PM eliminates the need for a lot of the coding details that are necessary when drawing to a printer or plotter.

Still, this is much better than how DOS does it (or doesn't do it, depending on how you look at it).

Background aside, this chapter will discuss the details of establishing a "connection" with a hardcopy device and the associated bells and whistles that can be done to ensure that your application has to do as little work as needed.

20.1 A Printer's Overview

Before we begin, a bit of overview of the design of the printing system is needed. As with the output device model, there is a layer of abstraction between the application and the printer. This is the "print queue," which is associated with a "print port," which can be a physical port or a networked logical port. The similarity stops here, however, since each print queue is also assigned a "printer driver." Applications "print" to the print queue, which stores the output in a device-independent format and relies on the printer driver to convert the device-independent graphics commands to device-specific ones. (Actually, the output goes to a queue processor, which uses the printer driver to assist it in converting the commands to the printer-specific ones.)

Additionally, there is also a spooler that is present. It constantly monitors the printer queues and serializes access to the printer port so that, for example, job 2 does not start printing in between pages of job 1. It also has the advantage of virtualizing access to the printer port so that your application can continue "printing" even though another print job is actually being sent to the printer port. If the spooler is bypassed, the output goes directly to the printer driver, meaning that your application will have to wait until printing has actually ended before receiving control back from the printer driver. See Figure 20.1.

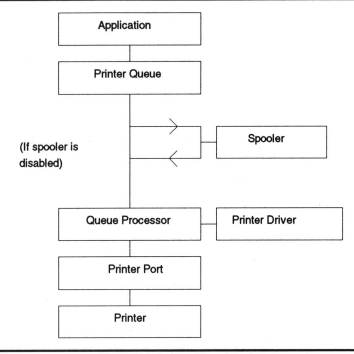

Figure 20.1. A view of the print subsystem.

Let us now look at the pseudocode on which we will initially base the sample code. This describes the strategy used for creating hardcopy output. "Draw page" is an abstract term that is defined by the application.

Initialize a DEVOPENSTRUC for the desired printer/plotter
Open a device context (HDC)
Create a presentation space (HPS) associated with the printer HDC

Tell the printer that we are starting a print job
Draw page 1
Tell the printer to start a new page
Draw page 2
   :
Tell the printer to start a new page
Draw page n
Tell the printer that we are finished with the print job

Destroy the HPS
Close the printer HDC

You might have noticed two things worth noting: the reference to the data structure DEVOPENSTRUC and the phrase "tell the printer that...". The DEVOPENSTRUC is explained below; how to tell the printer anything at all is explained later in this chapter.

The DEVOPENSTRUC structure describes the hardcopy device to PM. It contains the following nine fields:

```
typedef struct _DEVOPENSTRUC {
    PSZ pszLogAddress;
    PSZ pszDriverName;
    PDRIVDATA pdriv;
    PSZ pszDataType;
    PSZ pszComment;
    PSZ pszQueueProcName;
    PSZ pszQueueProcParams;
    PSZ pszSpoolerParams;
    PSZ pszNetworkParams;
} DEVOPENSTRUC;
```

pszLogAddress points to the name of the printer queue to print to. *pszDriverName* points to the name of the printer driver to be used when converting the output to printer-specific commands. *pdriv* points to printer-specific data to be used when printing, i.e., whether to print in portrait or landscape mode. This will be discussed in more detail later in the chapter. *pszDataType* points to the type of output being sent. This can be either PM_Q_STD or PM_Q_RAW, the latter indicating that the application has already converted the output to the appropriate commands for the printer and that the output should pass directly to the printer port. Using this is discouraged, since it does not fit into the strategy of output device independence discussed at the beginning of this chapter. *pszComment* points to a string describing the output being printed. *pszQueueProcName* points to the name of the queue processor to be used (OS/2 comes with two queue processors — "PMPRINT" and "PMPLOT"; see below for determining the default queue processor for a particular printer). *pszQueueProcParams*, *pszSpoolerParams*, and *pszNetworkParams* point to a set of queue processor parameters, spooler parameters, and network parameters. We will not be using these fields.

The initialized DEVOPENSTRUC is passed to *DevOpenDC* as the fifth parameter, with the number of fields that are initialized as the fourth parameter. As a rule, you should always initialize all nine fields, even though you don't use all of them.

"Telling" the printer to do certain things is accomplished by sending it an "escape code." An escape code is a method of accessing the capabilities of an output device for which there is no API. Two examples of this are starting and ending a print job.

```
LONG DevEscape(HDC hdcDevice,
               LONG lEscCode,
               LONG lSzInData,
               PBYTE pbInData,
               PLONG plSzOutData,
               PBYTE pbOutData);
```

hdcDevice is the handle to the device context. *lEscCode* is the DEVESC_* code that you want to issue to the device. *lSzInData* is the size of the data being passed in. *pbInData* points to the data being passed in. *plSzOutData* points to the size of the buffer to receive the results (if any). On return, this variable is updated to reflect the number of bytes actually copied into *pbOutData*. *pbOutData* points to the receiving buffer for the results of the call (if any).

For escape codes that do not have any data, you should specify 0 for *lSzInData* and NULL for *pbInData*, *plSzOutData*, and *pbOutData*.

So, substituting real code where possible in our pseudocode, we now have the following code that reflects the initialization steps to establish the connection between the application and the printer.

```
BOOL printDoc(HAB habAnchor,PCHAR pchName)
{
    DEVOPENSTRUC dosPrinter;
    HDC hdcPrinter;
    SIZEL szlHps;
    HPS hpsPrinter;

    //-------------------------------------------------------------
    // Initialize a DEVOPENSTRUC for the desired printer/plotter
    //-------------------------------------------------------------
    dosPrinter.pszLogAddress="LPT1Q";
    dosPrinter.pszDriverName="PSCRIPT";
    dosPrinter.pdriv=NULL;
    dosPrinter.pszDataType="PM_Q_STD";
    dosPrinter.pszComment=pchName;
    dosPrinter.pszQueueProcName="PMPRINT";
    dosPrinter.pszQueueProcParams=NULL;
    dosPrinter.pszSpoolerParams=NULL;
    dosPrinter.pszNetworkParams=NULL;
```

```
//-----------------------------------------------------------
// Open a device context (HDC)
//-----------------------------------------------------------
hdcPrinter=DevOpenDC(habAnchor,
                     OD_QUEUED,
                     "*",
                     9L,
                     (PDEVOPENDATA)&dosPrinter,
                     NULLHANDLE);
if (hdcPrinter==NULLHANDLE) {
   //-----------------------------------------------------------
   // An error occurred
   //-----------------------------------------------------------
   return;
} /* endif */

//-----------------------------------------------------------
// Query the width and height of the printer page
//-----------------------------------------------------------
DevQueryCaps(hdcPrinter,CAPS_WIDTH,1L,&szlHps.cx);
DevQueryCaps(hdcPrinter,CAPS_HEIGHT,1L,&szlHps.cx);

//-----------------------------------------------------------
// Create a presentation space (HPS) associated with
//   the printer HDC
//-----------------------------------------------------------
hpsPrinter=GpiCreatePS(habAnchor,
                       hdcPrinter,
                       &szlHps,
                       PU_PELS|GPIT_MICRO|GPIF_DEFAULT|GPIA_ASSOC);
if (hpsPrinter==NULLHANDLE) {
   //-----------------------------------------------------------
   // An error occurred
   //-----------------------------------------------------------
   DevCloseDC(hdcPrinter);
   return;
} /* endif */

//-----------------------------------------------------------
// Tell the printer that we are starting a print job
//-----------------------------------------------------------
if (DevEscape(hdcPrinter,
              DEVESC_STARTDOC,
              (LONG)strlen(pchName),
              pchName,
              NULL,
              NULL)!=DEV_OK) {
   //-----------------------------------------------------------
   // An error occurred
   //-----------------------------------------------------------
   GpiDestroyPS(hpsPrinter);
   DevCloseDC(hdcPrinter);
   return;
} /* endif */
```

```
//-------------------------------------------------------------
// Draw page 1
//---------------------------------------------------
if (!drawPage(hpsPrinter,1)) {
    //---------------------------------------------------
    // An error occurred so abort the print job
    //---------------------------------------------------
    DevEscape(hdcPrinter,
            DEVESC_ABORTDOC,
            0L,
            NULL,
            NULL,
            NULL);
    GpiDestroyPS(hpsPrinter);
    DevCloseDC(hdcPrinter);
    return;
} /* endif */

//---------------------------------------------------
// Tell the printer to start a new page
//---------------------------------------------------
if (DevEscape(hdcPrinter,
            DEVESC_NEWFRAME,
            0,
            NULL,
            NULL,
            NULL)!=DEV_OK) {
    //---------------------------------------------------
    // An error occurred so abort the print job
    //---------------------------------------------------
    DevEscape(hdcPrinter,
            DEVESC_ABORTDOC,
            0L,
            NULL,
            NULL,
            NULL);
    GpiDestroyPS(hpsPrinter);
    DevCloseDC(hdcPrinter);
    return;
} /* endif */

//---------------------------------------------------
// Draw page 2
//---------------------------------------------------
if (!drawPage(hpsPrinter,2)) {
    //---------------------------------------------------
    // An error occurred so abort the print job
    //---------------------------------------------------
    DevEscape(hdcPrinter,
            DEVESC_ABORTDOC,
            0L,
            NULL,
            NULL,
            NULL);
    GpiDestroyPS(hpsPrinter);
    DevCloseDC(hdcPrinter);
    return;
} /* endif */
```

```
//------------------------------------------------
// Tell the printer that we are finished with the print job
//------------------------------------------------
if (DevEscape(hdcPrinter,
              DEVESC_ENDDOC,
              0L,
              NULL,
              NULL,
              NULL)!=DEV_OK) {
   //------------------------------------------------
   // An error occurred so abort the print job
   //------------------------------------------------
   DevEscape(hdcPrinter,
             DEVESC_ABORTDOC,
             0L,
             NULL,
             NULL,
             NULL);
   GpiDestroyPS(hpsPrinter);
   DevCloseDC(hdcPrinter);
   return;
} /* endif */

//------------------------------------------------
// Destroy the HPS and close the printer HDC
//------------------------------------------------
GpiDestroyPS(hpsPrinter);
DevCloseDC(hdcPrinter);
}
```

Looking at the hard-coded values for *pszLogAddress* and *pszDriverName*, it is hard to imagine this as being the device-independent code discussed earlier. Well, you're right. There is actually a (huge) step before this to initialize the initialization — selecting the printer and any job-specific parameters.

20.2 Where's My Thing?

What we need is a way to figure out what printers and queues are defined so that we neither have to rely on hard-coded values, nor have to prompt the user for this information. Instead, we should simply retrieve the needed data and present the user with a choice of printers to print to. Fortunately, this information is obtainable through the spooler (Spl) functions and in particular *SplEnumQueue*.

```
(SPLERR)SplEnumQueue(PSZ pszComputer,
                     ULONG ulLevel,
                     PVOID pvBuf,
                     ULONG ulSzBuf,
                     PULONG pulNumReturned,
                     PULONG pulNumTotal,
                     PULONG pulSzBufNeeded,
                     PVOID pvReserved);
```

pszComputer is the name of the computer containing the queues to enumerate. This is for networked printing and can be NULL to specify the local computer. *ulLevel* specifies the amount and type of information to return. *pvBuf* points to a buffer to contain the results. If NULL, the number of bytes needed is returned in *pulSzBufNeeded*. *ulSzBuf* specifies the size of the buffer pointed to by *pvBuf*. If *pvBuf* is NULL, this is ignored. *pulNumReturned* specifies the number of queues returned, while *pulNumTotal* specifies the total number of queues. *pvReserved* is reserved and must be NULL.

The data returned is dependent on the value of *ulLevel* and can be one of the following:

ulLev Value	Data Returned in *pvBuf*
3	*pvBuf* points to an array of PPRQINFO3 structures
4	*pvBuf* points to a list of PPRQINFO3 structures, with each element of the list followed by 0 or more PPRJINFO2 structures describing the jobs currently in the queue
5	*pvBuf* points to a queue name
6	*pvBuf* points to an array of PPRQINFO6 structures

We will be interested in information level 3, which returns all of the information that we will need to eliminate the hard-coded values shown in the code above. Let's look at the PPRQINFO3 structure in detail:

```
typedef struct _PRQINFO3 {
    PSZ pszName;
    USHORT uPriority;
    USHORT uStartTime;
    USHORT uUntilTime;
    USHORT fsType;
    PSZ pszSepFile;
    PSZ pszPrProc;
    PSZ pszParms;
    PSZ pszComment;
    USHORT fsStatus;
    USHORT cJobs;
    PSZ pszPrinters;
    PSZ pszDriverName;
    PDRIVDATA pDriverData;
} PRQINFO3;
```

pszName is the queue name. *uPriority* is the default queue priority and is used to calculate the default job priority for the queue. *uStartTime* is the number of minutes past midnight when the queue becomes active. *uUntilTime* is the number of minutes past midnight when the queue becomes inactive. *fsType* specifies one or more flags describing any characteristics of the queue. *pszSepFile* points to the file name of the separator page. *pszPrProc* points to the name of the queue processor used. *pszParms* points to the default queue processor parameters to be used. *pszComment* points to the description string that is displayed in the Workplace Shell. *fsStatus* specifies one or more flags describing the status of the queue. *cJobs* specifies the number of jobs in the queue. *pszPrinters* specifies one or more printers, separated by commas, that use this queue (for printer pooling). *pszDriverName* specifies the printer driver and device (if the driver supports more than one device) separated by a period. *pDriverData* points to the default driver data to be used.

We will see later that the only information we really need for any printer is the corresponding DEVOPENSTRUC structure and the device name, if the printer driver supports more than one device. The function *createPrnList*, which enumerates the printers in the system and calls *extractPrnInfo* to initialize the DEVOPENSTRUC structure for the printer. Also included is *destroyPrnList*, which returns any consumed memory to the system.

The following is code for extracting the DEVOPENSTRUC information from a PRQINFO3 structure.

```
typedef struct {
    DEVOPENSTRUC dosPrinter;
    CHAR achDevice[256];
} PRNLISTINFO, *PPRNLISTINFO;

#define CPL_ERROR               (USHORT)0
```

```
#define CPL_NOPRINTERS              (USHORT)1
#define CPL_SUCCESS                 (USHORT)2

VOID extractPrnInfo(PPRQINFO3 ppiQueue,DEVOPENSTRUC *pdosPrinter)
//----------------------------------------------------------------
// This function extracts the needed information from the specified
// PRQINFO3
// structure and places it into the specifies DEVOPENSTRUC
// structure.
//
// Input:  ppiQueue - points to the PRQINFO3 structure
// Output: pdosPrinter - points to the initialized DEVOPENSTRUC
// structure
//----------------------------------------------------------------
{
    PCHAR pchPos;

    pdosPrinter->pszLogAddress=ppiQueue->pszName;

    pdosPrinter->pszDriverName=ppiQueue->pszDriverName;
    pchPos=strchr(pdosPrinter->pszDriverName,'.');
    if (pchPos!=NULL) {
       *pchPos=0;
    } /* endif */

    pdosPrinter->pdriv=ppiQueue->pDriverData;
    pdosPrinter->pszDataType="PM_Q_STD";
    pdosPrinter->pszComment=ppiQueue->pszComment;

    if (strlen(ppiQueue->pszPrProc)>0) {
       pdosPrinter->pszQueueProcName=ppiQueue->pszPrProc;
    } else {
       pdosPrinter->pszQueueProcName=NULL;
    } /* endif */

    if (strlen(ppiQueue->pszParms)>0) {
       pdosPrinter->pszQueueProcParams=ppiQueue->pszParms;
    } else {
       pdosPrinter->pszQueueProcParams=NULL;
    } /* endif */

    pdosPrinter->pszSpoolerParams=NULL;
    pdosPrinter->pszNetworkParams=NULL;
}

USHORT createPrnList(HWND hwndListbox)
//----------------------------------------------------------------
// This function enumerates the printers available and inserts them
// into the specified listbox.
//
// Input:  hwndListbox - handle to the listbox to contain the list
// Returns:  an CPL_* constant
//----------------------------------------------------------------
{
    SPLERR seError;
    ULONG ulSzBuf;
    ULONG ulNumQueues;
    ULONG ulNumReturned;
```

```
ULONG ulSzNeeded;
ULONG ulIndex;
PPRQINFO3 ppiQueue;
PCHAR pchPos;
PPRNLISTINFO ppliInfo;
SHORT sInsert;

//--------------------------------------------------------------
// Get the size of the buffer needed
//--------------------------------------------------------------
seError=SplEnumQueue(NULL,
                     3,
                     NULL,
                     0L,
                     &ulNumReturned,
                     &ulNumQueues,
                     &ulSzNeeded,
                     NULL);
if (seError!=ERROR_MORE_DATA) {
   return CPL_ERROR;
} /* endif */

ppiQueue=malloc(ulSzNeeded);
if (ppiQueue==NULL) {
   return CPL_ERROR;
} /* endif */

ulSzBuf=ulSzNeeded;

//--------------------------------------------------------------
// Get the information
//--------------------------------------------------------------
SplEnumQueue(NULL,
             3,
             ppiQueue,
             ulSzBuf,
             &ulNumReturned,
             &ulNumQueues,
             &ulSzNeeded,
             NULL);

//--------------------------------------------------------------
// ulNumReturned has the count of the number of PRQINFO3
// structures.
//--------------------------------------------------------------
for (ulIndex=0; ulIndex<ulNumReturned; ulIndex++) {
   //--------------------------------------------------------------
   // Since the "comment" can have newlines in it, replace them
   // with spaces
   //--------------------------------------------------------------
   pchPos=strchr(ppiQueue[ulIndex].pszComment,'\n');
   while (pchPos!=NULL) {
      *pchPos=' ';
      pchPos=strchr(ppiQueue[ulIndex].pszComment,'\n');
   } /* endwhile */

   ppliInfo=malloc(sizeof(PRNLISTINFO));
```

```
        if (ppliInfo==NULL) {
           continue;
        } /* endif */

        //------------------------------------------------------------
        // Extract the device name before initializing the
        // DEVOPENSTRUC structure
        //------------------------------------------------------------
        pchPos=strchr(ppiQueue[ulIndex].pszDriverName,'.');
        if (pchPos!=NULL) {
           *pchPos=0;
           strcpy(ppliInfo->achDevice,pchPos+1);
        } /* endif */

        extractPrnInfo(&ppiQueue[ulIndex],&ppliInfo->dosPrinter);

        sInsert=(SHORT)WinInsertLboxItem(hwndListbox,
                                         0,
                                         ppiQueue[ulIndex].pszComment);

        WinSendMsg(hwndListbox,
                   LM_SETITEMHANDLE,
                   MPFROMSHORT(sInsert),
                   MPFROMP(ppliInfo));
     } /* endfor */

     free(ppiQueue);
     return CPL_SUCCESS;
}

VOID destroyPrnList(HWND hwndListbox)
//------------------------------------------------------------------
// This function destroys the printer list and returns the memory
// to the system.
//
// Input:  hwndListbox - handle of the listbox containing the
// printer list
//------------------------------------------------------------------
{
     USHORT usNumItems;
     USHORT usIndex;
     PPRNLISTINFO ppliInfo;

     usNumItems=WinQueryLboxCount(hwndListbox);

     for (usIndex=0; usIndex<usNumItems; usIndex++) {
        ppliInfo=(PPRNLISTINFO)PVOIDFROMMR(WinSendMsg(hwndListbox,
                                           LM_QUERYITEMHANDLE,
                                           MPFROMSHORT(usIndex),
                                           0L));
        if (ppliInfo!=NULL) {
           free(ppliInfo);
        } /* endif */
     } /* endfor */

     WinSendMsg(hwndListbox,LM_DELETEALL,0L,0L);
}
```

20.3 I Want That with Mustard, Hold the Mayo, No Onions, Extra Ketchup, ...

Okay, so now we have the printer selection tools needed (you're going to have to write the dialog procedure!), but what if the user wants the printer output to go to a file, for example? In a restaurant, when you want to order an entree, you can usually see what it comes with ("a vegetable and a choice of salad or a dessert"). With printers, the same concept applies; it is referred to as the job-properties (or as the printer driver data). These are usually specific to the printer type and can include portrait/landscape mode, form used, etc. These job-properties are stored in the *pdriv* field of the DEVOPENSTRUC structure and are queried and changed via the *DevPostDeviceModes* function.

```
(LONG)DevPostDeviceModes(HAB habAnchor,
                         PDRIVDATA pddData,
                         PSZ pszDriver,
                         PSZ pszDevice,
                         PSZ pszPrinter,
                         ULONG ulOptions);
```

habAnchor is the anchor block of the thread calling the function. *pddData* is used to store the results. If NULL, this function returns the number of bytes needed to store the data. *pszDriver* is the printer driver name and corresponds to the *pszDriverName* field of the DEVOPENSTRUC structure. *pszDevice* is the device name and corresponds to the *achDevice* field of our PRNLISTINFO structure. *pszPrinter* is the key name passed to *PrfQueryProfileData* and is passed to the *queryPrinter* routine (and is stored in the *achPrinter* field). Finally, *ulOptions* can be one of three DPDM_* constants:

CONSTANT	DESCRIPTION
DPDM_QUERYJOBPROP	Returns the default data in *pddData*.
DPDM_POSTJOBPROP	Displays the printer-specific dialog box containing the job-properties and the forms list. If *pszPrinter* is NULL, the initial values displayed on the dialog box are taken from the *pddData* field.
DPDM_CHANGEPROP	Displays first the DPDM_POSTJOBPROP dialog box and then displays the "printer-properties" dialog box, allowing the user to change any permanent settings regarding the printer.

This information now allows us to provide a "Properties" button on a printer selection dialog box. Note that you won't normally need the DPDM_QUERYJOBPROP option since the *SplEnumQueue* returns this information. Now we have all of the tools needed to query the printers defined for the system and the data specific to each and also the job-properties.

20.4 Where Were We?

Looking back, we now know that somewhere before the initialization of the DEVOPENSTRUC structure, we need to display a dialog box allowing the user to select which printer to print the document on and any job-properties he or she wishes to use. From the values returned, we can properly initialize the DEVOPENSTRUC structure with non-hard-coded values, thereby increasing our device independence. To firm up our knowledge, the following is a simple example program that prints a box.

PRINT.C

```
#define INCL_DEV
#define INCL_DOSERRORS
#define INCL_SPL
#define INCL_SPLDOSPRINT
#define INCL_WINERRORS
#define INCL_WININPUT
#define INCL_WINLISTBOXES
#define INCL_WINMENUS
#define INCL_WINSHELLDATA
#define INCL_WINSYS
#define INCL_WINWINDOWMGR

#include <os2.h>
#include <stdio.h>
#include <string.h>
#include <stdlib.h>
#include <process.h>
#include "print.h"

#define CLS_CLIENT              "SampleClass"

#define CPL_ERROR               (USHORT) 0
#define CPL_NOPRINTERS          (USHORT) 1
#define CPL_SUCCESS             (USHORT) 2

typedef VOID ( * _Optlink PRNTHREAD ) ( PVOID ) ;


typedef struct {
  DEVOPENSTRUC    dosPrinter ;
  CHAR            achDevice [256] ;
} PRNLISTINFO, *PPRNLISTINFO ;
```

```
typedef struct {
    ULONG           ulSizeStruct ;
    HWND            hwndOwner ;
    DEVOPENSTRUC    dosPrinter ;
} PRNTHREADINFO, *PPRNTHREADINFO ;


typedef struct _CLIENTINFO {
    HWND            hwndListbox ;
} CLIENTINFO, *PCLIENTINFO ;


MRESULT EXPENTRY clientWndProc ( HWND hwndClient,
                                 ULONG ulMsg,
                                 MPARAM mpParm1,
                                 MPARAM mpParm2 );

VOID _Optlink printThread ( PPRNTHREADINFO pptiInfo );
BOOL drawPage ( HPS hpsDraw, USHORT usPage );
USHORT createPrnList ( HWND hwndListbox );
VOID destroyPrnList ( HWND hwndListbox );
VOID extractPrnInfo ( PPRQINFO3 ppiQueue,
                      DEVOPENSTRUC *pdosPrinter );

INT main ( VOID )
{
    HAB             habAnchor ;
    HMQ             hmqQueue ;
    ULONG           ulFlags ;
    HWND            hwndFrame ;
    BOOL            bLoop ;
    QMSG            qmMsg ;

    habAnchor = WinInitialize ( 0 ) ;
    hmqQueue = WinCreateMsgQueue ( habAnchor, 0 ) ;

    WinRegisterClass ( habAnchor,
                       CLS_CLIENT,
                       clientWndProc,
                       0,
                       sizeof (PVOID)) ;

    ulFlags = FCF_SIZEBORDER | FCF_TITLEBAR | FCF_TASKLIST |
              FCF_SHELLPOSITION | FCF_SYSMENU | FCF_MENU |
              FCF_ACCELTABLE ;

    hwndFrame = WinCreateStdWindow ( HWND_DESKTOP,
                                     WS_VISIBLE,
                                     &ulFlags,
                                     CLS_CLIENT,
                                     "Printing Sample Application",
                                     0,
                                     NULLHANDLE,
                                     RES_CLIENT,
                                     NULL ) ;
```

```
        if ( hwndFrame != NULLHANDLE ) {
            bLoop = WinGetMsg ( habAnchor,
                                &qmMsg,
                                NULLHANDLE,
                                0,
                                0 ) ;

            while ( bLoop ) {
                WinDispatchMsg ( habAnchor, &qmMsg ) ;
                bLoop = WinGetMsg ( habAnchor,
                                    &qmMsg,
                                    NULLHANDLE,
                                    0,
                                    0 ) ;
            } /* endwhile */

            WinDestroyWindow ( hwndFrame ) ;
        } /* endif */

        WinDestroyMsgQueue ( hmqQueue ) ;
        WinTerminate ( habAnchor ) ;
        return ( 0 ) ;
}

MRESULT EXPENTRY clientWndProc ( HWND hwndClient,
                                 ULONG ulMsg,
                                 MPARAM mpParm1,
                                 MPARAM mpParm2 )
{
    PCLIENTINFO    pciInfo ;

    pciInfo = WinQueryWindowPtr ( hwndClient, 0 ) ;

    switch ( ulMsg ) {
    case WM_CREATE:
        {
            //--------------------------------------------------------
            // Allocate and initialize the CLIENTINFO structure
            //--------------------------------------------------------
            pciInfo = malloc ( sizeof ( CLIENTINFO )) ;
            if ( pciInfo == NULL ) {

                WinMessageBox ( HWND_DESKTOP,
                                HWND_DESKTOP,
                                "An error occurred in initialization.",
                                "Error",
                                0,
                                MB_OK | MB_INFORMATION ) ;

                return MRFROMSHORT ( TRUE ) ;
            } /* endif */

            WinSetWindowPtr ( hwndClient, 0, pciInfo ) ;
```

```
                pciInfo -> hwndListbox = WinCreateWindow ( hwndClient,
                                                           WC_LISTBOX,
                                                           "",
                                                           LS_HORZSCROLL |
                                                           LS_NOADJUSTPOS,
                                                           0,
                                                           0,
                                                           0,
                                                           0,
                                                           hwndClient,
                                                           HWND_TOP,
                                                           WND_LISTBOX,
                                                           NULL,
                                                           NULL ) ;

            if ( pciInfo -> hwndListbox == NULLHANDLE ) {
                WinMessageBox ( HWND_DESKTOP,
                                HWND_DESKTOP,
                                "An error occurred in initialization.",
                                "Error",
                                0,
                                MB_OK | MB_INFORMATION ) ;
                free ( pciInfo ) ;
                return MRFROMSHORT ( TRUE ) ;
            } /* endif */

            WinSendMsg ( hwndClient,
                         WM_COMMAND,
                         MPFROMSHORT ( MI_REFRESH ) ,
                         0 ) ;
        }
        break ;
    case WM_DESTROY:
        //-----------------------------------------------------------
        // Return the resources to the system
        //-----------------------------------------------------------
        destroyPrnList ( pciInfo -> hwndListbox ) ;
        WinDestroyWindow ( pciInfo -> hwndListbox ) ;
        break ;
    case WM_SIZE:
        WinSetWindowPos ( pciInfo -> hwndListbox,
                          NULLHANDLE,
                          0,
                          0,
                          SHORT1FROMMP ( mpParm2 ) ,
                          SHORT2FROMMP ( mpParm2 ) ,
                          SWP_MOVE | SWP_SIZE | SWP_SHOW ) ;
        break ;
    case WM_INITMENU:
        switch ( SHORT1FROMMP ( mpParm1 )) {
        case M_SAMPLE:
            {
                SHORT             sSelect ;
                PPRNLISTINFO      ppliInfo ;
```

```
               sSelect = WinQueryLboxSelectedItem (
                   pciInfo -> hwndListbox ) ;

               ppliInfo =
                   (PPRNLISTINFO) PVOIDFROMMR (
                      WinSendMsg ( pciInfo -> hwndListbox,
                                   LM_QUERYITEMHANDLE,
                                   MPFROMSHORT ( sSelect ) ,
                                   0 )) ;

               //-------------------------------------------------------
               // If no printer is selected, disable the print
               // menuitem
               //-------------------------------------------------------
               if ( sSelect != LIT_NONE ) {
                   WinEnableMenuItem ( HWNDFROMMP ( mpParm2 ) ,
                                       MI_PRINT,
                                       TRUE ) ;
               } else {
                   WinEnableMenuItem ( HWNDFROMMP ( mpParm2 ) ,
                                       MI_PRINT,
                                       FALSE ) ;
               } /* endif */

               //-------------------------------------------------------
               // If no printer is selected or there is no driver
               // data, disable the setup menuitem
               //-------------------------------------------------------
               if (( sSelect != LIT_NONE ) && ( ppliInfo != NULL ) &&
                   ( ppliInfo -> dosPrinter.pdriv != NULL )) {
                   WinEnableMenuItem ( HWNDFROMMP ( mpParm2 ) ,
                                       MI_SETUP,
                                       TRUE ) ;
               } else {
                   WinEnableMenuItem ( HWNDFROMMP ( mpParm2 ) ,
                                       MI_SETUP,
                                       FALSE ) ;
               } /* endif */
           }
           break ;
        default:
           return WinDefWindowProc ( hwndClient,
                                     ulMsg,
                                     mpParm1,
                                     mpParm2 ) ;

        } /* endswitch */
        break ;
   case WM_COMMAND:
        switch ( SHORT1FROMMP ( mpParm1 )) {
        case MI_PRINT:
           {
               SHORT          sIndex ;
               PPRNLISTINFO   ppliInfo ;
               PPRNTHREADINFO pptiInfo ;
```

```
        //-----------------------------------------------------
        // Query the selected printer
        //-----------------------------------------------------
        sIndex = WinQueryLboxSelectedItem (
            pciInfo -> hwndListbox ) ;

        ppliInfo =
            (PPRNLISTINFO) PVOIDFROMMR (
                WinSendMsg ( pciInfo -> hwndListbox,
                             LM_QUERYITEMHANDLE,
                             MPFROMSHORT ( sIndex ) ,
                             0 )) ;

        //-----------------------------------------------------
        // Allocate and initialize the PRNTHREADINFO structure
        // to pass to the thread
        //-----------------------------------------------------
        pptiInfo = malloc ( sizeof ( PRNTHREADINFO )) ;
        if ( pptiInfo == NULL ) {
            WinMessageBox ( HWND_DESKTOP,
                            HWND_DESKTOP,
                            "An error occurred while"
                            " trying to print",
                            "Error",
                            0,
                            MB_OK | MB_INFORMATION ) ;
            return MRFROMSHORT ( TRUE ) ;
        } /* endif */

        pptiInfo -> ulSizeStruct = sizeof ( PRNTHREADINFO ) ;
        pptiInfo -> hwndOwner = hwndClient ;
        pptiInfo -> dosPrinter = ppliInfo -> dosPrinter ;

        //-----------------------------------------------------
        // Create the thread to do the printing
        //-----------------------------------------------------
        if ( _beginthread(( PRNTHREAD ) printThread,
                          NULL,
                          0x8000,
                          ( PVOID ) pptiInfo ) == - 1 ) {
                          WinMessageBox ( HWND_DESKTOP,
                            HWND_DESKTOP,
                            "An error occurred while"
                            " trying to print",
                            "Error",
                            0,
                            MB_OK | MB_INFORMATION ) ;
        } /* endif */
    }
    break ;
case MI_SETUP:
    {
        USHORT              usSelect ;
        PPRNLISTINFO        ppliInfo ;
```

```
        //----------------------------------------------------
        // Query the selected printer
        //----------------------------------------------------
        usSelect = WinQueryLboxSelectedItem (
            pciInfo -> hwndListbox ) ;
        ppliInfo =
            (PPRNLISTINFO) PVOIDFROMMR (
                WinSendMsg ( pciInfo -> hwndListbox,
                             LM_QUERYITEMHANDLE,
                             MPFROMSHORT ( usSelect ) ,
                             0 )) ;

        DevPostDeviceModes (
            WinQueryAnchorBlock ( hwndClient ) ,
                ppliInfo -> dosPrinter.pdriv,
                ppliInfo -> dosPrinter.pszDriverName,
                ppliInfo -> achDevice,
                NULL,
                DPDM_POSTJOBPROP ) ;
    }
    break ;
case MI_REFRESH:
    {
        USHORT      usResult ;

        destroyPrnList ( pciInfo -> hwndListbox ) ;

        usResult = createPrnList (
            pciInfo -> hwndListbox ) ;

        switch ( usResult ) {

        case CPL_ERROR:

            WinMessageBox ( HWND_DESKTOP,
                            HWND_DESKTOP,
                            "An error occurred while "
                            "refreshing the list",
                            "Error",
                            0,
                            MB_OK | MB_INFORMATION ) ;
            break ;

        case CPL_NOPRINTERS:

            WinMessageBox ( HWND_DESKTOP,
                            HWND_DESKTOP,
                            "There are no printers defined.",
                            "Warning",
                            0,
                            MB_OK | MB_INFORMATION ) ;
            break ;

        default:
```

```
                    WinSendMsg (
                        WinWindowFromID ( hwndClient, WND_LISTBOX ) ,
                                          LM_SELECTITEM,
                                          MPFROMSHORT ( 0 ) ,
                                          MPFROMSHORT ( TRUE )) ;
                    break ;

                } /* endswitch */
            }
            break ;
        case MI_EXIT:

            WinPostMsg ( hwndClient, WM_CLOSE, 0, 0 ) ;
            break ;

        default:

            return WinDefWindowProc ( hwndClient,
                                      ulMsg,
                                      mpParm1,
                                      mpParm2 ) ;
        } /* endswitch */
        break ;

    case WM_PAINT:
        {
            HPS         hpsPaint ;
            RECTL       rclPaint ;

            hpsPaint = WinBeginPaint ( hwndClient,
                                       NULLHANDLE,
                                       &rclPaint ) ;
            WinFillRect ( hpsPaint,
                          &rclPaint,
                          SYSCLR_WINDOW ) ;
            WinEndPaint ( hpsPaint ) ;
        }
        break ;
    default:
        return WinDefWindowProc ( hwndClient,
                                  ulMsg,
                                  mpParm1,
                                  mpParm2 ) ;
    } /* endswitch */

    return MRFROMSHORT ( FALSE ) ;
}
```

```
VOID _Optlink printThread ( PPRNTHREADINFO pptiInfo )
//------------------------------------------------------------------
// This function is the secondary thread which prints the output.
//
// Input:  pptiInfo - points to the PRNTHREADINFO structure
//                    containing needed information
//------------------------------------------------------------------
{
    HAB             habAnchor ;
    HMQ             hmqQueue ;
    HDC             hdcPrinter ;
    SIZEL           szlHps ;
    HPS             hpsPrinter ;

    habAnchor = WinInitialize ( 0 ) ;
    hmqQueue = WinCreateMsgQueue ( habAnchor, 0 ) ;
    WinCancelShutdown ( hmqQueue, TRUE ) ;

    //------------------------------------------------------------
    // Open a device context (HDC)
    //------------------------------------------------------------
    hdcPrinter = DevOpenDC ( habAnchor,
                             OD_QUEUED,
                             "*",
                             9L,
                             (PDEVOPENDATA) &pptiInfo -> dosPrinter,
                             NULLHANDLE ) ;

    if ( hdcPrinter == NULLHANDLE ) {
        //--------------------------------------------------------
        // An error occurred
        //--------------------------------------------------------
        WinAlarm ( HWND_DESKTOP, WA_ERROR ) ;
        WinMessageBox ( HWND_DESKTOP,
                        pptiInfo -> hwndOwner,
                        "Error creating the device context.",
                        "Error",
                        0,
                        MB_INFORMATION | MB_OK ) ;

        WinDestroyMsgQueue ( hmqQueue ) ;
        WinTerminate ( habAnchor ) ;
        free ( pptiInfo ) ;
        _endthread ( ) ;
    } /* endif */

    //------------------------------------------------------------
    // Query the width and height of the printer page
    //------------------------------------------------------------
    DevQueryCaps ( hdcPrinter, CAPS_WIDTH, 1L, &szlHps.cx ) ;
    DevQueryCaps ( hdcPrinter, CAPS_HEIGHT, 1L, &szlHps.cy ) ;

    //------------------------------------------------------------
    // Create a presentation space (HPS) associated with the printer
    // HDC
    //------------------------------------------------------------
```

```
    hpsPrinter = GpiCreatePS ( habAnchor,
                               hdcPrinter,
                               &szlHps,
                               PU_LOENGLISH |
                               GPIT_MICRO |
                               GPIA_ASSOC ) ;

if ( hpsPrinter == NULLHANDLE ) {
   //-------------------------------------------------------------
   // An error occurred
   //-------------------------------------------------------------
   DevCloseDC ( hdcPrinter ) ;

   WinAlarm ( HWND_DESKTOP, WA_ERROR ) ;
   WinMessageBox ( HWND_DESKTOP,
                   pptiInfo -> hwndOwner,
                   "Error creating the presentation space.",
                   "Error",
                   0,
                   MB_INFORMATION | MB_OK ) ;

   WinDestroyMsgQueue ( hmqQueue ) ;
   WinTerminate ( habAnchor ) ;
   free ( pptiInfo ) ;
   _endthread ( ) ;
} /* endif */

//-----------------------------------------------------------------
// Tell the printer that we are starting a print job
//-----------------------------------------------------------------
if ( DevEscape ( hdcPrinter,
                 DEVESC_STARTDOC,
                 strlen ( pptiInfo -> dosPrinter.pszComment ) ,
                 pptiInfo -> dosPrinter.pszComment,
                 NULL,
                 NULL ) != DEV_OK ) {
   //-------------------------------------------------------------
   // An error occurred
   //-------------------------------------------------------------
   GpiDestroyPS ( hpsPrinter ) ;
   DevCloseDC ( hdcPrinter ) ;

   WinAlarm ( HWND_DESKTOP, WA_ERROR ) ;
   WinMessageBox ( HWND_DESKTOP,
                   pptiInfo -> hwndOwner,
                   "Error starting the print job.",
                   "Error",
                   0,
                   MB_INFORMATION | MB_OK ) ;

   WinDestroyMsgQueue ( hmqQueue ) ;
   WinTerminate ( habAnchor ) ;
   free ( pptiInfo ) ;
   _endthread ( ) ;
} /* endif */
```

```
//---------------------------------------------------------
// Draw sample output
//---------------------------------------------------------

if ( !drawPage ( hpsPrinter, 1 )) {

    //---------------------------------------------------------
    // An error occurred so abort the print job
    //---------------------------------------------------------

    DevEscape ( hdcPrinter,
                DEVESC_ABORTDOC,
                0,
                NULL,
                NULL,
                NULL ) ;
    GpiDestroyPS ( hpsPrinter ) ;
    DevCloseDC ( hdcPrinter ) ;

    WinAlarm ( HWND_DESKTOP, WA_ERROR ) ;
    WinMessageBox ( HWND_DESKTOP,
                    pptiInfo -> hwndOwner,
                    "Error drawing the printer page.",
                    "Error",
                    0,
                    MB_INFORMATION | MB_OK ) ;

    WinDestroyMsgQueue ( hmqQueue ) ;
    WinTerminate ( habAnchor ) ;
    free ( pptiInfo ) ;
    _endthread ( ) ;
} /* endif */

//---------------------------------------------------------
// Tell the printer that we are finished with the print job
//---------------------------------------------------------
if ( DevEscape ( hdcPrinter,
                 DEVESC_ENDDOC,
                 0,
                 NULL,
                 NULL,
                 NULL ) != DEV_OK ) {

    //---------------------------------------------------------
    // An error occurred so abort the print job
    //---------------------------------------------------------

    DevEscape ( hdcPrinter,
                DEVESC_ABORTDOC,
                0,
                NULL,
                NULL,
                NULL ) ;

    GpiDestroyPS ( hpsPrinter ) ;
    DevCloseDC ( hdcPrinter ) ;
```

```
            WinAlarm ( HWND_DESKTOP, WA_ERROR ) ;
            WinMessageBox ( HWND_DESKTOP,
                            pptiInfo -> hwndOwner,
                            "Error ending the print job.",
                            "Error",
                            0,
                            MB_INFORMATION | MB_OK ) ;

        WinDestroyMsgQueue ( hmqQueue ) ;
        WinTerminate ( habAnchor ) ;
        free ( pptiInfo ) ;
        _endthread ( ) ;
    } /* endif */

    //-------------------------------------------------------------
    // Destroy the HPS and close the printer HDC
    //-------------------------------------------------------------

    GpiDestroyPS ( hpsPrinter ) ;
    DevCloseDC ( hdcPrinter ) ;
    WinAlarm ( HWND_DESKTOP, WA_NOTE ) ;
    WinDestroyMsgQueue ( hmqQueue ) ;
    WinTerminate ( habAnchor ) ;
    free ( pptiInfo ) ;
    _endthread ( ) ;
    return ;
}

BOOL drawPage ( HPS hpsDraw, USHORT usPage )

//-------------------------------------------------------------
// This function draws a box for page 1.  Any other page number
// returns an error.
//
// Input: usPage - specifies the page number to draw.
// Returns:  TRUE if successful, FALSE otherwise
//-------------------------------------------------------------

{
    switch ( usPage ) {
    case 1:
        {
            POINTL      ptlMove ;

            ptlMove.x = 10 ;
            ptlMove.y = 10 ;

            GpiMove ( hpsDraw, &ptlMove ) ;

            ptlMove.x = 100 ;
            ptlMove.y = 100 ;

            GpiBox ( hpsDraw, DRO_OUTLINE, &ptlMove, 0, 0 ) ;
        }
        break ;
```

```
       default:
          return FALSE ;
       } /* endswitch */

       return TRUE ;
}

USHORT createPrnList ( HWND hwndListbox )

//------------------------------------------------------------------
// This function enumerates the printers available and inserts them
// into the specified listbox.
//
// Input:  hwndListbox - handle to the listbox to contain the list
// Returns:  an CPL_* constant
//------------------------------------------------------------------

{
    SPLERR           seError ;
    ULONG            ulSzBuf ;
    ULONG            ulNumQueues ;
    ULONG            ulNumReturned ;
    ULONG            ulSzNeeded ;
    ULONG            ulIndex ;
    PPRQINFO3        ppiQueue ;
    PCHAR            pchPos ;
    PPRNLISTINFO     ppliInfo ;
    SHORT            sInsert ;

    //------------------------------------------------------------------
    // Get the size of the buffer needed
    //------------------------------------------------------------------
    seError = SplEnumQueue ( NULL,
                             3,
                             NULL,
                             0,
                             &ulNumReturned,
                             &ulNumQueues,
                             &ulSzNeeded,
                             NULL ) ;
    if ( seError != ERROR_MORE_DATA ) {
       return CPL_ERROR ;
    } /* endif */

    ppiQueue = malloc ( ulSzNeeded ) ;
    if ( ppiQueue == NULL ) {
       return CPL_ERROR ;
    } /* endif */

    ulSzBuf = ulSzNeeded ;

    //------------------------------------------------------------------
    // Get the information
    //------------------------------------------------------------------
```

```
    SplEnumQueue ( NULL,
                   3,
                   ppiQueue,
                   ulSzBuf,
                   &ulNumReturned,
                   &ulNumQueues,
                   &ulSzNeeded,
                   NULL ) ;

//------------------------------------------------------------
// ulNumReturned has the count of the number of PRQINFO3
// structures.
//------------------------------------------------------------

for ( ulIndex = 0 ; ulIndex < ulNumReturned ; ulIndex ++ ) {

   //------------------------------------------------------------
   // Since the "comment" can have newlines in it, replace them
   // with spaces
   //------------------------------------------------------------

   pchPos = strchr ( ppiQueue [ulIndex] .pszComment, '\n' ) ;
   while ( pchPos != NULL ) {
      *pchPos = ' ' ;
      pchPos = strchr ( ppiQueue [ulIndex] .pszComment, '\n' ) ;
   } /* endwhile */

   ppliInfo = malloc ( sizeof ( PRNLISTINFO )) ;
   if ( ppliInfo == NULL ) {
      continue ;
   } /* endif */

   //------------------------------------------------------------
   // Extract the device name before initializing the
   // DEVOPENSTRUC structure
   //------------------------------------------------------------

   pchPos = strchr ( ppiQueue [ulIndex] .pszDriverName, '.' ) ;
   if ( pchPos != NULL ) {
      *pchPos = 0 ;
      strcpy ( ppliInfo -> achDevice, pchPos + 1 ) ;
   } /* endif */

   extractPrnInfo ( &ppiQueue [ulIndex] ,
                    &ppliInfo -> dosPrinter ) ;

   sInsert = ( SHORT ) WinInsertLboxItem ( hwndListbox,
                            0,
                            ppiQueue [ulIndex] .pszComment ) ;

   WinSendMsg ( hwndListbox,
                LM_SETITEMHANDLE,
                MPFROMSHORT ( sInsert ) ,
                MPFROMP ( ppliInfo )) ;
} /* endfor */
```

```
      free ( ppiQueue ) ;
      return CPL_SUCCESS ;
}

VOID destroyPrnList ( HWND hwndListbox )

//------------------------------------------------------------------
// This function destroys the printer list and returns the memory
// to the system.
//
// Input:  hwndListbox - handle of the listbox containing the
//                       printer list
//------------------------------------------------------------------

{
    USHORT           usNumItems ;
    USHORT           usIndex ;
    PPRNLISTINFO     ppliInfo ;

    usNumItems = WinQueryLboxCount ( hwndListbox ) ;

    for ( usIndex = 0 ; usIndex < usNumItems ; usIndex ++ ) {
       ppliInfo =
          (PPRNLISTINFO) PVOIDFROMMR (
             WinSendMsg ( hwndListbox,
                          LM_QUERYITEMHANDLE,
                          MPFROMSHORT ( usIndex ) ,
                          0 )) ;

       if ( ppliInfo != NULL ) {
          free ( ppliInfo ) ;
       } /* endif */
    } /* endfor */

    WinSendMsg ( hwndListbox, LM_DELETEALL, 0, 0 ) ;
    return ;
}

VOID extractPrnInfo ( PPRQINFO3 ppiQueue,
   DEVOPENSTRUC *pdosPrinter )

//------------------------------------------------------------------
// This function extracts the needed information from the specified
// PRQINFO3 structure and places it into the specifies DEVOPENSTRUC
// structure.
//
// Input:  ppiQueue - points to the PRQINFO3 structure
// Output: pdosPrinter - points to the initialized DEVOPENSTRUC
//                       structure
//------------------------------------------------------------------

{
    PCHAR        pchPos ;

    pdosPrinter -> pszLogAddress = ppiQueue -> pszName ;
    pdosPrinter -> pszDriverName = ppiQueue -> pszDriverName ;
    pchPos = strchr ( pdosPrinter -> pszDriverName, '.' ) ;
```

```
     if ( pchPos != NULL ) {
        *pchPos = 0 ;
     } /* endif */

     pdosPrinter -> pdriv = ppiQueue -> pDriverData ;
     pdosPrinter -> pszDataType = "PM_Q_STD" ;
     pdosPrinter -> pszComment = ppiQueue -> pszComment ;

     if ( strlen ( ppiQueue -> pszPrProc ) > 0 ) {
        pdosPrinter -> pszQueueProcName = ppiQueue -> pszPrProc ;
     } else {
        pdosPrinter -> pszQueueProcName = NULL ;
     } /* endif */

     if ( strlen ( ppiQueue -> pszParms ) > 0 ) {
        pdosPrinter -> pszQueueProcParams = ppiQueue -> pszParms ;
     } else {
        pdosPrinter -> pszQueueProcParams = NULL ;
     } /* endif */

     pdosPrinter -> pszSpoolerParams = NULL ;
     pdosPrinter -> pszNetworkParams = NULL ;
     return ;
}
```

PRINT.RC

```
#include <os2.h>
#include "rc.h"

ACCELTABLE RES_CLIENT
{
   "^p", MI_PRINT, CHAR
   "^P", MI_PRINT, CHAR
   "^s", MI_SETUP, CHAR
   "^S", MI_SETUP, CHAR
   "^r", MI_REFRESH, CHAR
   "^R", MI_REFRESH, CHAR
   VK_F3, MI_EXIT, VIRTUALKEY
}

MENU RES_CLIENT
{
   SUBMENU "~Print", M_SAMPLE
   {
      MENUITEM "~Print sample\tCtrl P", MI_PRINT
      MENUITEM "Printer ~setup...\tCtrl S", MI_SETUP
      MENUITEM SEPARATOR
      MENUITEM "~Refresh list\Ctrl R", MI_REFRESH
   }
   SUBMENU "E~xit", M_EXIT
   {
      MENUITEM "E~xit sample\tF3", MI_EXIT
      MENUITEM "~Resume", MI_RESUME
   }
}
```

PRINT.H

```
#define RES_CLIENT              256
#define WND_LISTBOX             257
#define M_SAMPLE                256
#define MI_PRINT                257
#define MI_SETUP                258
#define MI_REFRESH              259
#define M_EXIT                  260
#define MI_EXIT                 261
#define MI_RESUME               262
```

PRINT.MAK

```
PRINT.EXE:                      PRINT.OBJ \
                                PRINT.RES
        LINK386 @<<
PRINT
PRINT
PRINT
OS2386
PRINT
<<
        RC PRINT.RES PRINT.EXE

PRINT.RES:                      PRINT.RC \
                                PRINT.H
        RC -r PRINT.RC PRINT.RES

PRINT.OBJ:                      PRINT.C \
                                PRINT.H
        ICC -C+ -Gm+ -Kb+ -Ss+ PRINT.C
```

PRINT.DEF

```
NAME PRINT WINDOWAPI

DESCRIPTION 'Printing example
Copyright (c) 1992 by Larry Salomon
All rights reserved.'

STACKSIZE 16384
```

This program illustrates the use of multithreading within a PM application. Due to the design of the system input model, all "well-behaved" PM applications should completely process every message within a certain amount of time (the guideline currently is 1/10th of a second) to avoid locking up PM (actually, applications continue to run, but none can respond to user input). Thus, for tasks that will exceed this limit, a secondary thread should be used.

Note that because many PM functions require the existence of a message queue, you will likely have to call *WinInitialize* and *WinCreateMsgQueue*.

Also, it is usually good to call *WinCancelShutdown* so that PM will not send the thread a WM_QUIT message if the user should shut down the system while processing is still in progress.

You will recognize the *extractPrnInfo*, *createPrnList*, and *destroyPrnList* functions from previous examples. *createPrnList* creates a DEVOPENSTRUC structure for each printer present and calls *extractPrnInfo* to initialize it. It also saves the device name for calls to *DevPostDeviceModes*.

drawPage is present only to separate the drawing from the print-job initialization (in *printThread*). Since it really does nothing, it could instead be placed directly in *printThread*. If your application does any complex drawing, it might be beneficial to keep the drawing separate so that (1) it allows you to reuse the code between printing and repainting and (2) it does not clutter up the print-job handling. Your mileage may vary.

printThread handles the creation of a queued device context and associated presentation space and the print-job creation. It calls *drawPage* to actually draw the output. With the exception of a few changes, it is the same code that was used earlier.

The client's window procedure (*clientWndProc*) provides the meat on the bones, so to speak. It utilitizes the window words to store a pointer to a structure containing any needed instance data. The instance data here contains the handle of a list box, to avoid using global variables instead. This list box, created in the WM_CREATE processing, contains the list of the printers defined for the system. It is resized in the WM_SIZE processing to match the size of the client, for maximum utilitization of "screen real estate."

Here we also see our first use of the WM_INITMENU message. This message is sent whenever the action bar or a pull-down menu is selected. This allows the application to disable menuitems according to the state of the application at the time the menu was selected instead of trying to doing this on a per-action basis (i.e., the user selected item A on the menu, so immediately disable item B and enable item C). Taking a snapshot of the application is frequently much easier to do than figuring out state tables and all sorts of third-order differential equations just to see if the "Save" menuitem should be selectable.

The WM_INITMENU has two parameters as well: SHORT1FROMMP(*mpParm1*) contains the resource id of the menu that was selected, and HWNDFROMMP(*mpParm2*) contains the handle of the menu that was selected. The client checks to see if a printer is selected and if it contains any driver data and enables or disables the menuitems as appropriate.

Of particular interest should be the processing of the menuitems. MI_PRINT indicates that something should be printed, and this should take place asynchronously, so a PRNTHREADINFO structure is allocated and initialized with the handle of the client window and a pointer to the PRNLISTINFO structure for the selected window. A second thread is finally created using *_beginthread* and is passed the pointer to the PRNTHREADINFO structure (the second thread is responsible for freeing the structure).

MI_SETUP has practically nothing to do since everything was done already by *createPrnList*. It simply queries the PRNLISTINFO structure and calls *DevPostDeviceModes*.

MI_REFRESH simply calls *destroyPrnList* followed by *createPrnList*. This is needed in case the user adds a new printer after starting the application. Unfortunately, yet understandably, there is no way to be notified instead whenever the system configuration changes, so we have to force the user to select this menuitem to update the list.

Appendix A

References

IBM [March 1991], Operating System/2™ Programming Tools and Information Version 1.3, *Programming Guide.* [91F9259]

IBM [March 1992], OS/2 2.0 Technical Library, *Control Program Programming Reference.* [10G6263]

IBM [March 1992], OS/2 2.0 Technical Library, *Presentation Manager Programming Reference Volume I.* [10G6264]

IBM [March 1992], OS/2 2.0 Technical Library, *Presentation Manager Programming Reference Volume II.* [10G6265]

IBM [March 1992], OS/2 2.0 Technical Library, *Presentation Manager Programming Reference Volume III.* [10G6272]

IBM [March 1992], OS/2 2.0 Technical Library, *Programming Guide Volume I.* [10G6261]

IBM [March 1992], OS/2 2.0 Technical Library, *Programming Guide Volume II.* [10G6494]

IBM [October 1991], Systems Application Architecture Library, *Common User Access Advanced Interface Design Reference.* [SC34-4290]

IBM [September 1991], Systems Application Architecture Library, *Common Programming Interface C Reference — Level 2.* [SC09-1308-02]

612 — The Art of OS/2 2.1 C Programming

IBM [April 1992], C Set/2, *Migration Guide*. [10G4445]

IBM [April 1992], C Set/2, *User's Guide*. [10G4444

IBM [April 1992], Red Book, *OS/2 Version 2.0 Volume 1: Control Program*. [GG24-3730-00]

IBM [April 1992], Red Book, *OS/2 Version 2.0 Volume 4: Application Development*. [GG24-3774-00]

Paul Somerson [June 1988], *PC Magazine DOS Power Tools Techniques, Tricks and Utilities*, Bantam Books, Inc., New York, New York.

H.M Deitel, M.S. Kogan [1992], *The Design of OS/2*, Addison-Wesley Publishing Company, Inc., New York, New York.

Robert Orfali, Dan Harkey [1992], *Client/Server Programming with OS/2 2.0 2nd Ed.*, Van Nostrand Reinhold, New York, New York.

Index

Order Form

QED Publishing Group
170 Linden Street
P.O. Box 812070
Wellesley, MA 02181-0013
Tel: 617-237-5656
Fax: 617-235-0826

Name _____

Company _____

Address _____

City, State, Zip _____

Telephone No. _____

❑ Please charge my credit card.   ❑ VISA   ❑ MC   ❑ AMEX

Card No. _____   Exp. Date _____

Signature _____
(Order invalid without signature)

Qty.	Order No.	Title	Price	Total
	44694469	The Art of OS/2 2.1 C Programming	$39.95	
	44694698	It's TIme to Clean Your Windows: Designing GUIs that Work	44.95	
	44694671	Thinking Person's Guide to OS/2 2.1	24.95	
	44694507	Testing Client/Server Applications	39.95	
		QED Book Catalog	FREE	
Please add $3.00 per book for shipping. Airmail, outside of US is $15.00.		**Subtotal**		
		5% sales tax (MA residents)		
		Shipping		
		7% GST (Canada only)		
		Total		